A Garden of

Table of Contents

Heritage Paint System	2
Making a Plan to Paint	5
Rendering an Image	6
Quick Sketch and Designing	9
Limited palette/ Color wheel	5
Lost Edges	10
Feathering Techniques	11
Consistency of Paint and Technique	15
Painting Techniques	16
Mixing Colors	21

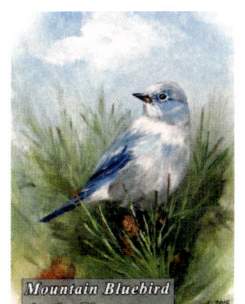
Lesson 1- 26

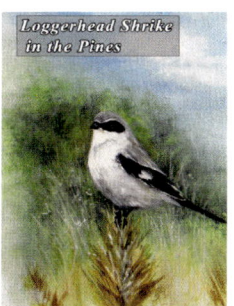
Lesson 2- 41

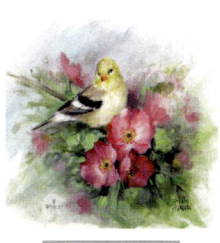
Lesson 3- 56

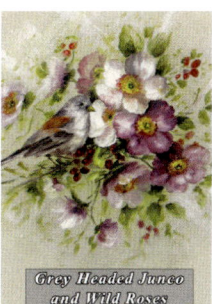
Lesson 4- 70

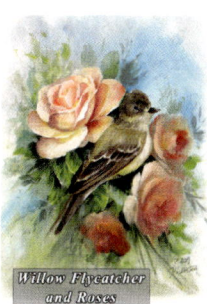
Lesson 5- 82

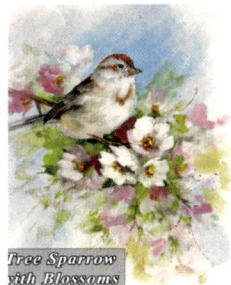
Lesson 6- 102

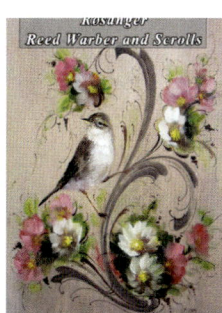
Lesson 7- 115

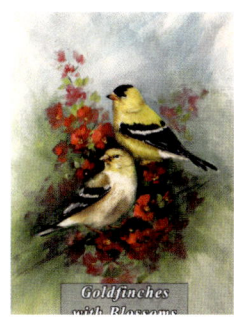
Lesson 8- 131

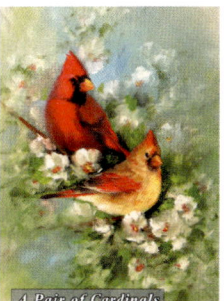
Lesson 9- 149

Published by
Jansen Art Studio Inc.
Elizabethtown, PA USA
David and Martha Jansen

Multimedia Content
Jansen Studio Productions
Silver Spring, PA USA
Jessica Jansen & Dave Parmer

Copyright Notice

No mechanical reproduction of any form may be used to reproduce the contents in this book. Those who lawfully purchase this book may print the designs and lessons for personal use only. Copies for any other reason are prohibited without written permission from Jansen Art Studio Inc. Copying this book or any of its contents without permission violates both US and International law. Those who wish to teach the content of this book must contact Jansen Art Studio Inc. for written permission. Failure to do so constitutes a violation of the copyright. U.S. Title 17 reserved.

Brushes Used in this Book

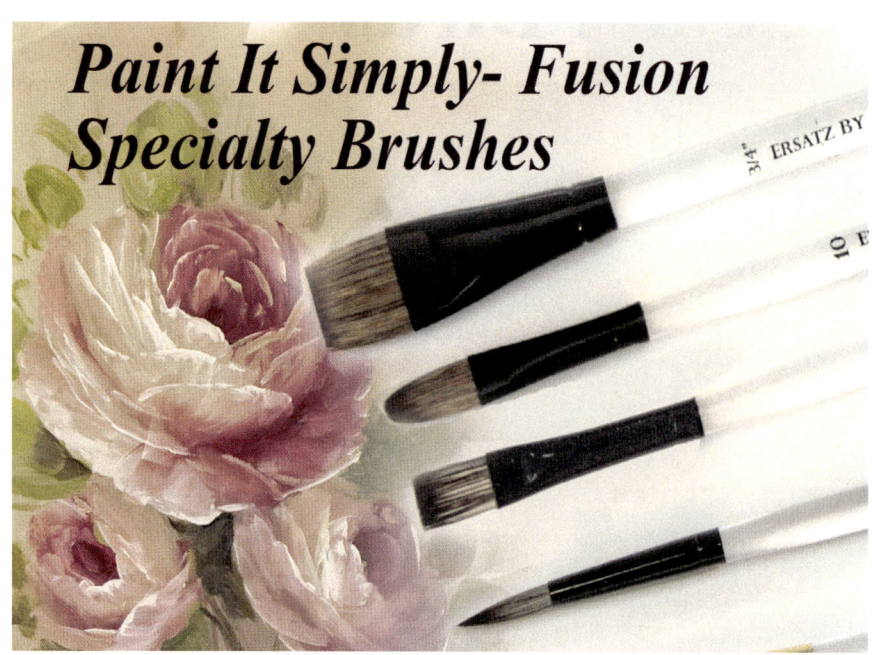

Brushes Used for These Lessons

Brushes by Global Art Supply
This lesson is painted with the fusion flats and filberts. You can use either the flat or filbert in these lessons.

Brushes I used in these lessons
Fusion Flat Size 4, 6, 8 and 10
Fusion Flat Size 3/4 inch.
Watercolor Round # 4 or # 8
Raphael 16684 # 3 Quill for some liner details.

Fusion brushes must be used for these techniques. Attempting to use other brands and types of brushes will only lead to frustration. This is an American made brush that is very versatile. The brush hair is a synthetic squirrel and is very soft. It is much softer than normal acrylic brushes. This allows the artist to achieve a softer look to the painting with fewer strokes. This is very desirable for the techniques shown here because, with the Paint It Simply lessons, we don't want to blend. Achieving a soft look quickly is desirable.

Heritage MultiMedia® Paint System

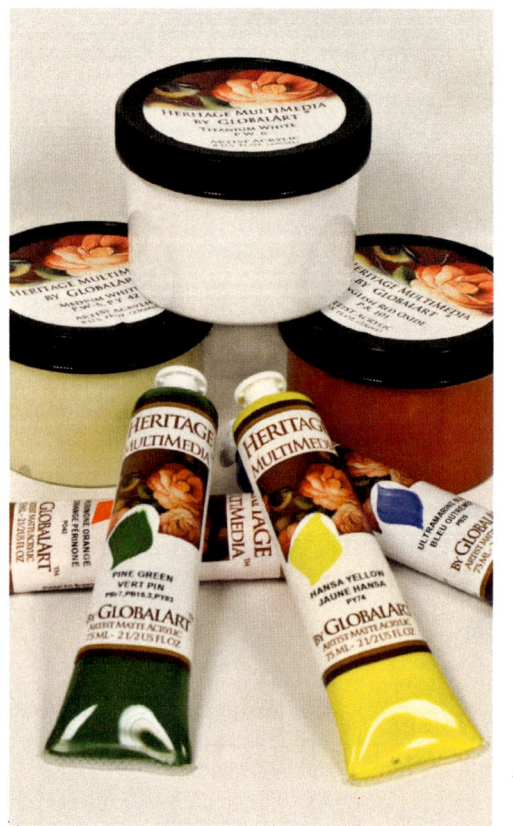

Not all acrylics are the same. As a matter of fact, industry standards dictate controls over the labeling of acrylics as to quality and durability. For example, most bottle acrylics are not "artist" quality. To be labeled "artist quality" the paint must have little to no filler added. The artist quality paints are designed to be mixed together to form new and traditional colors. Be careful when selecting paint and make sure you are using the best quality you can afford.

For this book we are using Global Art Supply's Heritage MultiMedia® Acrylics. The techniques described in this book have been formulated to work with this paint line. **Substitution of brands is not recommended** as the mixing and technique results will not be the same, and you will hinder your ability to learn the techniques.

Heritage MultiMedia® is a resin based acrylic that can be easily converted into watercolor, Global Colors (oil emulation), and tempera colors. Basically, the artist controls the paint film, not the company.

Preparing the Surfaces for These Lessons

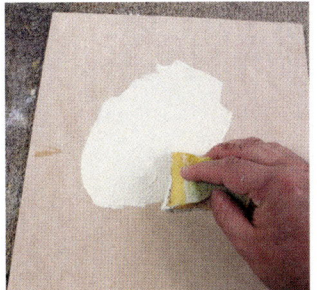

For these lessons I use Super MDF wood panels or Canvas Panels that I make. Please see GlobalArtSupply.com of detailed canvas making instructions. Whatever surface you choose to use, it should be semi-hard. We achieve this by mixing the base color with an equal amount of Heritage MultiSurface Sealer which will harden the paint layer making the techniques easier to accomplish.

Step 1
Mix White, or Medium White, with equal amount of MultiSurface Sealer and base the desired surface. Apply with soft brush or sponge shown here.

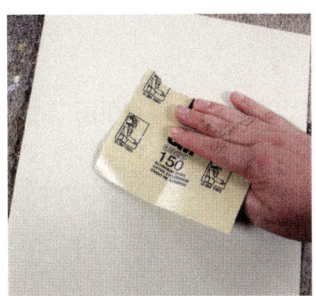

Step 2
Sand the surface with 150 to 220 grit sand paper to smooth. Do not use too fine a paper such as 400, because you will make the surface too slick.

Step 3
Transfer design or sketch with pencil. Follow next directions from each individual lesson. Give the surface a light transparent coat of paint and Extender.

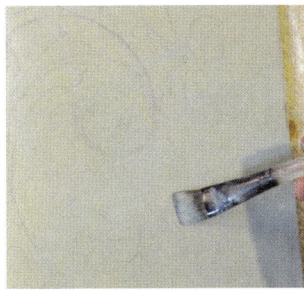

Step 4
When coating the surface do not have too much paint or too thin (watery). This will make painting the design more difficult. Just a light coat, stretch it out.

Varnishing Your Finished Painting

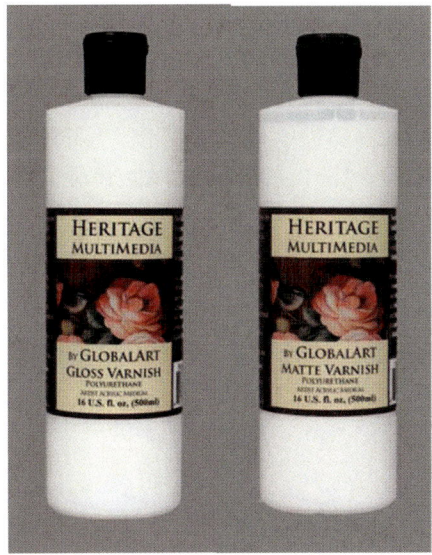

Heritage Varnishes are a state-of-the-art clear, non-yellowing, resin-based polyurethane varnish. They brush on smoothly and are self-leveling so that the artist doesn't have to stroke and stroke to smooth it out. It will give the quality protection of a Polyurethane varnish with the ease of application you have enjoyed from acrylics. Heritage Varnish is excellent for both interior and exterior use. When dry, it creates a hard, durable satin, gloss or matte finish that is ideal for artwork on a variety of surfaces. It dries quickly in 5 to 10 minutes, depending on weather conditions. You can slow that drying time with the addition of Extender Medium to the Varnish. For best results, thin the varnish with a little to equal amount of water. This makes application easier. Mix varnishes to create desired sheen. To make a Satin finish mix the Gloss and Matte Varnishes 1 to 1. Heritage Varnish is compatible with all Heritage paints and mediums. It is non-toxic and cleans up with soap and water. Because it is an acrylic product, it should not be used over oil based products.

Directions: Surface should be dust free and completely dry. Shake well then let the bottle stand for a few minutes. Apply with a brush or sponge. Varnish is easier to apply if thinned with water. Apply with a wet brush. Mist the surface with water if varnish begins to dry before you have finished varnishing. You can lengthen the drying time with the addition of Extender Medium. Additional coats can be applied as soon as the last coat is dry. Rinse brush thoroughly after use. Clean up with soap and water.

Two coats are sufficient for indoor use, three coats for exterior use. When applying multiple coats of varnish, allow NO MORE than 24 hours between coats. If you wait more than 24 hours, a light sanding with 400 grit sandpaper can be done to create better "tooth" for the final coat.

Making Global Colors using the Global Palette

To make Global Colors, we need to evaporate some of the water from the paint and replace it with our concentrated Extender Medium.

How long does it take?
This is a difficult question to answer because evaporation is different is different parts of the country. Generally, it takes 24 to 48 hours. The longer you leave the color open to evaporate water, the longer the open time of the final paints. You can achieve a 30 hour drying time if left open for 1 week.

How long can I store the Globals?
If you paint every few days, just put the lid on the palette and that is enough. If you are not going to paint for 1 week or 1 month, cover with press and seal before applying the lid. Properly stored the self life is indefinite. We have some Global Palettes that are perfect and 4 years old! Take care of your palette. With proper care and storage the paint will remain moist as in the tube. If you do not store properly, the paint will dry out!

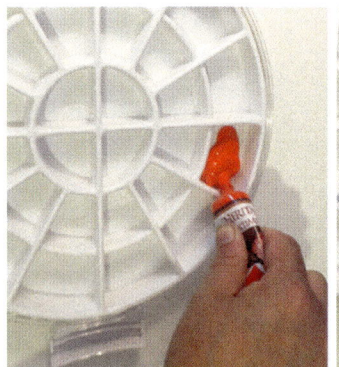
Step 1   Step 2

Step 1
Fill the desired well 1/2 to 3/4 full of with the desired color of paint.

Step 2
Add about 20% to 25% Heritage Extender. No need to be perfect! Close is ok!

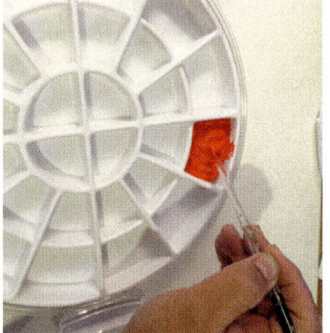 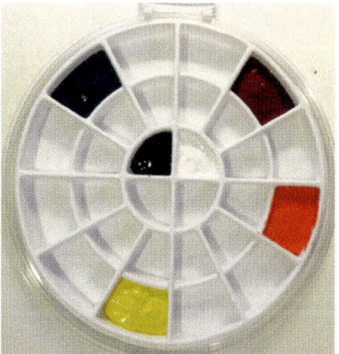
Step 3   Step 4

Step 3
Mix the color and Extender very well. This is important. Mix until the paint is creamy.

Step 4
Let the color stand for 24 to 48 hours while water evaporates. Stir the colors every 6 to 8 hours to help the evaporation of water.

Step 5
To store colors for a long time, cover the palette with Press and Seal before putting on the lid of the Global Palette.

Step 6
For longer storage you can mist the lid of the Global Palette with distilled water. Do not mist the paints.

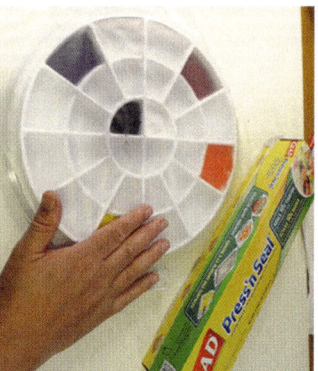 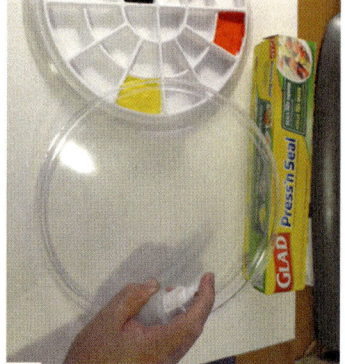
Step 5   Step 6

Rendering Your Painting and Making a Plan

When painting birds, there are several approaches one can use. You can take a small liner brush and render each feather in precise detail and give the bird the ultimate realism. I painted some of these years ago and, while the painting came out beautifully, it didn't feel like a painting because it had no stroke movement. It was just a thousand fine liner strokes. While technically appealing, it didn't satisfy the artist in me nor really look like a painting. Now, that being said, not everyone will agree with my feelings. That is ok. The art world is huge and there is room for many opinions. Even mine. When I use paint and brush, I want it to look like a painting.

For me, I love the power of the stroke and the movement of thick paint. I guess that comes from years of Rosemaling and Alla Prima painting. So, when I paint, I like to feel paint! I love paintings that go from found to lost. This means that there are areas that are "blurry" or unrefined. This is what happens in nature and we should do the same thing in our paintings in order to accurately capture the feelings of nature.

Which each painting, I start with a plan. That plan can be as simple as… let's paint a flower. But, it is still a plan. Allowing some freedom in this plan will increase your creativity. However, you must understand the elements of the plan and the necessity for those elements in your painting. I can start with a very detailed plan which outlines colors, brushes, and techniques or I can start with a very simple plan and develop the painting along the way. The simple plan will have the same elements to the painting as the more complicated plan.

Art is about refining and developing your plan. With the designs in this book, we will set a goal with each painting and then head toward that goal. If your goal is to paint exactly like I did then you will be copying. If your goal is to understand my thought process, then your painting will be a little different than mine and that is wonderful. Both are ok. What is important is to set the plan, the expectation, and stay with it to avoid frustration.

For these paintings I set some plan guidelines like this:
1. Which object is the most important? If this painting is about the bird, I must paint the bird with the most interest. This means using more color contrast, more detailed strokes and liner movements. Textures and mottled color generate even more interest.

2. Am I rendering a realistic bird or painting an artistic expression of the bird? This is one of the most important questions an artist should ask about each painting. As I grew in my artistic understanding, I went through several stages. First, I wanted to paint realistic. I studied blending and made all my paintings very smooth and plastic looking. Later, I wanted to paint more casual and impressionistic. Realistic paintings will have defined edges and precise color changes. When you relax the edges and allow for the strokes to show you create the feeling of a painting. Paintings have texture and strokes and give the viewer the definite feeling that it is a painting and not a photograph.

3. When painting the bird, first I will establish the undertone, then the darker and lighter areas. I slowly refine the bird until I add the amount of detail desired

4. Work and rework the painting and allow it to evolve. This is how I like to paint. I paint each painting for what it needs at any given time. I do not follow specific steps because this can lead to copying. Copying is ok, but when I create new, I need to make a plan.

So, to start a painting, your plan can be very simple. These are just a few guidelines to help you develop the painting. Do not plan too much. If a plan is too detailed, you will shut down your creativity. You always want to leave room for changes within the painting. Painting is about change.

Rendering the Bird Image

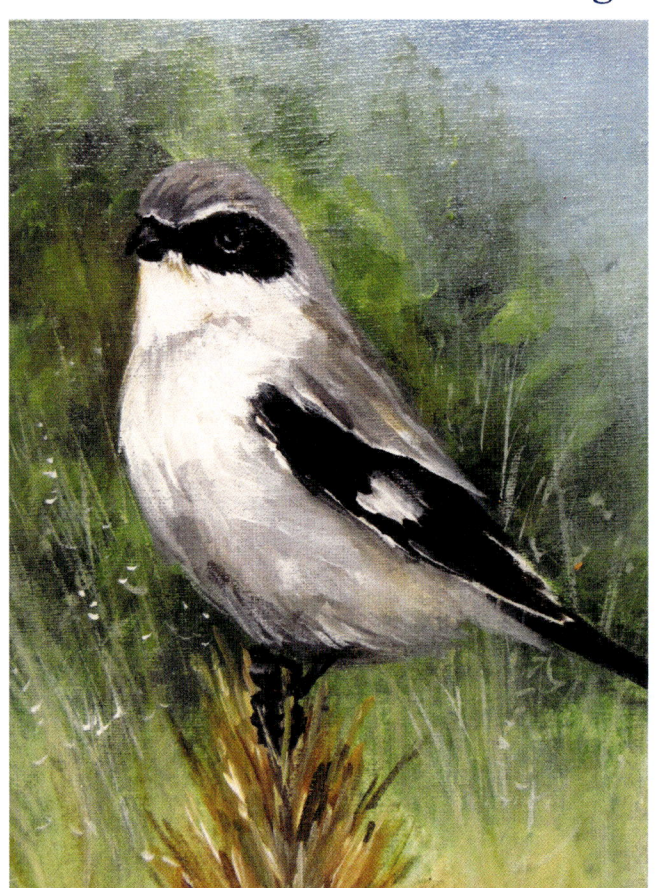
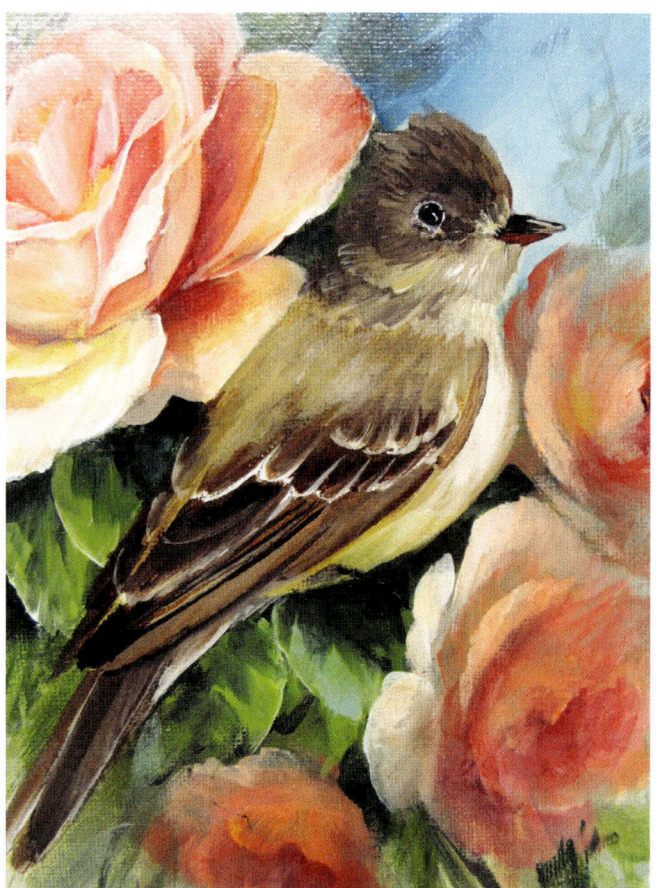

Here are 2 examples of paintings in the book and my thought process that goes with them.
The Shrike on the left is painted more casually. The image is rendered as a painting. Notice how casual the brush strokes are. The feeling of the feathers is loose and not perfect. I use a large brush to capture the movement in the painting.
The Flycatcher on the right is painted a little more perfectly. While not a realistic bird, I do take more time and care with the image. The details are more accurate with lines and details carefully applied.
I enjoy both looks when painting. Both are correct and both are fun to paint. One is loose, the other is more precise.

Creating a Vignetted Painting

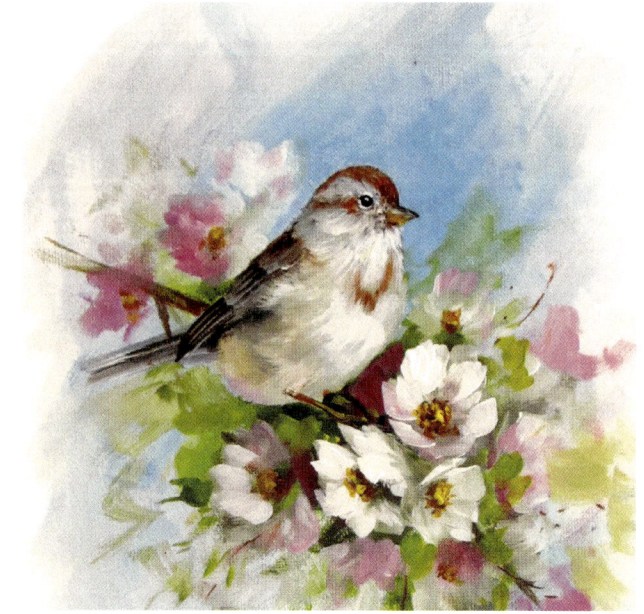

To vignette a painting is to apply color while maintaining some of the original background. I have read many rules over the years- such as 20% of the painting must be the white of the canvas. I don't know if agree with that, but it is a good place to start. Normally the artist chooses the interest area and contrasts it with a background color. That expression softens as the you move away from the center of interest. In this example, notice how the blue contrasts the head of the sparrow and then softens, even with strokes, to the white background. You can add other colors as needed. It is an artistic look that I love exploring. I am going to do more of them!

Anatomy of the Bird

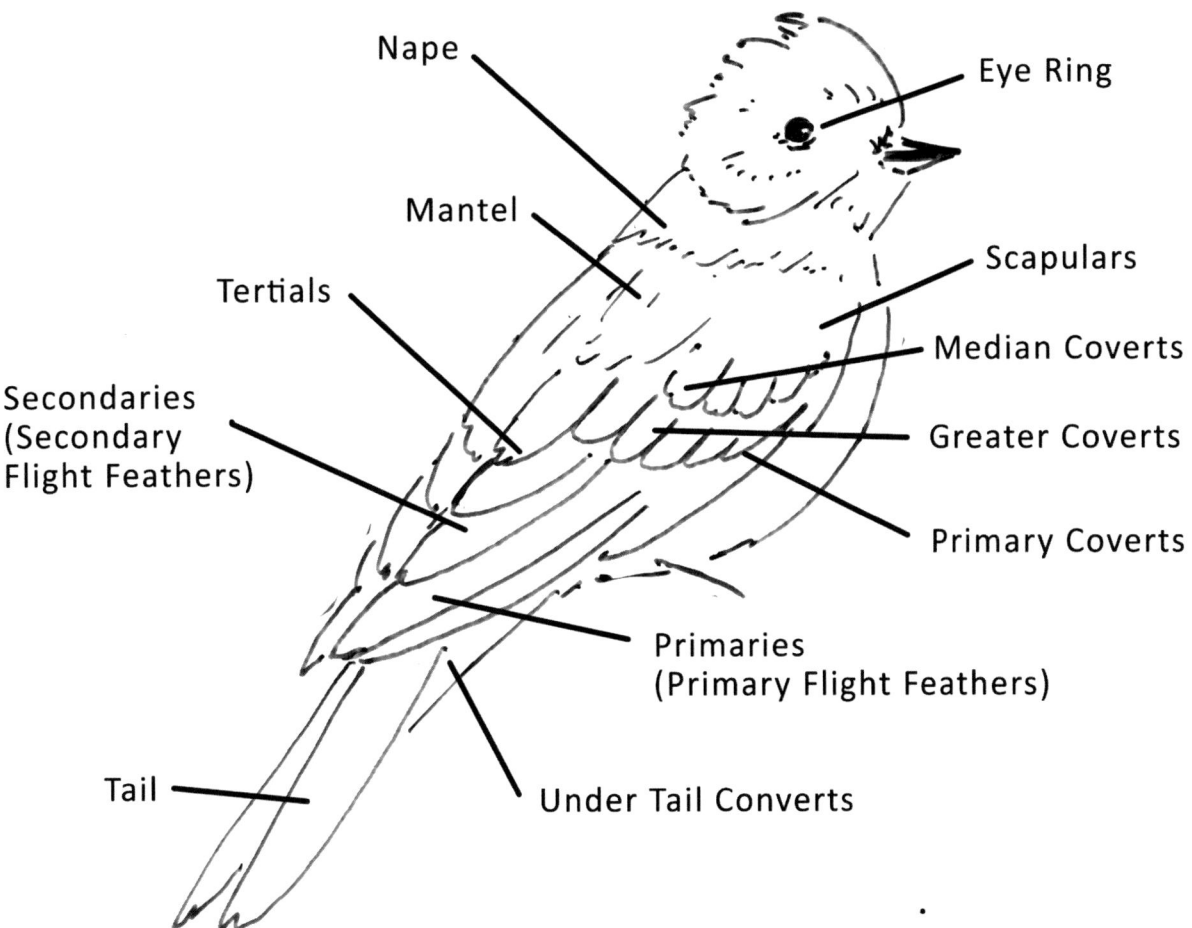

When painting birds, you must decide how you're going to render them. Are you creating a painting in which some of the anatomy will be lost to the art or a detailed study where you paint them a little more realistically. Anatomy is important. Each bird though is a little different and sometimes due to position you do not see all the feather groupings.

Just like I explain in flower painting, it is easier to paint something if you understand its structure. You do not have to memorize all the parts, just be aware of them because structure gives you ideas on how to paint the birds. It shows you how to move the brush. Let's take a brief look.

There are many parts to the bird, but I generally divide it into just a few areas for ease of painting. Flight Feathers, Mantle, Coverts, Tail, Head and Eye Ring. Head and tail are easy. Here are the others.

Flight Feathers-Primaries, Secondaries and Tertials.
These are the largest feathers on the bird and are on the wing. I paint them with the longest strokes.

Coverts
Median, Greater, Primary- These are smaller feathers that cover the flight feathers. They really make up a larger visual part of the wing and are stacked in layers.

Mantle
This represents the beginning of the back on the bird. I will call the top of the wing the mantle in the instructions for ease of understanding. The mantle sits on top the scapulars (on top of the front of the wing). I generally paint this area all as one movement for ease.

Making a Quick Sketch- See the Bird's Lines

Many times I work from photos of real birds, but it never hurts to know how to make a quick sketch. Any good plan starts with a quick sketch. Each artist is different in how the approach this quick sketch. I like to do the following. I vary the movement lines of the head and body to turn the head in different directions. Look at each pattern in the book and see if you can find the lines.

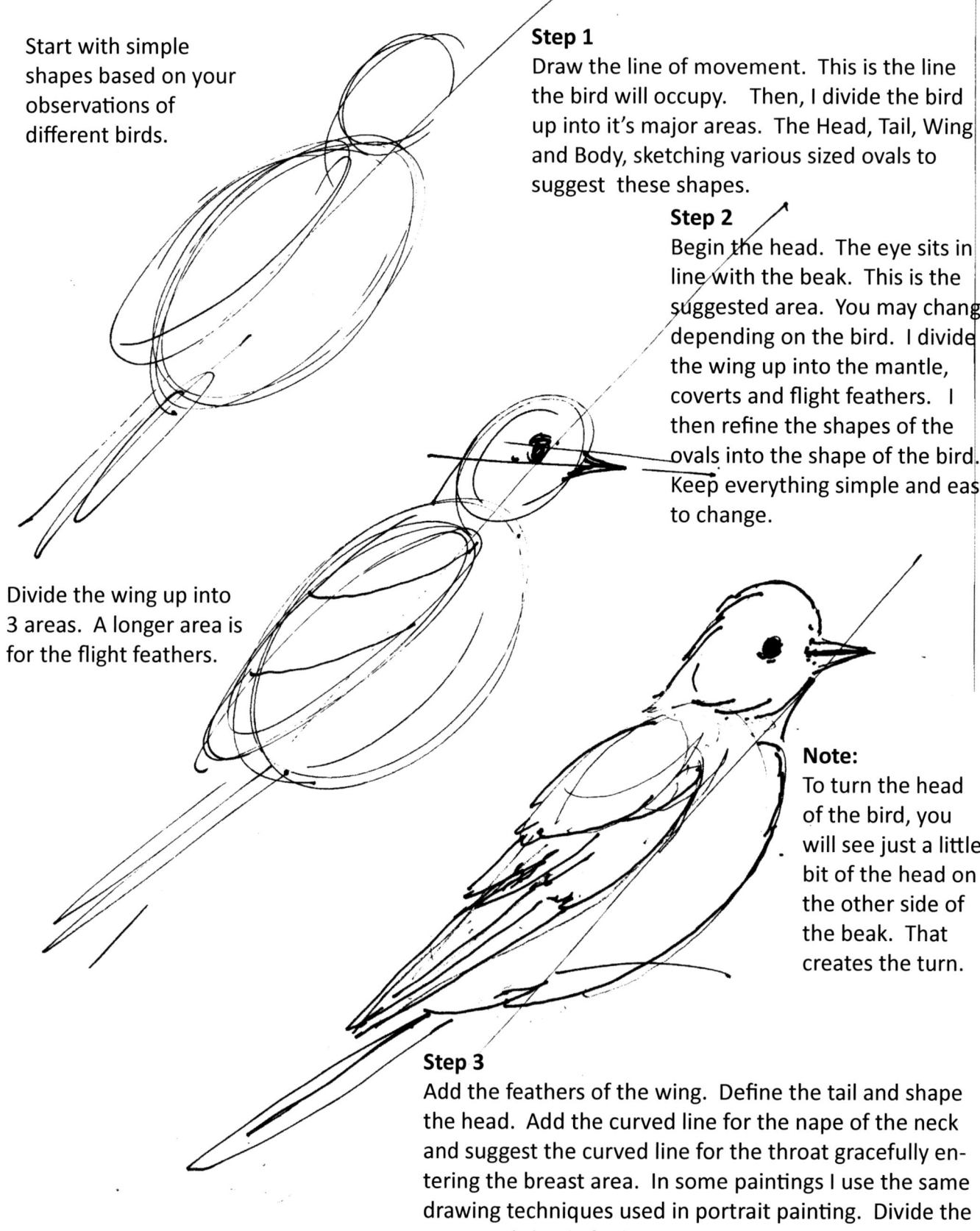

Start with simple shapes based on your observations of different birds.

Step 1
Draw the line of movement. This is the line the bird will occupy. Then, I divide the bird up into it's major areas. The Head, Tail, Wing and Body, sketching various sized ovals to suggest these shapes.

Step 2
Begin the head. The eye sits in line with the beak. This is the suggested area. You may change depending on the bird. I divide the wing up into the mantle, coverts and flight feathers. I then refine the shapes of the ovals into the shape of the bird. Keep everything simple and easy to change.

Divide the wing up into 3 areas. A longer area is for the flight feathers.

Note:
To turn the head of the bird, you will see just a little bit of the head on the other side of the beak. That creates the turn.

Step 3
Add the feathers of the wing. Define the tail and shape the head. Add the curved line for the nape of the neck and suggest the curved line for the throat gracefully entering the breast area. In some paintings I use the same drawing techniques used bin portrait painting. Divide the areas and slowly find and define the shapes of the bird.

A Quick Overview of Design

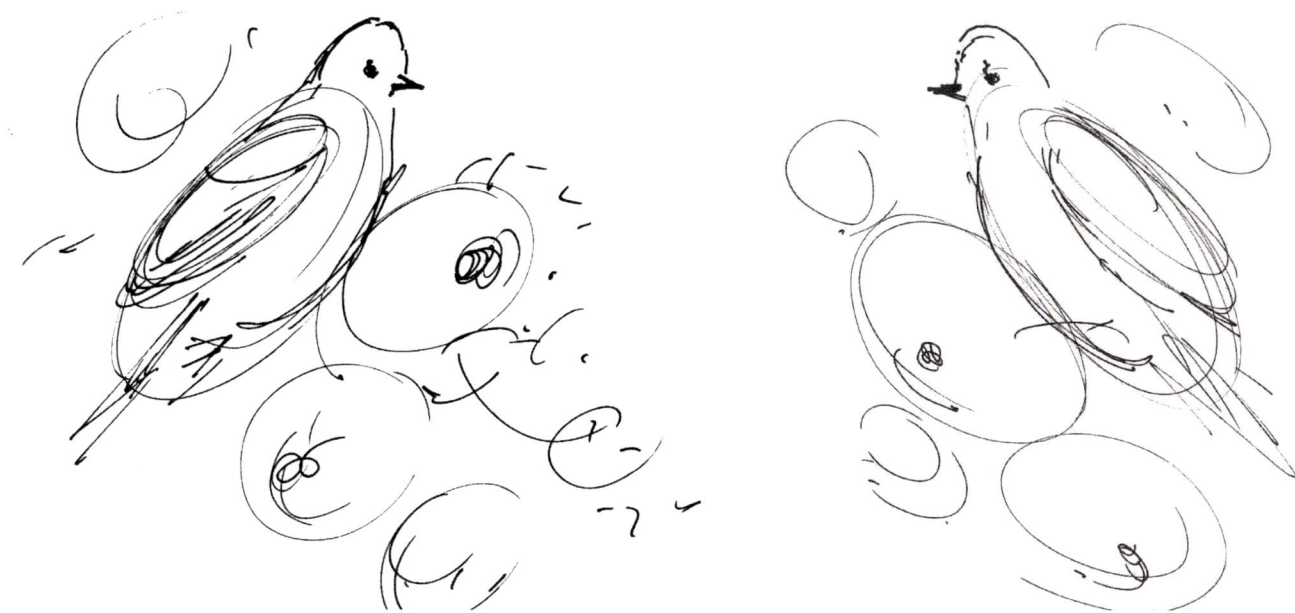

This book doesn't focus on design, but I feel the need to give you a few things to think about as you paint the lessons. If the bird is the center of interest in your plan, it needs to be the largest object in the design. This is called design weight. Secondly, the direction the bird is facing creates a journey in the painting. The viewer will look whereever the bird is looking. Try not to have everything facing in the same direction. Roses should angle differently than the bird. Stems and line movement should be in a different direction than the way the bird is facing. If you are interested in design and its many rules, please see our Youtube videos or our design series DVDs. Create your own paintings!

Contour Feathers and Length of Feathers

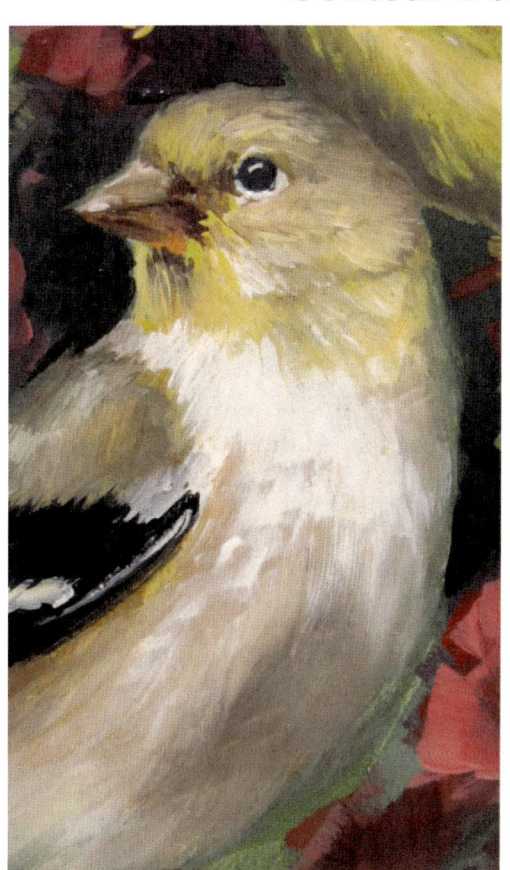

Feathering the birds with contour following strokes is very important because they give shape to the bird. Notice in the feathers how they flow around the head. The shorter feathers are always around the beak area. Sometimes they are just small taps of the brush. As you go down the body, the size and stroke length of the feathers increases. In the lessons you will see me feather the birds back and forth several times until I establish the look to the feathers that I want.

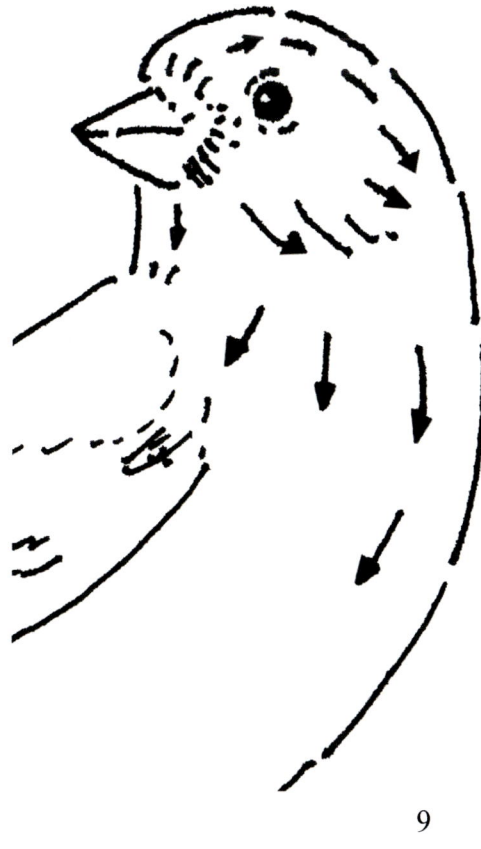

Rendering the Lost Edge

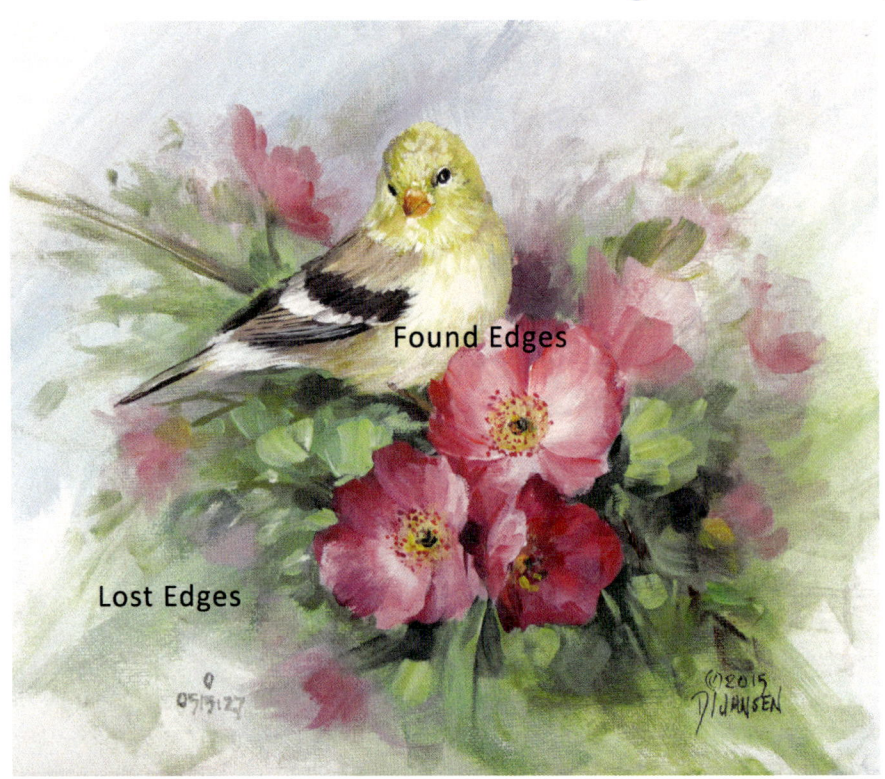

What makes a painting different from a photo? Painting represents the brush and how we use that brush defines the type of artist that we are. Every artist uses a brush differently and that is what makes a painting so unique and individual.

To render a painting realistically, there are techniques we use to define the edges of the painting. These techniques support the details that you would see in real life. Artists however create interest and capture depth of field. The artist compresses into a small area what we would see happen in a mile. So what you see in real life over a long distance, you see inside a painting. This creates a painting rather than realism. This beautiful addition to art is accomplished by what we call the lost edge. Lost edges develop the depth of field inside a painting.

When I was a decorative painter, I would transfer the design and then fill in the design with color, making sure I followed the design exactly. This always left a hard edge of color in all my paintings. That hard edge is something an artist controls for interest and depth in the painting. A pattern creates a repeated edge, but an artist will soften those edges to give depth and interest. As an object recedes in nature, the human eye loses the ability to see the edges clearly. Details become less defined and the edges become softer. It is like looking at a mountain in the distance. You can't see all the trees that are on that mountain, but they are there. The goldfinch painting above shows the lost edge technique. In real life, or in a photograph, she is so close to the blossoms that the viewer would see those blossoms in detail with defined edges. Because it is a painting, we soften them for interest.

Brushes for Feathering Techniques

When deciding which brushes to use, I think about the edges the brushes create as well as the details. The type of edges you want will depend on the plan you have developed. In most lessons here, I want detail feathers around the beak and eyes. Then they slowly soften as they go down the body of the bird. This will give the face more contrast which causes the viewer to be drawn to that area.

I break brushes down into the types of details they give the feathers. I use the Raphael 16684 #3 quill any time I want very fine details. It makes very small additions of color. However, it doesn't make soft edges so I only use it in the feather or face details. The # 4 watercolor round, or sometimes the # 8, is one of my favorite brushes for painting birds. It makes both soft and hard edge feathers depending on the pressure you use and the consistency of the paint. We will show you this in the feathering section. The next brushes are the Global Art Supply fusion flats in various sizes. They don't make as fine an edge as the rounds or liners so I use them to establish the movement of color and then detail more with the round if needed.

Basic Steps before Feathering Your Bird

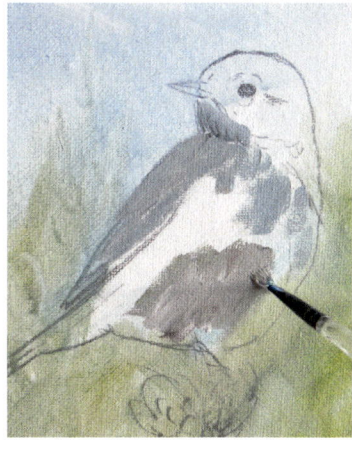

Before we go into feather details, we need to develop the techniques we will use in the painting. As I will show you in later, I use several painting techniques from alla prima to half tone, but we also need to develop the overall progression of colors. The technique is what you use to apply the paint to the surface and soften the edges. The overall technique gives you the main directions of the painting.

For example, with many decorative painting styles we follow: base coat, shadow, highlight, and liner work. For these lessons, we may use alla prima or half tones techniques, but we also need to have an overall approach to the painting. If this isn't clearly established, you will play and overwork areas. Work with a plan and keep moving through the painting and so you develop life and energy in your painting. Let's take a few minutes and look at the overall technique before we get into the feathering details.

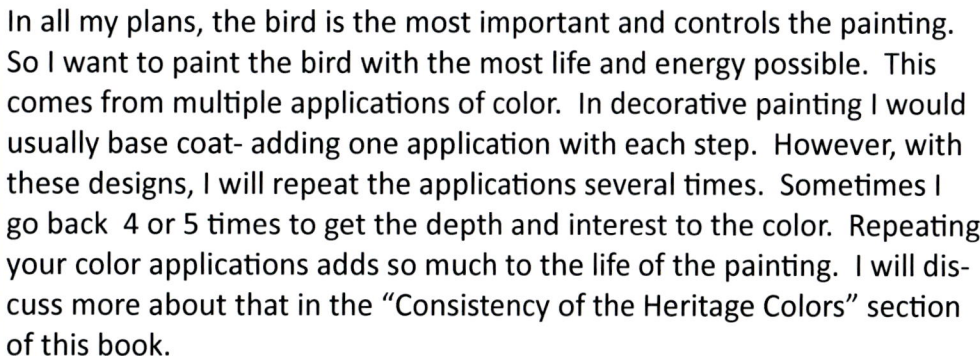

In all my plans, the bird is the most important and controls the painting. So I want to paint the bird with the most life and energy possible. This comes from multiple applications of color. In decorative painting I would usually base coat- adding one application with each step. However, with these designs, I will repeat the applications several times. Sometimes I go back 4 or 5 times to get the depth and interest to the color. Repeating your color applications adds so much to the life of the painting. I will discuss more about that in the "Consistency of the Heritage Colors" section of this book.

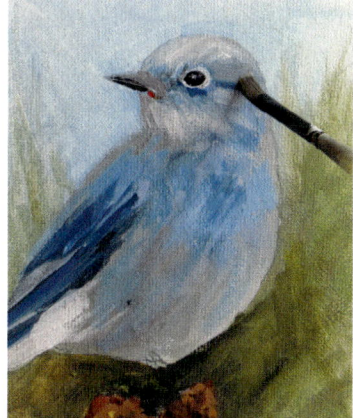

Basic Steps to Start the Painting. I alter slightly from lesson to lesson.
Step 1
Find the undertone for the bird or flower. This is like the base color but a little more. Most of this color will be covered up by the feathers. I try to look through the feather to see what colors that area might be. A tan color for a brown bird, cool toned red color for a bright red bird, and gray tones in this bluebird etc.

Step 2
I like to find some shadow tones. Not yet the darkest but this helps define the areas of the bird.

Step 3
Soften the shadow tones with a slightly lighter and warmer version of the undertone. I also begin to add some details and begin the feathers.

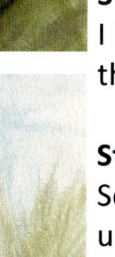

Step 4
Using your finger, soften the movement to the body of the bird. This adds soft flow between the shadows and mid tones. I will build more feathers on top of this movement with the feathering techniques.

Feathering Techniques
Fine Details & Small Feathers

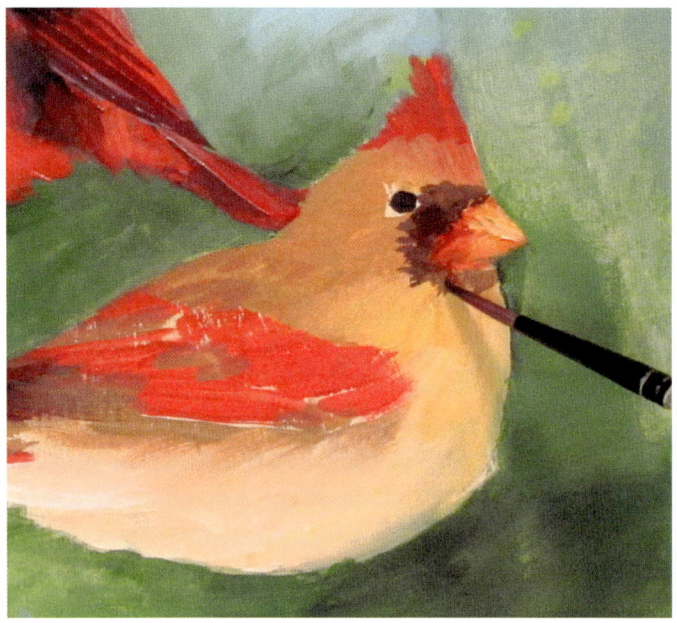

First apply the undertone. Then apply the light, if painting the light breast area, or shadow, if feathering around the beak as shown here. Use stiff or thick paint and not much Extender Medium. We want the paint to move together as we add more and more details. Use a # 4 round brush.

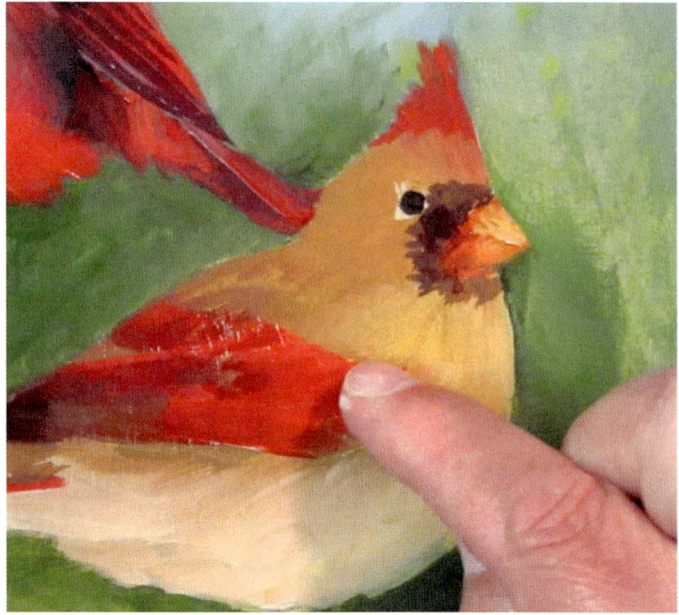

After applying the darks and lights, soften the colors together with your finger to create the base for the movement. Move your finger with the contours of the bird. Here I move up and down and slightly curve the edges for roundness.

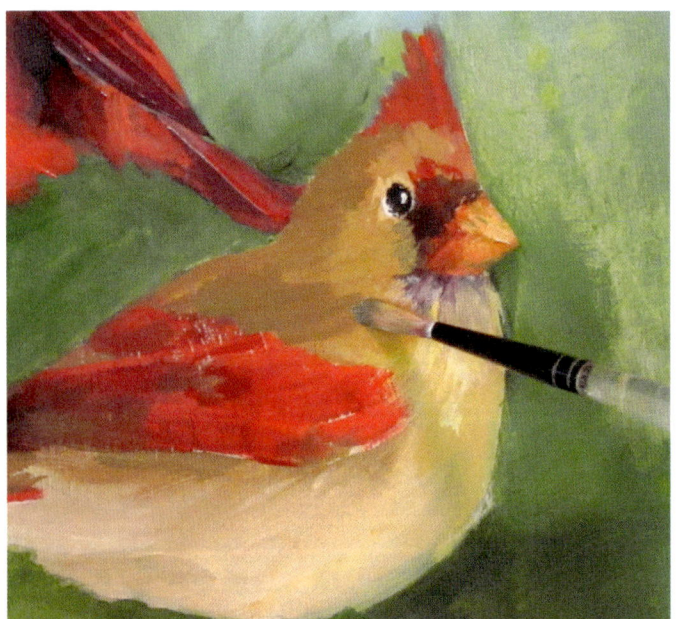

I flatten the round to begin making smaller strokes of color. Let the round "fan" out at the tip so it makes uneven strokes. Work back and forth with the lights and darks following the contours of the area you are feathering and the suggested lengths of the strokes. This build even more movement for the detailed feathers.

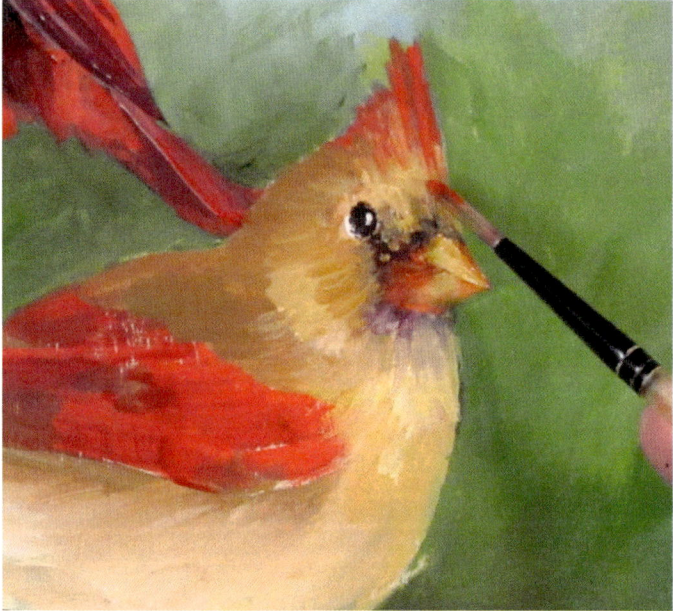

Now you can use the point of the # 4 round, or if adding small detail feathers around the eye and beak, the # 3 quill. Use the point and again work the colors back and forth establishing the movement. Sometimes I finish a feather pulling down, and sometimes pulling up. Vary directions so you get the most interest to your small feathers.

Feathering Techniques
Negative Feather Painting

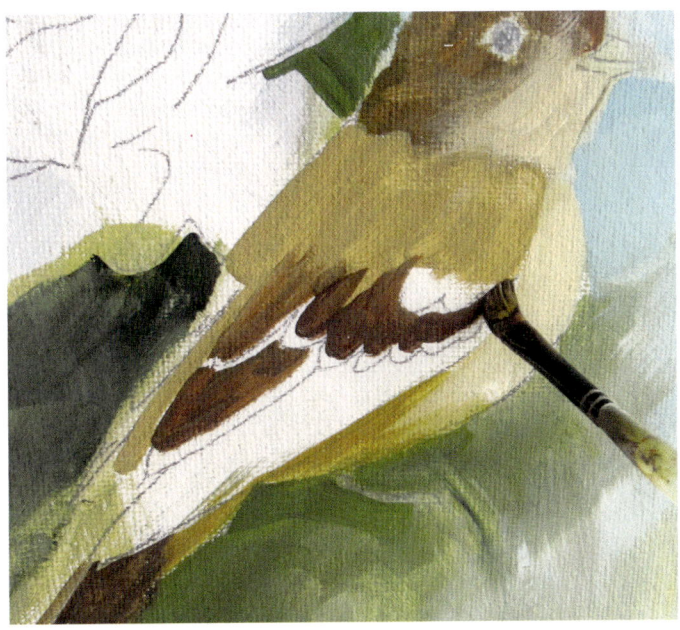

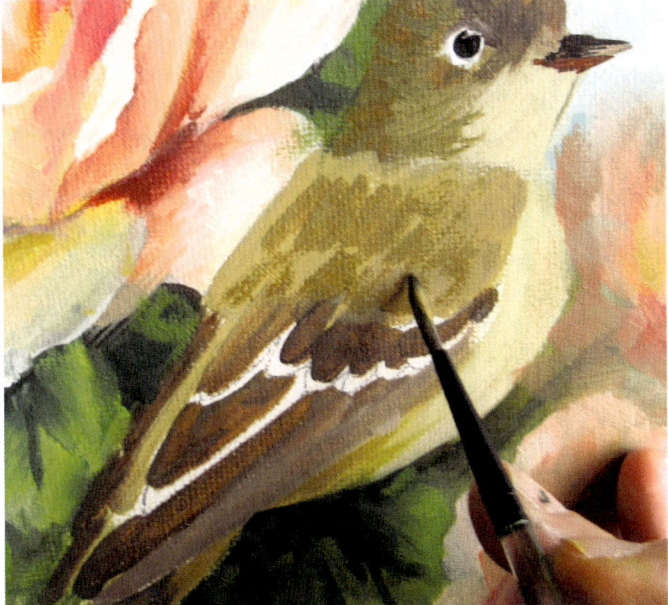

First apply the undertone. Then apply the light, if painting the light breast area, or shadow, if feathering under a wing. You can use the flat or the round brush for this technique. Base in the desired color of the area. I will sometimes leave a little light edge for the tip of the wing.

Mottle down the other colors of the wing. Many times when doing the negative technique, I paint the feathers in reverse as shown here. Stroke down the feather and stop short of the end of the feather. Leave light ends to the feathers, or you can apply these in the next step.

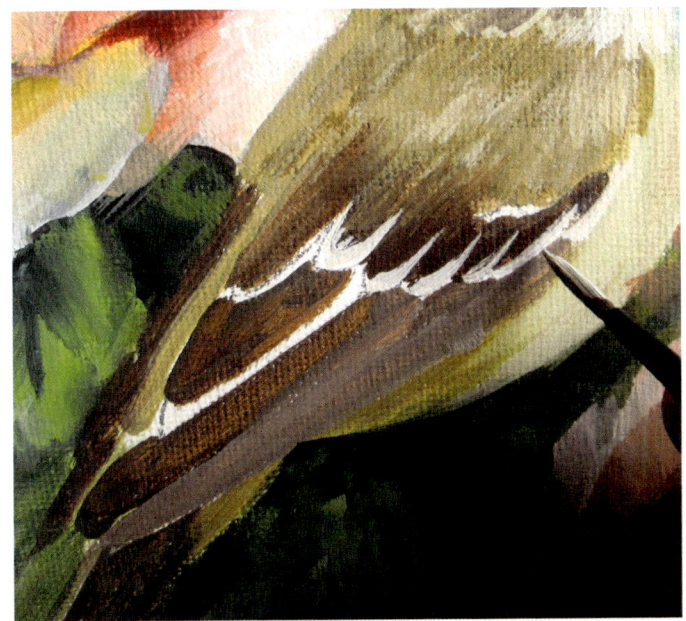

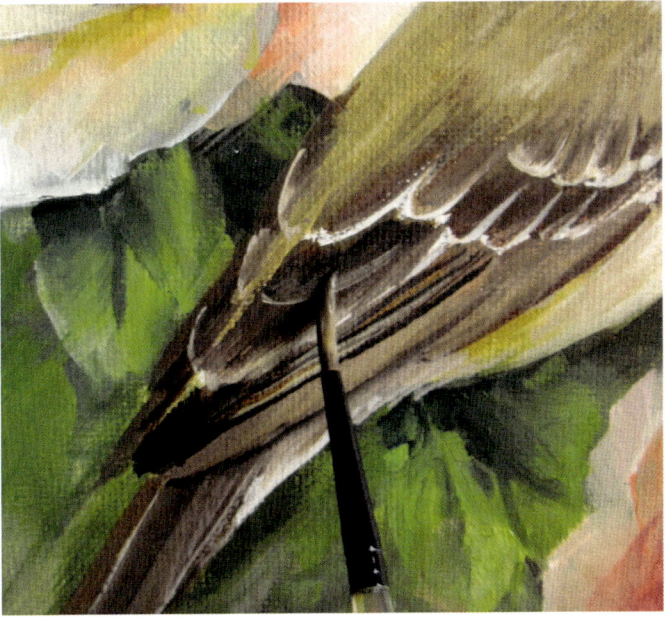

The next step is to apply the light ends to the feathers. The negative painting technique works well for birds that have light edges to the feathers. I do this for many varieties of birds of prey. Using the point of the round or even the liner brush for smaller feathers, add the white tips to the feathers. Apply more than needed.

Now using a dark color first, followed by a medium tone, begin to paint down the length of the feather stopping just a little before the end of the feather. You can put on a very detailed yet casual light end to the feather. I believe it looks more real than just applying light lines to the end of the feather with a liner brush. It is faster too.

Feathering Techniques
Large Areas

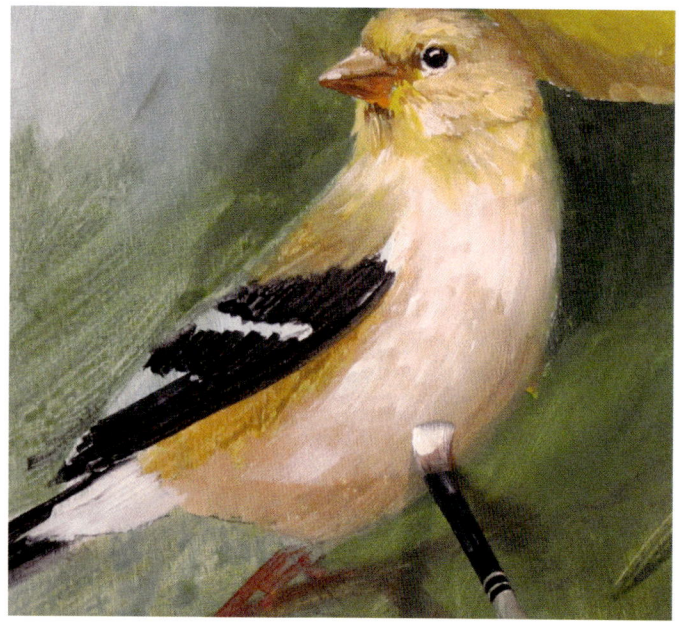

First apply the undertone. Then apply the light, if painting the light breast area, or shadow, if feathering under a wing. For larger areas of feathers I usually use a medium sized flat brush. Use stiff or thick paint and not much Extender Medium. We want the paint to move together.

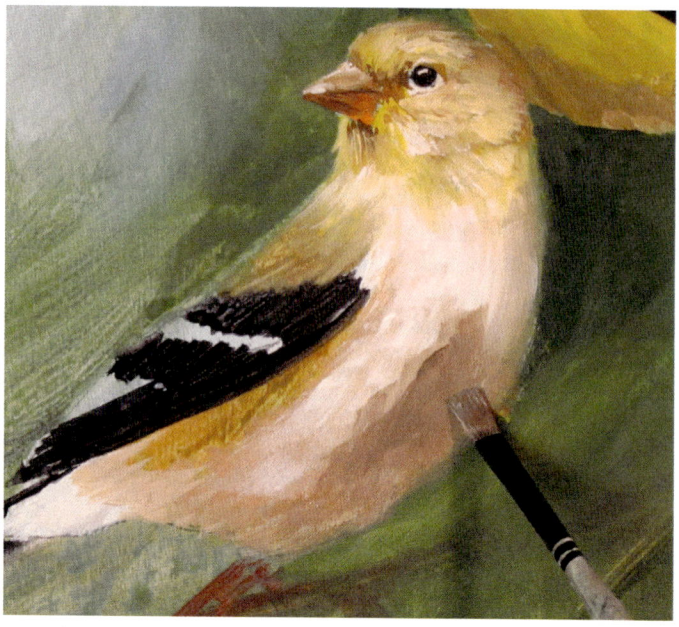

Apply some shadows with the larger brush. Use short strokes of the color so that you get some movement between the colors. This step I will repeat several times between the light and the dark tones creating movement between the colors and values.

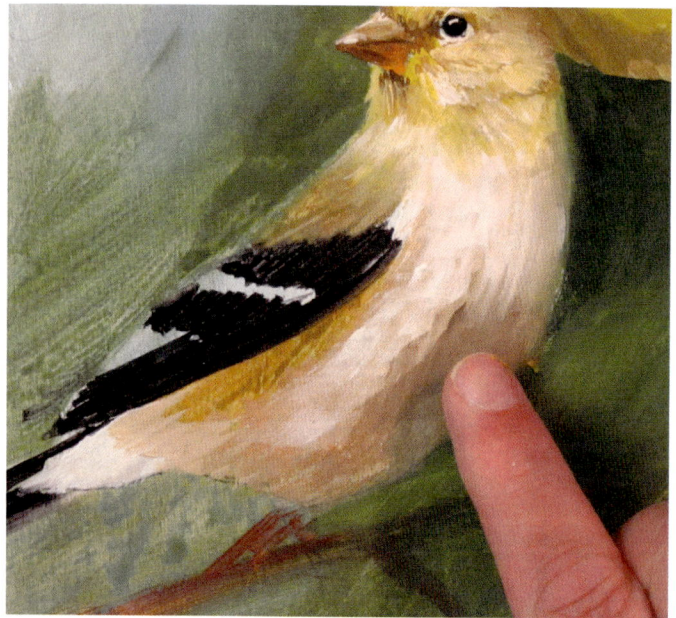

This is the most important step. Once you have added enough color to the surface of the bird and created the light and dark values, move the color around with your finger. Because the paint is so thick, it will not blend easy and the colors will "flow" together and mottle.

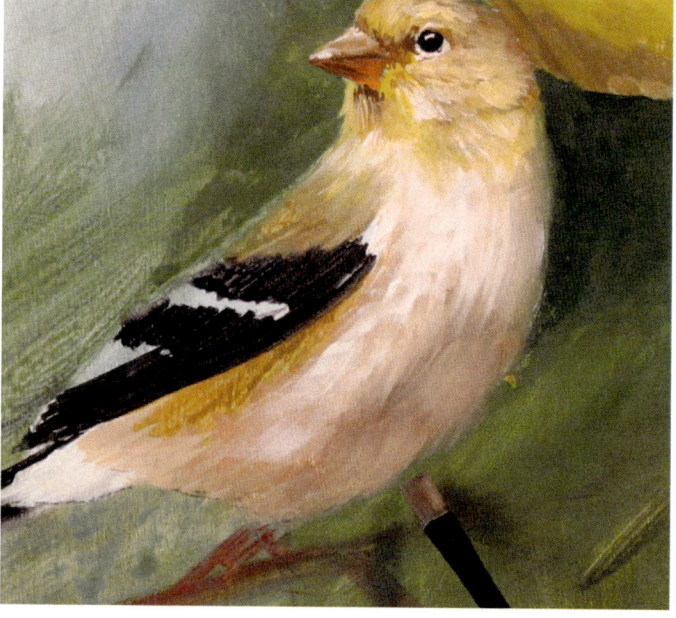

The last step is to use the small flat to add any final feather movement on top of the softened feathers. I usually keep this to a minimum. I will sometimes use the round or the liner to add a few smaller color highlights to finish the effect.

Consistency of the Heritage Paints

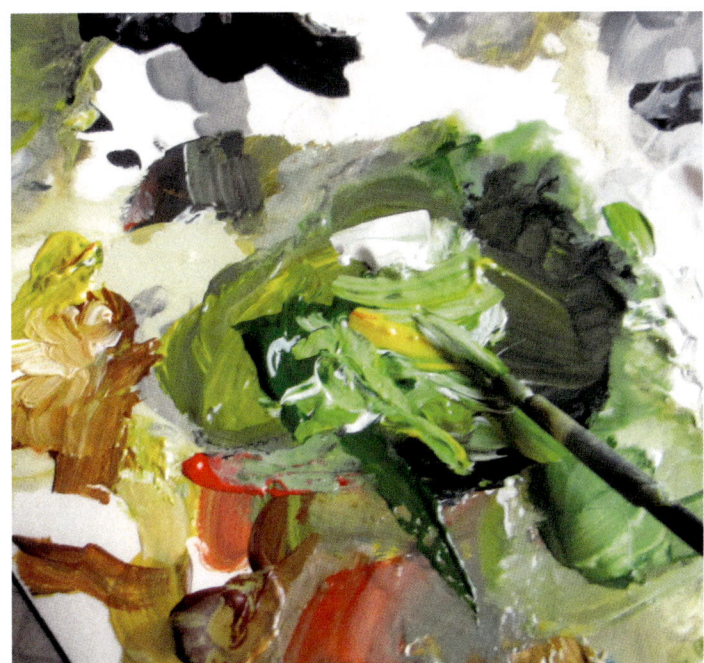

Notice The thick paint and how it does not "run" together on the palette. It "flows" around but keeps it's consistency

The Heritage Acrylics are thick bodied acrylics designed for professional artist painting. You can do a variety of techniques with the colors which we will introduce you to in this book.

Acrylic Painters

Today, many acrylic painters in the decorative painting industry are accustomed to using lower quality bottled acrylics and "flow" acrylics that are meant to be thin. Many acrylics used in decorative painting are designed for stroking and simple painting techniques.

Paint companies thin the acrylics to make them flow better. Because of this, if you have painted with bottles or used "flow" acrylics, you are used to thin paint. This can present a problem when you paint the techniques in this book. You may have the tendency to apply the color too thinly. This causes the paint to dry too quickly and prevents you from developing the depth of color necessary to add the interest to the painting. Keep this in mind as you paint through the lessons. For these techniques I use very thick color!

Application of Paint

One of the most common issues in new painters is the fear of using paint. This fear causes a new artist to use less paint, apply thin color or try to stretch their mixes with water. Over the years, while developing these techniques, I noticed I was slowly applying thicker and thicker paint. John Singer Sargent, who was one of the greatest Alla Prima painters of the 19th century, said that an "artist should apply the paint so it flows together. " I studied his paintings in several museums in Europe and the USA. They looked so thick and fresh and had huge amounts of paint. But what did he mean by "flow" together? My first thought was paint has to be thin in order to flow together. Many paintings later, I realized that the paint must be thick enough so that it "moves" together but doesn't blend. Thin paint "runs" together. Thicker paint moves together while keeping the color clarity intact. You want to be able to control the movement and the softness of the colors. To do this, you need thick paint. Lots and lots of thick paint. That is the secret!

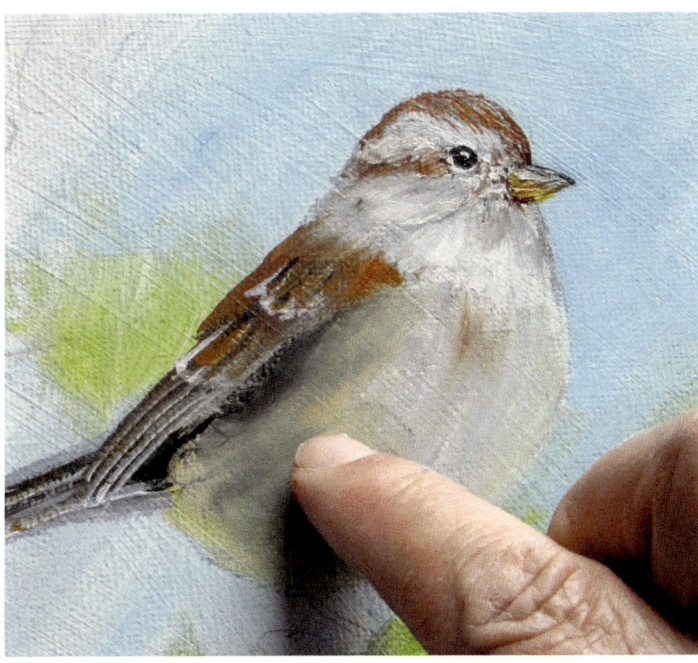

Paint must be used thick enough on the surface so you can use your finger to "push" it around and create the soft undertones for the feather. Blurry paint!

Alla Prima Painting Technique

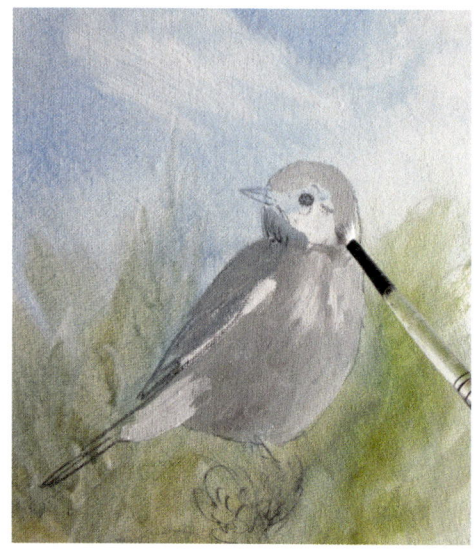

I work the entire painting first

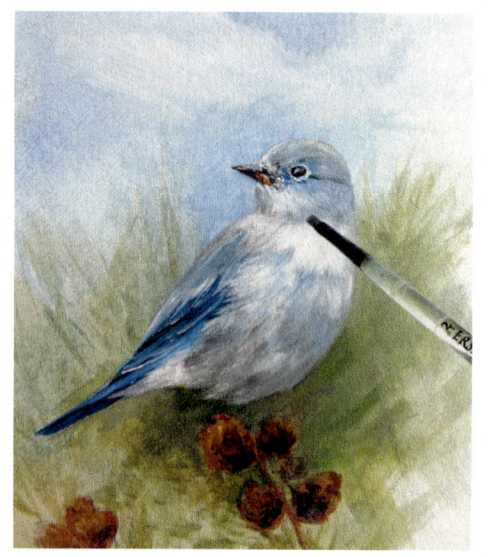

Repeat all objects several times

As stated earlier, I make a plan and follow it with a chosen technique. I use the Alla Prima technique for most of the lessons in this book. This technique requires a wet surface in which to paint your birds. We paint into a wet background for several reasons. One is the ability to quickly change a color and even erase a color just by rubbing it out with your finger. Another is the color variation that this technique gives. Many painters mix their colors in batches or buy premixed bottled colors because they do not want to mix. Brush mixing however is an essential key to learning to paint. Without that, you are just painting by number. The interest you develop in a painting is generated by the variations in color. So, artists look for techniques that allow them to quickly and effectively change the color while maintaining control. Alla Prima provides that vehicle.

First I wet the background with thinned color. Then I begin to casually state the undertone of the birds with mottled tones. The color on the background must not be too thick nor too lose. You will only find the correct amount through trial and error because everyone's hand and stroke pressure is different. If an area dries on you, simply re-wet the surface before continuing. It is that simple. Some like to work a small area at a time. I prefer to work the entire design. Wet the surface, casually establish the bird with the undertone and then step out and begin some of the other shapes in the painting. Add background leaves, shapes and colors. Do not work the elements with great detail. I think of it as slowly turning the focus knob on a camera. Start blurry and then slowly bring the painting into focus with refining.

With Alla Prima, you progress through the tones. You are slowly warming, cooling, brightening and dulling. I usually look for the undertone which is the basic tone of the bird. This means some mid value version of the bird. For example a white bird will be some grey color. I will describe this color to you in each lesson. Establish the mid tone. I then generally establish the dark tone. Not always, but most of the time I do this for both the birds and the flowers. Most of the backgrounds in this book are light, so the dark values give you contrast. Use them to establish some shape and form before the highlights. Work wet into wet.

Acrylic painters......

For years I had the problem of playing in my paint. Acrylic painters generally have this trouble. While you play, the colors and background will dry. Global colors can give you longer working times, but be careful. Establish the colors and move on. Think of the camera. Work the definitions in the birds and flowers with the knowledge that you will return to it again and refine it further. There is no need to paint a perfect bird right from the beginning. So please follow this rule.... Don't Play! Move and keep moving. Slowly build the strokes. Read through the lesson. How many times to you see me rework and area of feathers? 5, 6 ? I do it many times, each time adding more and more movement. You cannot get some of the beautiful looks that I achieve with the birds in just one application.

Half Tone Technique

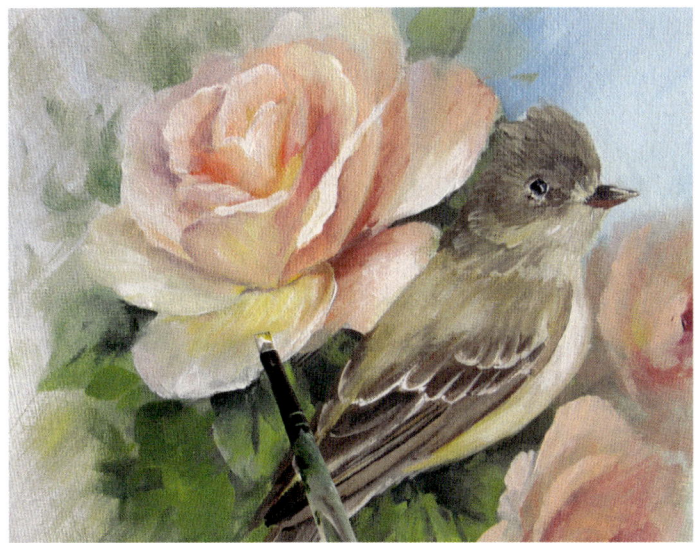

Set multiple tones next to each other with very little blending. Use optical blending to make softer.

The half tone technique is one of the first techniques I used as I moved away from painting with just acrylic techniques. It is a very fun technique and can render some extremely realistic flowers and birds very easy. I choose however not to render them very realistically because I like the look of a painting.

Start by basing in part of an object. This can be with a light or dark tone. Normally it is a dark tone. The next step is to make the opposite tone. So if you make a dark tone first, make a light tone second. Apply both tones in the areas they will occupy. This gives the artist a look at the painting of light and dark. The next step is to soften the effect. We soften with the half tone. Brush mix the dark value and the light value together on the palette making a tone in between the 2 values. Next apply that tone between them. Do not blend together. Just stroke on the tone. Next, make a tone halfway between the middle tone and the light value. Apply that between those two tones. Then make a tone between the dark and the middle tone and apply it in that area. Slowly refine the tones each time making a half tone between the two colors you want to soften. Finally you can soften the effects with a brush if you want or use you finger like I do. Many times however I do not, leaving the brushwork which will visually blend when you step back from the painting. This is why many artists paint at an easel. They can easily step back to see if the tones blend with the eye. This is called optical blending.

Painting the Sfumato Technique

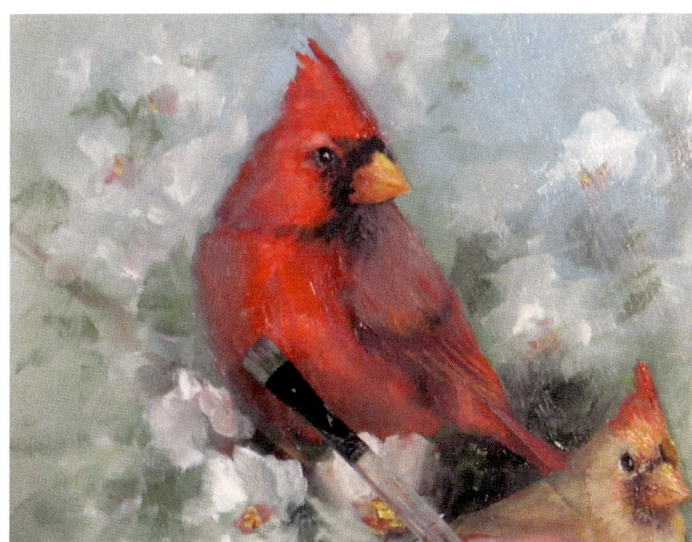

Set multiple tones next to each other with very little blending. Uses optical blending to make softer.

Sfumato is a technique made famous by Leonardo da Vinci on the Mona Lisa. The word is from the Italian word sfumare, which means "to tone down". With this technique the artist presents no harsh lines. Tones are softened with small strokes of a cloudy or compliment color which causes them to recede. This can also be used to create better realism in a painting. For the Cardinals lesson I used this technique to push the male Cardinal behind the female.

This is very similar to chiaroscuro which I have used many times in Dutch paintings to push the receding edges of objects back towards the background. With Sfumato you use a cloudy-color or complimentary color to the object you want to push back. This is a wonderful technique that we can use in many situations. It really works on the reds of the Cardinal. I hope you take some time to explore it.

Additional Techniques Used In This Book

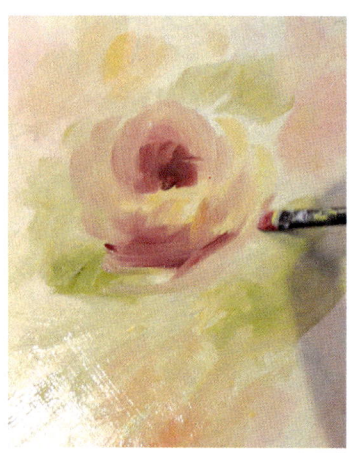

Transparent Color Washes- Sketching Shapes
Throughout the lessons we will add lots of interest through the use of color washes and creating a mosaic of colors. Artists for hundreds of years have concentrated on paint consistencies to enhance the designs.

With these lesson you will see several times where you should add various colors into the background and also within the petals. This is called a "mosaic" of color. When you apply this mosaic of color please vary the consistency of the paint by thinning some colors with additional Extender Medium. Varying the consistency of the colors will increase the variation within the blossoms.

The basic control or soft blending that occurs as you move the brush around the surface is controlled by the paint consistency. If a certain lesson is not working, I highly suggest changing the consistency of the paint for a better result.

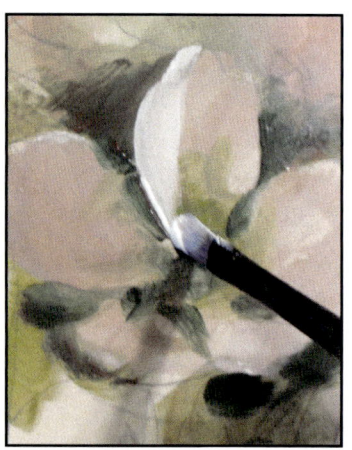

Light Color Petal Edging
One area that the fusion brush excels is in the application of white edges, and then softening them with other strokes. Throughout the lessons, we will edge the brush with various Whites, and then use the brush to "draw" the petal before filling it in with color.

To do this technique, tap one edge of the brush into the White or suggested light color. Sometimes I use the chisel edge, flat edge or at an angle as shown in this photo. Wiggle the brush as you draw the outside edge of the petal. Varying the amount of paint will create different petal effect. Once I have drawn the outside edge of the petal, I then stroke the brush back and forth to fill in the petal with color. If anything gets too harsh or too much, I soften with my finger.

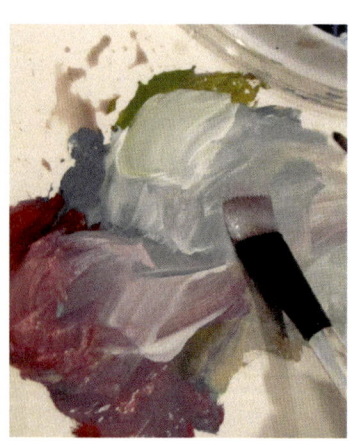

Brush Mottling
This is a technique we use extensively in this book. When you use colors that have a substantial difference in light and dark and brightness from each other it creates more interest in the final flower. To create a mottled brush you need to have colors about the same consistency. Place the colors right next to each other on the palette. Tap the brush up and down on the palette to load into the brush. Do not stroke the brush on the surface of the palette because this will cause them to blend and soften. Tap the colors on the palette just enough to cause them to load into the tip of the brush. Apply the colors to the flower or blossom with a light tapping motion. Use a very light pressure on the brush so that the tapping doesn't continue to blend the colors. A great technique for interest in the flowers.

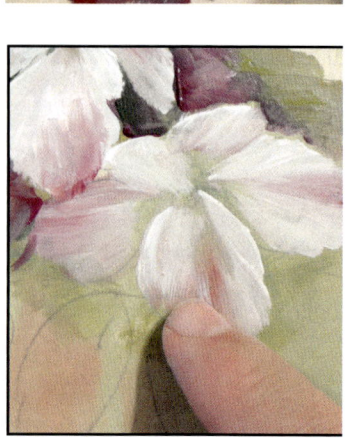

Lost Edge of the Petal
Artists are painters of edges. We fill in pattern lines or paint objects with edges that give them form and structure. The edges though are very important for dimension within the painting.

In real life, the human eye can not see all the details in objects that are further away. What happens is the edges of the objects "blur" as you get farther away from them. Our eyes are used to seeing this concept everyday. To capture this normal vision depth, the artist will paint a very clear edge to objects that they want to come forward, such as the front petal of a flower. They will soften or blur the back ones so they recede. I use my finger for this. Softening the edges of objects that are not important brings forward the others.

Additional Techniques Used In This Book

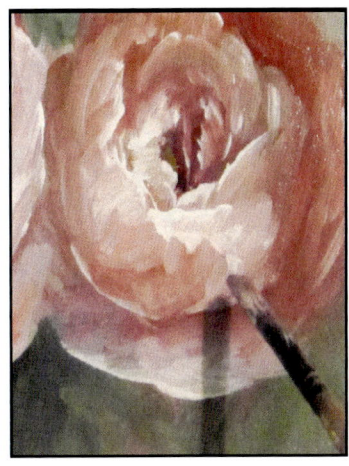

"Push Strokes"

Many artists tend to get trapped in one direction painting.

Paint It Simply is based on simple painting in multiple directions. Painting in multiple directions add more interest. The fusion brush is a very soft brush. It can be used in many different ways to create many beautiful looks. One look that I love is to "push" the brush instead of stroke the brush. Stroking can give a stiff look if you do it too much. By pushing the brush, the soft hairs of the fusion spread out, and apply the paint in a very casual manner that can not be created by stroking. Pushing strokes can be used with soft finger blending and stroking to create a wide variety of looks on a petal.

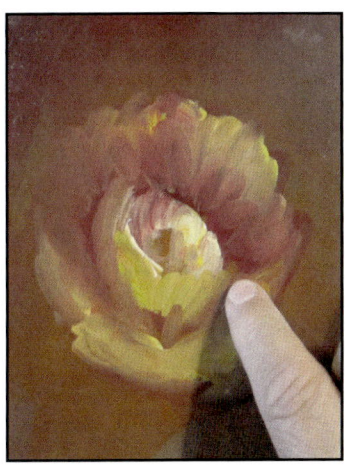

Pushing Color

For hundreds of years artists have used their fingers in painting. Since I started Painting Simply, I have used my finger more in painting than any other tool! I love the casual look that is created with the fingers.

Apply color to the surface. Mottle the colors with many others. Pushing color works the best if the background is wet with thick paint. Most techniques require thicker paint so make sure you have it on the surface. Apply the paint with the fusion. Then using good pressure with your finger, push the paint around into the shape of the object you are painting. I love to do this technique on the fronts of roses, where you want the colors to mottle and swirl, but not to blend. Too much brushwork can blend the color where pushing them around with your finger preserves the color.

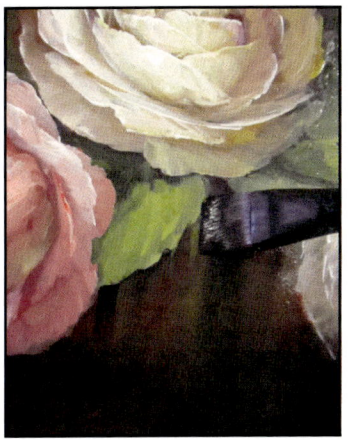

Negative Painting

In this technique, you use the background colors to clean up the edges of an object, rather than applying the edges again to the object.

This technique works very well when you are working on a wet background. Paint the desired object. Sometimes I will paint the object, a petal for example, then wipe my finger over the petal to soften and carry some background color into the petal. Then come back with a slightly larger brush with background in it and paint the background which will clean up the edge of the object. This also makes the object look more transparent. When painting, you can make edges with the objects color, and also in the reverse with the background. Negative painting in another great technique to add interest.

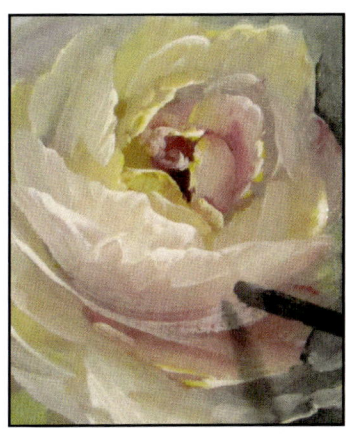

Lifting Off

Many times we paint the object with layers of color. With most decorative techniques with add colors that are needed to the object. With lifting off, you paint, then cover it, then lift the second color off revealing the first color. I love this technique and it is one of my favorites to use on rose shadows.

Apply base color. Then apply the shadow as needed on the object. For example at the bottom of the bowl. Then apply the mid value and highlight as desired. Many times you need to reapply or "restate" the shadow because we lose it. But, with the fusion brush, and sometimes your finger, you can start at the shadow and push up to lift off some of the base color and highlight, revealing the shadow again. Variation!!!

Additional Techniques Used In This Book

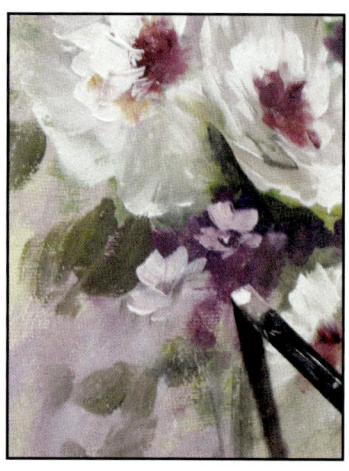

Optical Blending

This is a concept made famous by the Impressionist painters of the late 19th century. With this, the artist leaves portions of the painting "unblended" allowing the viewers eye to blend the tones from a short distance. Usually the artists take a step back of about 3 feet to view the painting. This softens the effect. The photographic cameras usually soften the effects of a photo. When artists paint from that photo, the result is an overblended painting. To combat this, we leave more areas of color exchanges. Try not to stroke more than 3 times in any area. Do not stroke many times! Leave streaks.

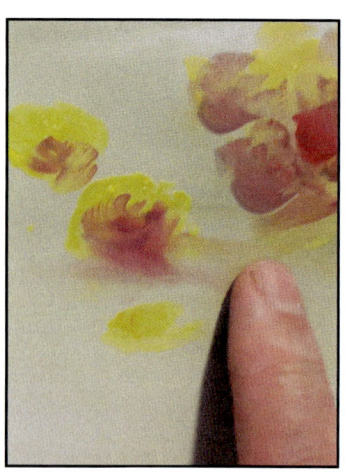

Blur Objects for Depth

This is a technique that is very important to the lessons in this book. Here we will start large areas of color. Do not paint each object perfectly. We leave edges undefined. I describe this to students in this way.... We start the painting like we are looking through a camera that has not focused on the subject. Do not find the edges.... Move colors and strokes around without finding perfect shaped. Think of it as slowly turning the focus ring on your camera, bringing it into focus. This will help develop tremendous depth in your painting. Start soft and undefined. Slowly add more edges to object.

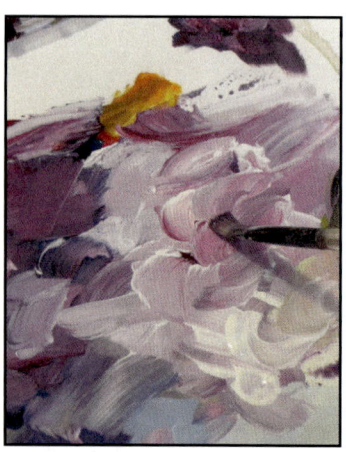

Flow Texture

The secret to a successful painting is paint. We say in the Program.."It is easier to paint with paint!" This is so true. When painting the lessons you need to use a lot of paint and use if fast. One of the greatest painters during the 19th century said that the artist should use paint so thick that is flows together, rather than mixing. This is the technique! Do not mix, let the color "swirl" and flow together, then optical blending will soften the colors when view from a short distance.

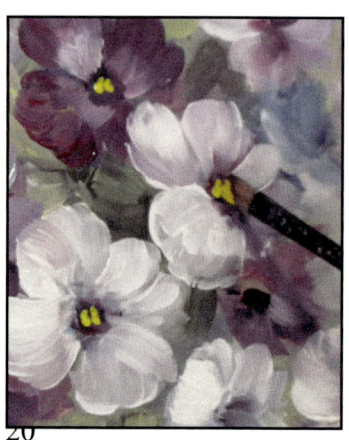

Corner Detailing

For the majority of the lessons in this book, I used the flat brush. With the filbert, we learn to use the edge of the brush, creating the "edging" technique used to draw petals. With the fusion flat brush, we use the corner of the brush to create edges and add the small details. The corner of the flat does not make the details as perfect as a round brush so it is perfect for this look. Pick up thick paint on the corner of the brush, use different pressures of the brush to make different effects. I usually like to mottle the color on the palette, then corner the flat with the mottled color before detailing.

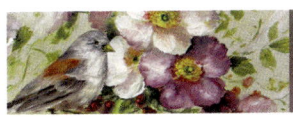
The Colors of Burnt Sienna and Pine Green

Next we need to talk about some various colors and color ideas. I mix for variation of color. This is why I use limited palettes. Below are 2 pigments you can add the Paint It Simply

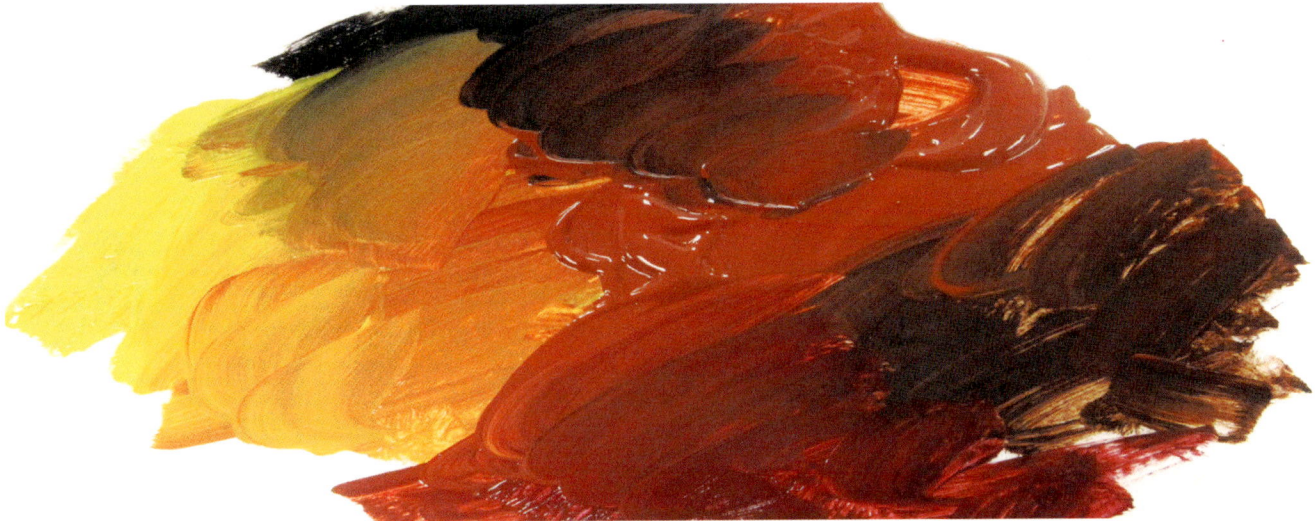

Burnt Sienna is a wonderful pure pigment and is in the earth color category of pigments. It is extremely warm in temperature but can be cold with several methods. It is more like a burnt orange color so if you think of it as a toned orange, you can easily mix it with other colors and obtain the expected results. Mixing Burnt Sienna with Hansa as shown on the left will yield a wide range of toned yellow. You can easily cool those yellow mixes with a tiny touch of black as shown at the top, or a little Red Violet. Add a touch of black to the Burnt Sienna alone will give you beautiful browns and Burnt Umbers. The colors you can make are endless and it is a wonderful color to expand the variation to our palette colors. Add a touch of blue will give beautiful greys when lightened with white.

Pine Green is not a pure color. It is made from several pure pigments so it can still give you beautiful mixing results. Many newer artists have trouble mixing the greens so the addition of Pine Green to your limited palette of painting will make green mixing overall easier. Pine Green is a warm green that can be made brighter with the addition of Hansa Yellow as seen on the left side above. Beautiful yellow greens. Adding a touch of the Phthalo Blue as shown on the top will make bright teal and blue greens. It tones and greys very well with the Burnt Sienna to make brown greens and well as the Red Violet which will make the color cooler as well. Dark greens can be made easily with a small addition of black. Very beautiful benchmark green for your limited palette.

Color Theory and Song Bird Color Mixing Techniques

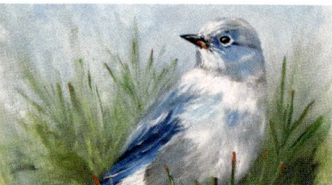

Greens- Leaves, Scrolls

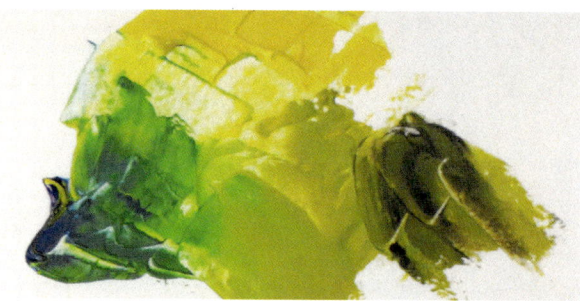

Hansa Yellow will make a wide variety of greens. On the left you can see Hansa mixed with Phthalo Blue on the right tiny touch of Carbon Black. Combine both for more greens!

Blues- Flowers, Leaves, Scrolls

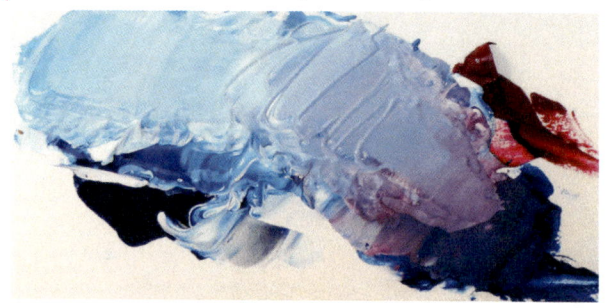

Phthalo Blue on the palette is a dark blue which leans to the green side. If you add a tiny touch of Red Violet, then lighten with white, you will make a wide variety of blues and blue violets.

Yellows- Flowers, Leaves, Scrolls

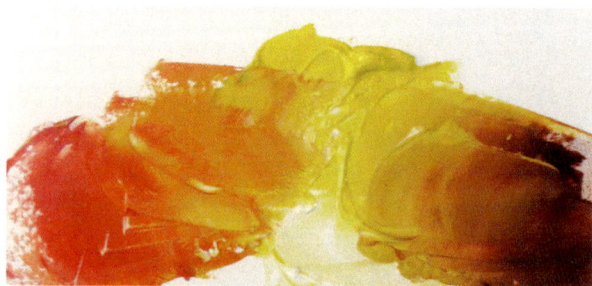

Hansa is a bright yellow. I like to use it softer. Add some browns (shown below) and touches of Red Violet and red add more variety. White lightens and opaque the yellow.

Oranges- Flowers, Leaves

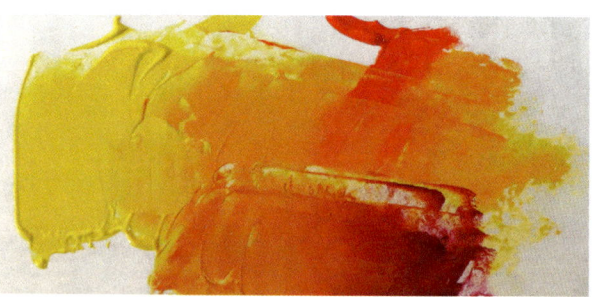

Hansa can also be used as a base for a wide variety of oranges. Tiny touches of Naphthol Red Light make warm oranges while touches of Red Violet make cooler oranges.

Reds- Flowers, Leaves

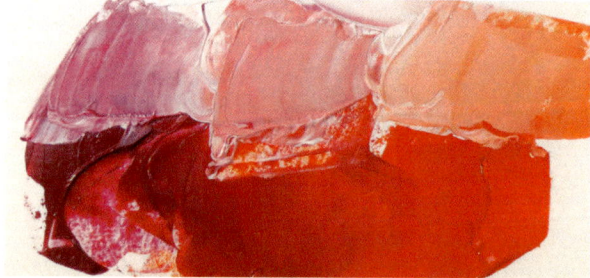

Naphthol Red Light is a warm red orange. Red Violet is a cool Red Violet. Mix together to make a wide range of reds and lighten with white to make soft pinks.

Browns- Flowers, Leaves

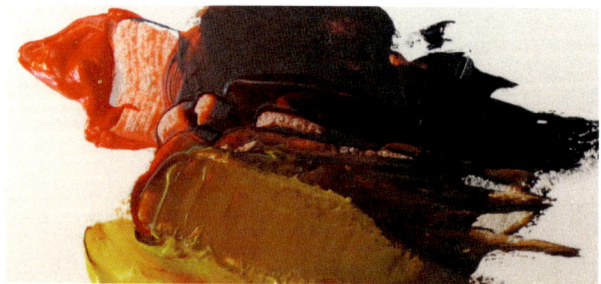

Base Brown is 2 parts Naphthol Red Light and 1 part Carbon Black. I vary this color in many brush mixes with additions of Hansa Yellow which lightens and make more sienna colors.

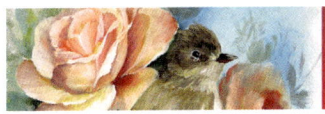

Temperature of Your Colors

Temperature is one of the most important principles in our Paint It Simply program, but also the hardest concept to "see" and understand. To make this concept easier to understand, we selected very limited colors, each one chosen with temperature in mind. You can easily paint temperature, without "seeing" it if you follow these principles. Lets take a look at temperature.

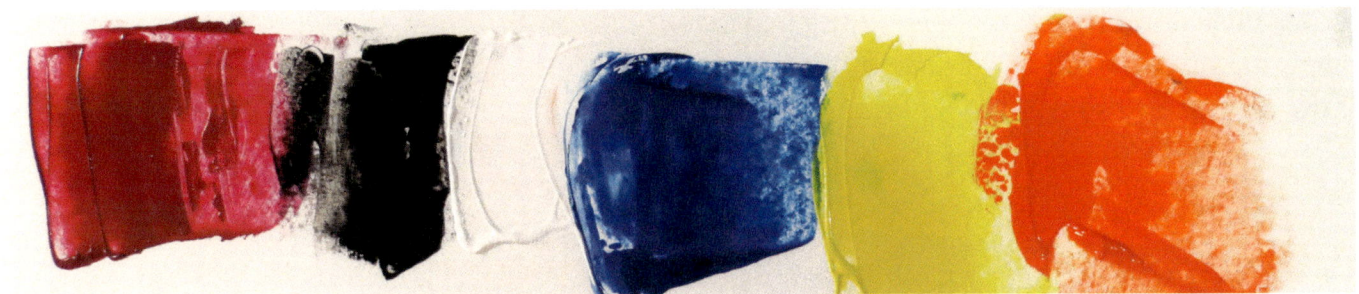

| **Cool Color** | | **Neutral Temperature** | | **Warm Temperature** |

Red Violet   Carbon Black   Titanium White   Phthalo Blue   Hansa Yellow   Naphthol Red Light

Red Violet is the coolest color in this palette. Many think that blacks are the coolest. This is not true. Some blacks are even warm. Our Carbon Black is considered a neutral leaning cool. White is a Neutral. Many also think that Phthalo Blue is cool. This is not true. Ultramarine Blue and Phthalo Blue are warm colors. There is not a manufacturer today of a cool Ultramarine Blue. Blues however will look cool when you use them in association with warmer colors. For example, look above. Then Phthalo Blue is slightly warm of neutral, however, according to the scale it is cooler than the Naphthol Red Light. So, if both are used in a painting, the Phthalo Blue will look cool and the Naphthol Red Light will look warm. The human eye is constantly balancing colors. You may see the blue as cool in a painting, but it only appears that way based on the colors that surround. it. Trust the scale above, and you can paint temperature in any Paint It Simply lesson.

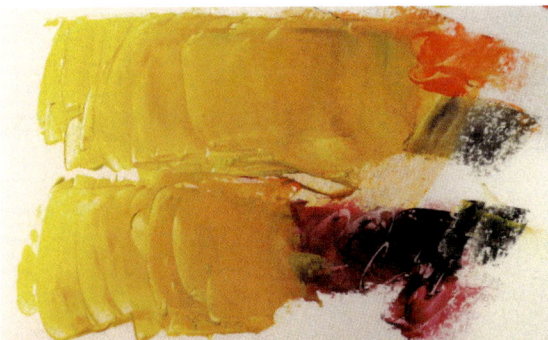

Here the top is mixed with Naphthol Red Light and tiny touch of Carbon Black. What happens to the Yellow? The red will warm, but the black will cool. If you increase the black, the color becomes greener and cooler. If you increase the red, the color become more orange and warmer.

The second mix shows Red Violet and Carbon Black. Here you will always make the color cooler since both colors are cool. So both colors cool slightly moving from left to right. There are many ways to cool a color.

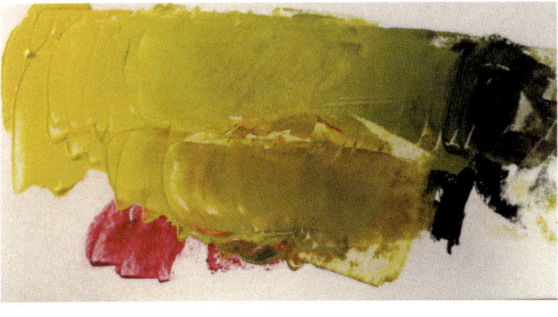

The last shows Hansa Yellow and Black making some greens. The green cools from left to right because Black is cooler than Hansa. Adding Red Violet cools the color even further.

Tonal Qualities of Color

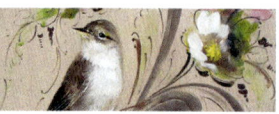

Color tone refers to the mixing of a neutral color with a pure color. For example, if I take Hansa Yellow which is a bright, slightly warm yellow and add a touch of light grey, I have made a tone of Hansa or a tonal color of Yellow. This is a broad definition of the term.

More precisely, in this book we will not use the grey tonal values of color. We will not mix black and white to make grey and then add that to a pure color. To make the tones in this book, I use complimentary colors, which also make greys, but they are greys that have more life and better harmony with the other colors in the palette. Lets look at some examples and how we can add some "tonal harmony" to our colors.

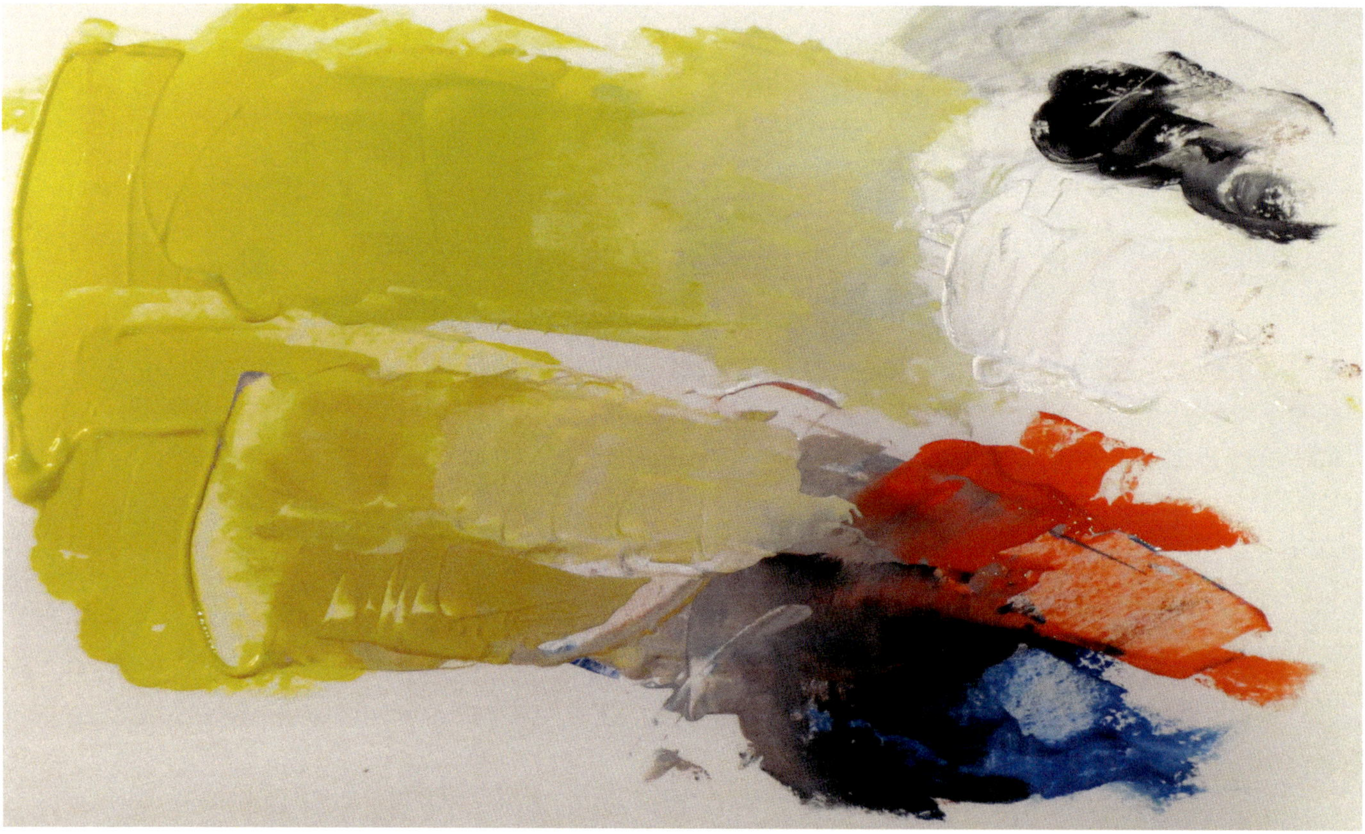

Here I have mixed Hansa Yellow with the tonal range of white and black. This is the broad definition of tonal color-making a yellow tone which is a softer, less dramatic tone of the Hansa Yellow. We would say this is a Tone of Yellow.

The second example uses Phthalo Blue and Naphthol Red Light with Titanium White. This makes what we call a "tertiary color. Tertiary means 3. The three primary colors are red, yellow, and blue. When these 3 colors are combined in any variation, they make a "tone" of a color because they make a "tertiary"grey. Add white to lighten the color to the value of Hansa, thus making a grey tone or tonal yellow.

In the lessons, when I want to mix a tonal variation of a color I use the "tertiary" tone. For example, to make a tonal variation of red, I will add greens. Greens are blue and yellow, thus red, yellow and blue. Making tonal colors is easy in these lessons, just combined everything to make a tonal color!!!

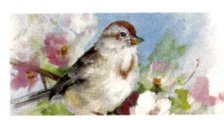 ## *Adjusting Brightness or Intensity*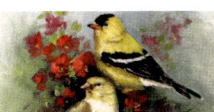

Brightness or Intensity in a color is also referred to as Saturation. There is a scale for this brightness that is used by many companies to establish a language of color. For Paint It Simply, we just need to understand a few principles. Lets take a look at some color……

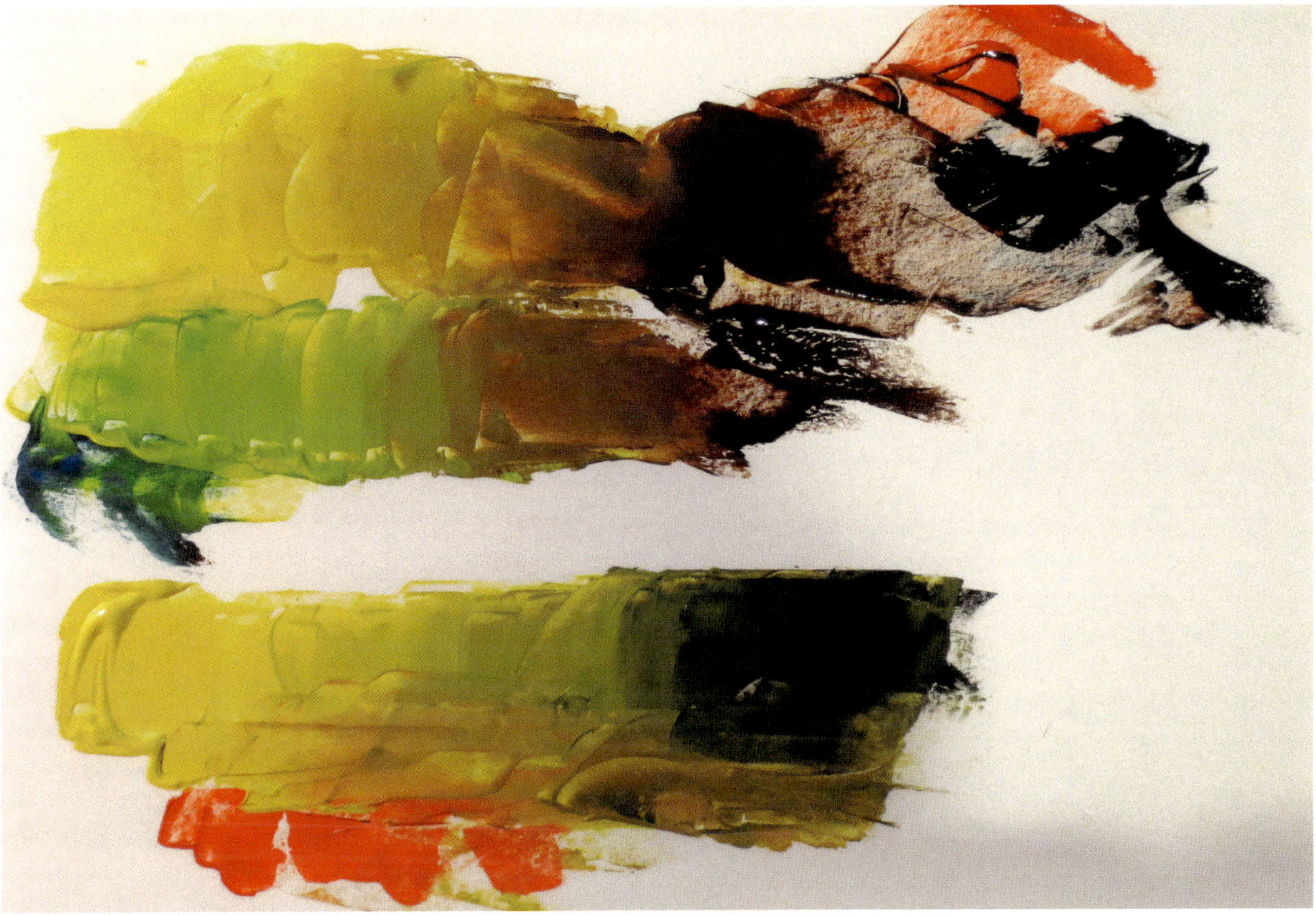

Here we have several mixes with Hansa Yellow. We know from the tonal lesson that we can use any tertiary color or grey to tone a color. Any tertiary will work. In painting, I like to create harmony. Harmony is when all the colors go together. This is easy to achieve when you use a limited palette. To adjust the brightness of a color we need to tone it and if you use a common color we will add harmony.

In the example above I used brown (2 parts red to 1 part black). The top line you can see Hansa Yellow mixed with brown. This reduces the intensity or saturation of the yellow as it moves to the right. Under that, I made a green with Hansa and tiny touch Phthalo Blue. Again, the intensity reduces as it moves to the right. Both colors have wonderful harmony because I am toning with the same color so they "go" together.

If you follow the "grey" method of toning where the greys and blacks are added to colors to lower the intensity, you can see that the yellow turns green. Adding small touches of red, will bring the yellow back to a lower intensity yellow. Blacks are wonderful to tone with and do add wonderful harmony. However, sometimes, they change the "hue" or color, as in this case, yellow becomes green. Using tertiary colors can lower intensity while keeping the colors from changing hue.

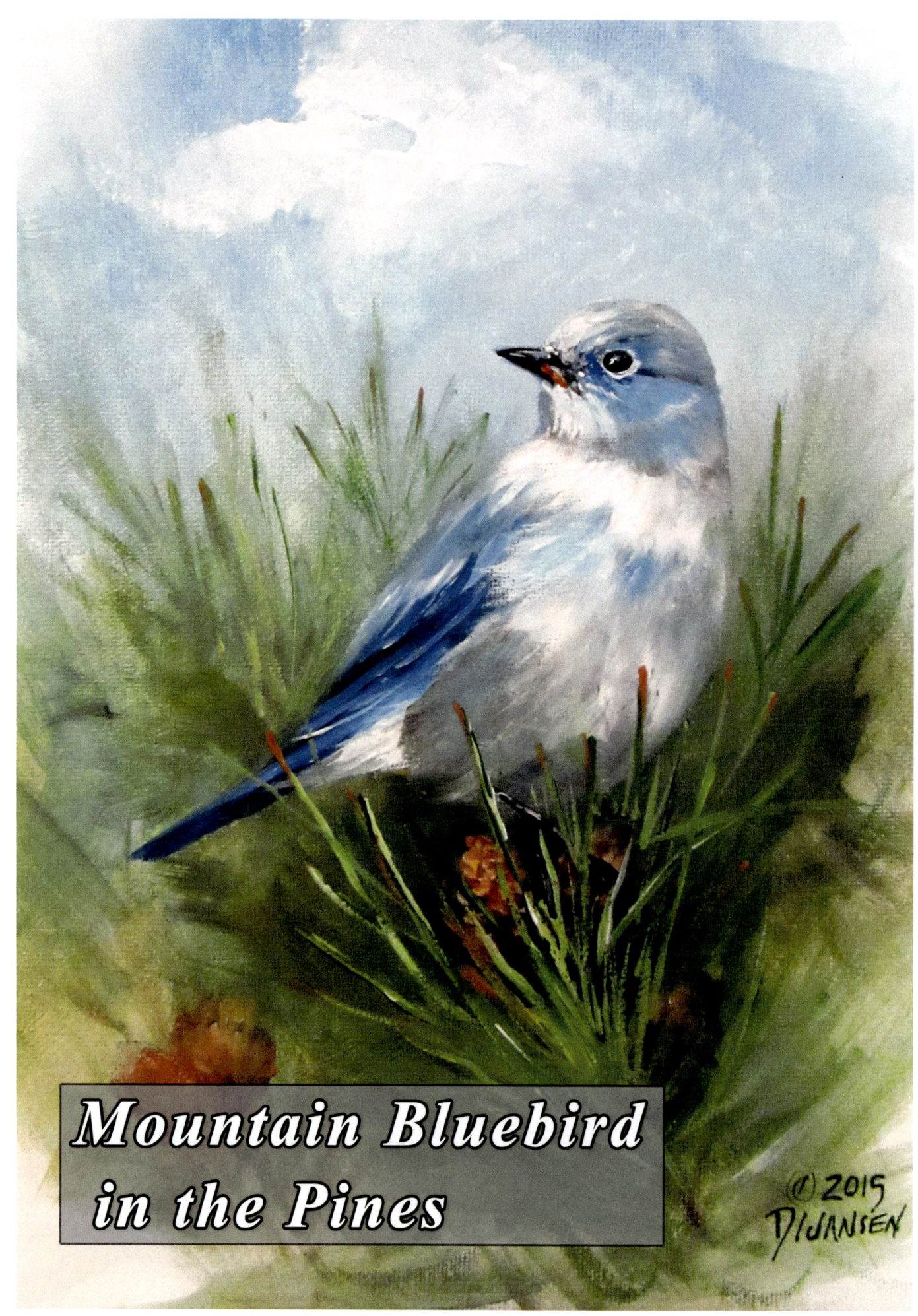

Mountain Bluebird in the Pines

Welcome to our first lesson. This is a wonderful lesson because we will use the soft colors of the mountain bluebird to teach us how to vary the look of the feathers. When I first started painting birds, I looked at them as a folk artist. I used strokes to set all the areas and create the details. Now, years later, I have slowly developed several techniques that I like to vary on birds.

The bird needs to be part of the composition. You need to paint him so that he is the center of interest and then decorate the supporting areas. Each painting in the book will present you with a ever increasing design complexity. The most complex are saved for the last where you must paint the male and female of each species. It can be challenging to flow the design and paint complexity together.

As we have stated earlier in the book, feathers can be made with a variety of brushes. Learning the different looks and where to apply them is essential to interest and uniformity. Remember your feathering lessons. Feathers on the top of the head are smaller. The feathers follow the shapes of the bird anatomy. The most important area is the head and the small feathers around the beak. This is the center of interest and where the viewers eye is drawn to first.
Pine needles are dangerous in that they have a lot of line movement. We need to establish and then soften them based on the details of your bird. Remember the face of the bird is the focal area or center of interest so other areas are presented with less detail. Wings are also areas that should be rendered with lots of thought. The primary flight feathers should suggest length, however, they should not lead the viewers eye for too long. Breaking the longer strokes with some mottled color is essential to keep the interest in the facial area of the bird. Follow the steps closely, soften constantly with your finger when you are painting outside the facial area. Remember, feathers are suggestions of movement. They all do not need to be exact.
Let's give it a try!

Paint It Simply Palette
Base Color- Medium White from Mixes

Palette Colors

Naphthol Red Light	Hansa Yellow
Red Violet	Titanium White
Carbon Black	Medium White
Phthalo Blue	Burnt Sienna
	Pine Green

Wood Surface
Super MDF Wood Panel about 11 Inch X 14 Inch to fit picture frame. Can also use canvas panel.

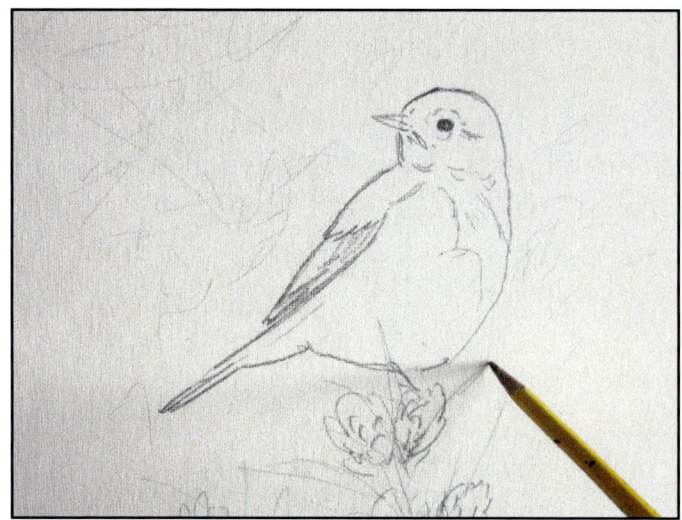

Step 1 Base board white and then transfer or sketch on the design with dark lines.

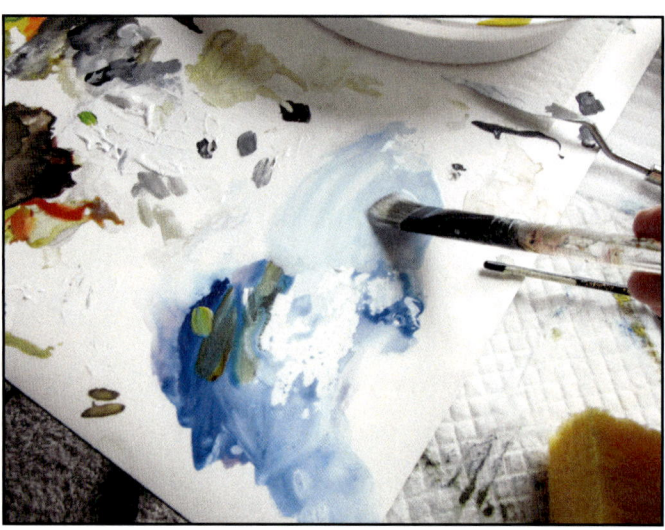

Step 2 Mottle the 3/4 inch flat brush with Phthalo Blue and lighten with some white.

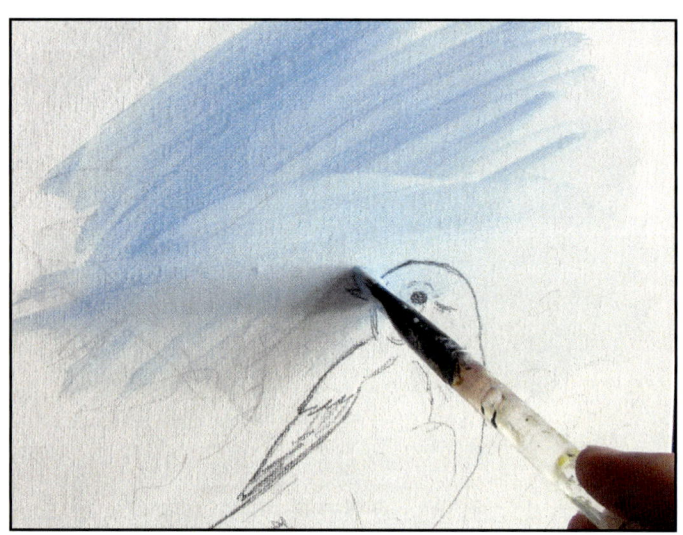

Step 3 Thin with Extender Medium and go over the top of the canvas. Go through the bird with transparent color.

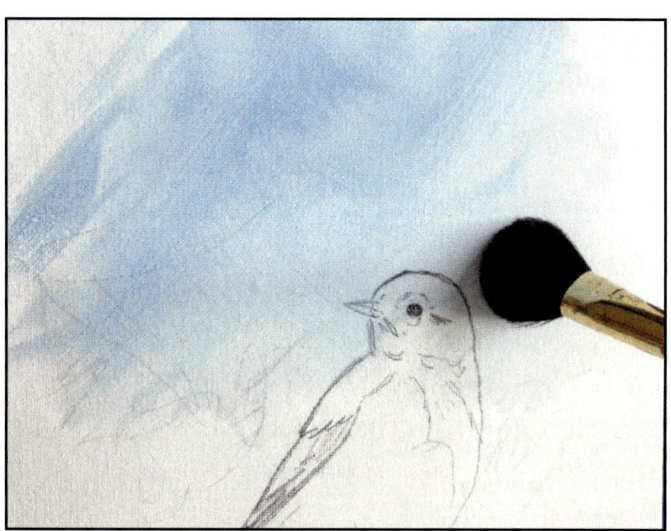

Step 4 You can use a mop brush to soften or use the 3/4 inch fusion. I don't use a mop very often, but it does soften really easy.

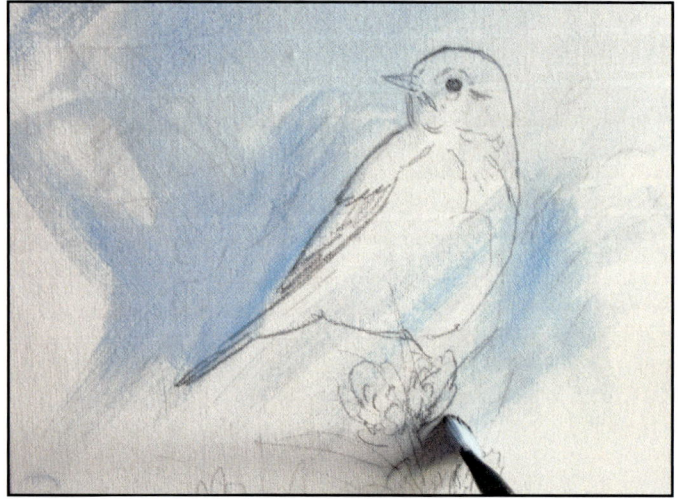

Step 5 Add more light blue around the bird and down his sides, softening color.

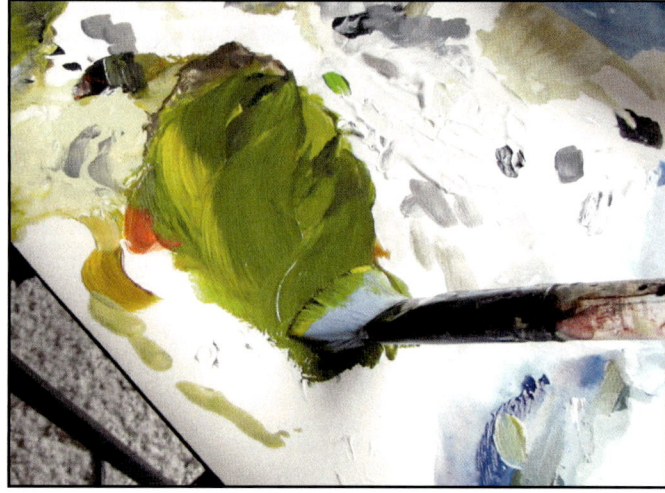

Step 6 Mottle a green with the blue in the brush and Hansa Yellow with touch black.

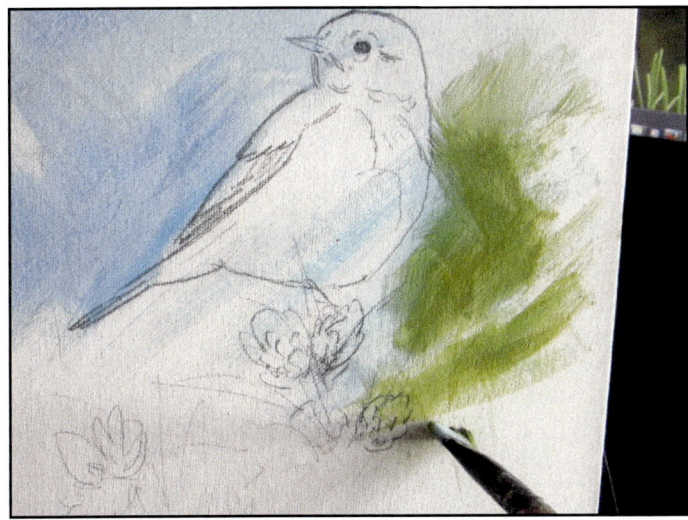

Step 7 Using the same flat, add this to the side of the bird and mottle the color for interest. Reload and continue to add green.

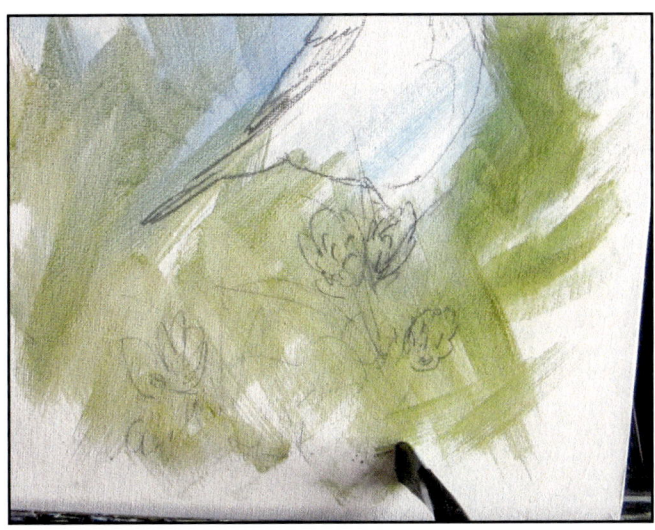

Step 8 Use the chisel of the brush to add some steaks of color on both sides of the bird. Let the sides soften to white background.

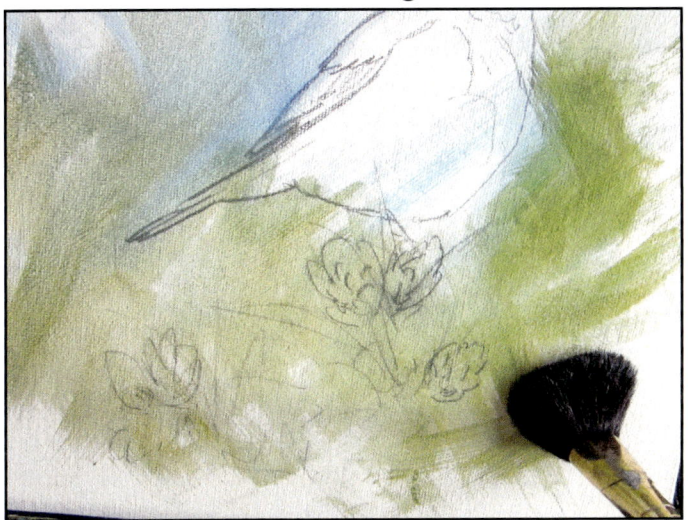

Step 9 You can soften the green color on the side with the mop.

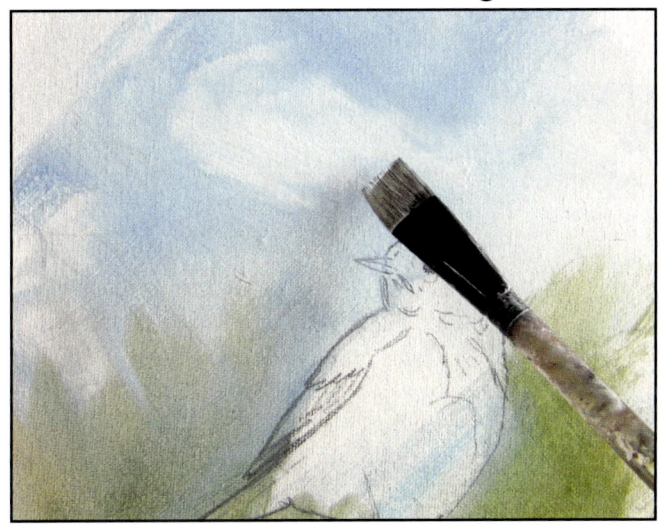

Step 10 Mottle the larger flat with some white and then add the suggestion of a cloud above the bird.

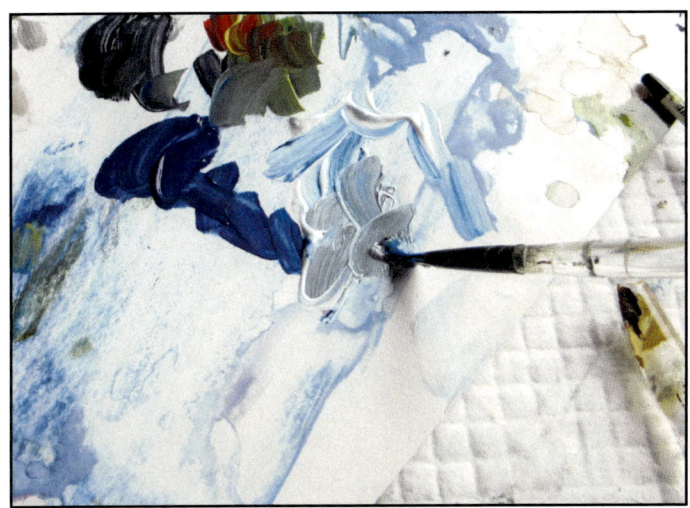

Step 11 Add a touch of black to the blue and white to make a lighter soft grey color.

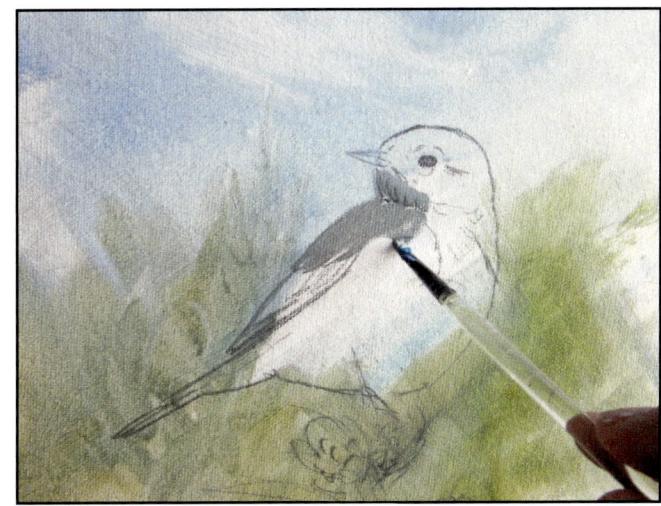

Step 12 Using a small flat, begin to base in the body of the bird near top of wing.

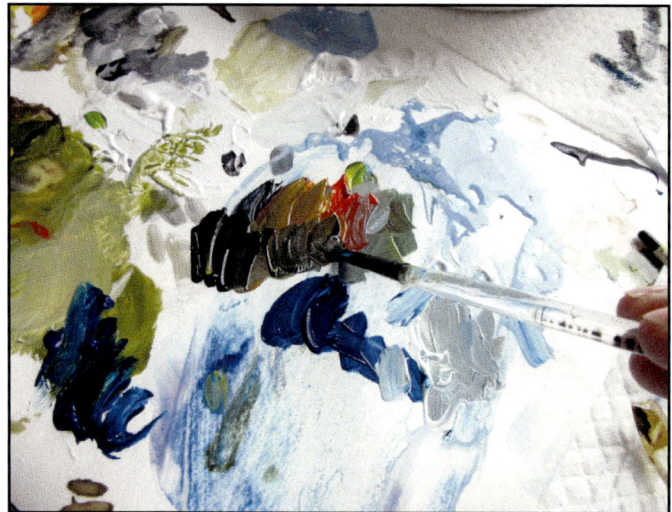

Step 13 We will vary the greys of the bird with reds, yellows, greens and blues. Start grey with black & white then vary with colors.

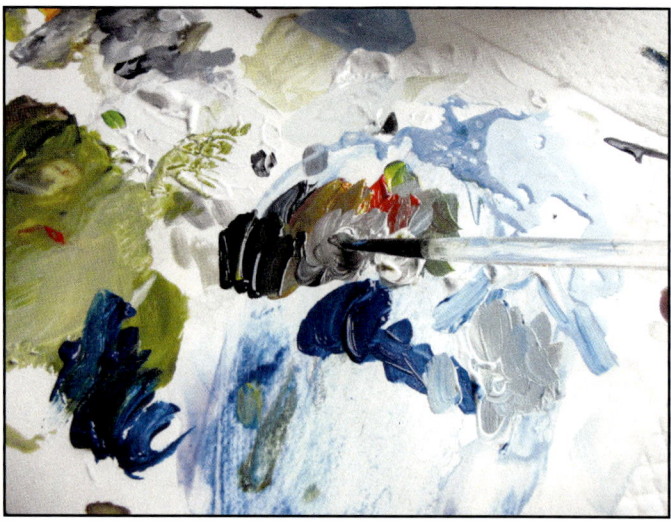

Step 14 Lighten the grey with the smaller flat. Vary with some Nap. Red Light which will warm color slightly.

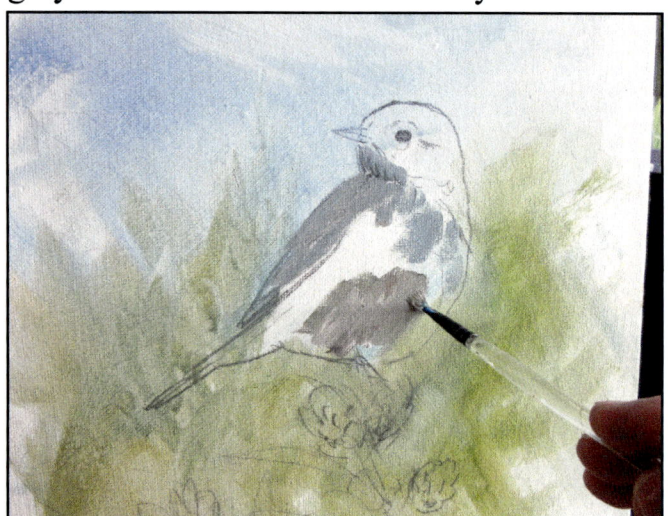

Step 15 Add this with short choppy strokes to the bottom of the breast of the bluebird.

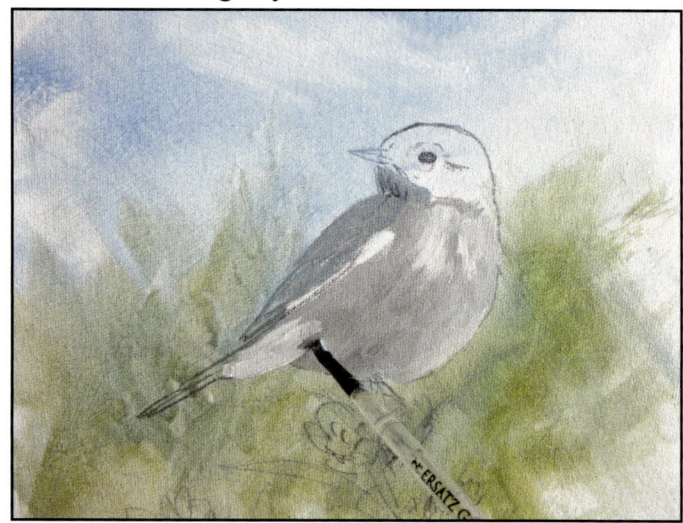

Step 16 Lighten the grey with more white and warm with touch of Hansa. Begin top of breast and bottom of tail with light grey.

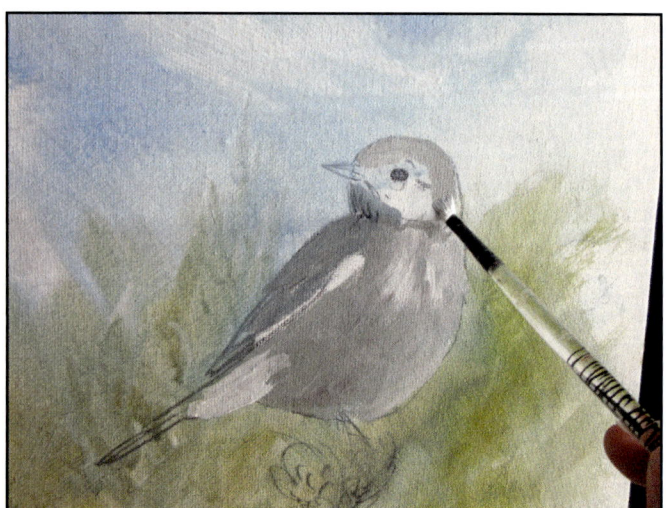

Step 17 Lighten with more white and add some light grey to the head.

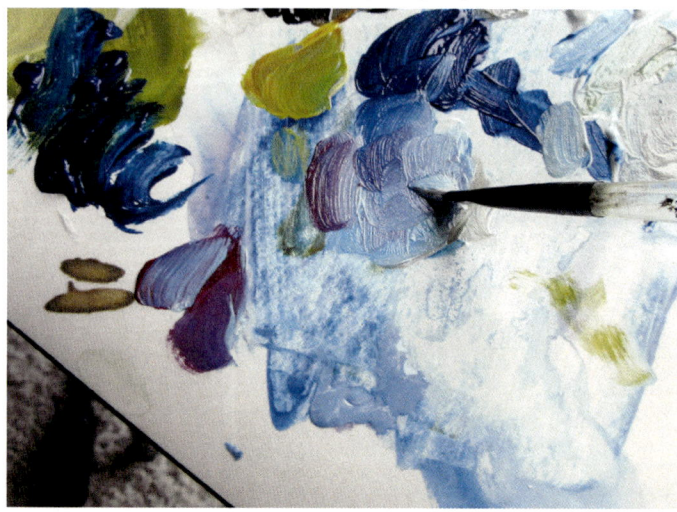

Step 18 Mottle the blues with blue and white, vary the blues with touches of Red Violet.

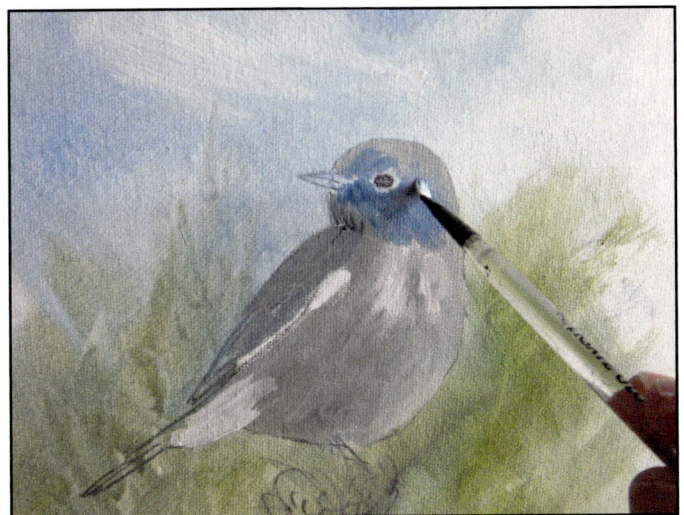

Step 19 Add some light blue, touch Red Violet to center of the bird with small flat. Use short choppy strokes. Pull light blue down breast.

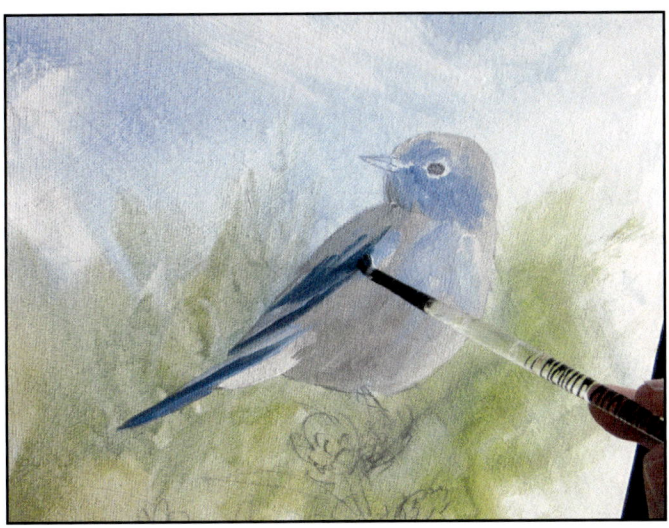

Step 20 Darken the color with more blue and touch Red Violet and add the strokes for the wing flight feathers. (Primary, secondary)

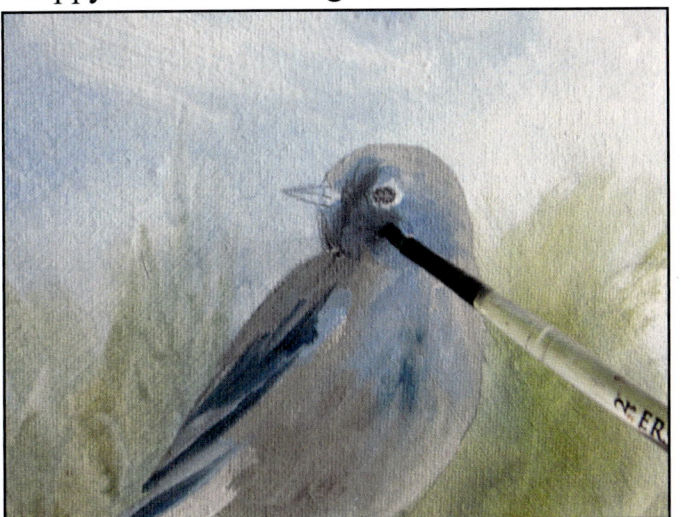

Step 21 Using a smaller flat, add darker grey around the eye and between the eye & beak. This will contrast the light small feathers.

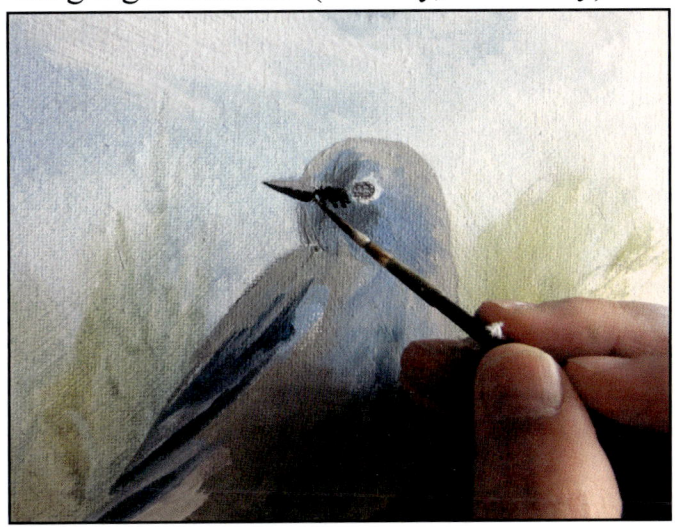

Step 22 Using favorite liner, add the dark black lower beak and then grey upper beak. Carry color toward the eye.

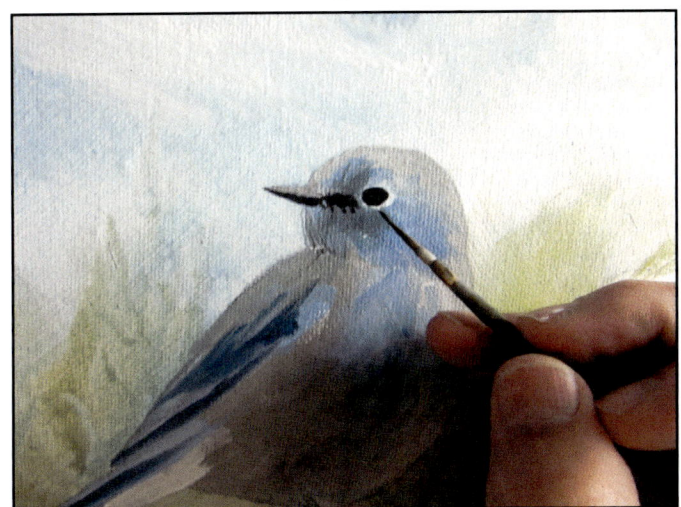

Step 23 Add the eye with the black and then the white eye ring.

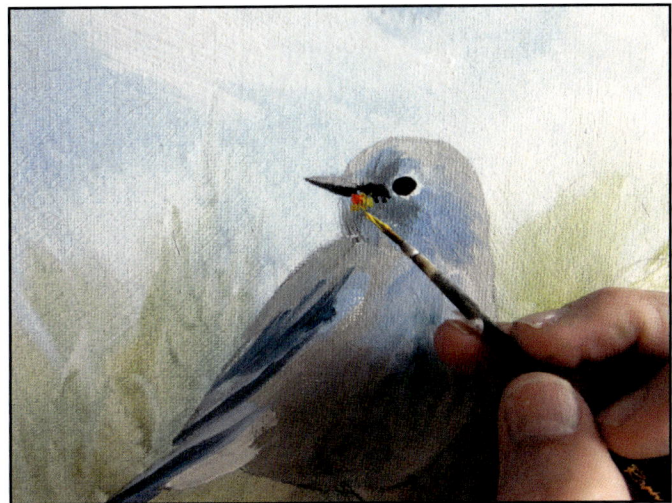

Step 24 Add some small touches of Nap. Red Light and Hansa to the beak area.

31

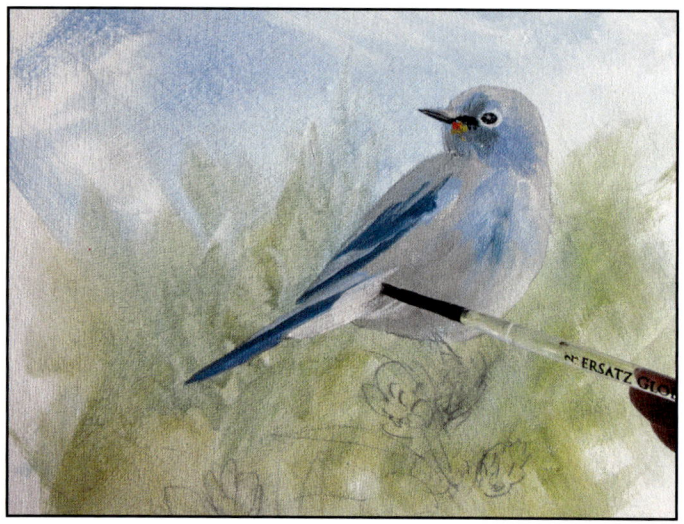

Step 25 Add some medium blue to the body and breast, then add more white to the tail area. We slowly develop colors.

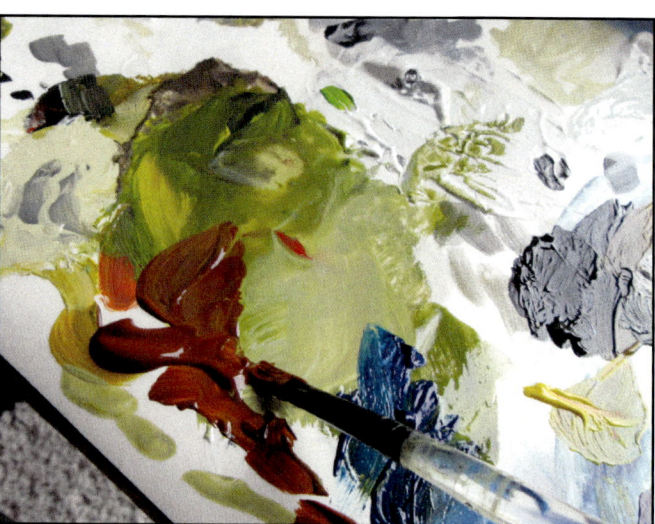

Step 26 Mottle Burnt Sienna with some greens and blues. Use medium size flat.

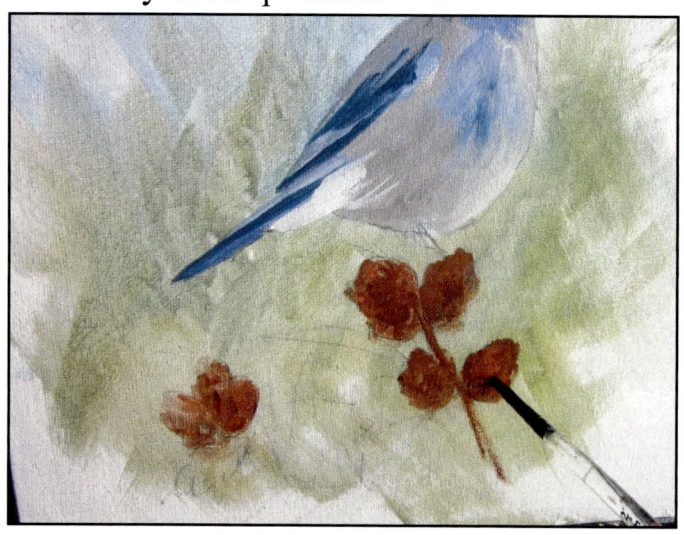

Step 27 Begin basic shapes of the pine cones and use the chisel to begin the suggestion for the stems.

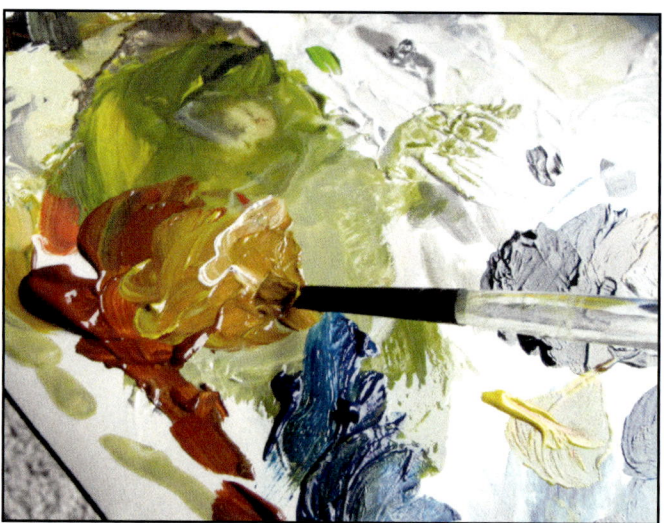

Step 28 Mottle the Burnt Sienna with some Hansa and then white to make a lighter toned yellow. Do not over mix the color.

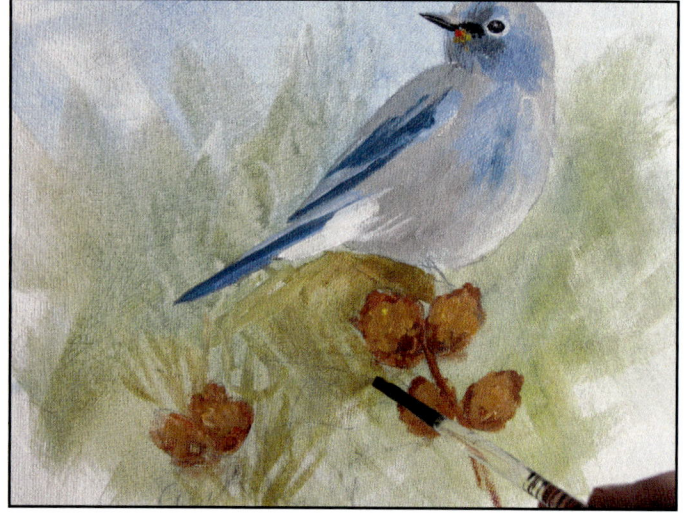

Step 29   Add the yellows to the pine cones and then add some into the green areas.

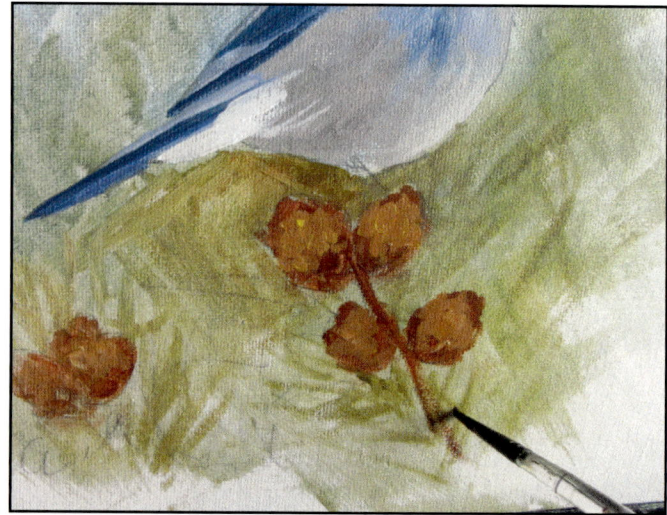

Step 30 Mottle with more greens and then use the chisel of the brush to make pine needles.

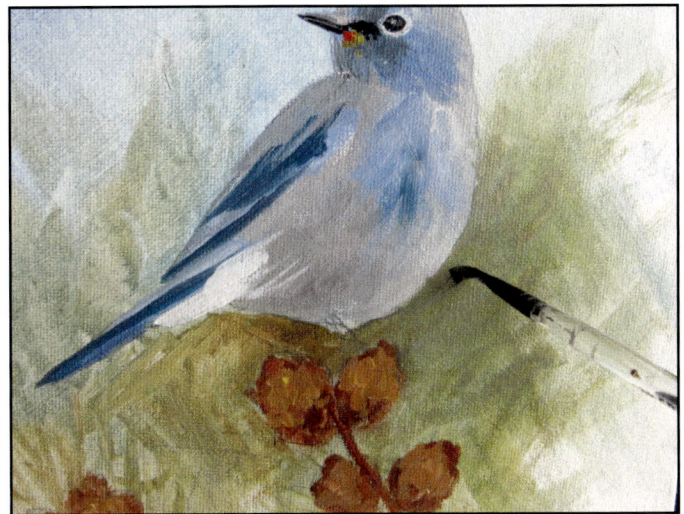

Step 31 Add some softer yellow greens around the bird. This builds the background color more opaque and pushes bird forward.

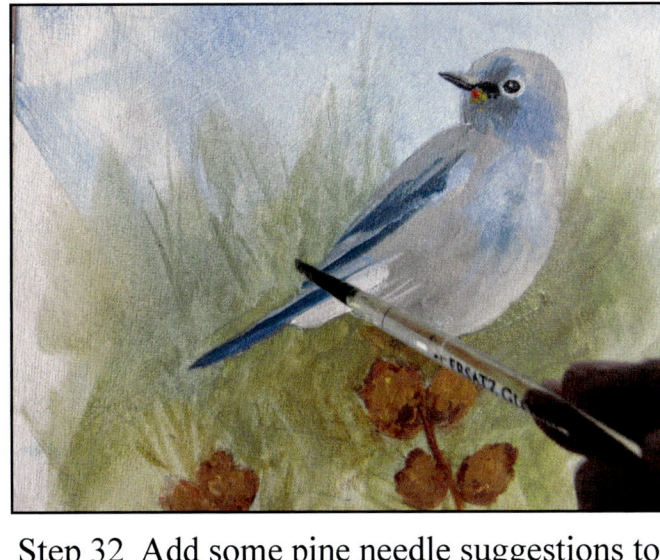

Step 32 Add some pine needle suggestions to the areas behind the bird. Keep soft.

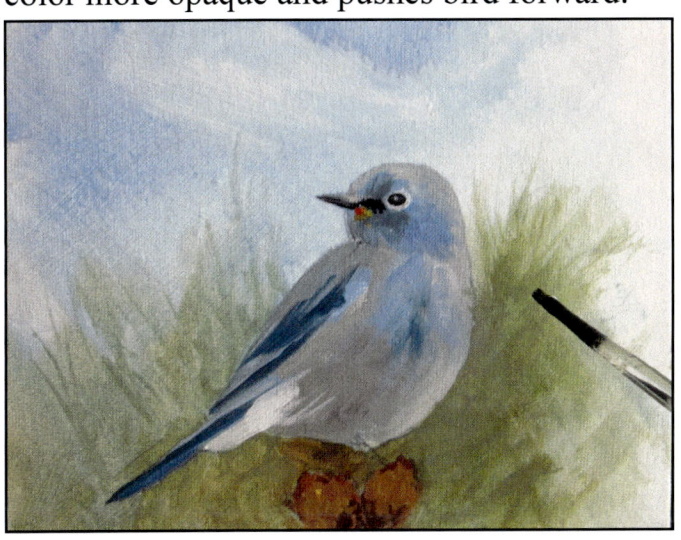

Step 33 Chisel some up and into the sky varying the greens slightly for interest.

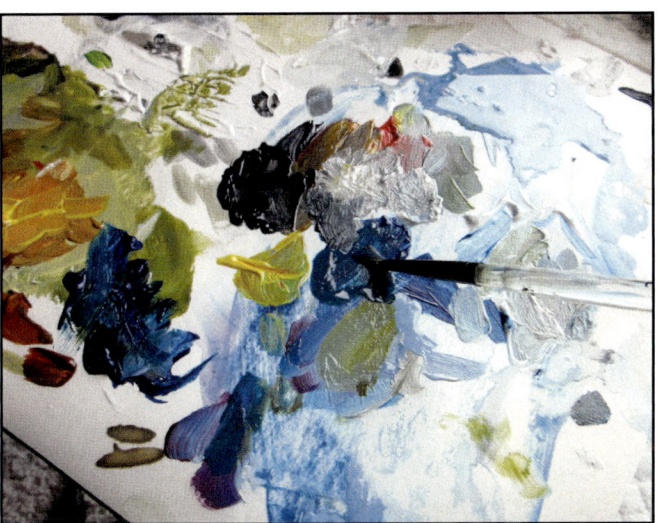

Step 34 Mottle the brush back into the blues. Make a medium blue from the Phthalo, greys and touch white.

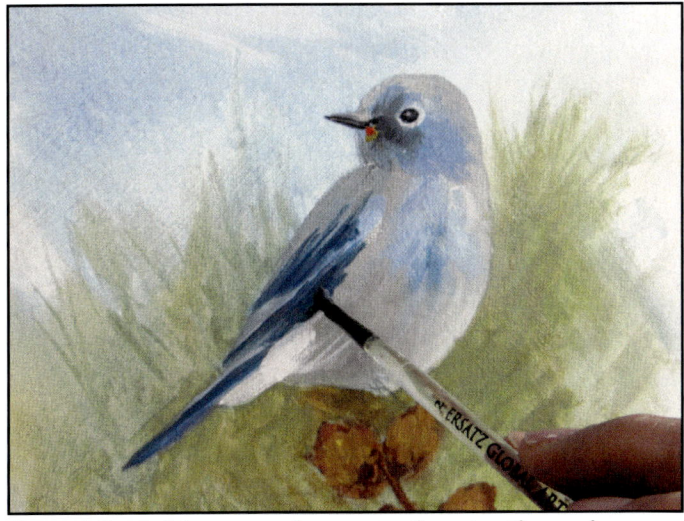

Step 35 Add some short strokes to the primary and secondary feathers.

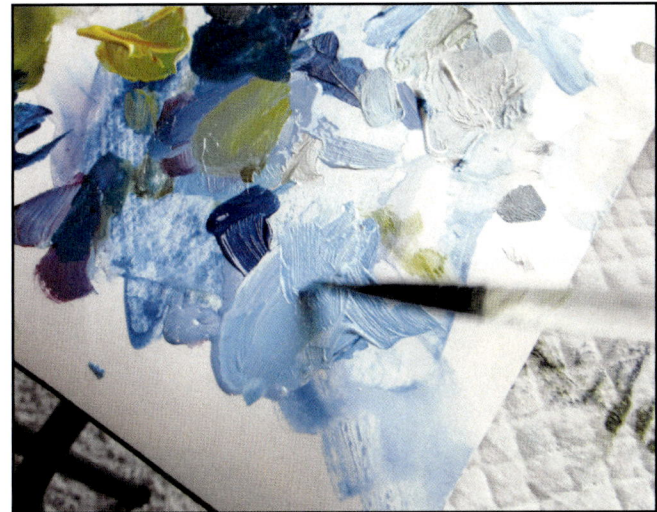

Step 36 Mottle the color a little lighter with more white and tiny touch greens.

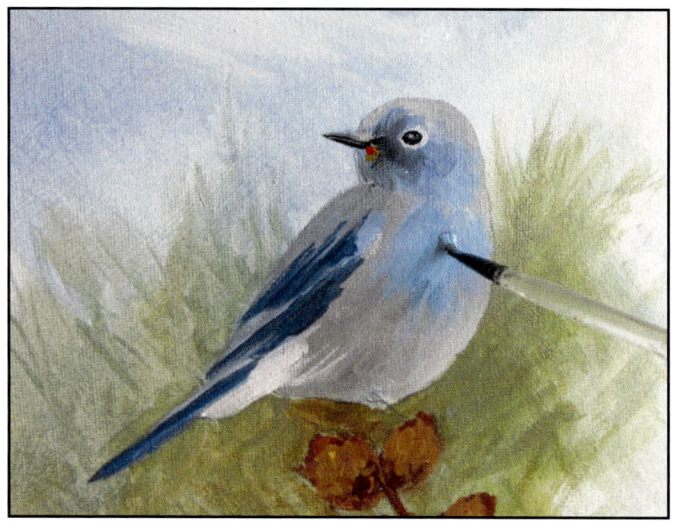

Step 37 Using short, shape following strokes, add this to the breast area. Remember that strokes down the breast are larger.

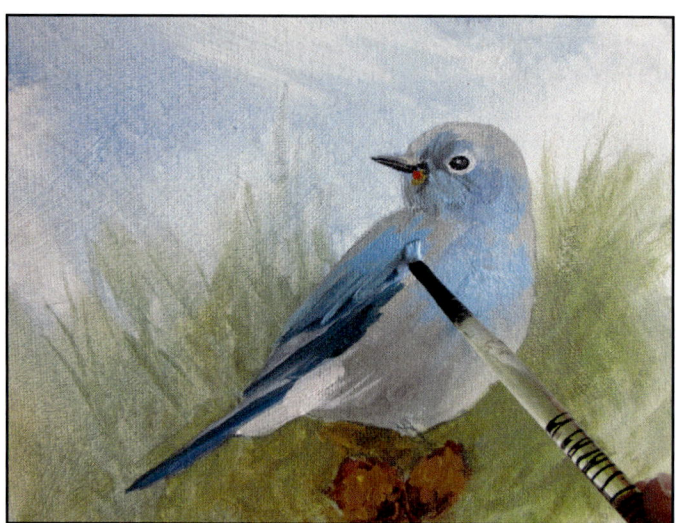

Step 38 Add the shorter covert strokes to the top of the wing with the light blue.

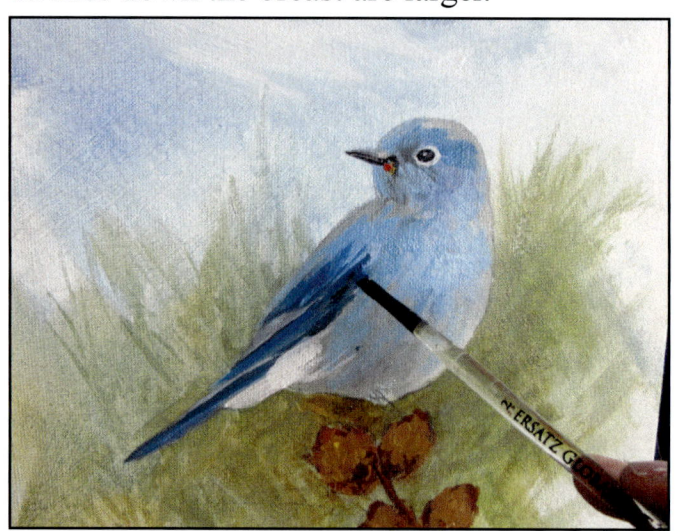

Step 39 Mottle the blue a little darker and add some half tones strokes to the primary and secondary feathers of the wing.

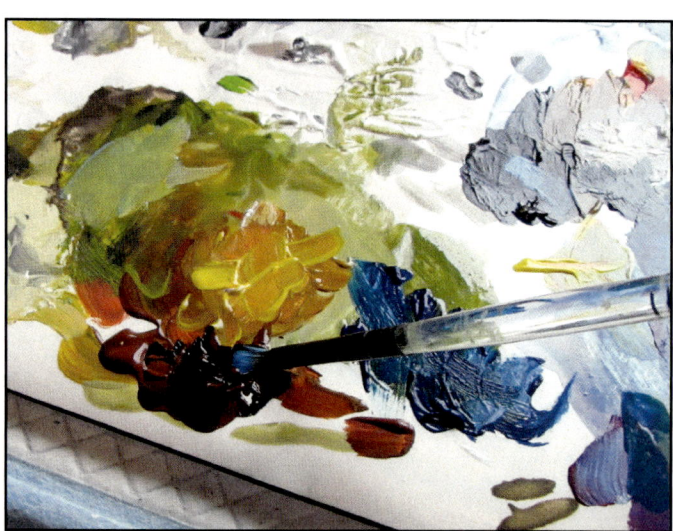

Step 40 Begin the pine cones with Burnt Sienna mottle with reds and black to make various browns. Notice blue still on the brush.

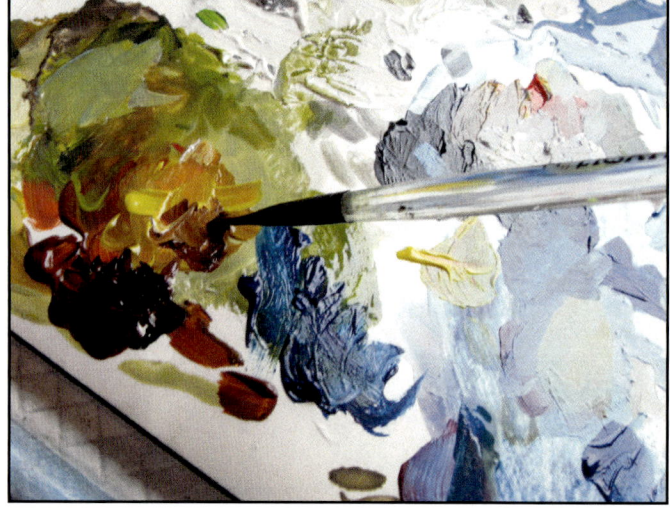

Step 41 Off to one side mottle the color lighter with some Hansa and white. Work into greens.

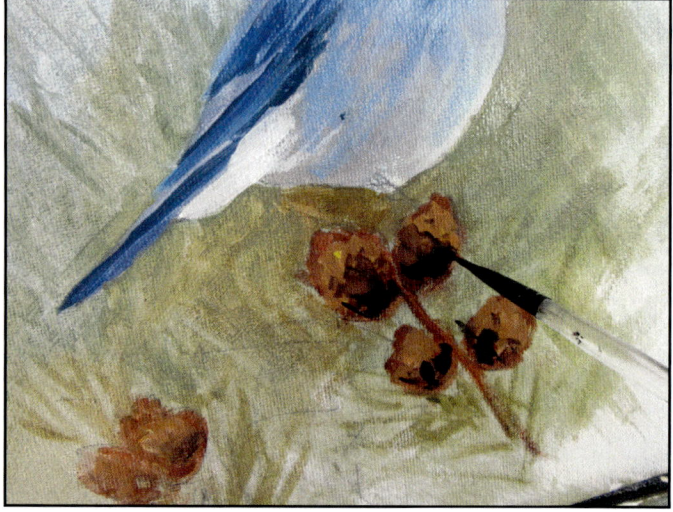

Step 42 Begin shapes with darker browns on the bottom and lighter yellows on top.

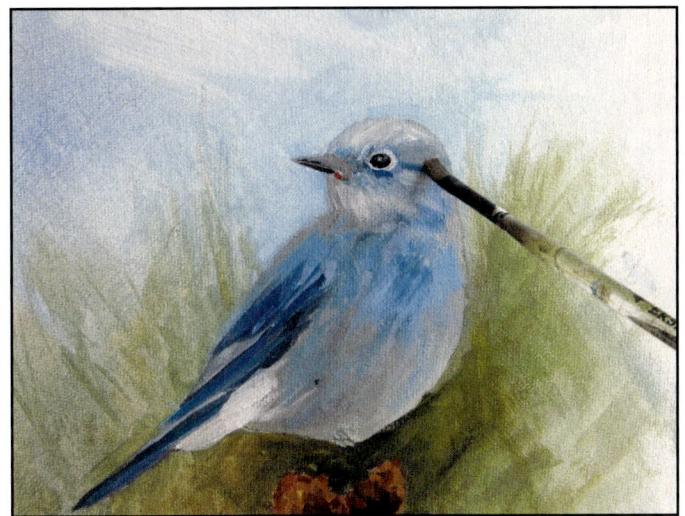

Step 43 Mottle the head with more grey colors in through the center, behind the eye area.

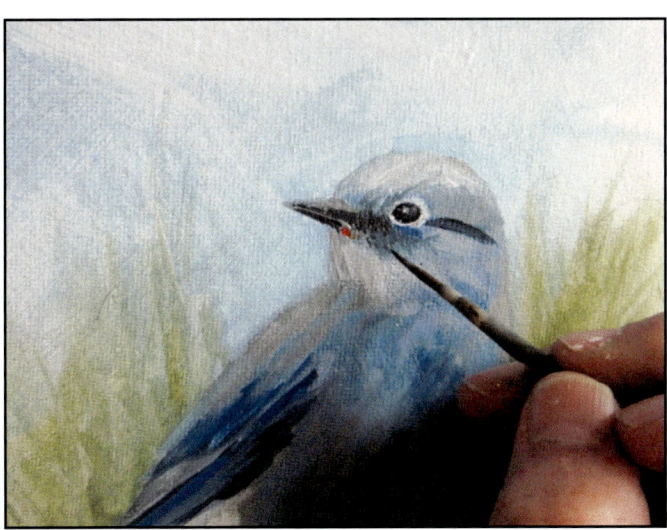

Step 44 Using a small detail brush add the smaller darker feathers around the beak. This will contrast the light in the next step.

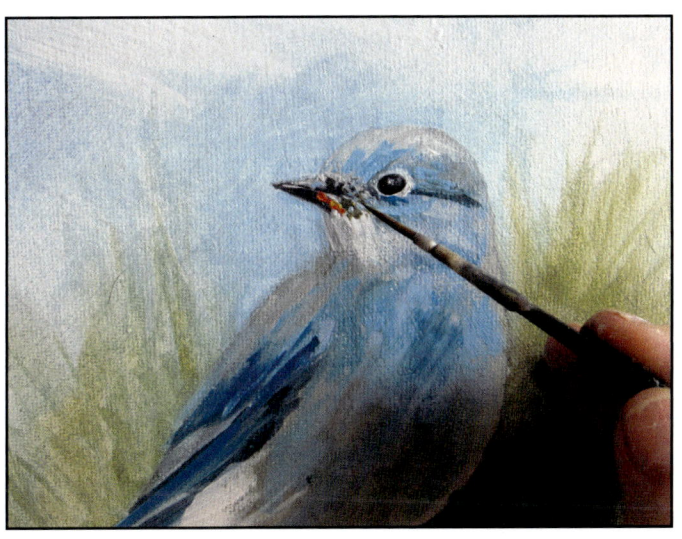

Step 45 Lighten the color with blues and whites and add some smaller touches to the feathers around the beak.

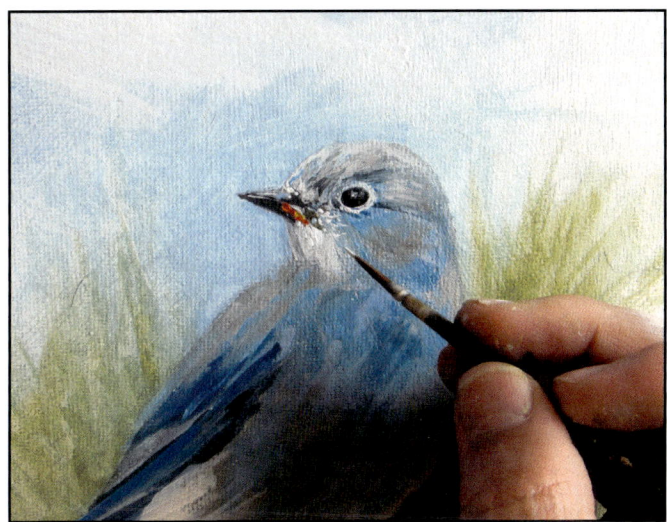

Step 46 Lighten the color with more white and add some very small touches around the beak. Work some around the head. Shape following.

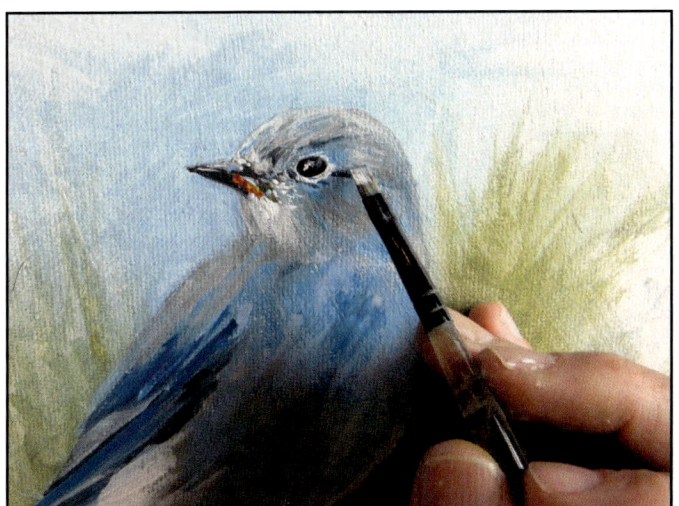

Step 47 Restate some of the blues and white around the eye. I use a larger brush for difference.

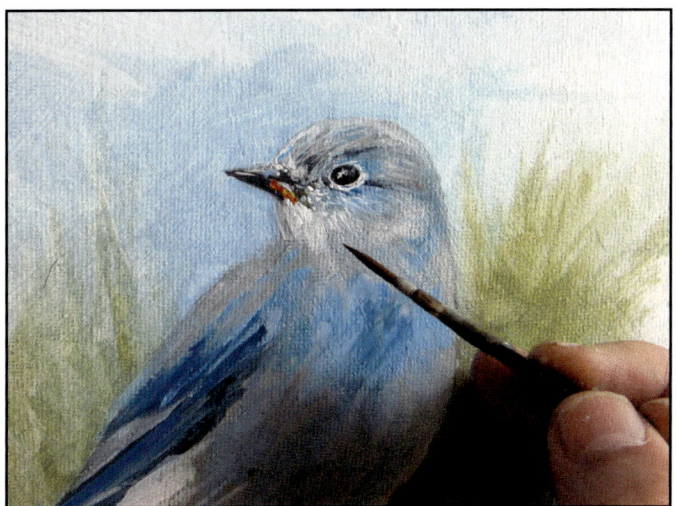

Step 48 Pull some additional lighter feathers down the neck area for details.

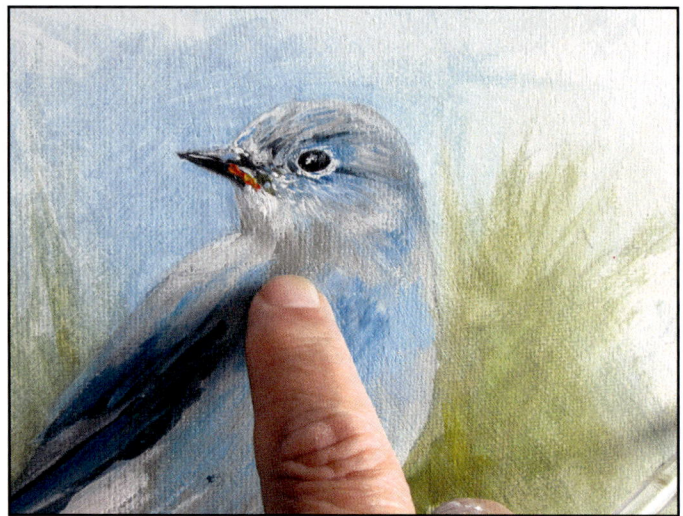

Step 49   Many times I use my finger to soften the strokes of the feathers. Try not to blend, that will destroy the movement.

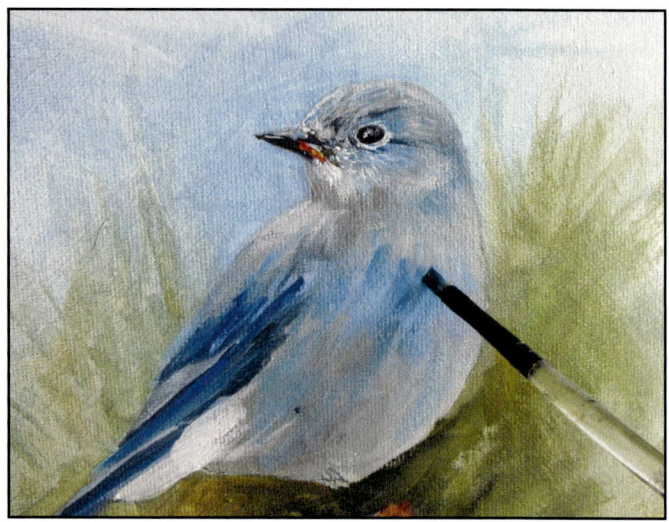

Step 50 Mottle the small flat with more medium blue and then continue to add the breast feathers and soften with your finger.

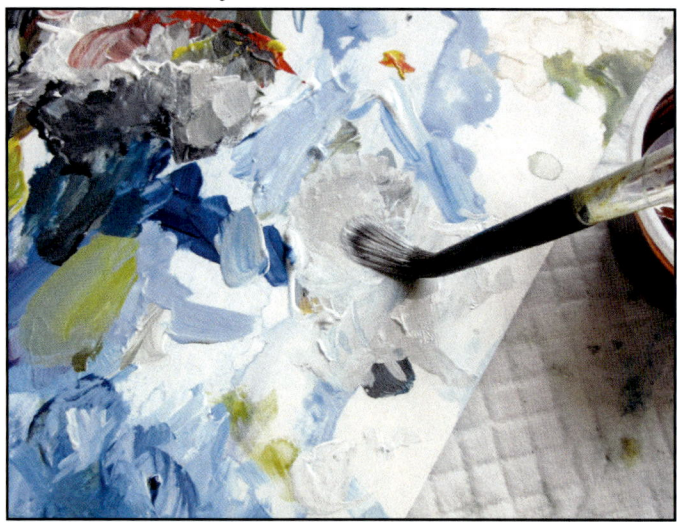

Step 51 Mottle a little larger filbert or flat with some grey color from the palette. White with touch black and blue.

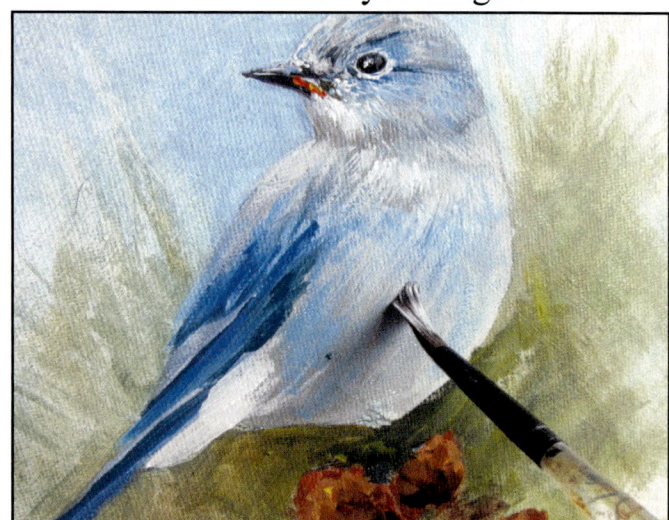

Step 52 Add some feather strokes to the breast area. Remember as you go down the feathers are larger.

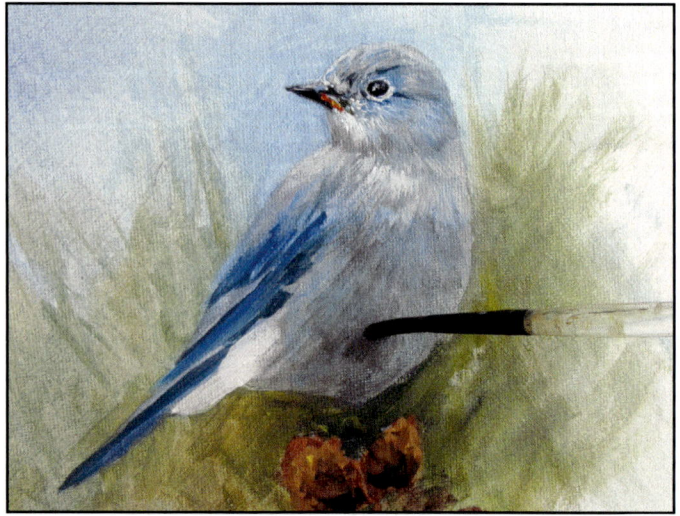

Step 53   Change to smaller brush and add some darker greys to reduce the breast feathers.

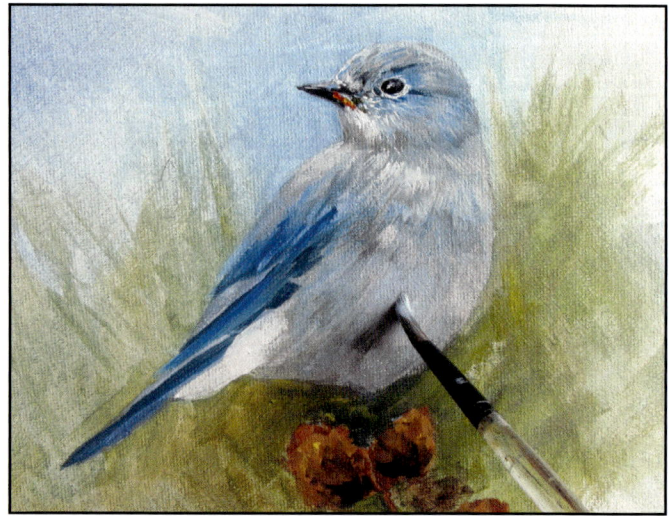

Step 54 Lighten the color with more white and blue and add some smaller lights.

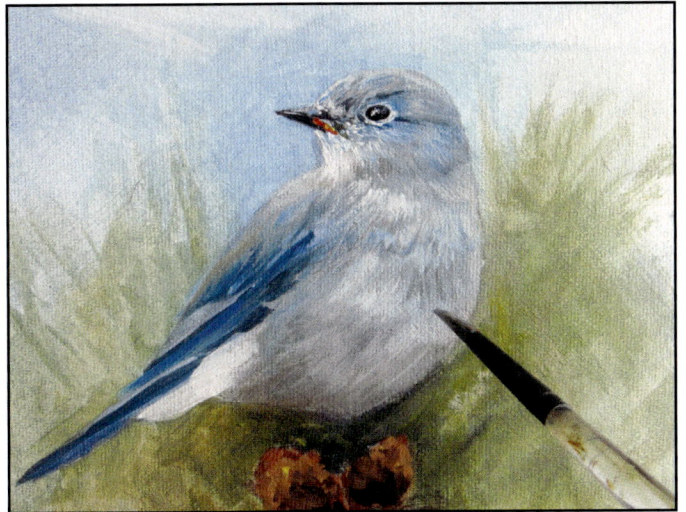

Step 55 Continue to work the breast area. Remember that the breast feather need to be softer and less movement than head feathers.

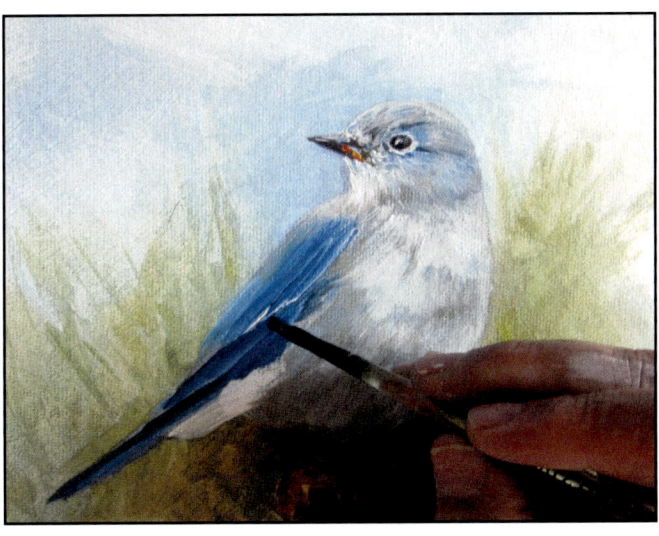

Step 56 Mottle the brush with blues and corner with white. Use this to edge the feathers. See the video for techniques.

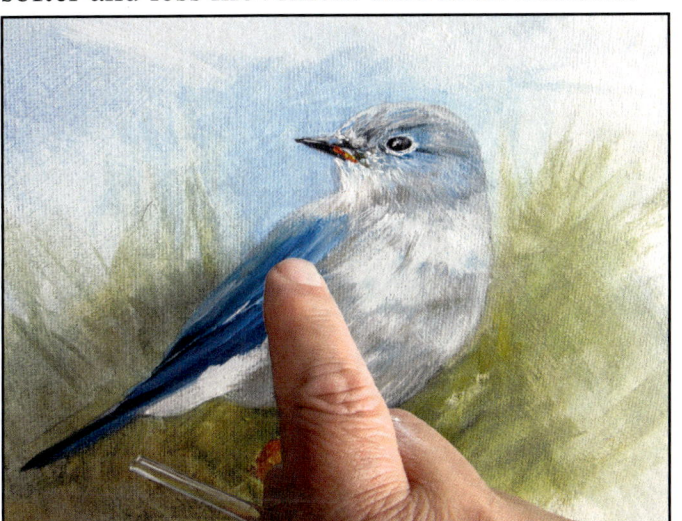

Step 57 I will soften sometimes with my finger to add movement, but keep the feathers softer so not to compete with head feathers.

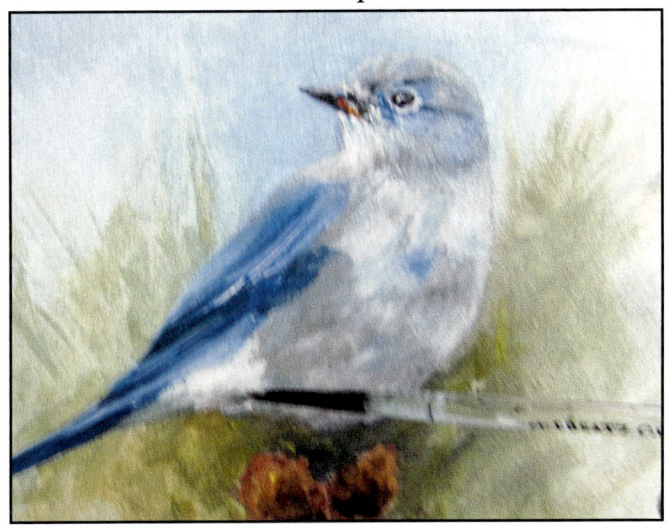

Step 58 Add white to the tail area. Keep light and choppy.

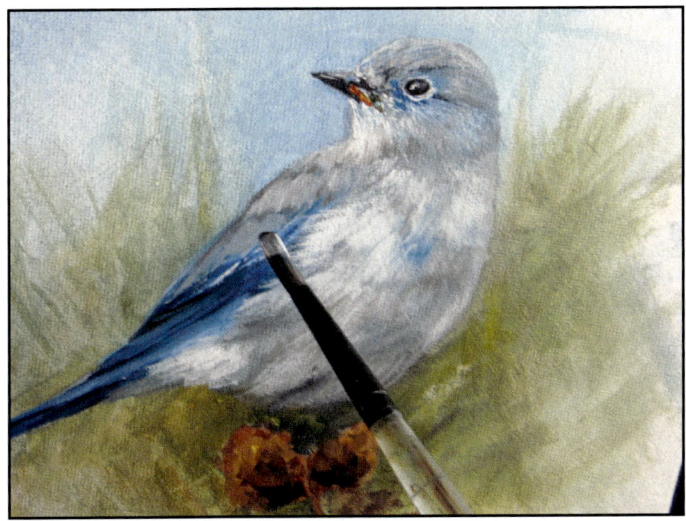

Step 59 Add some lighter greys to the coverts and mantle on top of the wing.

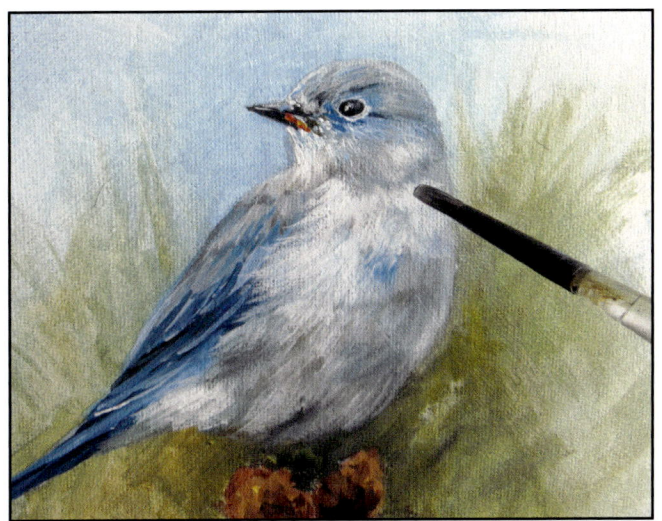

Step 60 Add some lighter greys to the neck and then add some smaller white strokes.

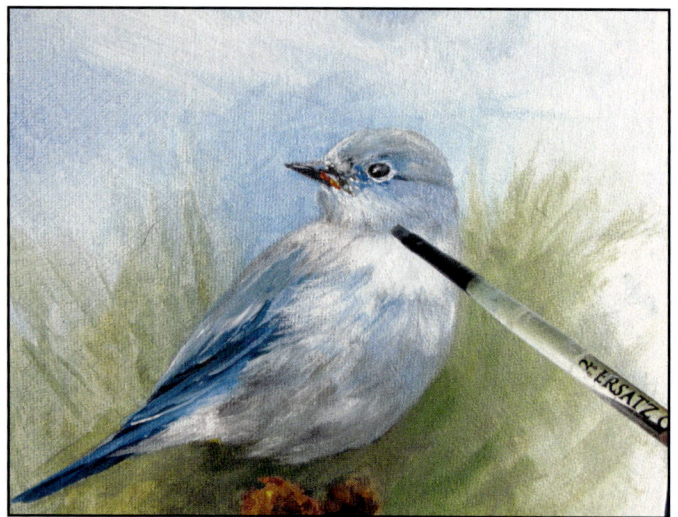

Step 61 Restate some medium and shadow strokes to push back the highlights. This softens the strokes keeping interest to head.

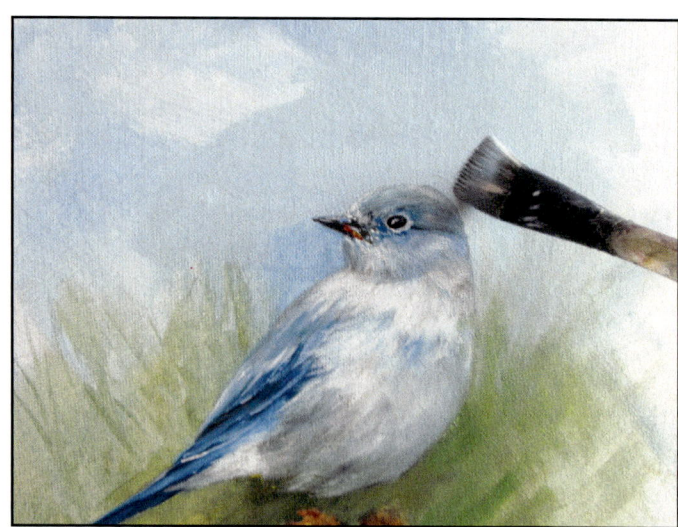

Step 62 Soften the sky around the head with more grey and blue paint. Keep paint heavier to provide backdrop for the head.

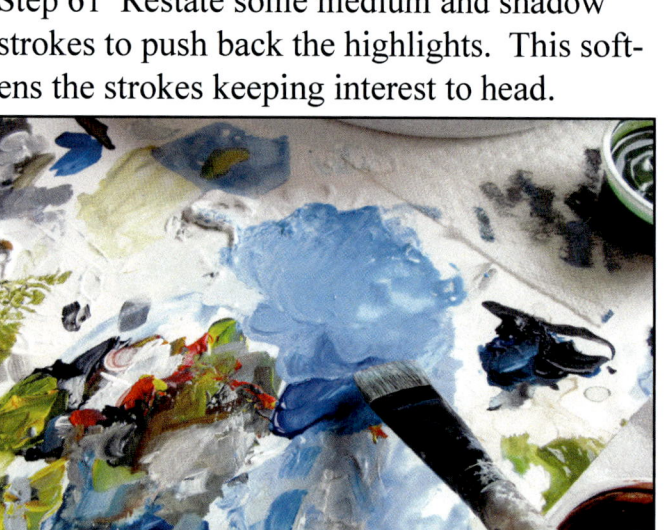

Step 63 Mottle the larger brush with some blue and white. Keep mottled for the sky.

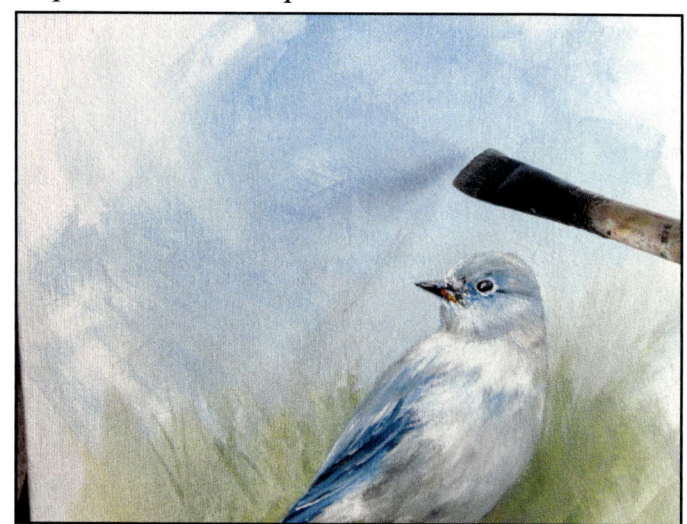

Step 64   Add additional blue into the sky area where you will place the cloud.

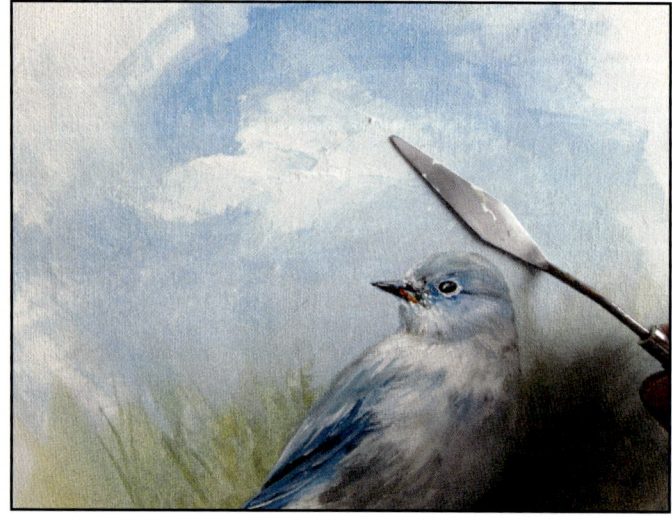

Step 65 Using the palette knife, add the cloud to the sky. Keep the knife flat and press down.

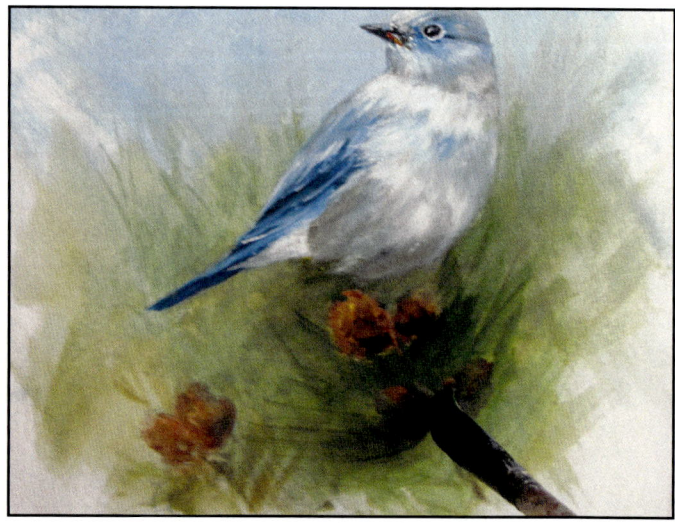

Step 66 Add some darker greens to the pine needle areas with the chisel of large brush.

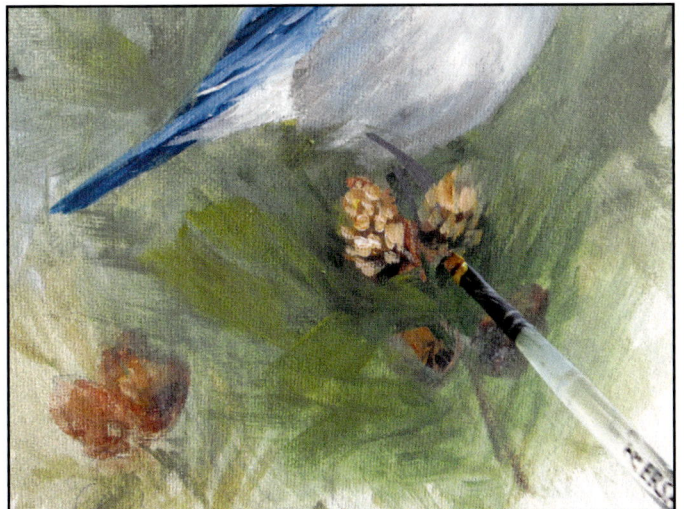

Step 67 Lighten the Burnt Sienna with yellow and white. Mottle on small flat and tap in the shapes of the pine cones.

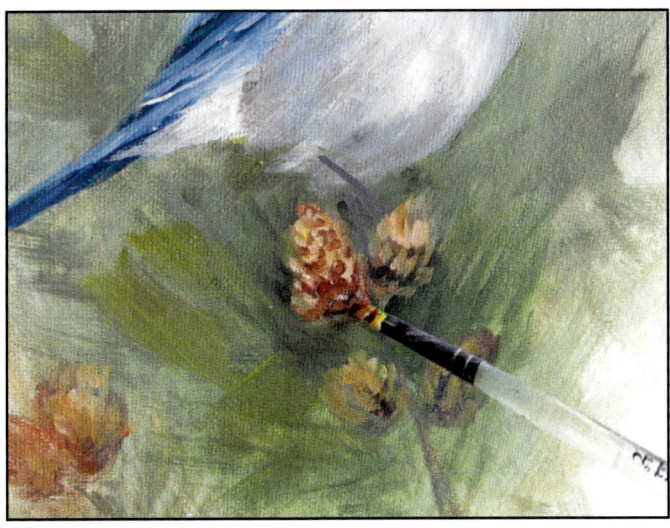

Step 68 Mottle with more Burnt Sienna and restate some shadows. Keep the lights soft by pushing back with the Burnt Sienna.

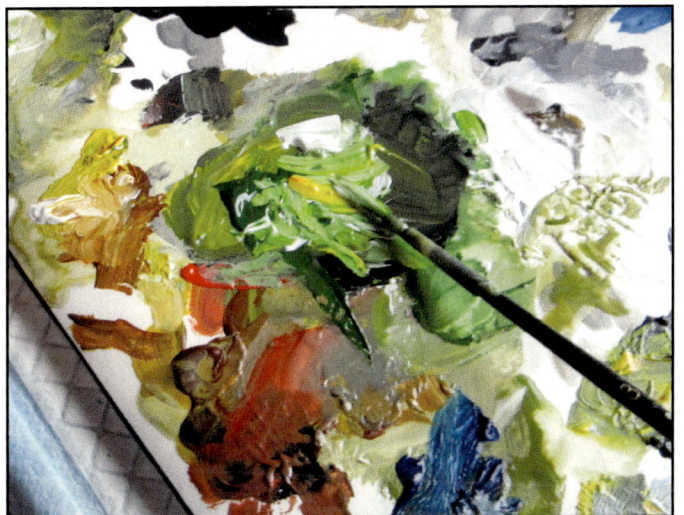

Step 69 Mottle liner with Pine Green and lighten with some Hansa and White. Keep mottled so colors come off brush varied.

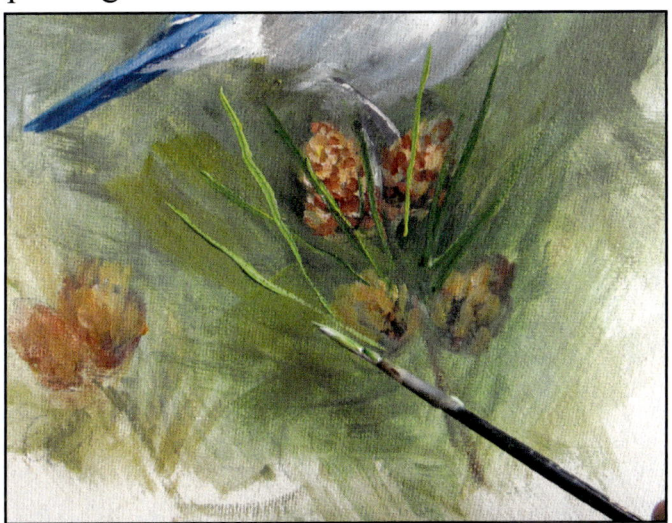

Step 70 Stroke on pine needles and roll the brush as you pull down the needle. This will release the colors more varied.

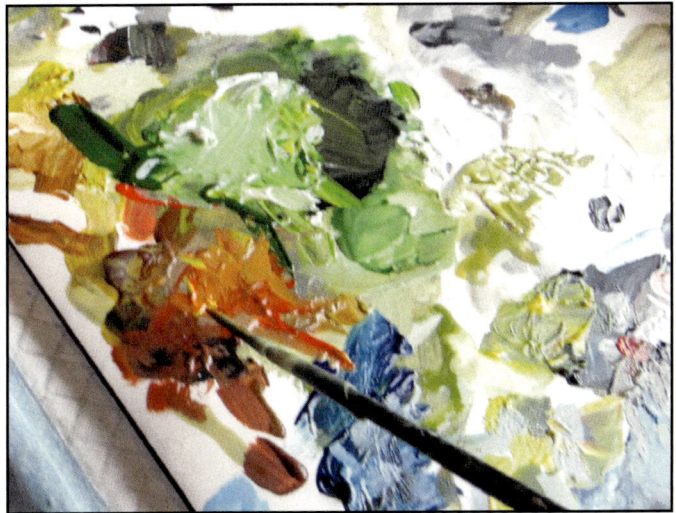

Step 71 Mottle the brush with reds, yellows and Burnt Sienna. Vary colors.

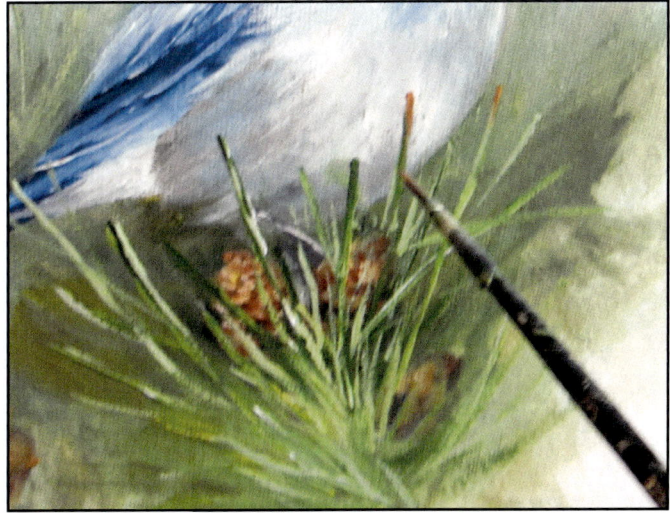

Step 72 Add to top tips of needles to finish. Vary colors. Enjoy!

Mountain Bluebird- Original Size

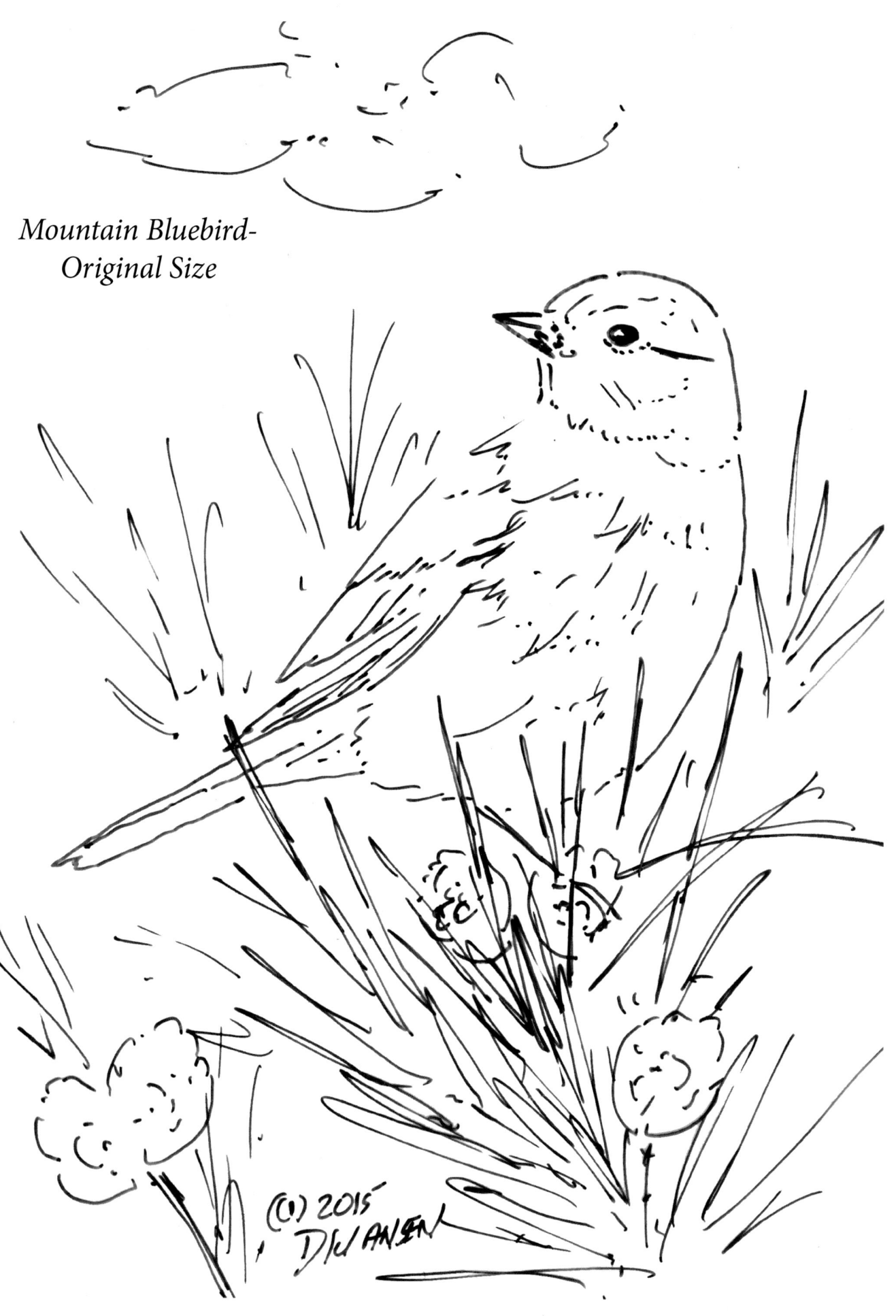

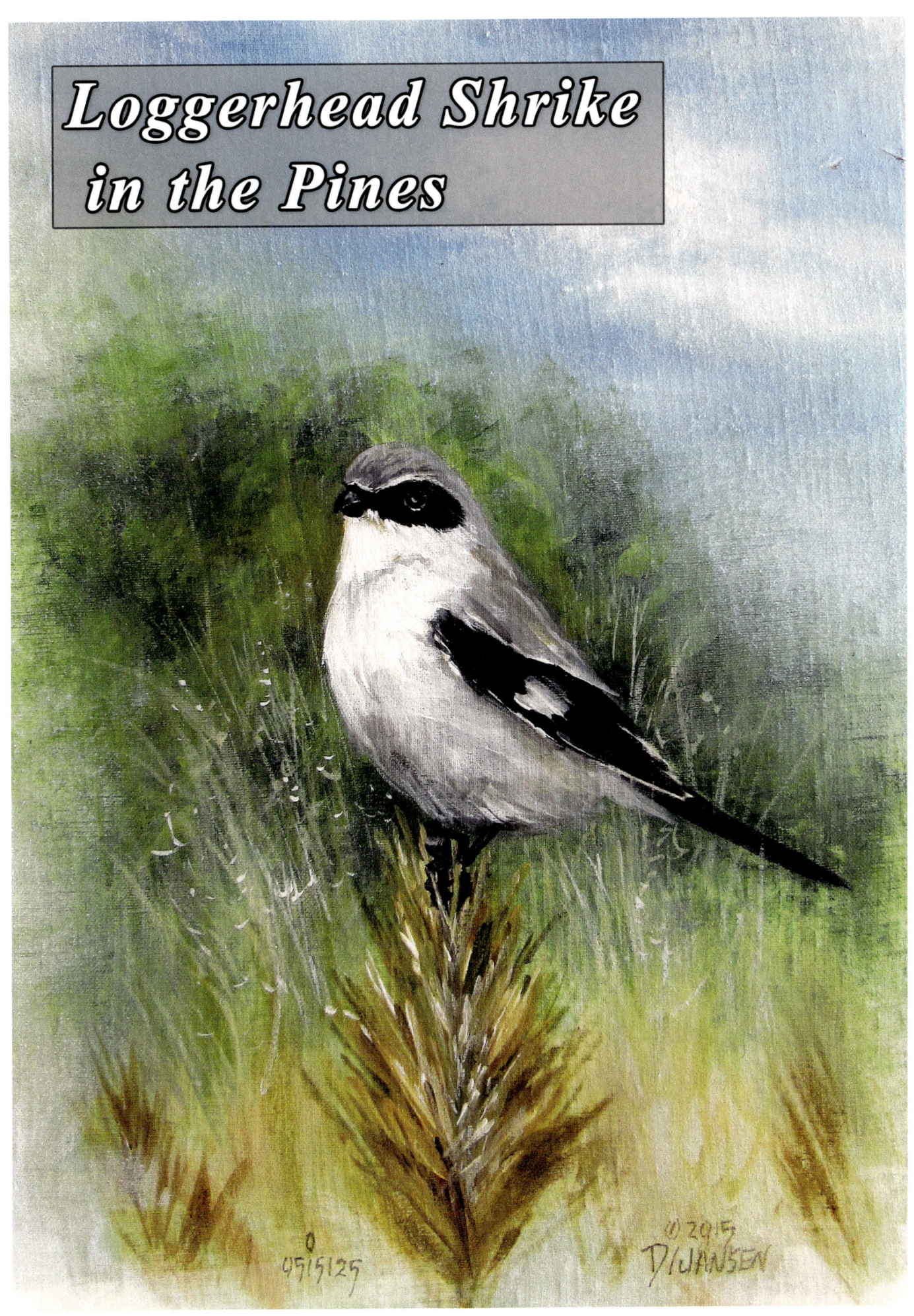

Loggerheaded Shrike in the Pines

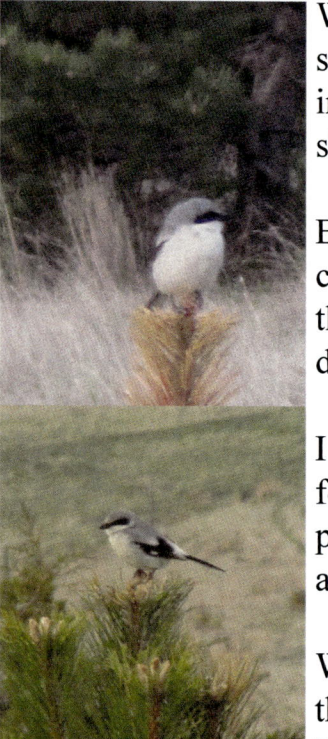

When I was in Nebraska for several weeks and painting many of the lessons in this book, I took hundreds of photos of birds that we do not have in Pennsylvania. One is the Shrike. It is a beautiful and powerful mid sized bird that graces the plains of Nebraska.

Each morning just after sun up I would go outside with my coffee and camera. He would be there, sitting on the top of a pine tree, waiting for the grasshoppers. I watched him swoop down grab one then return to his duty on top the pine tree.

I have included a couple of photos so you can get the feeling that I had for the painting. See him sit on top of the pine with the long grass of the plains growing up on the sides. Sometimes he would sit on a taller pine and there would be beautiful blue behind him.

With this lesson we must render the light and dark and create feathers in the black areas while still keeping them black. Not an easy thing to do. We will use negative feathering to make this happen.

Negative feathering allows you to paint back with the colors of an area, changing the colors back to the desired color, while leaving just enough of a contrast color to give definition.

One other area that will present some trouble is the eye. The shrike has a black eye on a black band in his head. The shrike doesn't have a white eye ring, which helps add interest to the eye. The eye almost disappears into the black band. I will add some white for this painting, just a little to add interest. This is what makes it a painting and not a photo. Let's give it a try!

Paint It Simply Palette
Base Color- Medium White from Mixes
Palette Colors

Naphthol Red Light	Titanium White
Red Violet	Medium White
Carbon Black	Base Brown
Phthalo Blue	Pine Green
Hansa Yellow	Burnt Sienna

Wood Surface
Linen covered wood panel about 14 Inch X 18 Inch to fit picture frame. Can also use canvas panel.

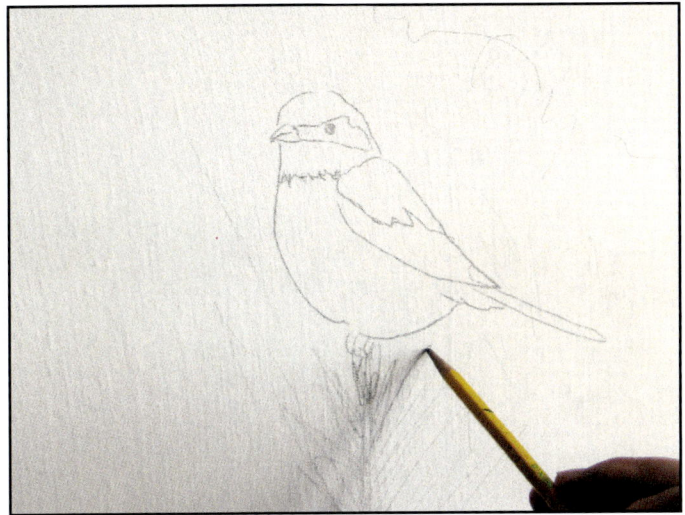

Step 1 Base the linen panel or canvas white, dry and then transfer or sketch the design with dark pencil.

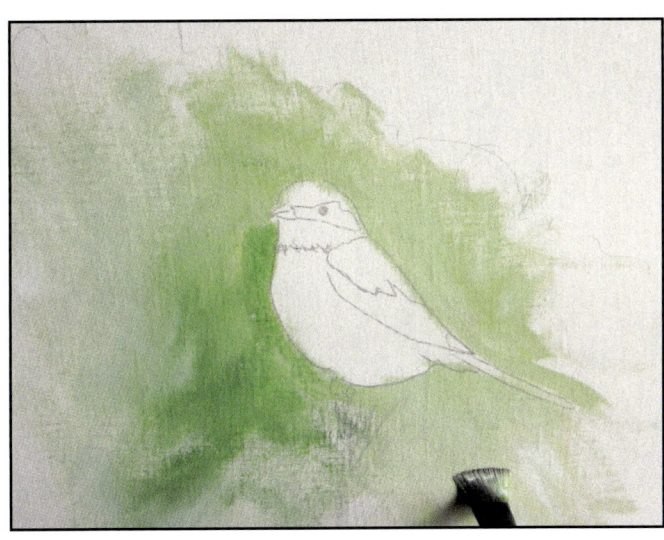

Step 2 Mottle the 3/4 inch brush with Pine Green and Extender and go around the bird. Heavier on the bottom.

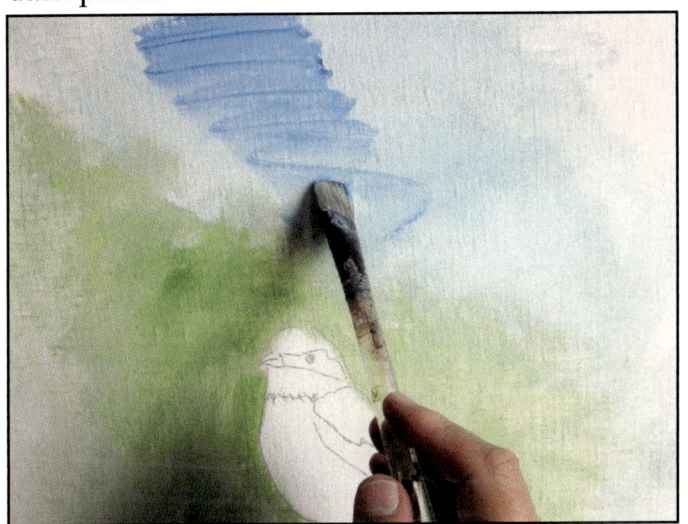

Step 3 Mottle the brush with some blue and touch white to lighten. Go over the sky area.

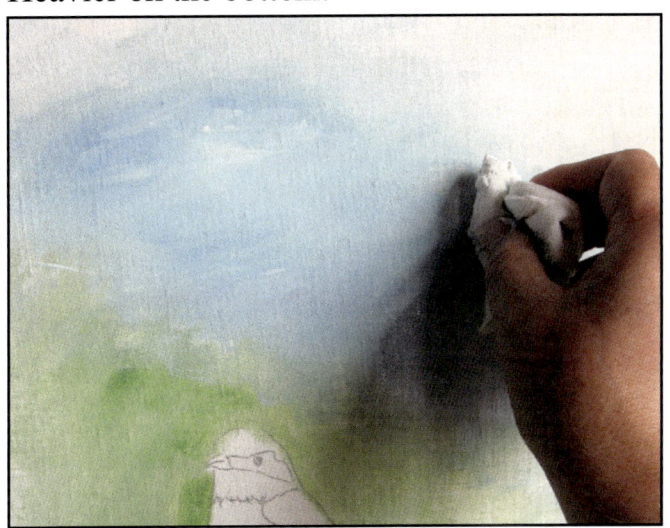

Step 4 I use many different techniques to soften the sky areas. Here I am using a paper towel with a little Extender.

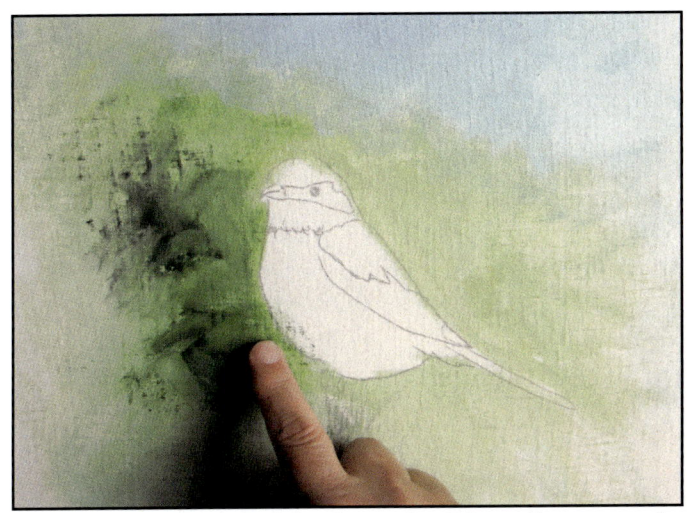

Step 5 Add some black to the Pine Green and then push around the bottom for interest.

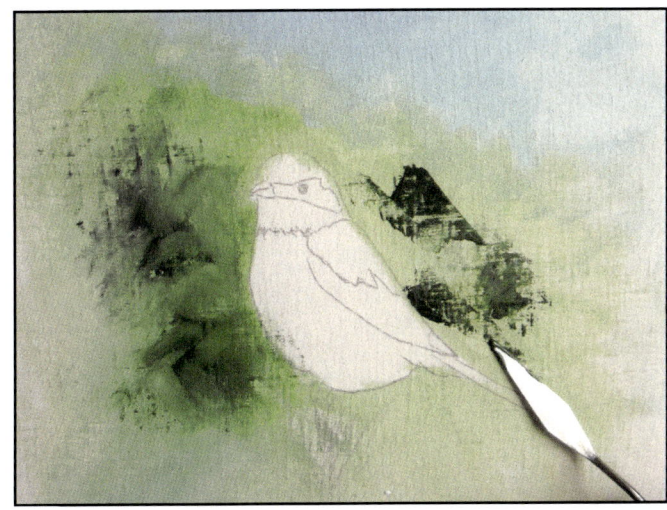

Step 6 Sometimes you can add the dark with the knife and then push around with finger.

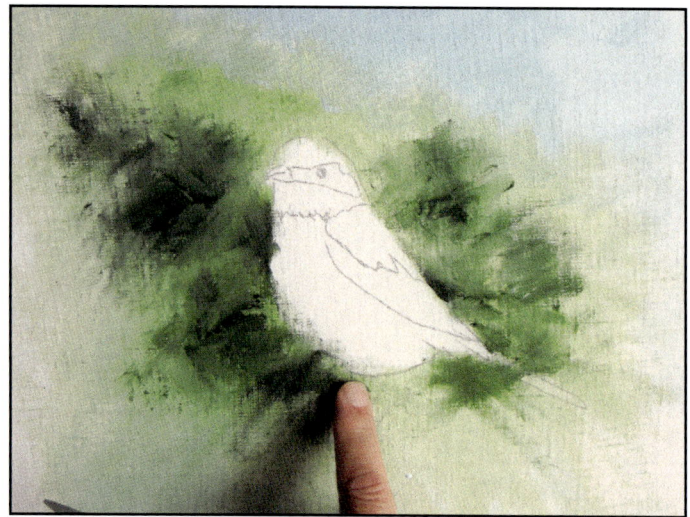

Step 7 Mottle in the Pine Green and black with the palette knife and then soften into the base with your finger.

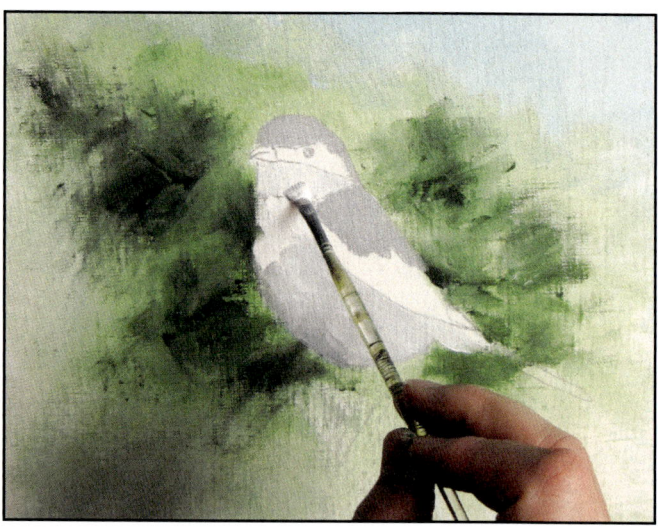

Step 8 Mottle white with touch black and blue to start grey color. Begin with small flat and base in the head and mantle.

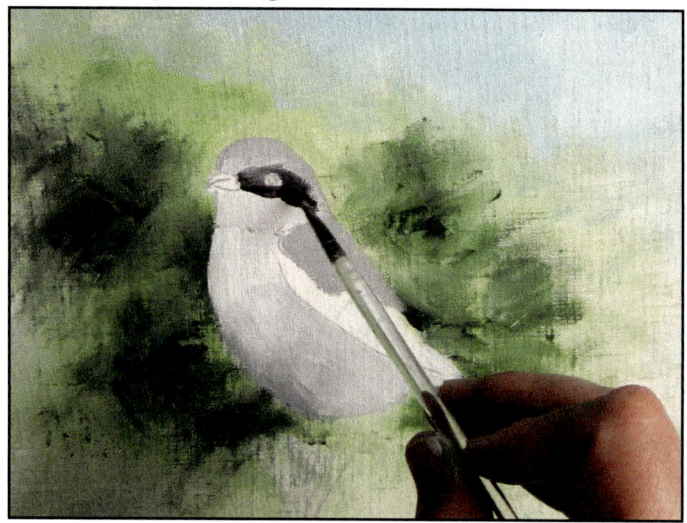

Step 9 Lighten grey with white and base neck and breast. Use smaller flat or round to base in the area around the eye.

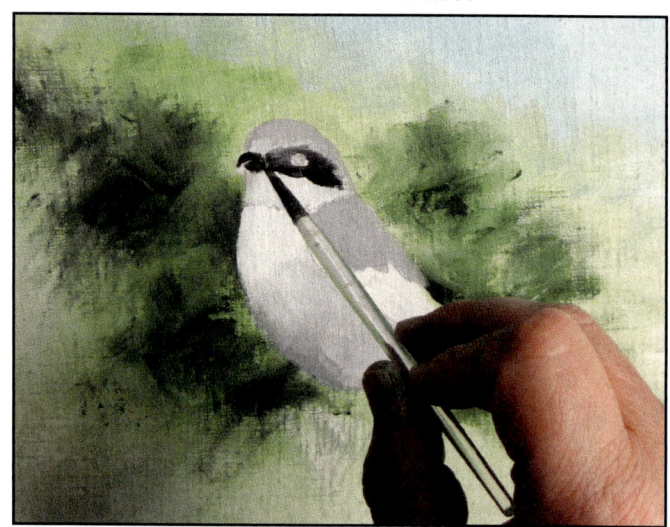

Step 10 Add the beak with the black. Leave small spaces so you do not lose all the pattern in the black paint.

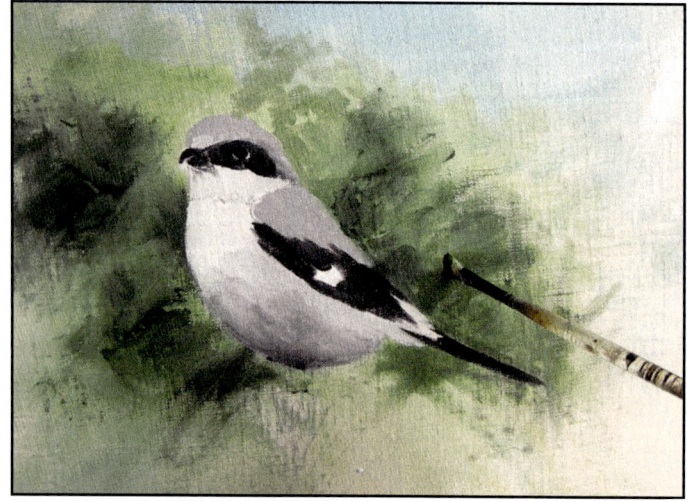

Step 11 Add the eye and the black primary and secondary flight feathers.

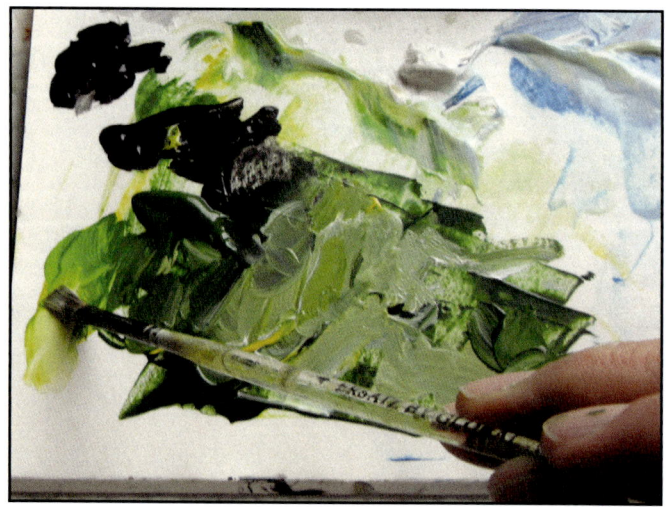

Step 12 Mottle the greens with a touch more Hansa and touch white.

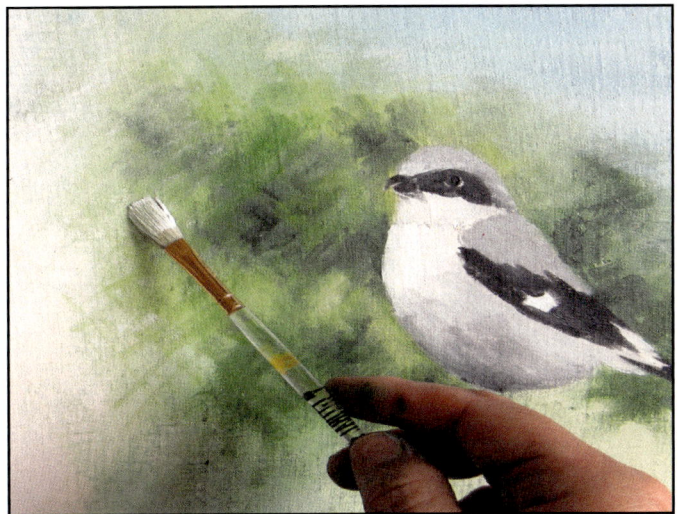

Step 13 Here I am using the bristle brush to add some lighter greens to the darker ones we applied earlier.

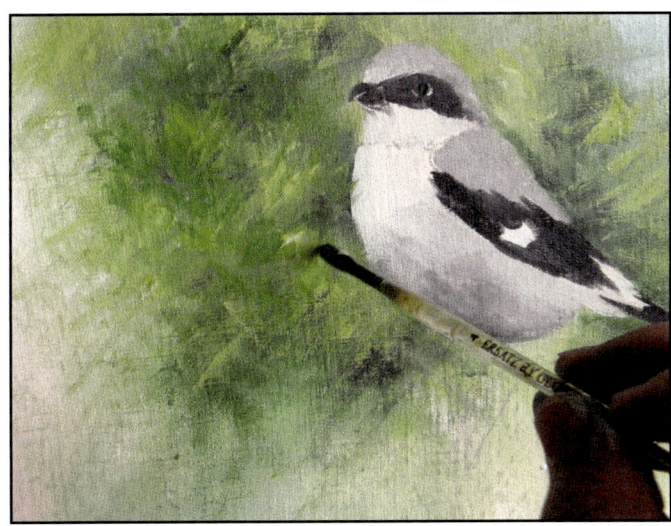

Step 14 Add some smaller movement to the greens with small flat and very light green. Drag over the surface to add interest.

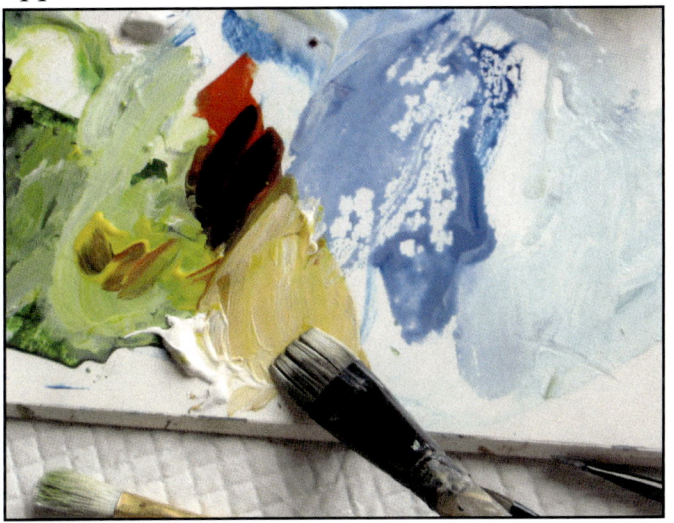

Step 15 Mottle the large brush with some red, black and yellow to make brown color. Lighten with some white.

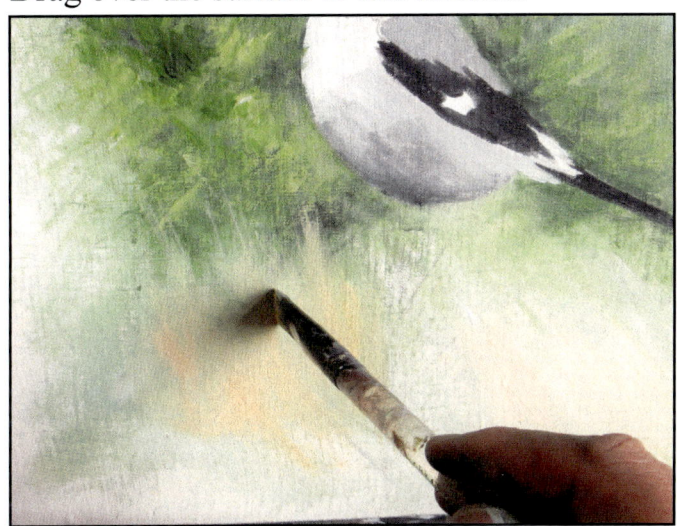

Step 16 Use the chisel of the brush to add the movement of the top of the pine. Think soft and movement only. No needles.

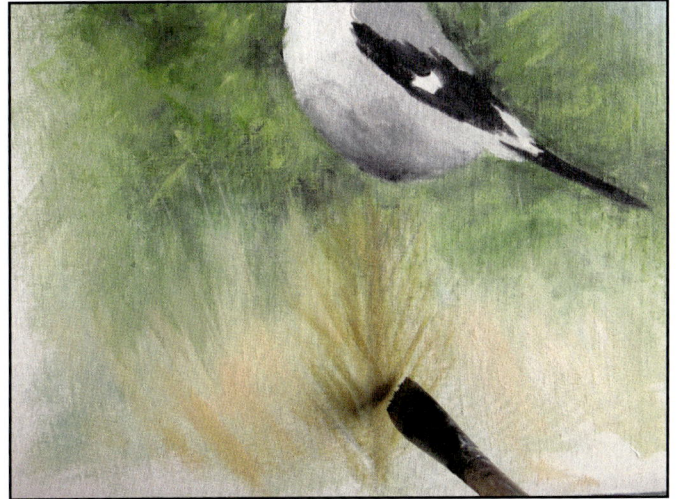

Step 17 Darken the color a little with some more brown and touch green add needles.

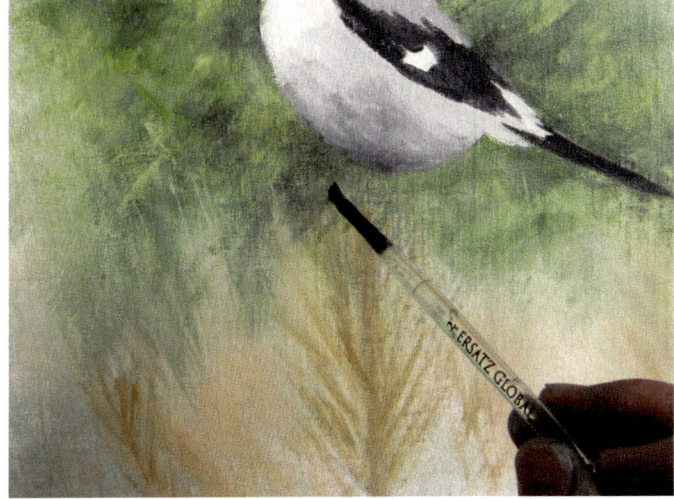

Step 18 Use the small flat to add more dark green and shape the needles with greens.

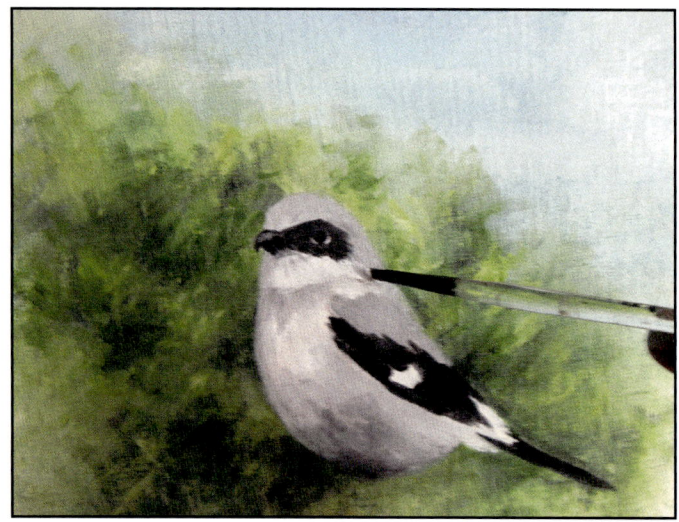

Step 19 Begin to break up the head feathers with some lighter greys and shape following strokes. Add light touch to beak.

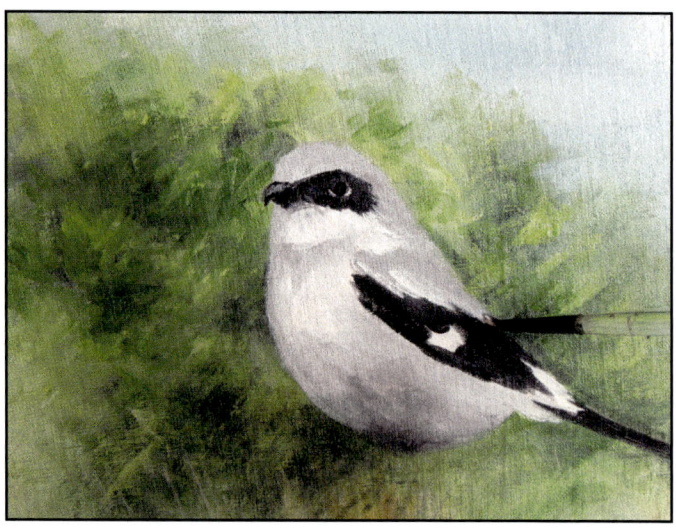

Step 20 Add some strokes of white down the mantle to add feather direction. Use chisel of the brush edged in white.

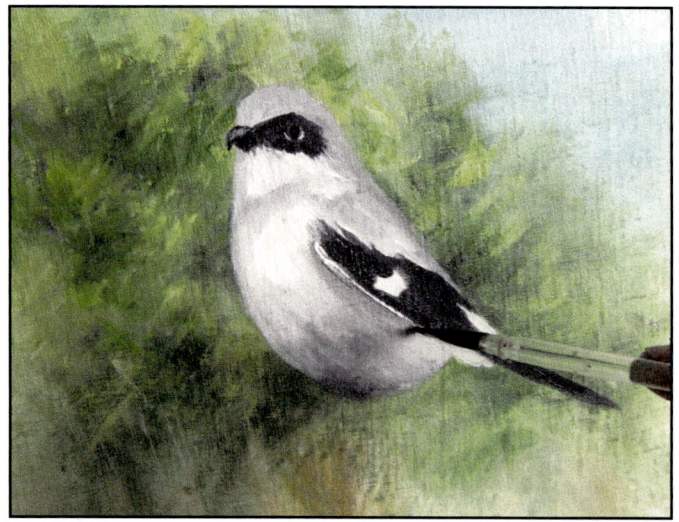

Step 21 Edge the brush with some white and using the chisel apply the front edge of the wing.

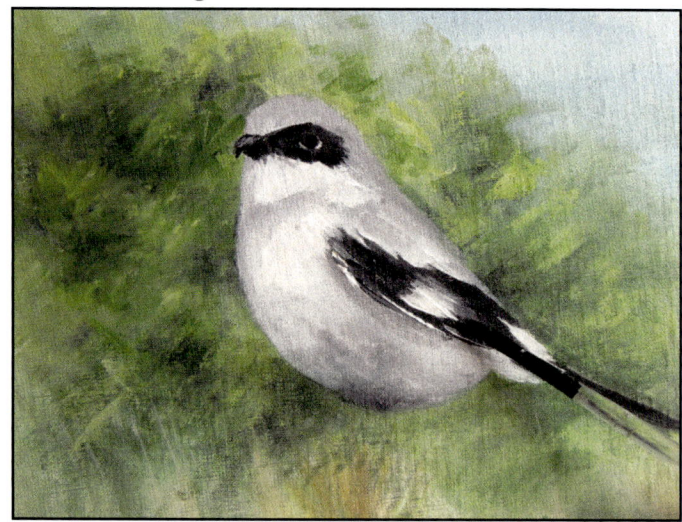

Step 22 Streak some white darkened with a little grey to suggest the coverts and flight feathers.

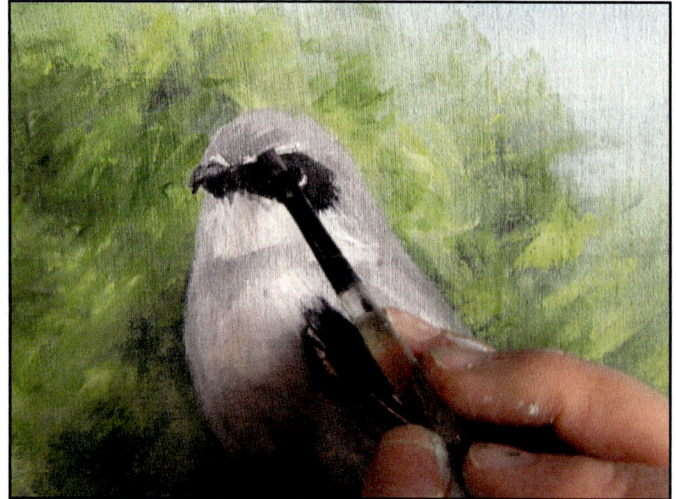

Step 23 Use the chisel of the flat with the darker grey to add some feathers to top of his head.

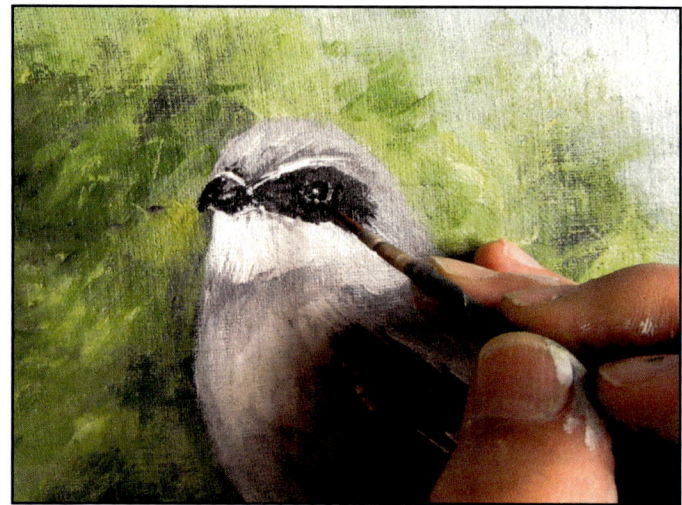

Step 24 Use the liner brush to add some detail to the eye ring and add small feathers.

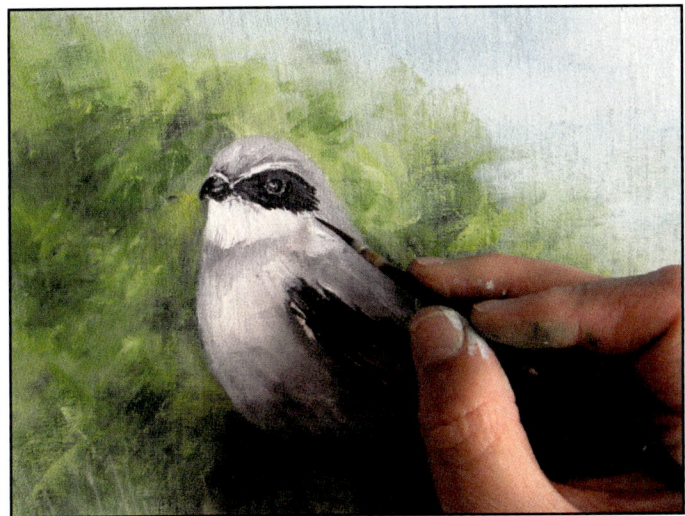

Step 25 Restate some of the black around the eye and then work the white again. I work the colors back and forth to establish the look.

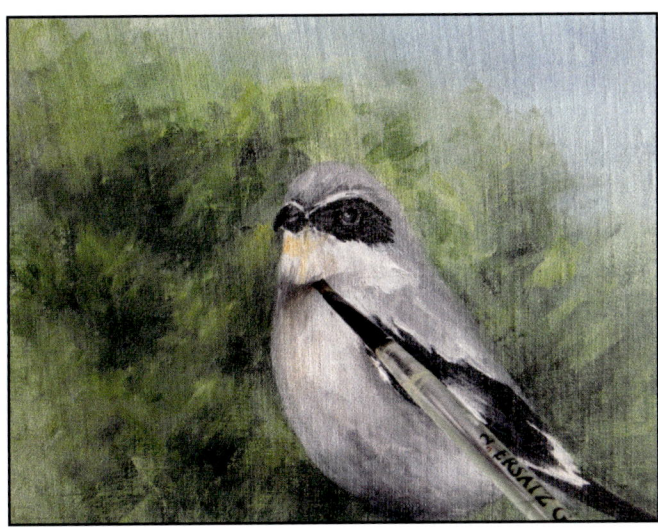

Step 26 Add some strokes of warm Hansa Yellow and touch red to warm the feathers of the neck and breast.

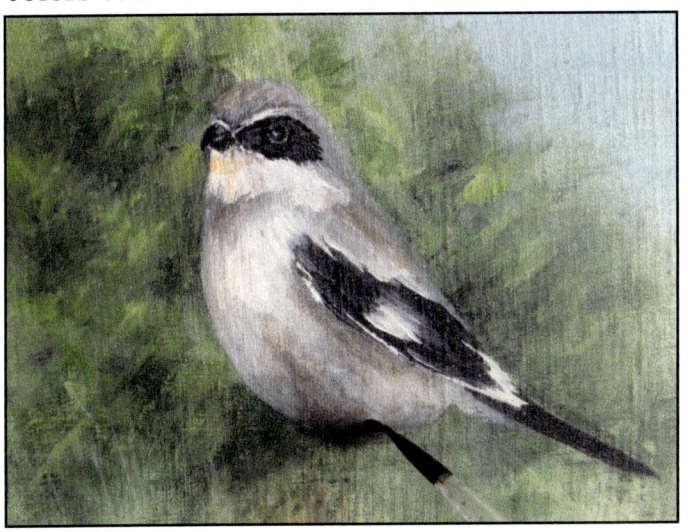

Step 27 Add some darker shadow strokes of darker grey to the bottom of the body where we will put the legs later.

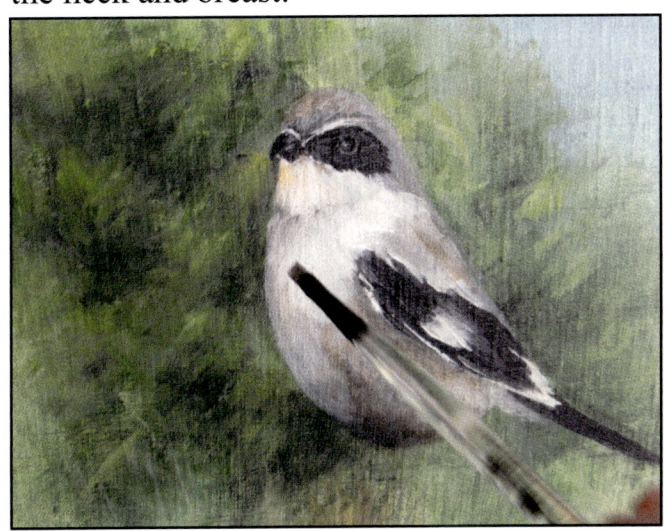

Step 28 Build some lights strokes of white on the breast and the neck with the small flat.

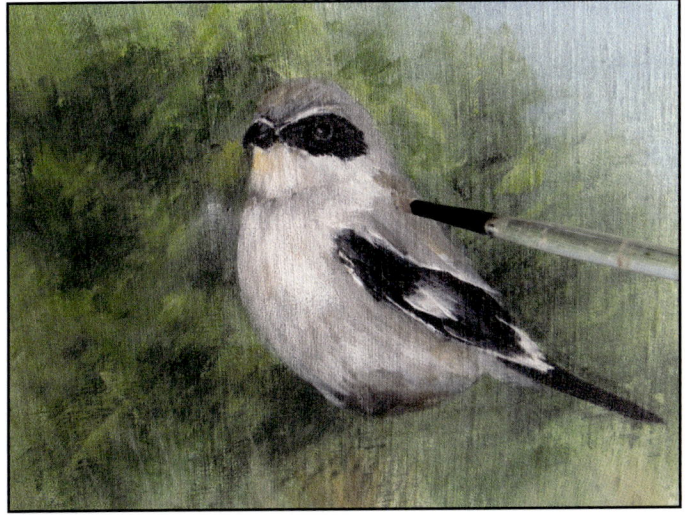

Step 29   Add some darker grey to the back of the body and the mantle of the wing.

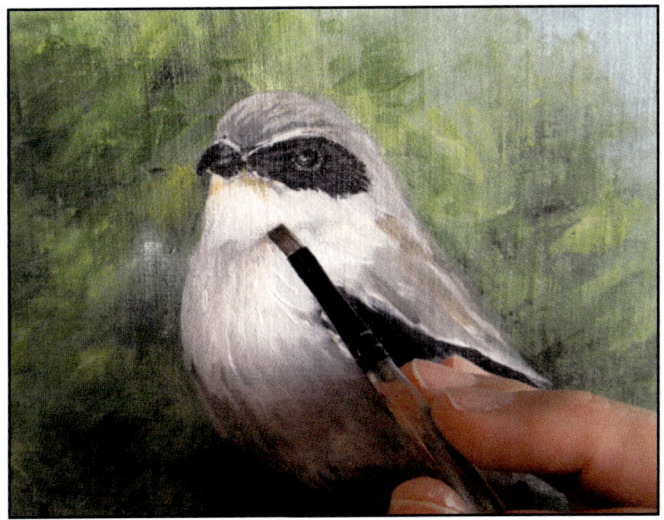

Step 30 Begin detailing around the neck. Remember the size of the strokes.

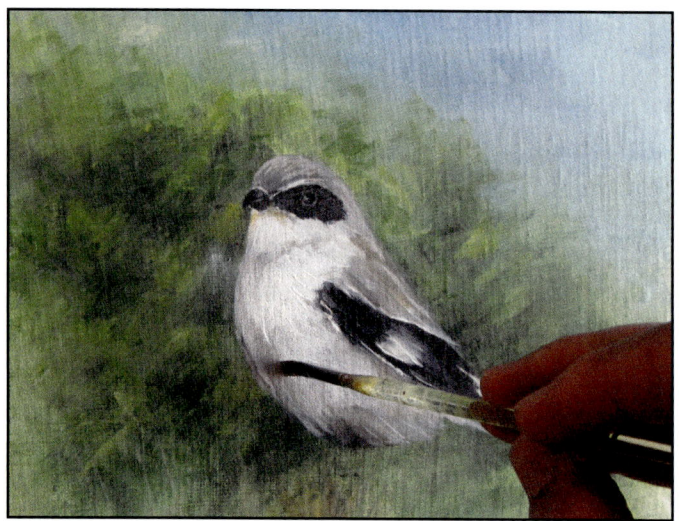

Step 31 Add some darker greys to the left side of the body and walk into the middle a little. Medium sized strokes in the body.

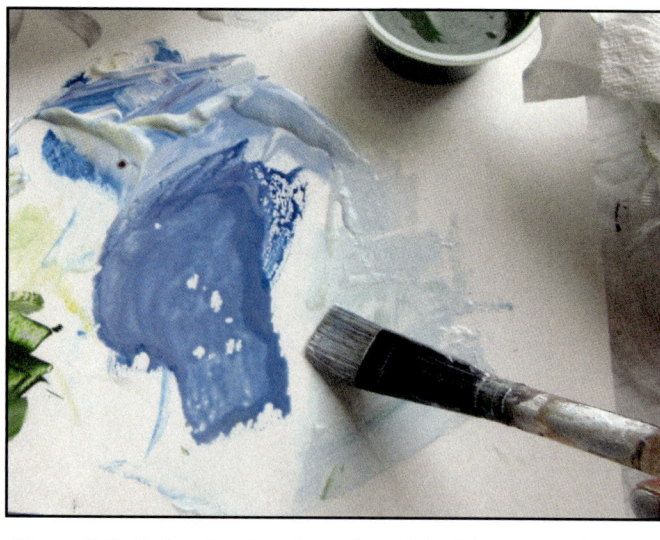

Step 32 Mottle the brush with blues and white to make light sky color.

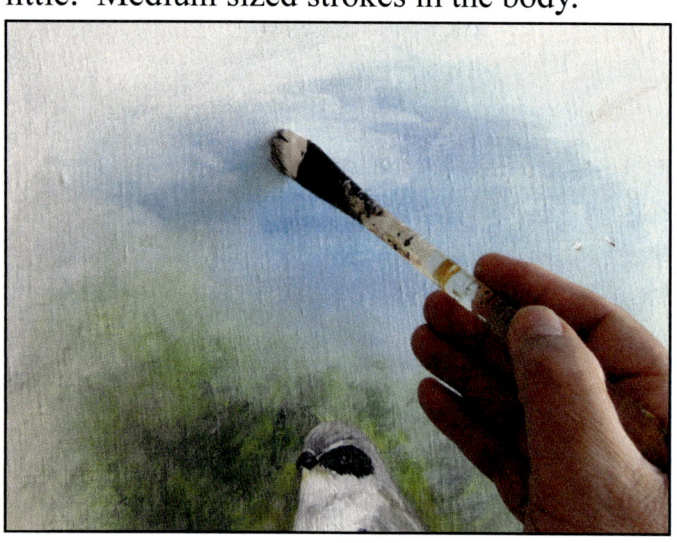

Step 33 Apply with Extender to the sky to moisten and get ready for the cloud in the next step. Make as dark as desired.

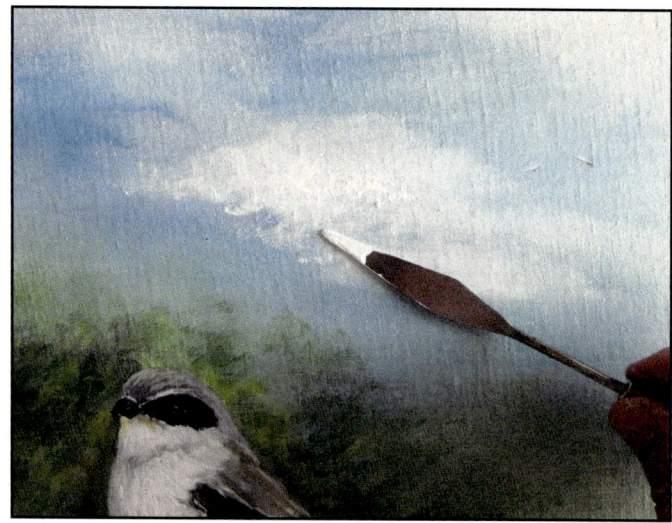

Step 34 Using the palette knife and white apply the cloud. Keep knife flat and slide from side to side to apply the paint.

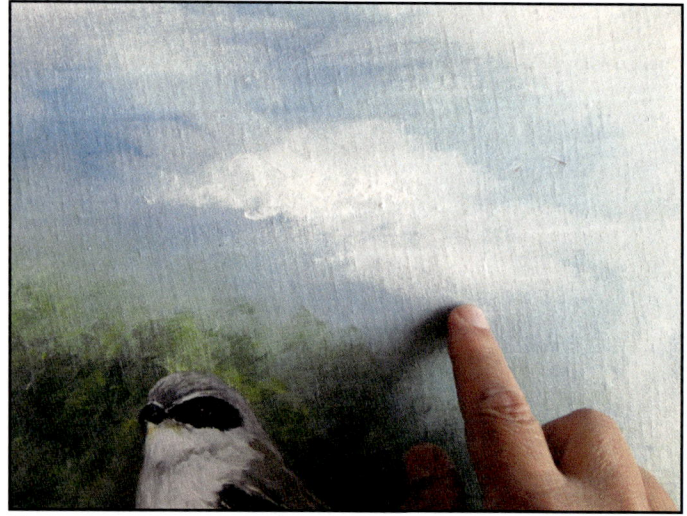

Step 35 Use your finger to soften the cloud into the wet sky. Soften right side.

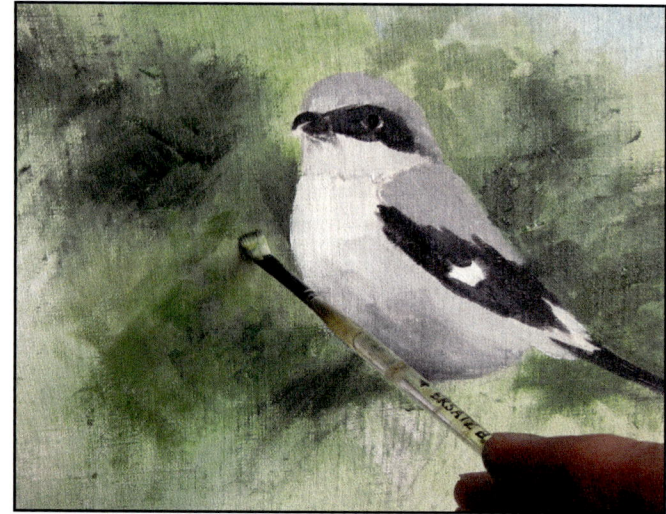

Step 36 I returned to the greens to work around the bird to make more opaque.

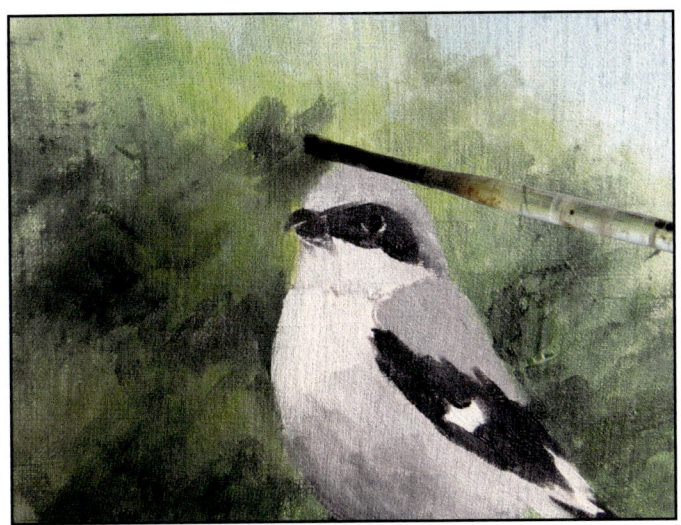

Step 37 Add some darker greens around the head. Make color more opaque. This will play against the head bringing him forward.

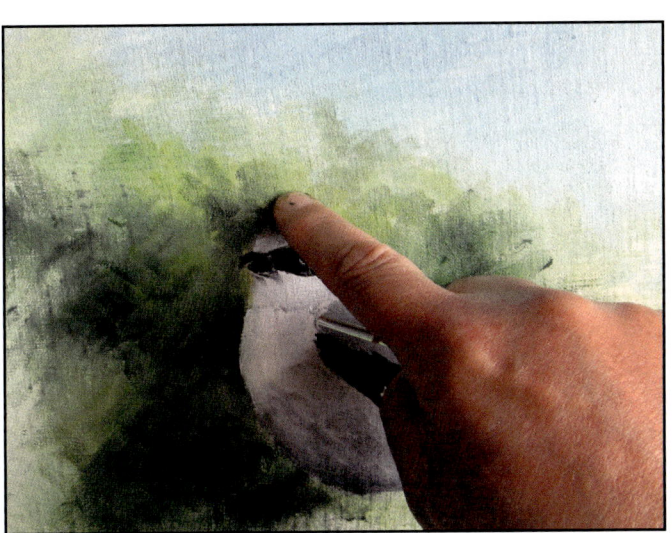

Step 38 Soften the outer edges with your finger to reduce the contrast and soften the green into the blue.

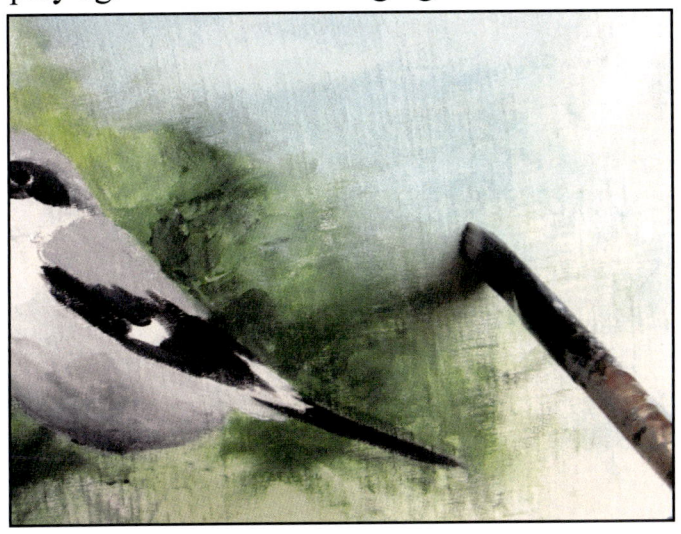

Step 39 Using the 3/4 inch brush and the sky colors, soften the greens into the sky. This will keep him as the center of interest.

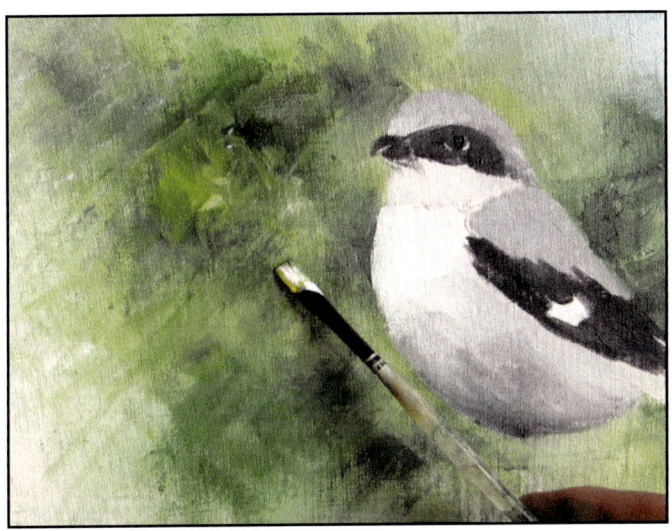

Step 40   We do however want to mottle some various values of greens around him to create some depth to the greens.

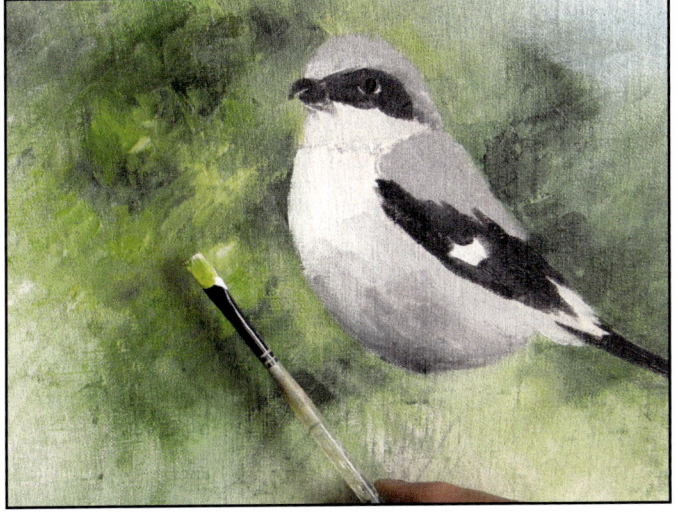

Step 41 Add some warmer Hansa and touch black to vary the green.

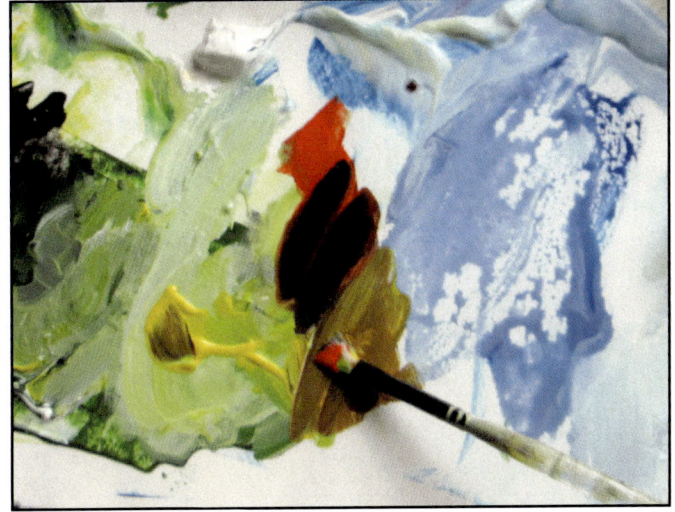

Step 42 Mottle a brown with red, black and some Hansa.

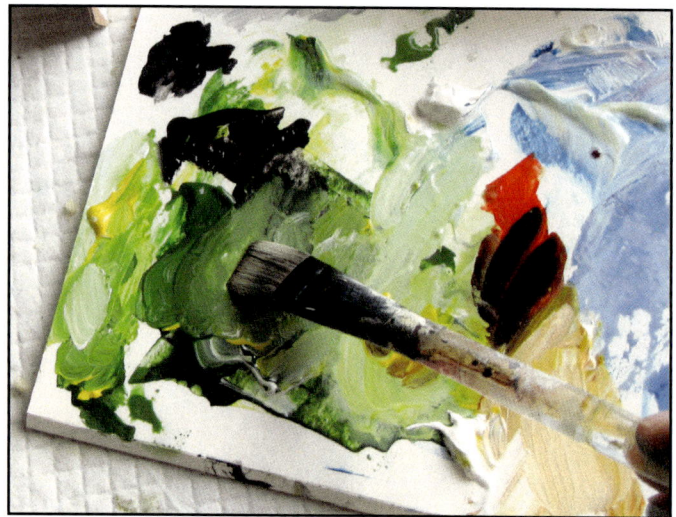

Step 43 Add some browns to the pine needles, like we did with the first lesson, then mottle some greens with the larger brush.

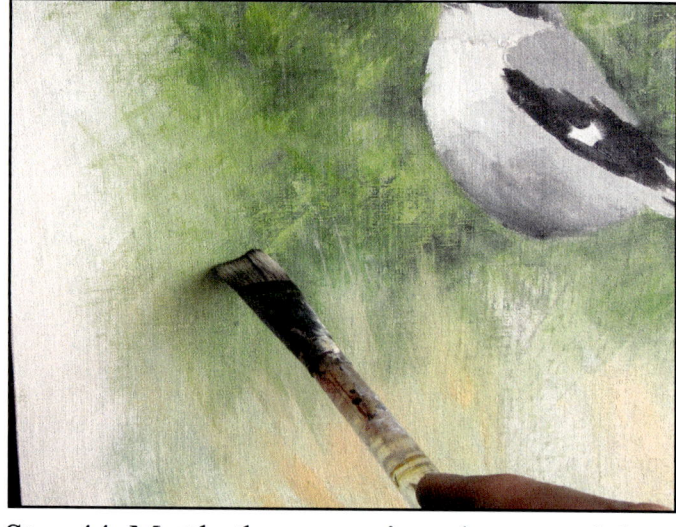

Step 44 Mottle the greens into the tops of the pine working up and down to make the movement of the pine top.

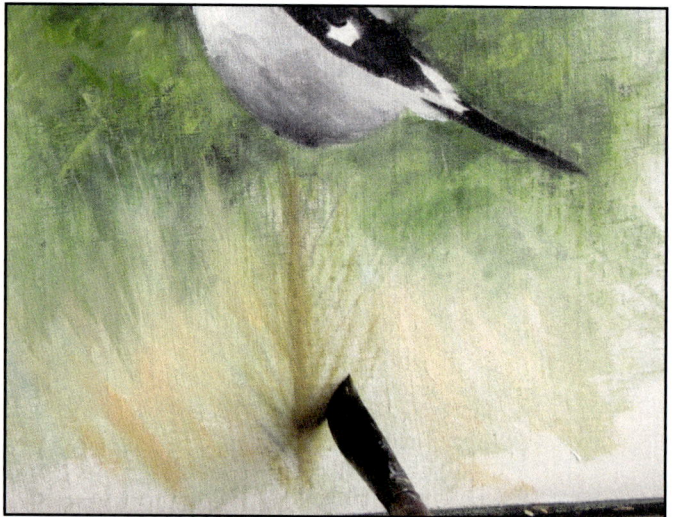

Step 45 Use the chisel of the brush to begin the shapes of the pine needles.

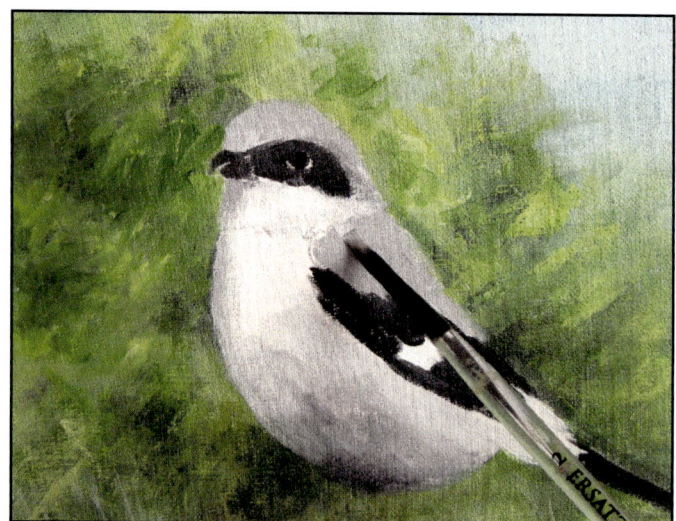

Step 46 Return to the mantle area of the wing and begin to add more greys for increased movement.

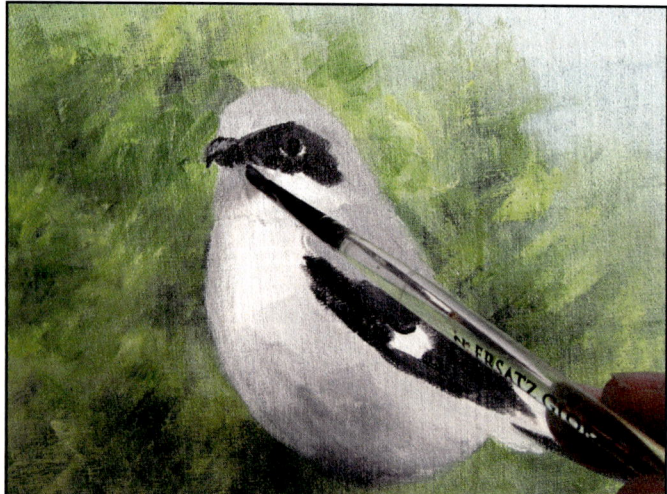

Step 47 Work some additional shadows under the beak with the small flat.

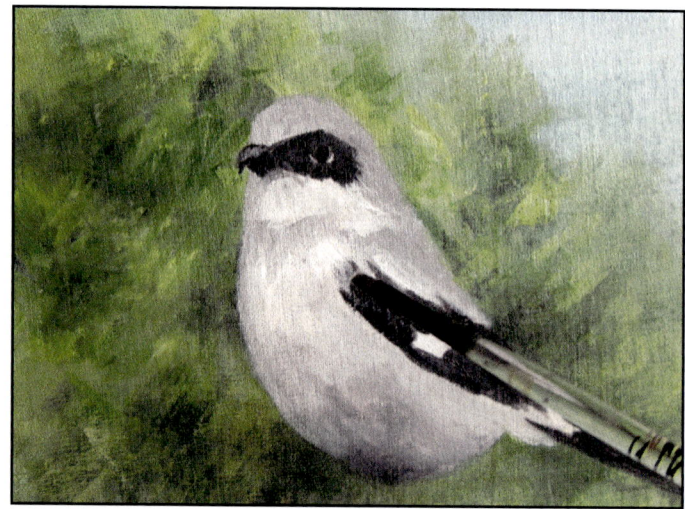

Step 48 Add some streaks from the mantle or top of the wing over the flight feathers.

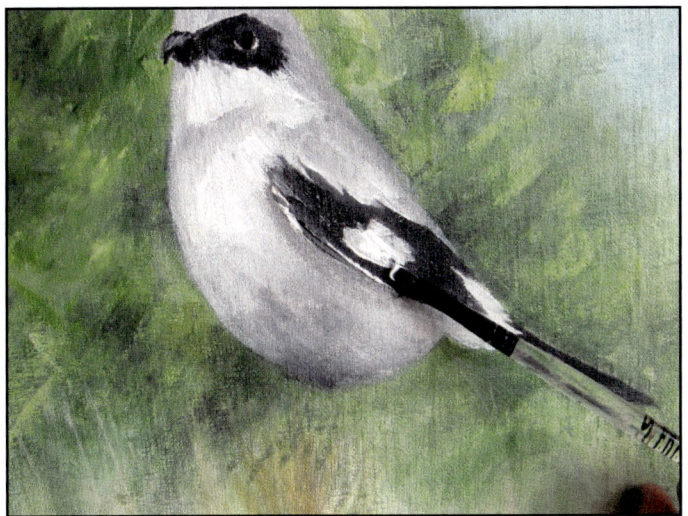

Step 49 Add some additional streaks of white to the coverts to add more interest.

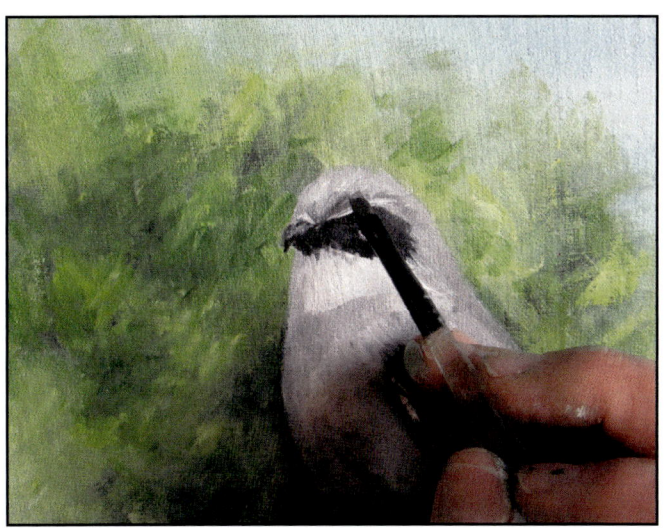

Step 50 Rework the greys on to the head using shape following darker greys and then add some white feathers.

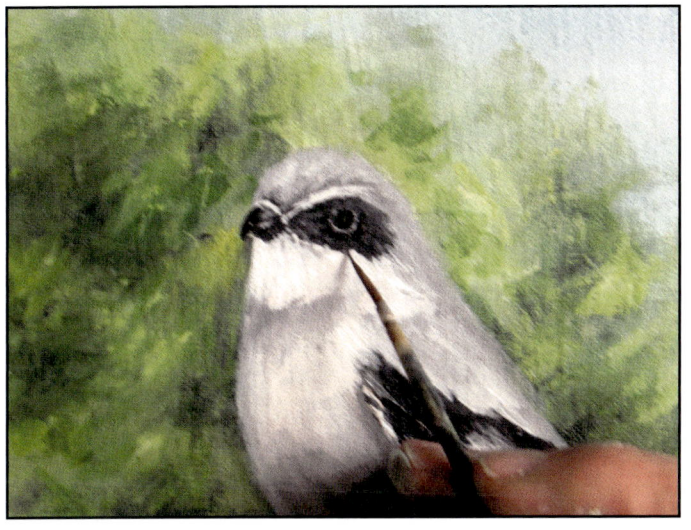

Step 51 Add some smaller touches with the liner and white to add some additional detail feathers around the head.

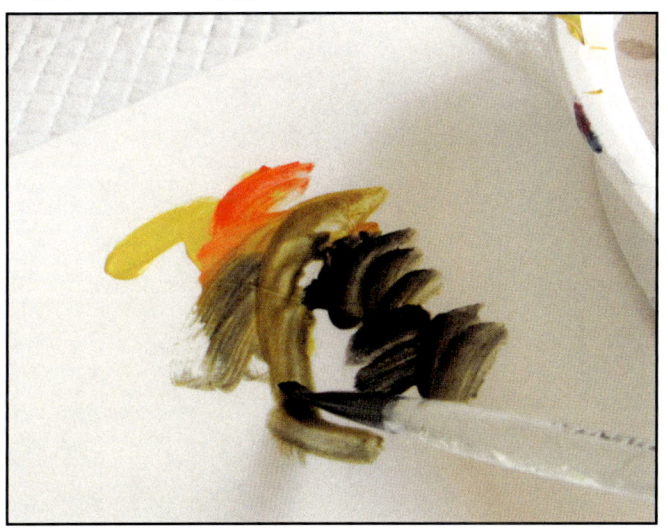

Step 52 Mottle a soft brown from the red, black and yellow.

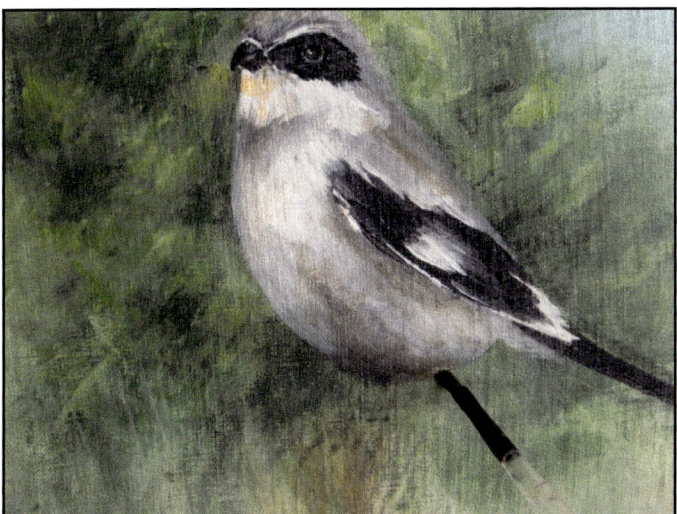

Step 53 Add this to the bottom of the bird where the feet go. We are restating this.

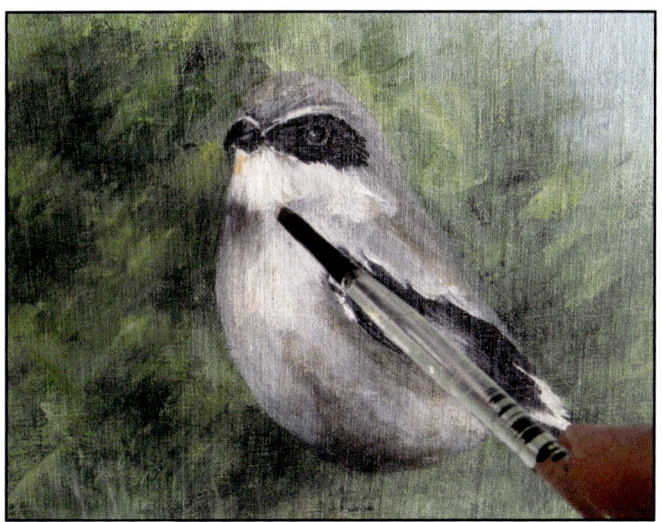

Step 54 Build the white one more time in the neck and down the breast. Small flat brush.

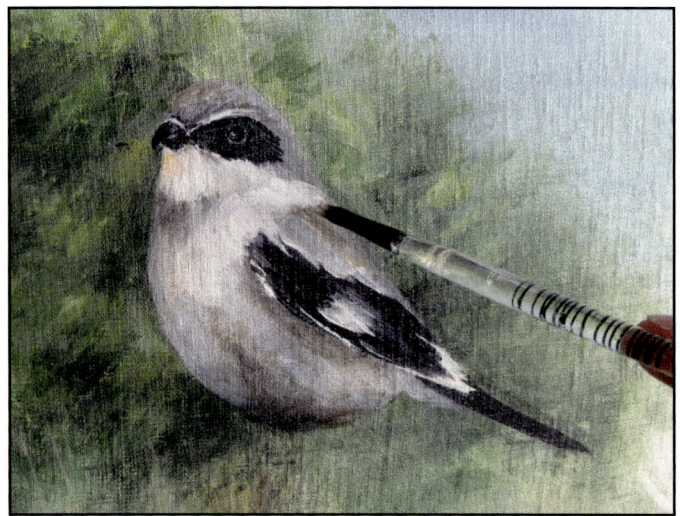

Step 55 Add some smaller strokes of light down the back. Remember length of the stroke in relation to the body.

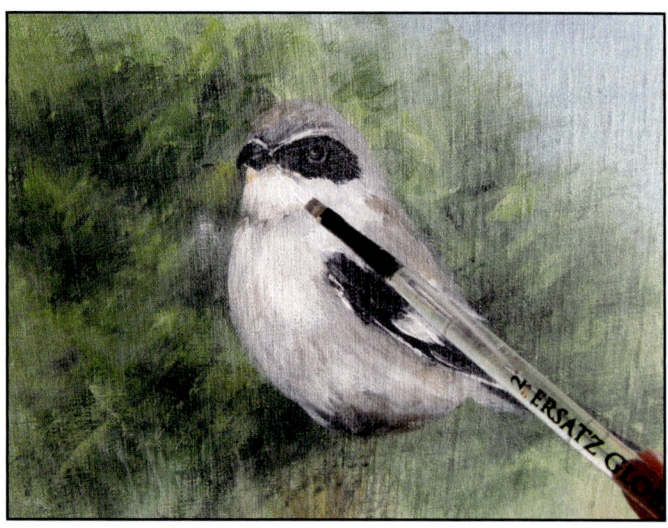

Step 56 Continue to build around the head. Each time I add something to the bird, I revisit the head with more detail.

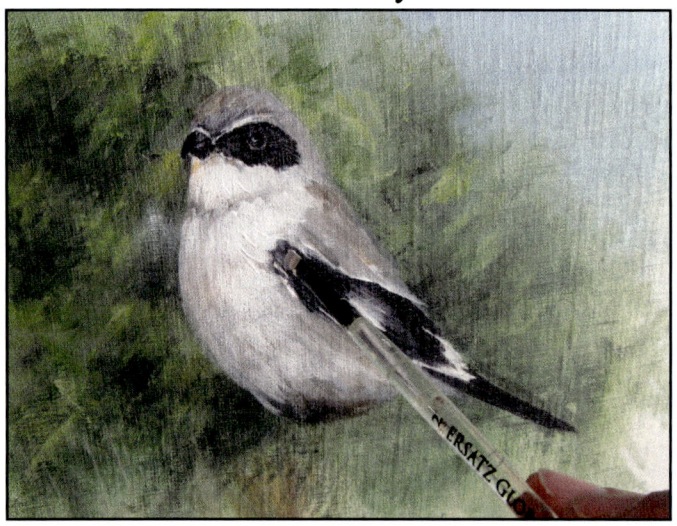

Step 57 Add some additional darks to the wings. Pull slightly longer strokes.

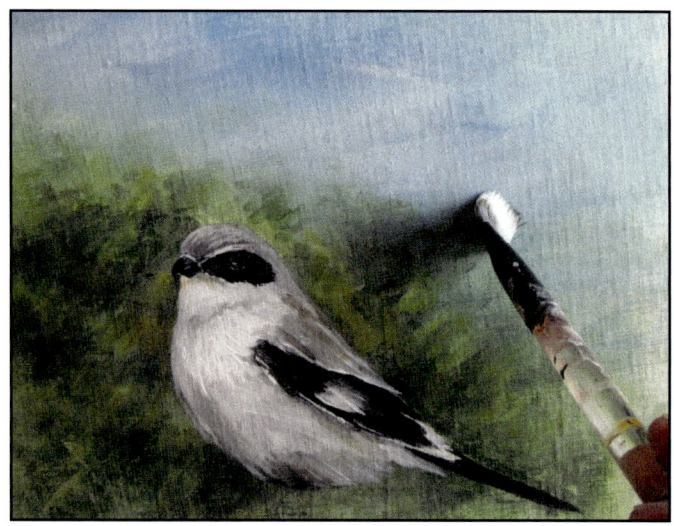

Step 58 Add some additional color to the sky and soften if needed to make the shrike come forward.

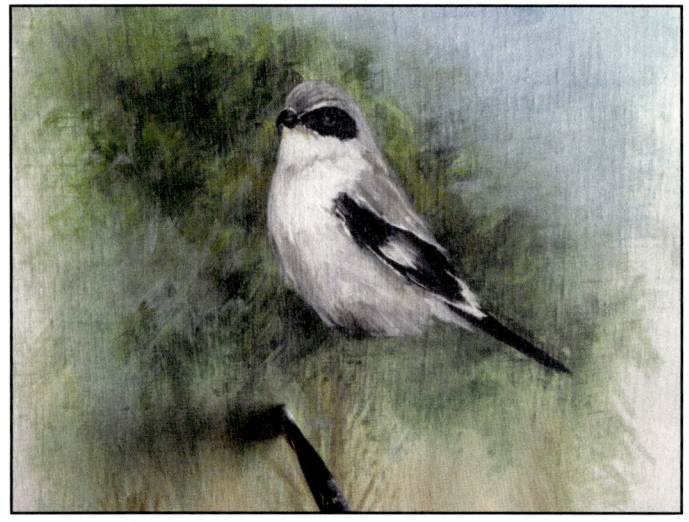

Step 59 Work some of the sky color down into the greens to soften and push back.

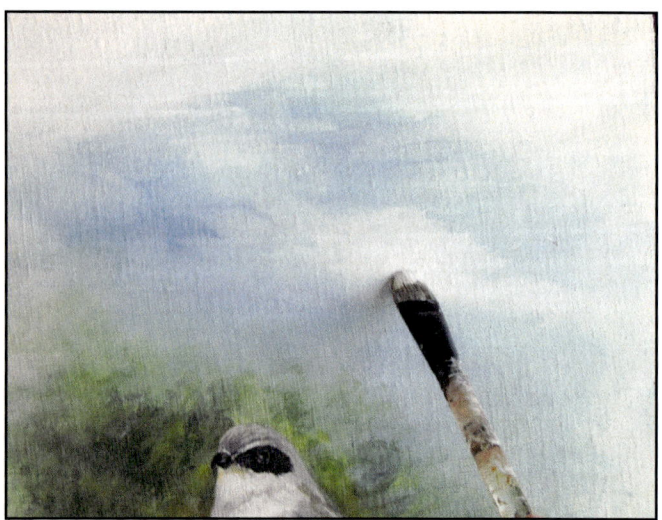

Step 60 Add more white to center of cloud and soften edges.

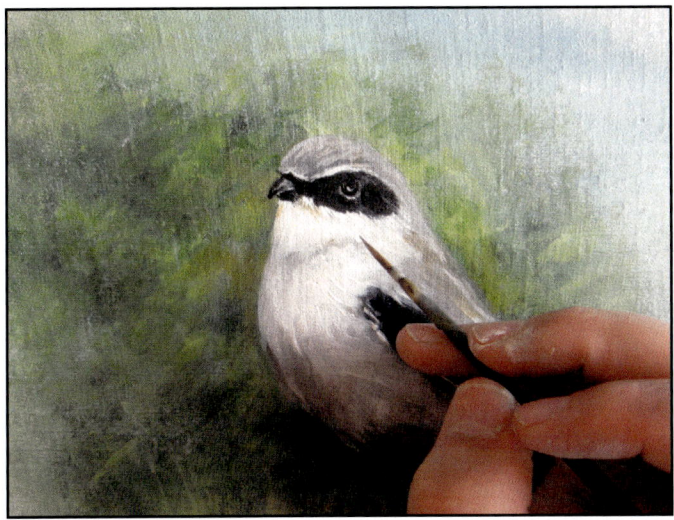
Step 61 Add final smaller feathers around the head area with the liner and white.

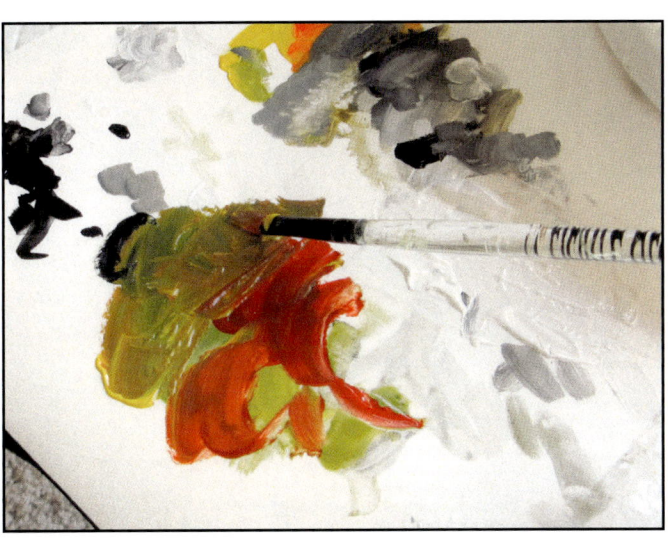
Step 62 Mottle a brown again with the red, yellow and touch black. Use small flat brush.

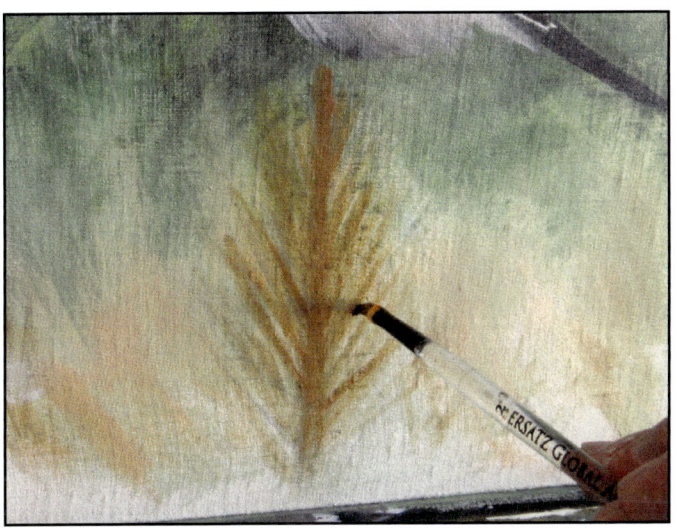
Step 63 Begin to build the shape of the pine top with the chisel.

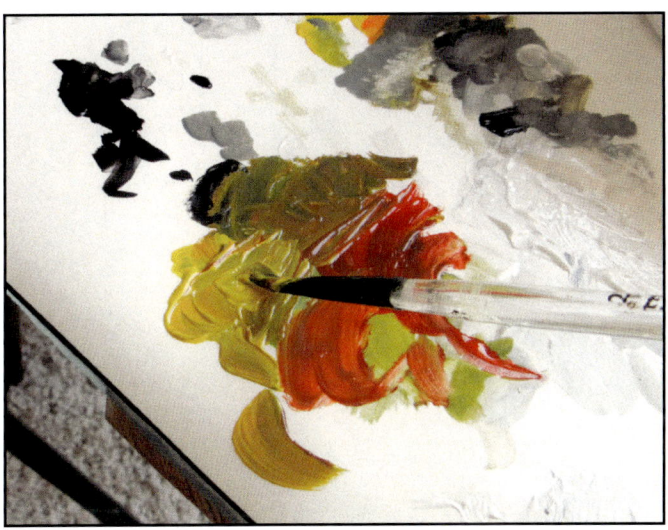
Step 64 Mottle the color lighter with some Hansa Yellow.

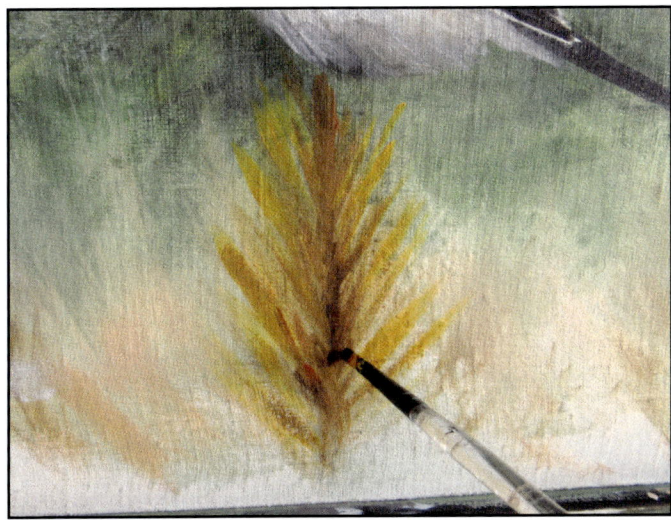
Step 65 Add to the pine needles and then add some mottled red colors.

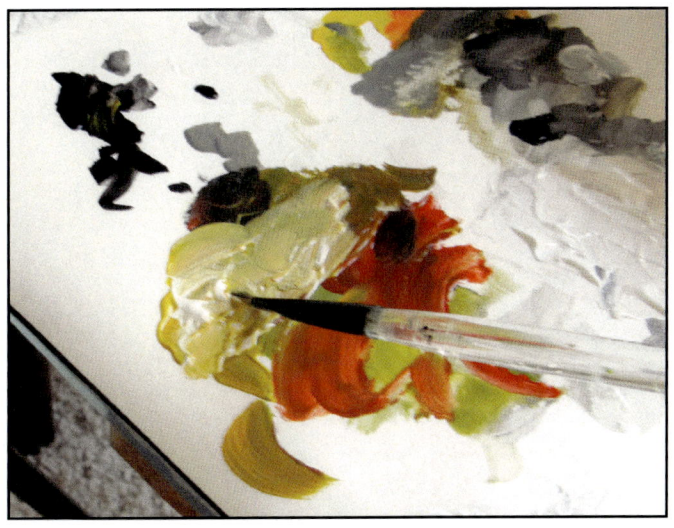
Step 66 Lighten the color with some whites and more Hansa.

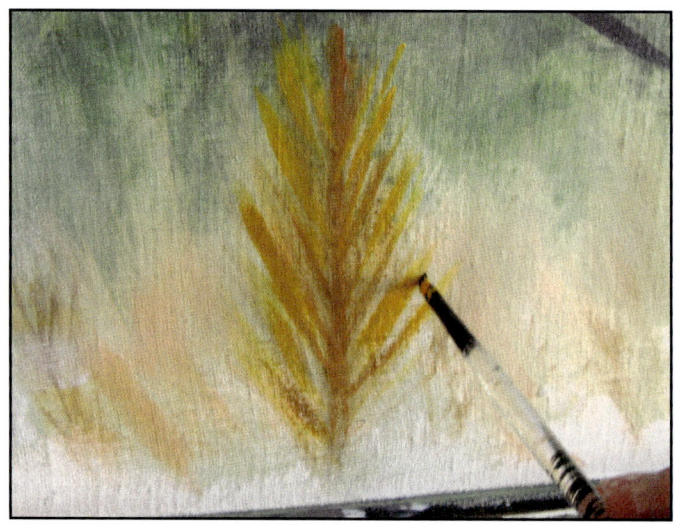

Step 67 Add this to the pine needles, slowly lightening in ever smaller areas.

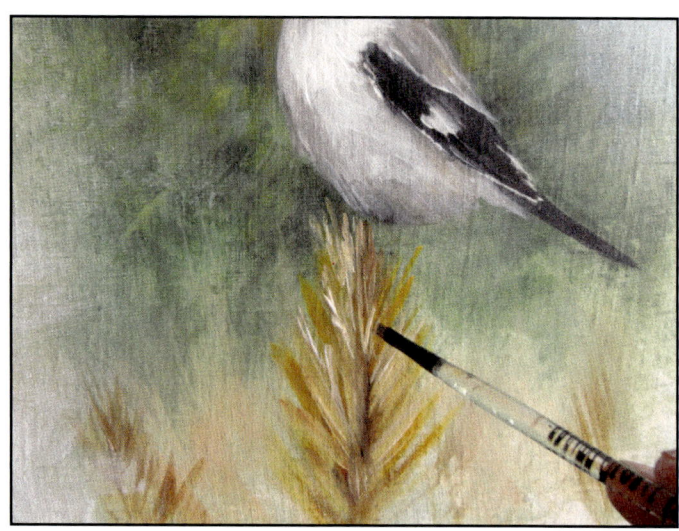

Step 68 Use the chisel and touches of white to add some small details to the pine needles.

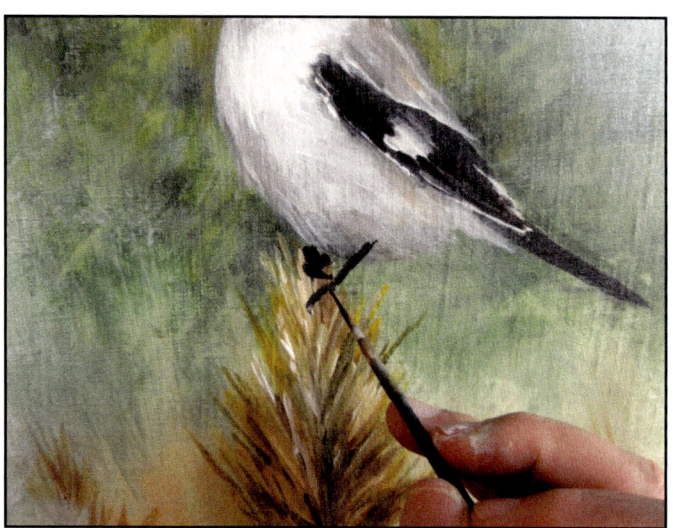

Step 69 Use the liner and some various greys to add the suggestions of the feet grabbing the top of the pine. I repeated several times.

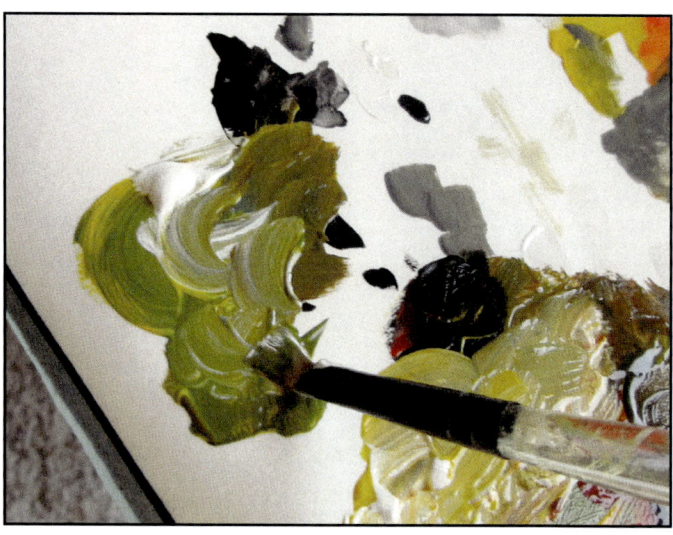

Step 70 Mottle more greens to add to outer pine needles tops. Vary colors. Slowly lighten the color to build highlights.

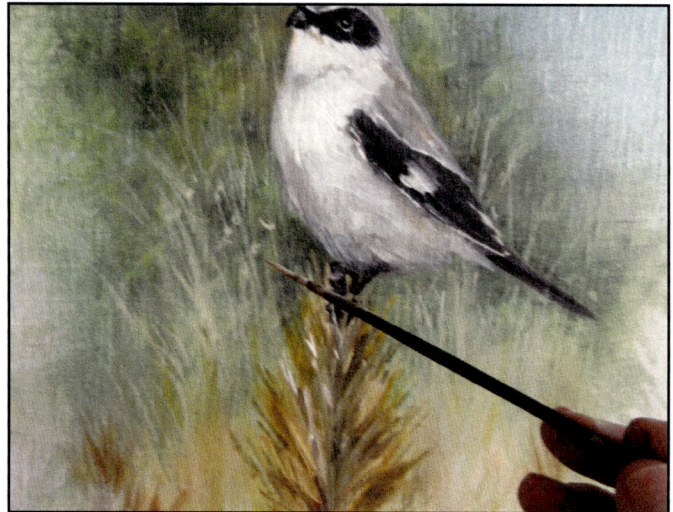

Step 71 Add liner of light yellow to make grasses and then tap to make small shines.

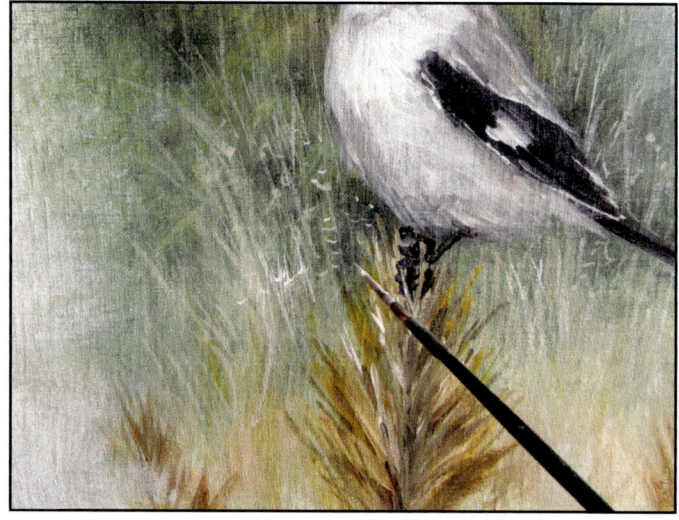

Step 72 Add more white shines and small touches of interest to finish. Enjoy!

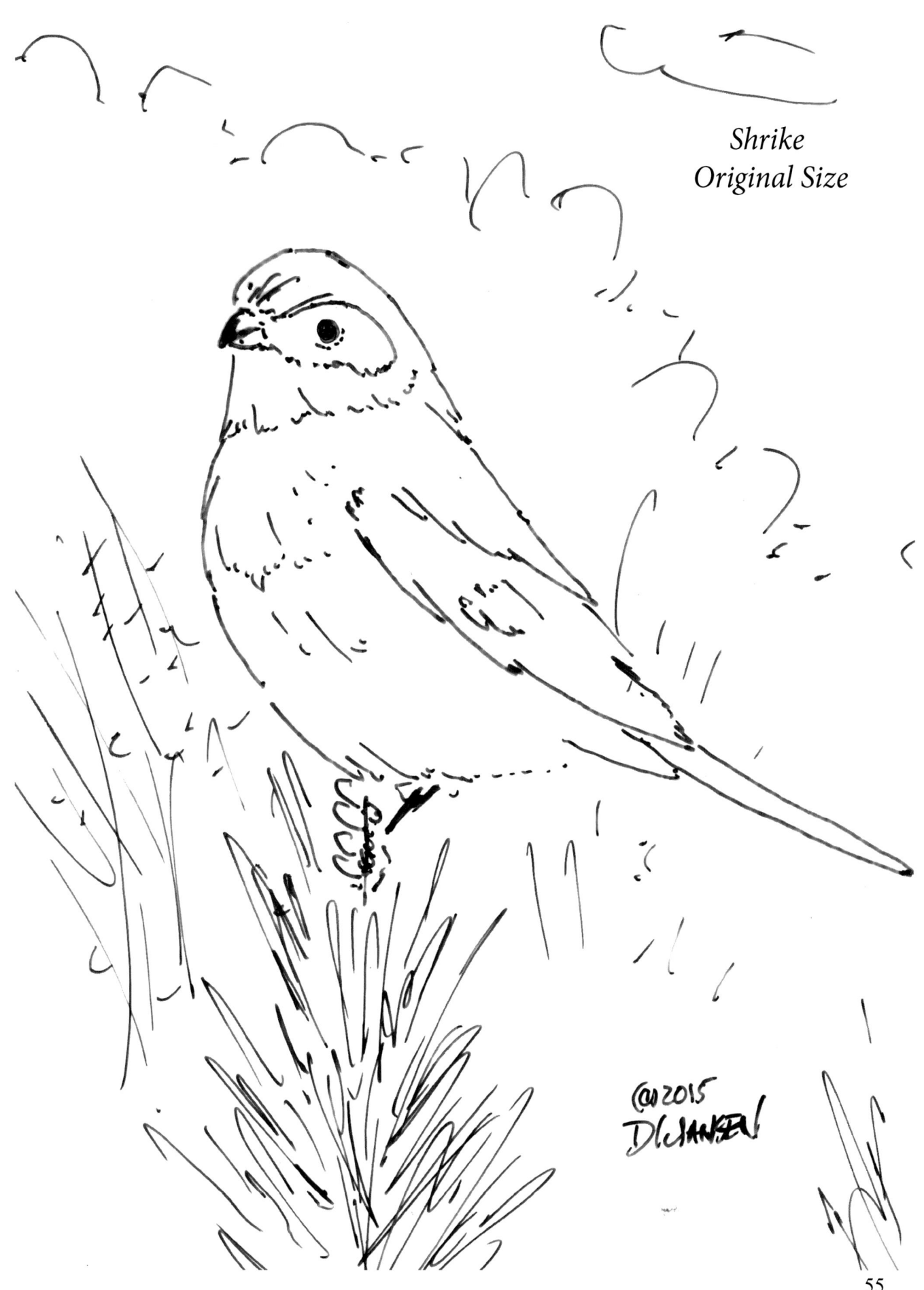

*Shrike
Original Size*

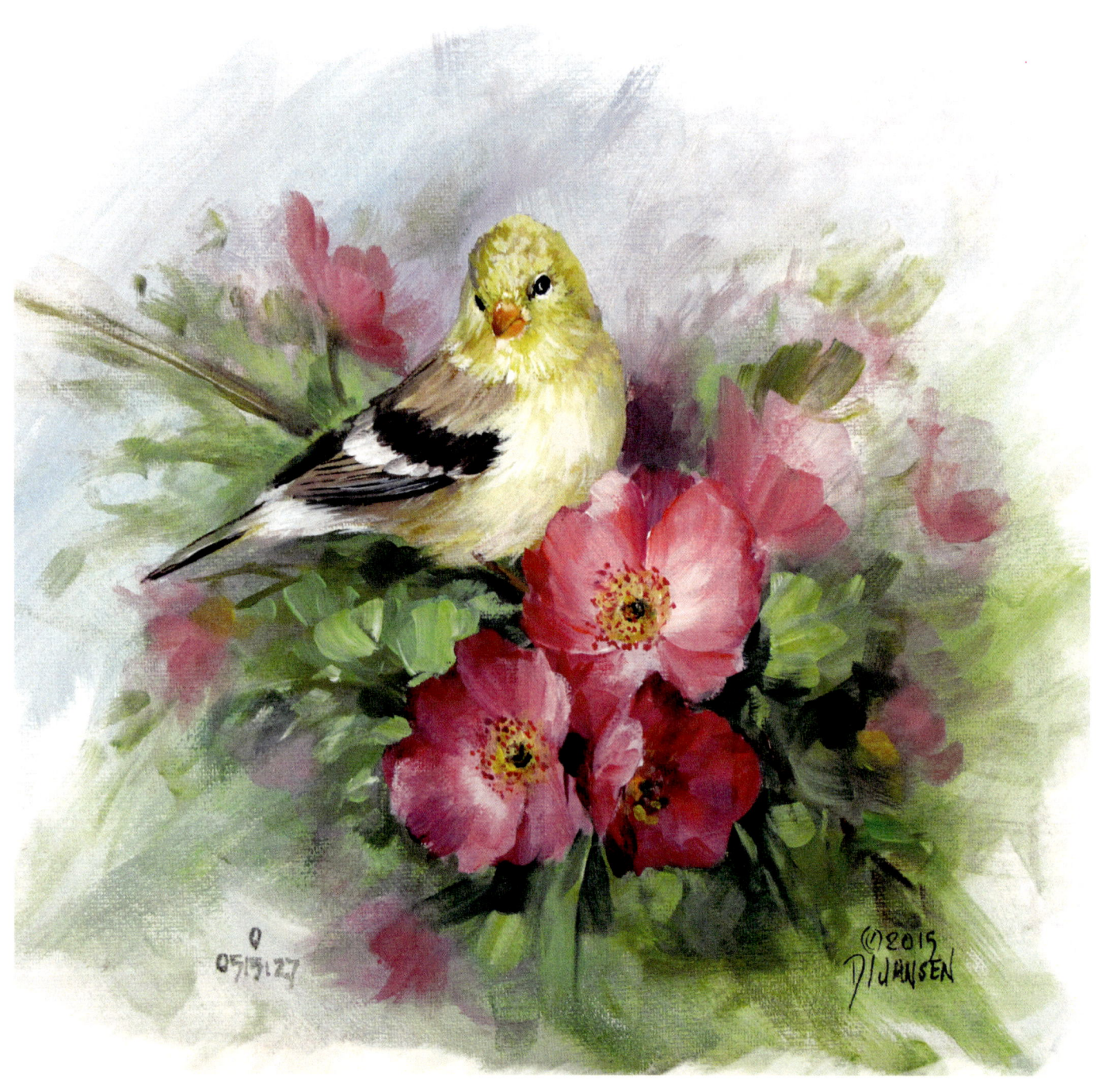

Goldfinch with Wild Roses

Goldfinch and Wild Roses

The female goldfinch is my favorite bird to paint. I love her soft yellows and tan colors. Her soft and gentle face. We will also paint our bird this time with some lovely wild roses. The first step in building a painting such as this is to decide the bird. Done, female goldfinch. Step 2 is to choose the composition. Here, I wanted her more horizontal to the painting surface and to look back over her shoulder for a different effect. Done. Next is to decide what kind of flowers to paint.

I break flowers into several different types. There are blossoms such as the wild rose. There is the rose which we will paint with the flycatcher. Also, there are multi petaled flowers like wild flowers or daisies. Wildflowers and daisies have a lot of directional motion to them and require a painting that has a lot of interest of movement. If you want to paint the goldfinch softly, you will not be able to paint her with a group of daisies. She would need lots of contrasting feathers so she can confront of the many petaled daisy. She would look great when painted with larger softer flowers.

So wild roses would be a good choice, angled through many planes of the design, with some flowers having strong petal edges while others are softer and recede into the design.

Now for color choices. She is a soft yellow, so following the rules of color contrast, she will stand out better if we used a version of the compliment. She would look great with any violet, blue violet or red violet wild blossoms. Her colors are warm, being to the yellow side, so we will make some cool red violets and cool greens to blue greens. She will contrast with the blossoms and leaves and you will see her more in the painting. Notice the "purple" or violet stroke just behind her breast area. This is a contrast color that brings her forward. Many times when I design a painting I look at the bird colors, amount of feathering interest and then decide on accent objects that will enhance the bird giving them the most interest. Let's give it a try!

Paint It Simply Palette
Base Color- Medium White from Mixes

Palette Colors

Naphthol Red Light	Hansa Yellow
Red Violet	Titanium White
Carbon Black	Medium White
Phthalo Blue	Base Brown
	Pine Green

Wood Surface
Super MDF Wood Panel about 11 Inch X 14 Inch to fit picture frame. Can also use canvas panel.

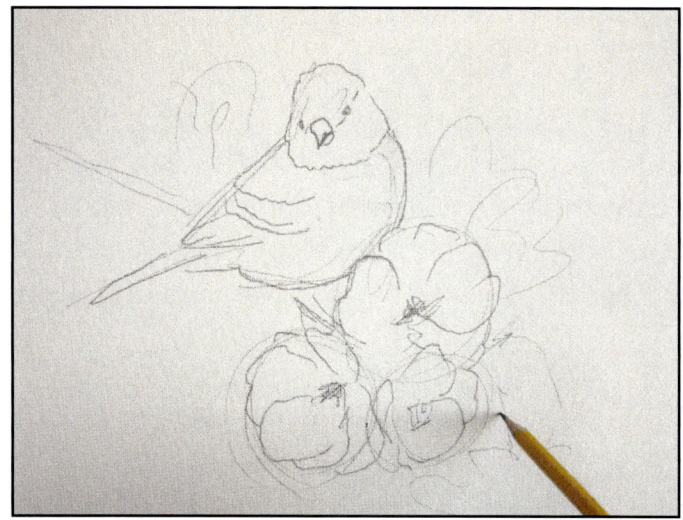

Step 1 Same step. White base canvas, transfer the design or sketch with pencil. Keep lines dark so you can see them through the paint.

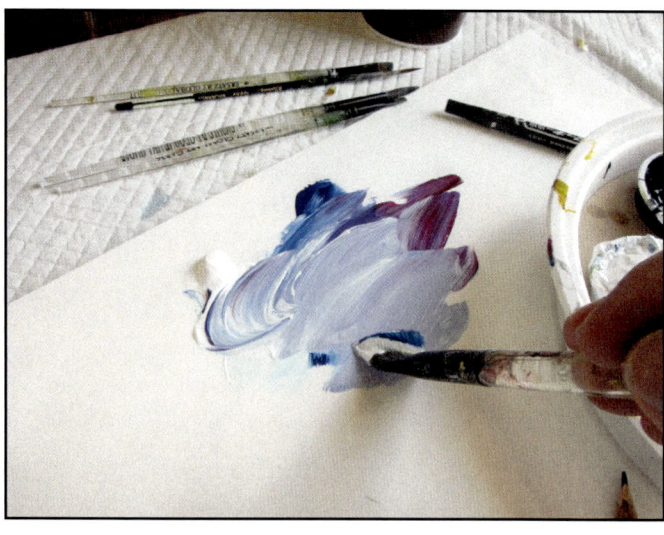

Step 2 Mottle a light blue violet with blue and Red Violet. Lighten with white and add Extender Medium.

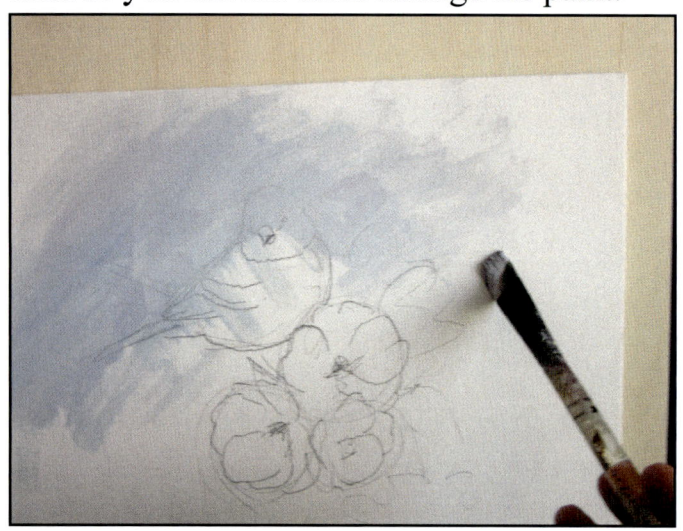

Step 3 Start working this across the top of the sky and down around the bird and flower tops.

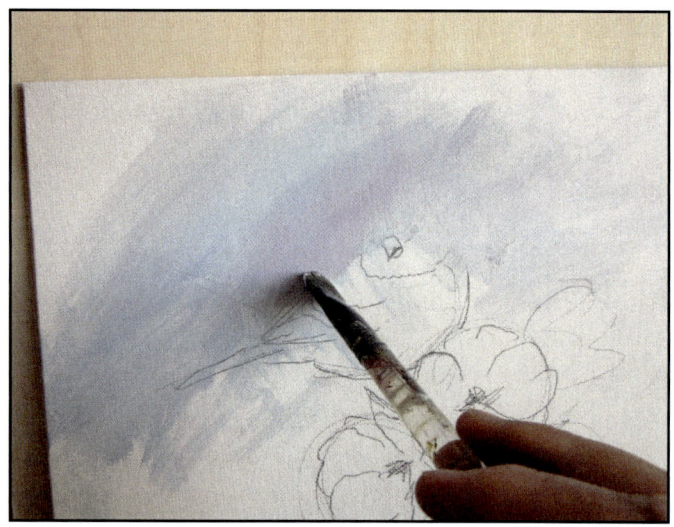

Step 4 Build the color a little more opaque around the bird to bring it forward when we apply color to the bird.

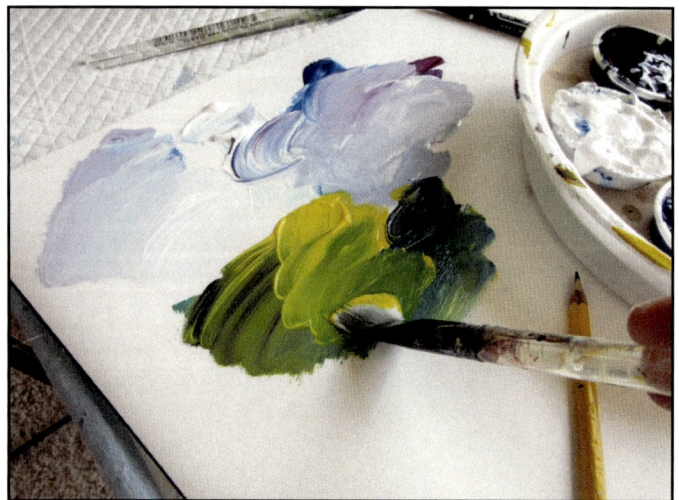

Step 5 Mottle a lighter yellow green with Hansa, black on one side add touch blue.

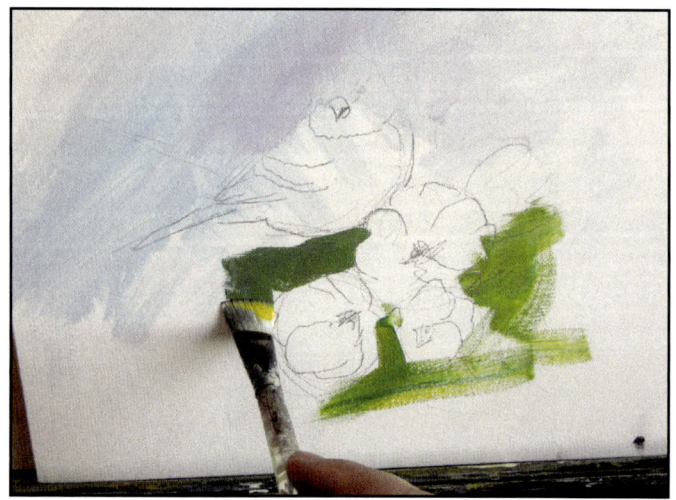

Step 6 Add around the flowers as a light green base for the leaves.

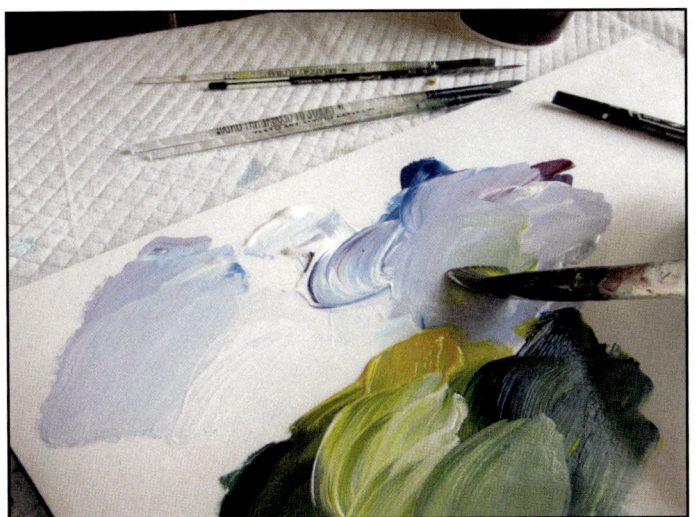

Step 7 Mottle the brush back into the blues and lighten with touch more white.

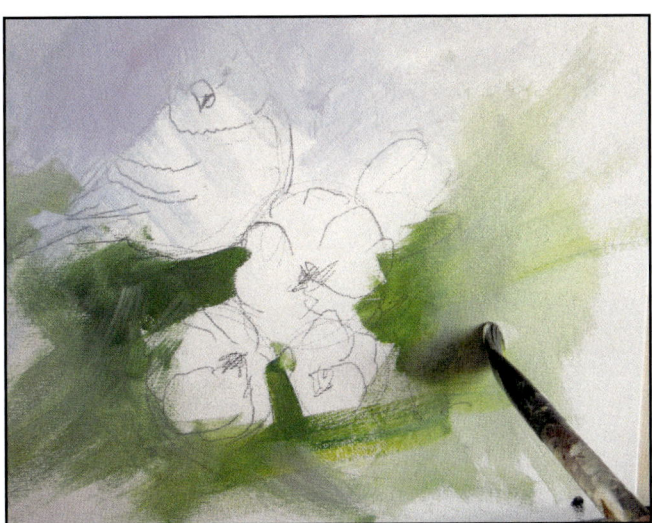

Step 8 Stroke the light blues into the greens and drag the color out to soften the outer edges.

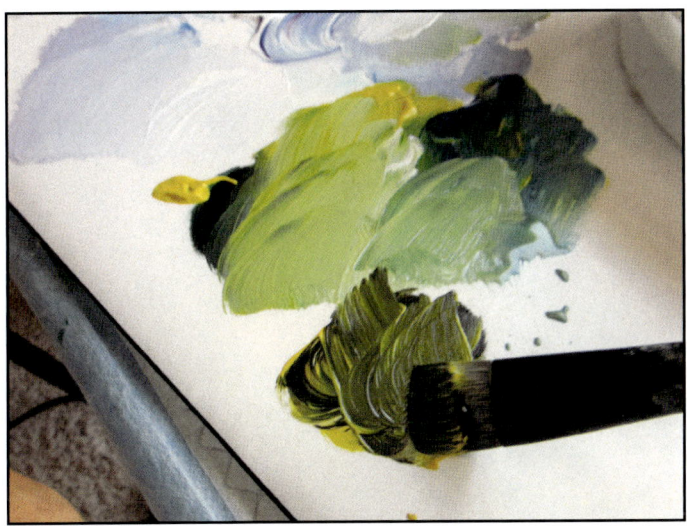

Step 9 Change the green by mottling with some black.

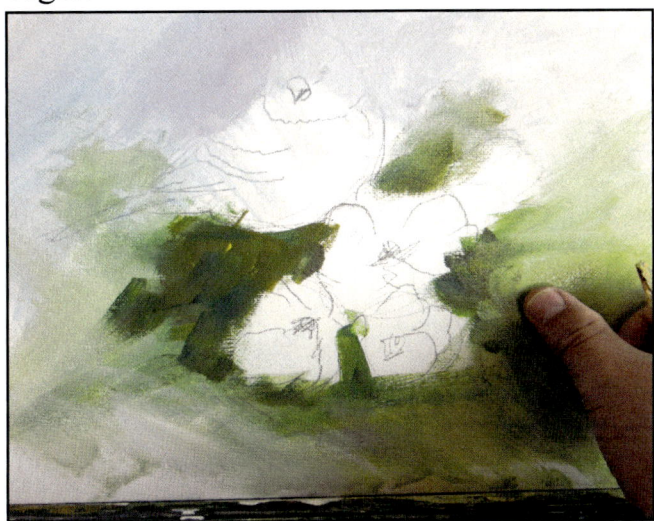

Step 10 Add around the flowers and drag out with your finger to soften the greens.

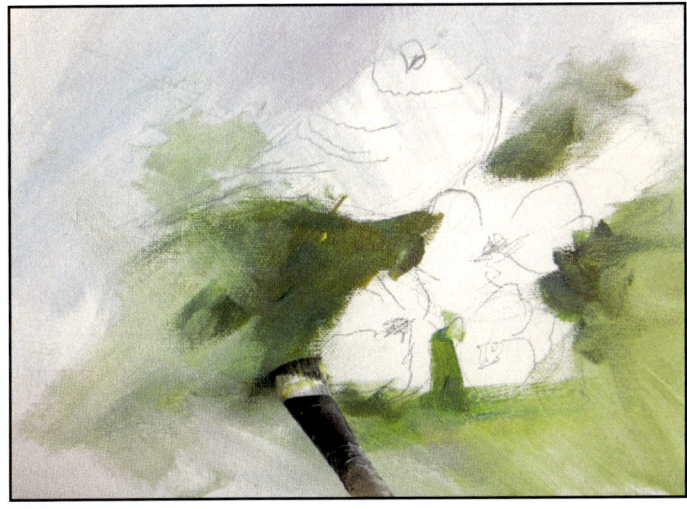

Step 11 Increase the color between the flowers which will make more opaque for contrast.

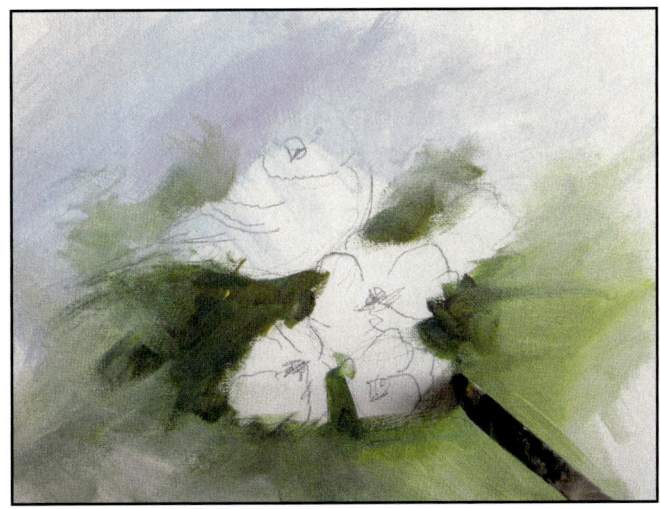

Step 12 Cool the color with some blue and touch black and add between flowers.

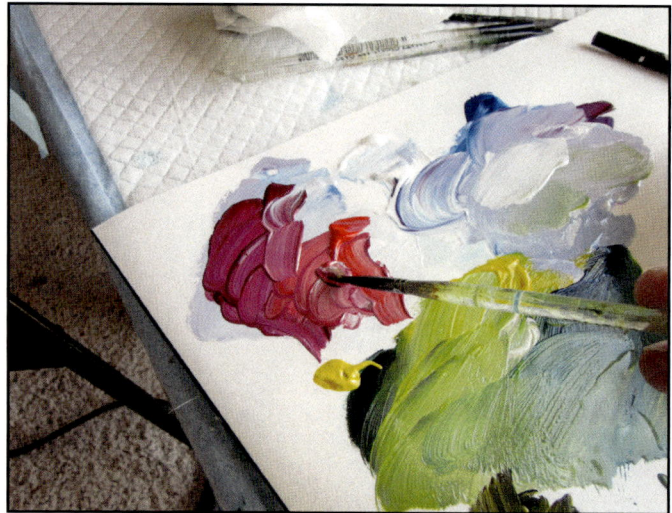

Step 13 Mottle Red Violet and Nap. Red Light together, then add touch sky colors to lighten.

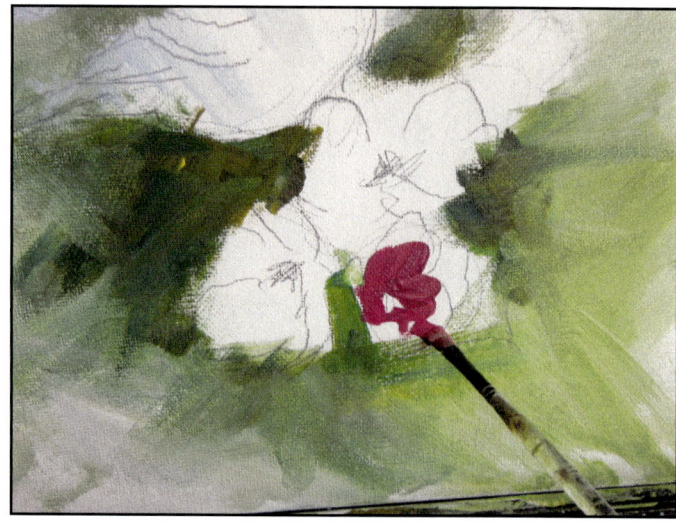

Step 14 Begin to base in the wild rose shapes. Use short strokes of the brush to make the shapes.

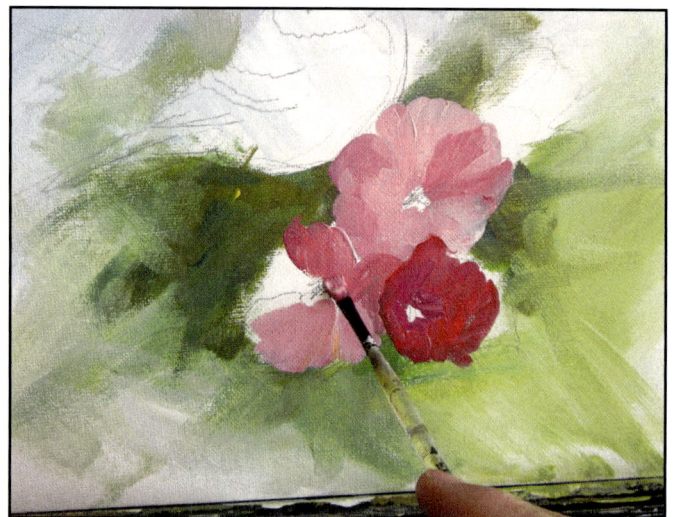

Step 15 Lighten the color with more white and add the other flowers. Vary the white to make various values of light pink.

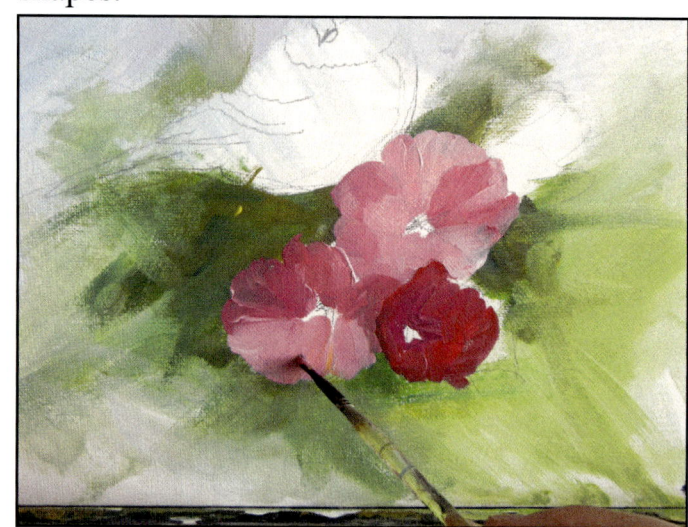

Step 16 Pull the strokes out from the center of the flower to give the petals some movement.

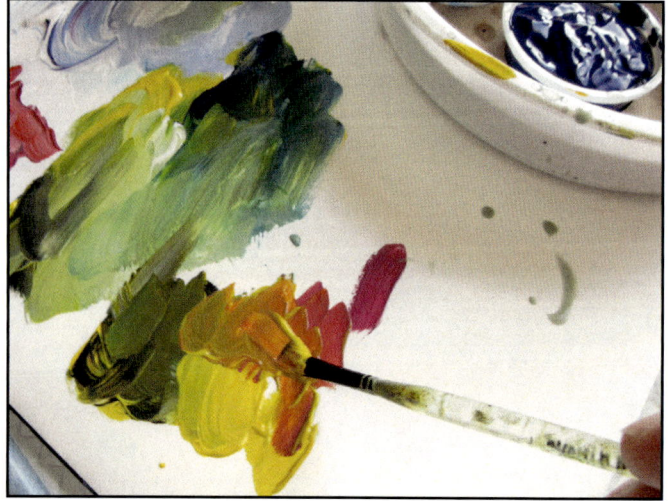

Step 17 Mottle the brush with the reds in the brush and then Hansa with touches of greens.

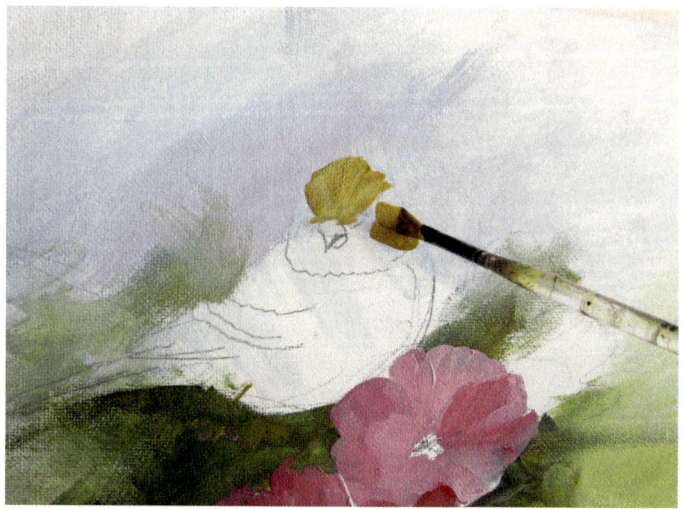

Step 18 Begin to base in her head with this toned yellow. Darken for side of her head.

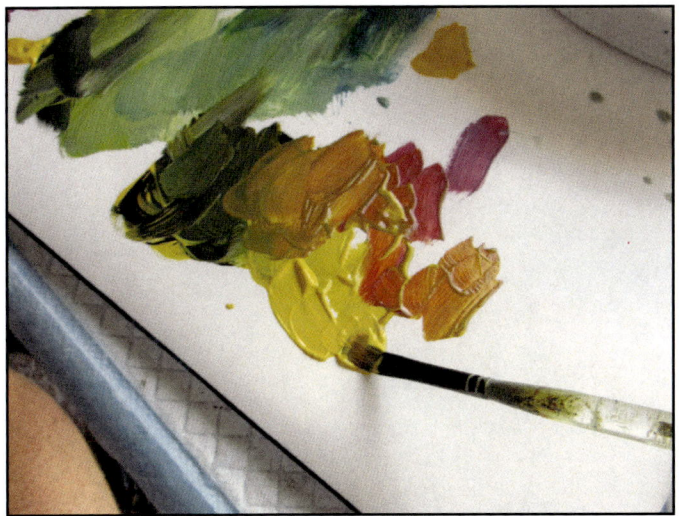

Step 19 Mottle with more Hansa Yellow to make a little brighter.

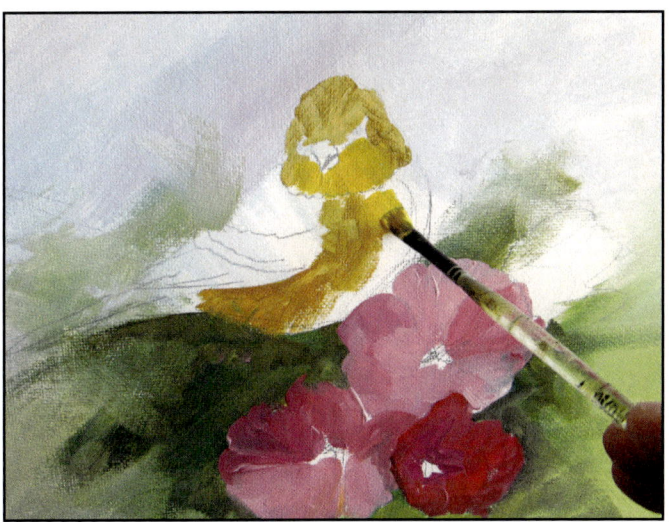

Step 20 Begin the front of her. Use the darker toned color under the wings and bottom of her body for roundness.

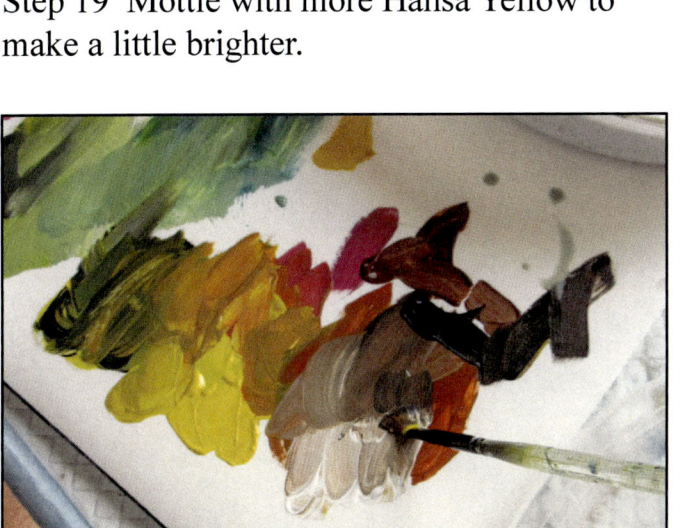

Step 21 Mottle the reds with a little white, black and touch yellows to make light tan color.

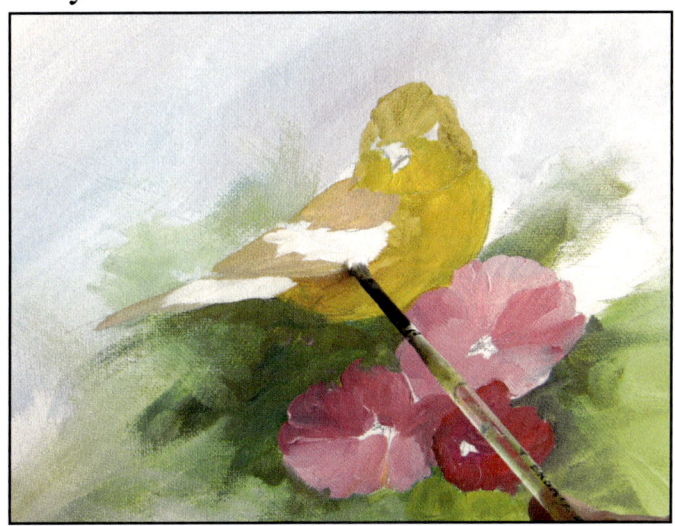

Step 22 Mottle this into the mantle and coverts of the wings. Long strokes for the primary flight feathers. Add white convert feathers.

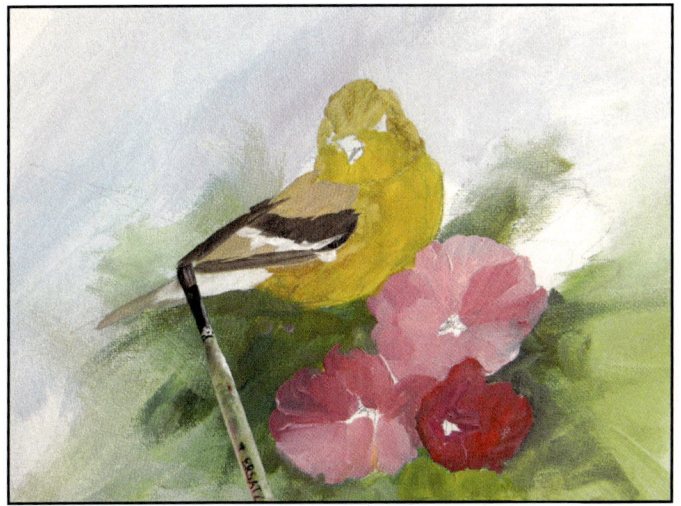

Step 23 Mottle the brush darker with touch black and add the darker coverts to the wings.

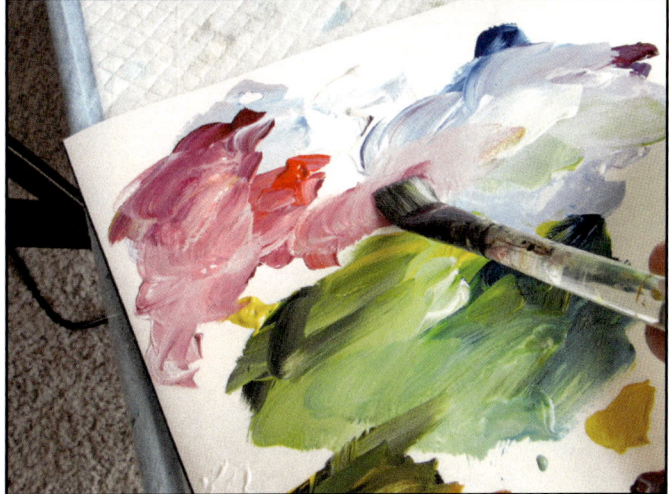

Step 24 Mottle the pinks with some soft sky colors using the 3/4 inch brush.

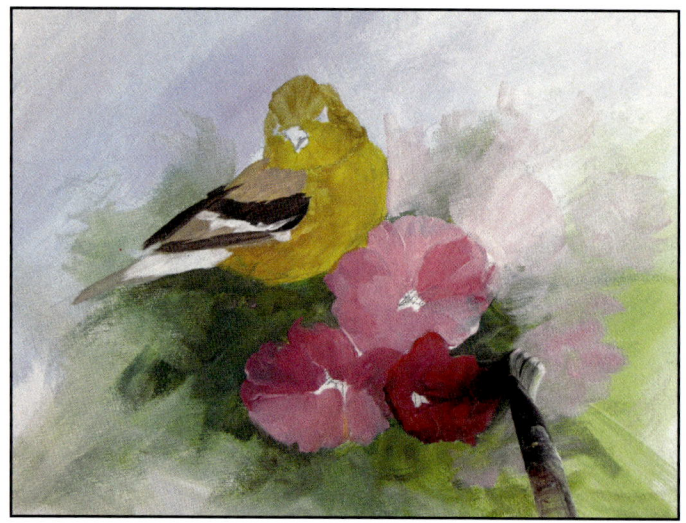

Step 25 Add some suggestions of back flowers with this transparent soft pink. Just suggest shapes for now.

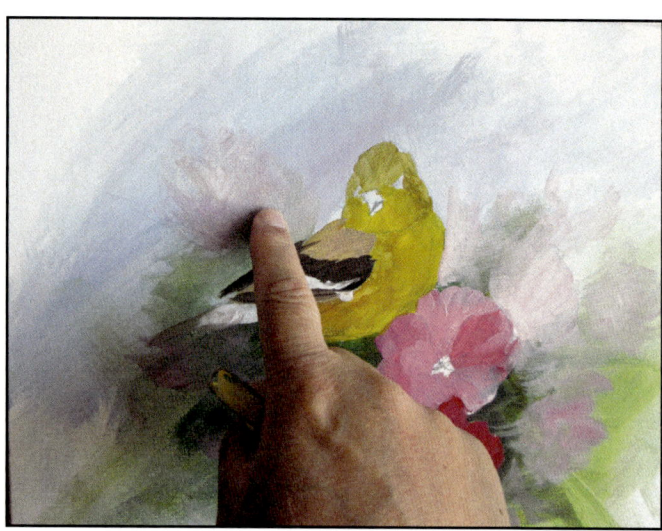

Step 26 Use your finger to suggest some soft movement to the flowers.

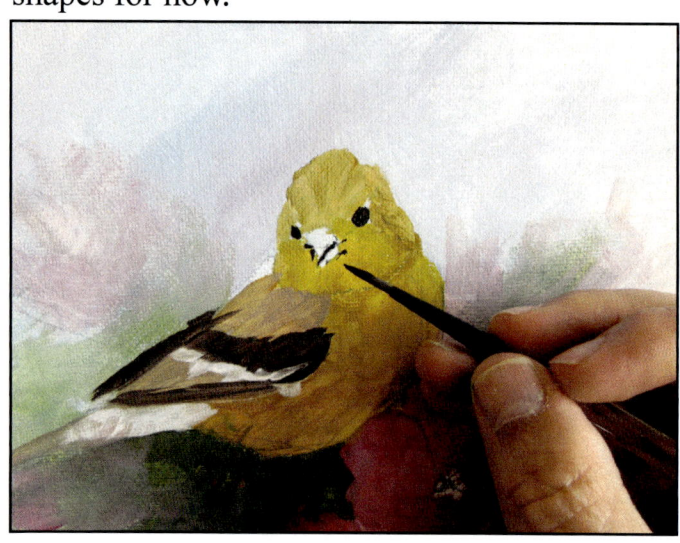

Step 27 Use the liner or round to add the eyes and the shadow lines of the beak. Use black.

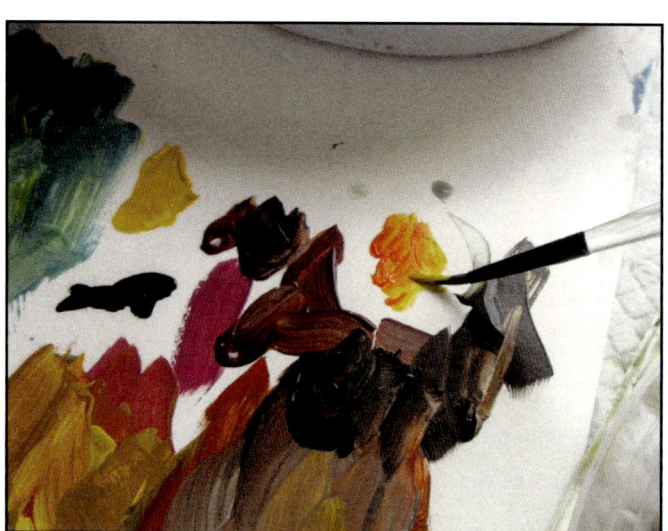

Step 28 Mottle an orange with red and Hansa. Lots of Hansa and just a touch of Nap. Red Light.

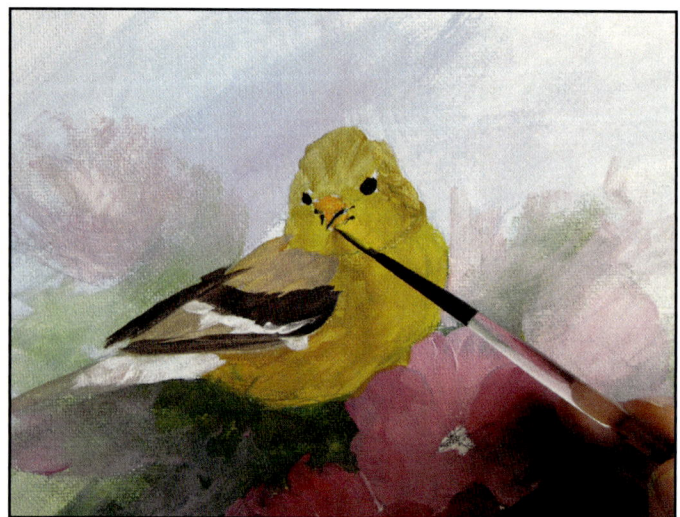

Step 29   Add this to the beak with the liner or round.

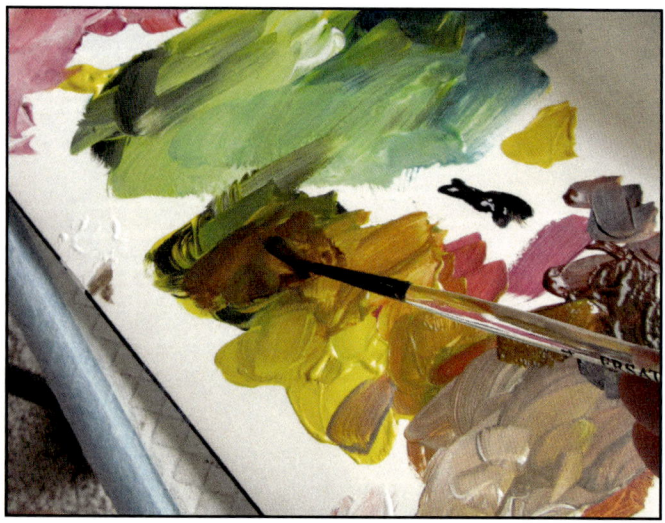

Step 30 Back to the toned yellow. Add more yellow and tone with green and red.

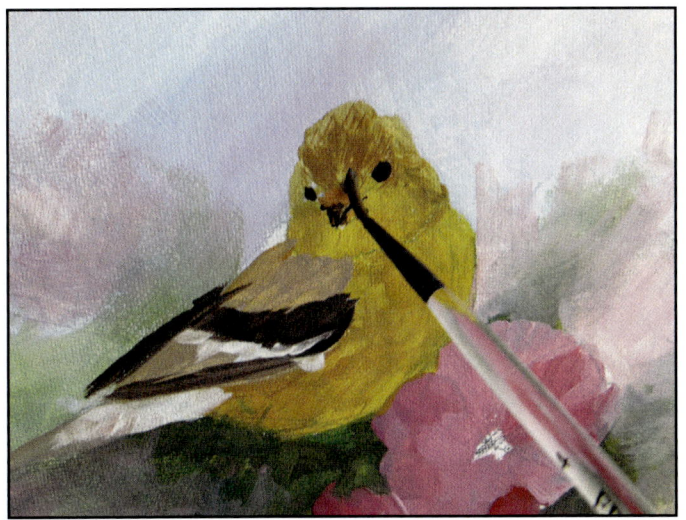

Step 31 Add this shadow yellow to the top of her head. Remember follow the contour and use smaller touches around the beak.

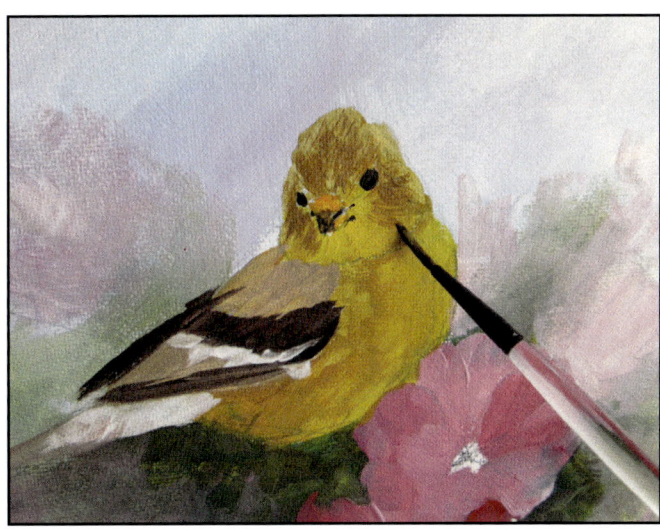

Step 32 Stroke down the sides of the head softening into the yellow of the body.

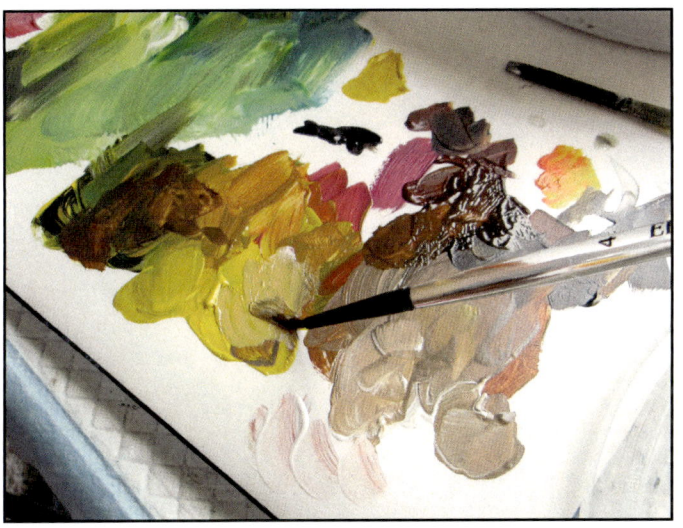

Step 33 Mottle the round brush back into the tan colors from earlier and add to touch more Hansa to brighten the color.

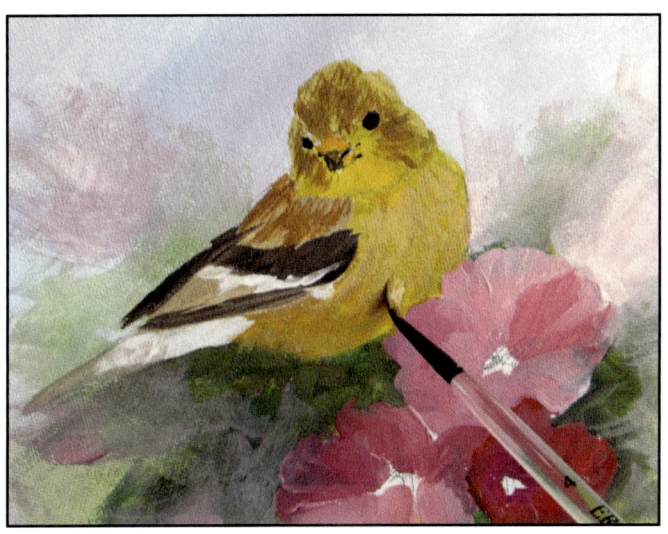

Step 34 Add this color with strokes to the breast. Soften the strokes down the breast with your finger like the first lesson.

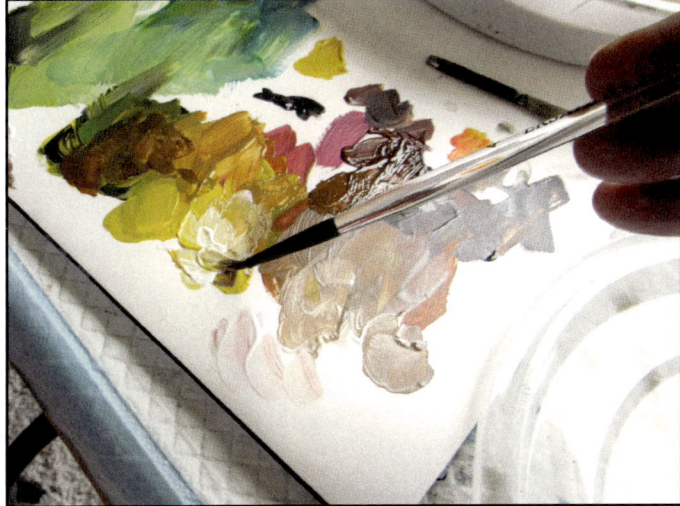

Step 35 Mottle the color a little lighter with some more Hansa and then white.

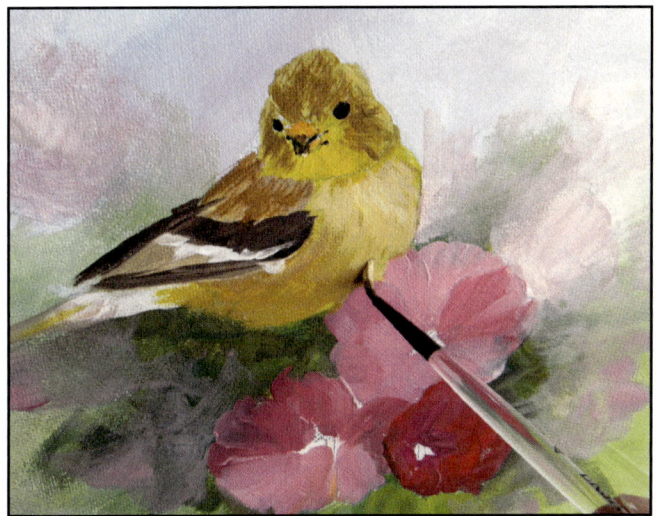

Step 36 Add the feathers to the breast area with strokes of light yellow tan.

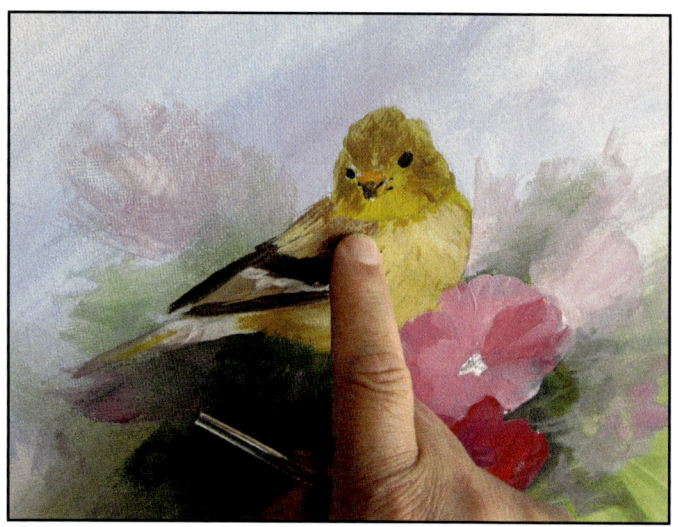

Step 37 Add some strokes of the light tan to the mantle on top the wings and then soften the feathers with your finger.

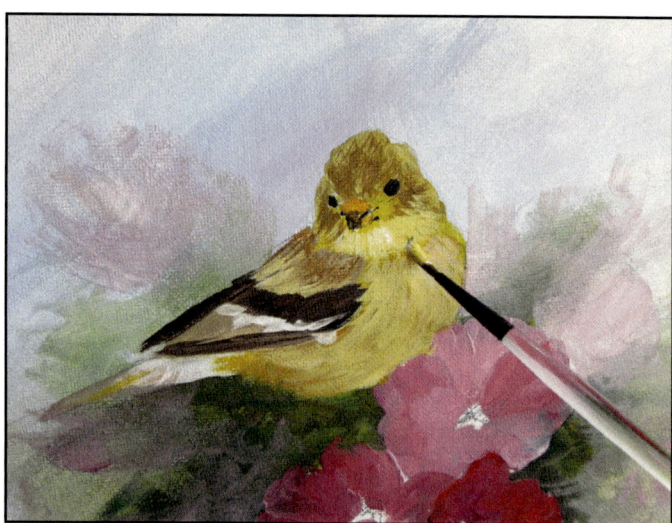

Step 38 Lighten the color again with more Hansa and white and add some smaller lighter feather strokes to the neck.

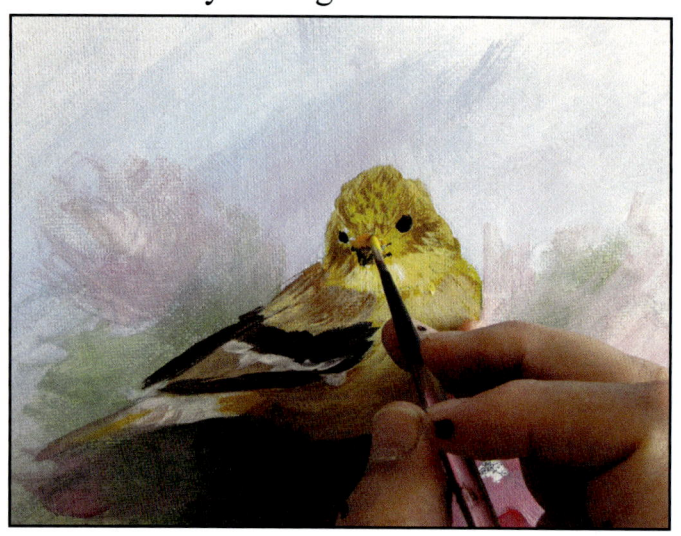

Step 39 Lighten the color and add some smaller touches of feathers around the neck and beak of the bird.

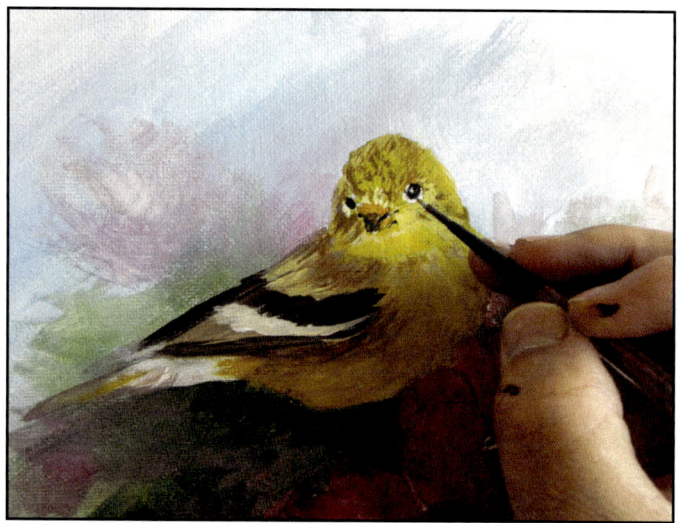

Step 40 Using a liner brush, add the light white eye ring around the eye and the small touch of shine to make the eye sparkle.

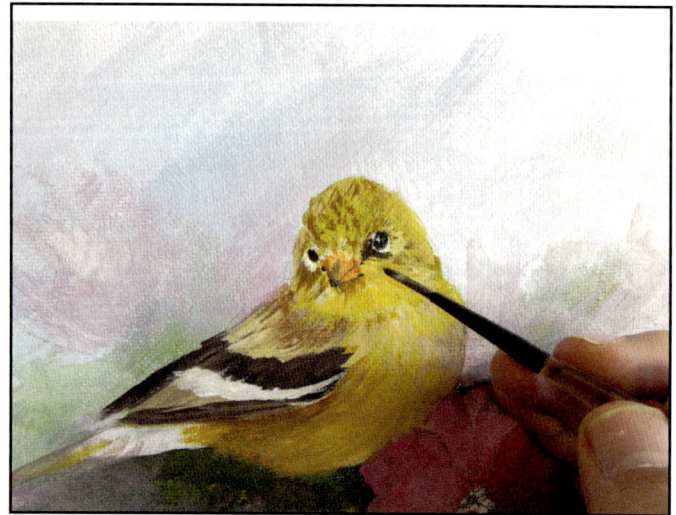

Step 41 Restate some darker brown and black shadow around the eye

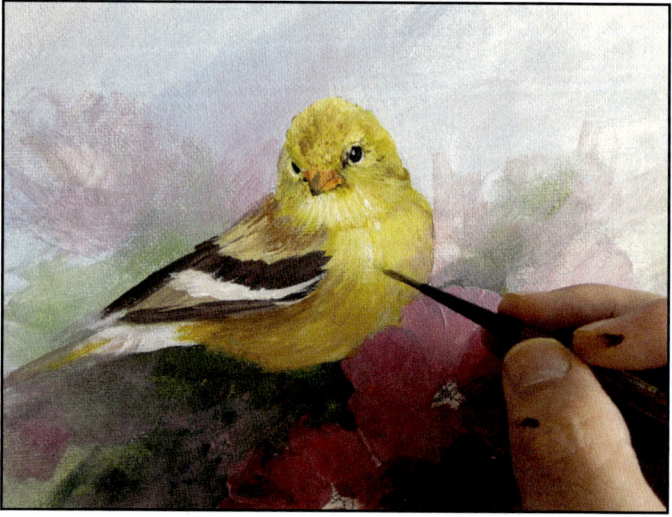

Step 42 Soften the shadows with light strokes. Continue to build light strokes.

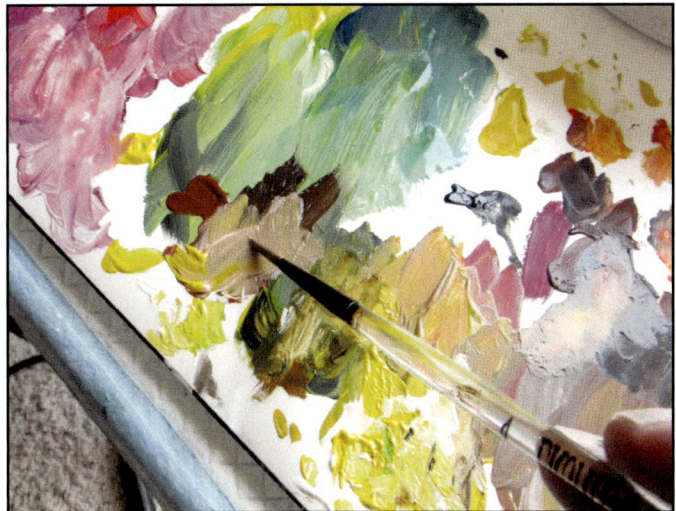

Step 43 Mottle the brush back into the tan colors.

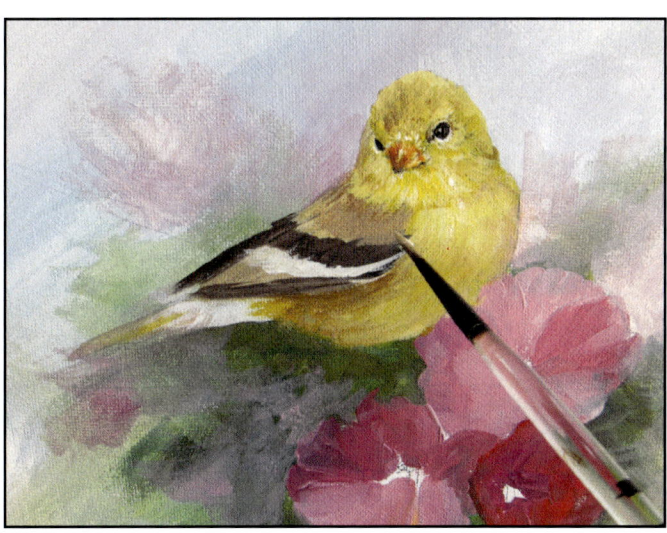

Step 44 Restate the mantle area on top the wing to add more stroke interest.

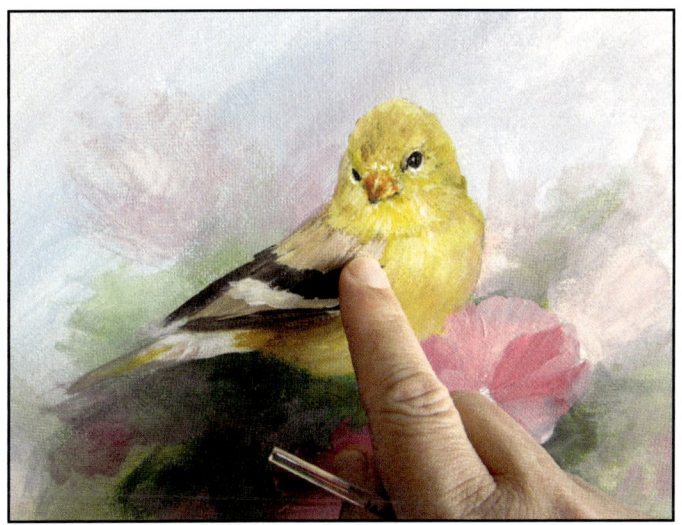

Step 45 Soften the mantle with your finger. I do this several times to create interesting movement in the feathers.

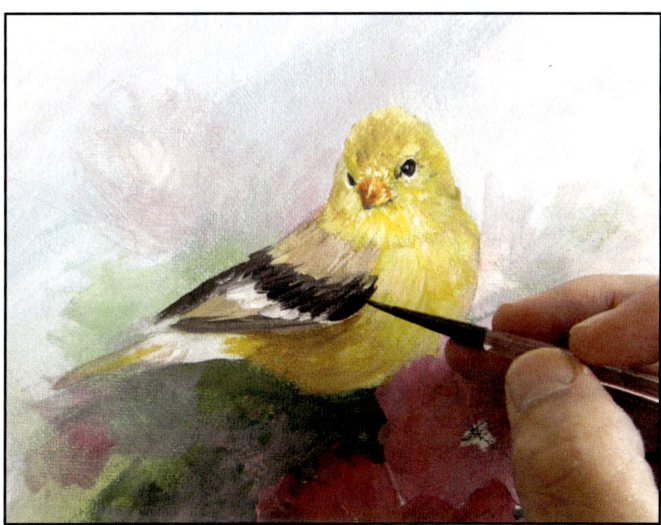

Step 46 Using a small round or flat add the darker, almost black, secondary flight feathers with medium sized strokes.

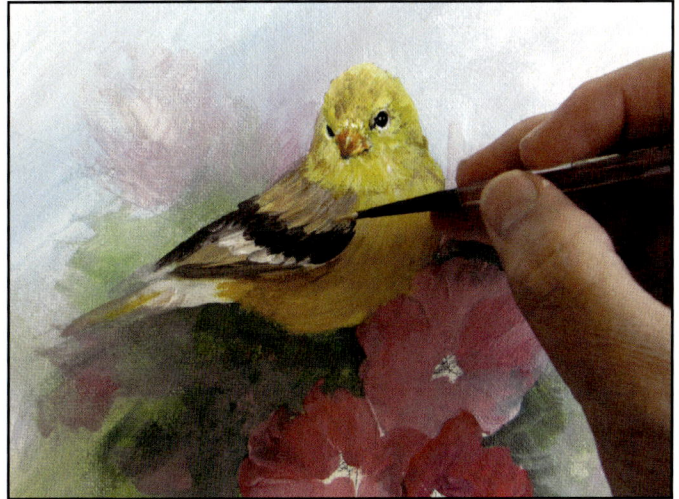

Step 47 Pull some tan color on top to suggest the lighter mantle on top the flight feathers.

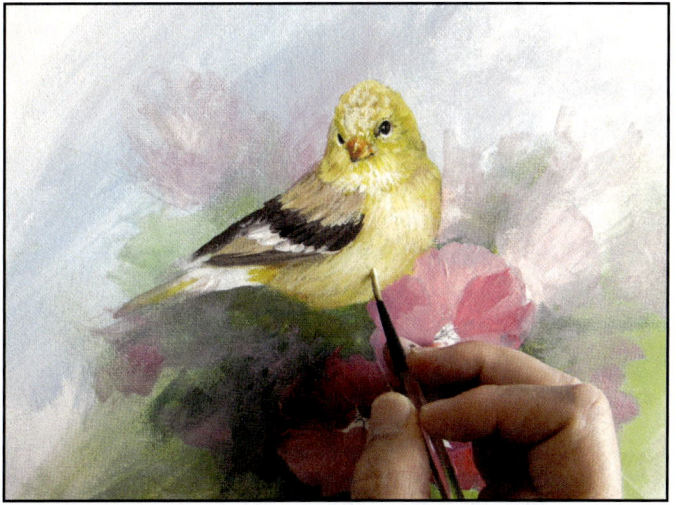

Step 48 Restate the lights on the breast area adding some smaller feather details.

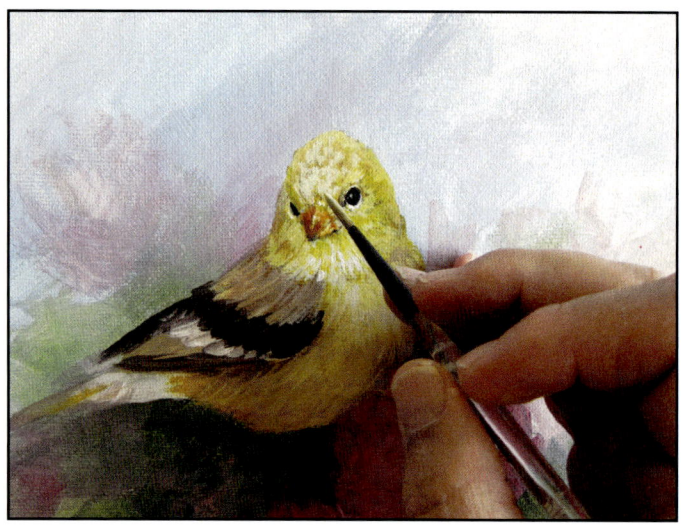

Step 49   Lighten the yellow with more white. Almost pure white and add some smaller touches to the top of her head.

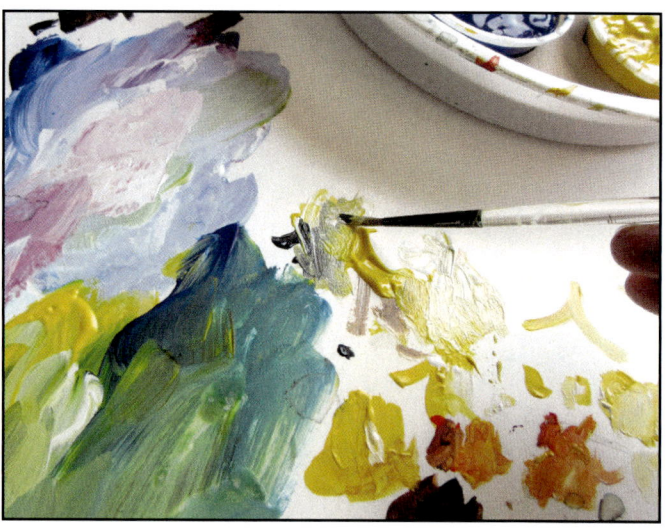

Step 50   Mottle the yellow with touch black and blues to create a cool light color. Almost grey.

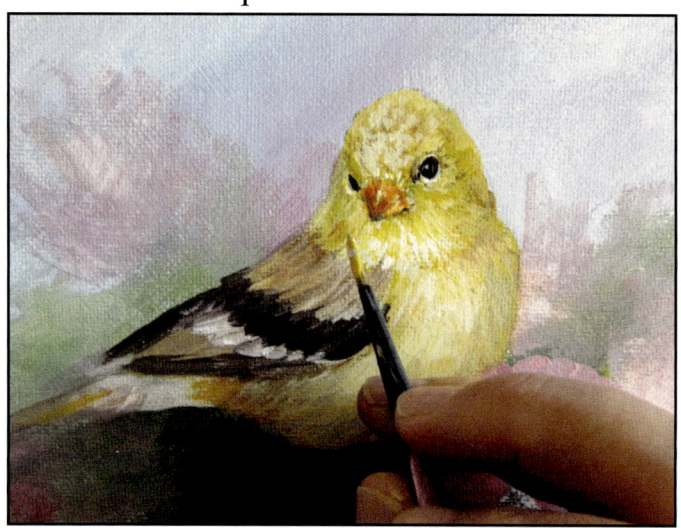

Step 51   Add to the left side of her face to tone he yellow and cause her face to turn down. This is a cool light color.

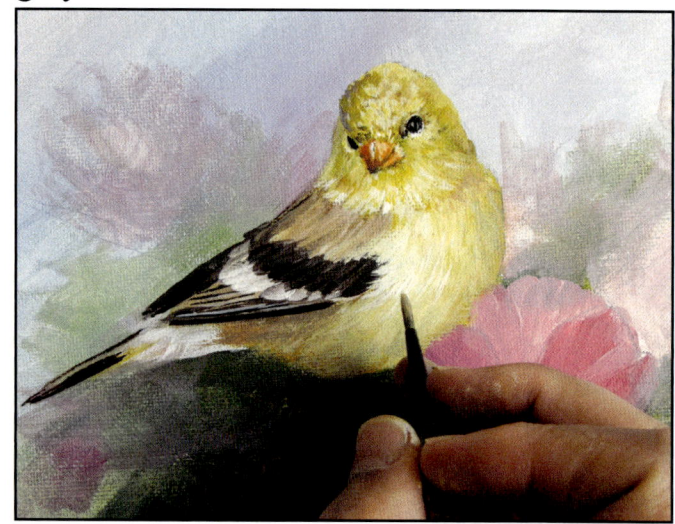

Step 52   Add some light feathers to the breast areas and dray over the wing. Add some dark and light details to the primary flight feathers.

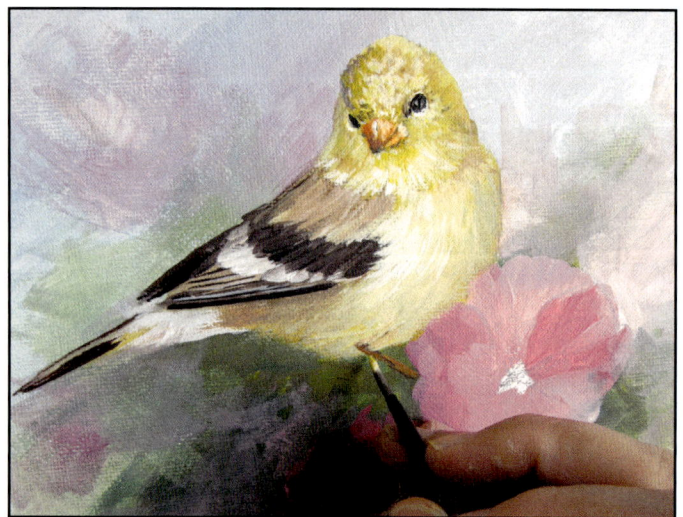

Step 53   Add her leg with some toned orange and then add some light feathers over it.

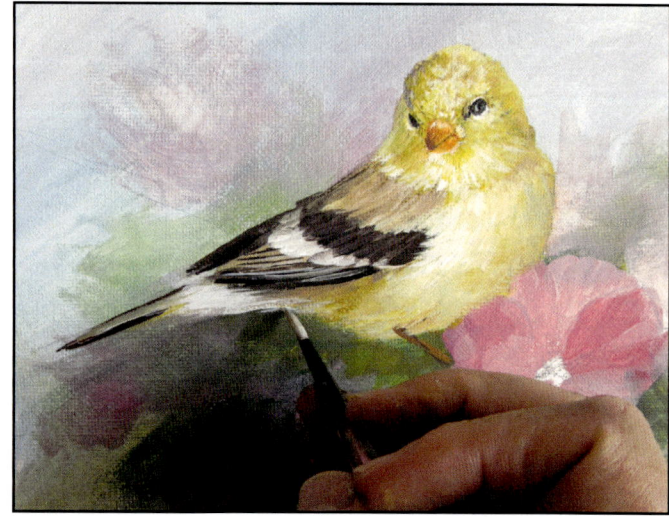

Step 54 Add some small strokes of white to the base of the tail to make feathers.

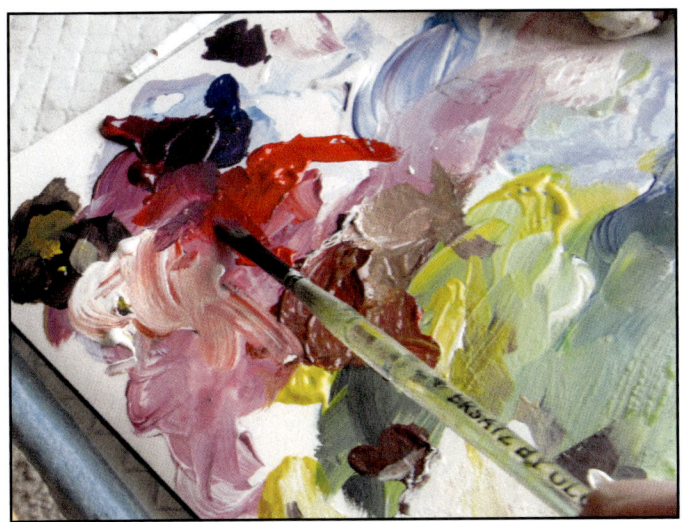

Step 55 Mottle the brush back into reds with touch blue to make darker. Keep mottled.

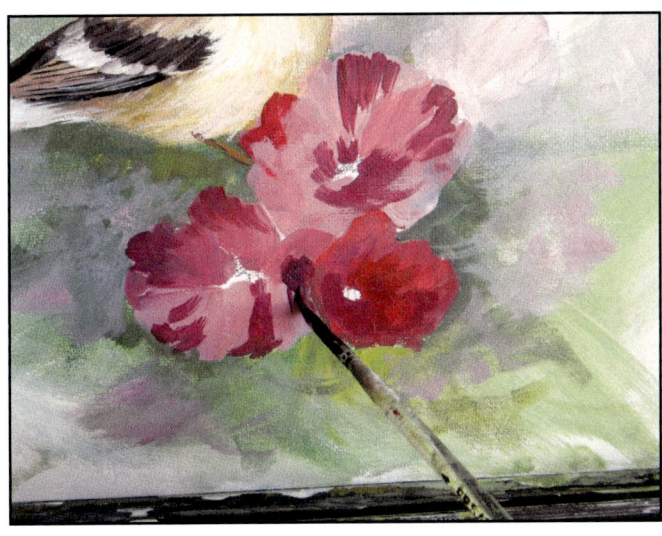

Step 56 Add some shadows and darker strokes from the tips of the petals in. Notice they don't go to the center. Short strokes.

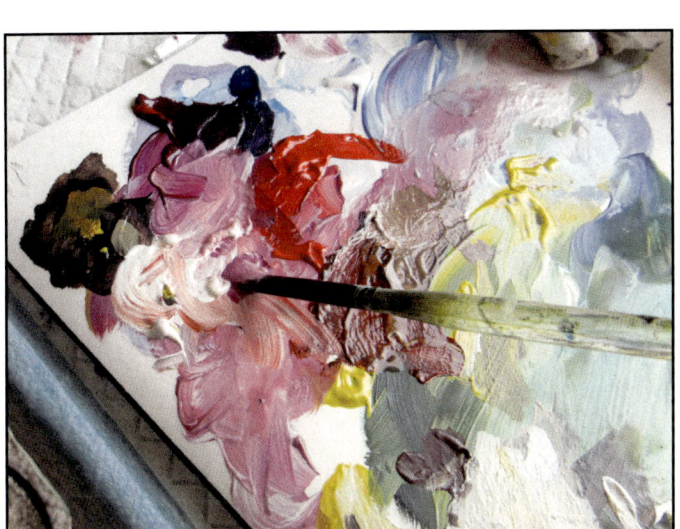

Step 57 Mottle the brush a little lighter with some white and touch Hansa to make just a little warmer orange color.

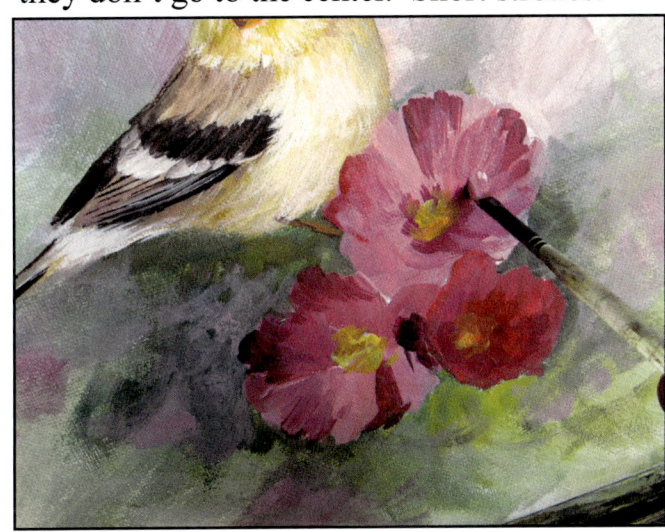

Step 58 Add this to the petals of the wild roses in the centers to build the streaky interest. Add Hansa centers to the roses.

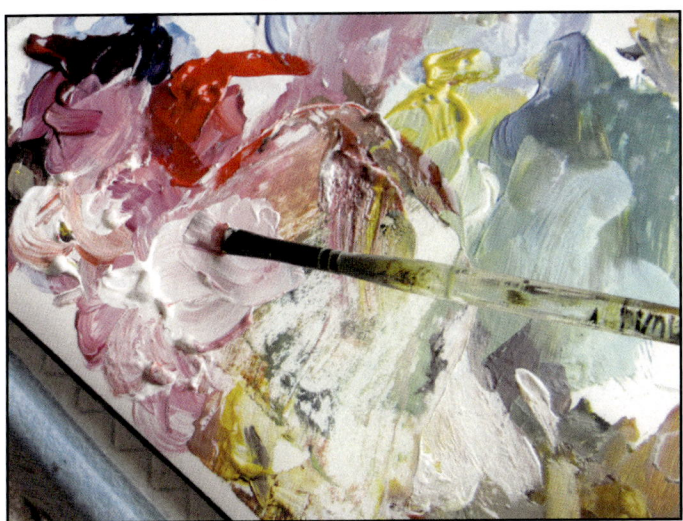

Step 59 Mottle the color a little lighter with some white.

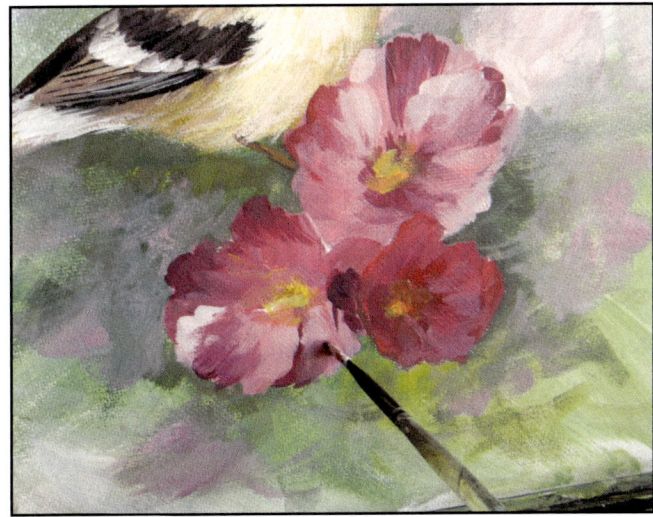

Step 60 Add some short strokes of white to the petals to make them more "streaky".

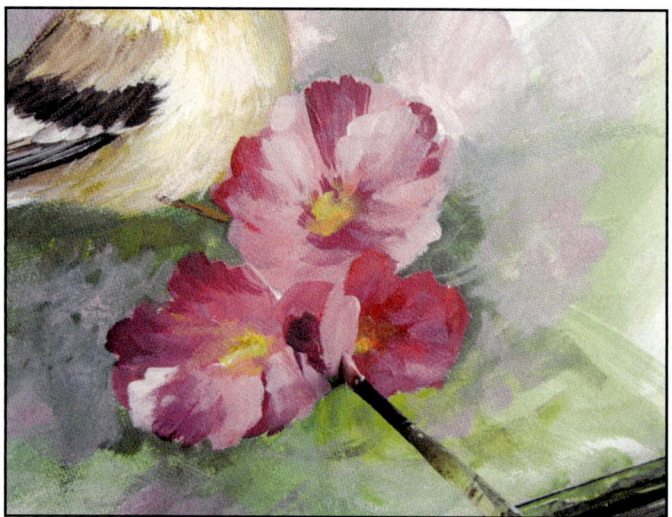

Step 61 Add the strokes to the front of the smaller front rose to turn the petal.

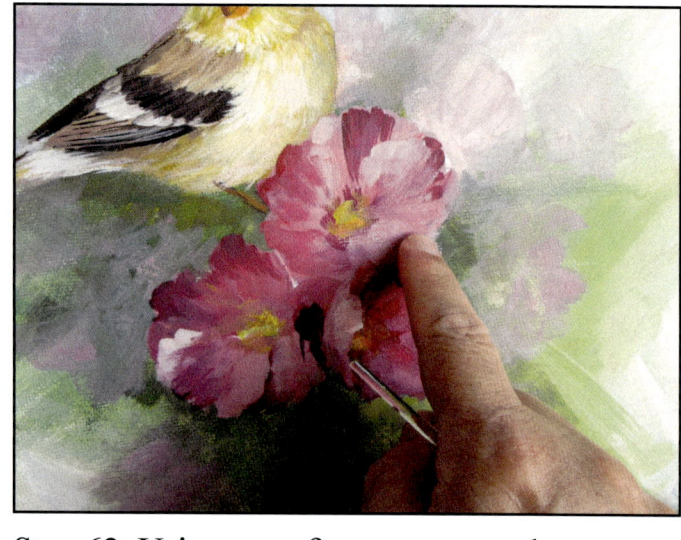

Step 62 Using your finger, go over the petals to soften the colors while still keeping the movement.

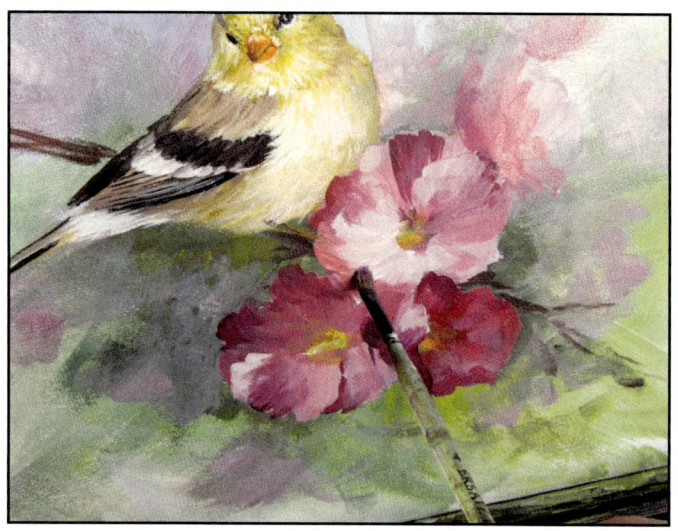

Step 63 Mottle the brush back into the light colors and restate the light colors around the centers. Add centers with some Hansa.

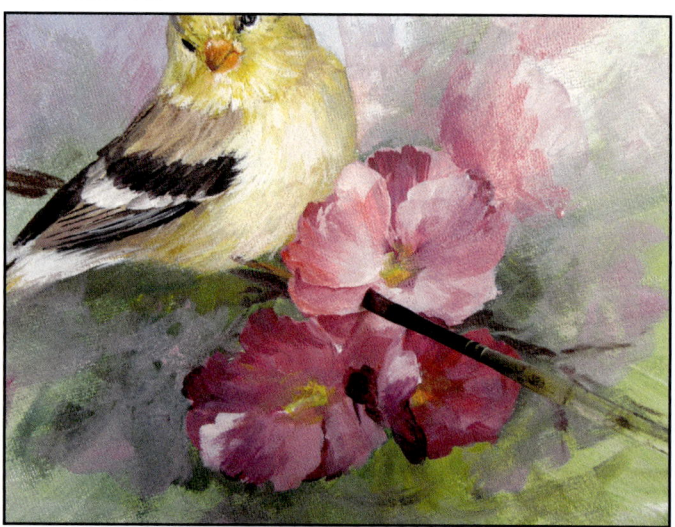

Step 64 Mottle the brush with some warmer Nap. Red Light and touch white. Pull in from petal edge to soften colors.

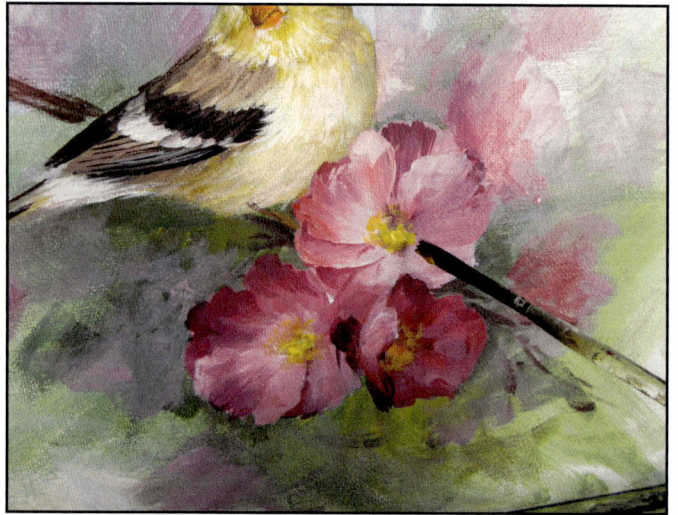

Step 65 Tap the centers of the flowers with more Hansa to restate the color.

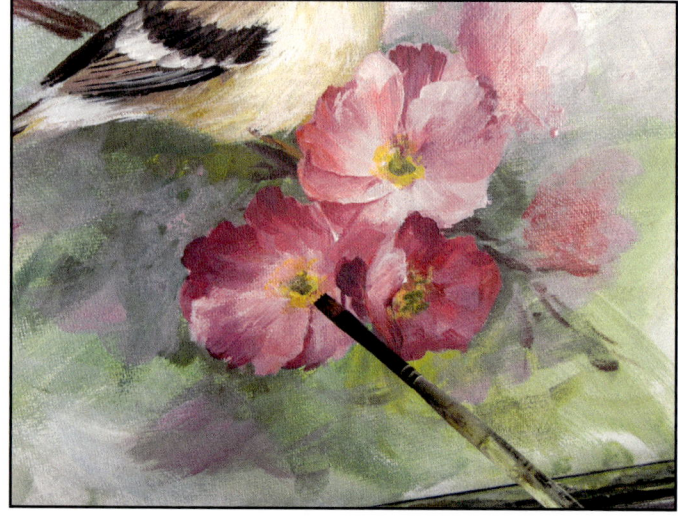

Step 66 Add a little green leaf color in the centers of the flowers.

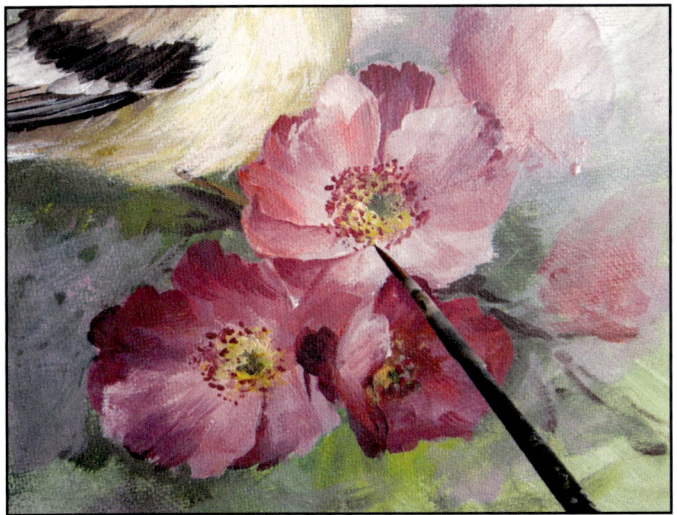

Step 67 Using the point of the liner add some small dark red pollen dots in the center of the roses.

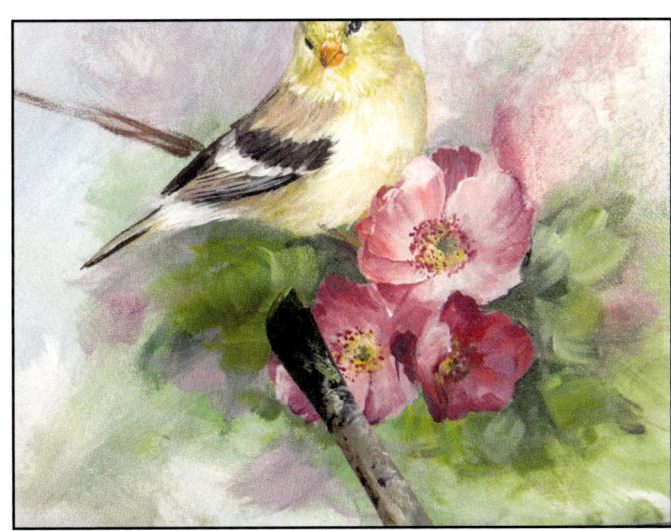

Step 68 Mottle the greens on the larger brush and add some around the flowers and below her to push her forward.

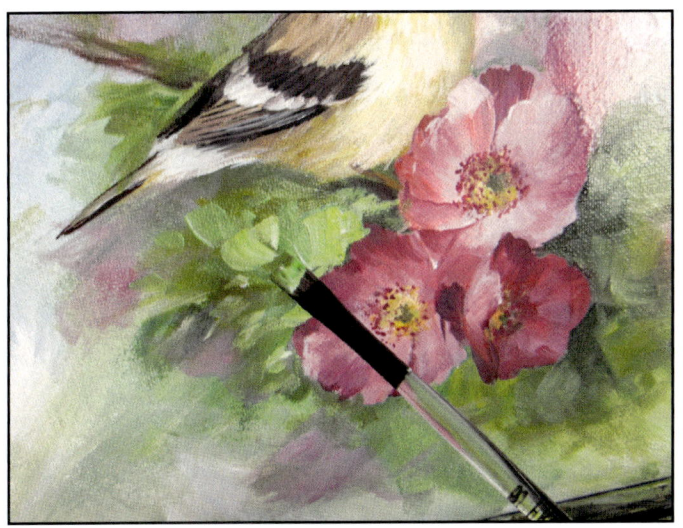

Step 69 Mottle a flat with green and lighten with some Hansa and White. Add strokes of light green to the leaves to add interest.

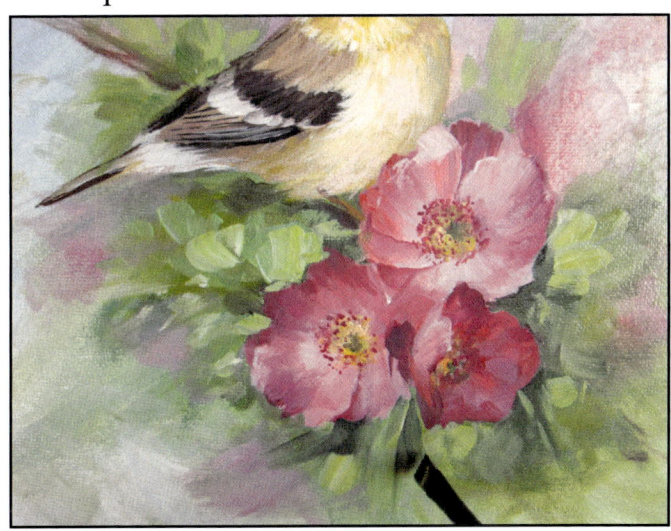

Step 70 Add suggestions of darker leaves and strokes below the center flowers. Add suggestions of back flowers with soft reds.

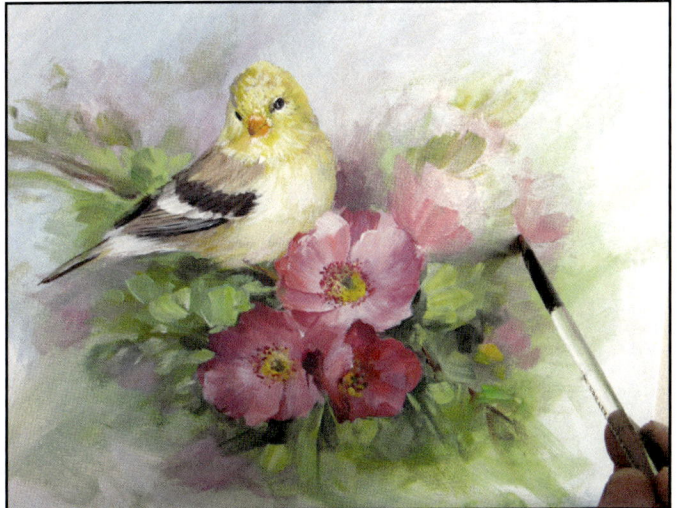

Step 71 Work the outside colors into the wet sky and greens to soften. Add brown stems.

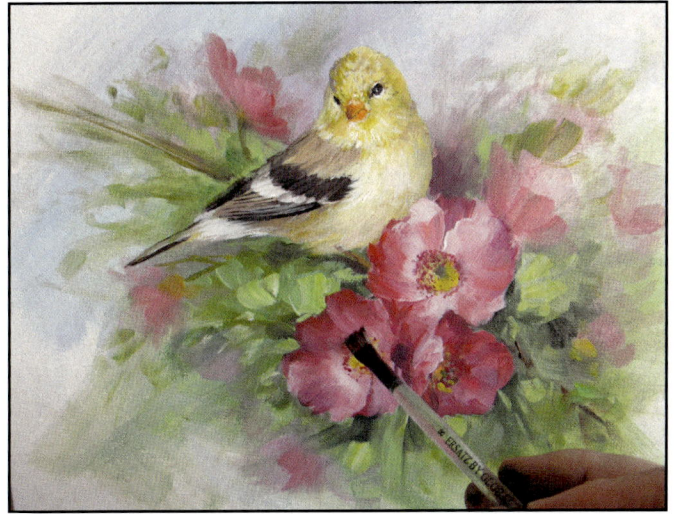

Step 72 Redefine the main roses with more dark reds to finish. Enjoy!

*Female Goldfinch
Enlarge Pattern
110% for Original
Size*

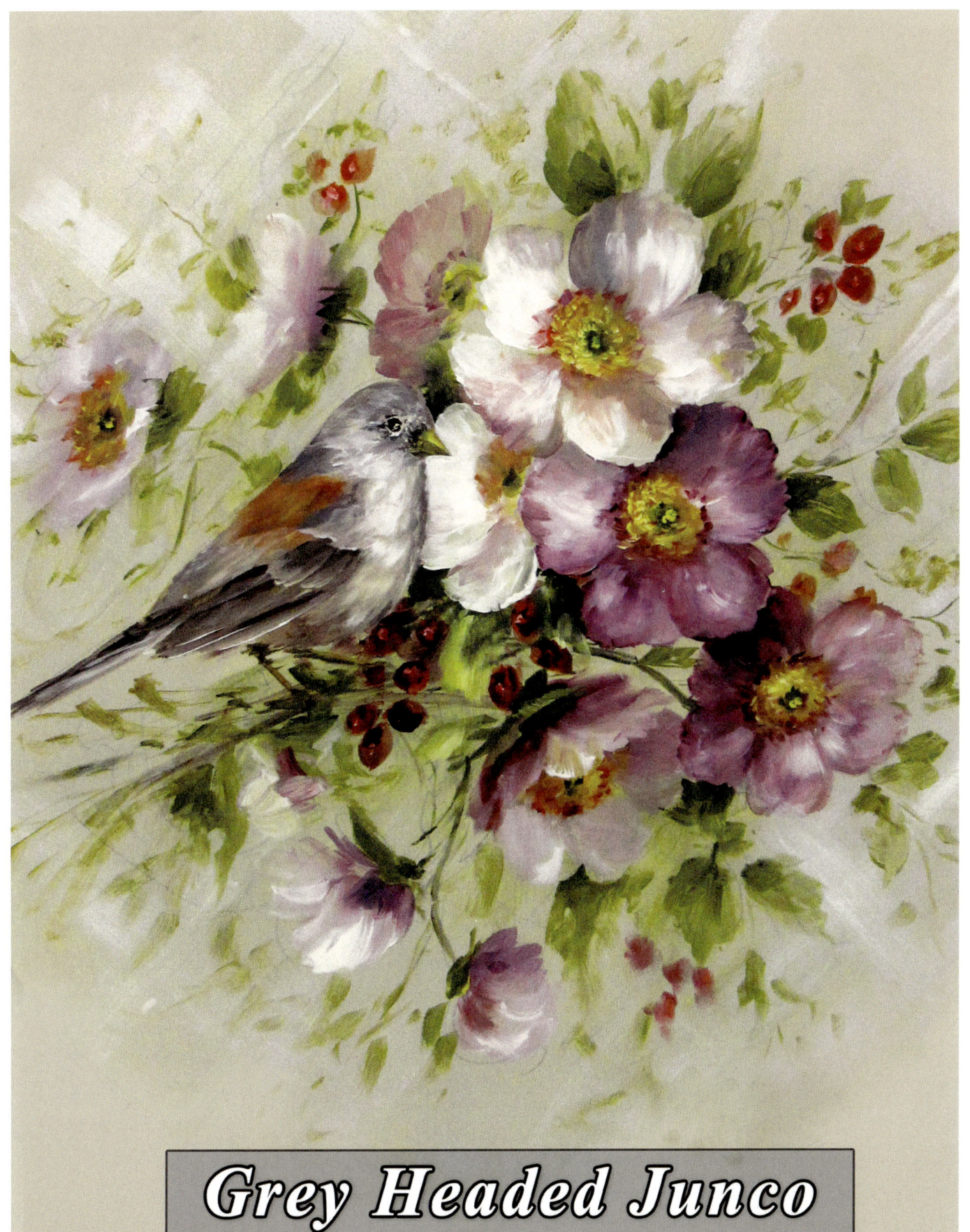

Grey Headed Junco and Wild Roses

Greyed Headed Junco and Wild Roses

I have been decorative painting for over 35 years and I love to paint on wood surfaces. No book is complete in my opinion without a few painted plates or trays! The grey headed junco is perfect for painting on a large round plate with some wild roses in various colors.

Decorative artists can have a bit of a problem when it comes to painting something that is real. Just how real do you make it? You can create a realistic painting or an artistic one by letting some realistic effects go for the look of a painting. That is what I wanted to do with this one. Also, you have to decide, is this a painting of the bird or the flowers? Often, when painting a design that contains both a bird and flowers, I make the painting about the flowers and let the bird sit in the background. Sometimes, the viewer doesn't notice the bird for several minutes, because I keep the color soft and compress bird into the background.

For this painting, we will paint the bird and flowers with contrast so that they sit together. This is not always a good setup, but this is a large plate and the overall size can support the contrast of movement.

We will start by casually applying a background and establishing movement in the background and the bird. Then, before finishing the bird, we will begin the objects in the painting. We set in the flowers and leaves, then return to the bird for details. Then we return to the flowers for their final details.

For this painting we will work the entire design by balancing color and contrast, then work the layers again. Since I have started painting with Alla Prima techniques, I enjoy this approach. I really never finish an object right from the start. I approach the painting like turning to focus lens on a camera. Work an area then turn the lens and bring things slowly into focus with ever increasing details. It is such a fun way to paint. Let's give it a try!

Paint It Simply Palette
Base Color- Medium White from Mixes

Palette Colors

Naphthol Red Light
Red Violet
Carbon Black
Phthalo Blue

Hansa Yellow
Titanium White
Medium White
Base Brown

Wood Surface
18" or 20" Wood plate available from JansenArtStudio.com

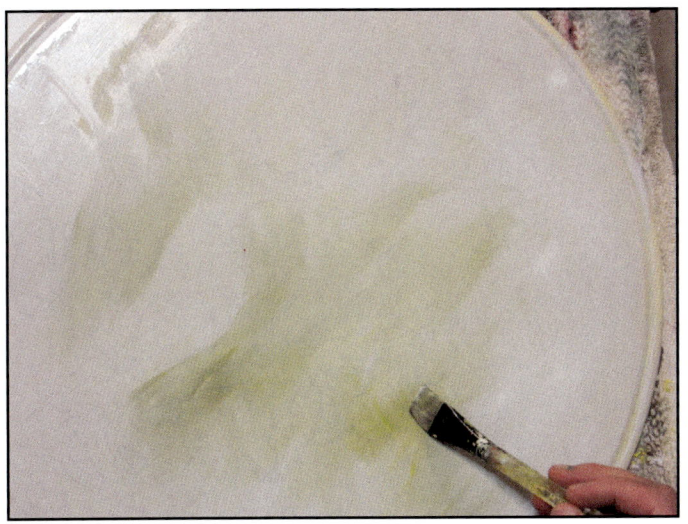

Step 1 Base plate or desired surface with Medium White and Extender after transferring your pattern. Mottle center with soft greens.

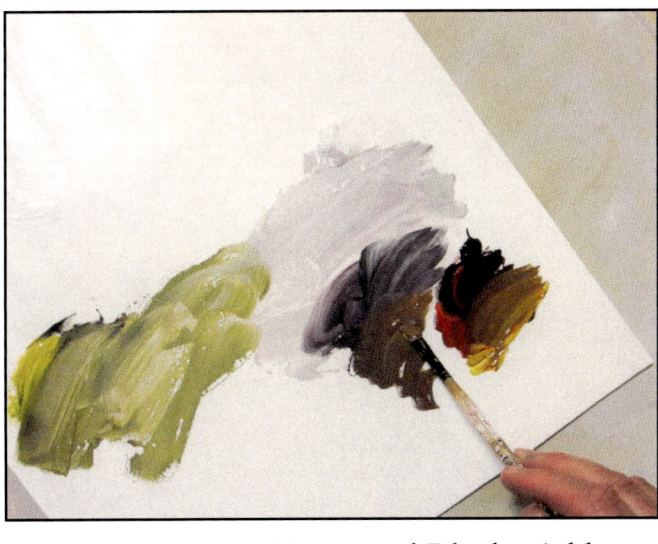

Step 2 Greens are Hansa and Black. Add whites, reds, yellows and black to make browns. Lighten with touch white.

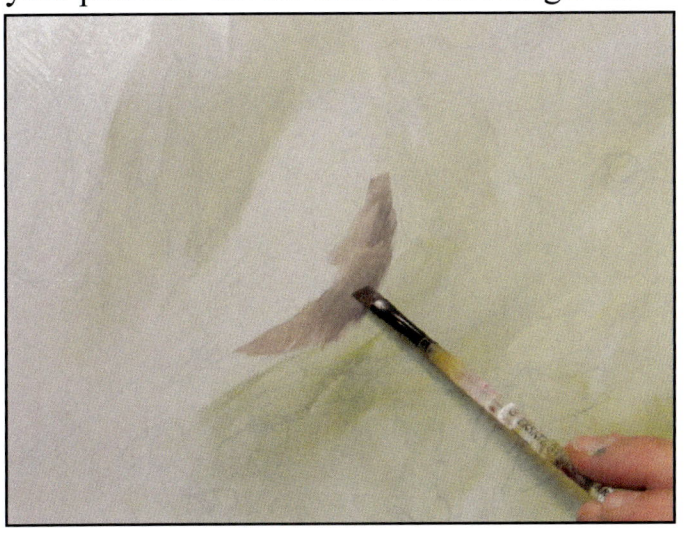

Step 3 Using a medium brown color begin the breast area of the Junco. I keep the brown slightly grey with more black and white.

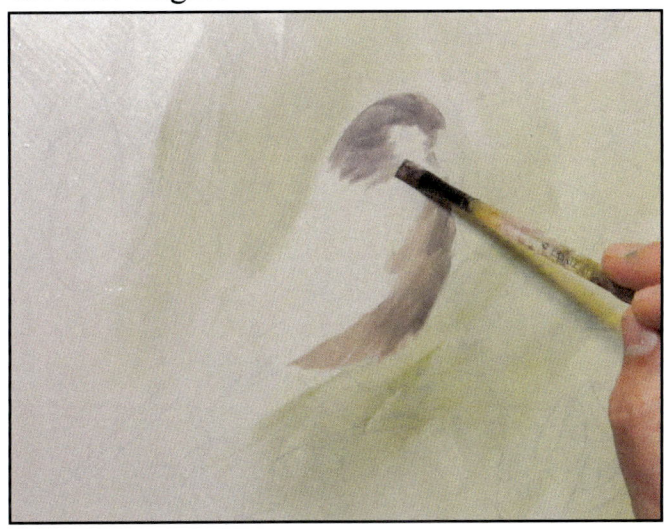

Step 4 Vary the brown/grey with more black and then start the top of the head. Use various sizes of strokes depending on area.

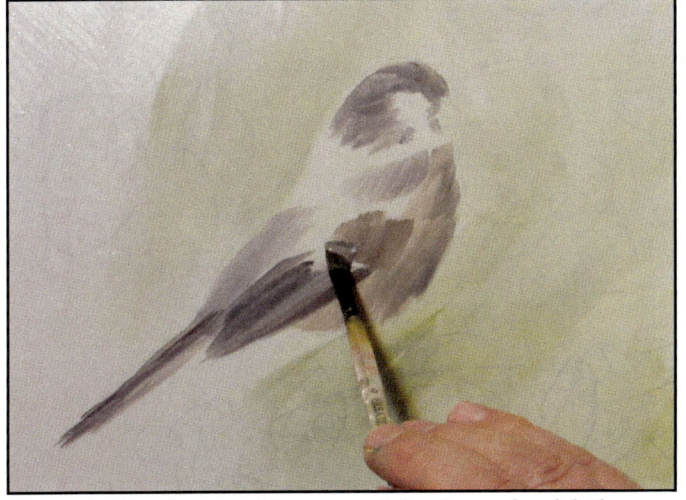

Step 5 Darken with more black and add the wing, tail and the mantle to the wing.

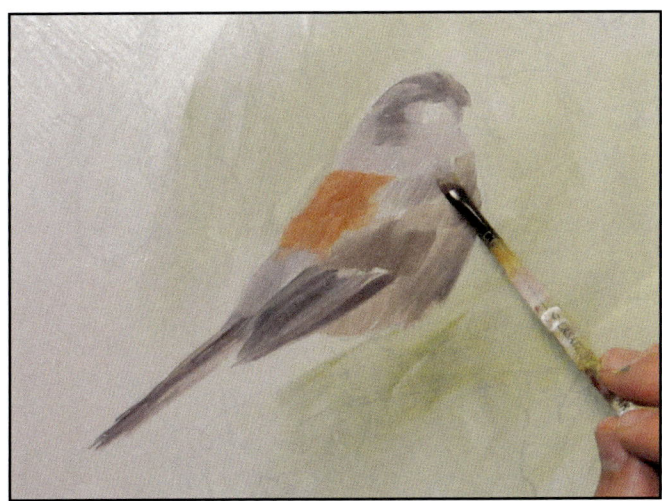

Step 6 Mottle soft orange with red and yellow and add to the back. Then continue with more medium greys.

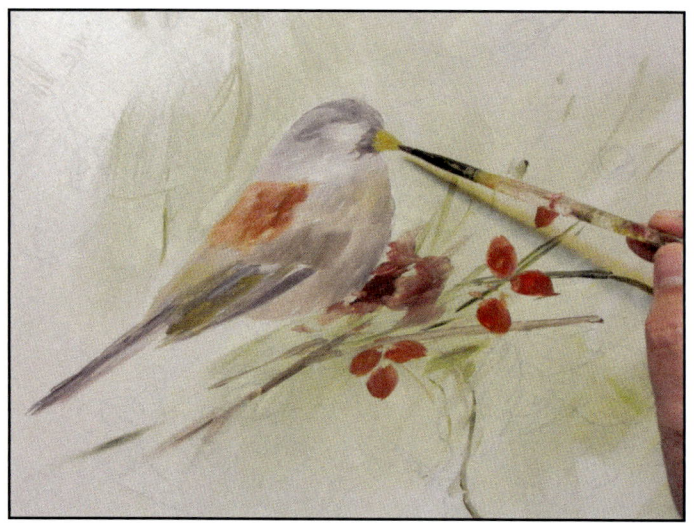

Step 7 Add berries with mottled reds and round brush. Add stems with browns. Add beak with Hansa and touch brown.

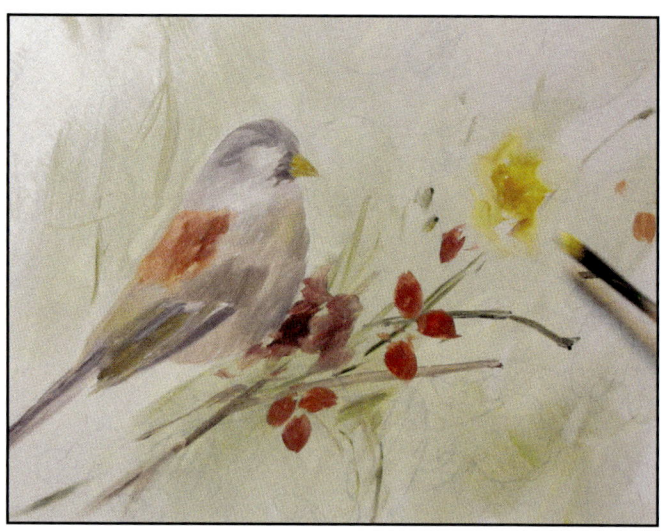

Step 8 Mottle the centers of the flowers with toned Hansa. Tone Hansa with the browns from the stems. (red + black).

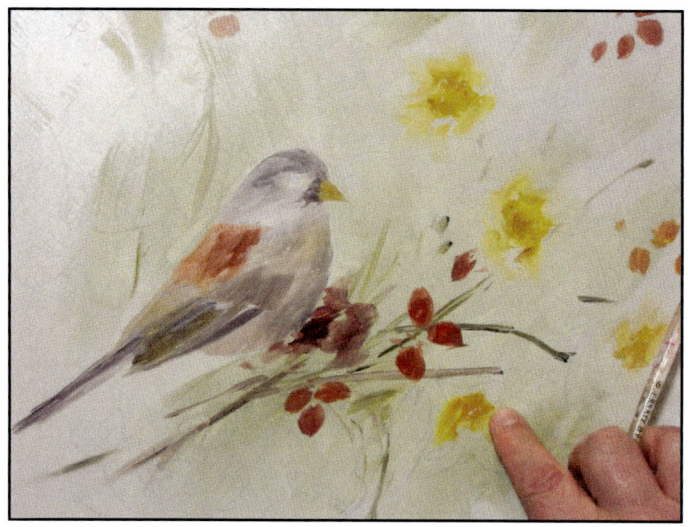

Step 9 Soften the centers of the flowers into the background with your finger.

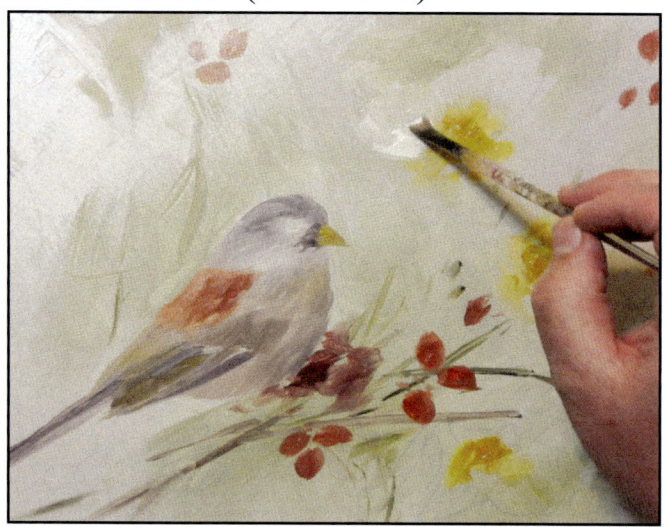

Step 10 Mottle the brush with some greys from the Junco and then lighten with white. Begin petals pulling strokes to the centers.

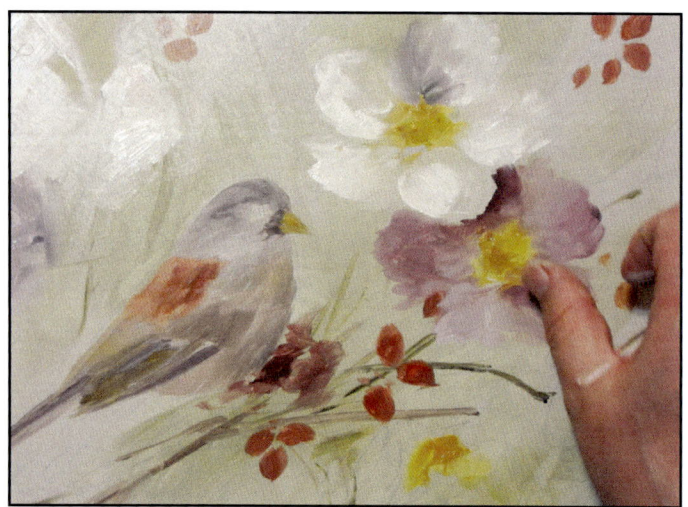

Step 11 Mottle a soft violet with Red Violet, grey and white and begin next flower shape.

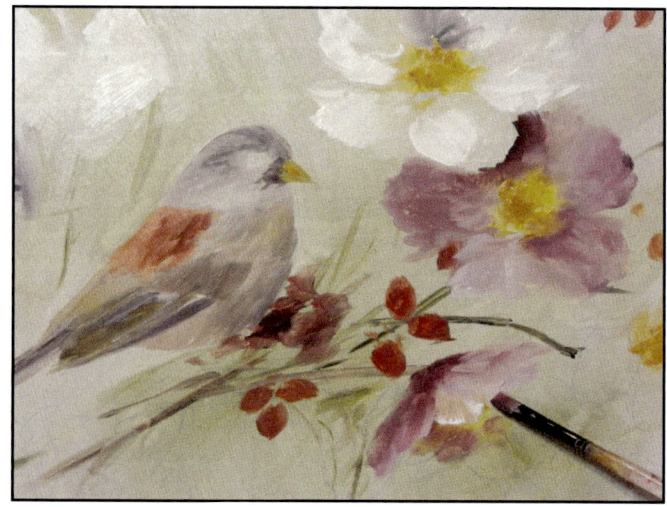

Step 12 Shadow with more Red Violet and then lighten fronts with touch more white.

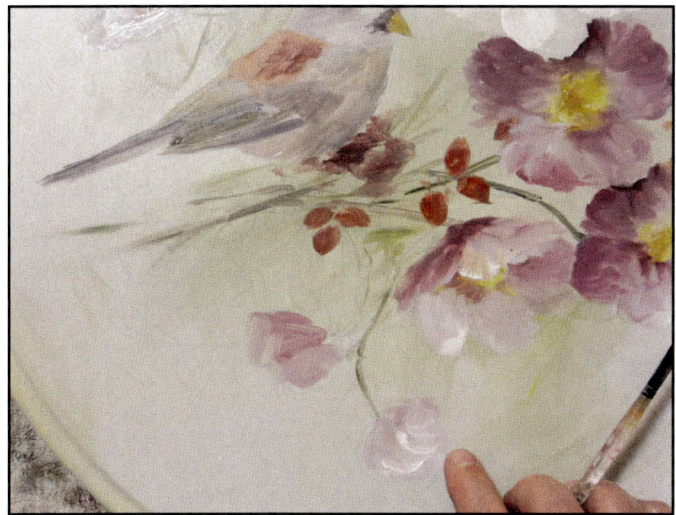

Step 13 Add the outside blossom buds and then soften them into the background with your finger.

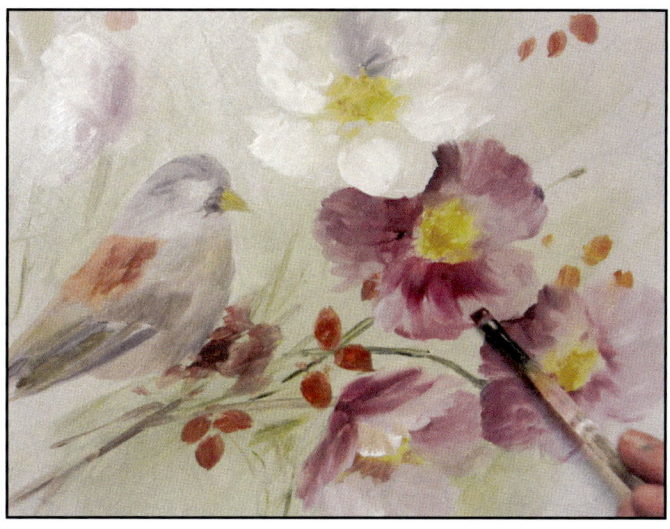

Step 14 Add some darker shadow colors to the roses around the centers and pull out. Vary color with Red Violet and touch blue or black.

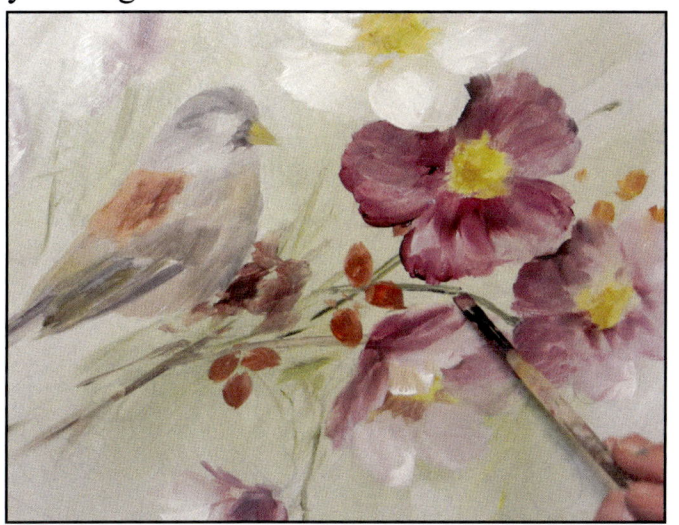

Step 15 Add some darks around the outside edges of the petals. Add the stems with greens made from Hansa and touch black.

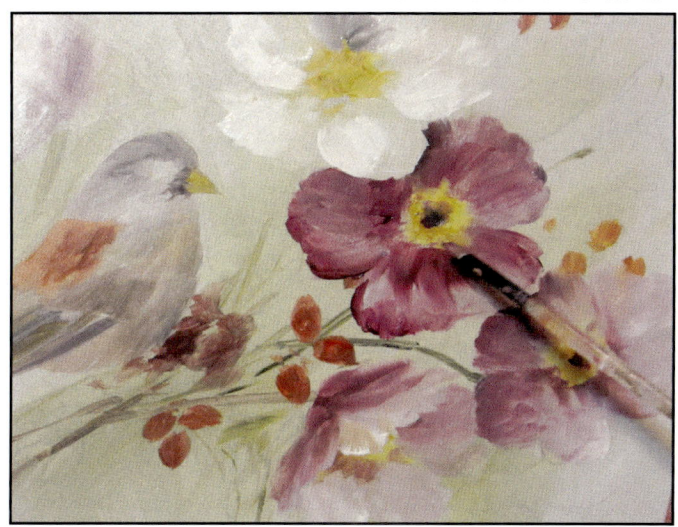

Step 16 Add the center of the roses with dark greens and browns.

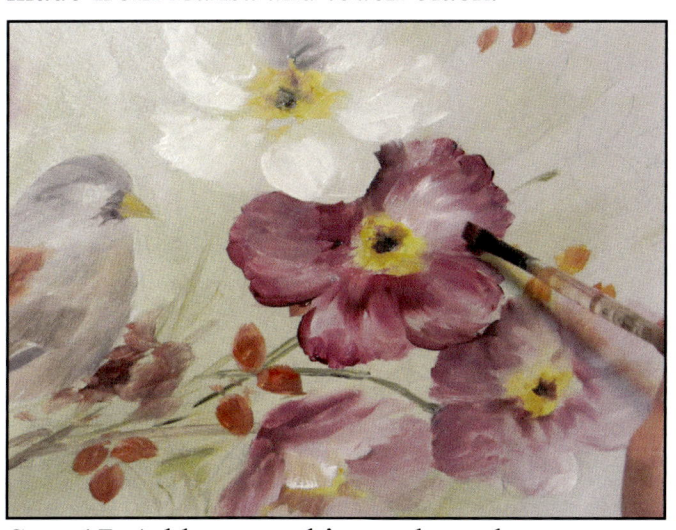

Step 17 Add some white to the red roses around the center and pull out to incorporate.

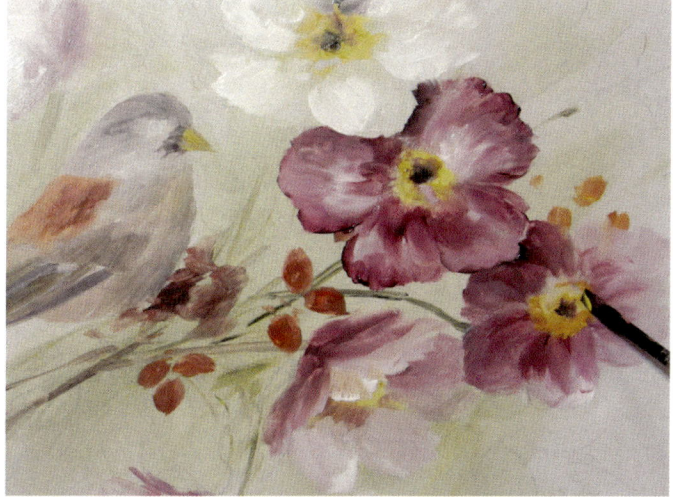

Step 18 Tap some lighter yellows around the center with the corner of the flat.

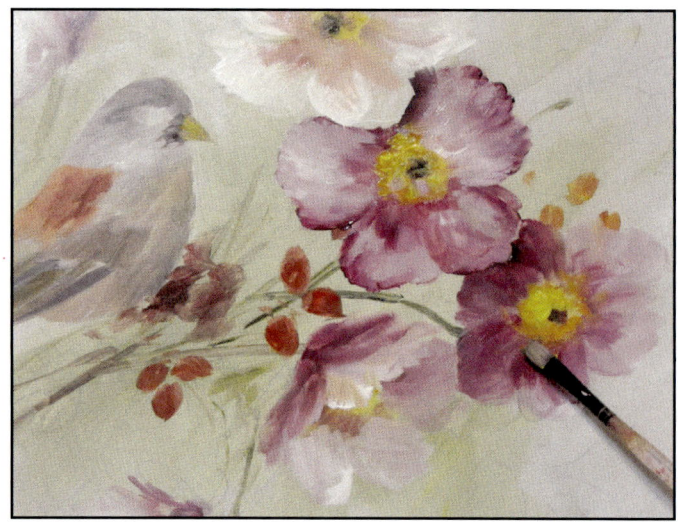

Step 19 Streak out some darker violets on some petals for more interest. See final photos for suggestions.

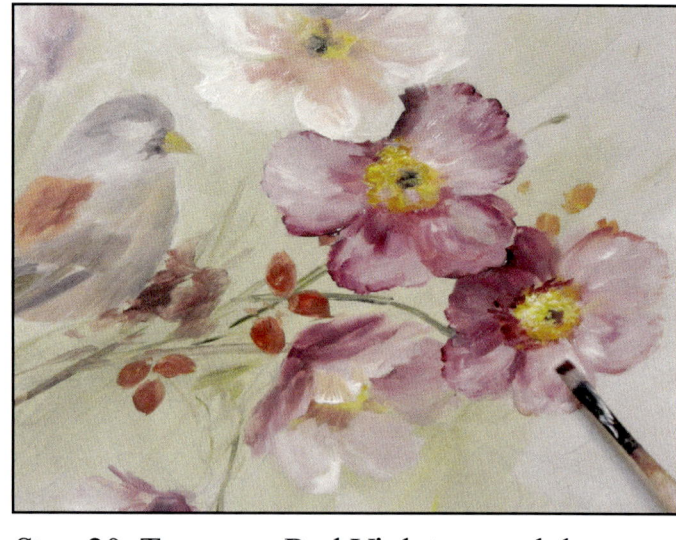

Step 20 Tap some Red Violet around the centers of the roses to add some shadow contrast and interest.

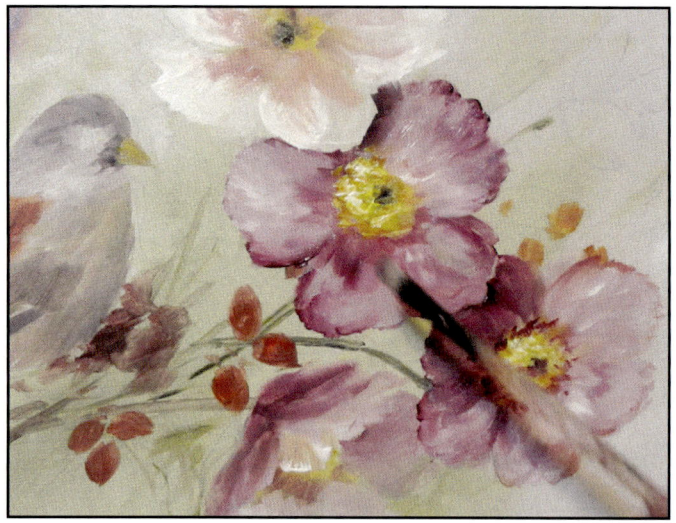

Step 21 Tap some light yellow into the center of the roses and then pull some additional light and dark colors out from the center.

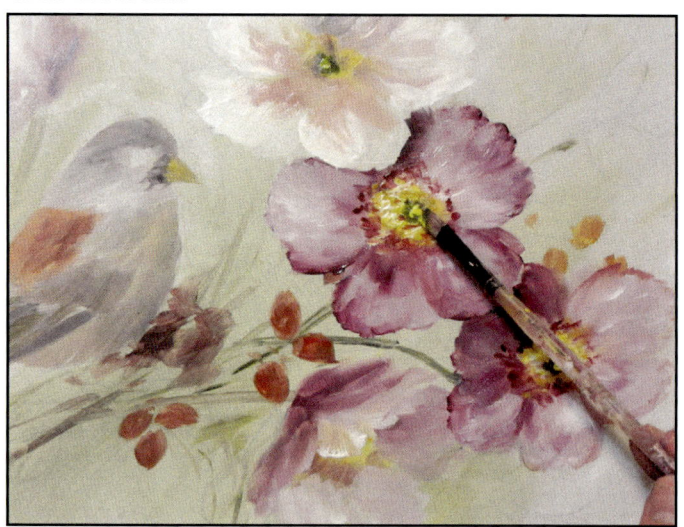

Step 22 I added more Red Violet around the center and then tapped in some lights into the center.

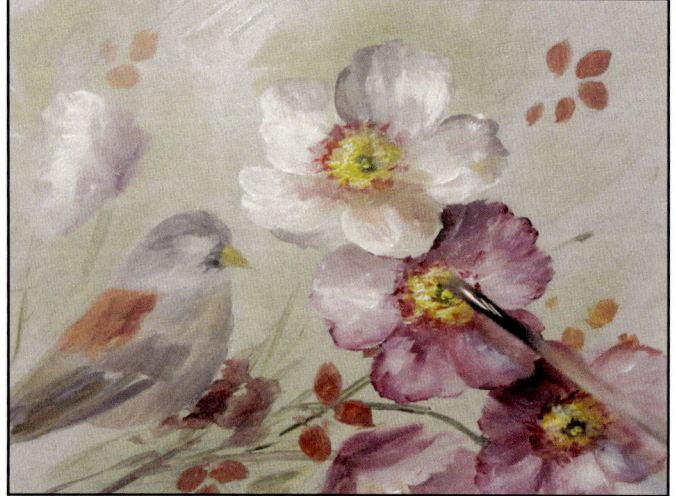

Step 23 Lighten the petals around the center and then pull out to soften the colors.

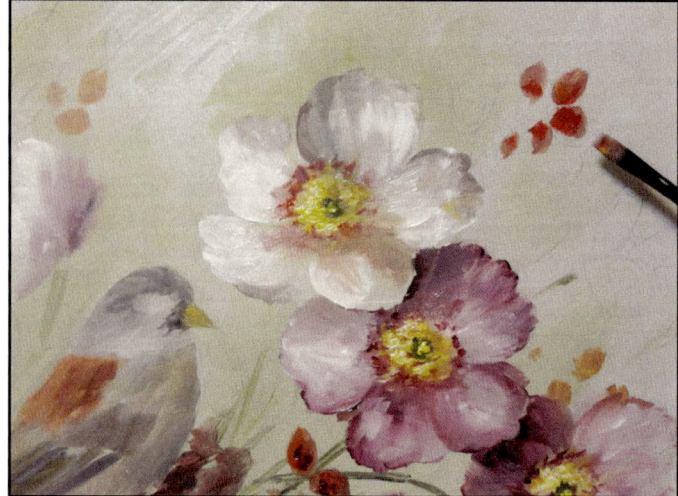

Step 24 Add more reds to the berries as shadows. Not too much dark. Keep soft.

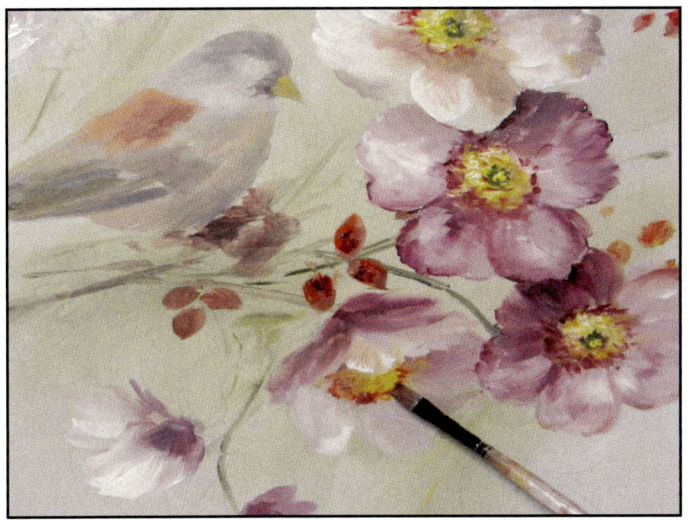

Step 25 Work the reds through the centers to carry the colors from the berries.

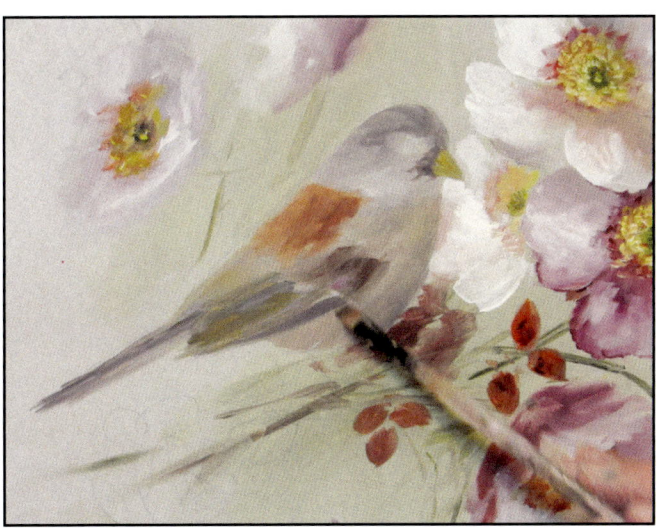

Step 26 Using the chisel of the flat and some darker greys, start the flight feathers on the wings.

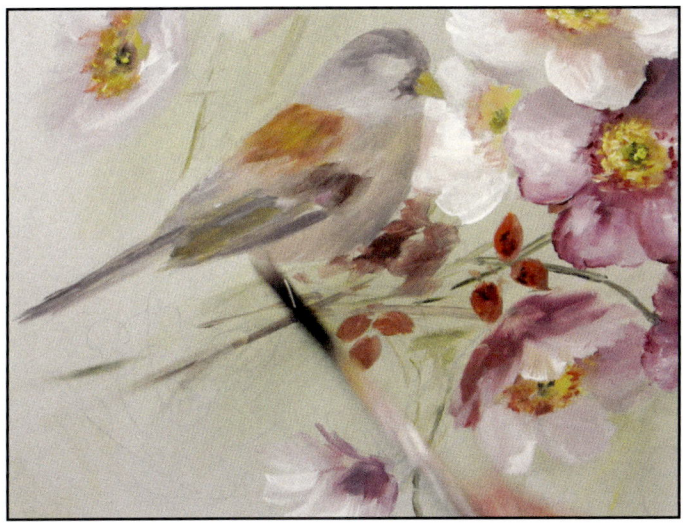

Step 27 Clean up the edges of the wings with the body color grey.

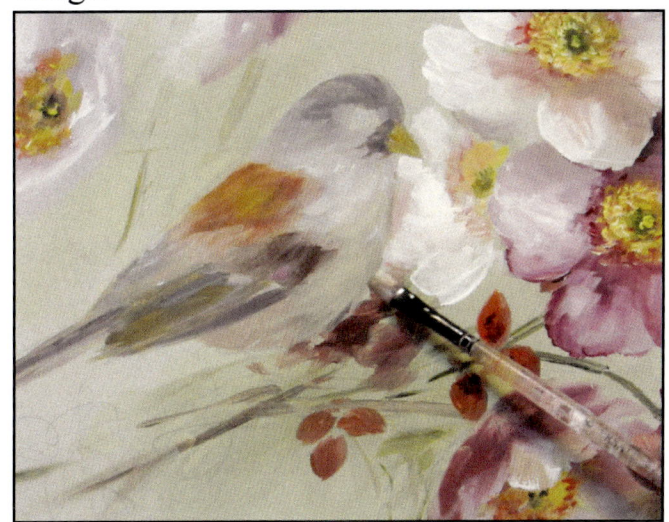

Step 28 Lighten the grey with more white and using shorter strokes near the neck start the feathers with the chisel of the flat.

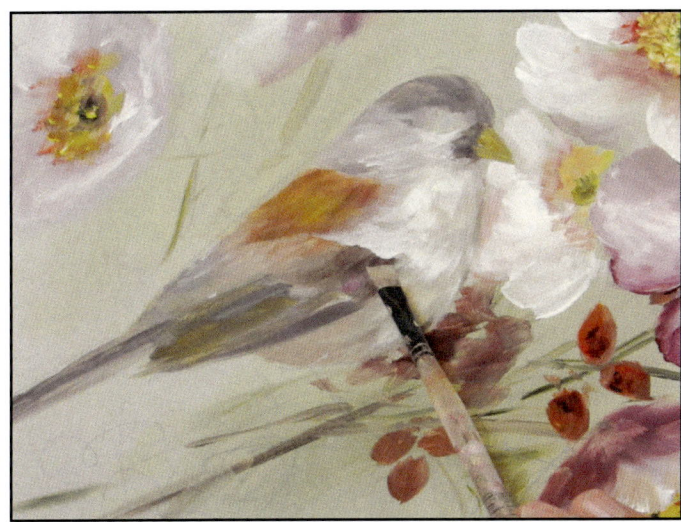

Step 29 Add the white to the top coverts of the wings. Keep color very light.

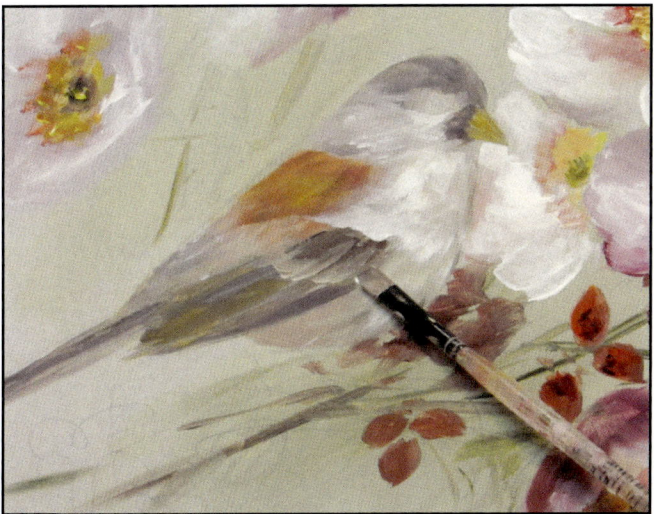

Step 30 Use the corner of the brush and white to make the secondary feathers.

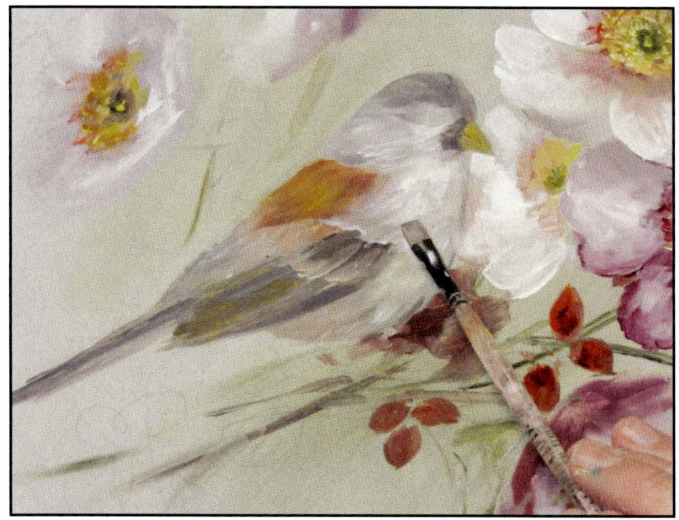

Step 31 Using the flat of the brush and some greys, stroke back removing some of the white and shaping the feathers.

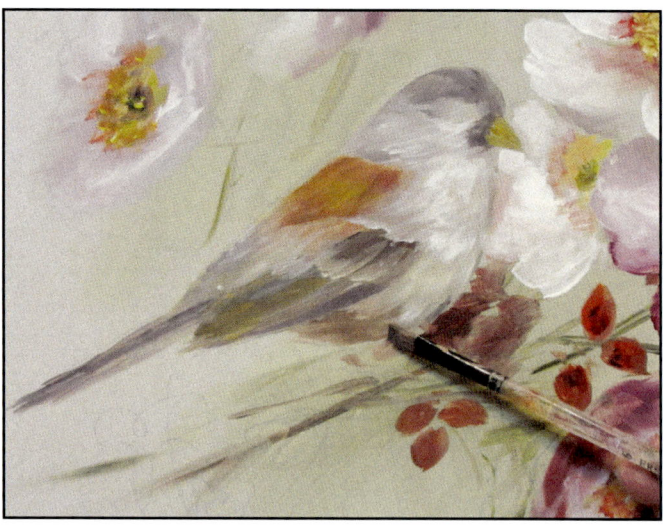

Step 32 Stroke lights down the breast and then stroke darks from the bottom up. Mottle them together to create the look of feathers.

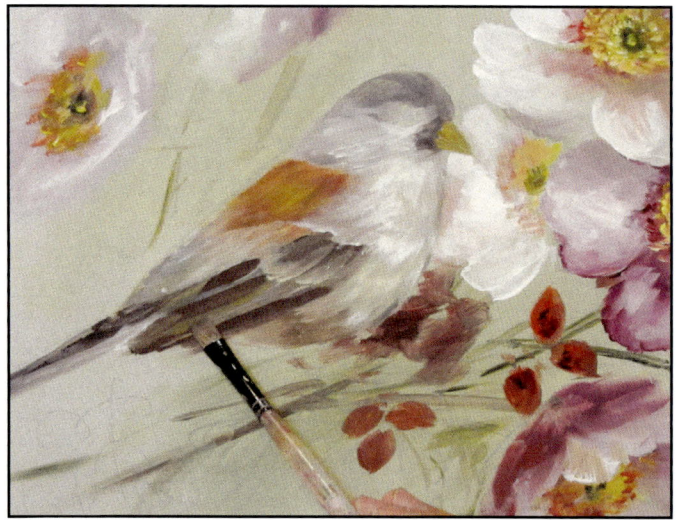

Step 33 Restate the darks of the primary flight feathers using the chisel of the brush and some darker colors.

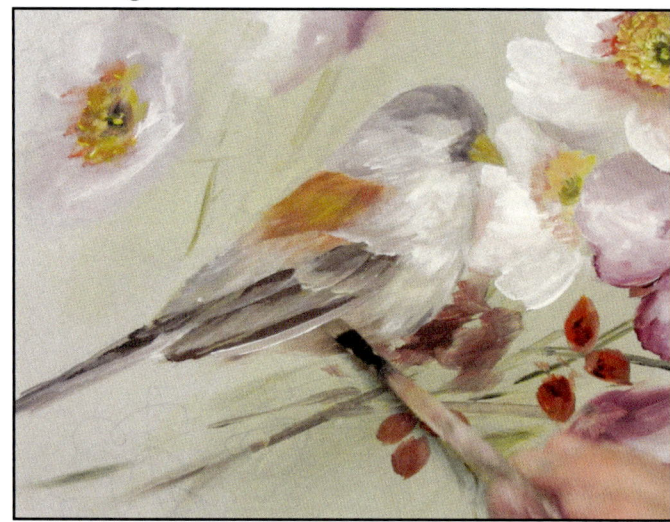

Step 34 Use the chisel of the small flat to shape some of the lower body feathers. Keep the area soft however so it recedes.

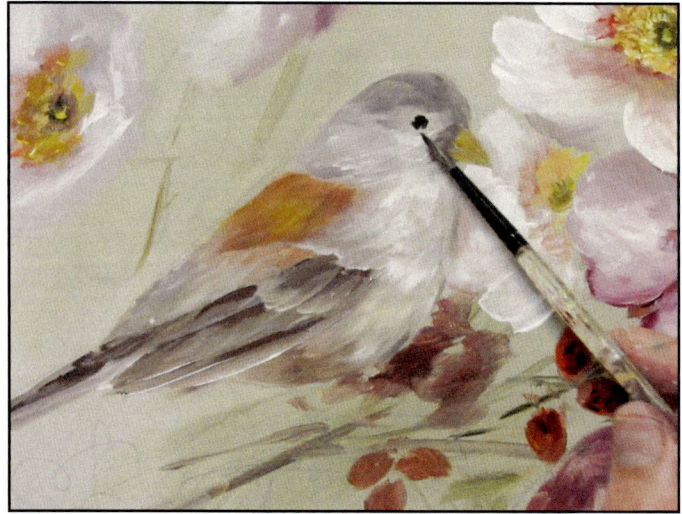

Step 35 Add the eye with the round and some black. Leave some white around for eye ring.

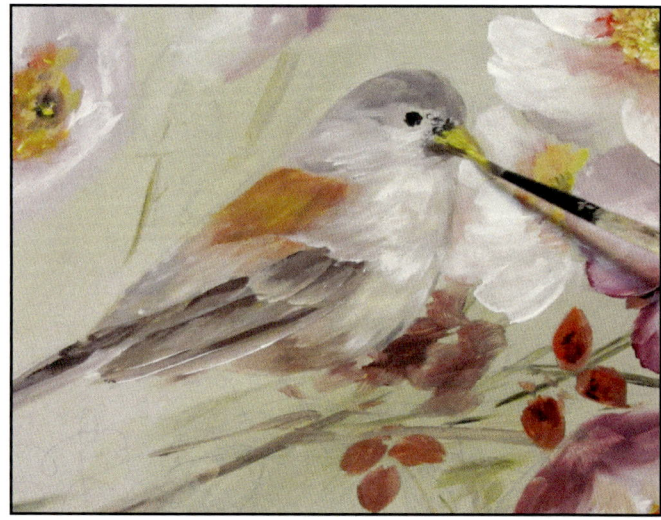

Step 36 Add some lighter Hansa to the top of the beak and shadow lower with grey/brown.

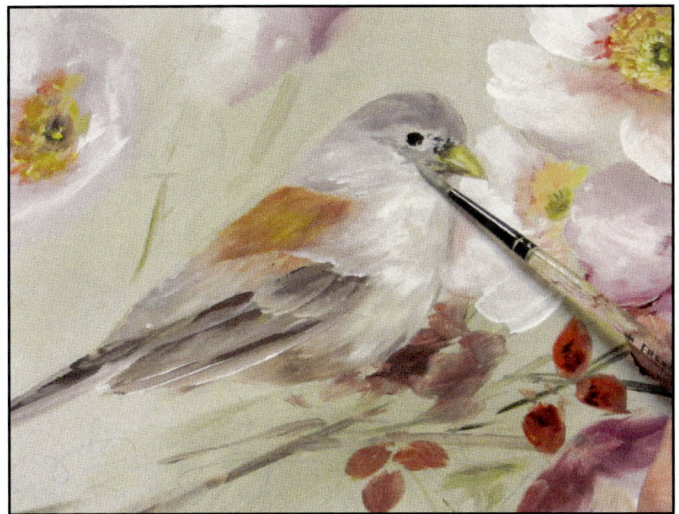

Step 37 Add some darker grey strokes around the beak to shadow. Pull some small strokes to set movement of the neck feathers.

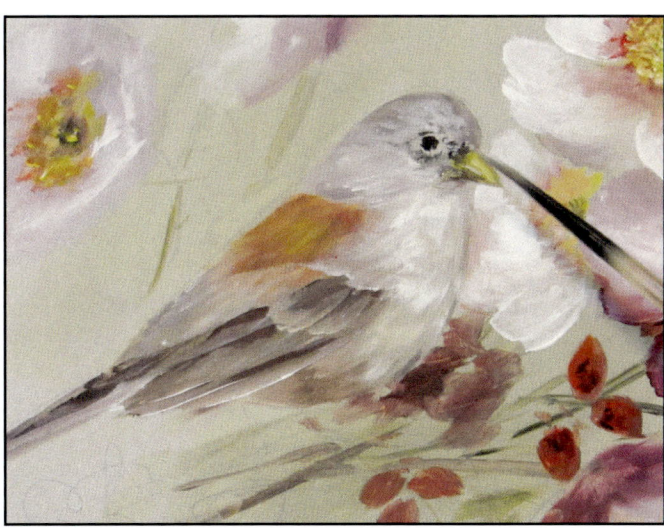

Step 38 Using the tip of the round, tap in some white around the top of the head to add the smaller lighter feathers.

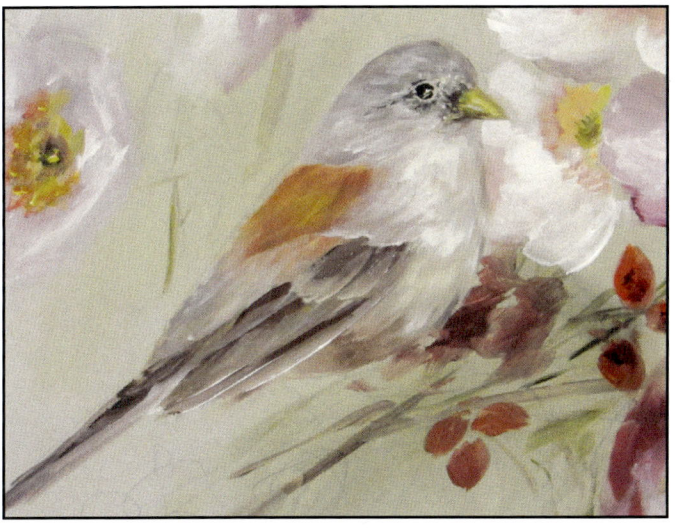

Step 39 Add more smaller feathers around the eye. Shadow under the eye ring and add the small shine to the eye.

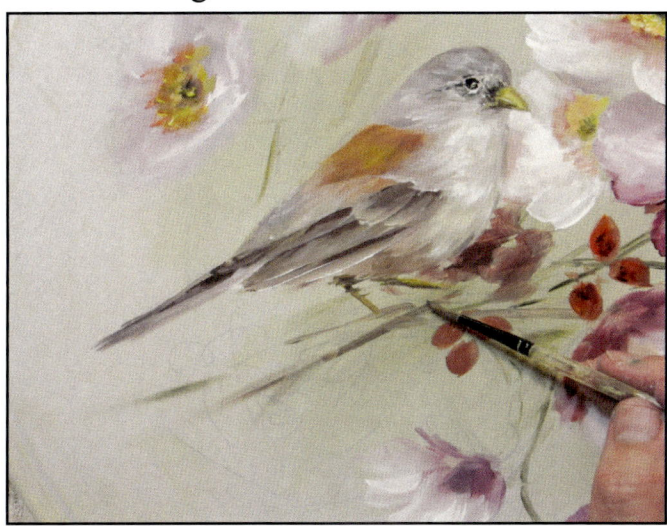

Step 40   Redefine the stems and legs of the Junco.

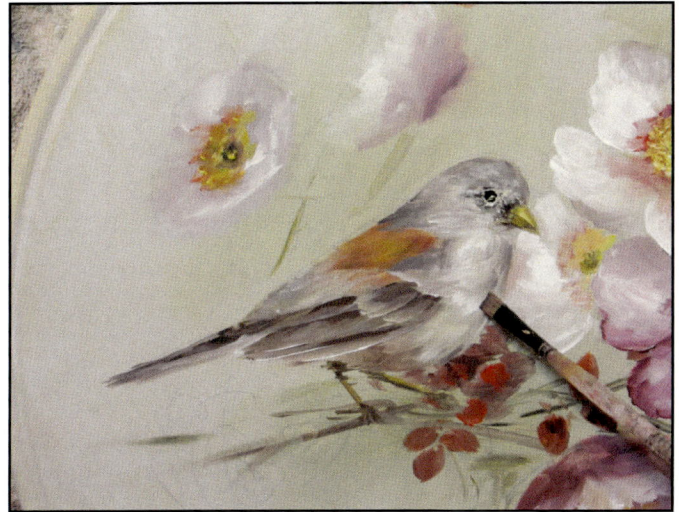

Step 41 Use the chisel to add final feathers to the light area of the breast.

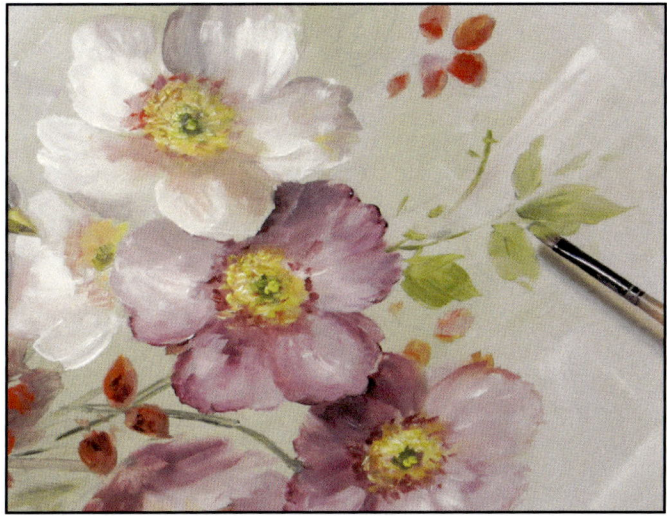

Step 42 Mottle soft greens and casually begin some smaller leaf shapes around design.

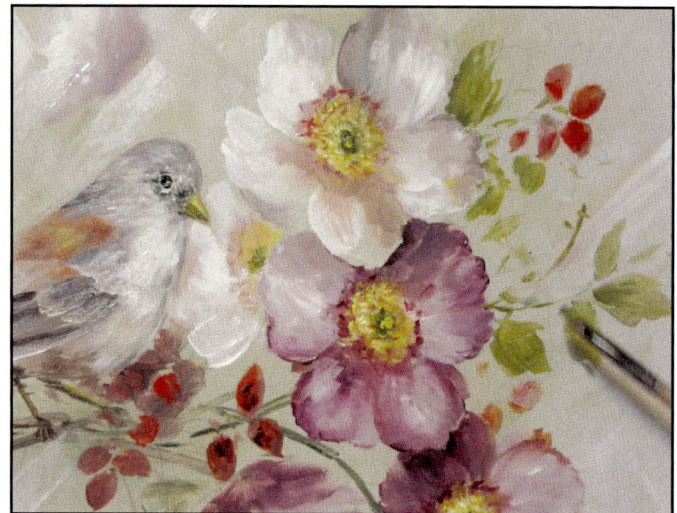

Step 43 Fill up around the design with some very simple leaf shapes. See final photo for some suggested placement and shapes.

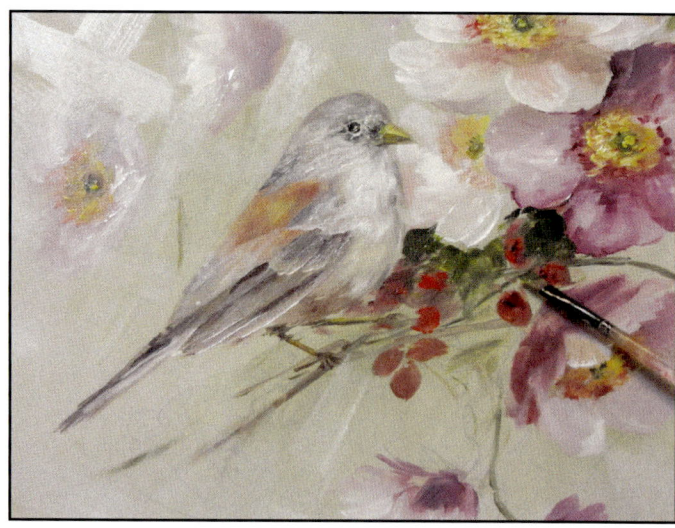

Step 44 Darken the leaves in the center with additional touches of black and yellow. Add some reds to the berries for more contrast.

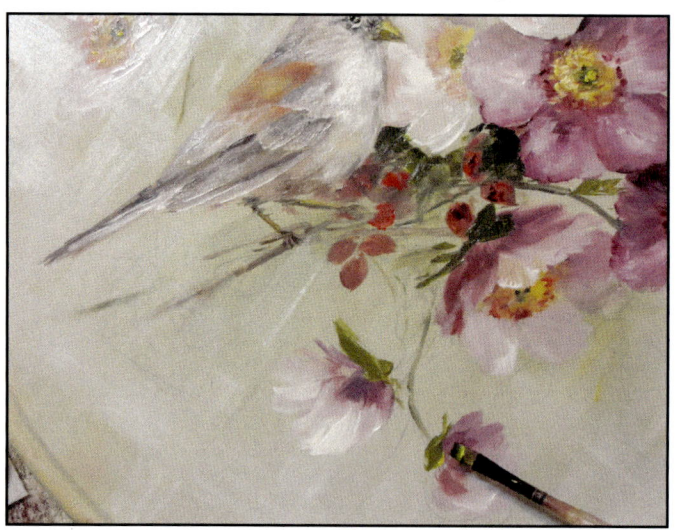

Step 45 Add smaller touches and details to the stems and sepals of the roses. Add some smaller light red shines to berries.

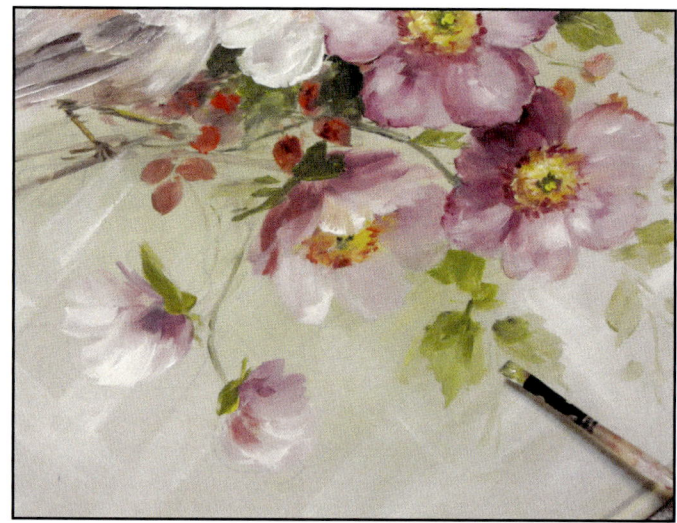

Step 46 I added some light cross hatching to the background with 3/4 brush. Then add additional leaves with various greens.

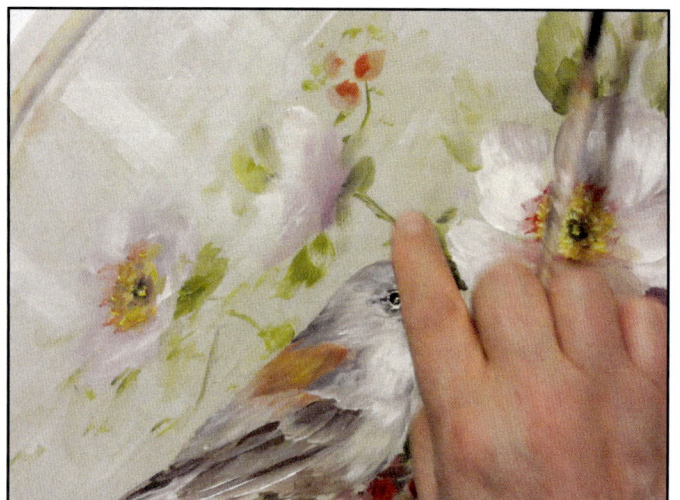

Step 47 Soften the greens back and add final touches and shines. See final photos.

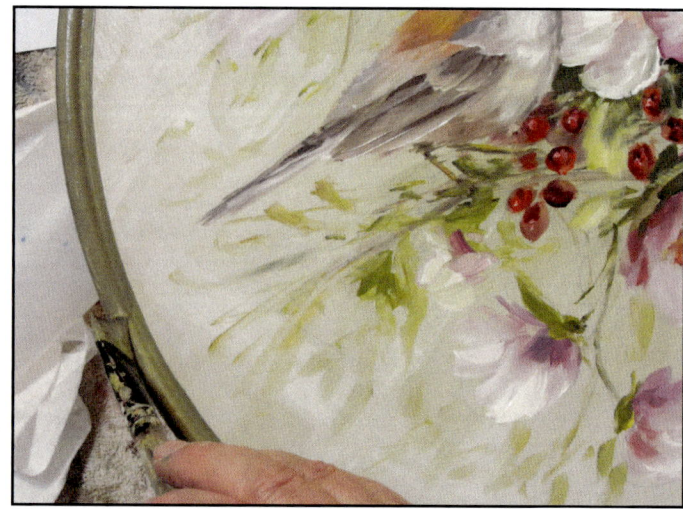

Step 48 Mottle soft green for rim or use color of choice to finish. Enjoy.

Junco Enlarge Pattern 185% for Original Size

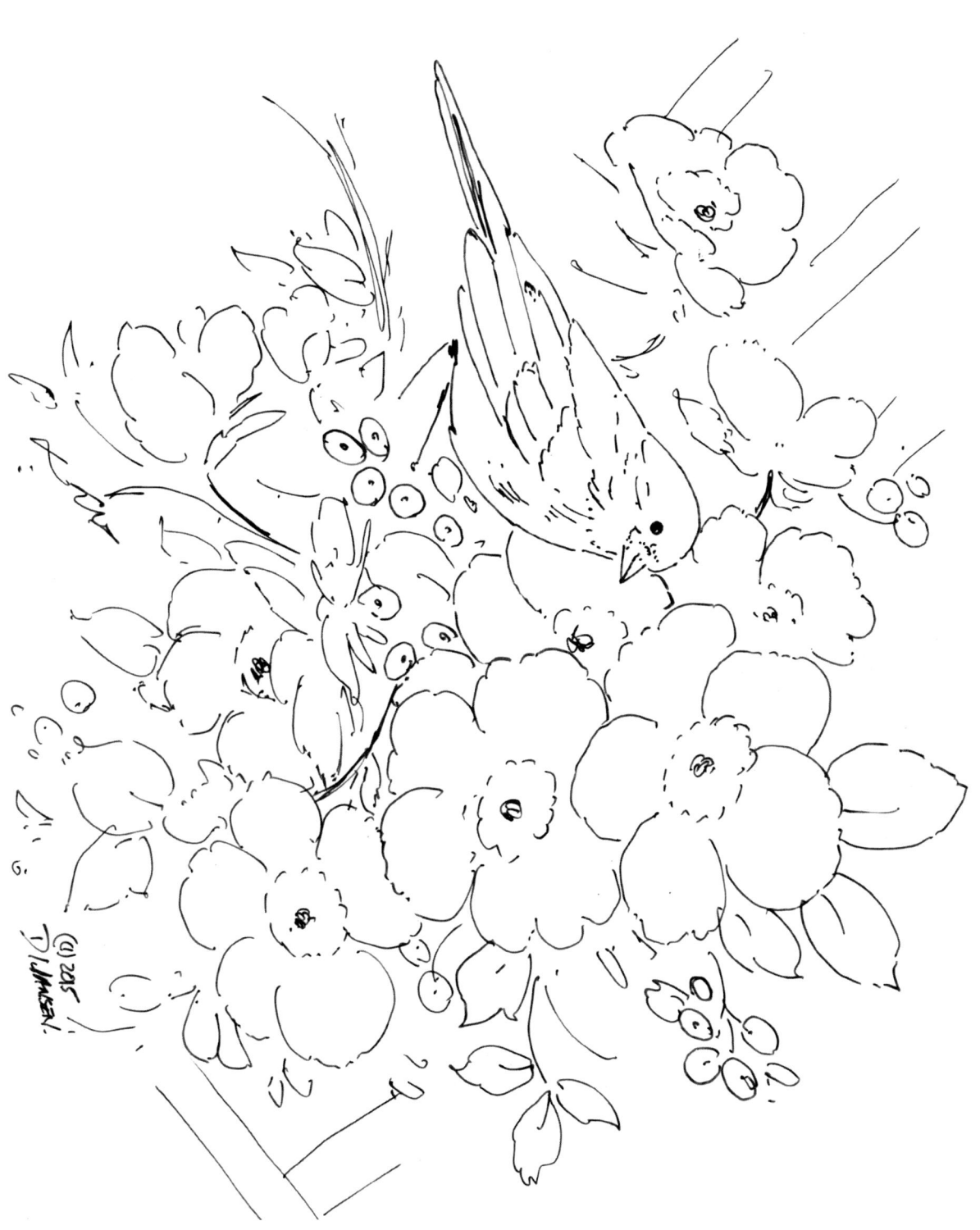

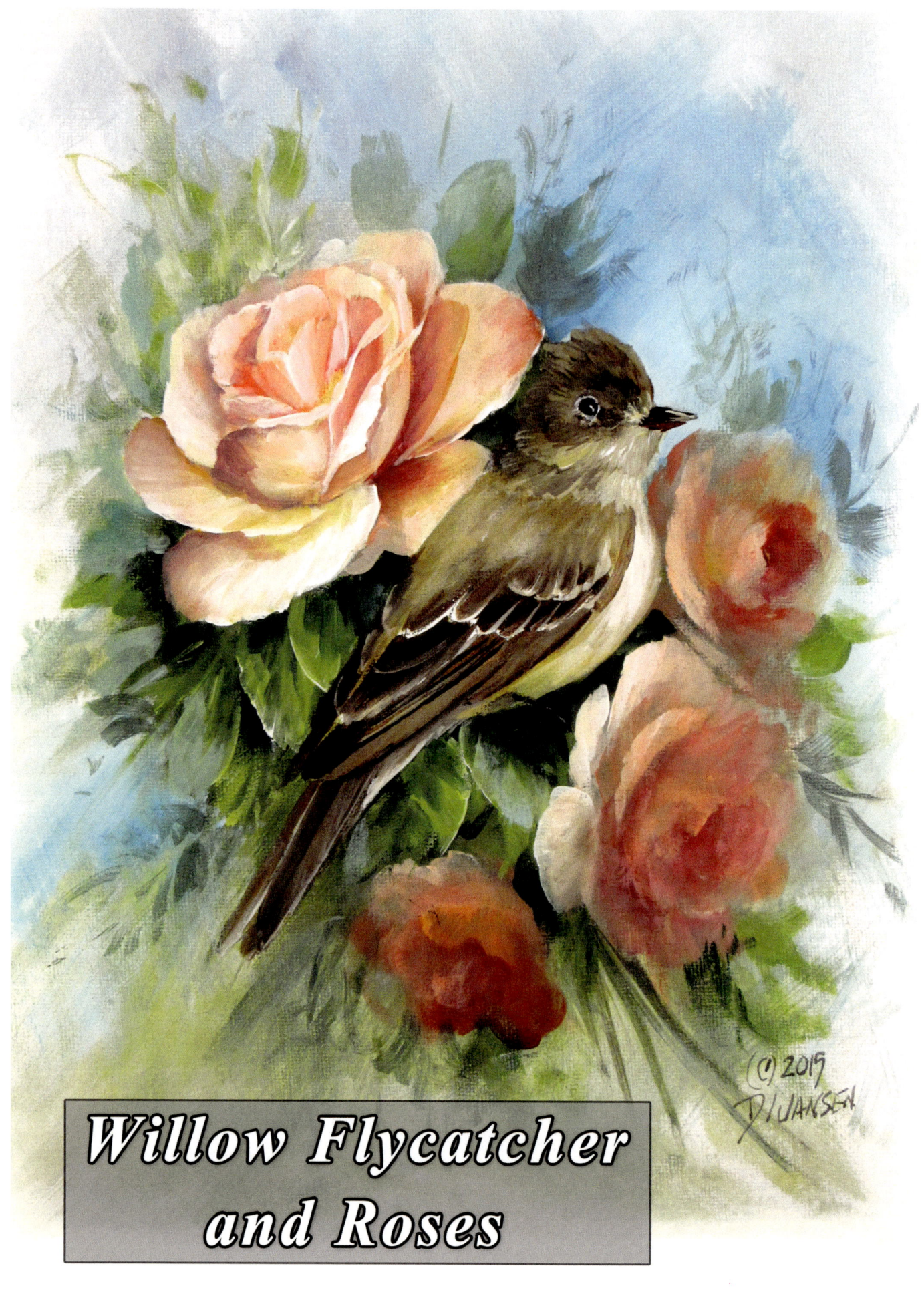

Willow Flycatcher and Roses

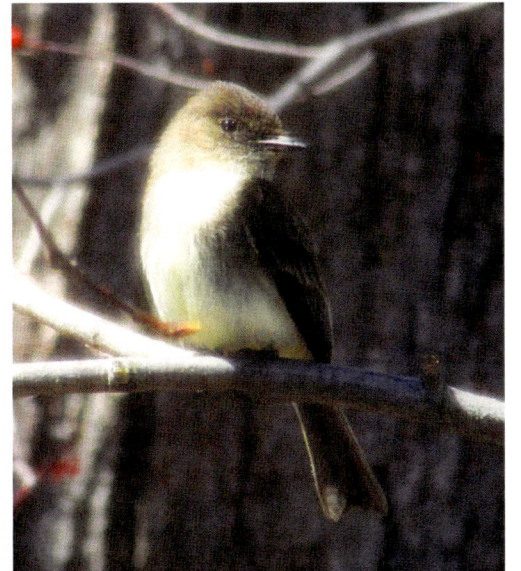

The flycatchers are birds I just love to paint. They are very aerobatic and not really afraid of humans once they get to know you. Here are just 2 of the hundreds of pictures I have taken of the flycatchers. The top one is the mother and the bottom are her babies this year. She built her nest under our deck and this is the picture of the little ones on the day she taught them how to fly. We watched them grow and hope they return to nest again next year.

For this painting I will render the flycatcher a little more realistically and paint the roses with a beautiful 1/2 tone technique. We will use some negative feathering techniques to paint the primary and secondary converts on the wings so they look a little more realistic.

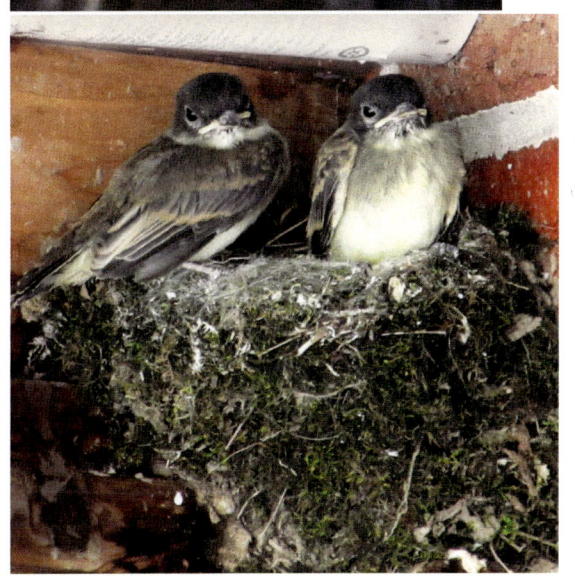

The 1/2 tone technique is a wonderful technique to paint this style of rose. You will establish one tone of dark, then apply the tone of light, then mix the tone right between the two tones you just applied and strike that in between them to soften. If you need to soften further, make a tone between the two areas you want to soften. You do not blend. Try to keep the color tones as clean as possible with to many strokes. Sometimes we blend so much that the life is taken away from the object and it looks plastic. The 1/2 tone technique will help you avoid this. Let's give it a try!

Paint It Simply Palette
Base Color- White

Palette Colors

Naphthol Red Light   Hansa Yellow
Red Violet   Titanium White
Carbon Black   Medium White
Phthalo Blue   Base Brown

Wood Surface
Super MDF Wood Panel about 11 Inch X 14 Inch to fit picture frame. Can also use canvas panel.

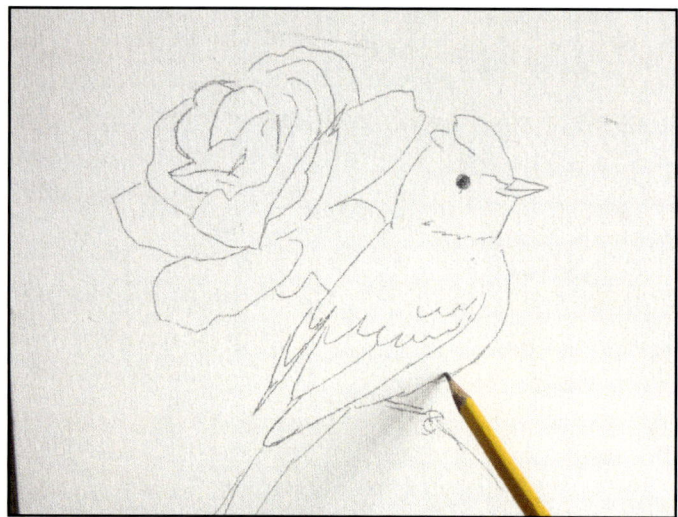

Step 1 Same start. Base canvas or board white, transfer or sketch the main lines of the design with transfer paper or pencil.

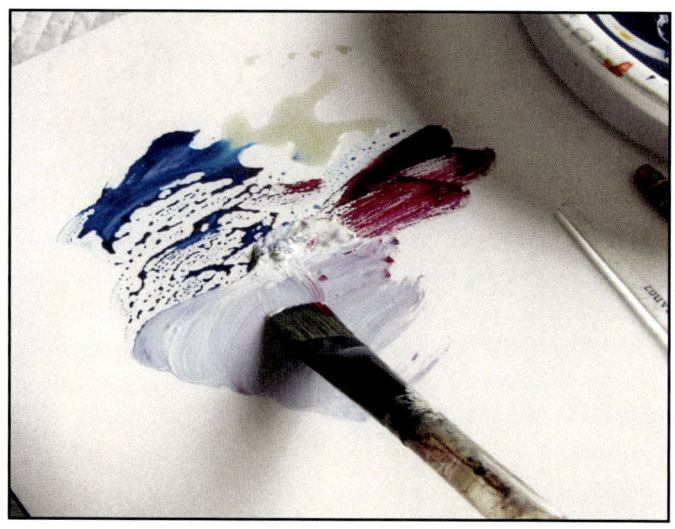

Step 2 Mottle a soft blue violet for the sky area with Phthalo Blue and touch Red Violet. Lighten with some white. 3/4 inch brush.

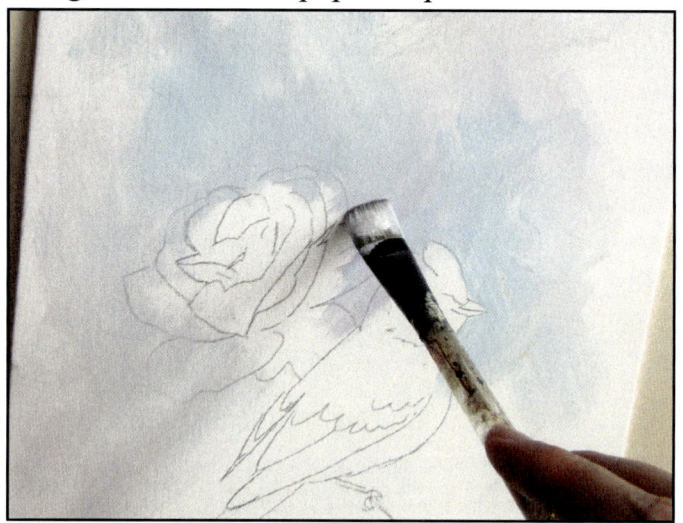

Step 3 Go over the sky with the blue and Extender Medium. Work around the bird and rose, but drag some color into them.

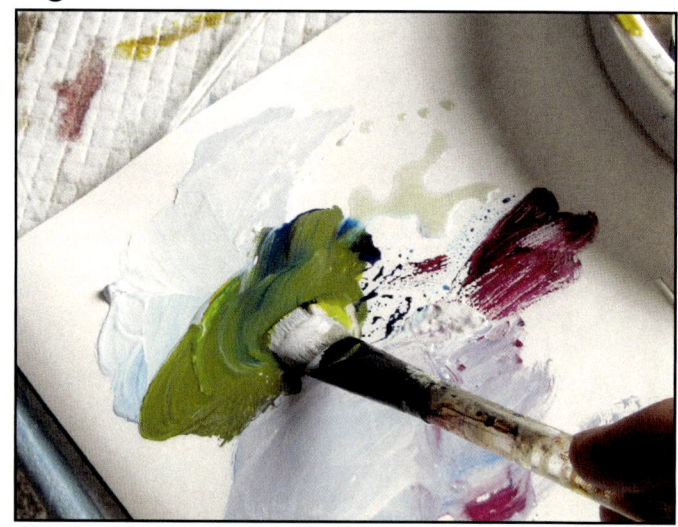

Step 4 Mottle the greens with Hansa and black, then add a touch blue to make brighter blue green.

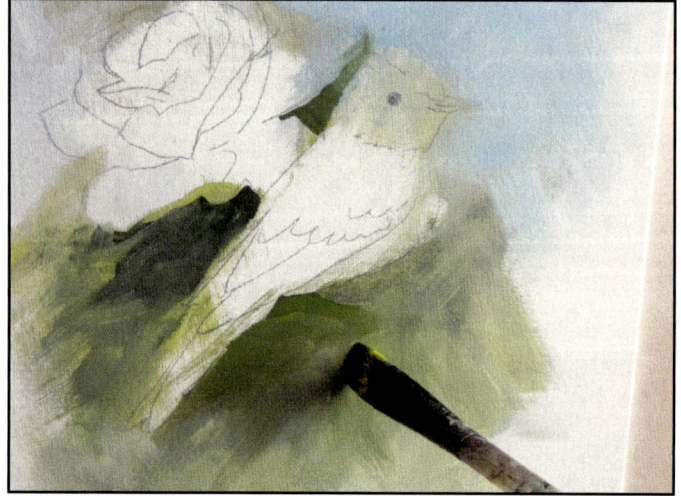

Step 5 Begin working the greens around the lower rose and bird. Vary the greens.

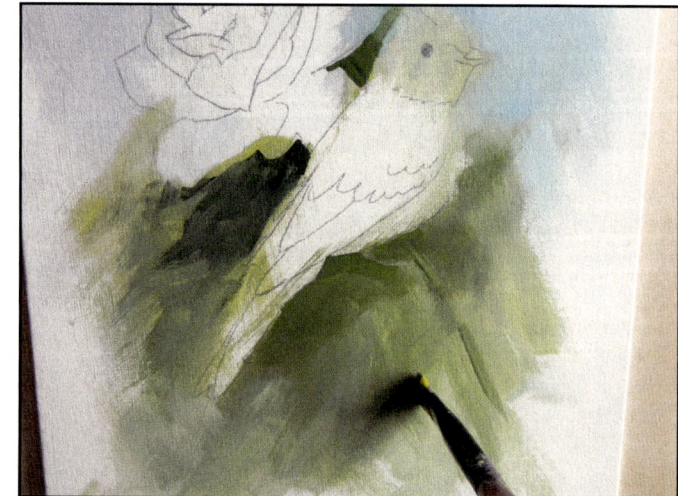

Step 6 Drag some of the color down for movement. Darken between rose and bird.

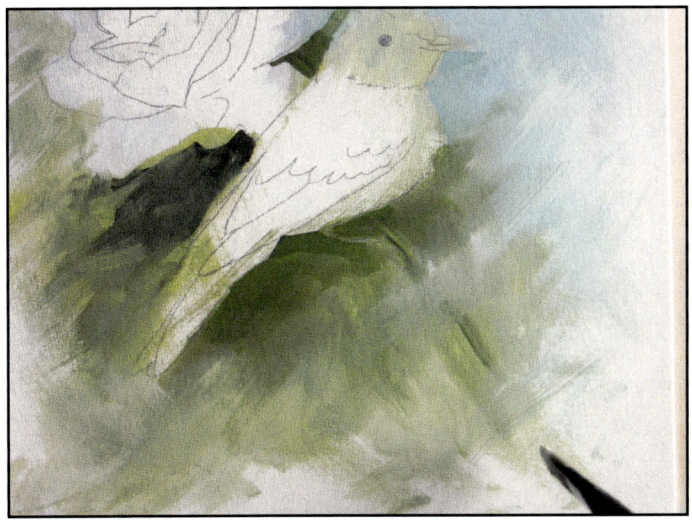

Step 7 Use the chisel of the brush to give the impression of some stems pulling down from the bird. These are rose stems.

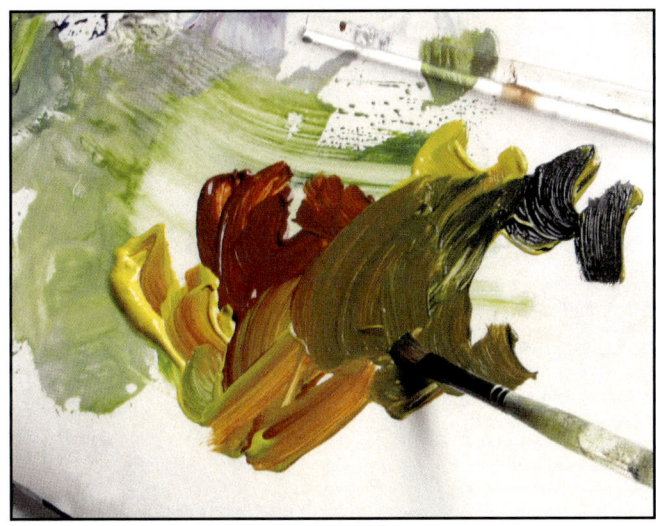

Step 8 Bird colors. Mottle Hansa and black, add some Burnt Sienna to tone the colors, keeping the reddish brown very toned.

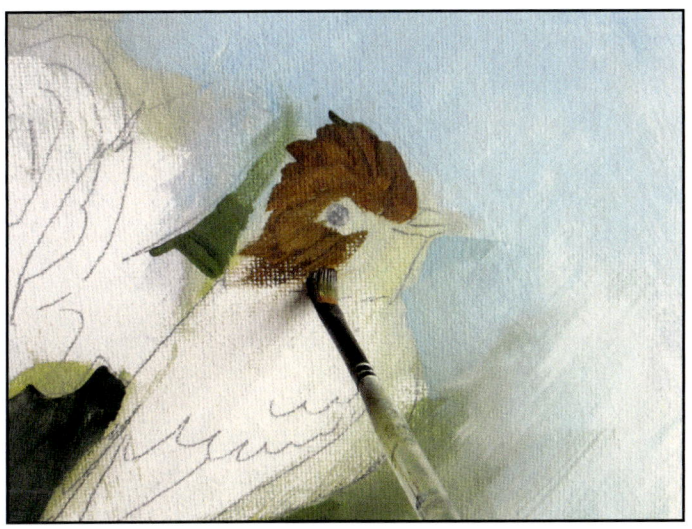

Step 9 Using small flat brush add the feathers to the top of head and work around the eye area following the contour of the body.

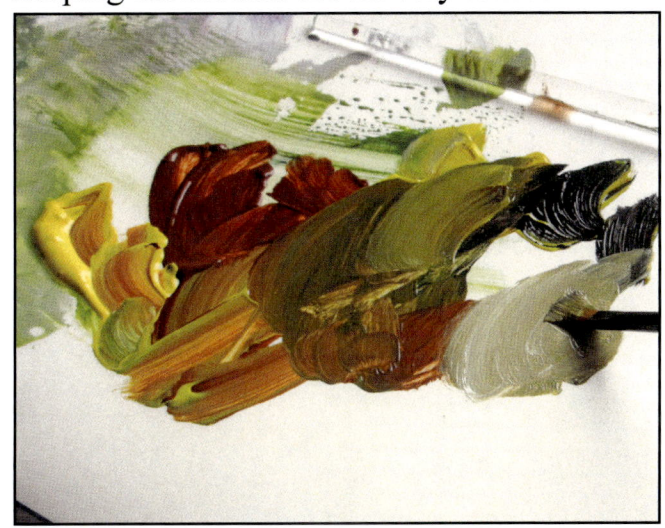

Step 10 Mottle the color a little lighter and add touch more black to make a little more grey.

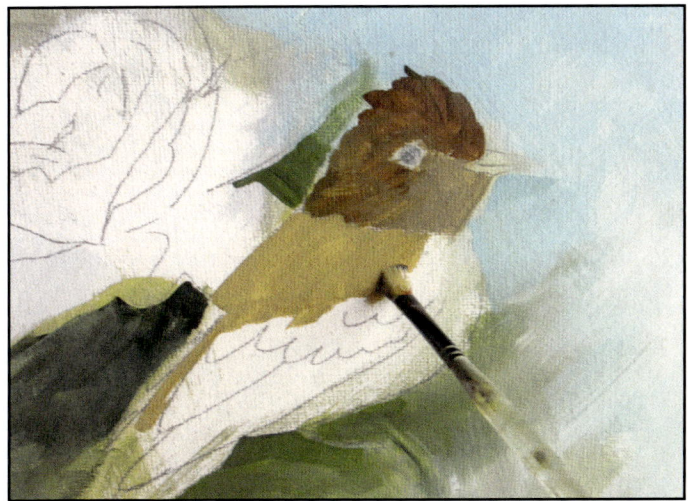

Step 11 Add this in the neck area, then make touch more red/yellow and add to mantle.

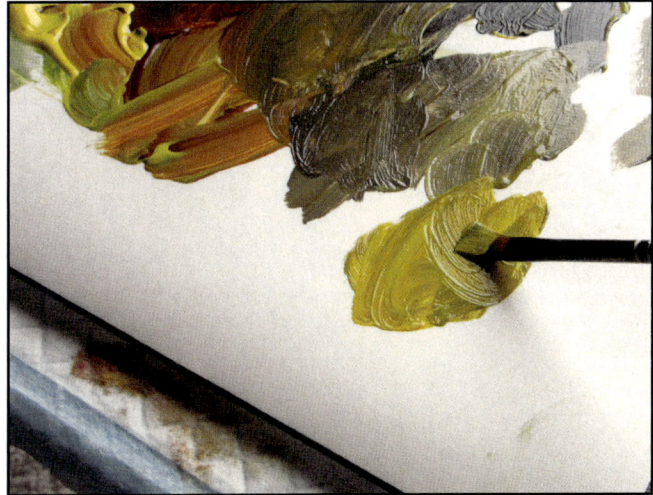

Step 12 Add a little Hansa to one side and mottle in the brush with other colors.

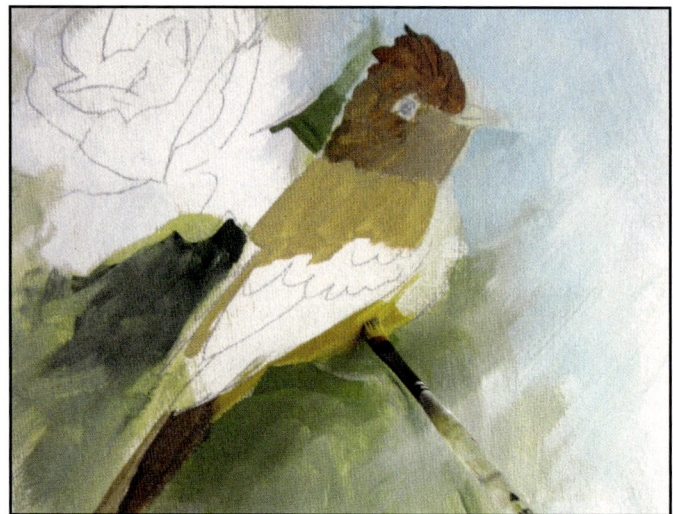

Step 13 Add this to the lower part of his body. Remember as you are applying these strokes, the size in relation to position in the body.

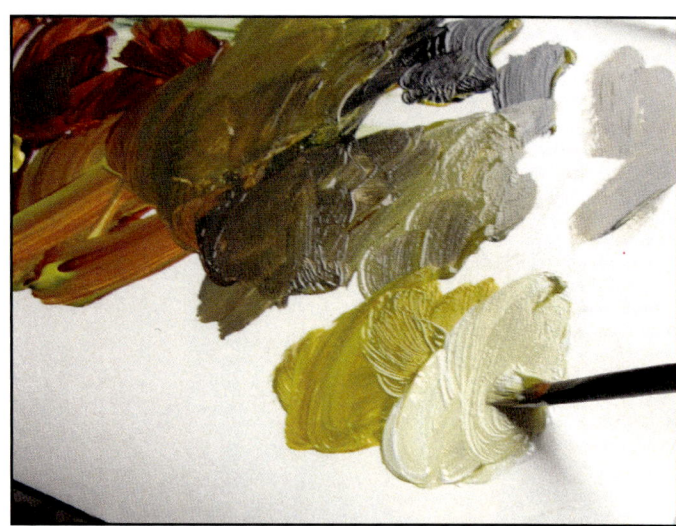

Step 14 Mottle the yellow color a little lighter with some white.

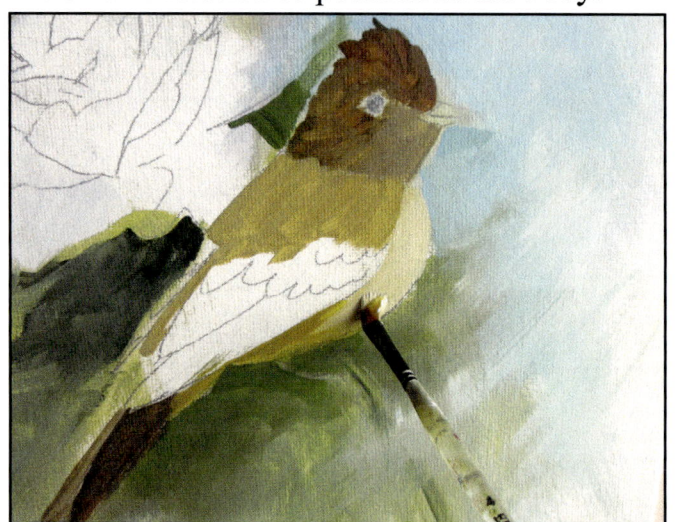

Step 15 Add this to the top of his breast under his chin. Pull down and mottle the color into the wet yellow we just applied.

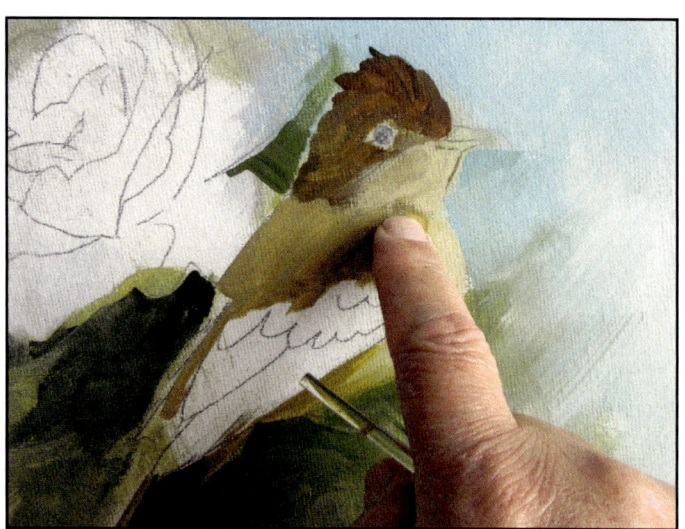

Step 16 I use my finger to bring the color together. Use short movements of the brush depending on the position in the body.

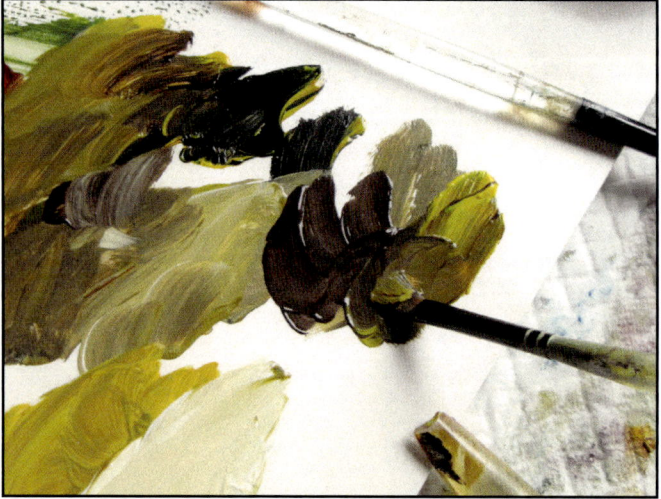

Step 17 Mottle the brush with some brown or here I added a touch of Burnt Umber.

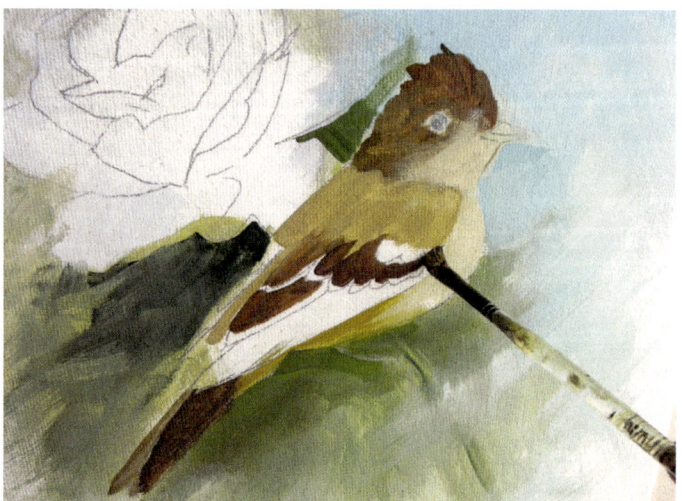

Step 18 I used this brown color to start the primary and secondary, leave some white.

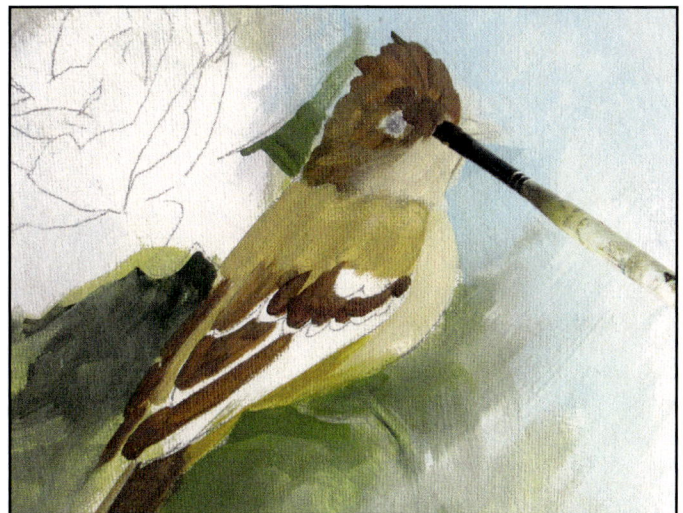

Step 19 Add some strokes to the top of the head and to the tail. Notice the white tips on the wings.

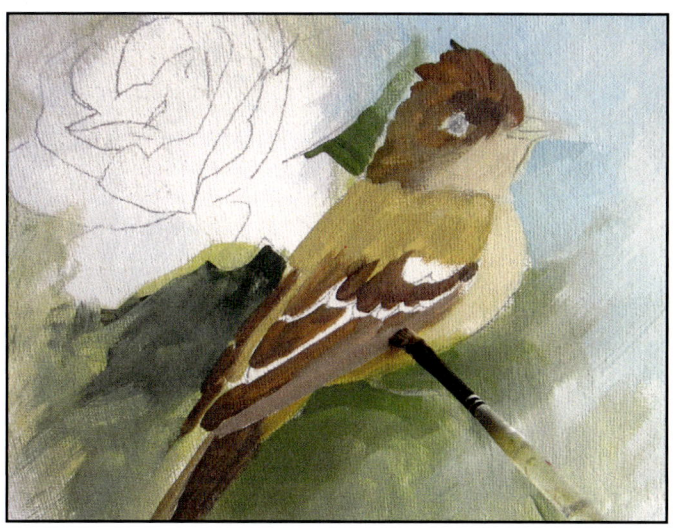

Step 20 Add a little more Burnt Umber and touch red to the tan to darken. Using the chisel add the front edge of the wing.

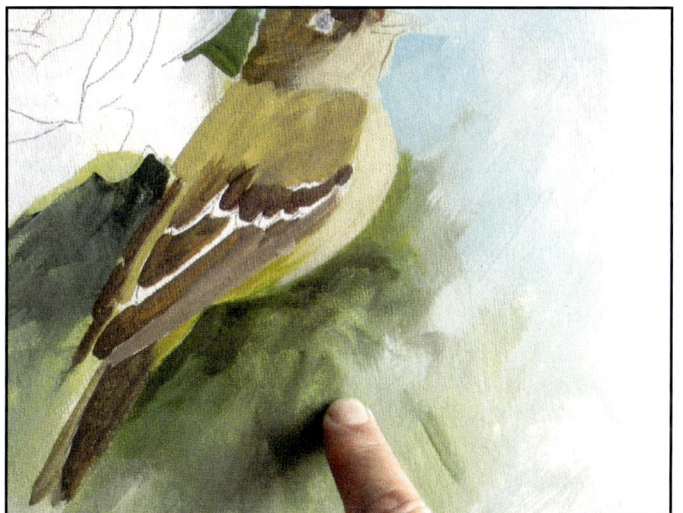

Step 21 Add some additional greens under the bird and soften with your finger. Keep some movement in and out for the stems.

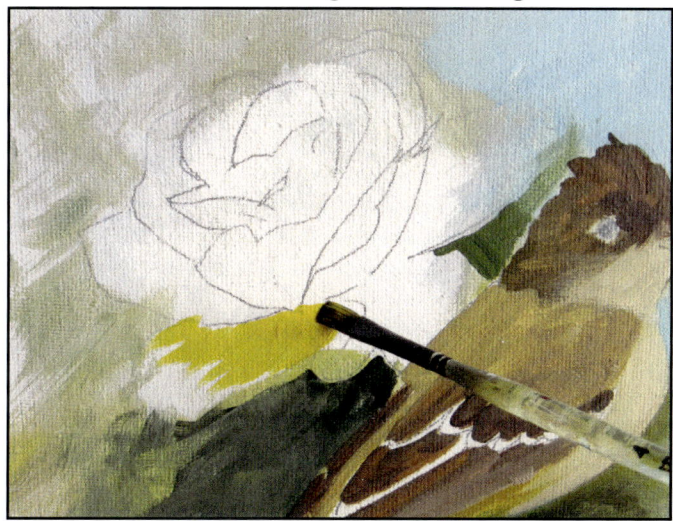

Step 22 Mottle the brush with Hansa and then begin to state the lower area of the rose. We will use the 1/2 tone technique.

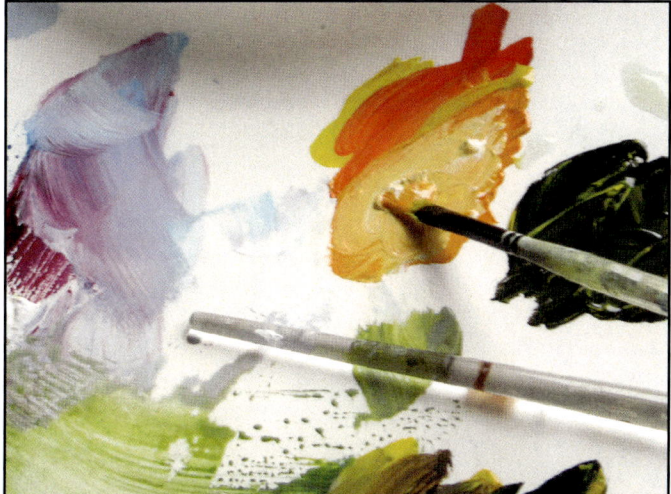

Step 23 Mottle the brush on the palette with Hansa and Nap. Red Light to make orange.

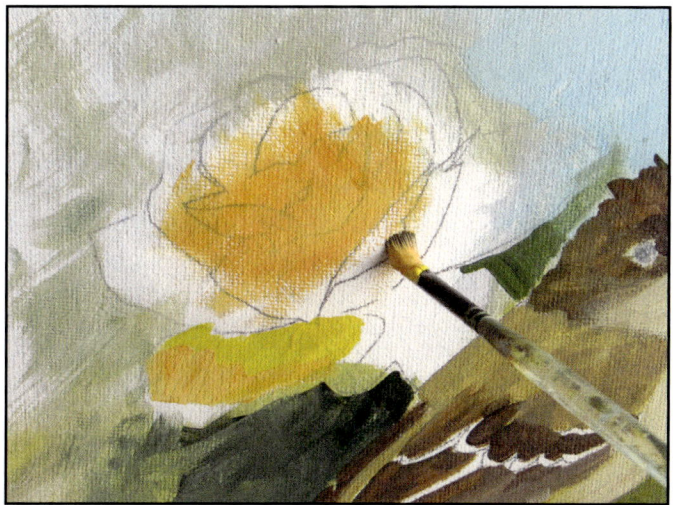

Step 24 Add Extender and go over the front of the rose allowing pattern to show through.

87

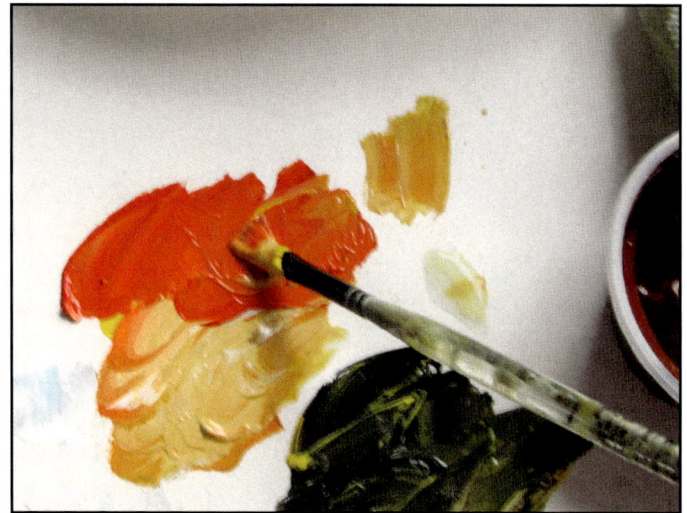

Step 25 Mottle the color with additional red to darken and shift the hue more red.

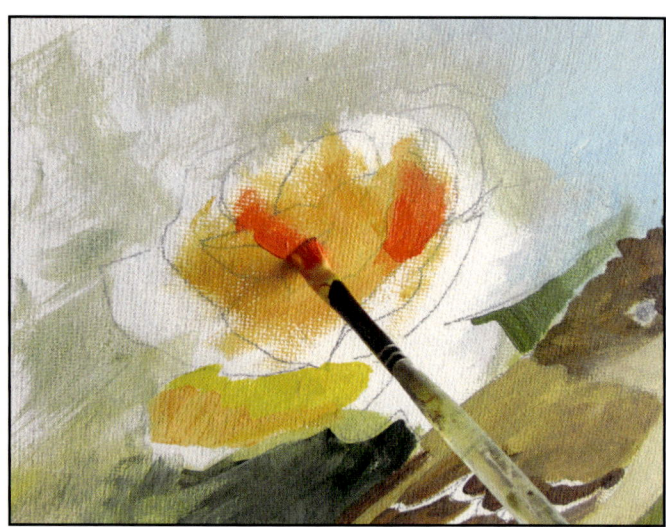

Step 26 Add some strikes of red. These represent the bright color spots I found in the original inspiration photo.

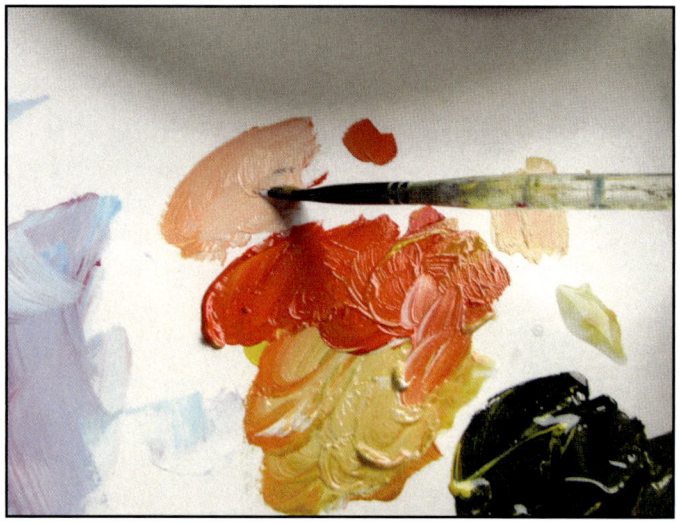

Step 27 Mottle the reds, yellow and then lighten with white to make a peach color. Add a little Extender to thin, just a little.

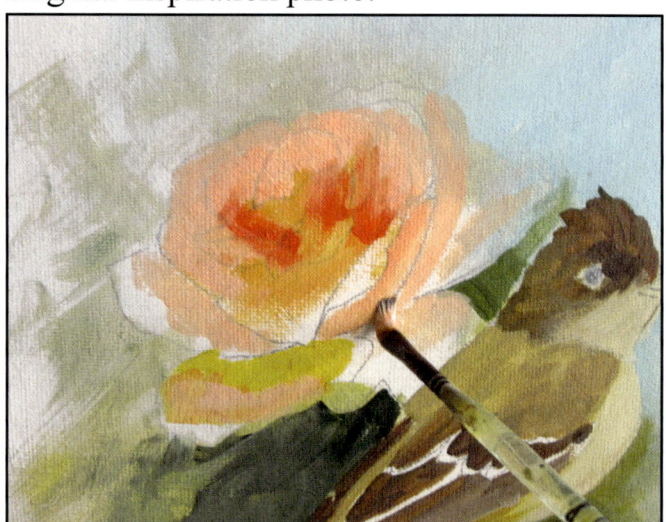

Step 28 Strike this into the rose pull the petals towards the base of the rose.

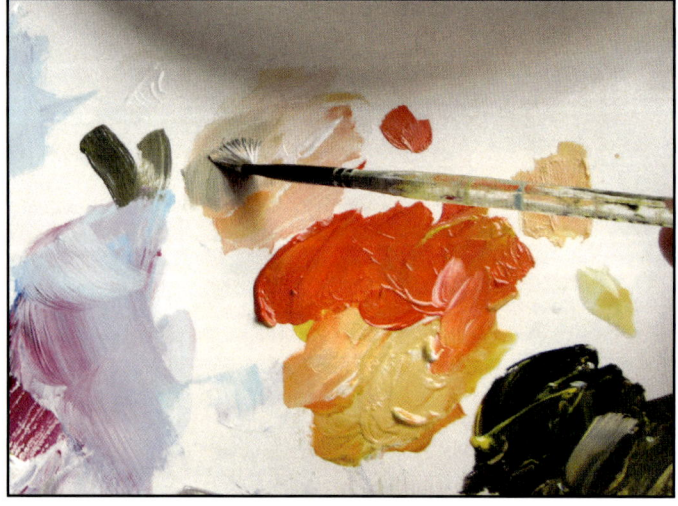

Step 29 Add a tiny touch green to tone then lighten with some white.

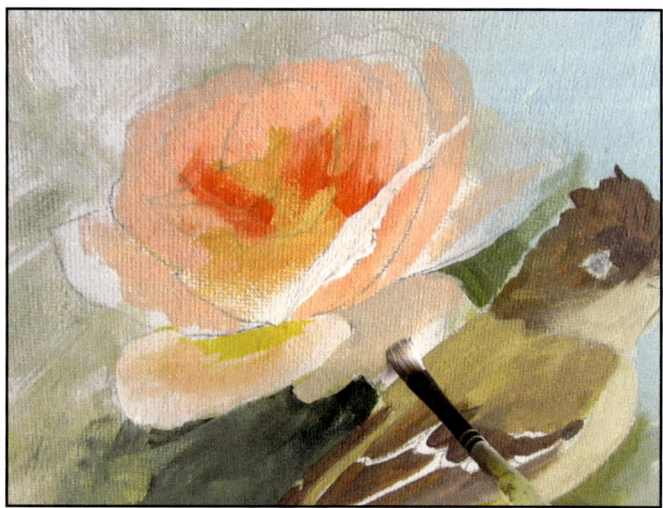

Step 30 Add the lighter slightly more toned petal in the front of the rose.

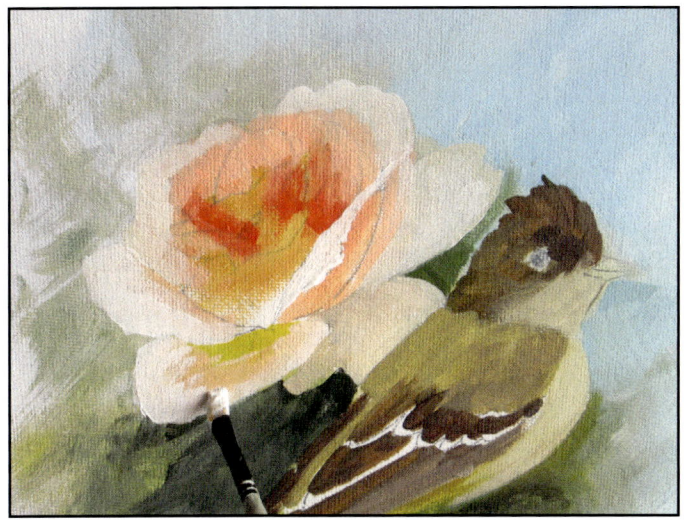

Step 31 Add the light edges of the petals with some white and mottled with the peach color.

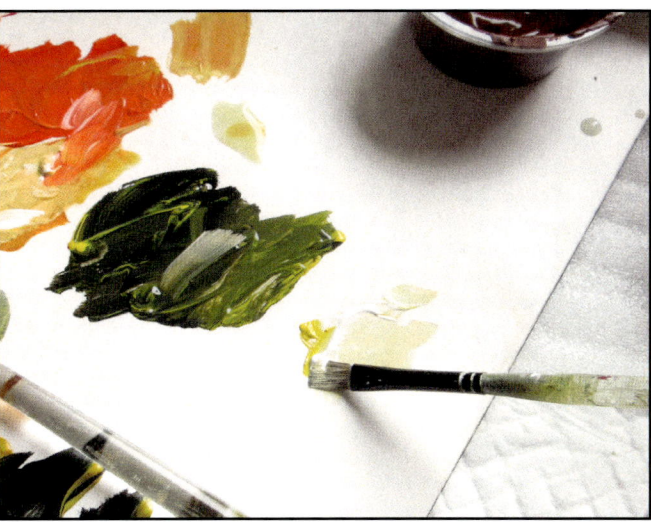

Step 32 Mottle the brush with some Hansa and then lighten with some white.

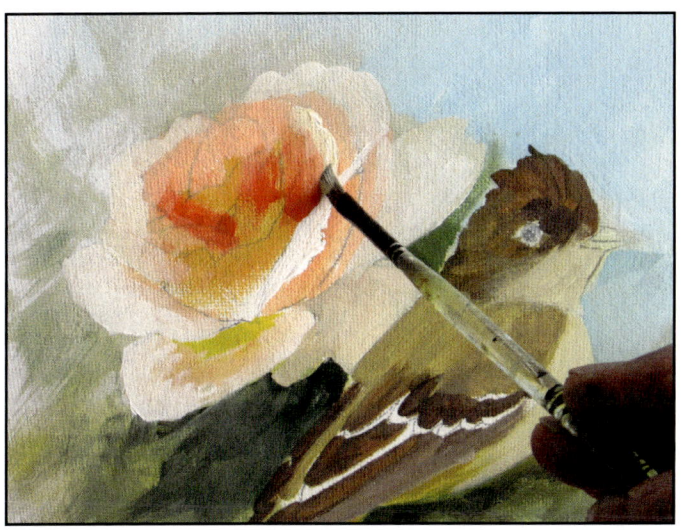

Step 33 Use the chisel of the brush to draw on the edges of the petals and then pull in towards the center a little.

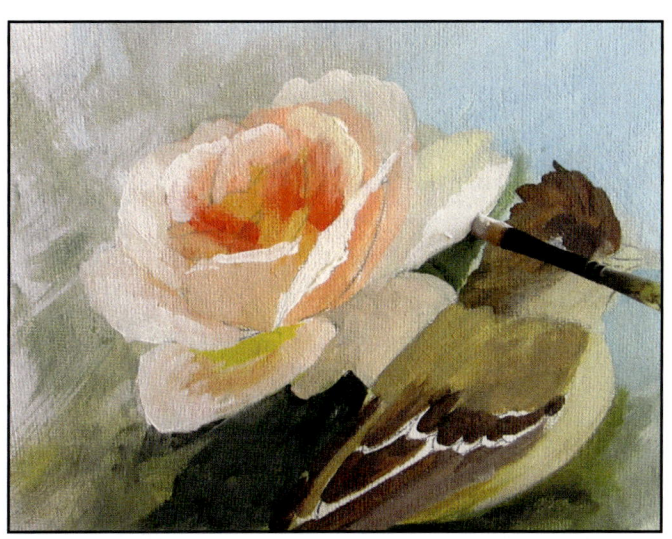

Step 34 Add some light color to the tips of the petals in the front petals.

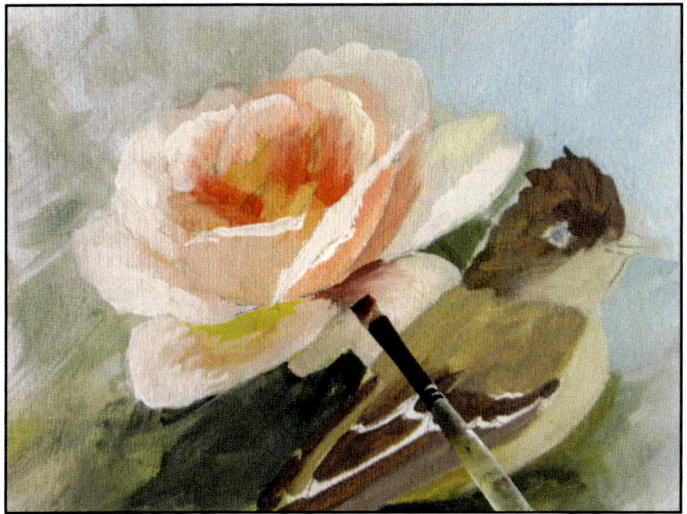

Step 35 Add some darker Burnt Sienna and touch Red Violet as shadow in front petal.

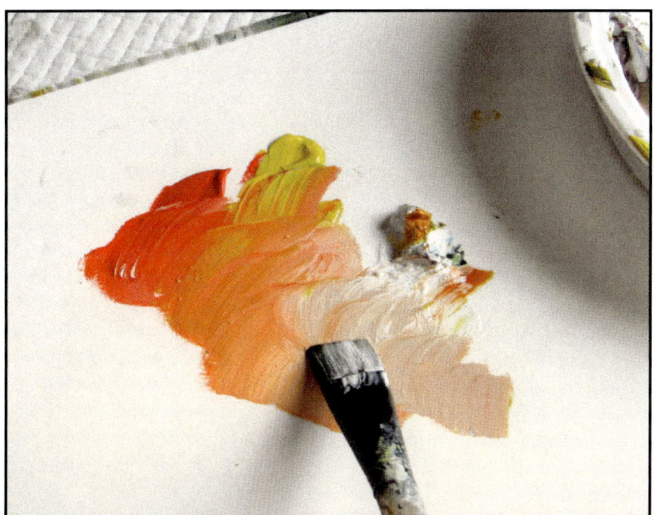

Step 36 Mottle the brush with the reds, yellows and lighten with white.

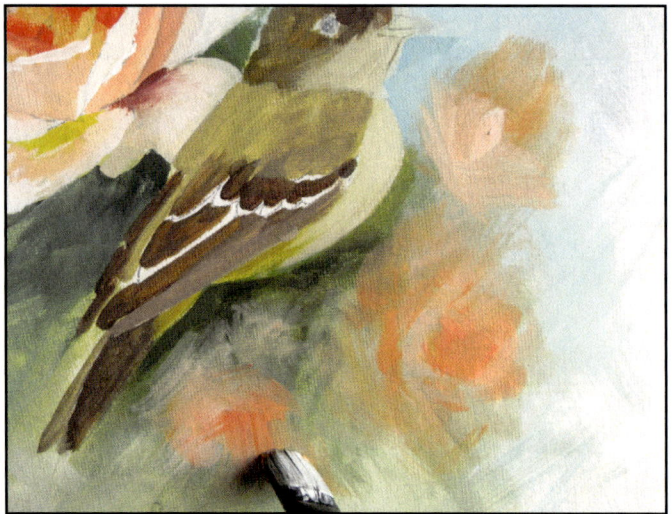

Step 37 Add some suggestions of shapes for other roses with the light peach color and larger flat brush.

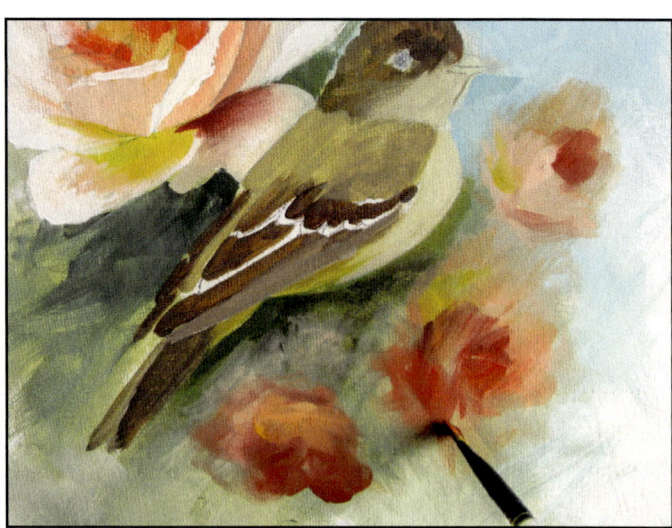

Step 38 Add some reds and then Red Violet shadows to the roses for suggested form.

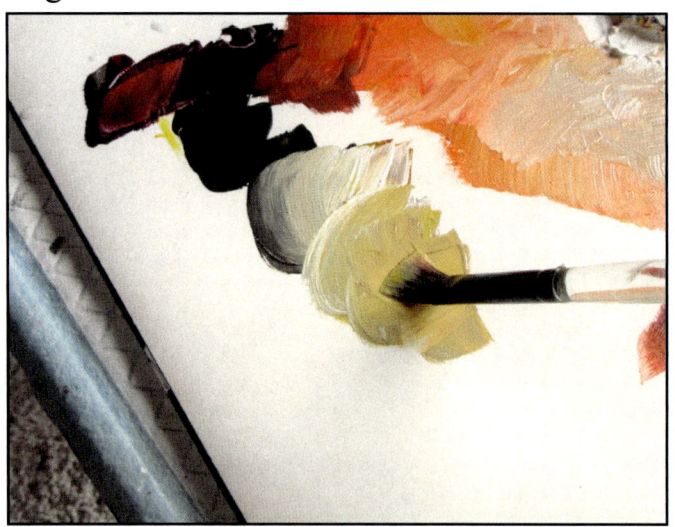

Step 39 Mottle brush with yellow, black and lighten with some white. Tan color.

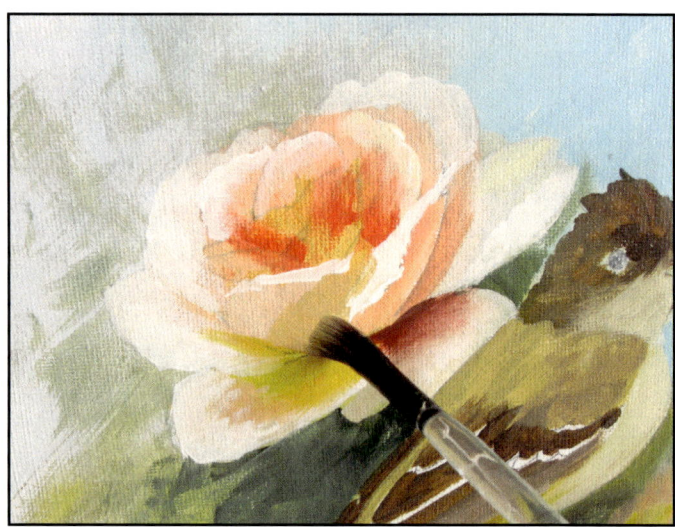

Step 40   Add some as toned 1/2 shadow to the bottom of the bowl in front of the rose.

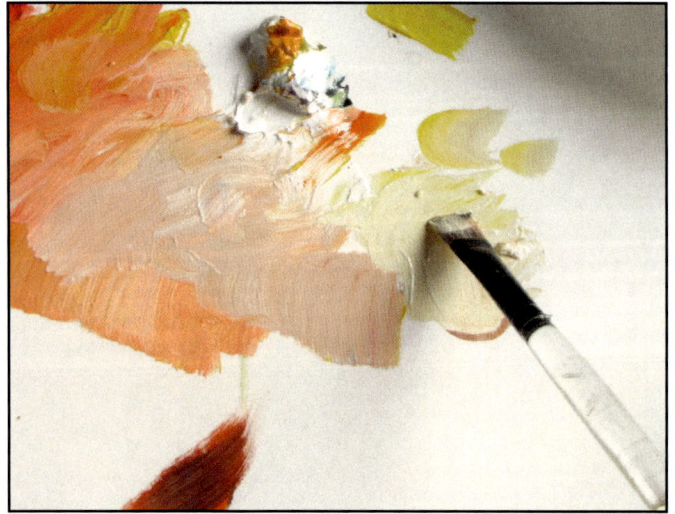

Step 41 Mottle brush with Hansa, white and touch peach color from earlier.

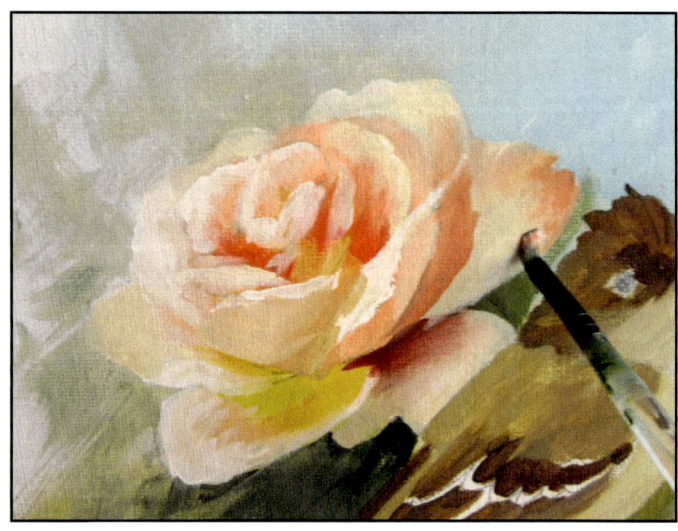

Step 42 Add to the inside of the rose where the bowl comes out.

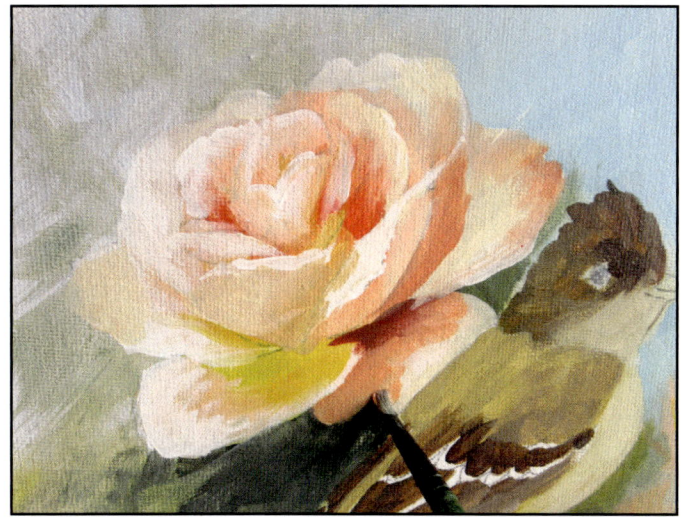

Step 43 Add some 1/2 tone shadow to the lower petal in front of the flower. 1/2 tone is half between the highlight and shadow.

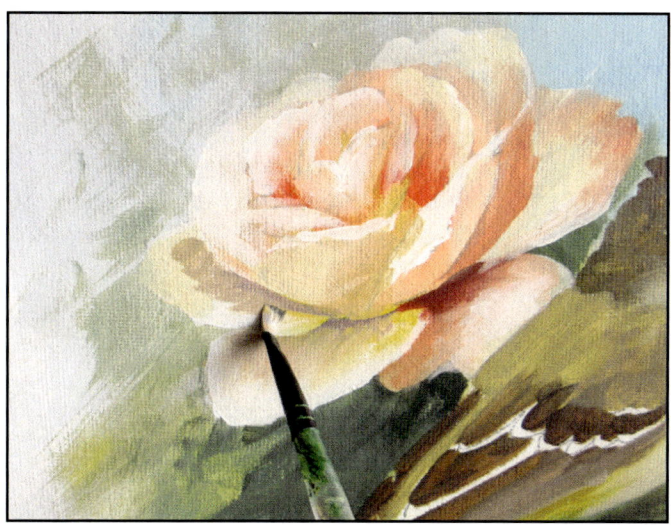

Step 44 Add some greyed 1/2 tone shadow next to the bowl on the left side.

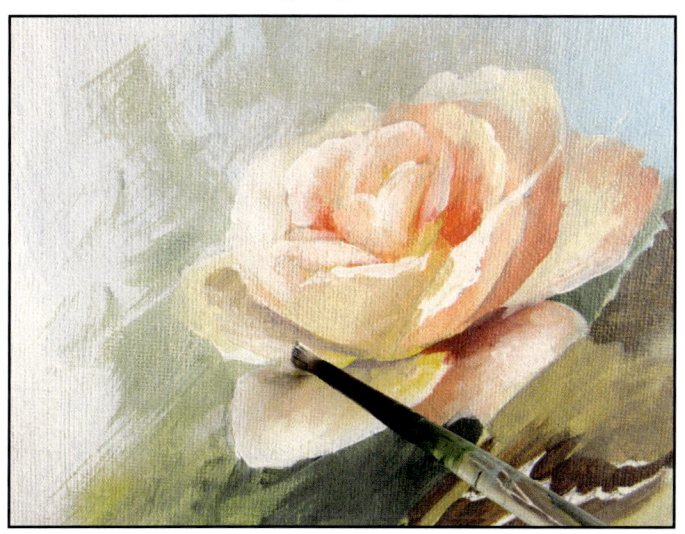

Step 45 Lighten color to make another 1/2 tone. Between the shadow and highlight we applied earlier. Stroke and soften color.

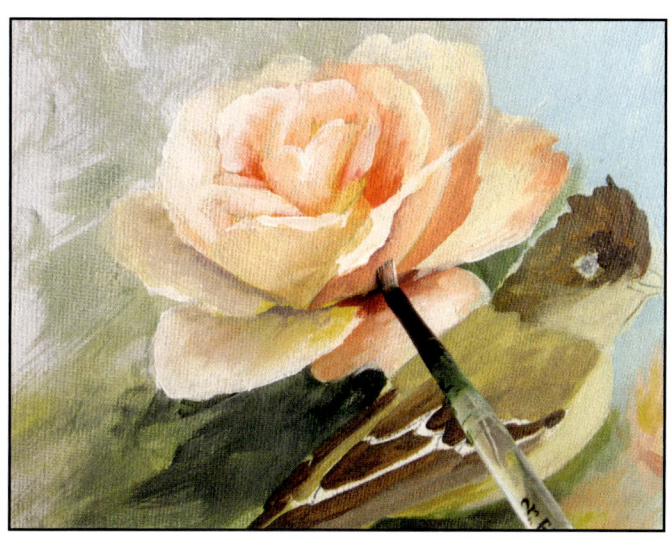

Step 46 Add some light to the underside of the top front petal. Just a little lighter than what you have there already.

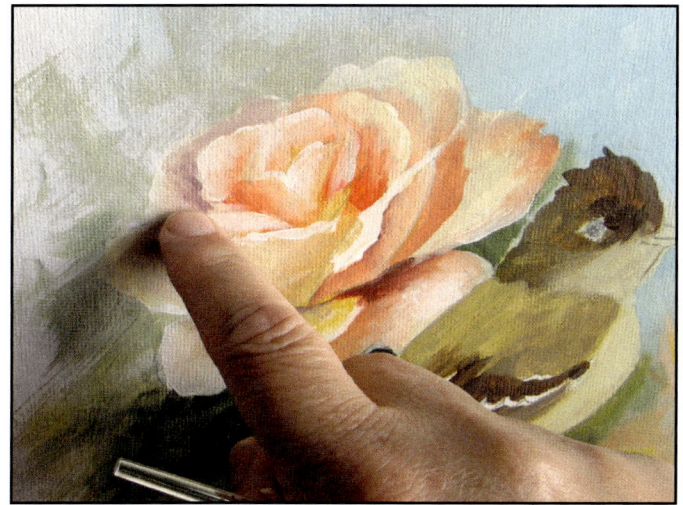

Step 47 For the back of the rose I use my finger to soften the edges to recede the petal.

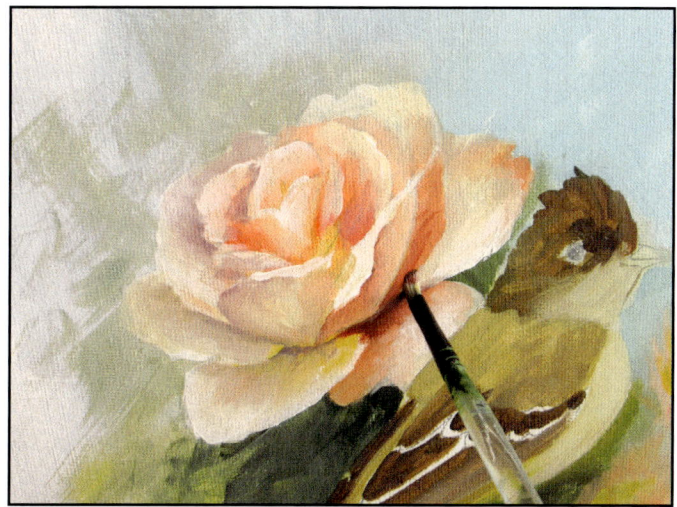

Step 48 Increase the dark in the bowl with more Burnt Sienna and touch Red Violet.

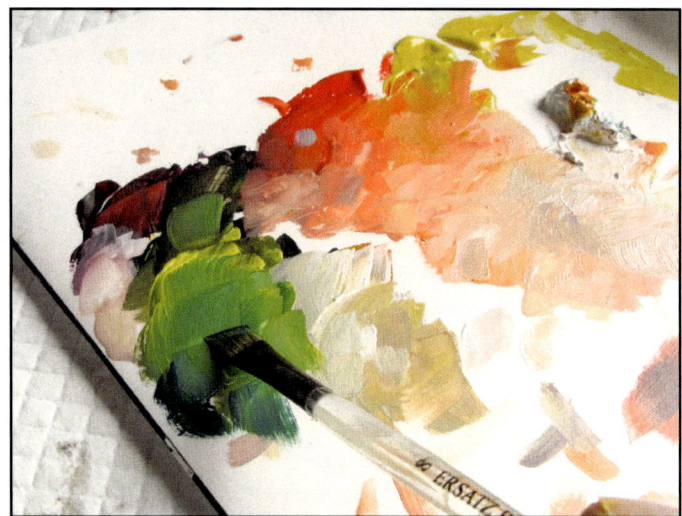

Step 49 Mottle green with Hansa and black, add touch blue. Always vary the greens with the different blue and black.

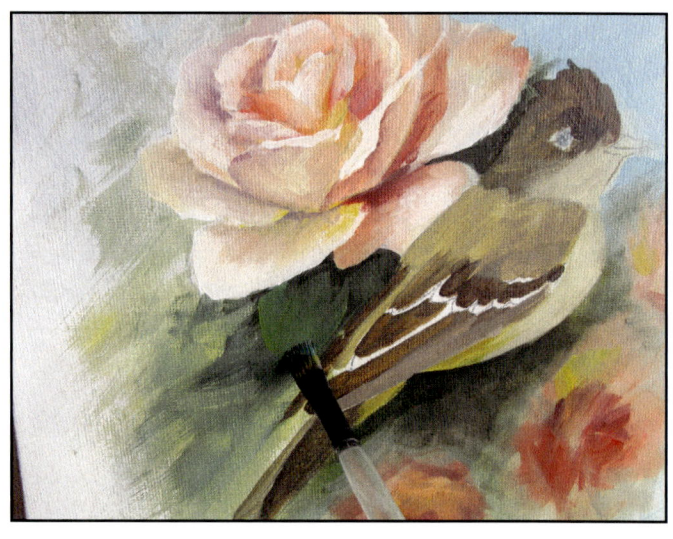

Step 50 Begin the leaves with a slightly darker value of the green. Small flat and make casual oval shapes.

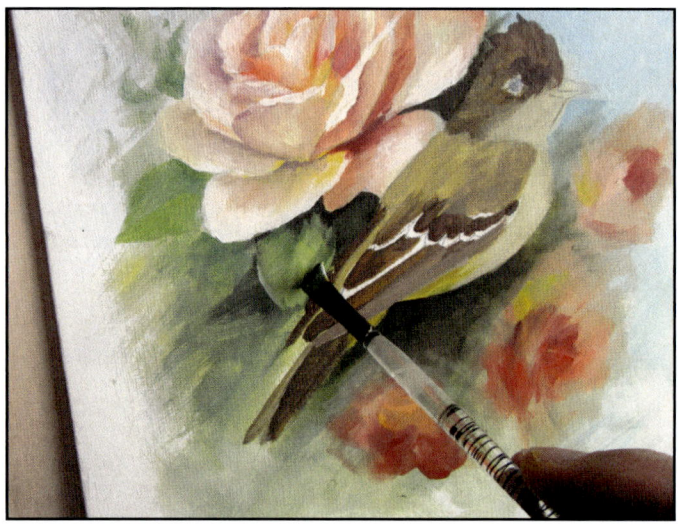

Step 51 Lighten the color with a little more Hansa and white. Add some light strokes from the center of the leaf out to the tip.

Step 52 Use the chisel of the small flat to add some stems to the flowers. Vary greens.

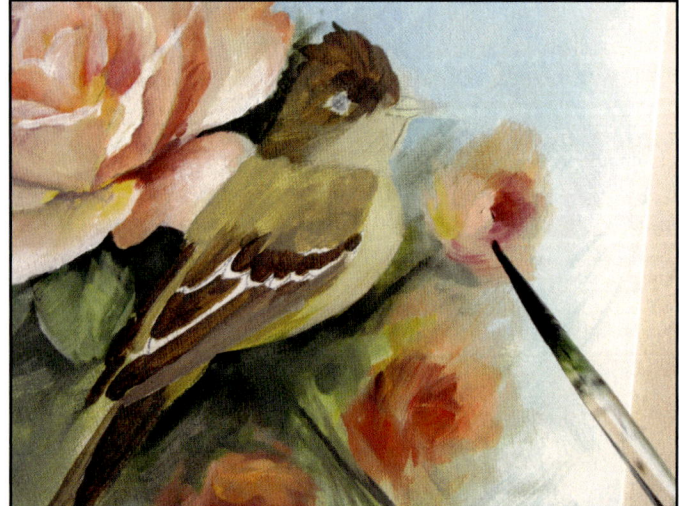

Step 53 Add some shadows of red and Red Violet to begin to shape the roses.

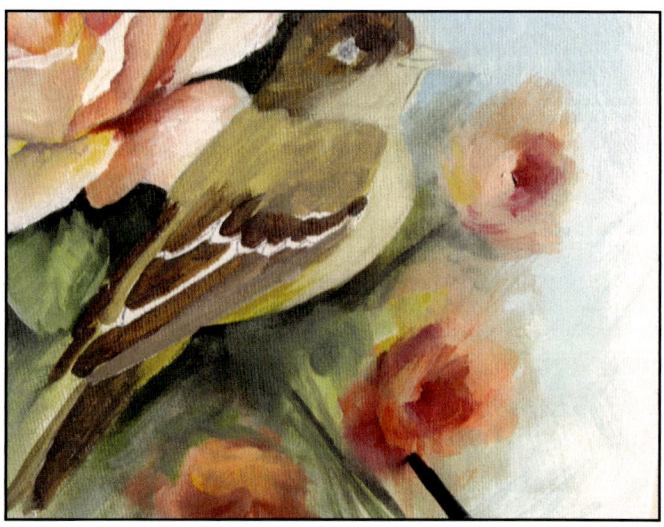

Step 54 Continue the shadows on the next flowers adding some casual shapes.

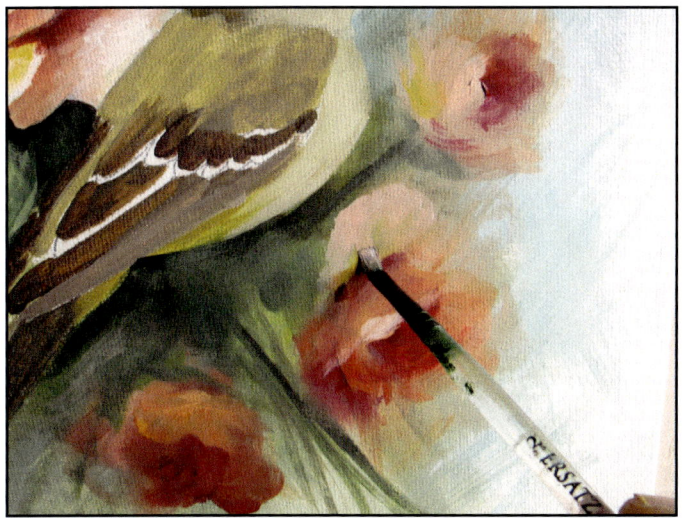

Step 55 Lighten the color to a peach color with reds, yellows and white. Begin some casual highlights. Soften with half tone.

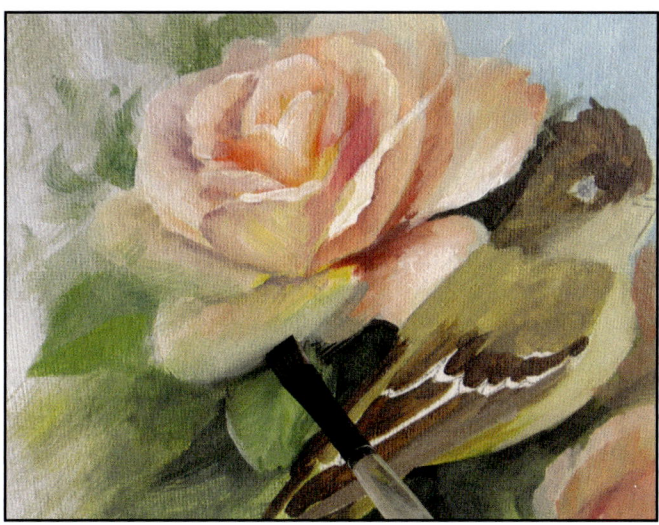

Step 56 Soften the edges of the main rose with some green from leaves. This makes the petals a little transparent if you want.

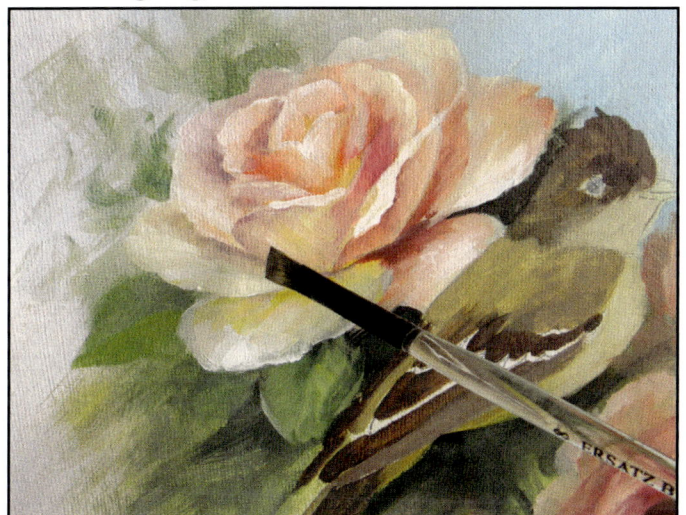

Step 57 Add some lights to the edges of the petals. Leave some of the greens showing if you want to make the petals transparent.

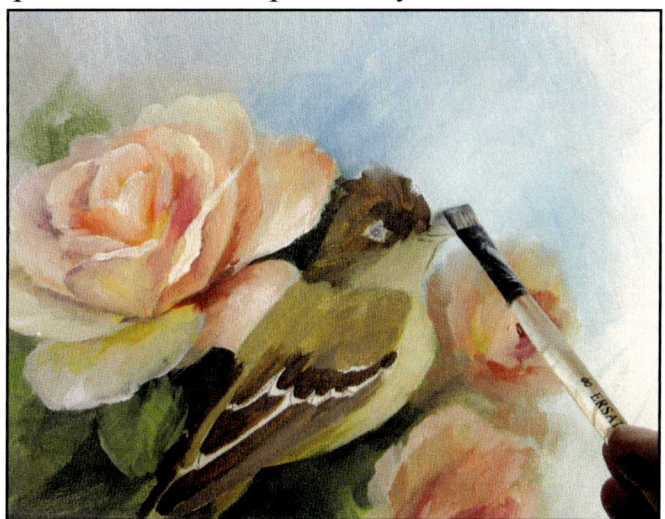

Step 58 Opaque the light blue color around the bird's head. This is important to make him come forward.

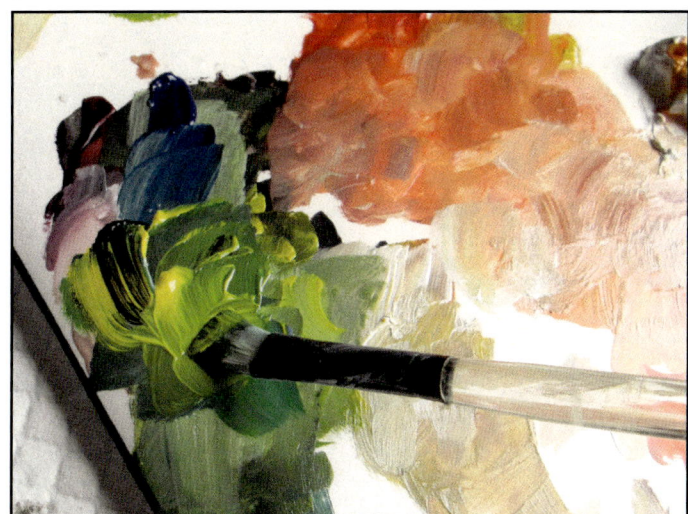

Step 59 Return and mottle the greens again, this time more Hansa to make brighter.

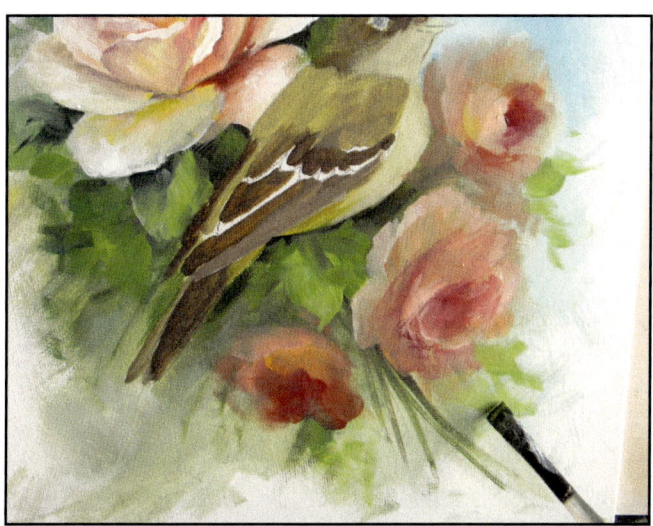

Step 60 Use this to suggest some leaf shapes out from the other roses.

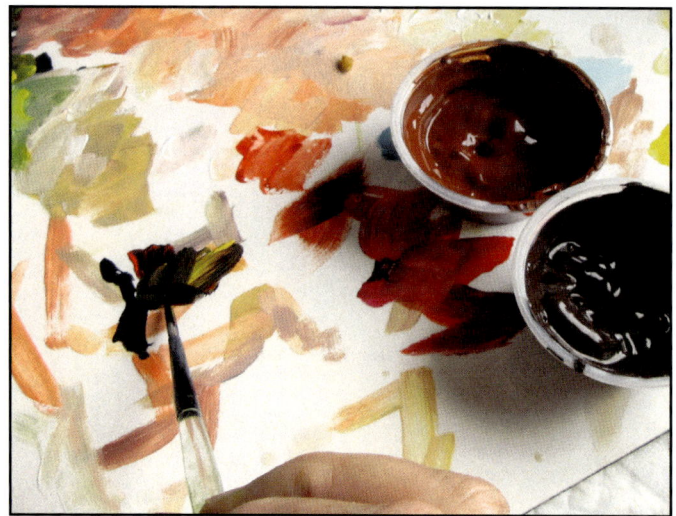

Step 61 Using round brush, mottle the Burnt Sienna, Burnt Umber and Hansa to make some various browns.

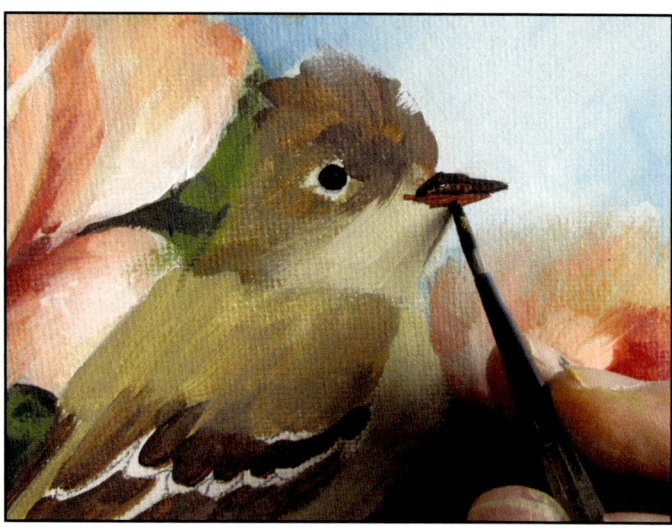

Step 62 Add a lower beak with more Burnt Sienna and an upper beak with more Burnt Umber. Add a black eye. Leave eye ring.

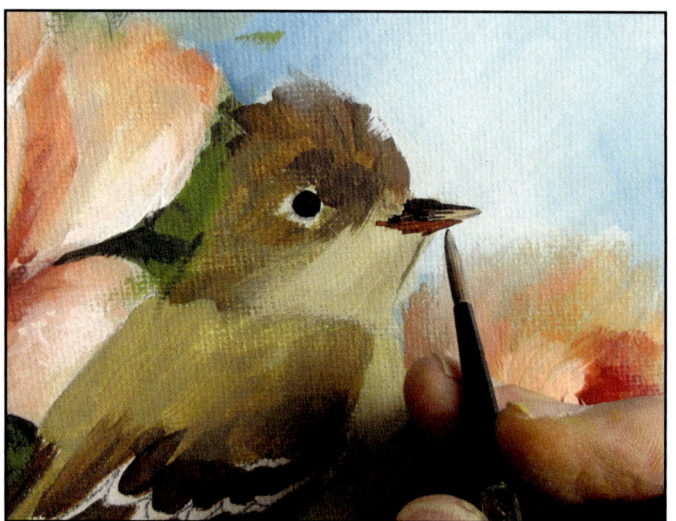

Step 63 Add a touch of tan highlight to the front of the beak.

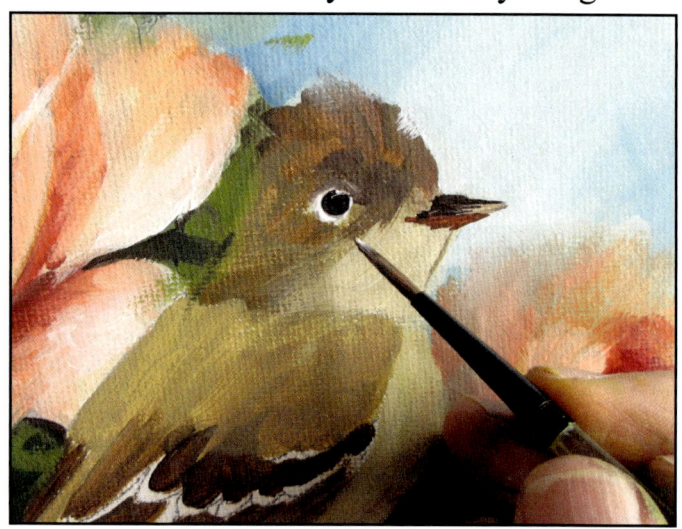

Step 64   Reinforce the white eye ring with more white and then begin to add some feather strokes.

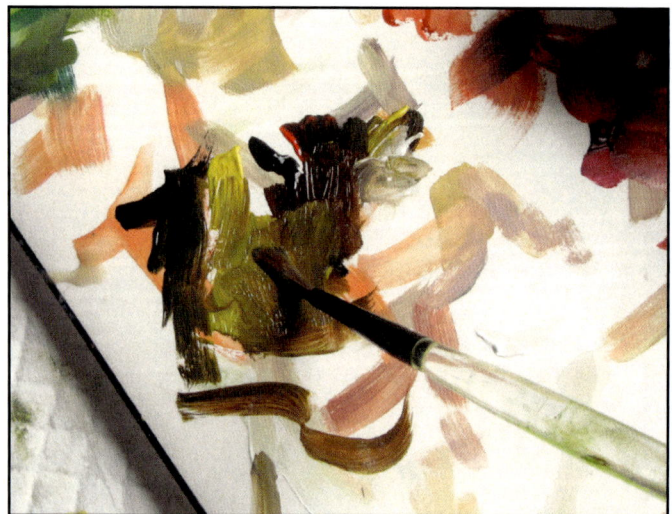

Step 65 Mottle browns with black and then add Hansa to lighten.

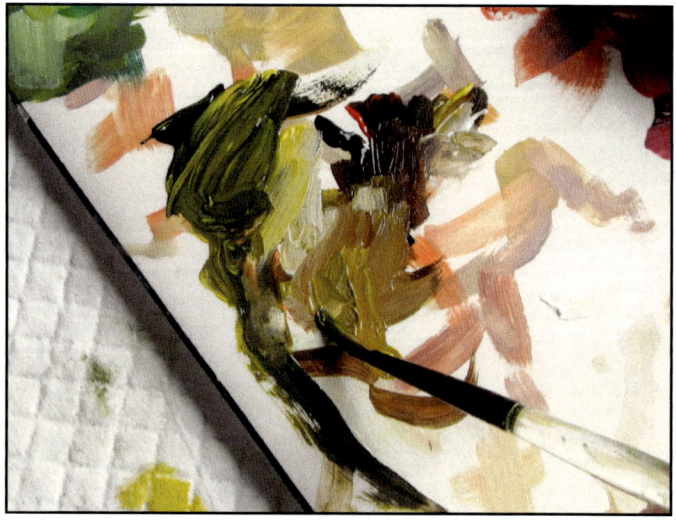

Step 66 Add a touch green to tone and then lighten with some white.

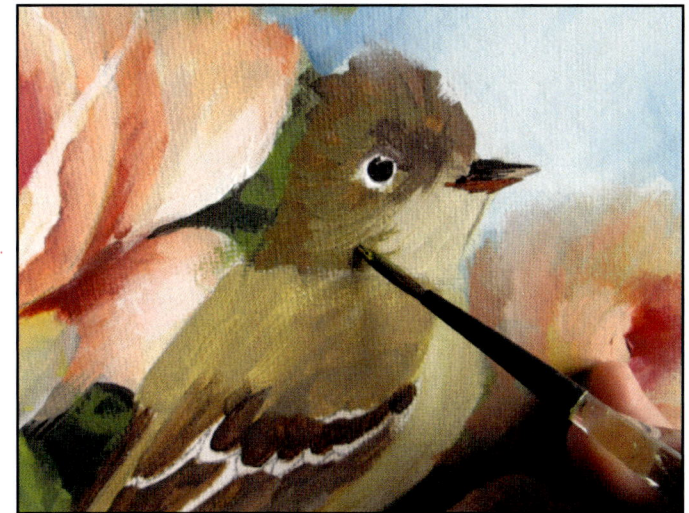

Step 67 Using the half tone technique, the feather color should come between the color already there and the light. A 1/2 tone.

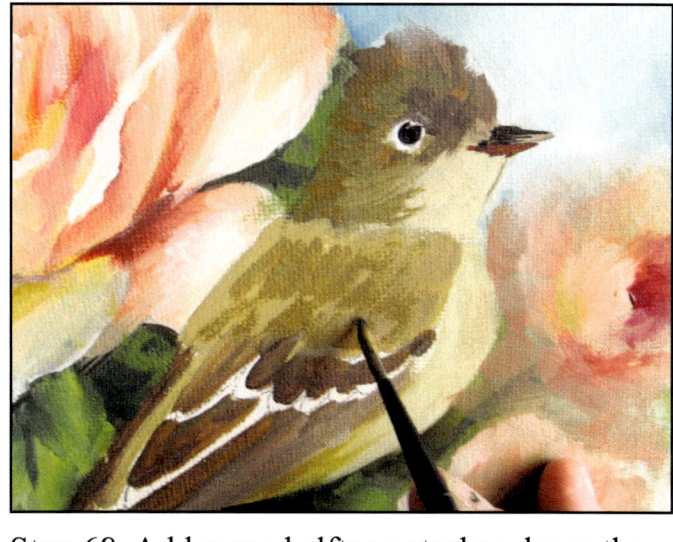

Step 68 Add some halftone strokes down the mantle of the wing which will add the feather movement.

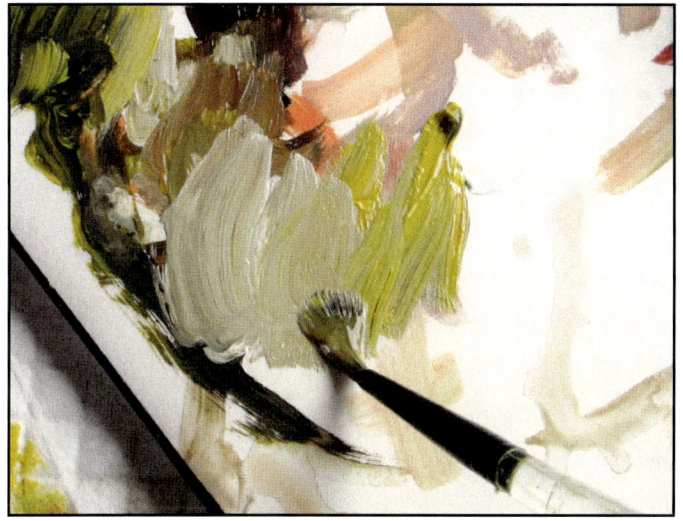

Step 69 Lighten the color with more Hansa and white using round brush. For these feathers push brush flat to spread out hairs.

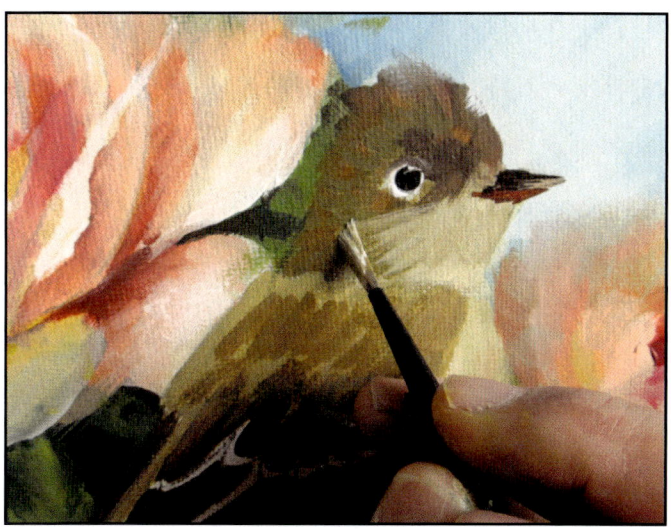

Step 70 Stroke on the feathers letting the brush open. This give a different look. Remember stroke length for head.

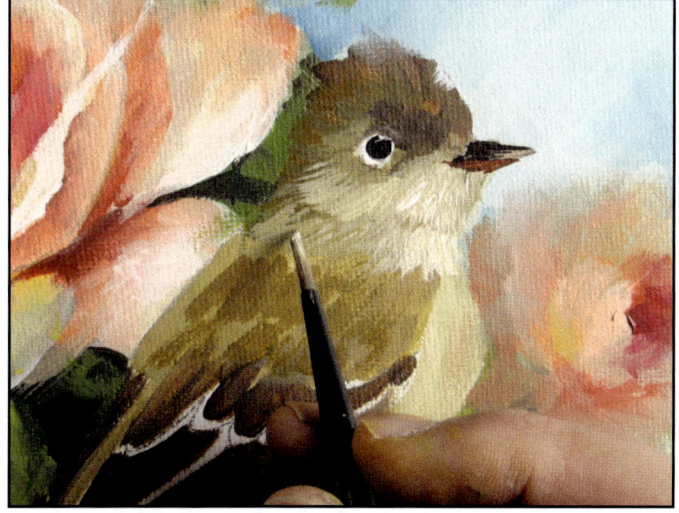

Step 71 Point the brush up and apply some smaller detailed strokes to the neck feathers.

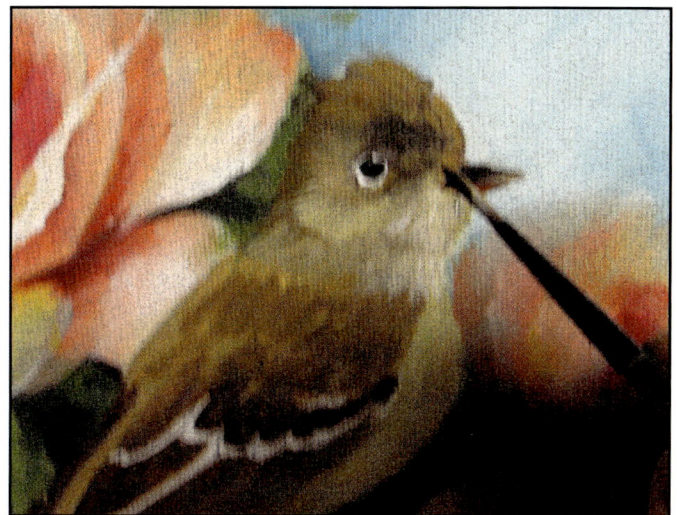

Step 72 Add some short strokes around the beak.

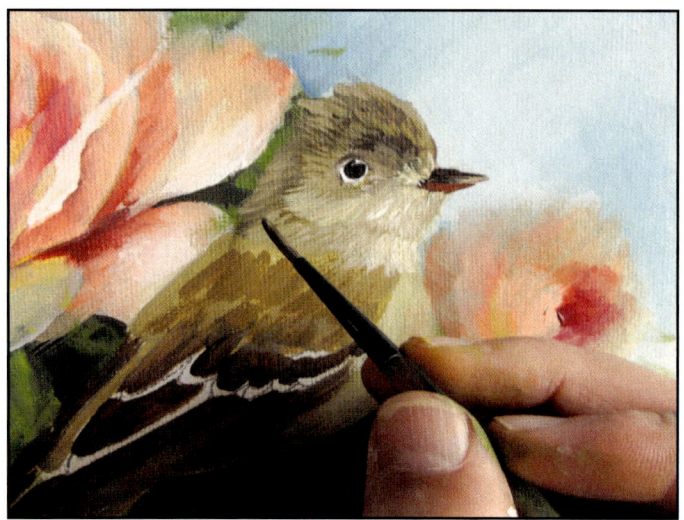

Step 73   Use the pointed brush to add the smaller feather details around the face. Notice the break around the cheek area.

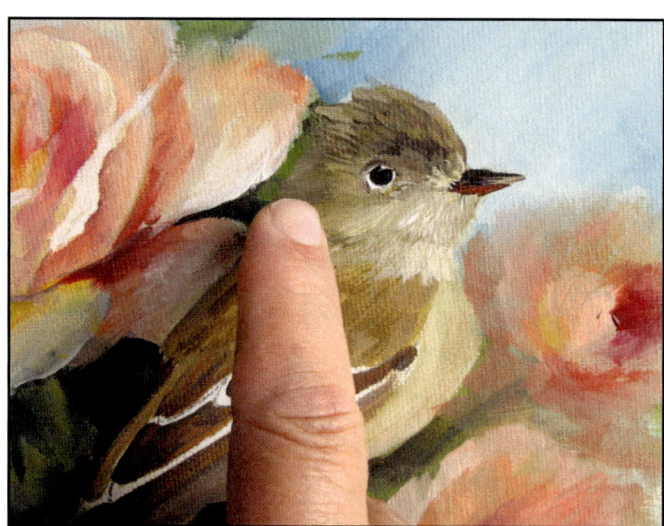

Step 74   Soften the back edges of the feathers to the side of the face recedes.

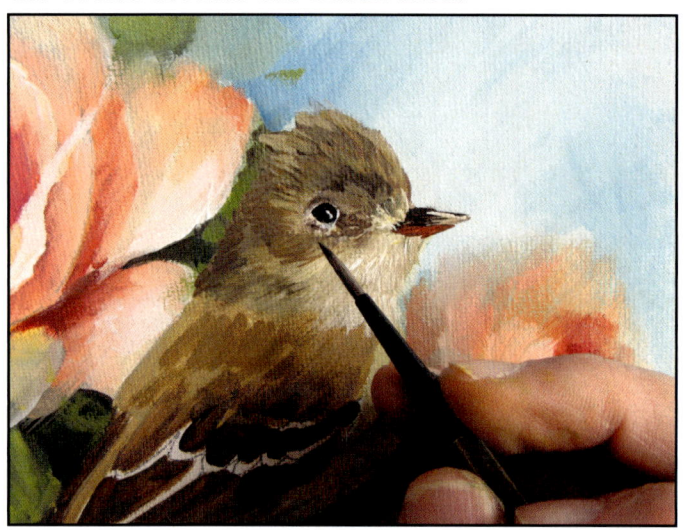

Step 75   Add small detail feathers around eye. I repeat lights and shadows several times until I get a good look to the eyes. Add eye shine.

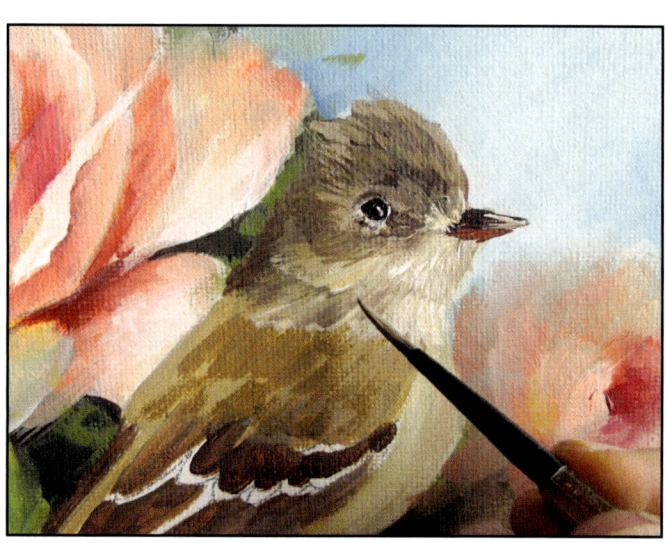

Step 76   I add light strokes as shown, then apply a darker stroke lifting off the brush to leave light ends on the feathers.

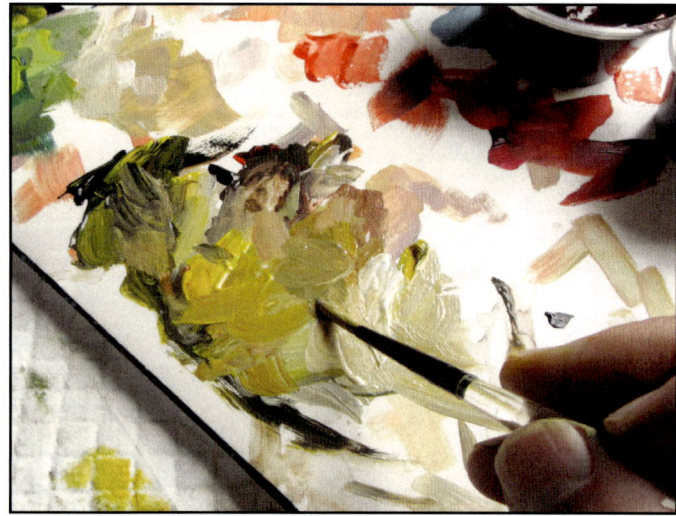

Step 77   Darken the color a little but it is still on the light side.

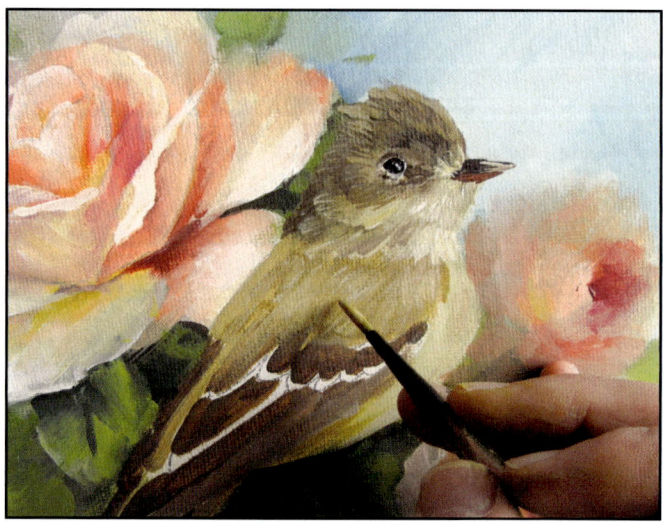

Step 78   Add some strokes to the coverts over the secondary flight coverts.

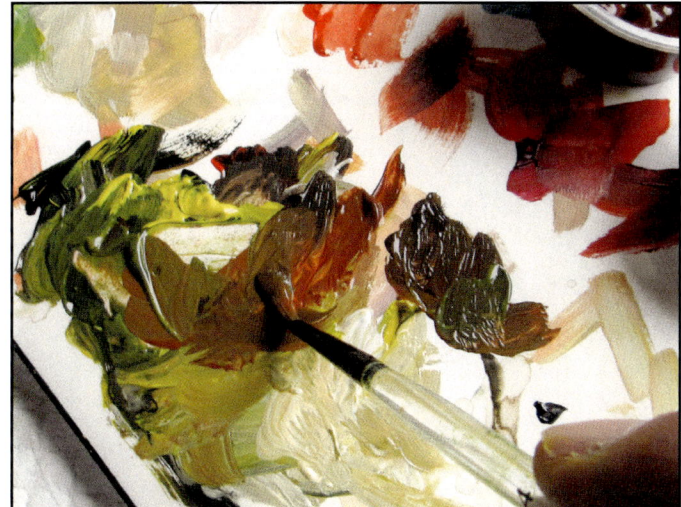

Step 79 Mottle browns, Burnt Sienna and Burnt Umber on the palette. I add a touch of greens as well.

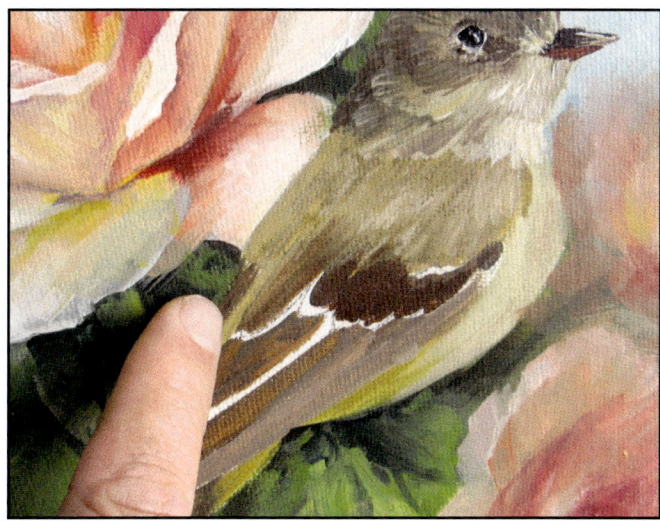

Step 80 Add to the back wings to recede and then soften with your finger so they recede.

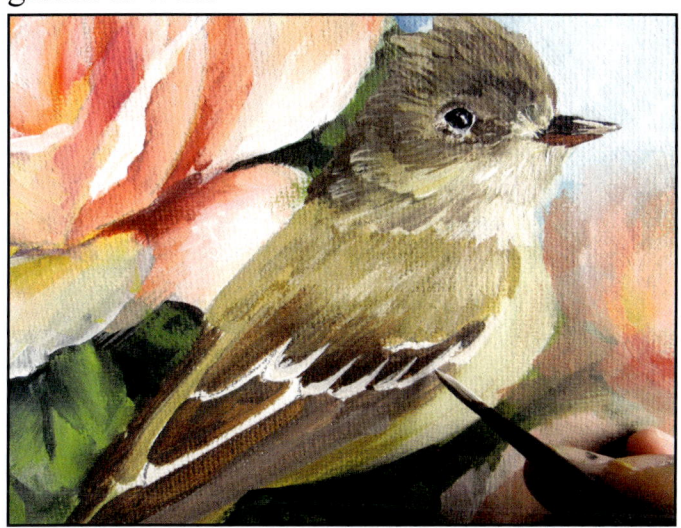

Step 81 Add light strokes to the tips of the flight coverts pulling up towards the mantle cover of the wing.

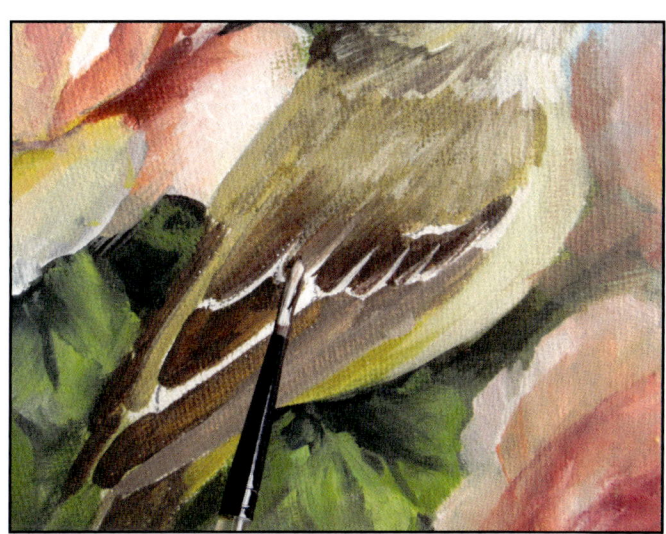

Step 82 Mottle the brush with some browns and pull down from the mantle towards the flight coverts leaving the white edges.

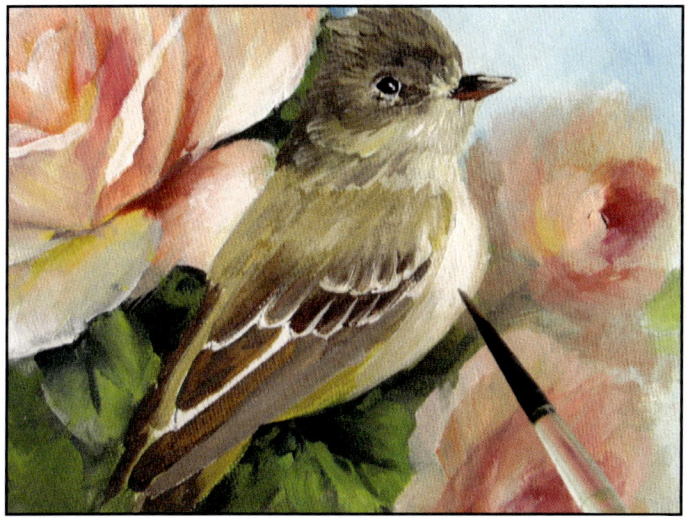

Step 83 Mottle the brush with light colors and add some strokes to the breast.

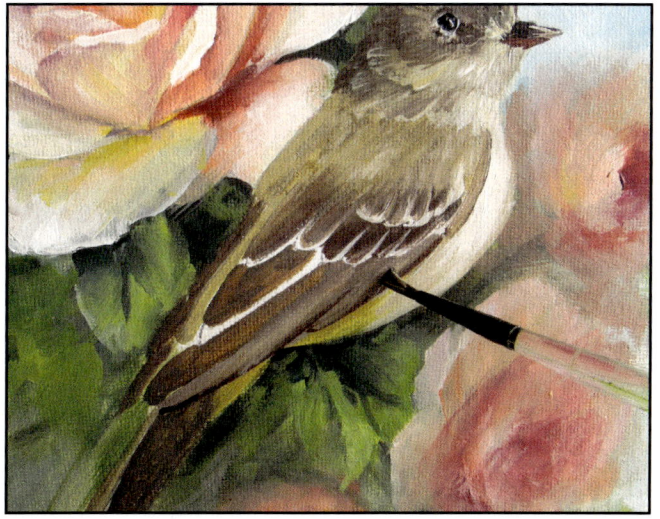

Step 84 Switch back to the tan and streak the front of the flight feathers.

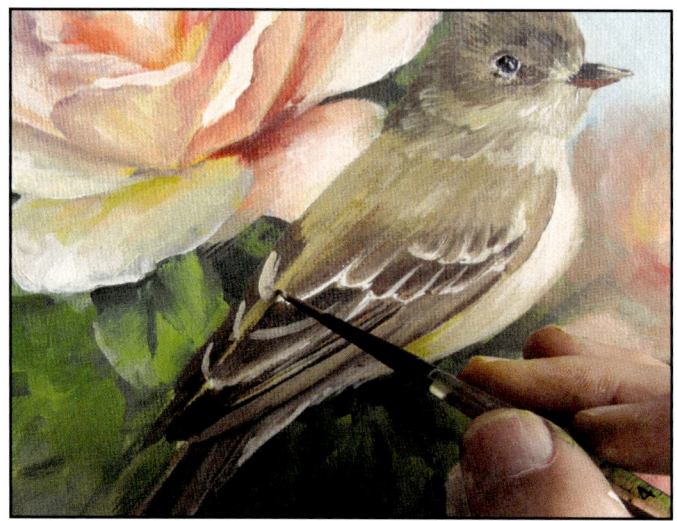
Step 85 Add the light tips to the back wings on the other side with light tan. Lighten color and add to wing on near side.

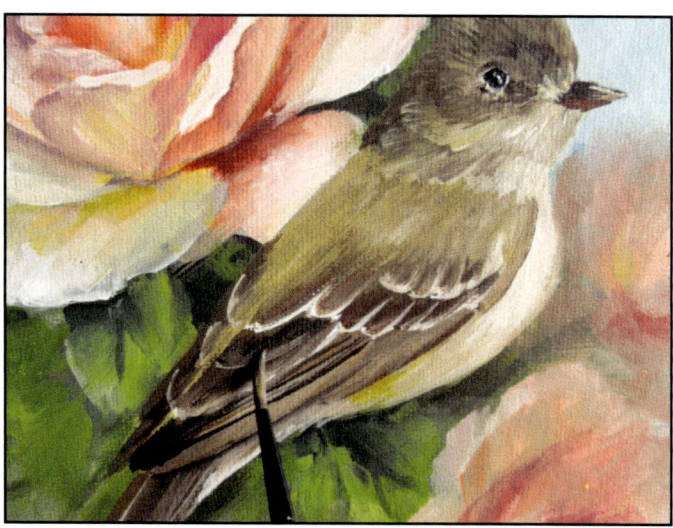
Step 86 Mottle the brush with brown and stroke down the wing setting in some of the light tips on the wings.

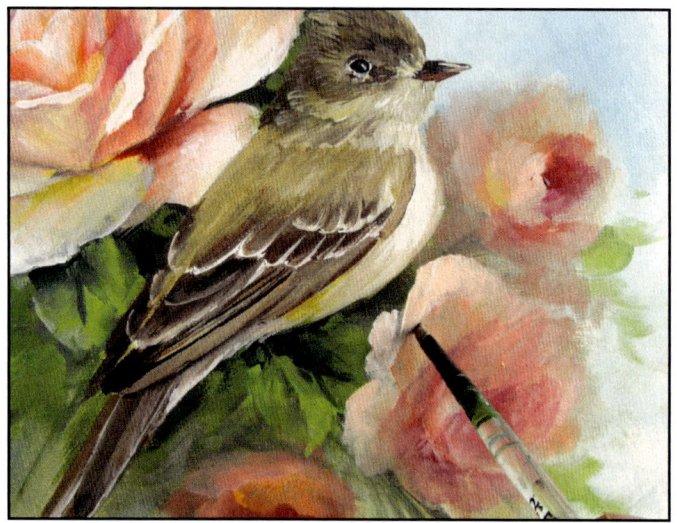
Step 87 Return to the roses and start to add some details to them now that we have the bird feathered.

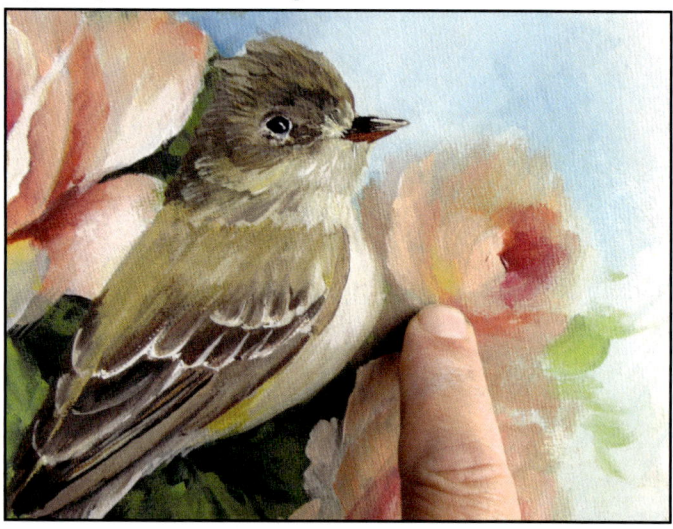
Step 88 Soften some of the back flowers. Always relate your rose to the center of interest bird and try to make it softer than the bird.

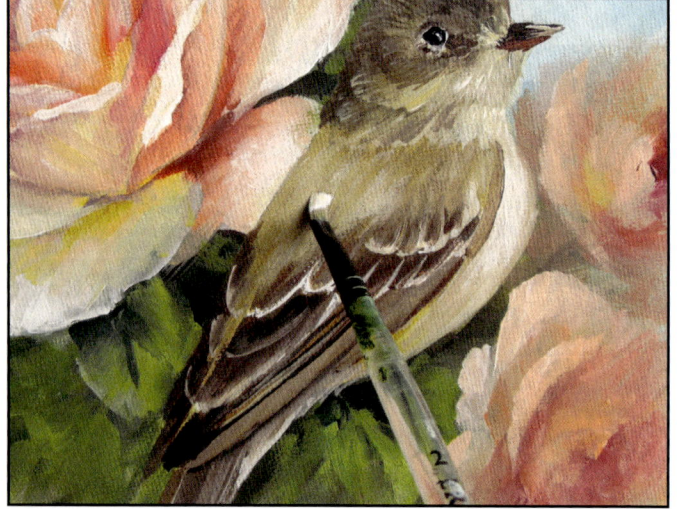
Step 89 If you need, add some additional lights to the mantle covering the bird's wing.

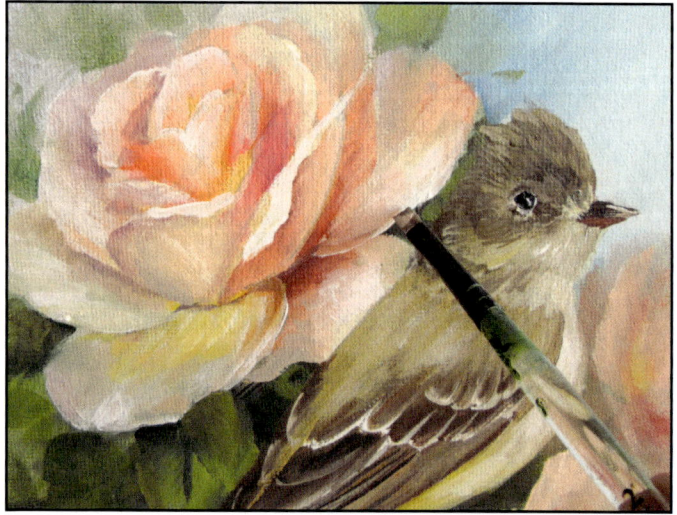
Step 90 Add some light edge detail to the main rose where it is next to the bird. Detail.

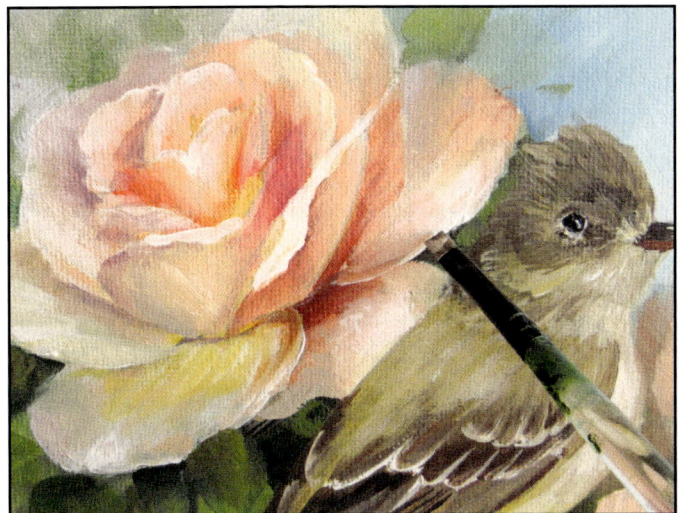

Step 91 Stroke out with some shadow to remove some of the light. This is the same we did on the birds wing. Same technique.

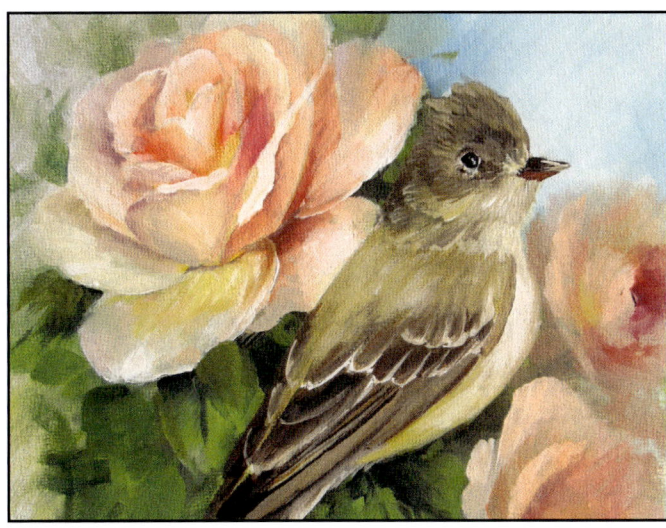

Step 92 Reflect on the bird and rose to make sure he comes in front. If he doesn't , add more light and dark feather contrast.

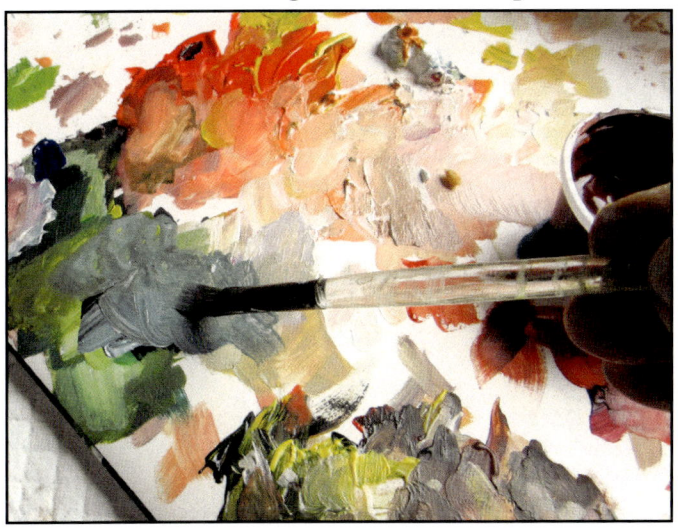

Step 93 I mottled some blue into the reds and greens to make a soft blue grey. Lighten with some white.

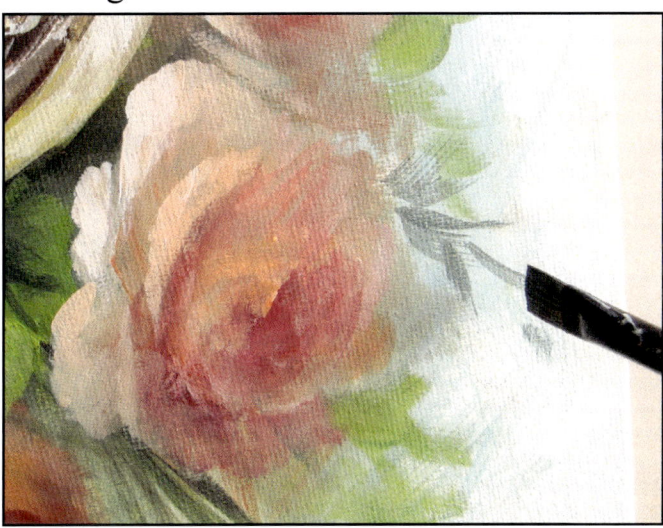

Step 94 Add this softly to the outside of the design. Contrast for the outside roses.

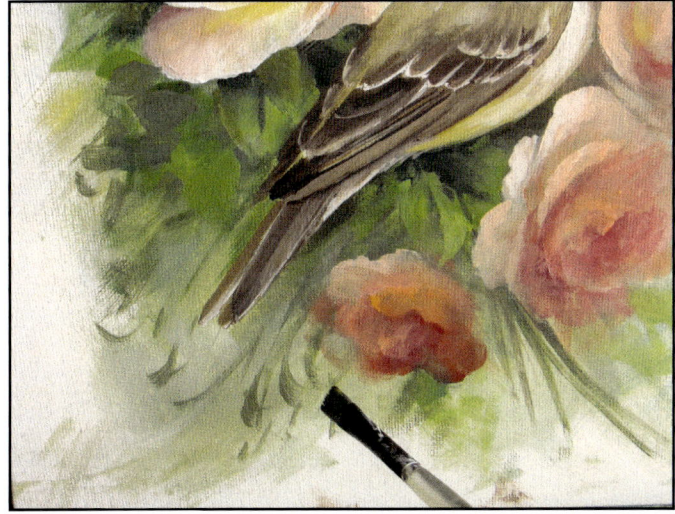

Step 95 Mottle a softer green and add some accent strokes around the roses.

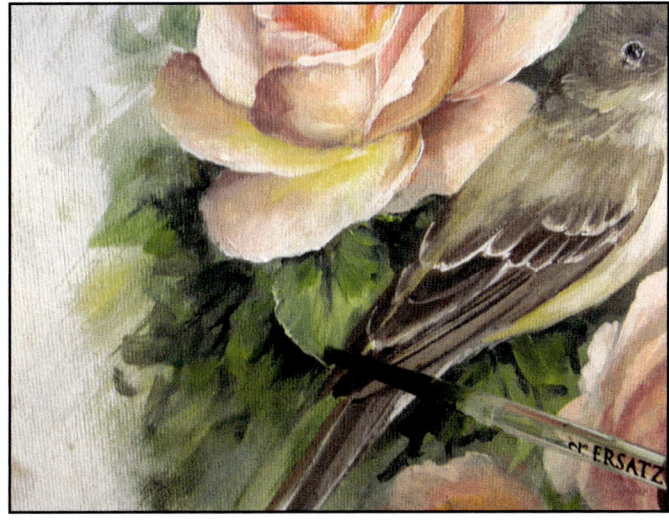

Step 96 Mottle a lighter green , corner the brush and begin to shape leaves.

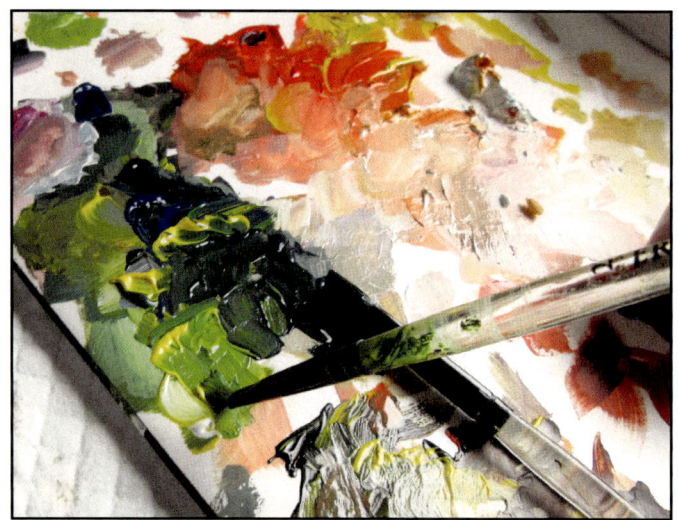

Step 97 Here is the palette area I use to create the green leaves. Notice the mottled colors and the warm yellow greens and cool greens.

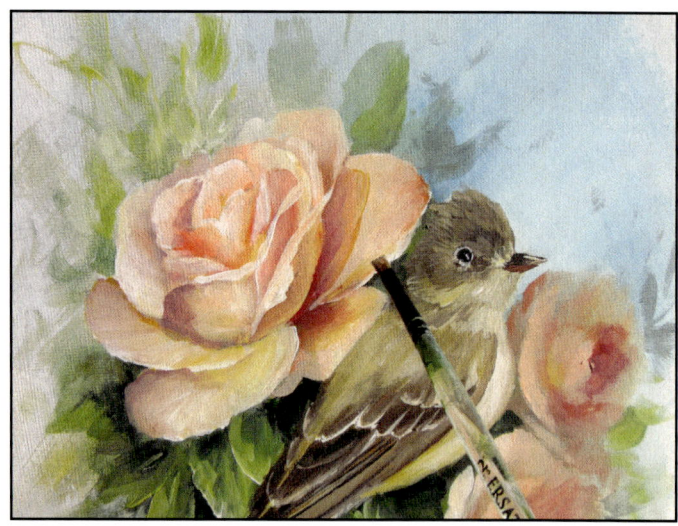

Step 98 Begin to edge and clean up the petals on the rose and other flowers. This brings them forward.

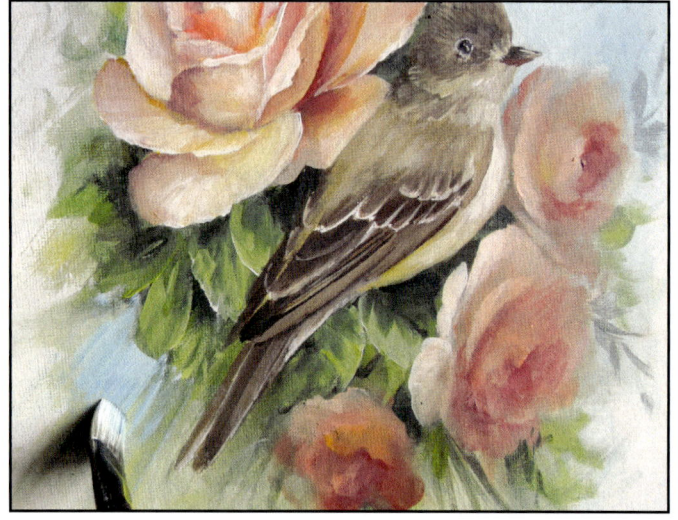

Step 99 Mottle a lighter blue and using the 3/4 inch brush, add this with some strokes to the bottom of the design for additional contrast.

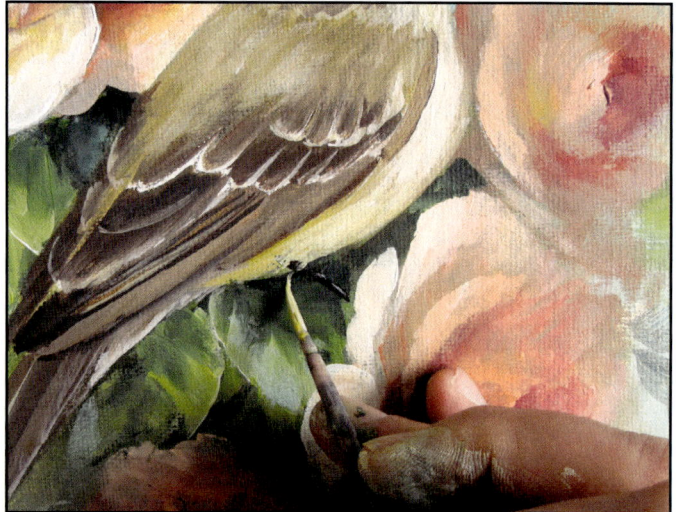

Step 100 Add final details line his leg with darks. Add any final light feathers for interest with liner.   Enjoy!

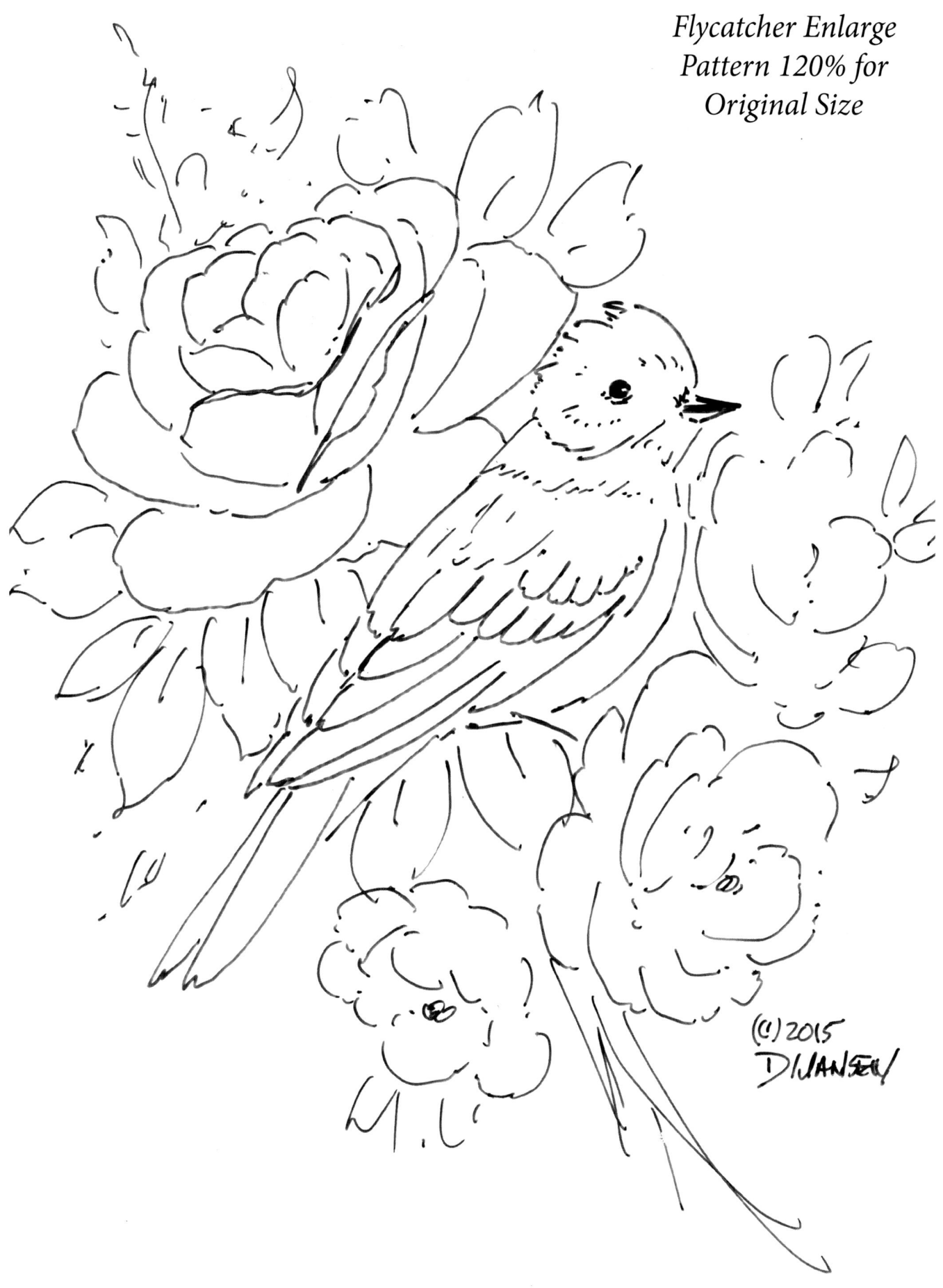

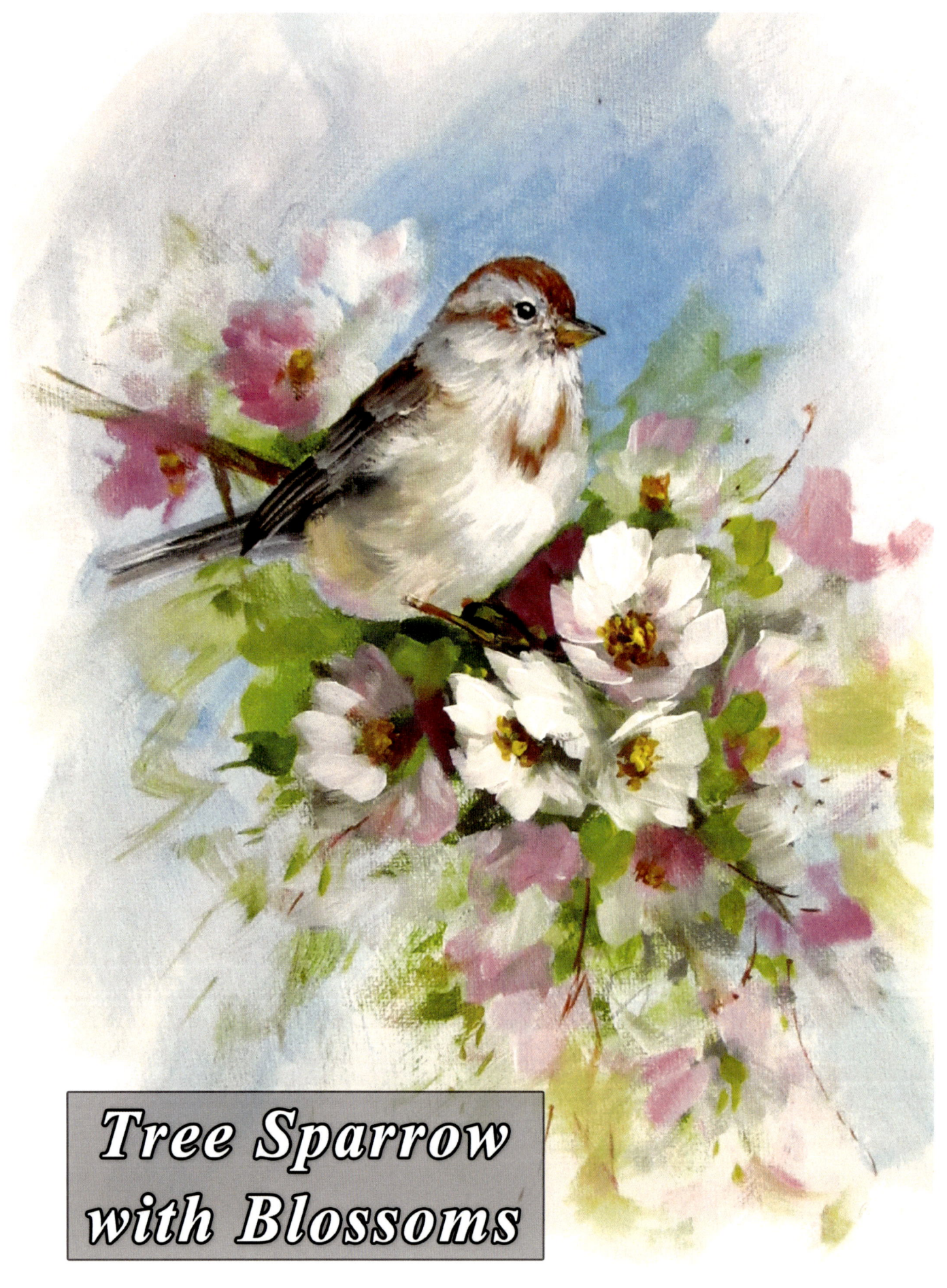

Tree Sparrow with Blossoms

Tree Sparrow and Blossoms

This little bird visits us all the time. There are many of them here in Pennsylvania. I love this little design. We will leave a lot of the white canvas. As I explained earlier, I like to vignette many of my paintings. It is a wonderful look and very artistic. I will paint the tree sparrow, then bring him forward with a splash of bright opaque blue right behind his head. This adds complimentary color contrast. The darker toned orange of his head contrasts with the bright blue.

The flowers are painted in softer white and cool Red Violet tones which also contrasts with the warmer colors on the sparrow. I am constantly searching for those color interactions when I choose a subject. Many times I like to place the bird against the sky or version of the sky. I do not always place them against the trees and bushes like I did with the cardinal lesson. The sky is a very important element for color and negative space. It adds not only color contrast but a breath of fresh air to the painting. Add the sky and breath!

We need white blossoms in the painting, but how do you paint white blossoms on a white background? With the leaves! Notice how the blossoms are framed by leaves. This helps break them away from the background. If you paint your blossoms and feel like they are a little lost, add more leaves. Also, notice that some blossoms appear lighter than others. In conjunction with the lightest blossoms you will see the darkest leaves. The dark color in the leaves make the light blossoms appear lighter. So, when you want more light in the blossoms, add dark and cool greens to frame them. This is a rule in painting called simultaneous contrast. One color effects the appearance of another color.

As you move away from the center of interest, let the details, strokes and colors become more like the white background. Many times I just rub the flower with my finger to push back the edges and make them lost. It is fun and fast! Let's give it a try!

Paint It Simply Palette
Base Color- Medium White from Mixes

Palette Colors

Naphthol Red Light
Red Violet
Carbon Black
Phthalo Blue
Hansa Yellow
Titanium White

Medium White
Base Brown
Burnt Sienna
Burnt Umber
Pine Green

Wood Surface
Super MDF Wood Panel about 11 Inch X 14 Inch to fit picture frame. Can also use canvas panel.

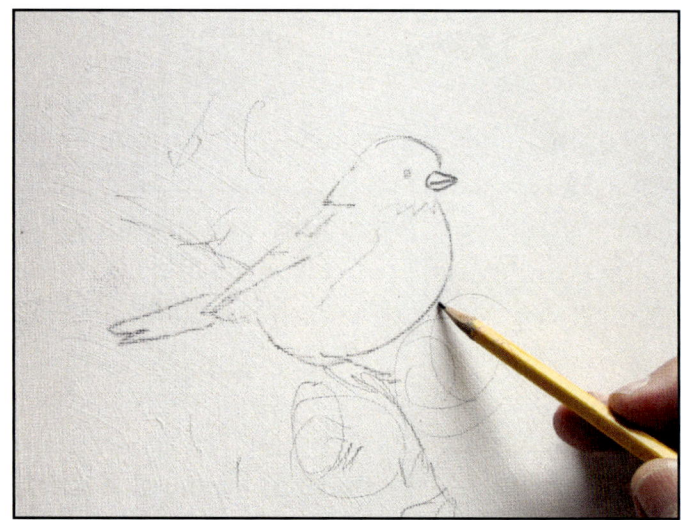

Step 1 As before, base board white and then sketch or transfer the design dark. This will help you see pattern through paint layers.

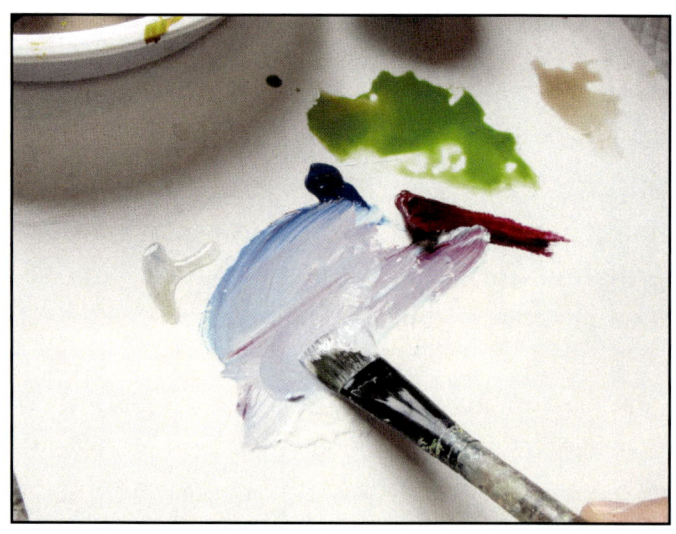

Step 2 Mottle a soft sky color with Phthalo Blue and touch Red Violet. Lighten with some white.

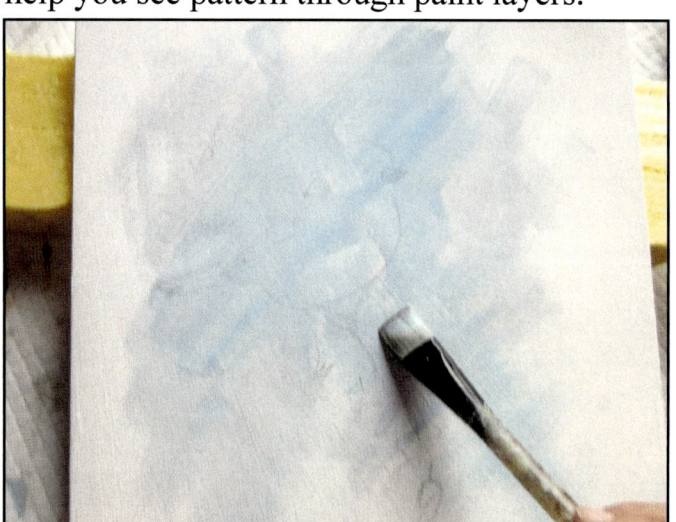

Step 3 Add Extender and casually apply this to the surface with brush movements in all directions. Leave some white canvas showing.

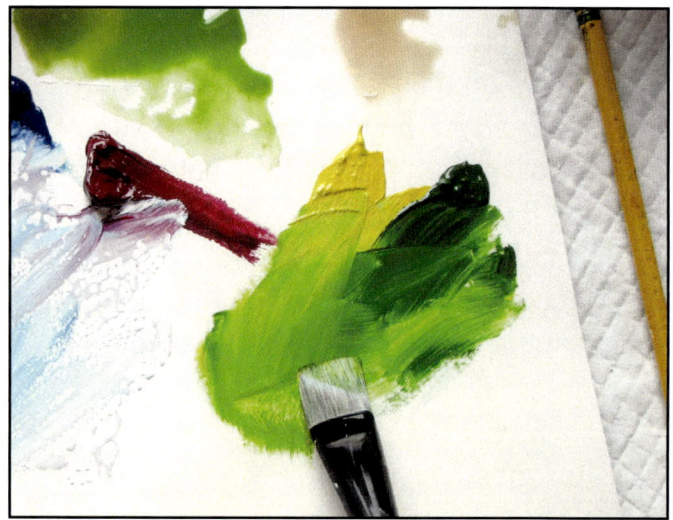

Step 4 Mottle some yellow greens with Pine Green and Hansa. Nice bright green. You can tone with some sky color if desired.

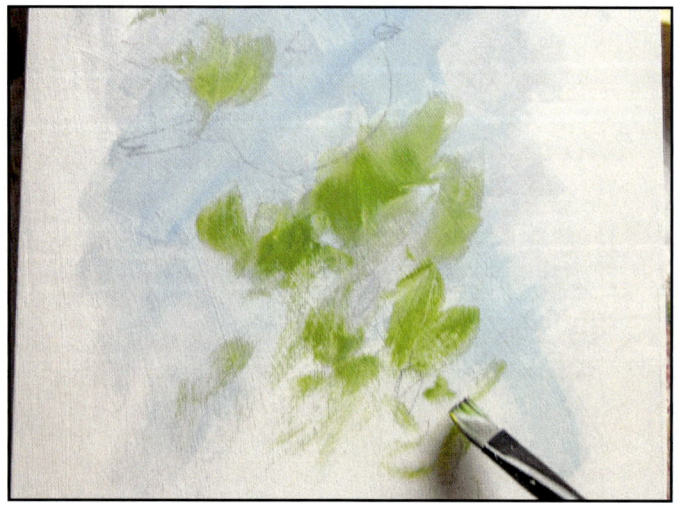

Step 5 Casually brush this through and around the design where the leaves will be. Just suggestions of shapes. No perfect leaves.

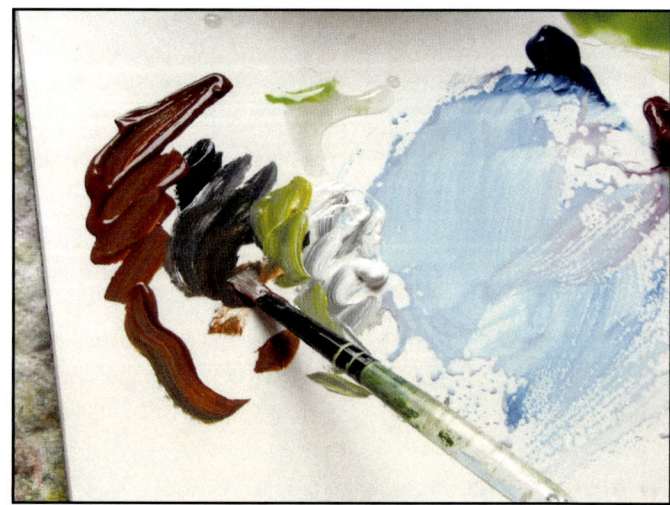

Step 6 Mottle some Burnt Sienna, black and Hansa to make grey brown. This is the color for his beak. We use later also.

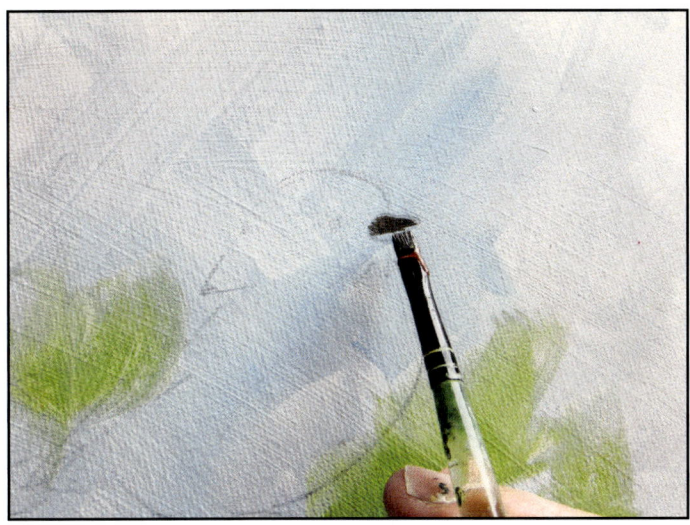

Step 7 Add dark top of the beak, then lighten with Hansa Yellow and add the bottom of the beak. I used small flat. Round works too.

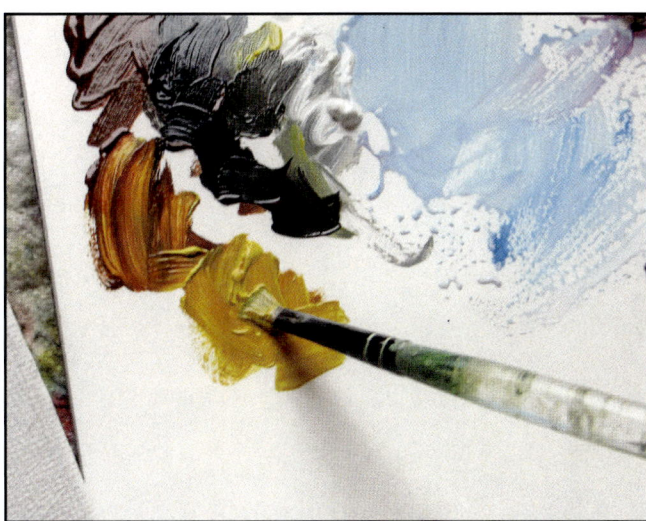

Step 8 Mottle the color lighter and more yellow with additional Hansa Yellow.

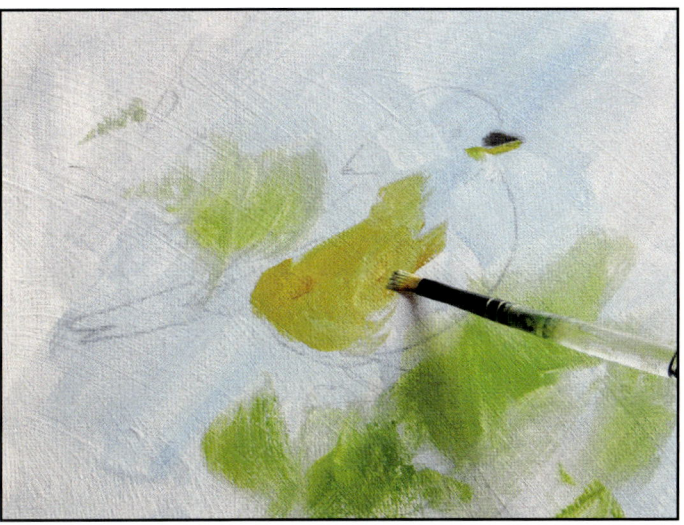

Step 9 Add this to the back of the body and under the wing as the dark for the body.

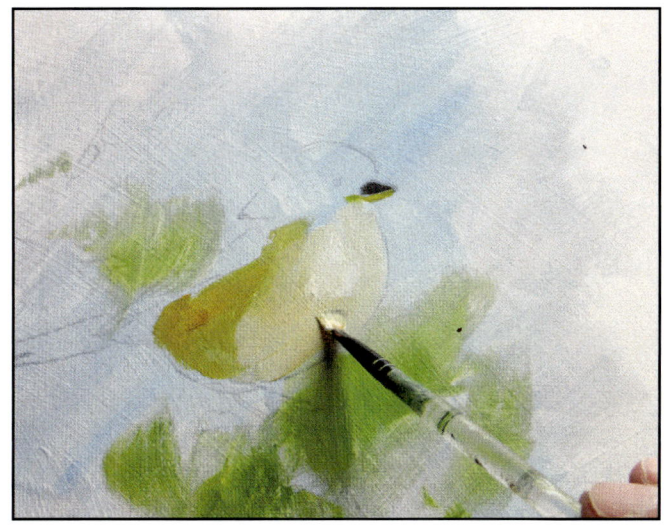

Step 10 Lighten the color with some white and add lighter strokes and then even lighter strokes with more white.

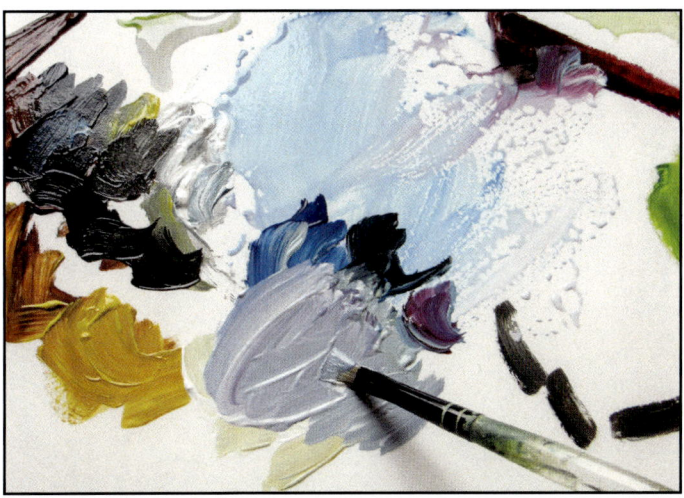

Step 11 Mottle the browns, yellows, blues, black and violet, then lighten with white to make a beautiful blue grey.

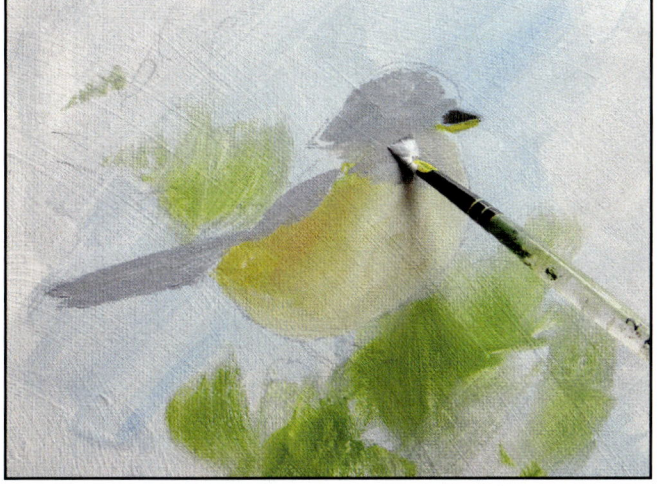

Step 12 Use this on top of his body and then stroke down into the light color to cross the colors.

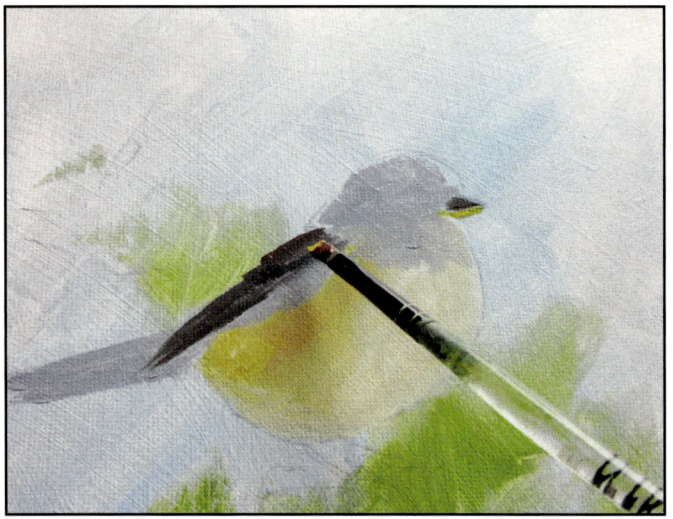

Step 13 Mottle the color with more Burnt Sienna and touch blue and black then add the suggestion of the wing.

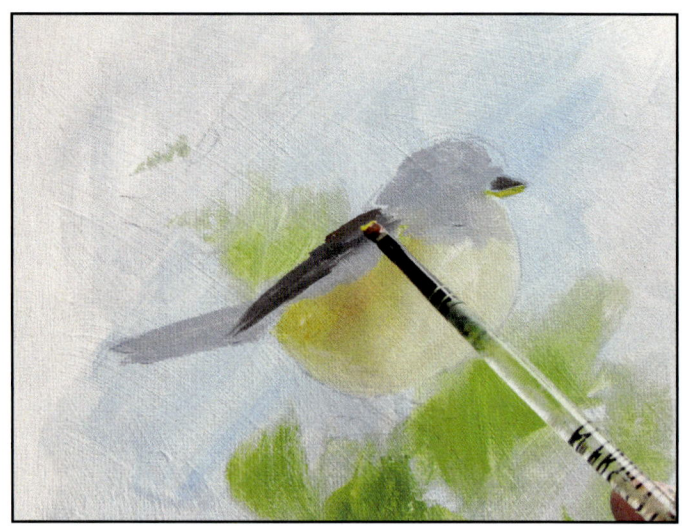

Step 14 Notice the mottled palette colors on the tip of the brush as I add some interest to the mantle area of the wing.

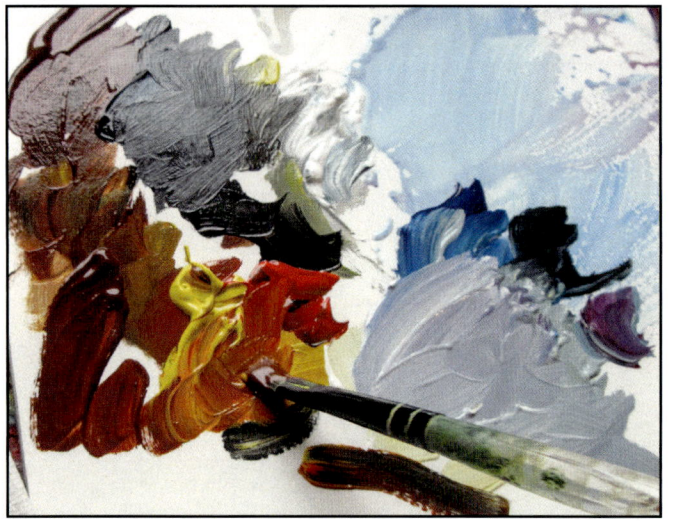

Step 15 Mottle the brush with some yellows and reds, along with the Burnt Sienna and light colors.

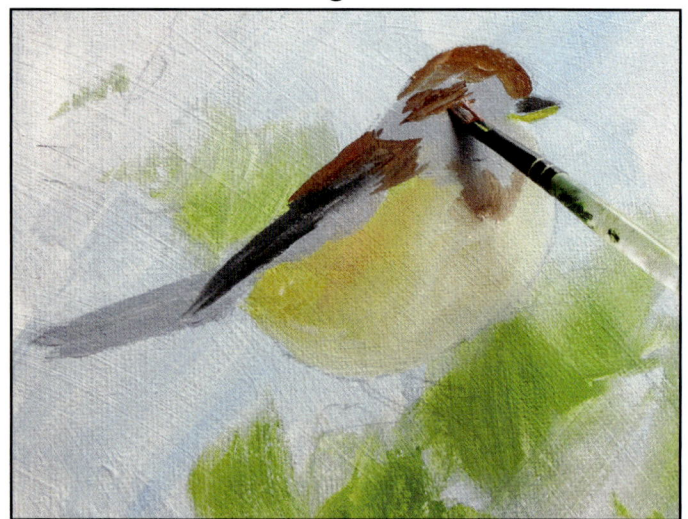

Step 16 Add this as the cap on top his head. Remember the shape following strokes and then the sizes of the strokes as you paint.

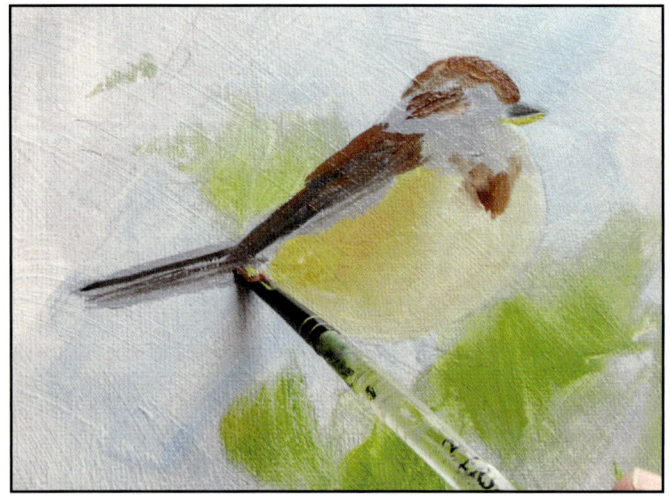

Step 17 Add smaller touches and strokes of the reddish brown down the wing area. Add a V shape to the chest with browns.

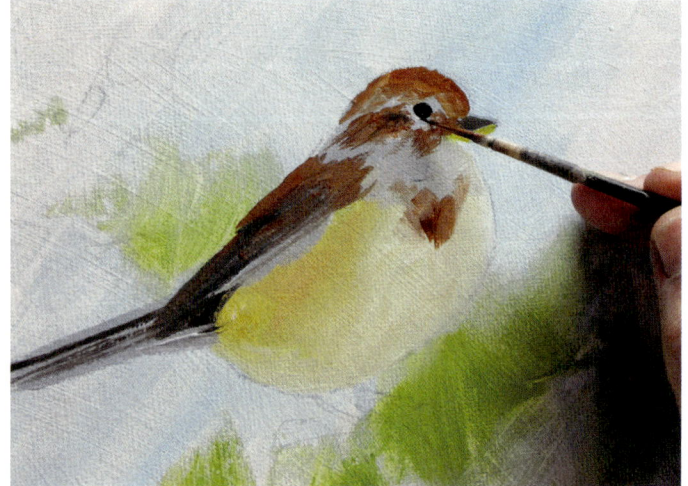

Step 18 Add some small strokes around the eye and face, then add the eye with a liner and black.

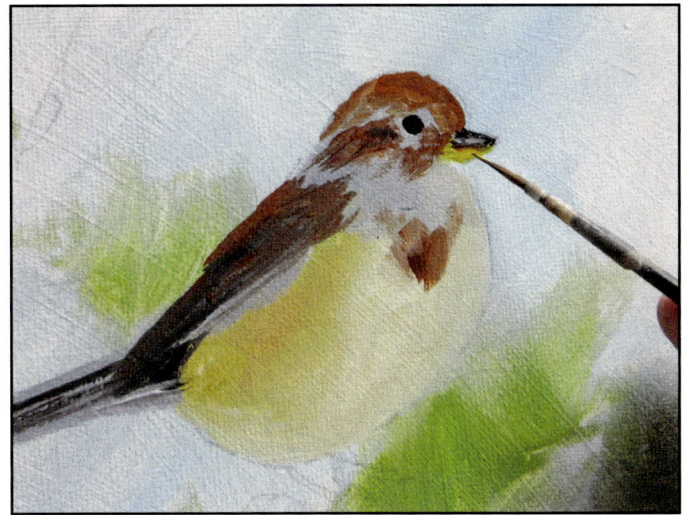

Step 19 Mottle the liner with some lighter brown and yellow and add some detail to lower beak. Add a light grey shine to the upper beak.

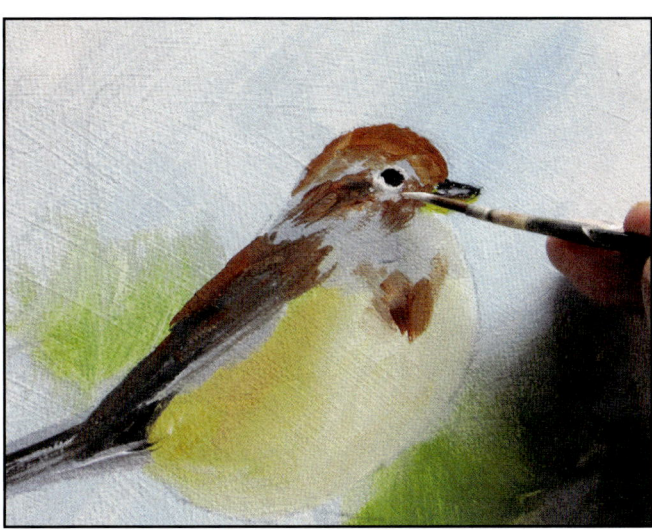

Step 20 Add the white eye ring to the area around the eye. Tap some of the color to add interest.

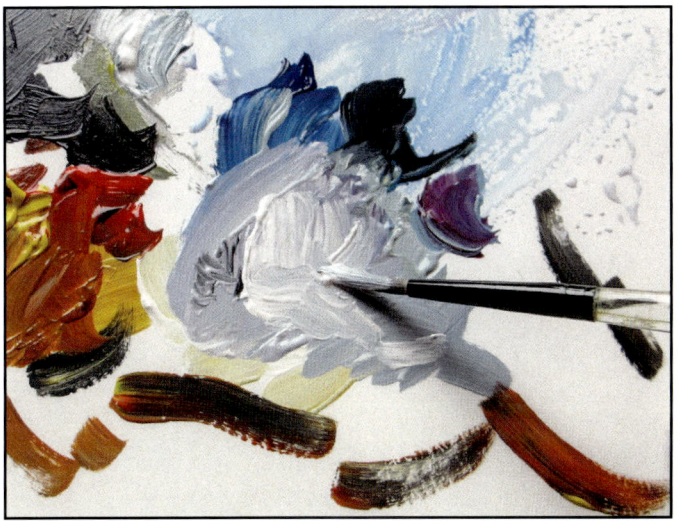

Step 21 Mottle the # 4 round with some of the grey from earlier and then lighten with some white.

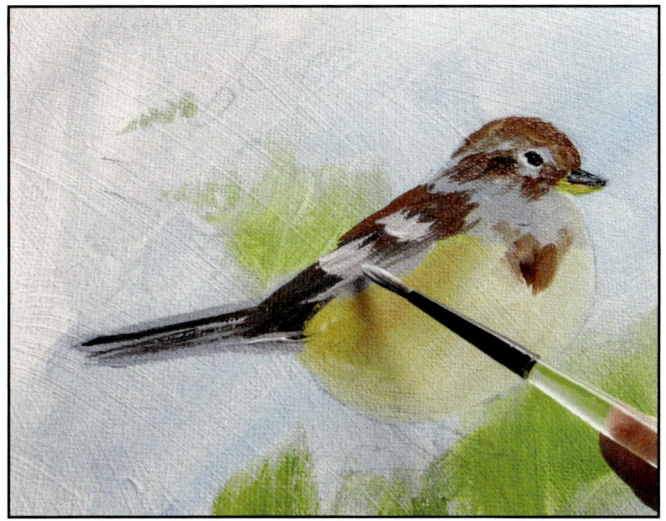

Step 22 Add the suggestions of the primary and secondary coverts with short strokes of the light color.

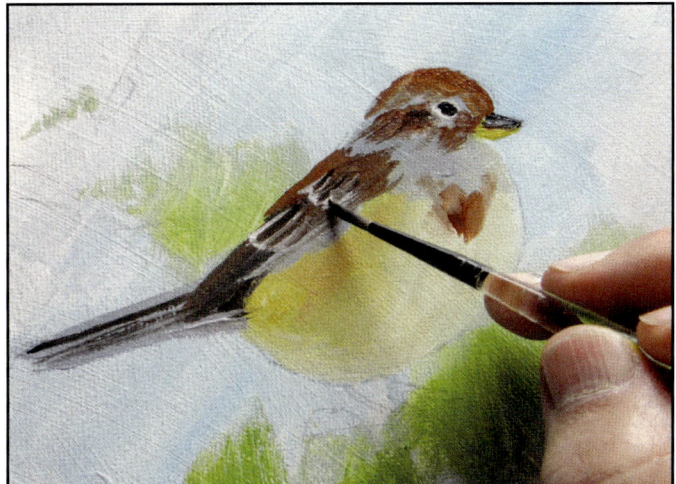

Step 23 Mottle the brush with dark and then stroke down the covert stroke to leave a little light grey showing on the tips.

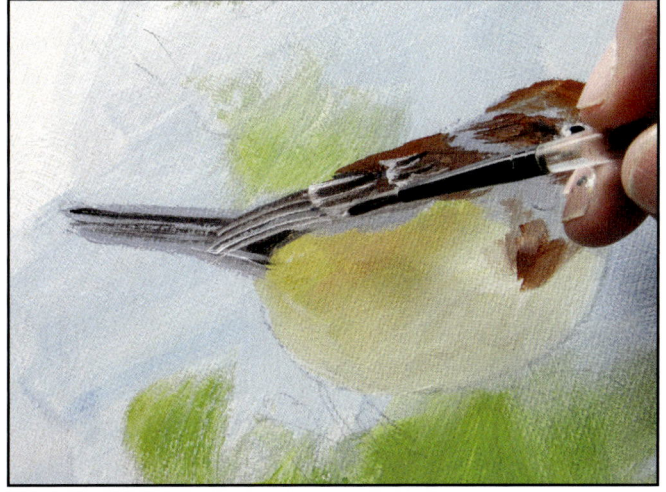

Step 24 Add some short strokes to the longer flight feathers at the end of the wing.

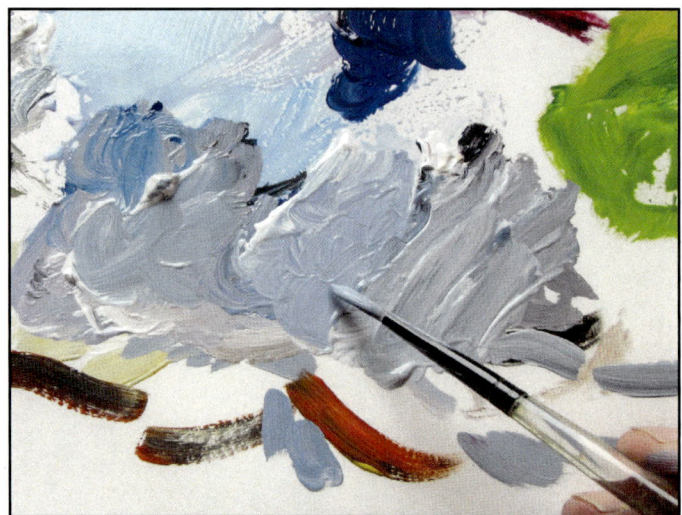

Step 25 Mottle the grey again with some grey and little light blue sky color.

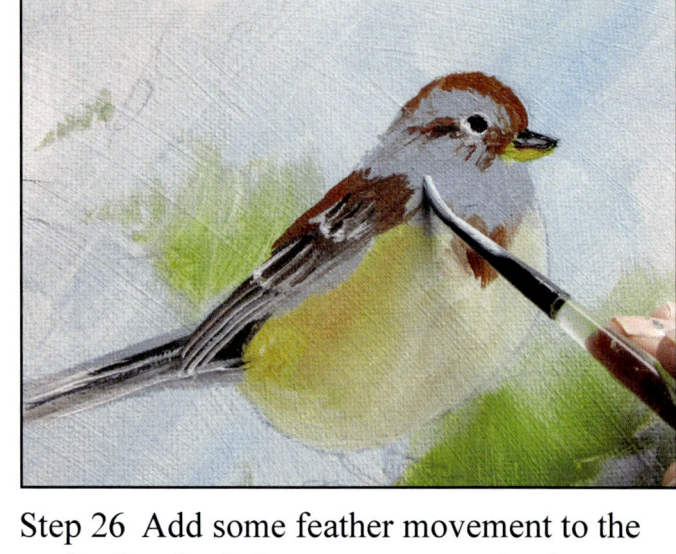

Step 26 Add some feather movement to the neck. Just look for movement and colors, Keep it simple.

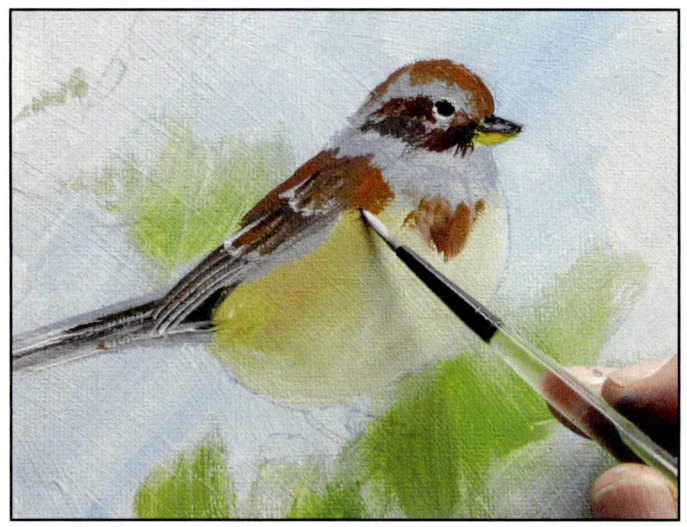

Step 27 Add some strokes of brighter reds and browns to the front of the mantle covering the wing.

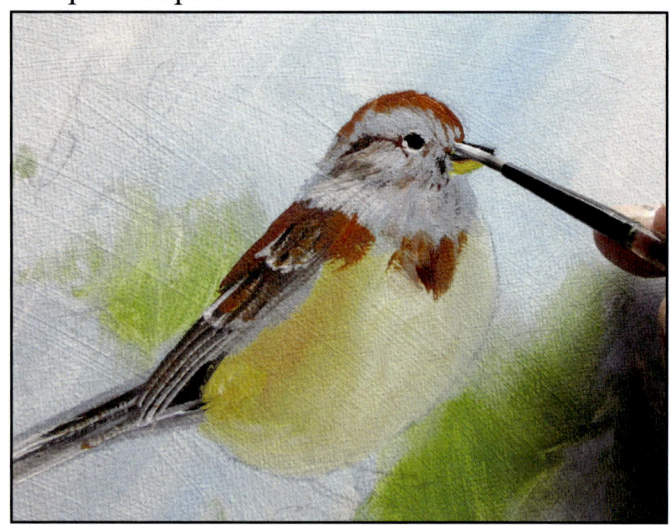

Step 28 Lighten the color with more white and add some smaller light detail strokes and feathers to the head area.

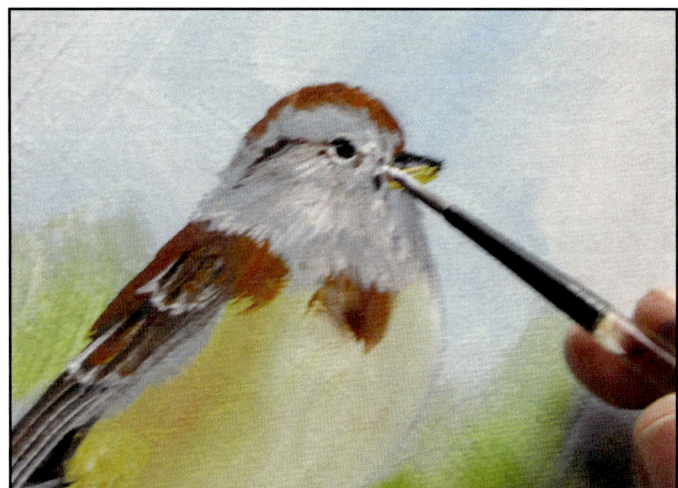

Step 29   Use just the tip of the brush and add the light touches around the beak. Tap brush.

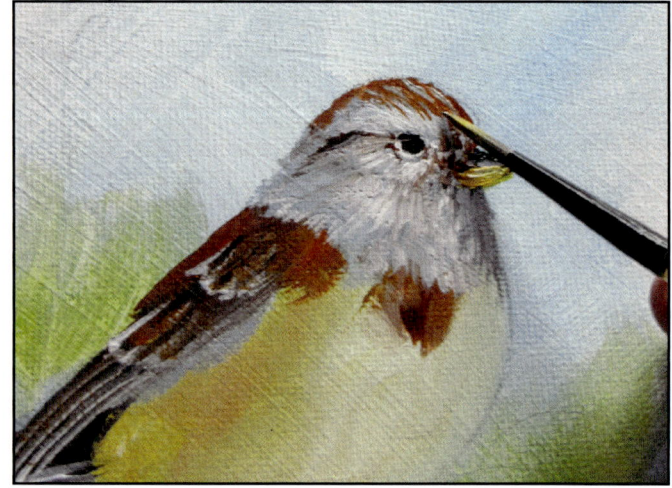

Step 30 Add some light strokes to the top of the head. If you get too much stroke back with some brown.

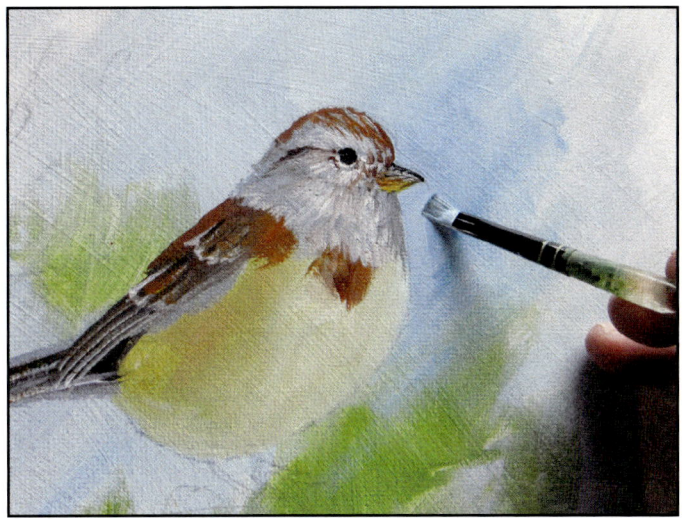

Step 31 Mottle the brush with some blue and white and add additional opaque color around the face to bring him forward.

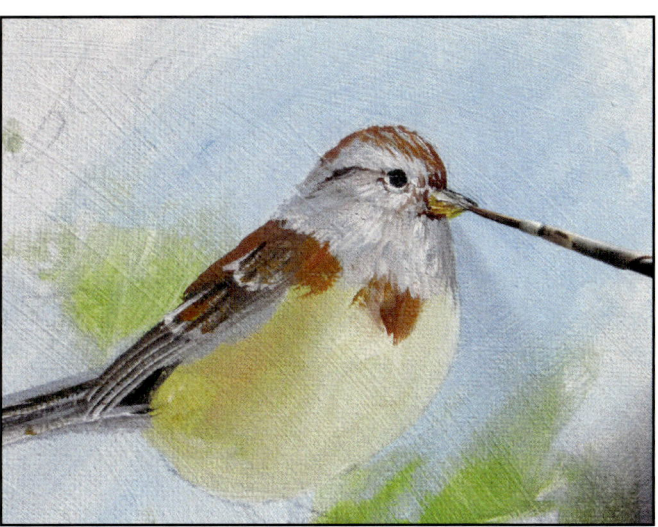

Step 32 Detail the beak and small feathers one more time to make him come forward.

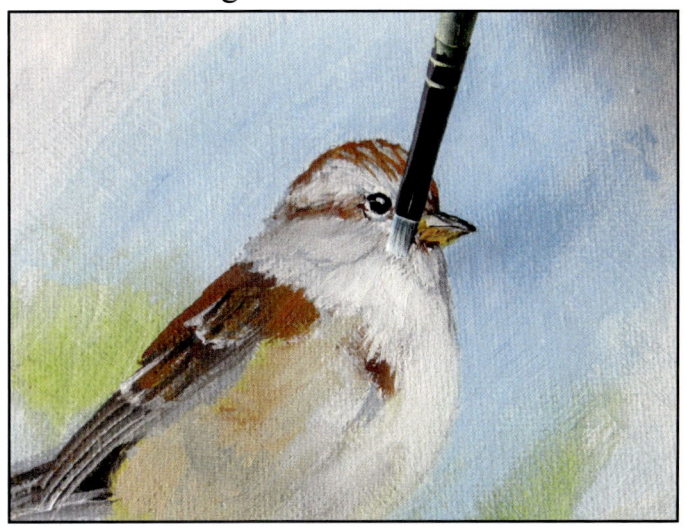

Step 33 Add some medium sized strokes of white around the neck using white. A little longer than face strokes. Small flat brush.

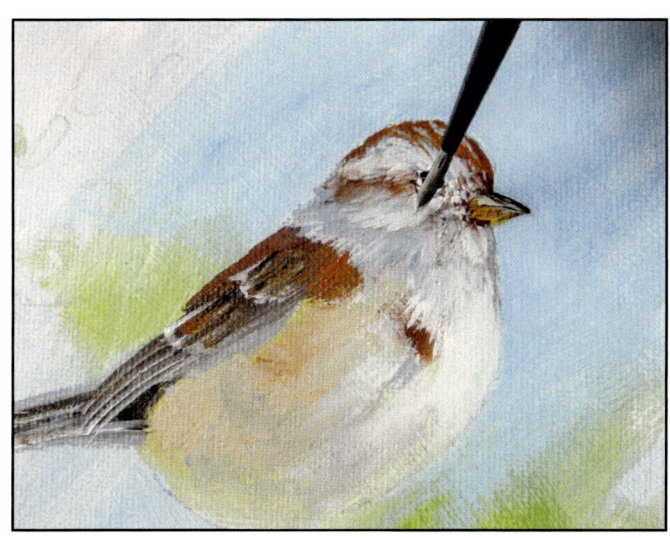

Step 34 Add the cheek feathers with the point of the round and mottled grey white.

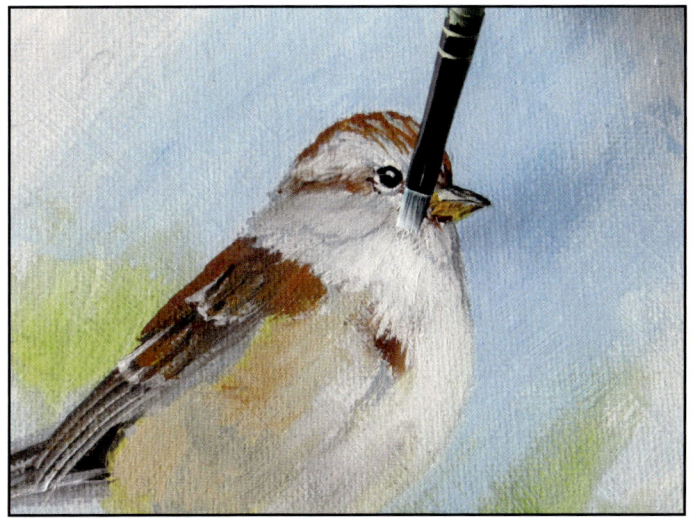

Step 35 Add some additional white to the neck feathers. I over paint a little.

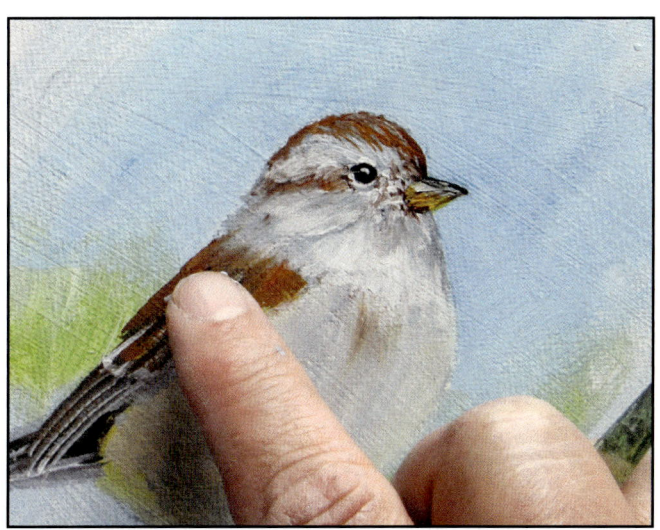

Step 36 Once I painted too much, I then soften the colors together with finger.

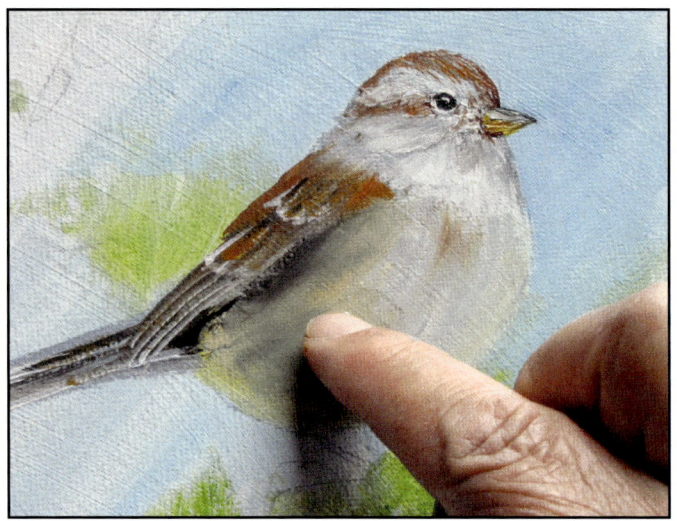

Step 37 Add some greys, browns and then whites to the body and soften with your finger. Just add movement of feathers.

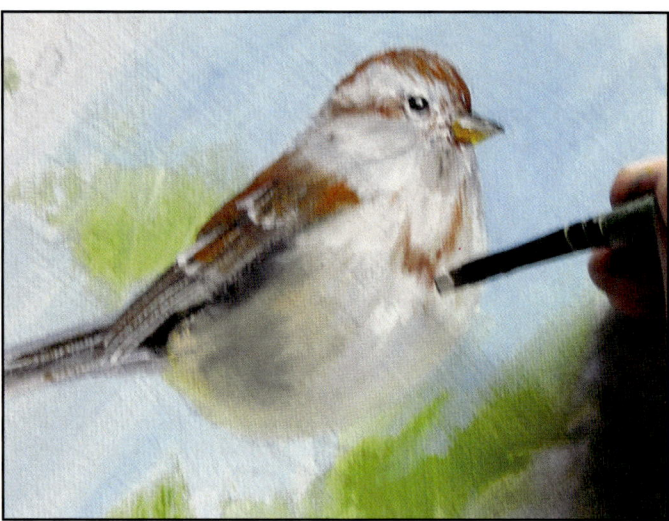

Step 38 Use the chisel of the brush and add Burnt Sienna mottled with yellow to define the V shape on his chest.

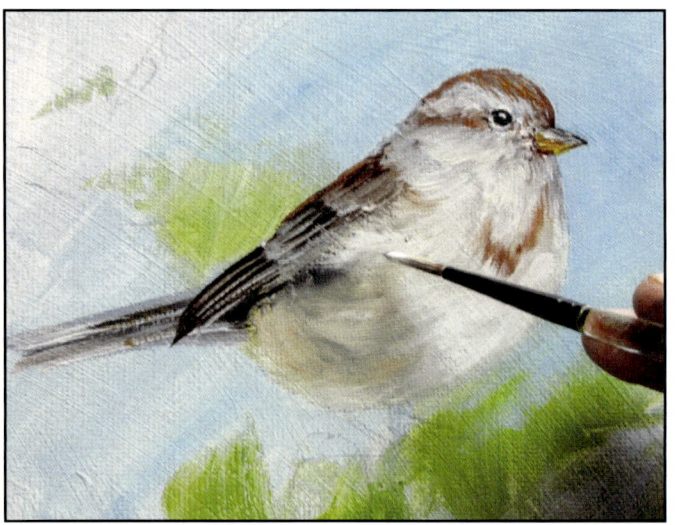

Step 39 Add the short strokes of the white decorative feathers to the breast and then stroke some over the mantle of wing.

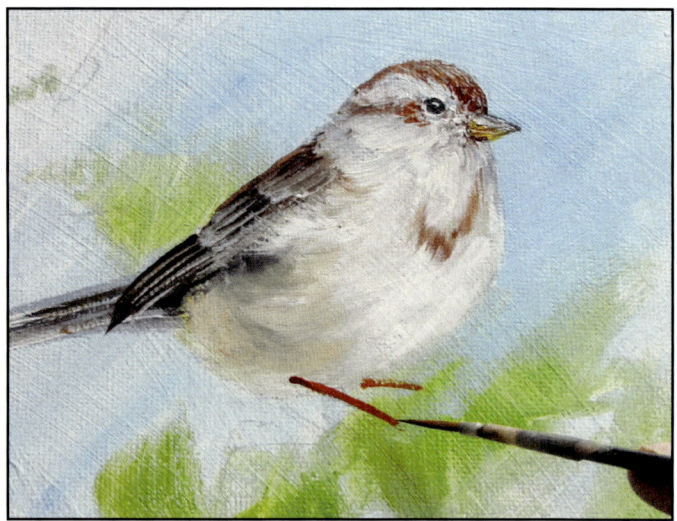

Step 40 Add his feet and legs with a liner and some reddish Burnt Sienna. I always mottle color, even on small strokes like this.

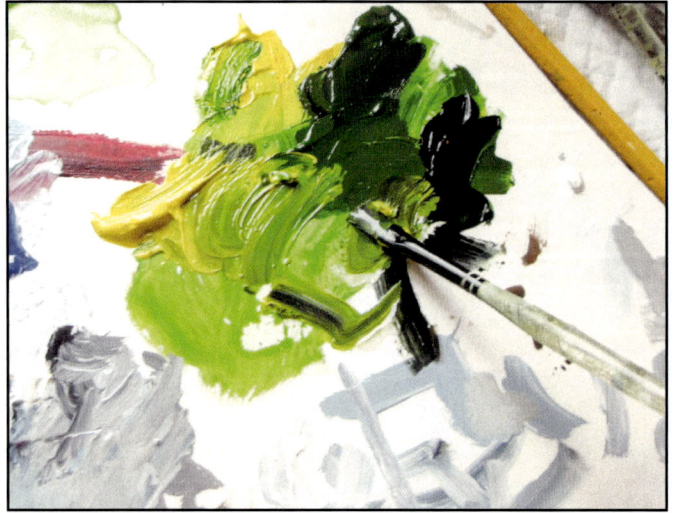

Step 41 Mottle some Pine Green, black and Hansa on the small flat.

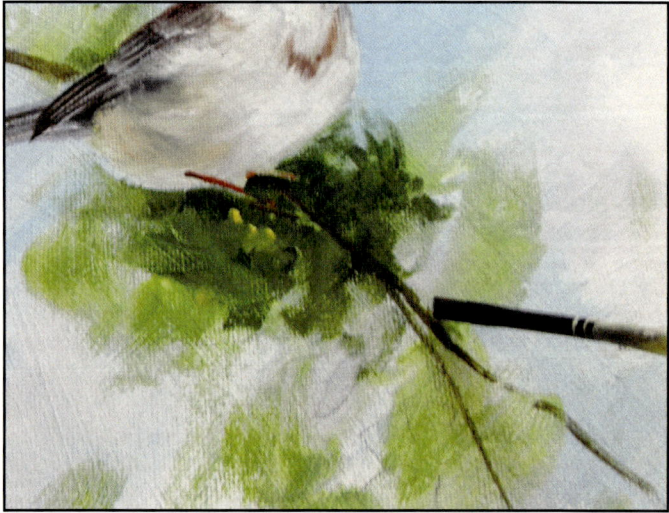

Step 42 Add shadows under bird, then use chisel and mottled Burnt Sienna for stems.

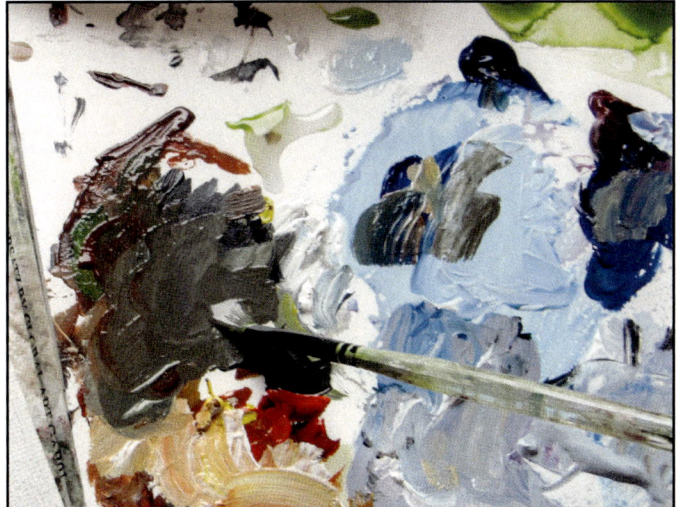

Step 43 Mottle the blues and Burnt Sienna together to make a grey and then add touch sky color to lighten.

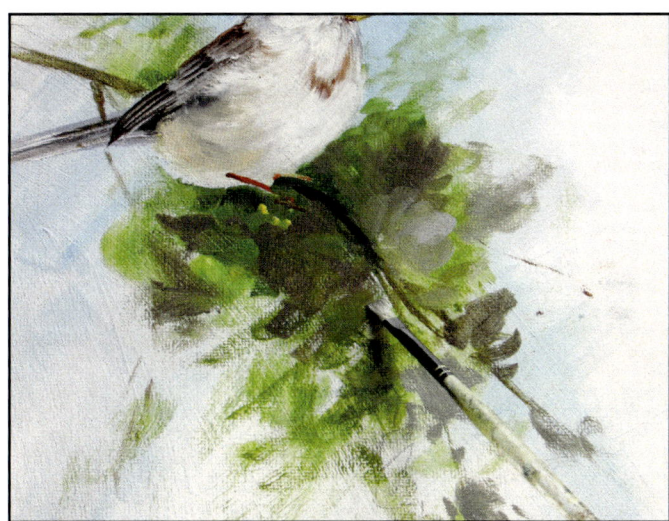

Step 44 This makes a mottled base color for the blossoms. Mottle through the green areas as the dark blossoms.

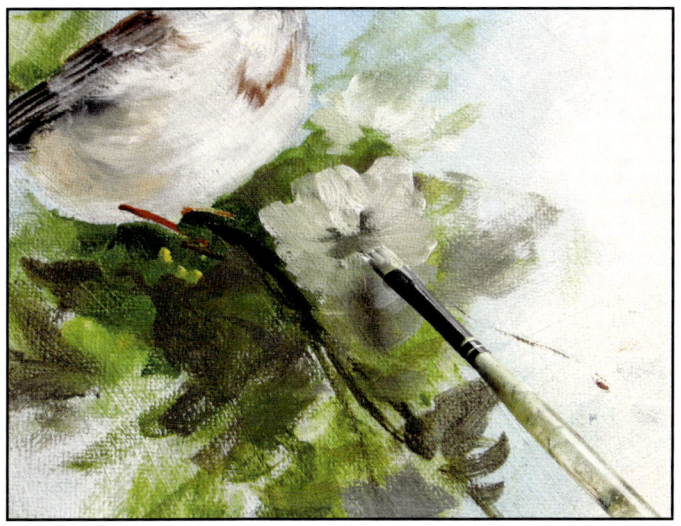

Step 45 Mottle the brush with some whites and then add the shapes of the blossoms with some strokes. Keep casual.

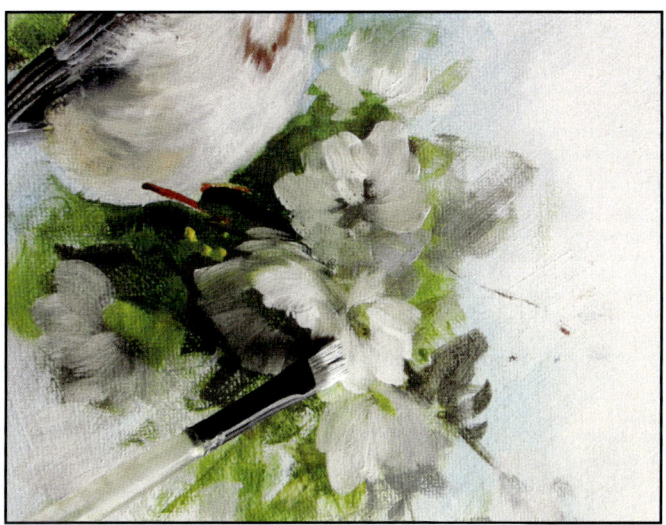

Step 46 Mottle the color with more white to lighten and then add more petals and petal strokes to the blossoms.

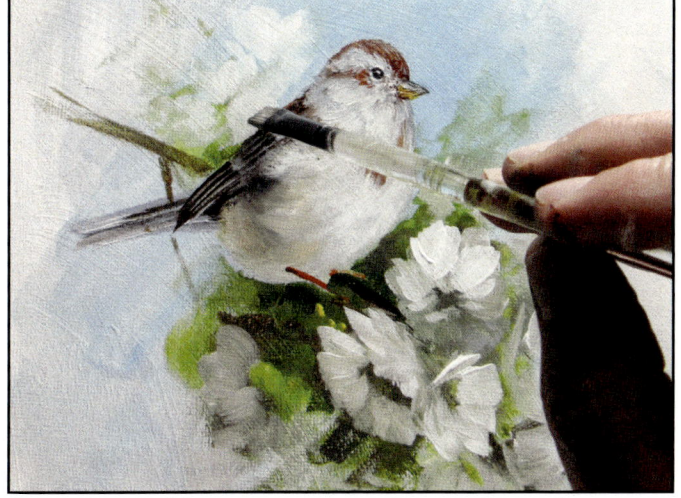

Step 47 Add some suggestions of petals to the blossoms behind the bird.

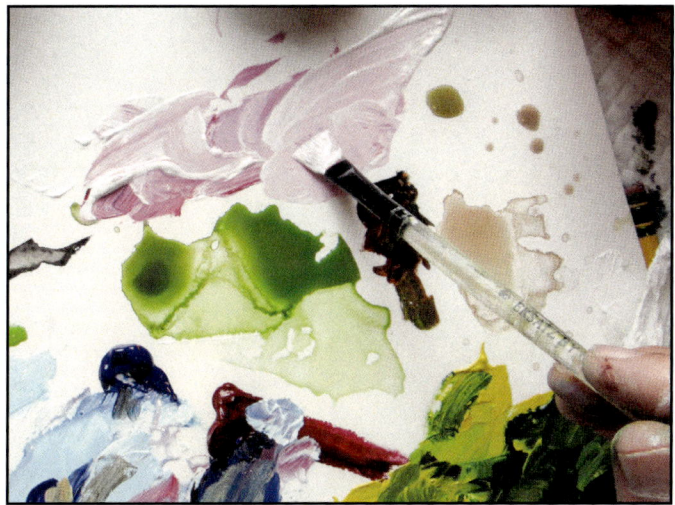

Step 48 Mottle the white with some Red Violet. Cool light pink color.

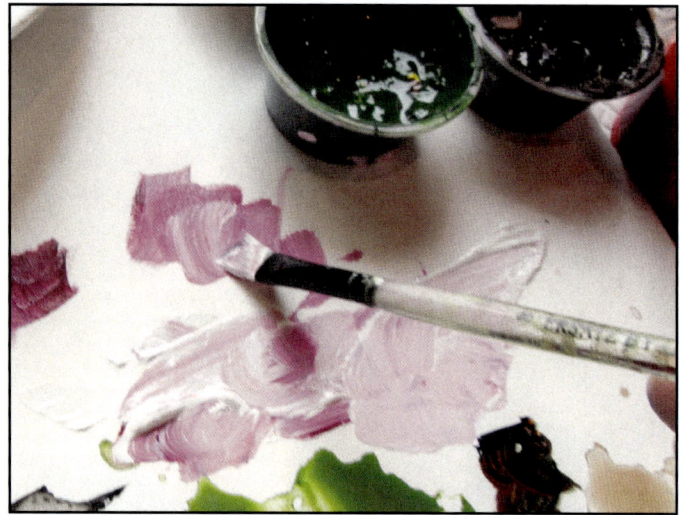

Step 49 Paint the next blossoms with mottled values of the Red Violets and white. Always vary the colors with mottled brush.

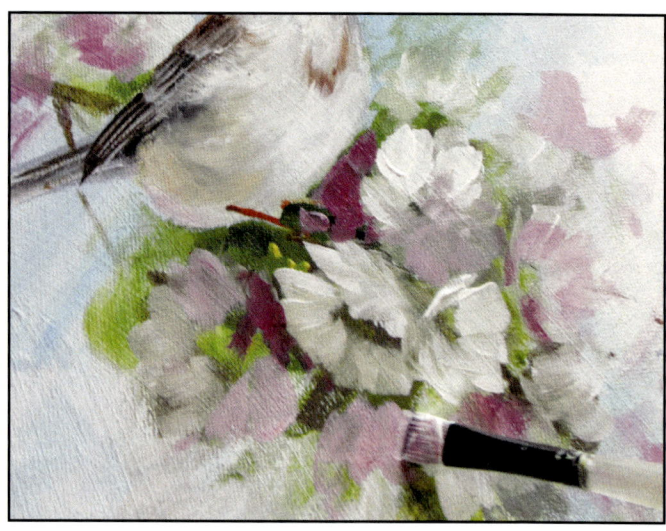

Step 50 Mottle the blossoms with the color. Notice all the lights and darks of the Red Violet blossoms. This makes it interesting.

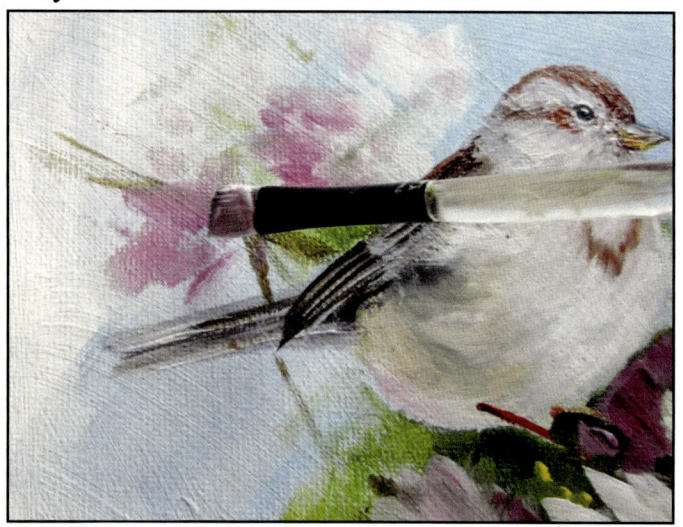

Step 51 Add some suggestions of the blossoms in the back. Do not use very dark values. Soft lights so they recede.

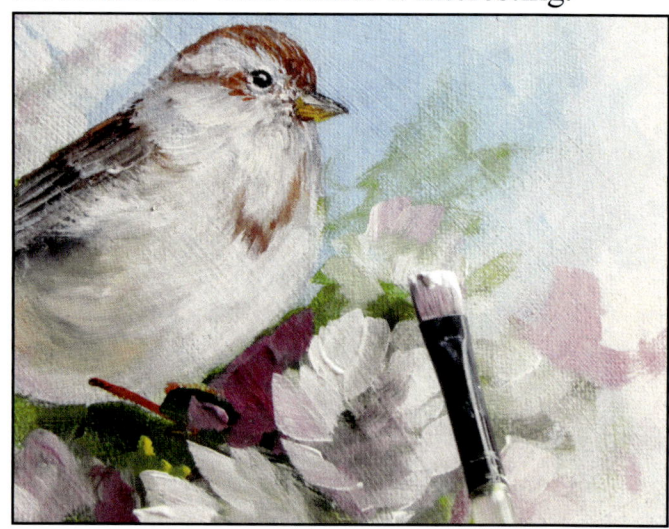

Step 52 Mottle the brush with lots of light texture and then add to the blossoms in front to make them come forward.

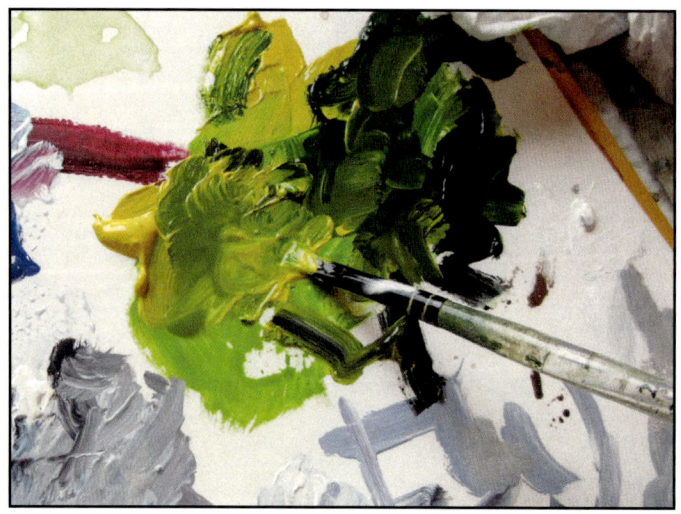

Step 53 Mottle the small flat back into the greens on the palette.

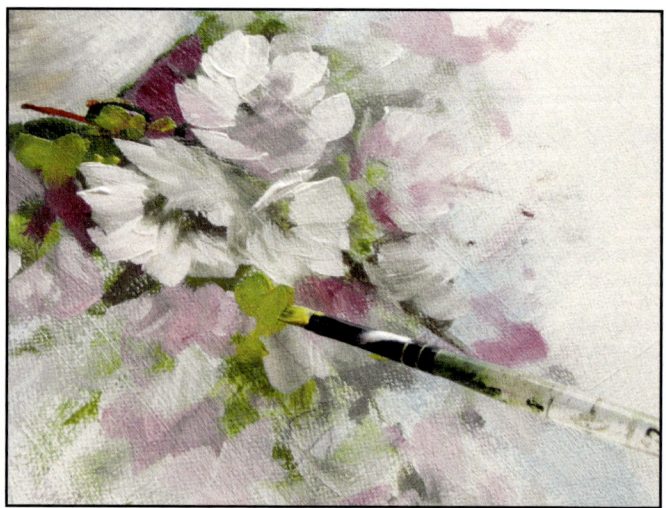

Step 54 Add the mottled greens leaves with short strokes of the brush.

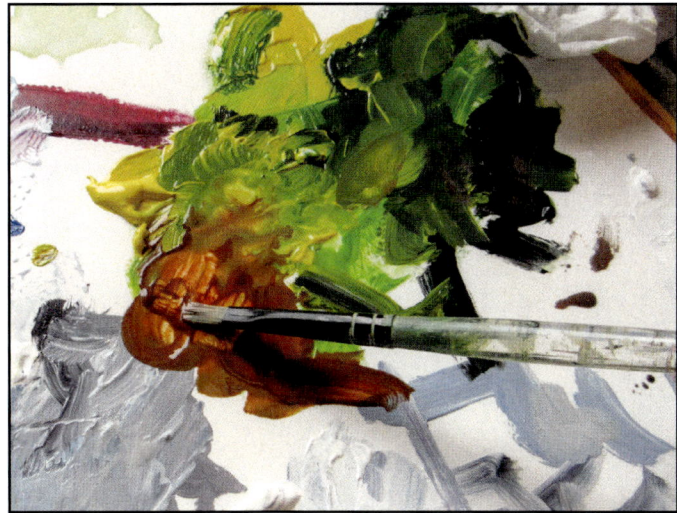

Step 55 Mottle the greens with some Burnt Sienna.

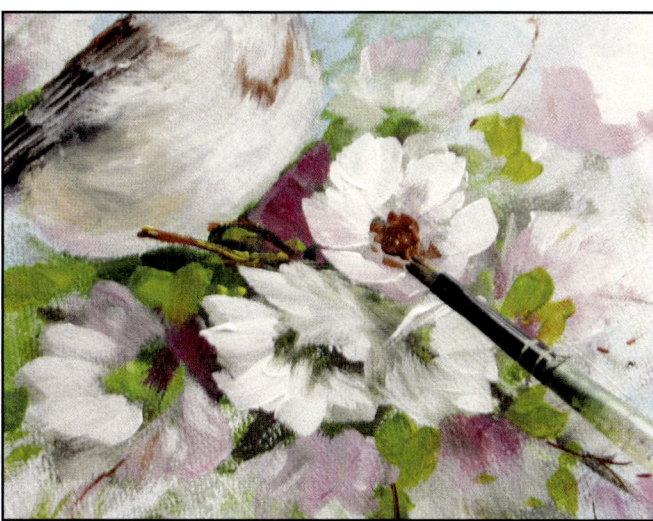

Step 56 Add the dark to the center of the blossoms to add interest contrast.

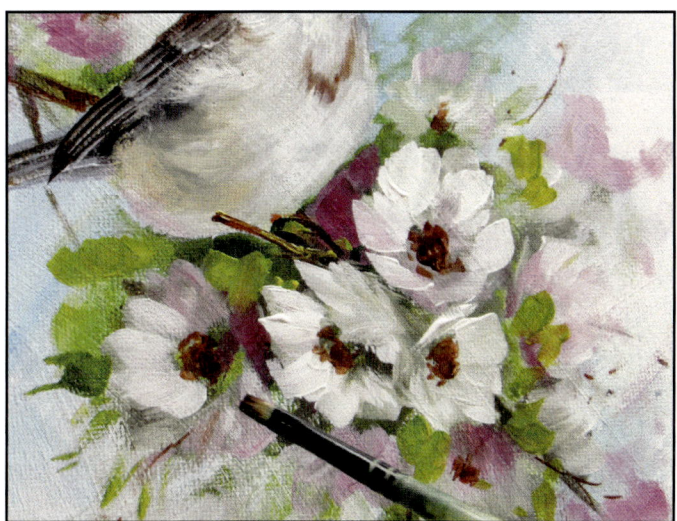

Step 57 Continue to add to the other blossoms and make the ones in the back very soft and transparent.

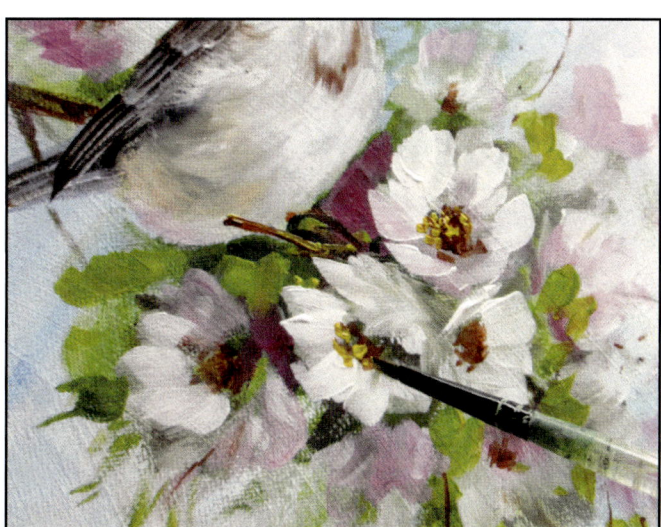

Step 58 Tap the corner of the brush into some Hansa and then add to the center of the blossoms for interest.

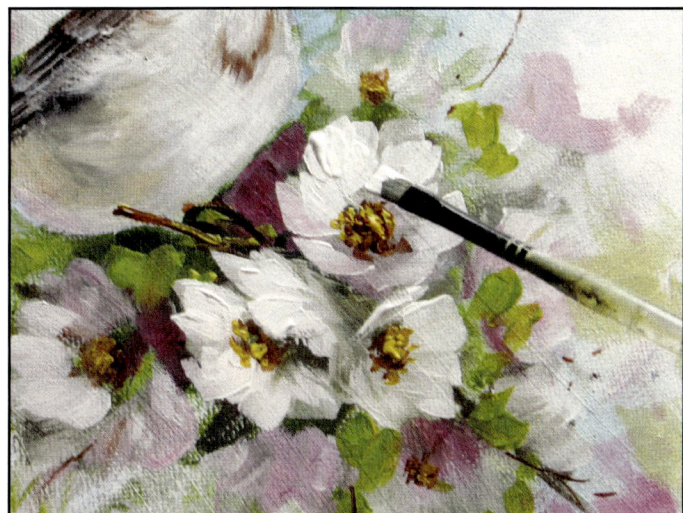

Step 59 Add some thick strokes of white to bring the blossoms by the bird forward.

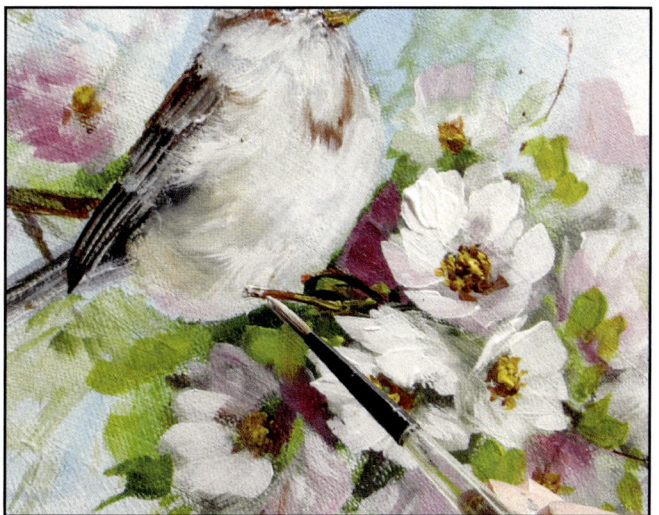

Step 60 Add some light finishing feathers with liner. Enjoy!

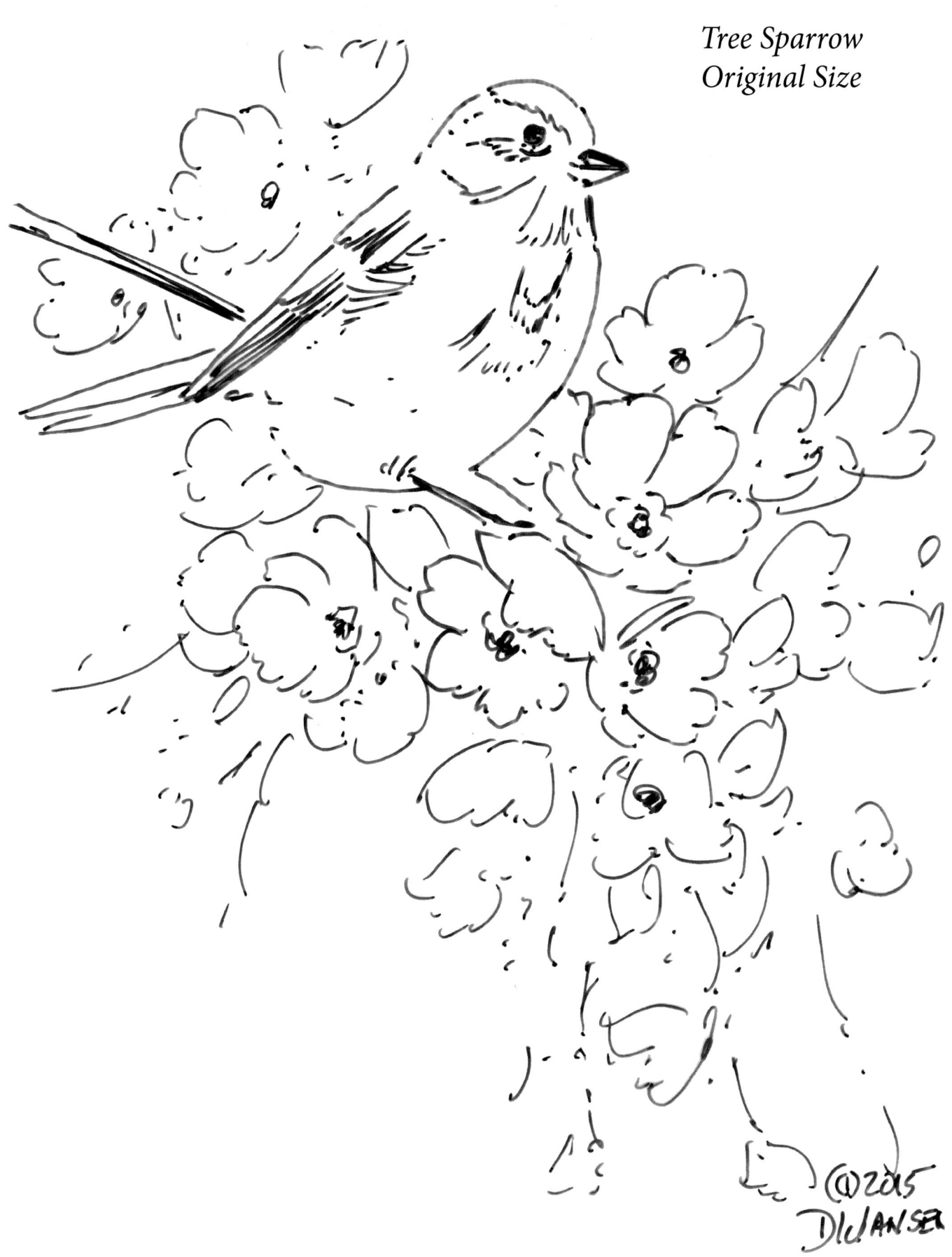

*Tree Sparrow
Original Size*

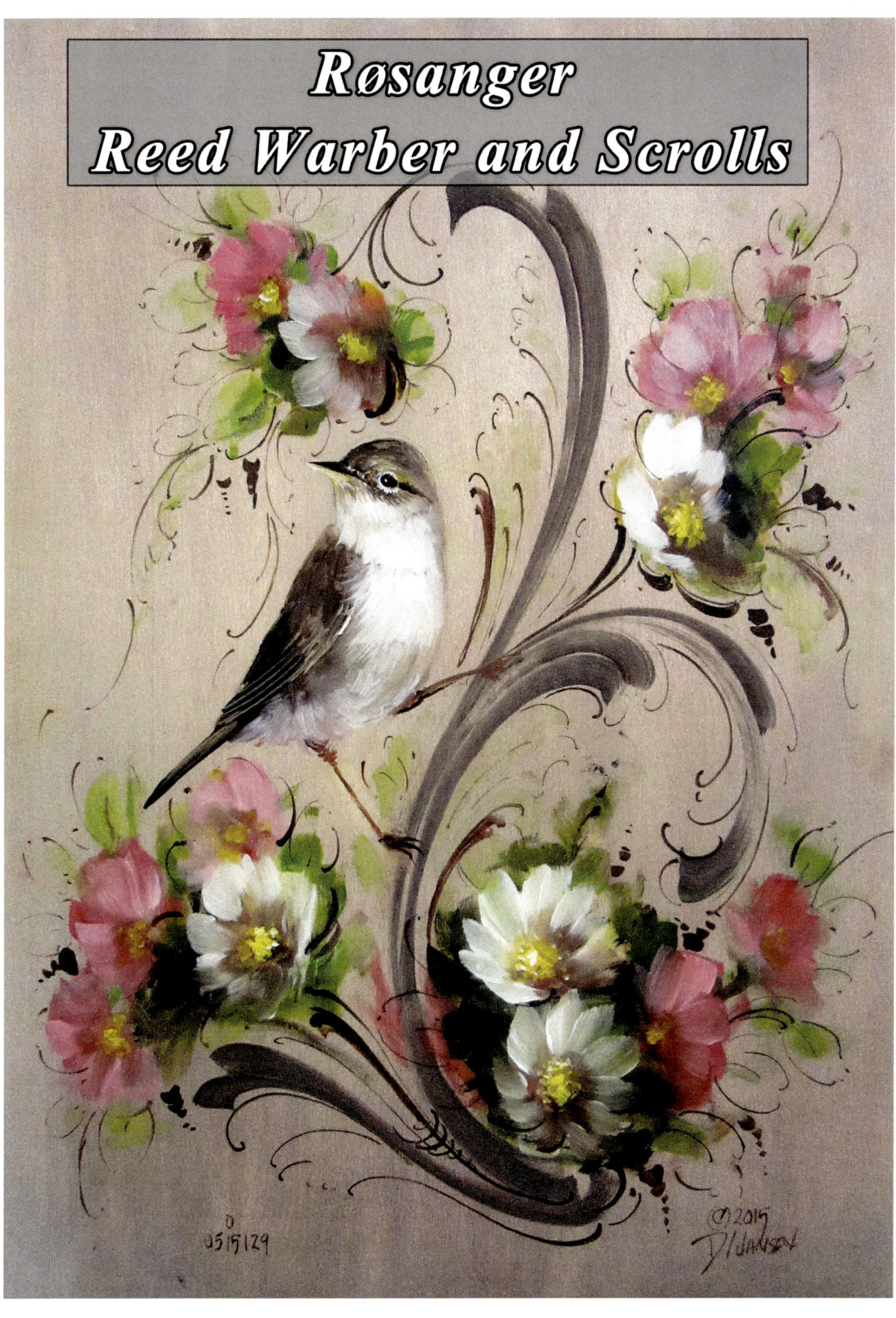

Røsanger
Reed Warber and Scrolls

Rørsanger-Reed Warbler and Scrolls

When I joined the decorative painting industry in the late 1970's I painted a lot of Rosemaling. I started with my mothers book *"Rosemaling Primer"* which was painted in oils and then took some classes with some noted international teachers. For years I studied the history and the colors of the styles. I learned there were really 2 types of Rosemalers. There was the professional that created new forms and styles. Then there was the craftsman who was more of a rural painter- uneducated in traditional art forms and color theory, but carried on the traditions of the styles.

A few years ago, a teacher that really impacted me for years passed away. I decided to read his book again. His book was a Rosemaling textbook written in 1974. This time I read the book as a teacher and artist, and not one who was copying the older styles. I was amazed just how much information he had placed in that book about creating your own style and advancing the art of Rosemaling.

Here are some thoughts: Art always changes. Without change it become stagnant and dies. He wrote that Art and Rosemaling must change and grow with society. I believe that. I continued to reread his book and found many passages that changed my feeling about Rosemaling and the beautiful art form it represents. Professional Rosemalers traveled to schools in Europe to learn the new ways of decorating with acanthus. They returned to Norway and incorporated those ideas and styles into the Norwegian culture. Thus, they created new looks and styles. This is how the art form grows. One style influences and pushes another forward and creates yet another style.

After reading that textbook again and again, I came up with new directions for my Rosemaling. I found birds that live in Norway and incorporated them into the Rosemaling style. The Rørsanger is a reed warbler with long skinny legs. I made the acanthus scrolls skinny to catch the feeling of the little bird. Thus, the style is presented with new ideas! Let's give it a try!

Paint It Simply Palette
Base Color- White
Palette Colors

Naphthol Red Light
Red Violet
Carbon Black
Phthalo Blue
Hansa Yellow

Titanium White
Medium White
Base Brown
Pine Green
Burnt Sienna

Wood Surface
Super MDF Wood Panel about 14 Inch X 18 Inch to fit picture frame. Can also use canvas panel.

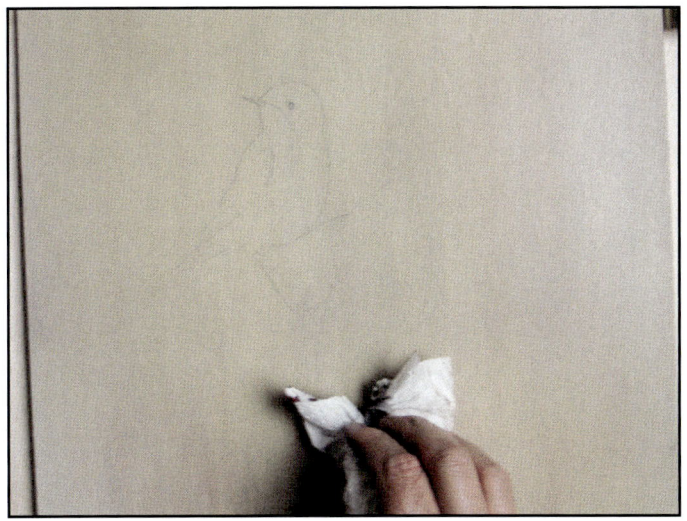

Step 1 Base board white and transfer design. Give surface coat of Extender and using paper towel wipe some greens and browns over.

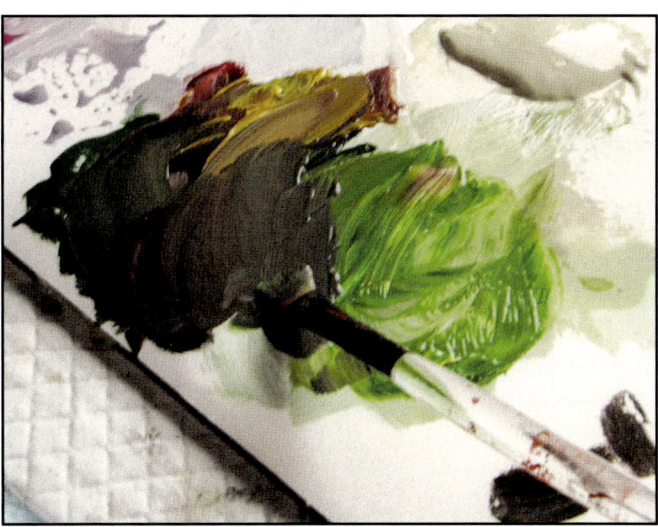

Step 2 Mottle a grey with Burnt Sienna, greens, black and white.

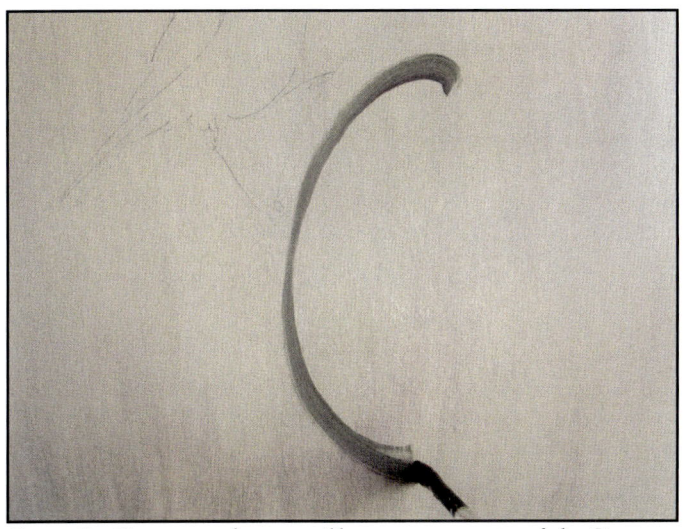

Step 3 Start main scroll movement with C shape. Start on flat of brush, stroke to chisel and then return to the flat to widen the scroll.

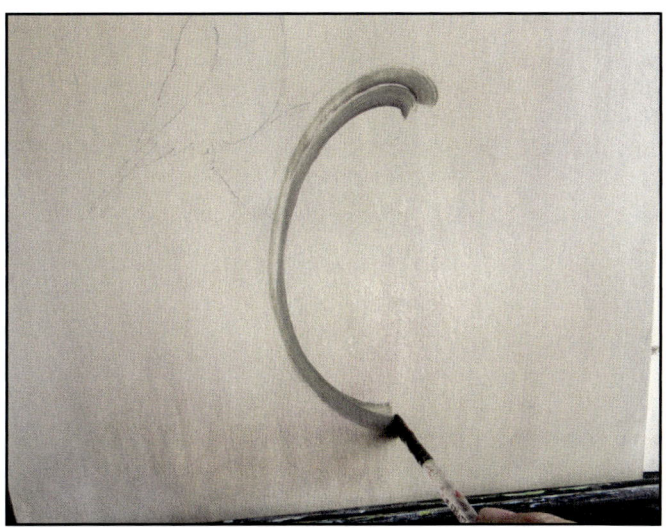

Step 4 Stroke a second slightly smaller stroke inside the first one to widen the scroll and add more weight to the scroll.

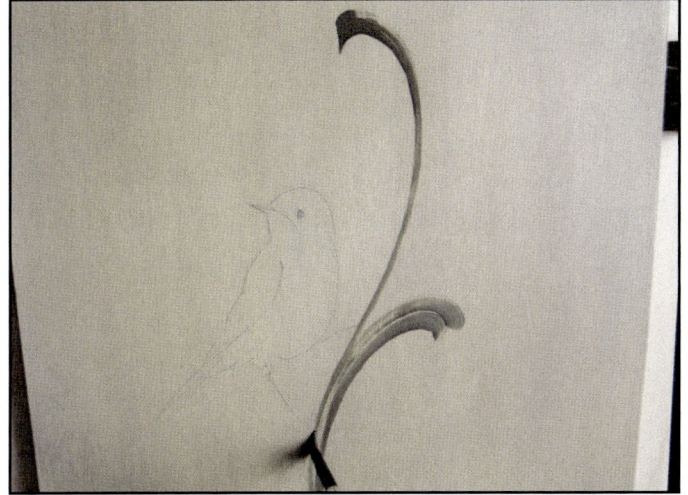

Step 5 Start the long S on the flat and stroke down to the chisel as it hits the C scroll.

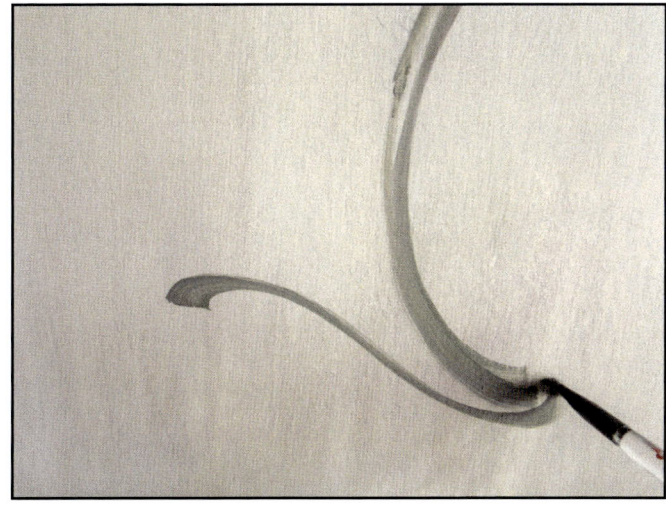

Step 6 On the bottom make a small S with the flat, chisel then flat to finish.

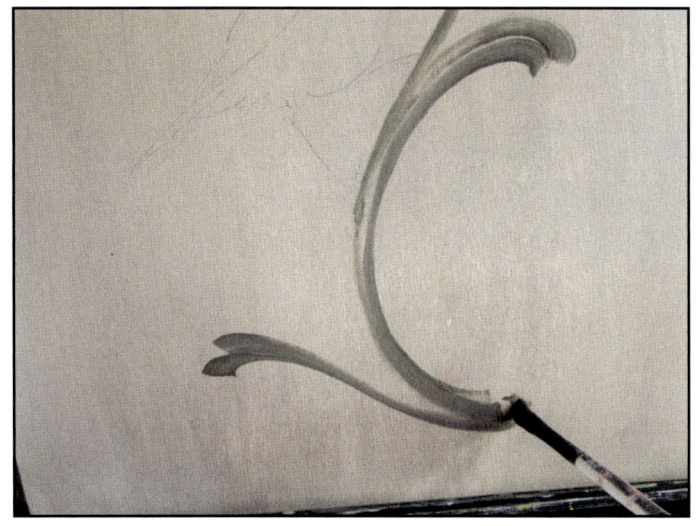

Step 7 Add second stroke to the bottom S to widen it out.

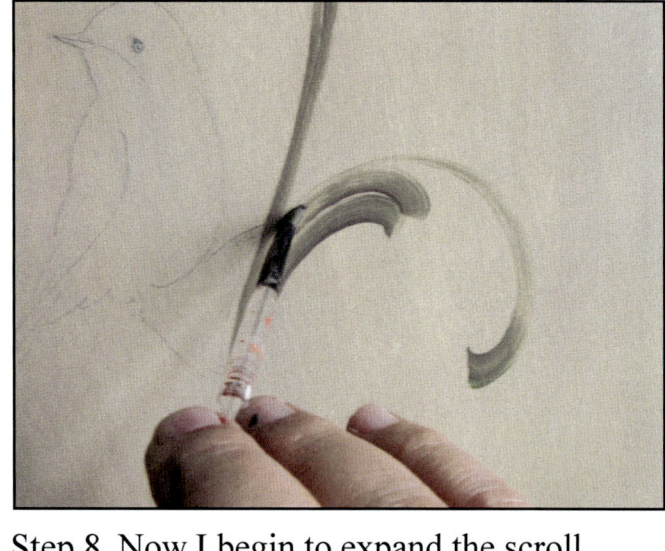

Step 8 Now I begin to expand the scroll, adding the curl or knob to the main C scroll. Start flat and then go to chisel joining scroll.

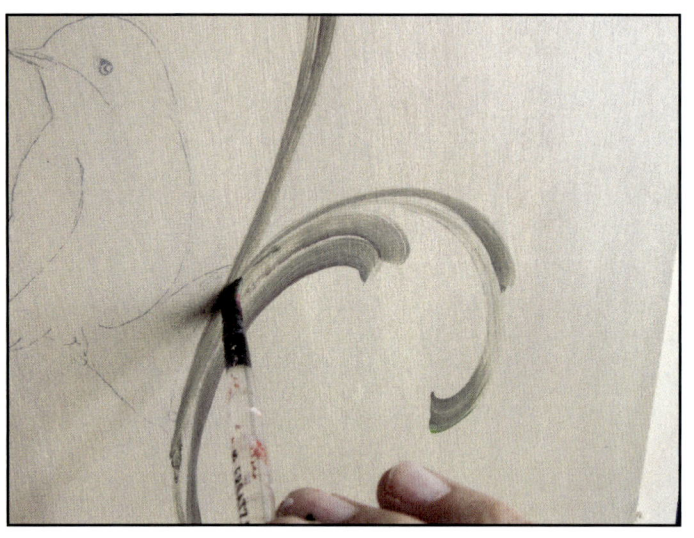

Step 9 Add second stroke to the knob with a flat to chisel motion. Just like a large comma stroke.

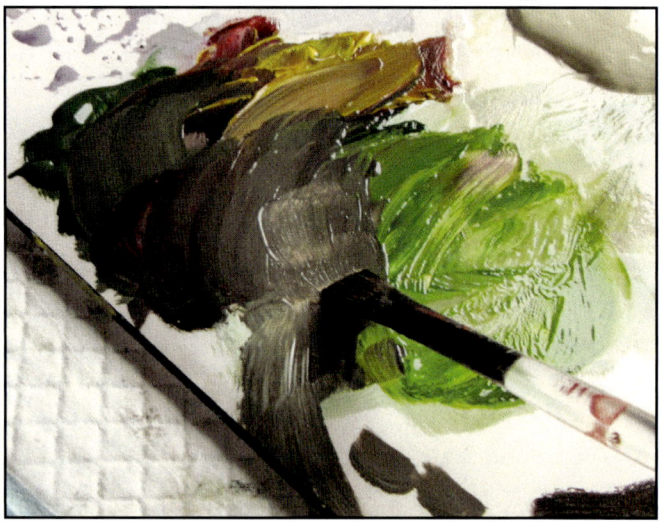

Step 10 Always return to the palette for more paint with each stroke. This can also make each stroke slightly different colors...GOOD!

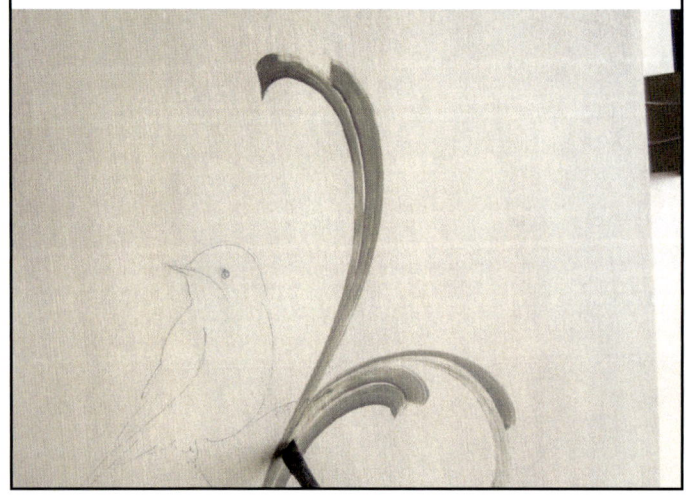

Step 11 Add a second stroke to the top S scroll. This widens the scroll.

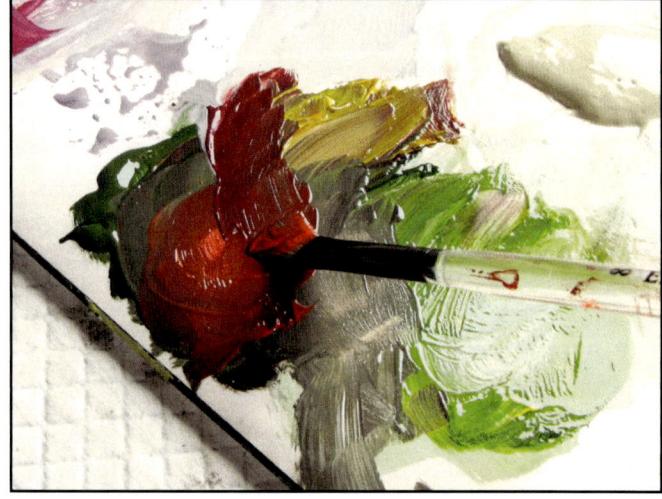

Step 12 Place some Red Violet and red in the colors and mottle to tone reds.

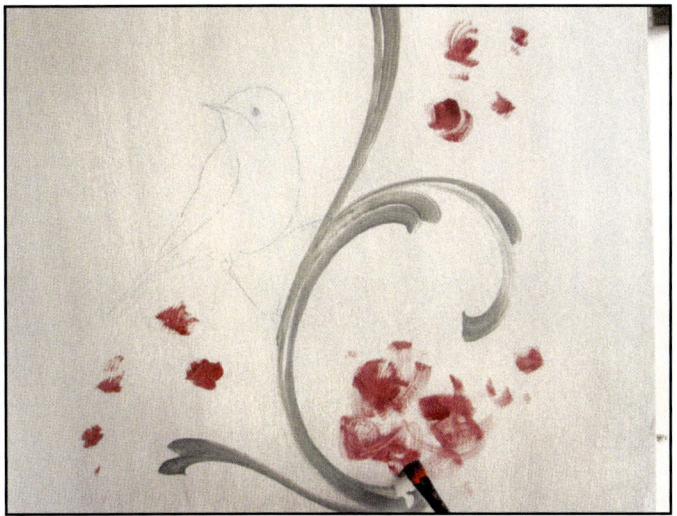

Step 13 Using smaller flat, casually add some touches of red where you may want to see the flowers. Keep loose.

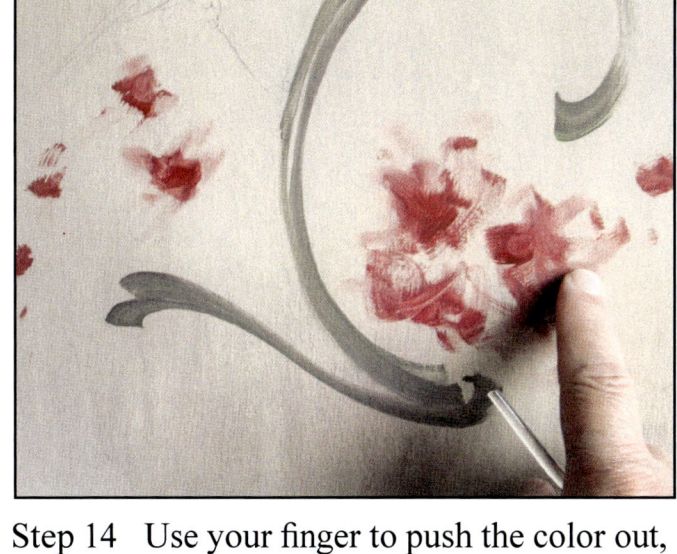

Step 14   Use your finger to push the color out, making the shapes more casual.

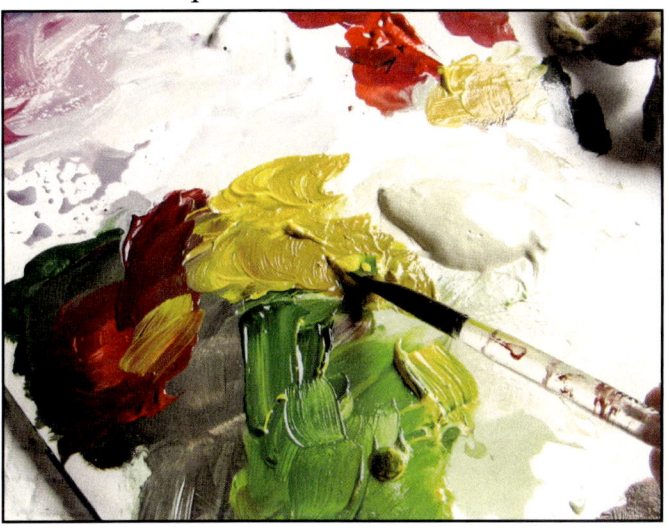

Step 15 Mottle the greens with some yellows to vary the color of greens.

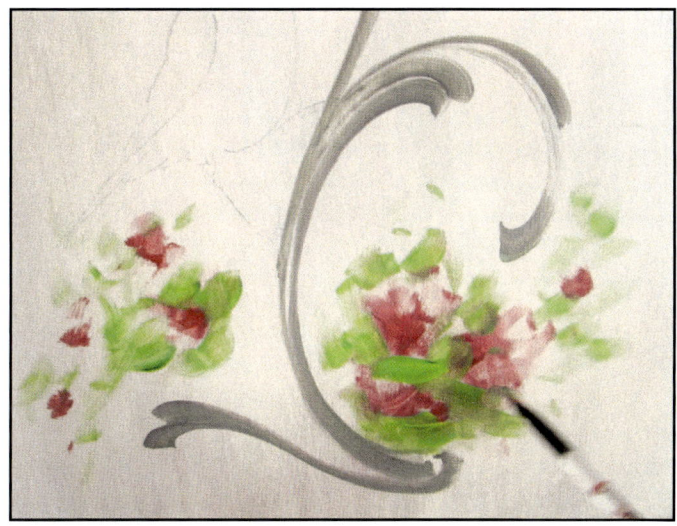

Step 16 Add some various greens and toned yellows to the areas around the red. Keep very casual.

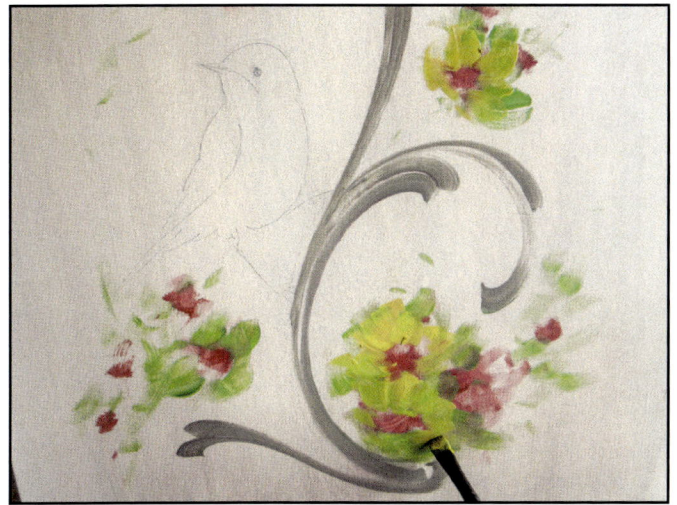

Step 17 Begin to add the yellows to the shapes of the blossoms. Keep casual for now.

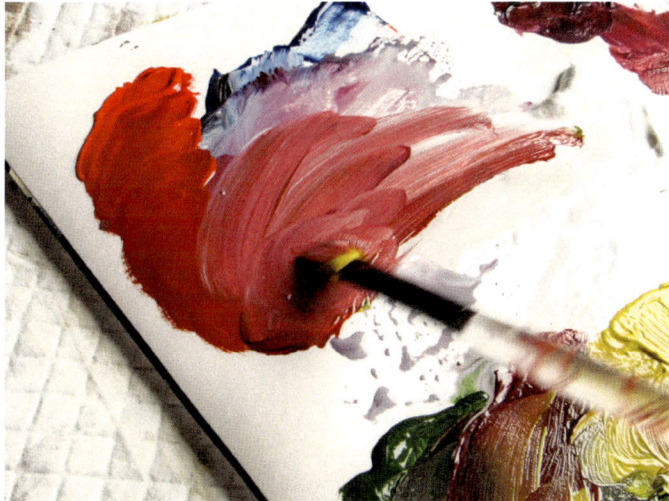

Step 18 Mottle the brush into the reds, vary with some white and touch blue. Add to the flowers for interest.

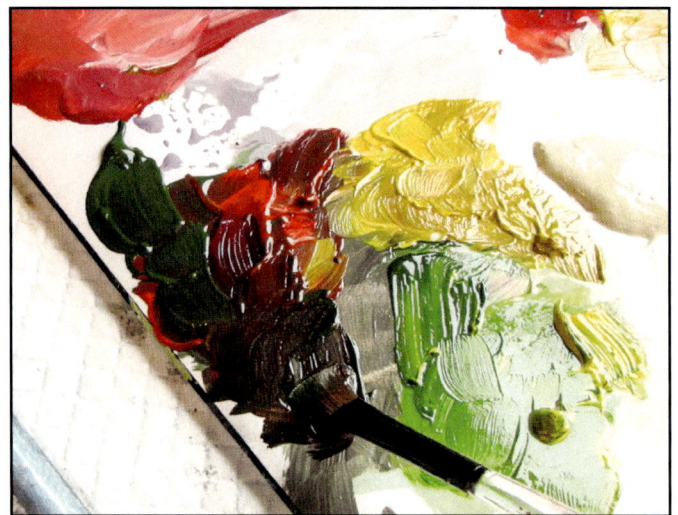

Step 19 Mottle some greens and blacks into the reds to make dark toned brownish grey.

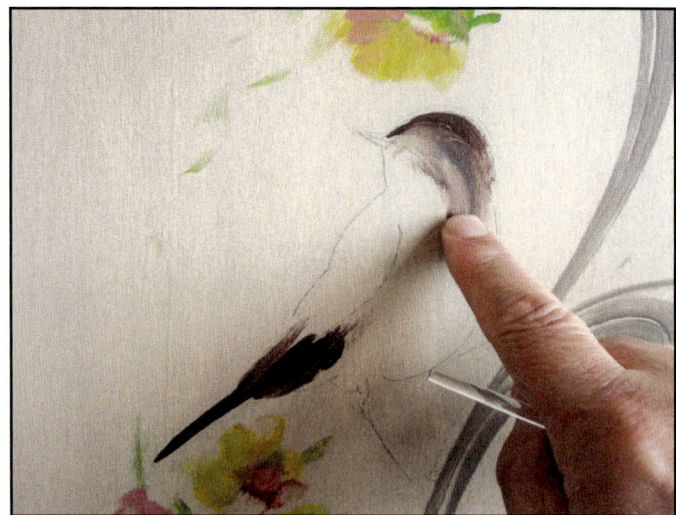

Step 20 Add some strokes to the birds head and tail and then soften the movement with your finger.

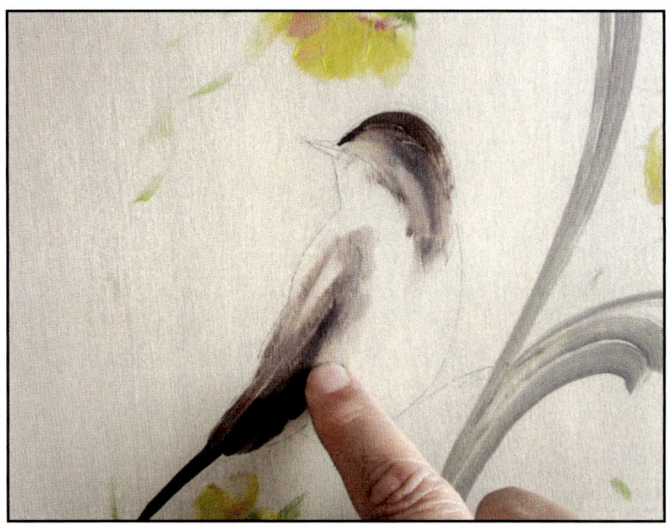

Step 21 Add some to the area of the wing and soften with your finger. Just look for some movement in paint, no exact shapes.

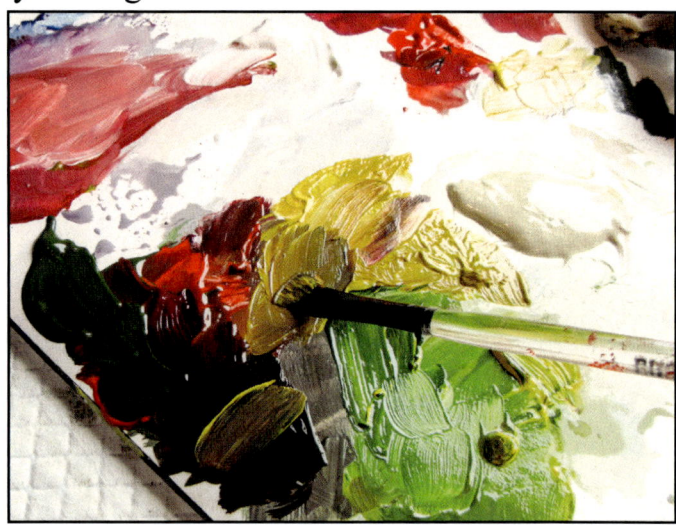

Step 22 Mottle the brush with some toned yellows. Reds and black. Almost a brown.

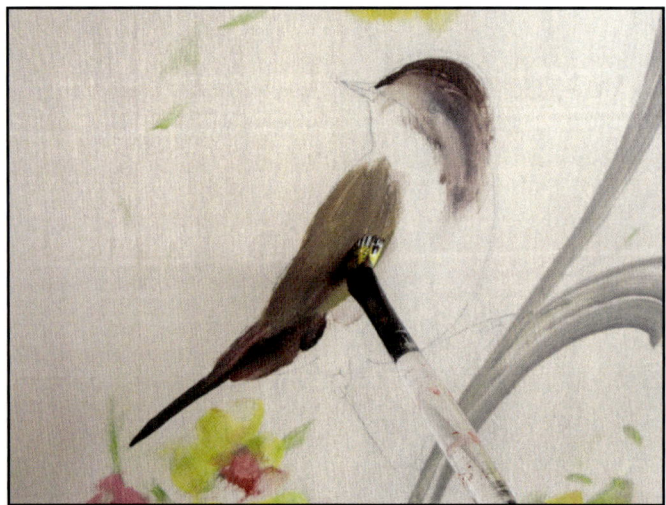

Step 23 Add this to the top of the wing. The mantle area of the bird.

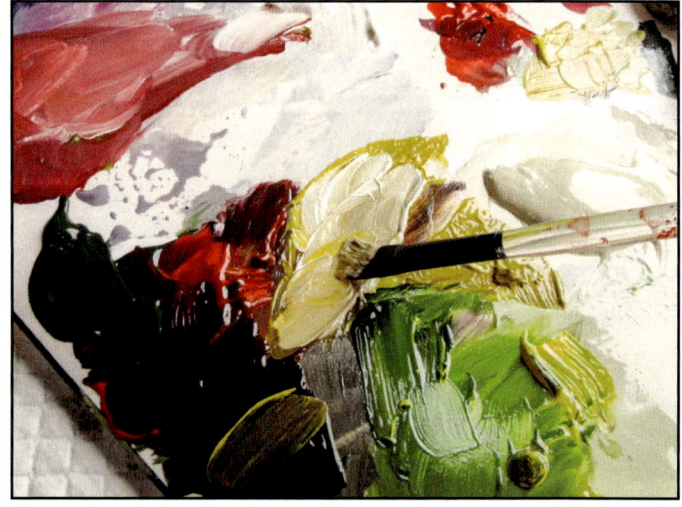

Step 24 Mottle the color with some additional Hansa and then lighten with some white.

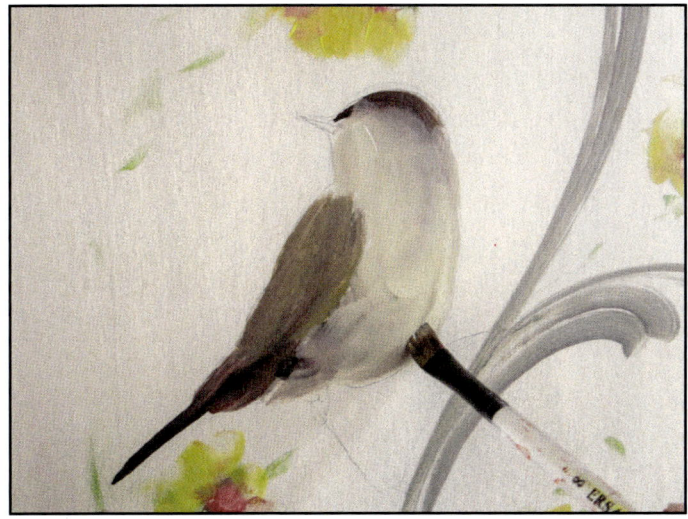

Step 25 Add this to the neck and body to add interest. Remember the shape following stroke to add the direction to the feathers.

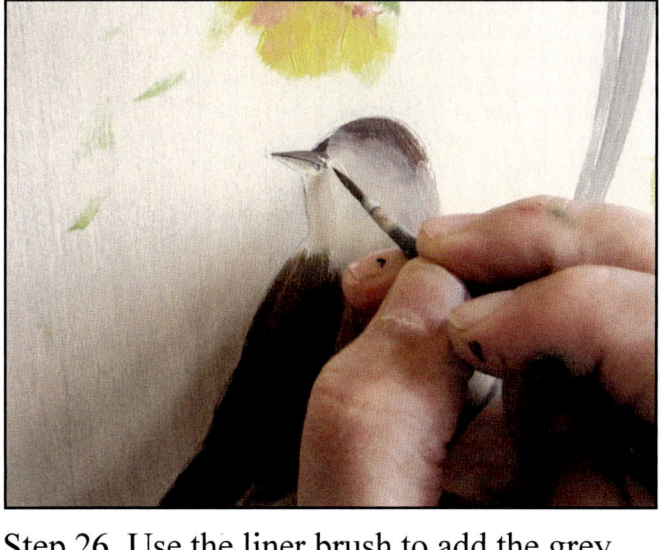

Step 26 Use the liner brush to add the grey beak and then light small feathers around the beak.

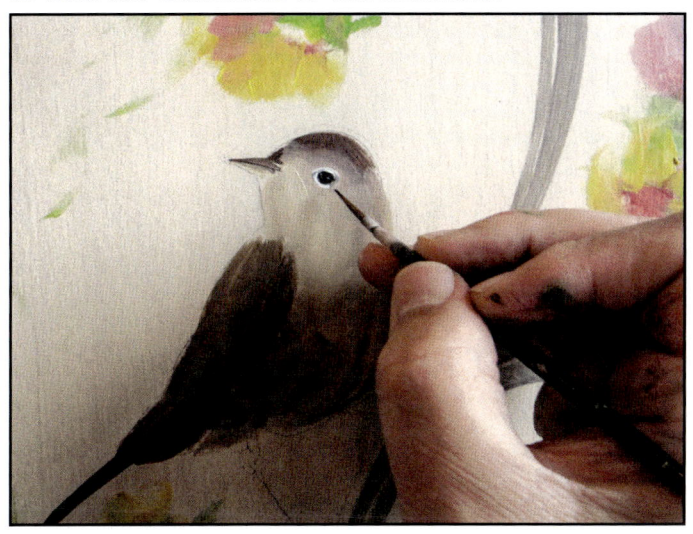

Step 27 Use the liner brush to add the white eye ring around the eye. Add the eye with black.

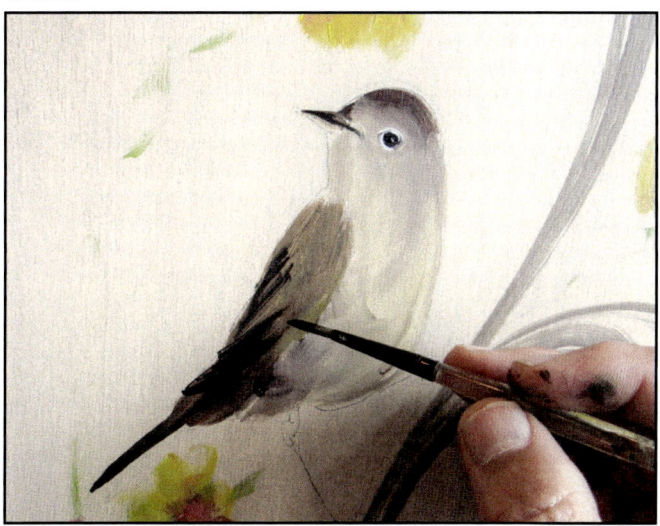

Step 28 Mottle into dark grey brown and add the motion of flight feathers to the bottom of wing and then some tail feathers.

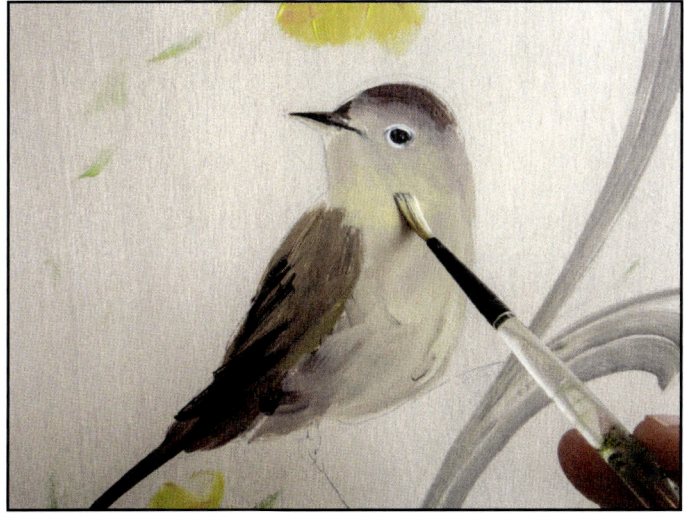

Step 29 Lighten the color with some Hansa and then add the tone to the neck feathers.

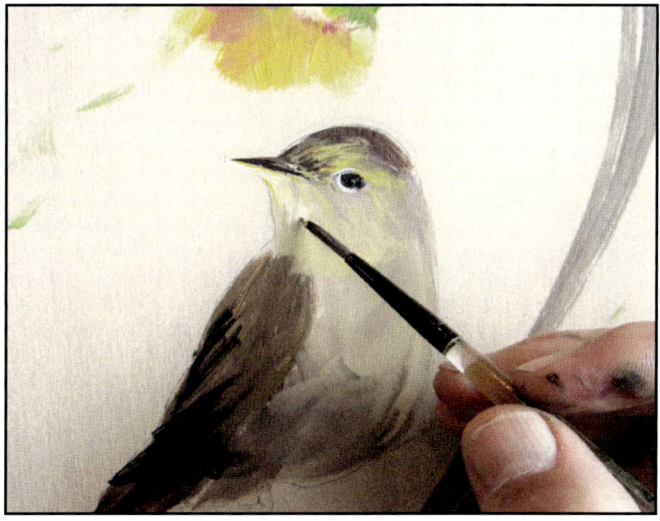

Step 30 Add more darks and lights to beak and then add smaller whites to neck feathers.

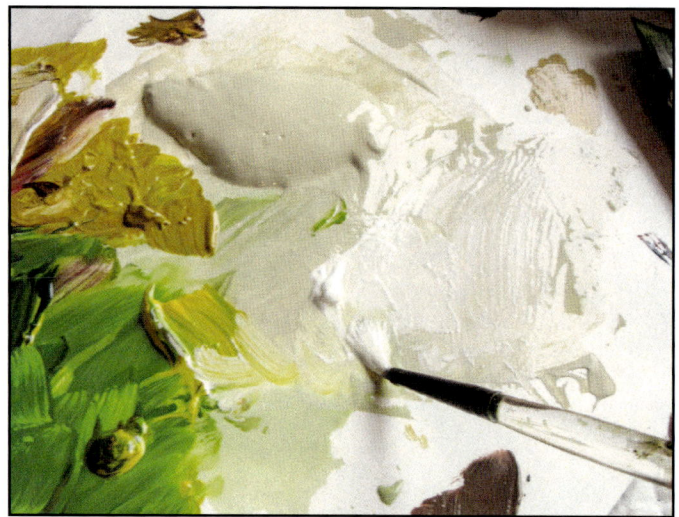

Step 31 Mottle the color lighter on the palette with more white. Notice all the variations to the colors. This adds interest.

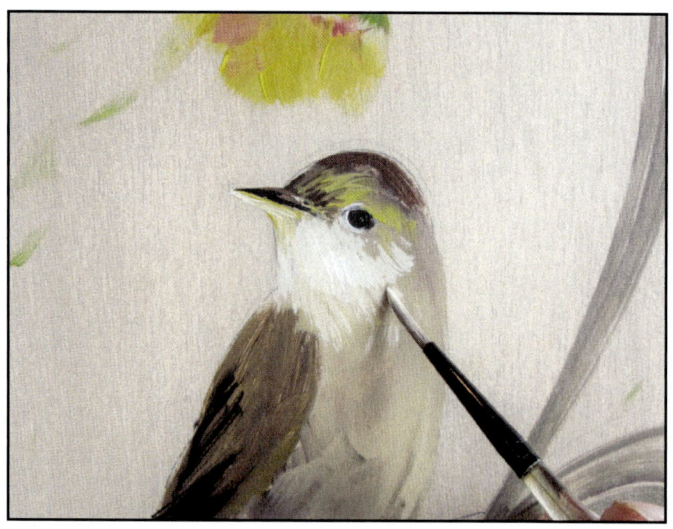

Step 32 Add some shorter strokes of white to neck and cheek area. Soften with grey strokes if needed.

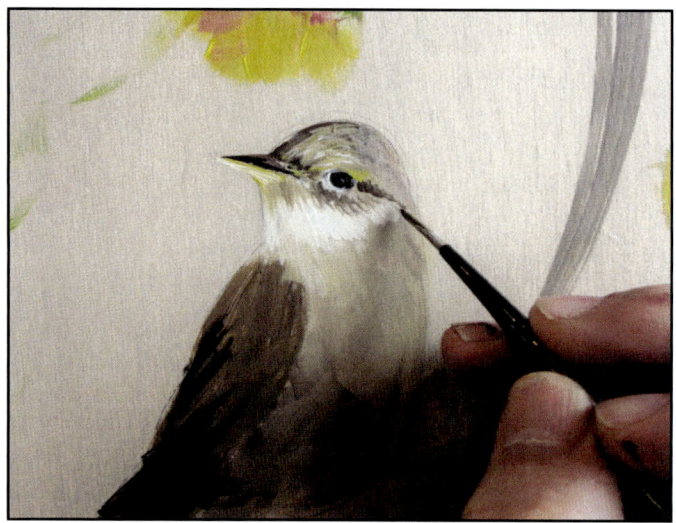

Step 33 Add the dark details behind the eye with darker greys.

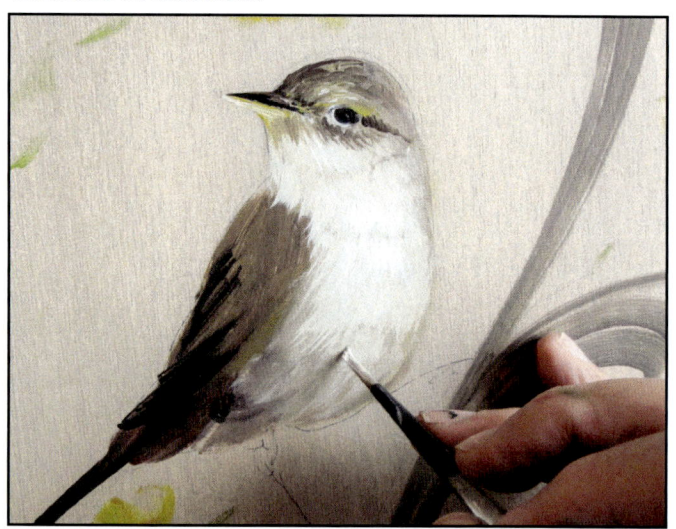

Step 34 Stroke down the body with more whites, soften with finger so you just have some movement.

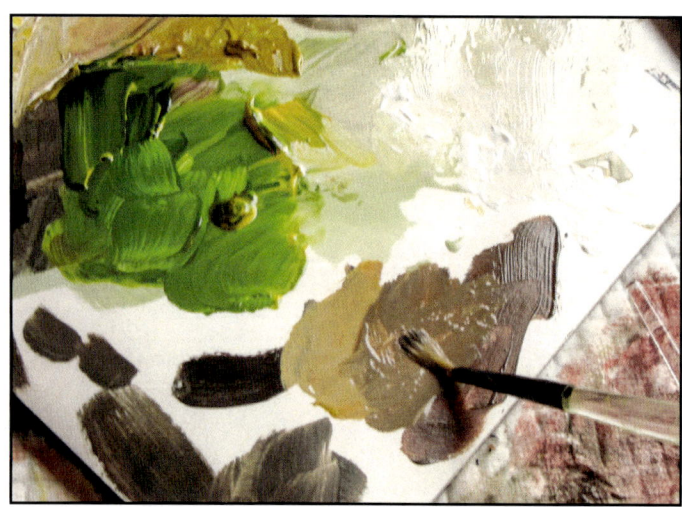

Step 35 Mottle the greys with touch more Hansa and touch reds. Lighten with white.

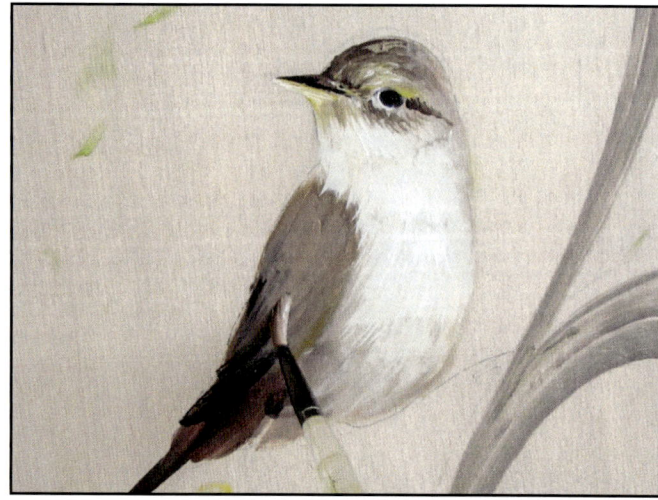

Step 36 Add this to the top mantel area of the wing. Pull down to make soft coverts.

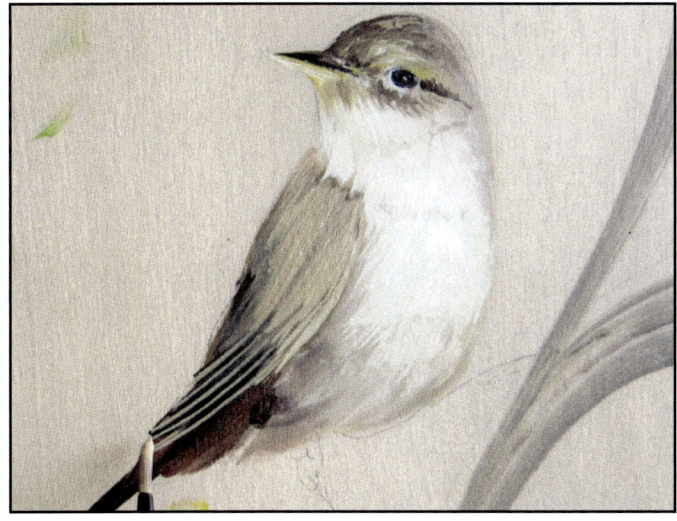

Step 37 Add some light and dark streaks to make the flight feathers. I used # 4 round brush.

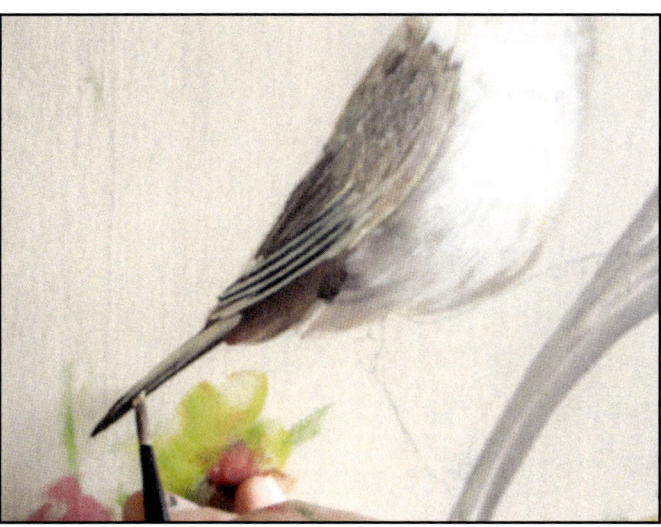

Step 38 Add some softer lights and darks to the tail to make those feathers.

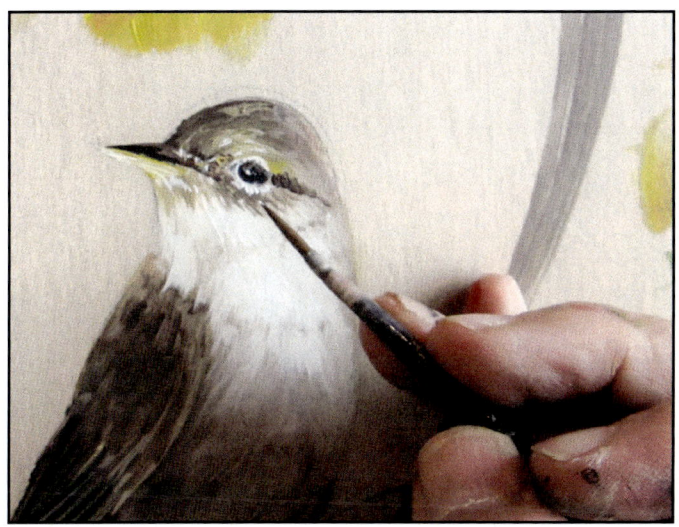

Step 39 Add some small touches of white to the face and around the eye for more interest. I used a liner brush.

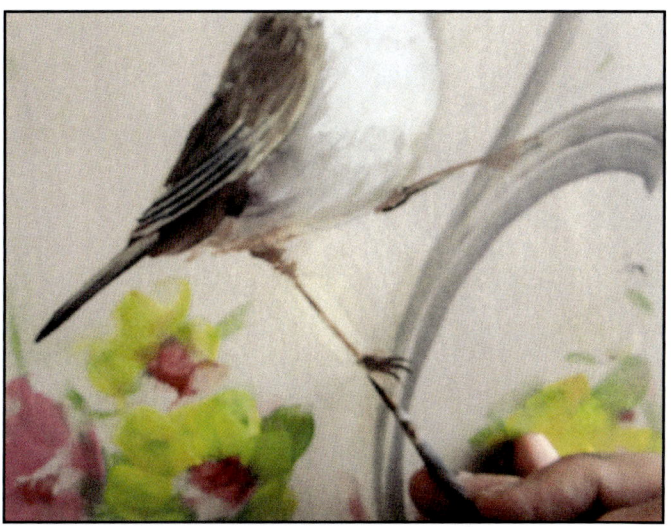

Step 40   Add the feet and legs with some brown/ greys. I love the long thin legs of this bird. Works great with the scrolls.

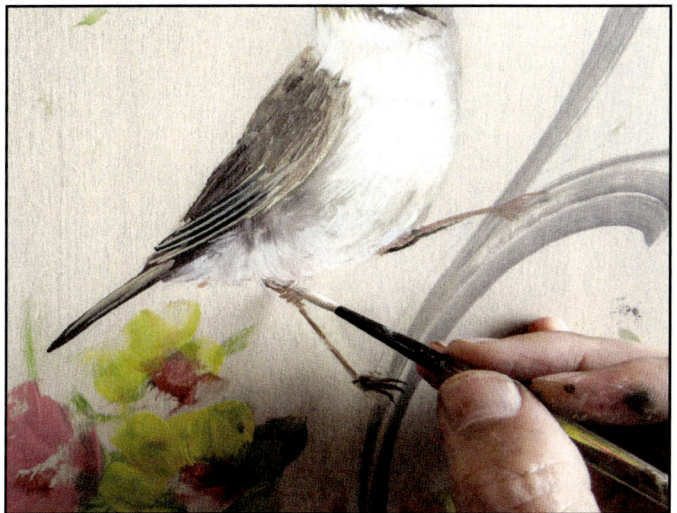

Step 41 Add some shorter strokes of white to the bottom of the body with # 4 round.

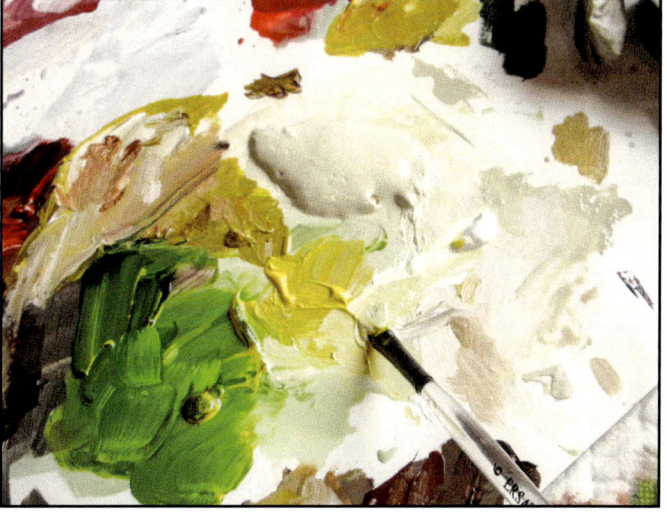

Step 42 Mottle the brush with some Hansa and white. I used small flat.

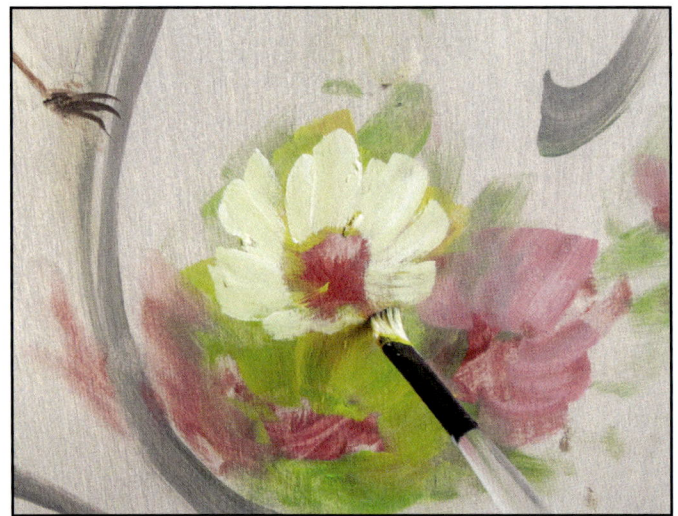

Step 43 Add the strokes to the flowers to begin the blossom shapes. Pull towards center varying the sizes.

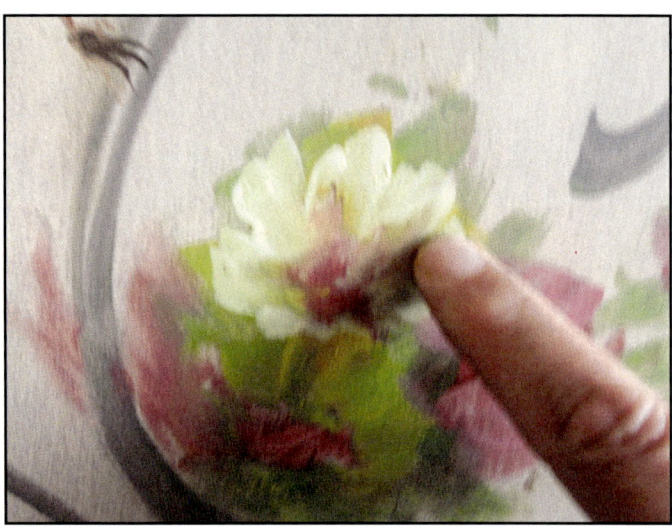

Step 44 Use your finger in and out of the center to soften the movement between the reds and yellows.

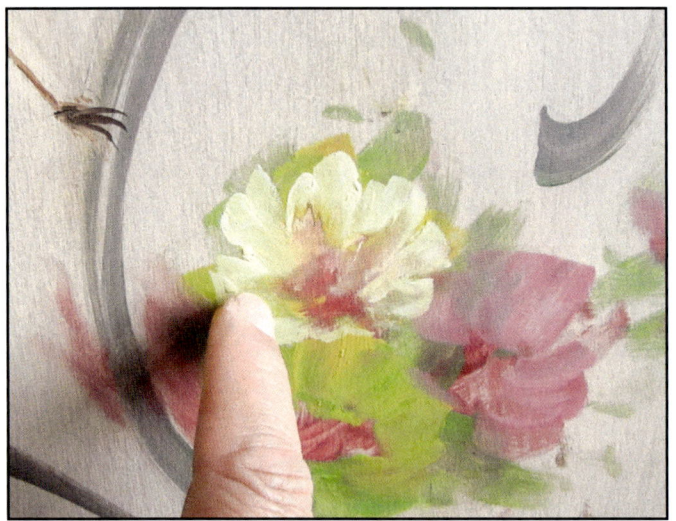

Step 45 Push out towards the greens. I repeat this several times to make the blossoms.

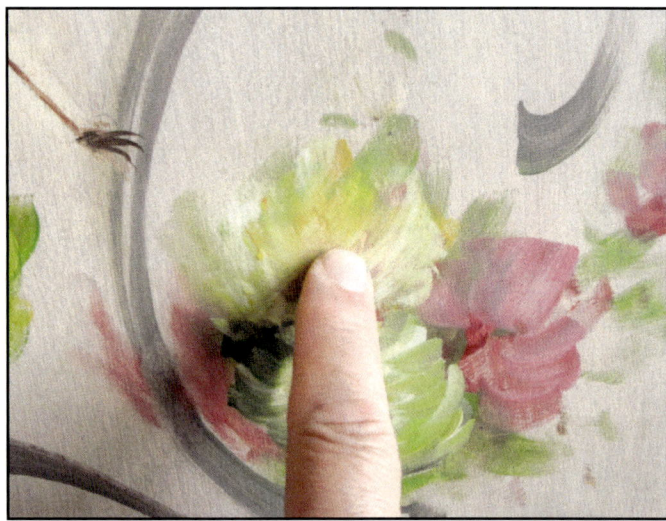

Step 46 Add some pink blossoms and restate white blossoms and push in and out again with your finger.

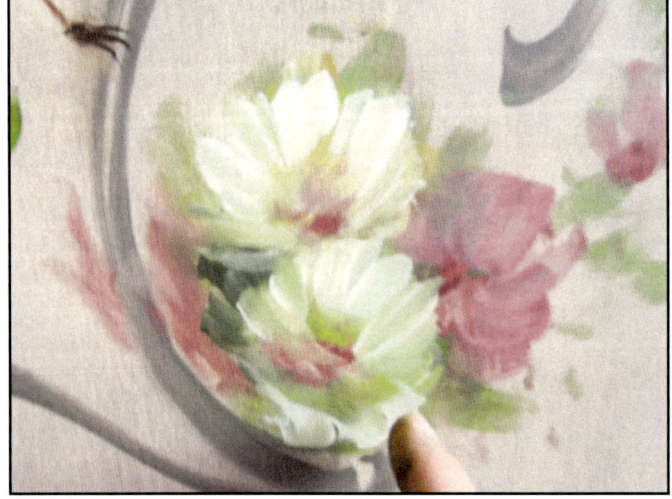

Step 47 Add some greens to the center of the blossoms and push in and out with finger.

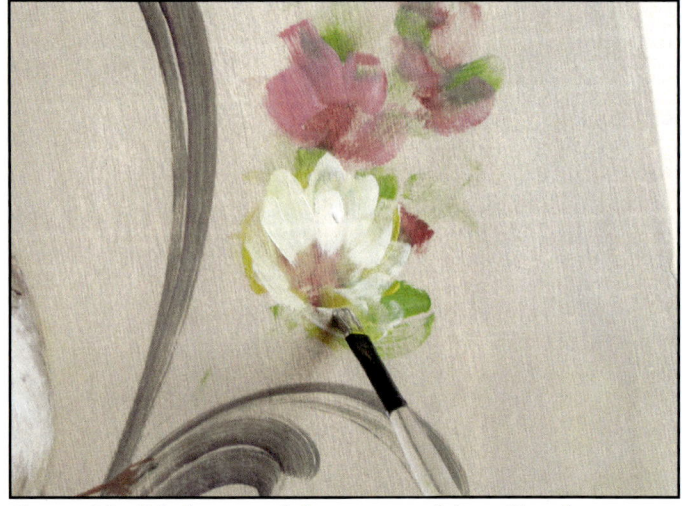

Step 48 Lighten with more white. Stroke on some smaller petals for more interest.

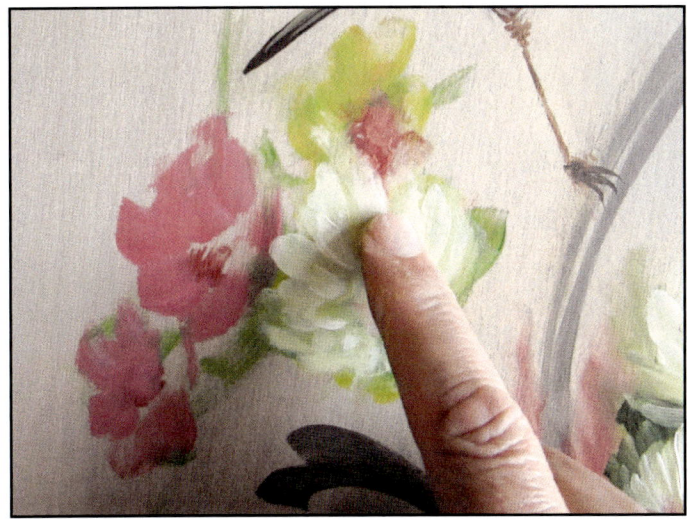

Step 49 Soften the colors with your finger leaving the movement for interest.

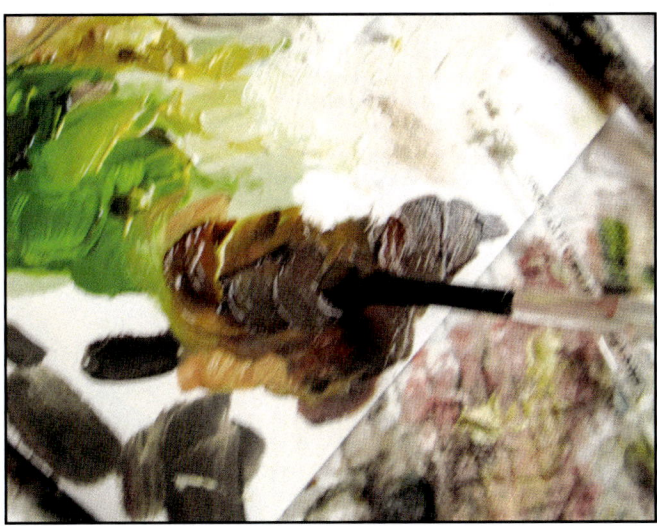

Step 50 Mottle the brush with some greys and browns. This will be the shadows for the light blossoms.

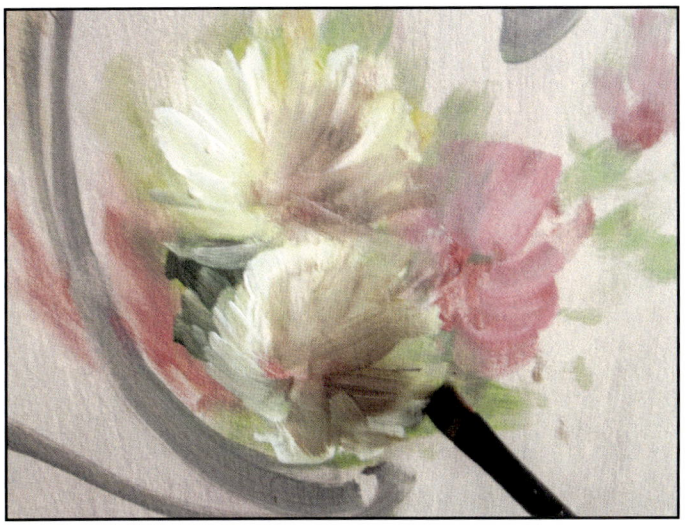

Step 51 Move the color in and out of the blossom. When I paint blossoms, I work them many times for interest.

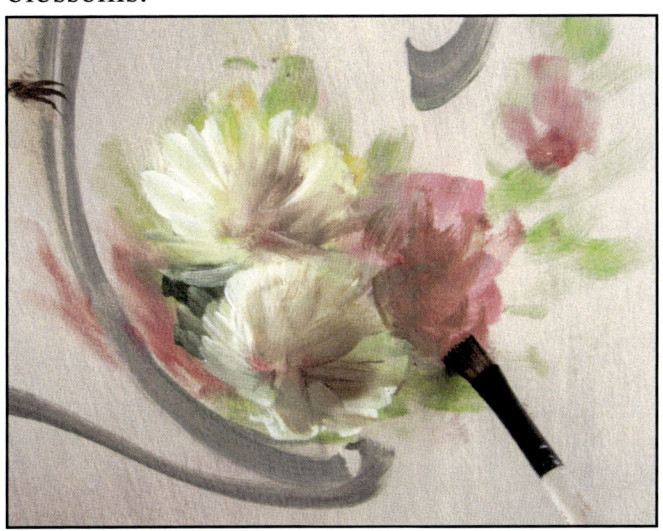

Step 52 Add some of the greys and browns to the other blossoms for interest and harmony.

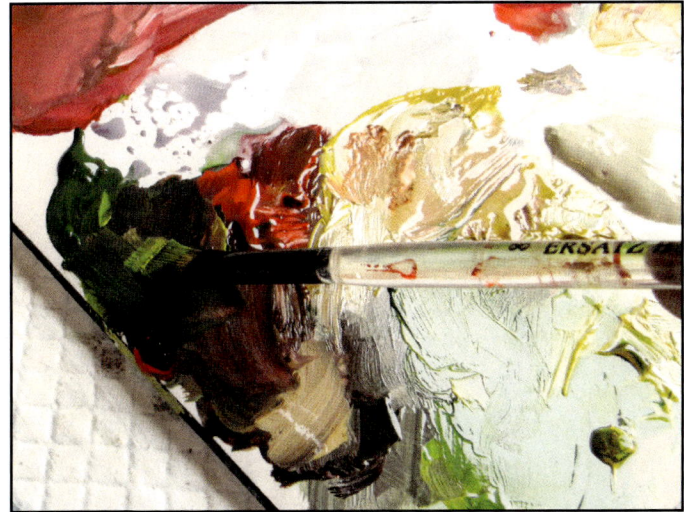

Step 53 Mottle the brush with some greens and tone with the greys.

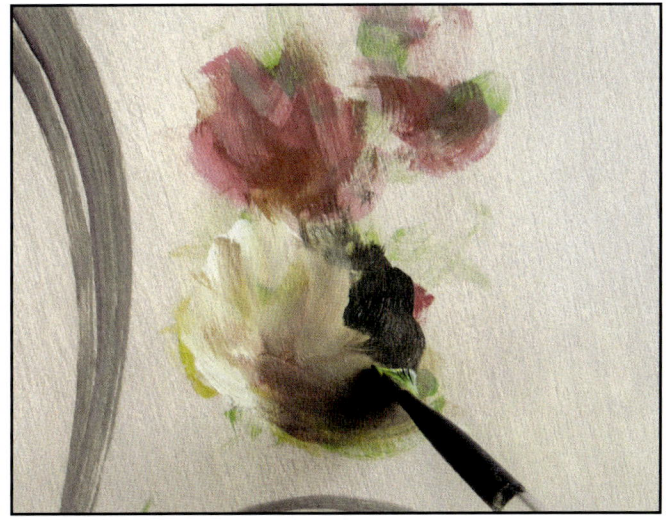

Step 54 Add this around the blossoms for shadow interest.

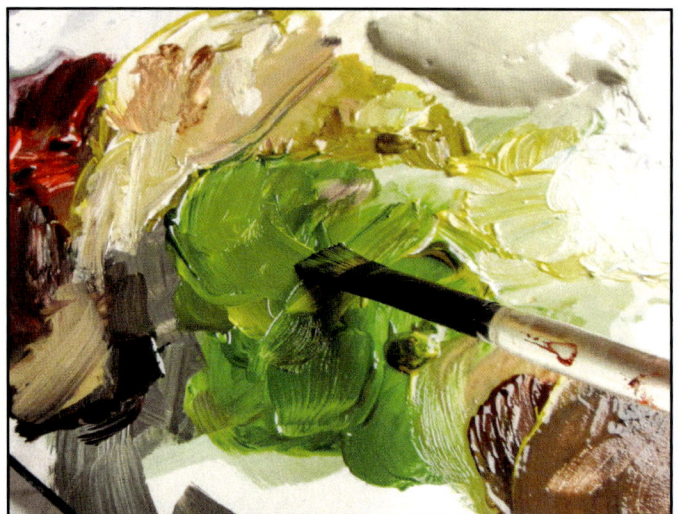

Step 55 Mottle the brush with some Pine Green, Hansa and then into the other colors for variation.

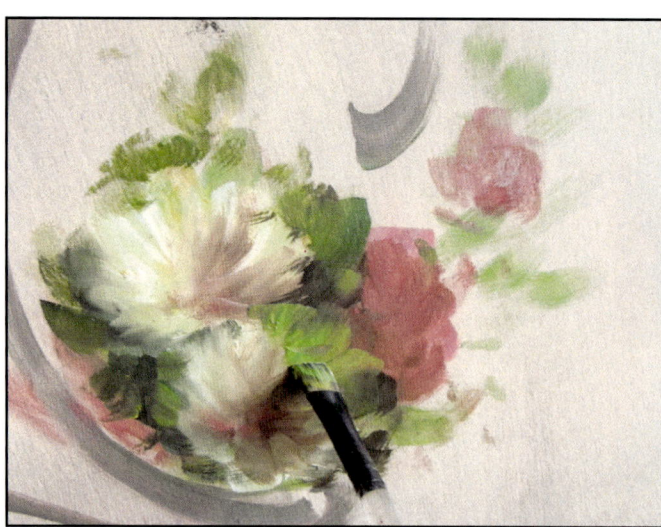

Step 56 Add some lighter mottled strokes to begin the shapes of the leaves.

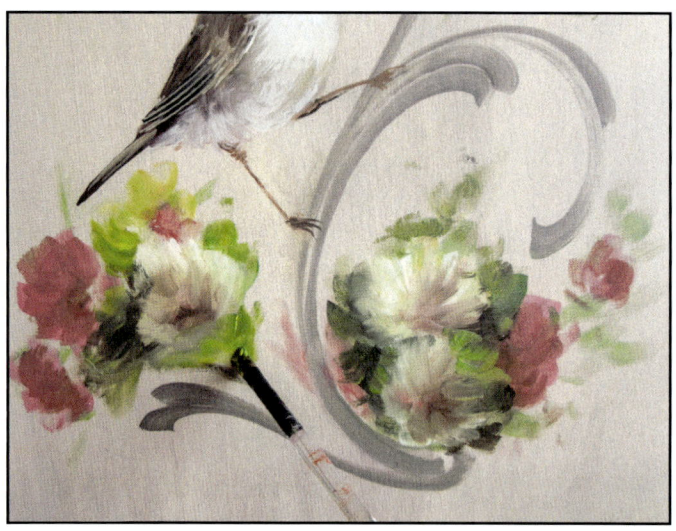

Step 57 Work around the design adding more shapes and leaves with mottled greens.

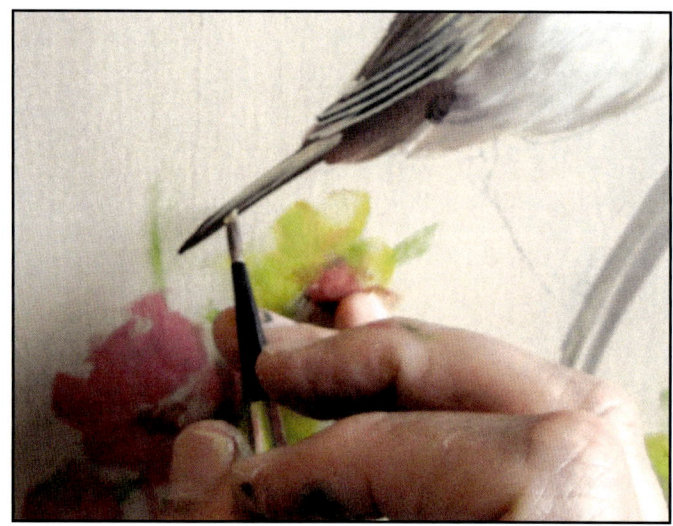

Step 58 Return to the bird to add some additional detailed strokes to make sure he is the center of interest.

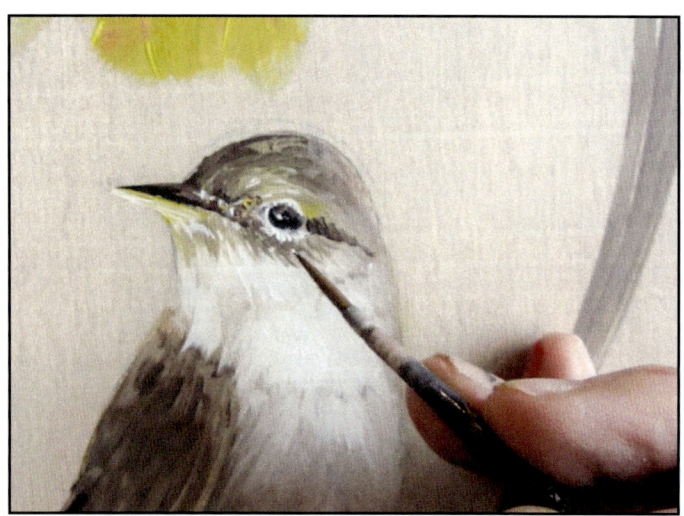

Step 59 Add some tiny strokes of yellows and white as details around eye.

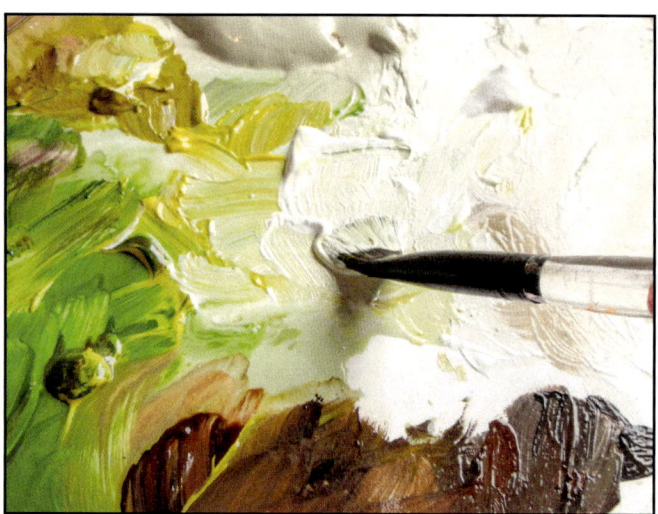

Step 60 Mottle the small flat with some white. Thick white paint.

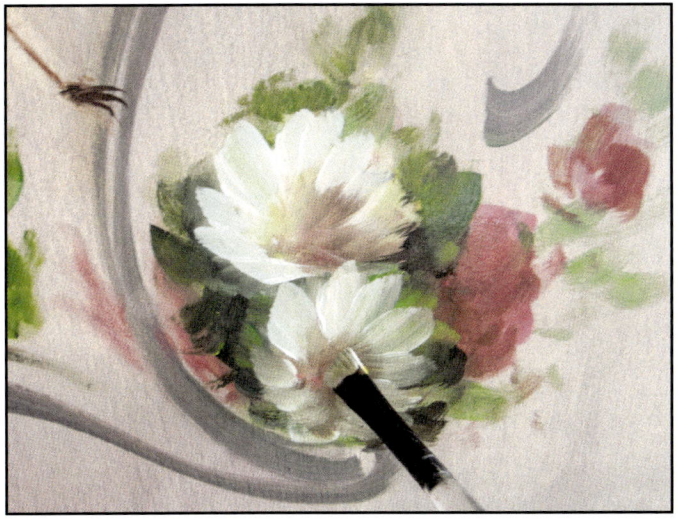

Step 61 Stroke the petals with more details. Use the corner of the brush to make the petal edges.

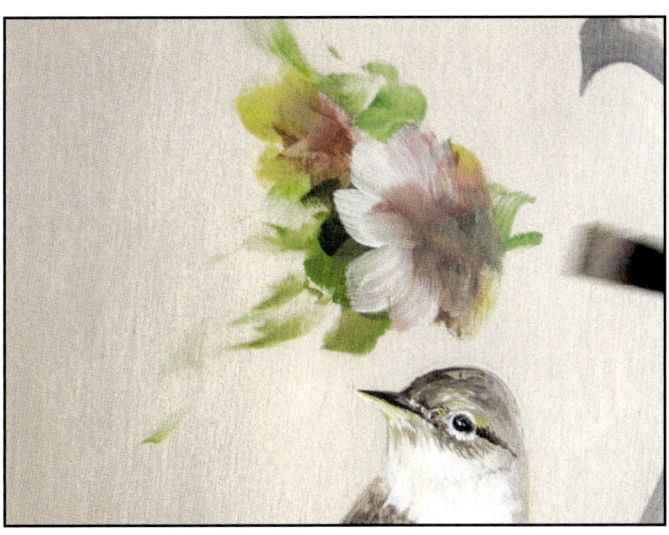

Step 62 Keep the flowers above him a little softer so that his details come forward.

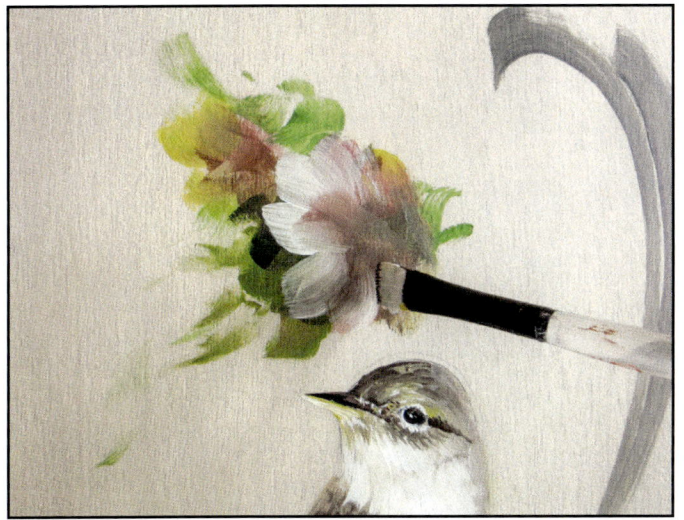

Step 63 Add petals with softer whites.

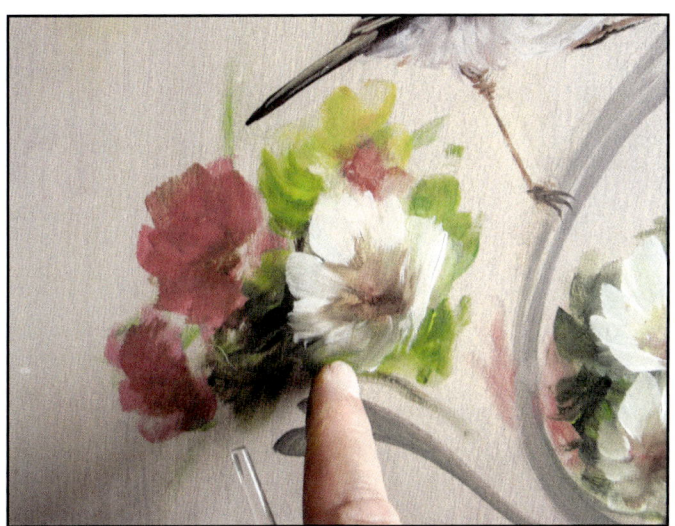

Step 64 Work around the design and watch the movement. Keep it soft with your finger.

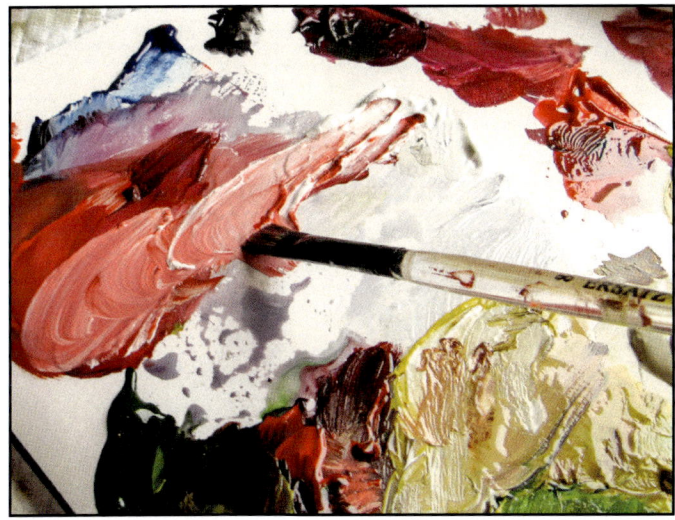

Step 65 Mottle the reds, keep warmer with more Nap. Red Light and lighten with white.

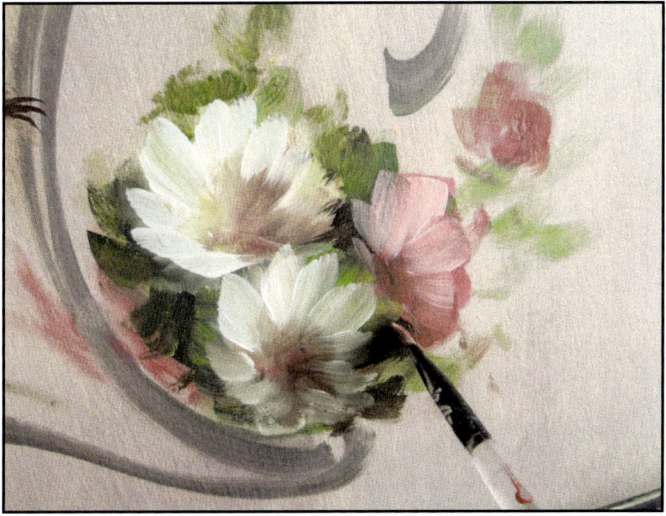

Step 66 Add some lighter pink blossom petals.

Step 67 Use your finger to soften the petals into the background.

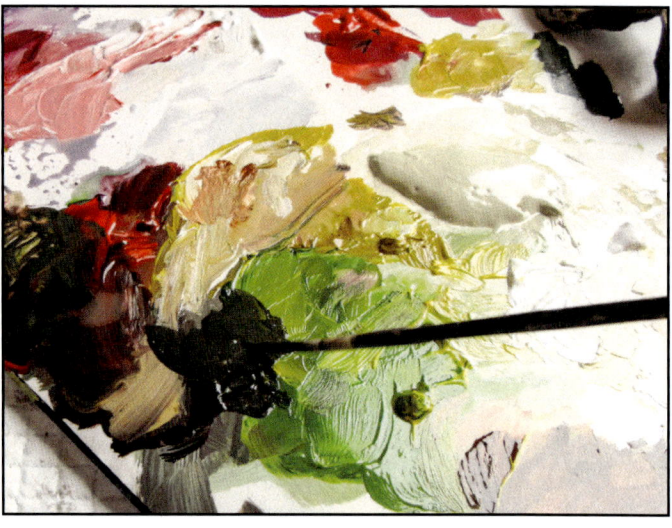

Step 68 Mottle the liner brush with some greens and touches black and browns to darken and tone the color. Thin with some water.

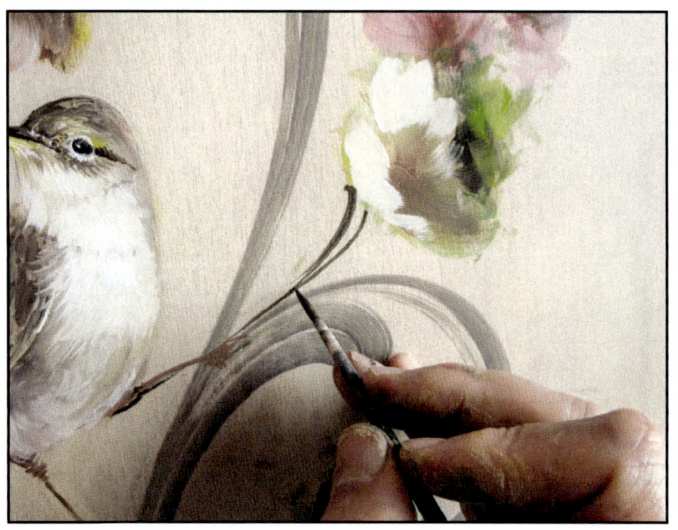

Step 69 Add the stems to the flowers to begin the liner decoration.

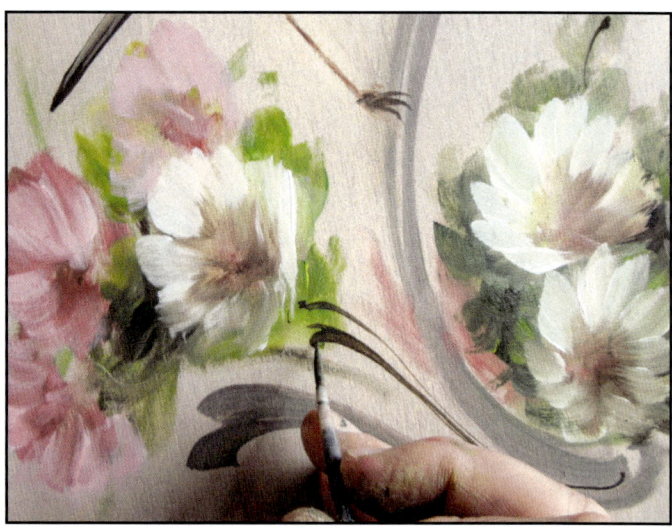

Step 70 I add at least 2 strokes to the main flower groups to give weight to the stem which gives more support the the flowers.

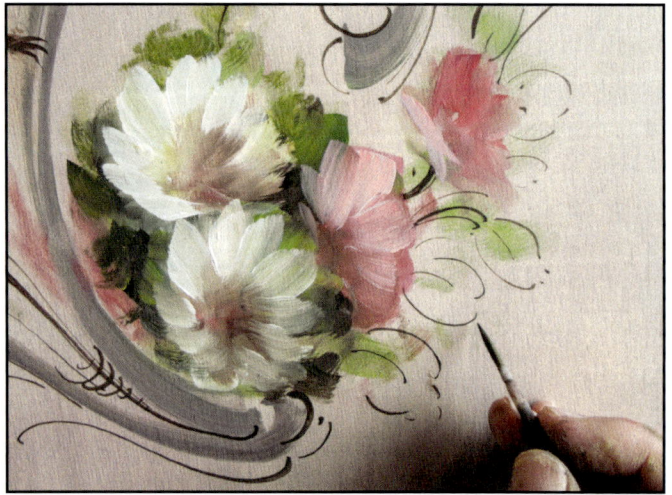

Step 71 Lightly and casually add some leaf shapes to the design.

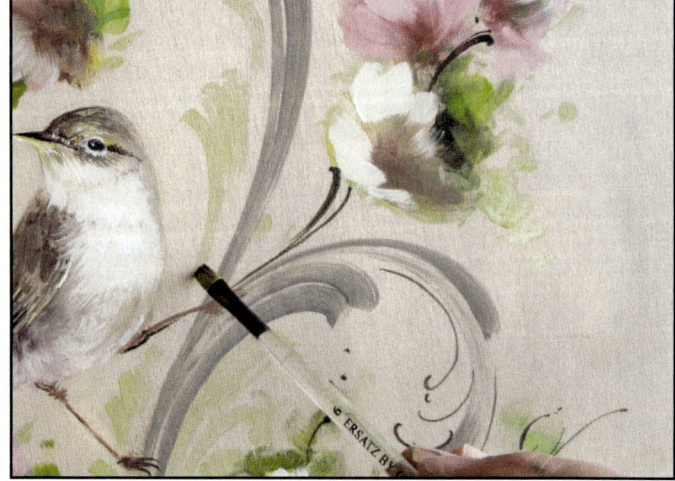

Step 72 Add soft green scrolls leaves. Keep light & loose. Frame them with liner work

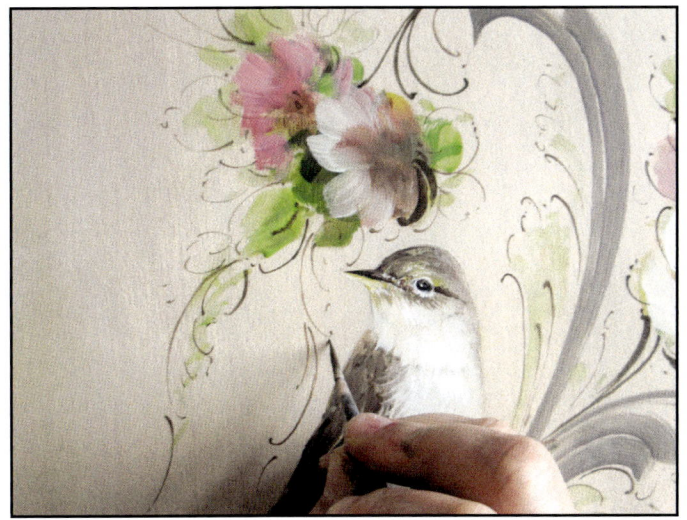
Step 73 Add longer strokes to make the suggestions of stems.

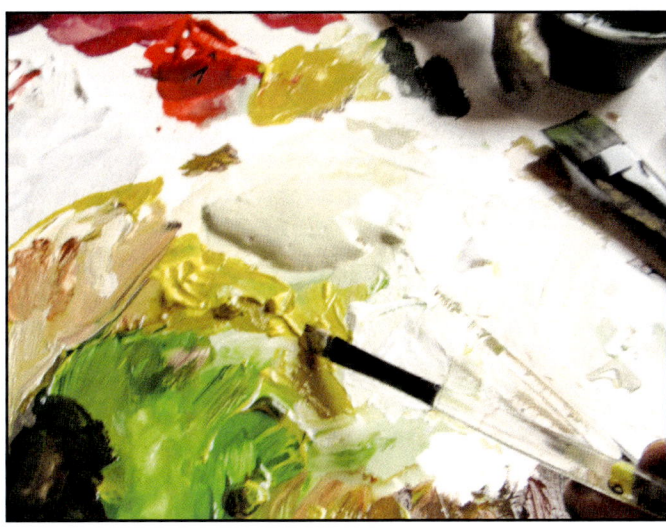
Step 74 Mottle the brush with some yellows and white to lighten.

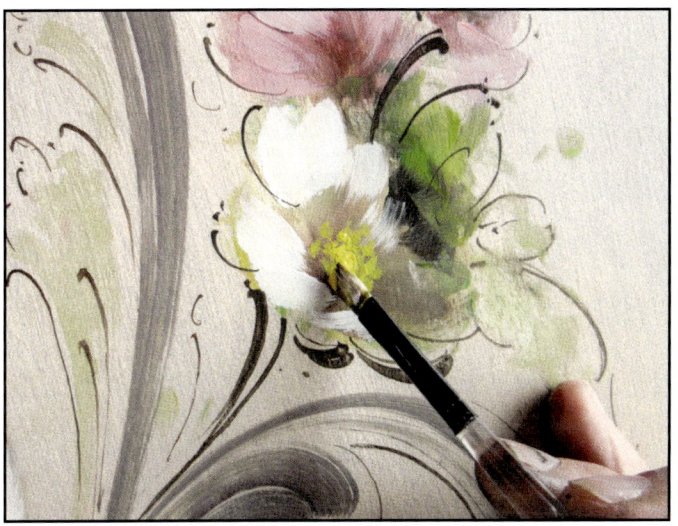
Step 75 Tap into the centers of the blossoms to add some interest. Soften as you go to the edges of the petals.

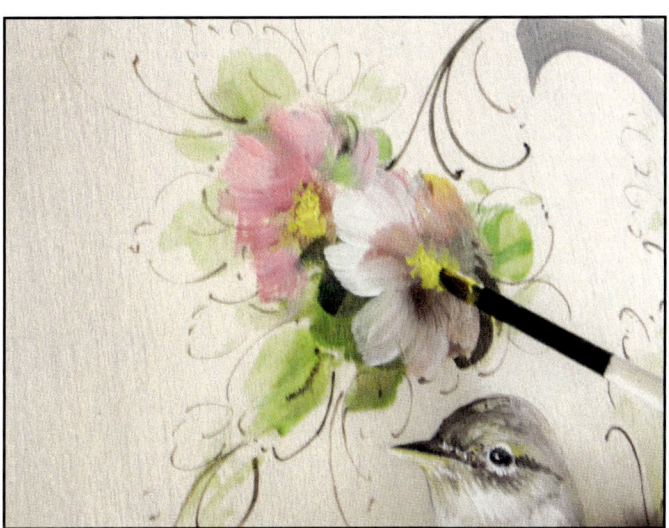
Step 76 Keep the centers softer near his head so they do not distract from him.

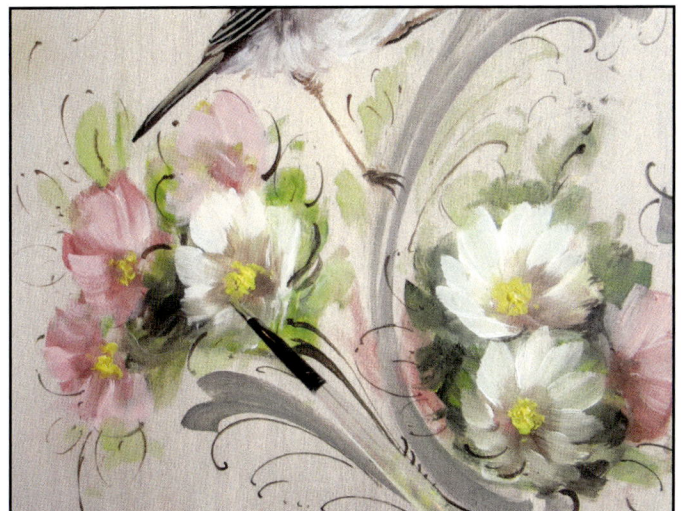
Step 77 Vary amounts of light for interest as you work through the design.

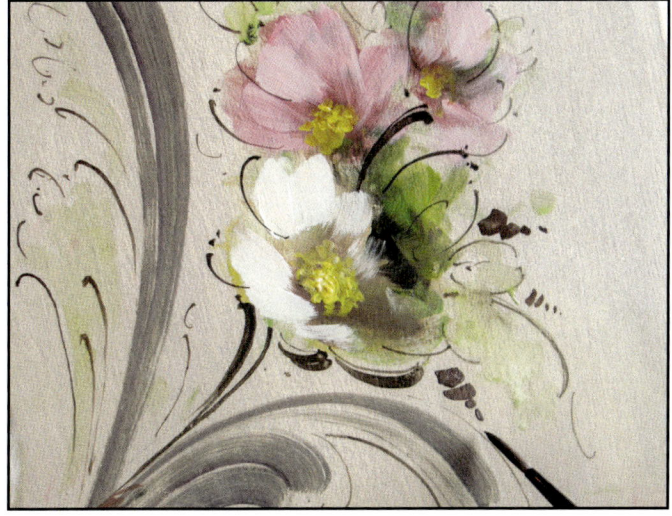
Step 78 Add final decorations with the round to finish. See photo for ideas..... Enjoy.

Rørsanger Enlarge Pattern 155% for Original Size

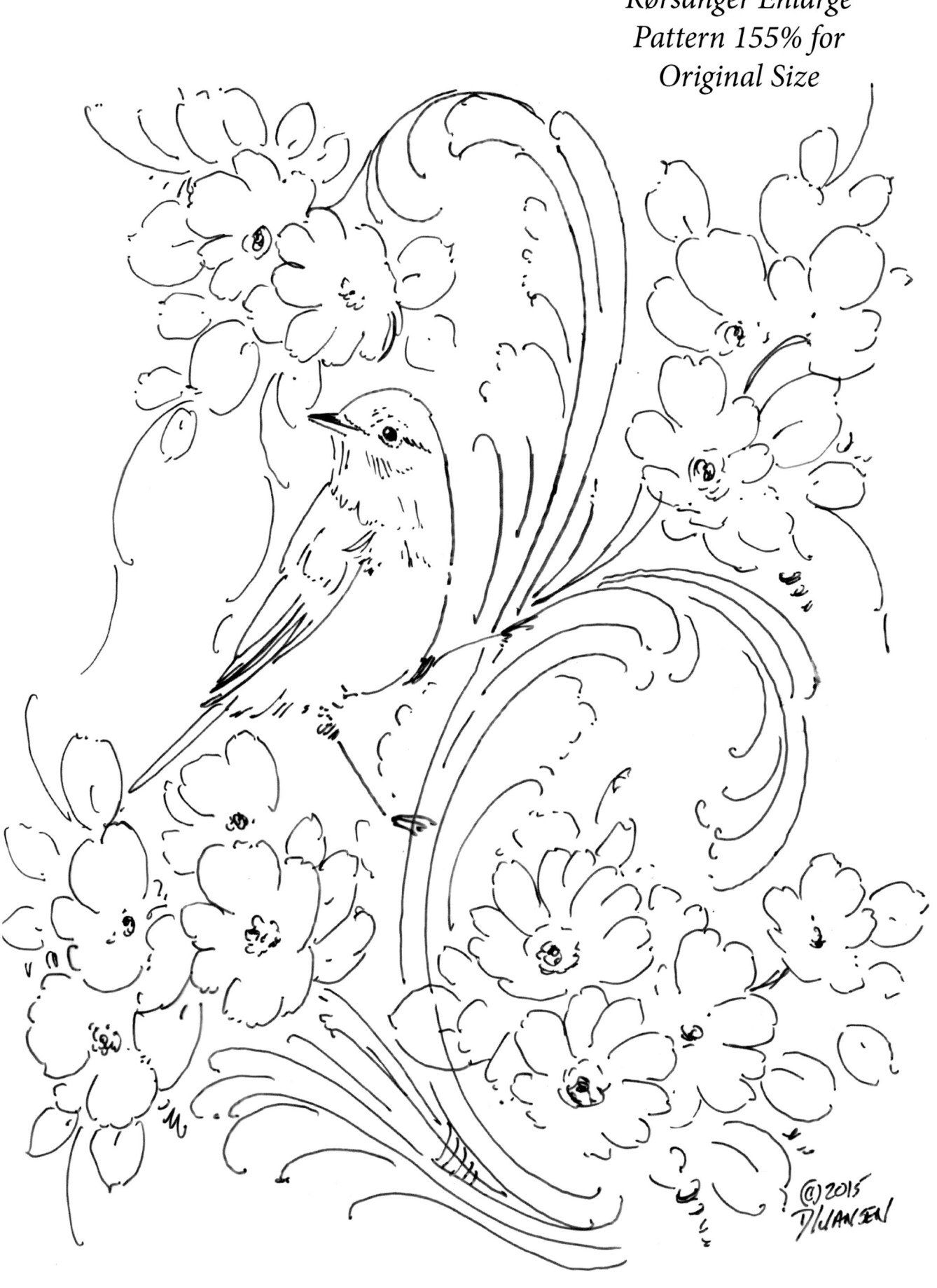

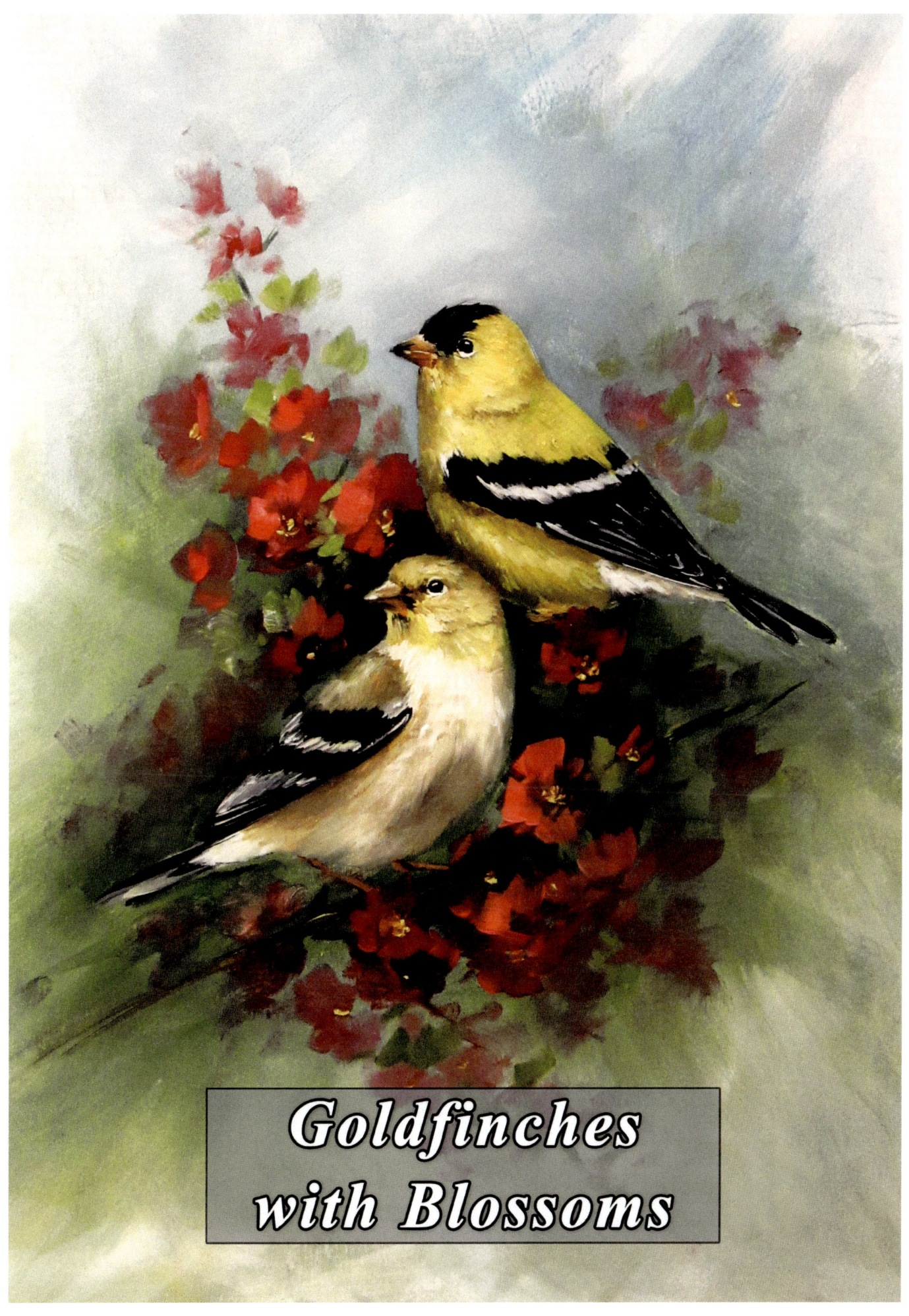

Goldfinches with Blossoms

I love the goldfinch. They are my favorite birds to paint. With this lesson, we put the male and the female together for the first time. When I designed this, I wanted the female to be closer to us. In nature, she is softer and more delicate looking than the male. I like softer colors and I guess this is one reason why I love to paint her. For the lesson, putting the brighter male behind the softer female will present some challenges. We want to make sure we can give her enough interest to sit in front.

As you paint the birds, always think about the relationship between the two. When you paint the beak for example, add just a little more to the female than the male. That will help her come forward. Notice the feathers on the birds. Both need feathers and we need to focus the feathers around the head, adding the most detail in that area. As an artists, you must always set a goal in the painting and constantly reflect back on that goal to make sure you are following your plan.

In this painting, he is brighter, but she controls the painting. Add details to her and then add the details to him. Return to her and make sure her details are more than his so she comes to the front. If he needs more details, make sure you paint them on her first, and use more. He must be softer in all details than her. If you get into trouble balancing the look between the pair, you can use the sfumato painting technique that I use on the last cardinal lesson. That will always help to adjust and control the interest.

The goal is to paint her a little softer, but with more detail and then place him, brighter, behind her and making him recede. It is important for the artist to learn to paint the objects in the painting and control the visual journey through those objects. Watch the application of your blossoms towards the end of the painting. Don't just stroke them. Apply them with thought and purpose. Paint them in relationship to the female Goldfinch. Let's give it a try!

Paint It Simply Palette
Base Color- White
Palette Colors

Naphthol Red Light	Titanium White
Red Violet	Medium White
Carbon Black	Base Brown
Phthalo Blue	Pine Green
Hansa Yellow	Burnt Sienna

Wood Surface
Super MDF Wood Panel about 14 Inch X 18 Inch to fit picture frame. Can also use canvas panel.

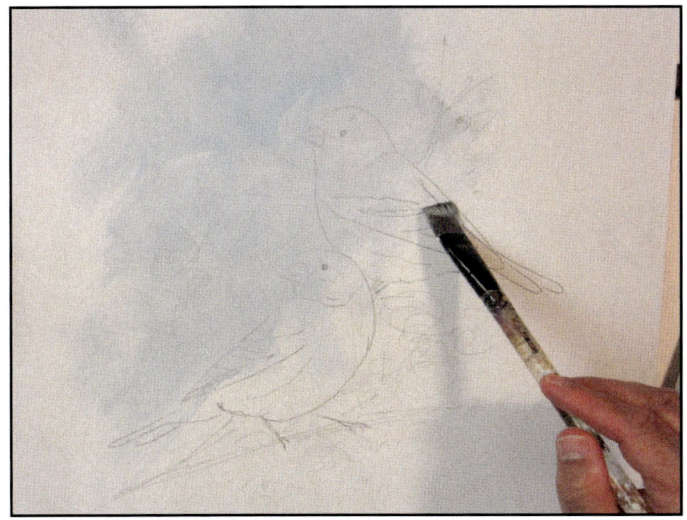

Step 1 Base board white and transfer design. Mottle blue, Red Violet and white to make sky color and go over the top of design.

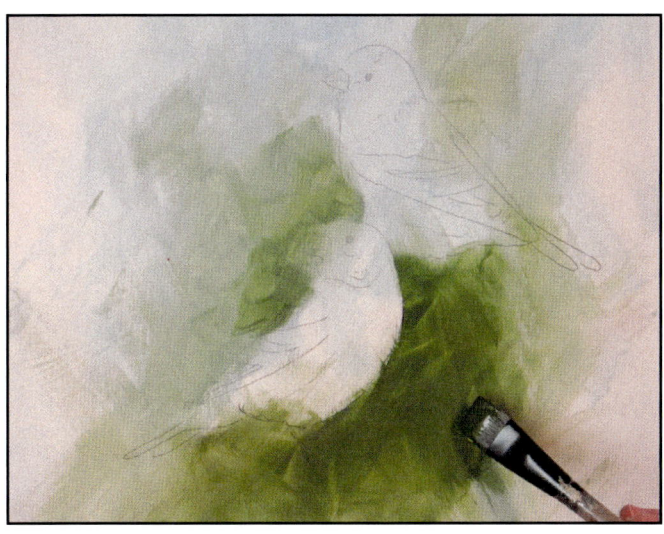

Step 2 Mottle greens, Hansa and black. Add some greens below the birds to help add contrast and add interest.

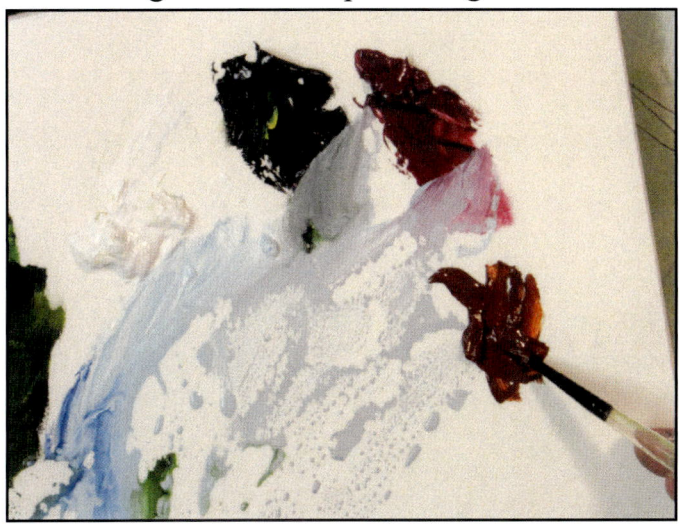

Step 3 Mottle the brush with Burnt Sienna.

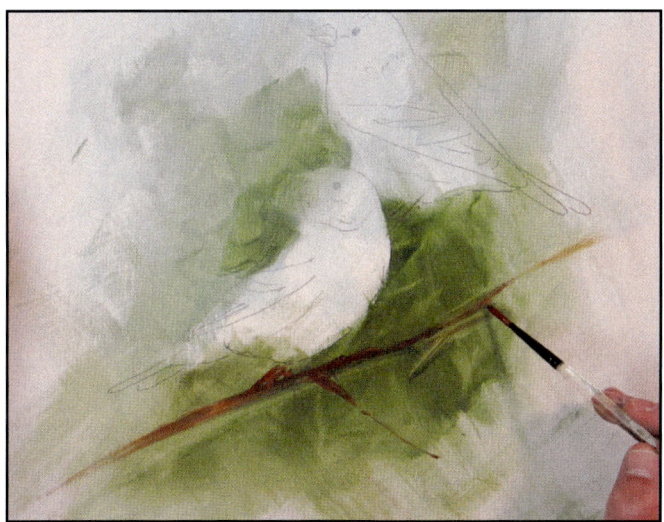

Step 4 Using the round add the branches under the birds. Most of this will be painted out later.

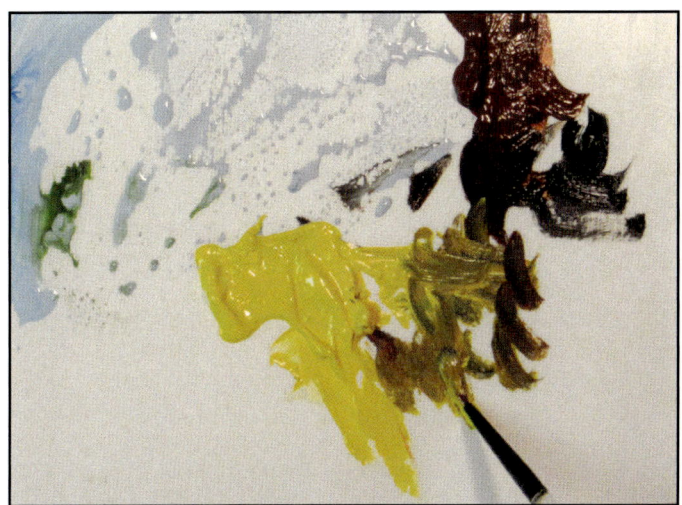

Step 5 Mottle Hansa with Burnt Sienna and touch black to tone. This is the color for the yellow golden finch.

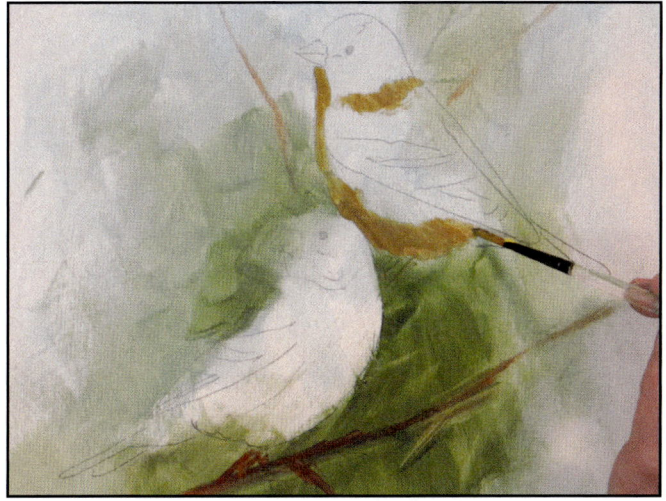

Step 6 Start with shadows under the male goldfinch. I used # 4 round brush.

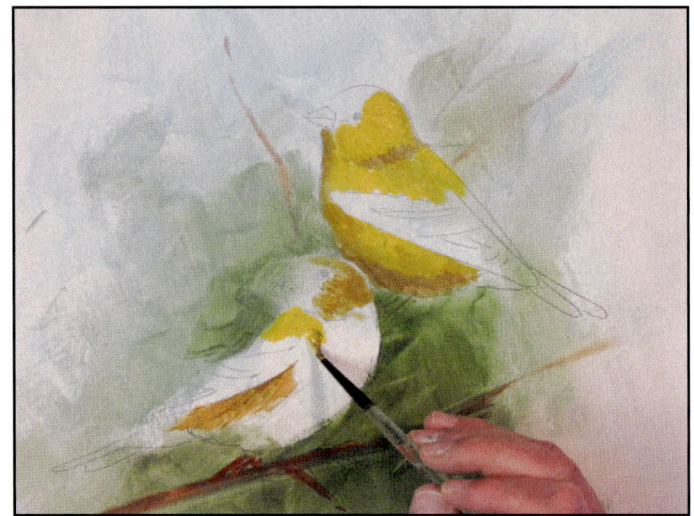

Step 7 Add some to her and then mottle brighter with additional Hansa and begin the body.

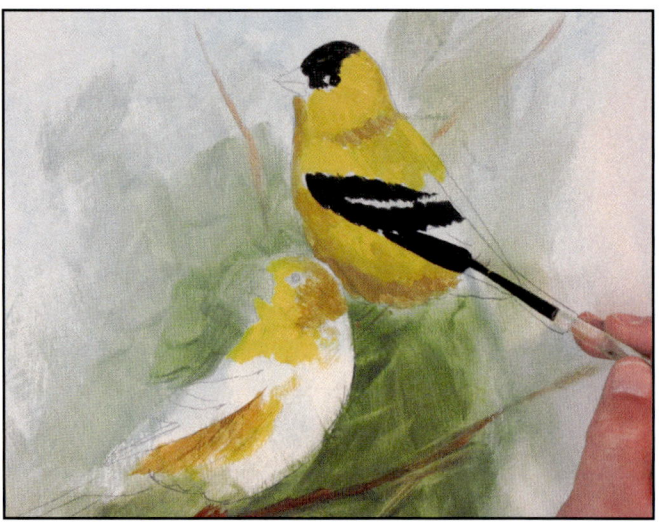

Step 8 Don't clean brush, mottle into black to darken and begin to base the dark areas of the male.

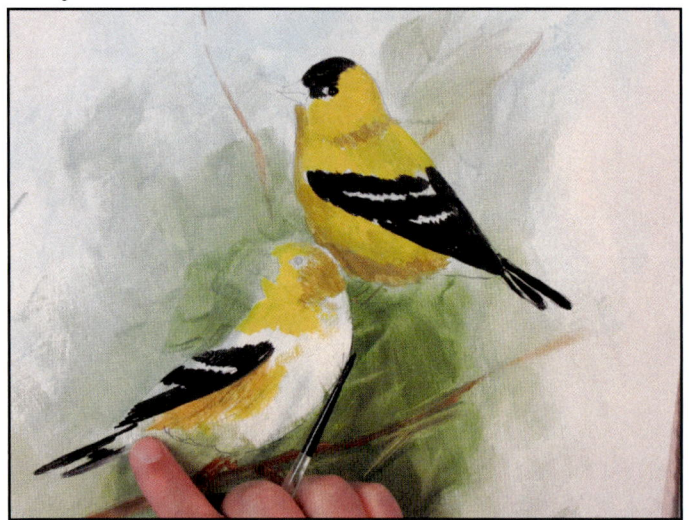

Step 9 Add the dark areas of the female and soften the colors with your finger. Add black to eyes.

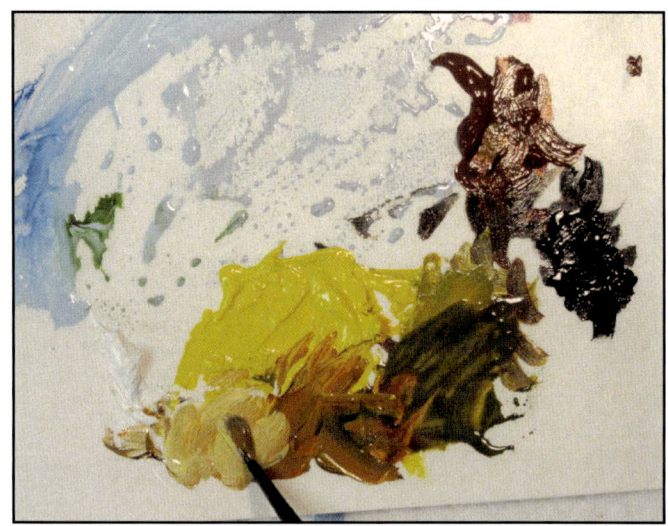

Step 10 Soften the Hansa with some of the Burnt Sienna and black, then lighten with some white to make tan color.

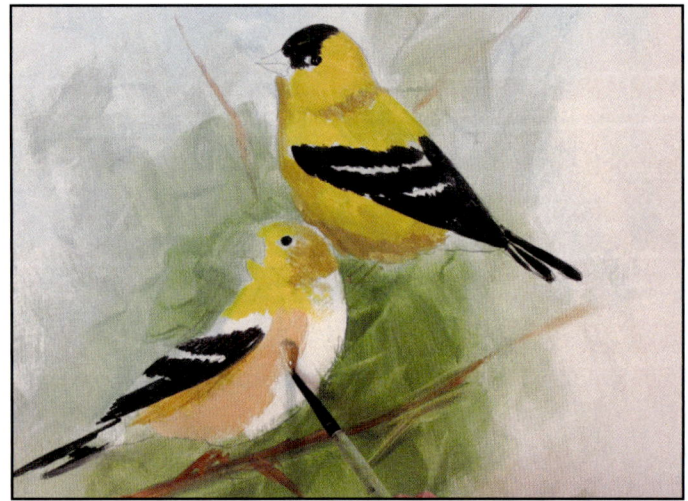

Step 11 Use this for the body of the female. Male is Hansa Yellow, female is tan color.

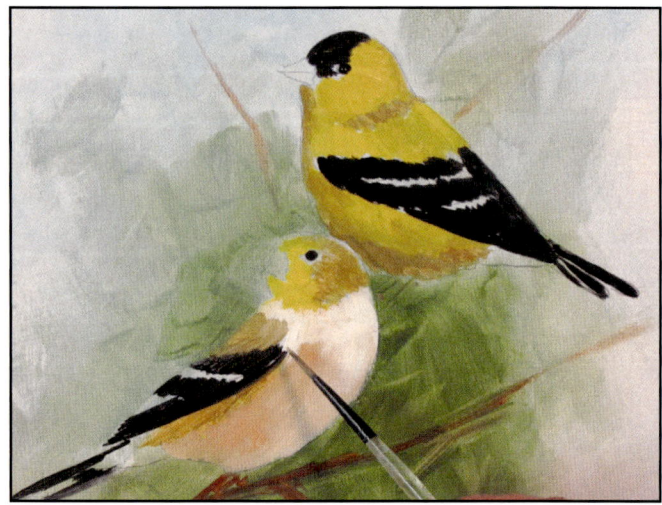

Step 12 Lighten the color with more white and add the neck area.

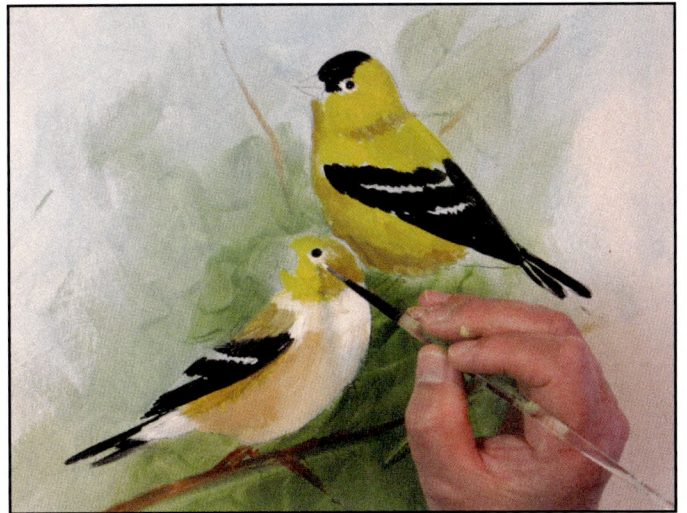

Step 13 Add some brighter yellows to the head of the female. Watch direction and size of strokes and you feather the head.

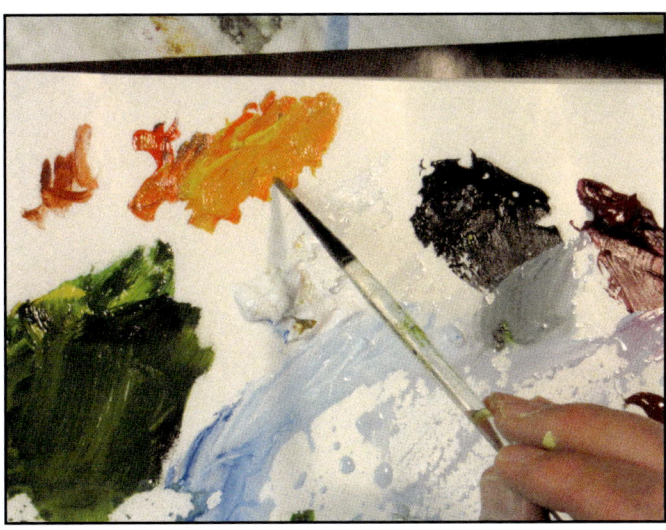

Step 14   Mottle an orange with reds and yellows using the small round or liner brush.

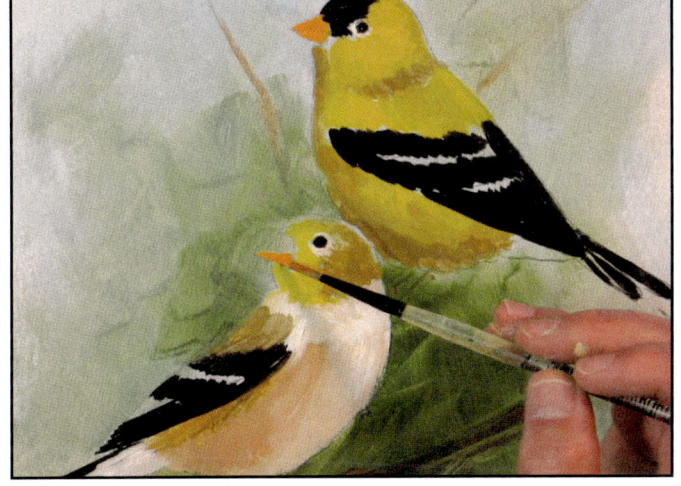

Step 15 Add the beaks of the birds. Top and bottom are the same color for now.

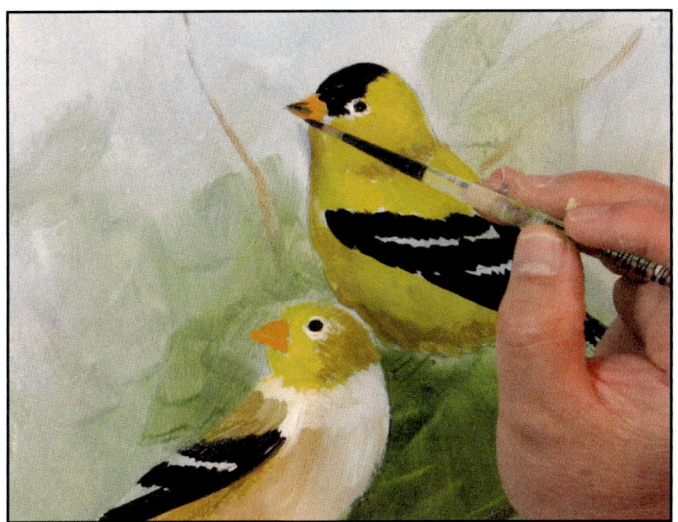

Step 16 Add some dark brown shadow to the top of the beak and pull just a little on the bottom of each one.

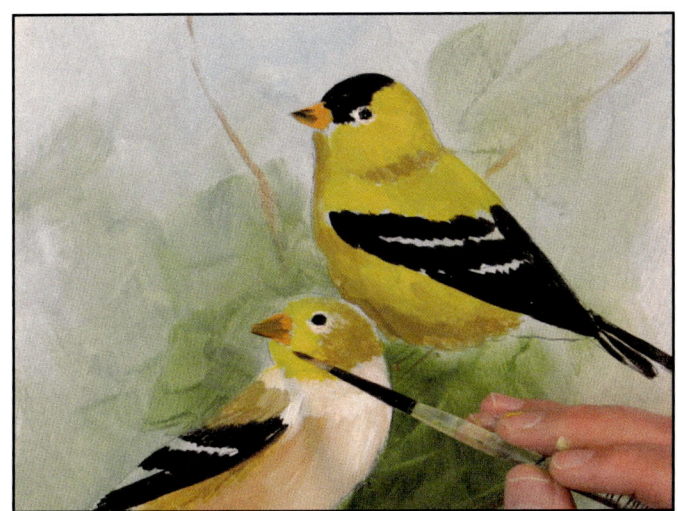

Step 17 Apply the shadow, we will develop further a little later.

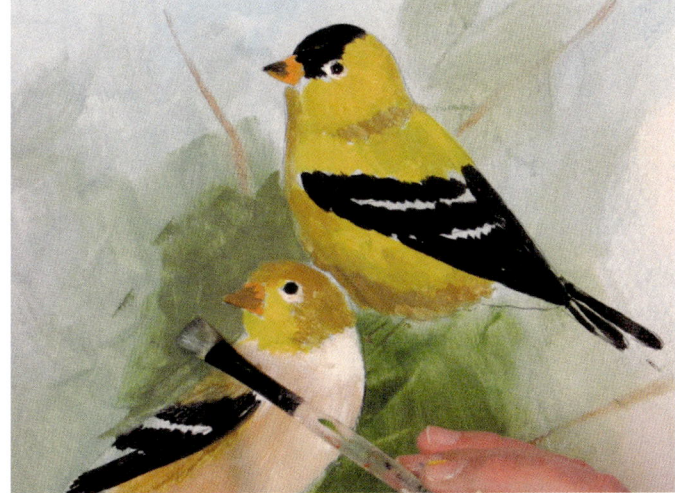

Step 18 Mottle some greens and add around the birds to help bring forward. More later.

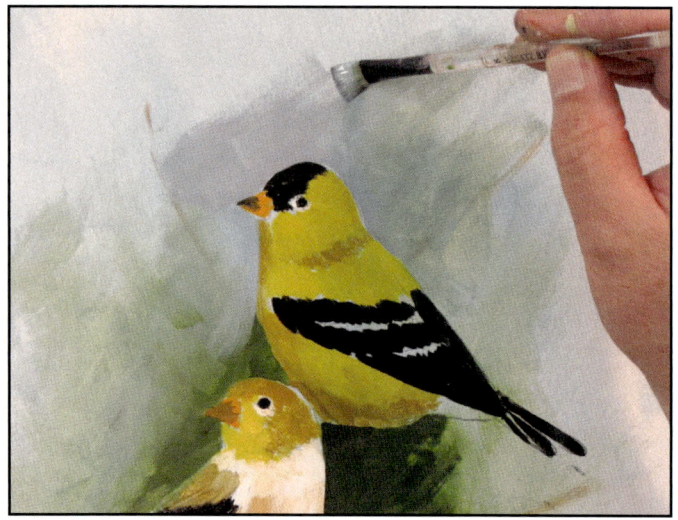

Step 19 Mottle a soft blue sky color, blues, violets and sometimes greens and lighten with white. Add around male to bring forward.

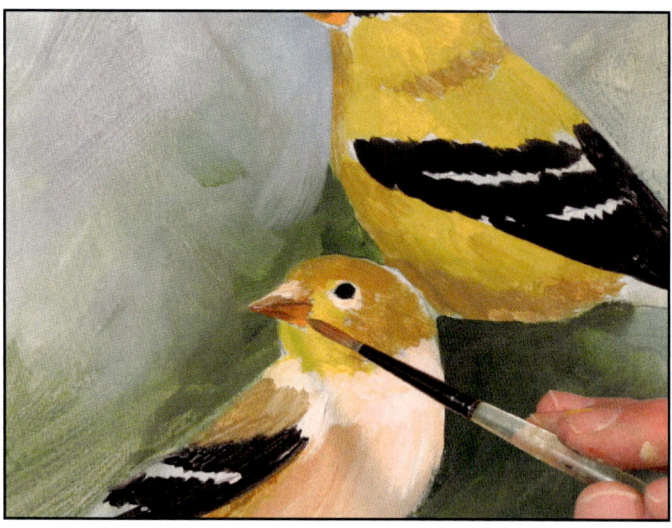

Step 20 Mottle oranges with lights and yellows and add to beak to define and break away from the greens and blues.

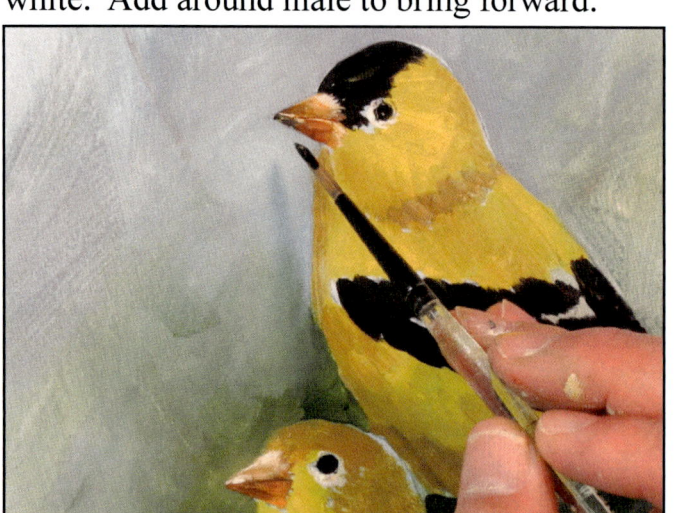

Step 21 Add some smaller touches of highlight to the beaks. Add thin line of light as separation of top and bottom beak.

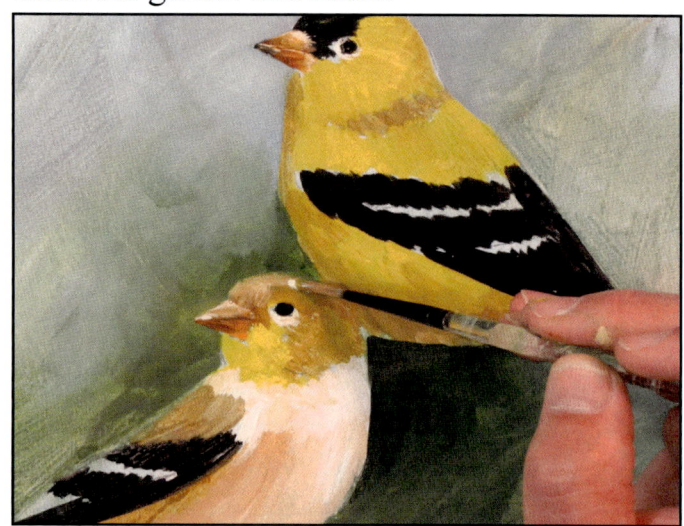

Step 22 Lighten the tan color with some more white and begin to feather the top of her head, following the contours of the head.

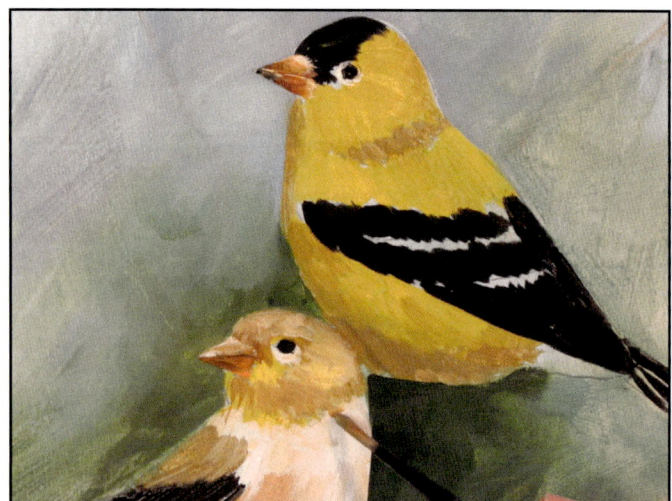

Step 23 Mottle with more Hansa and add some feathers to the head.

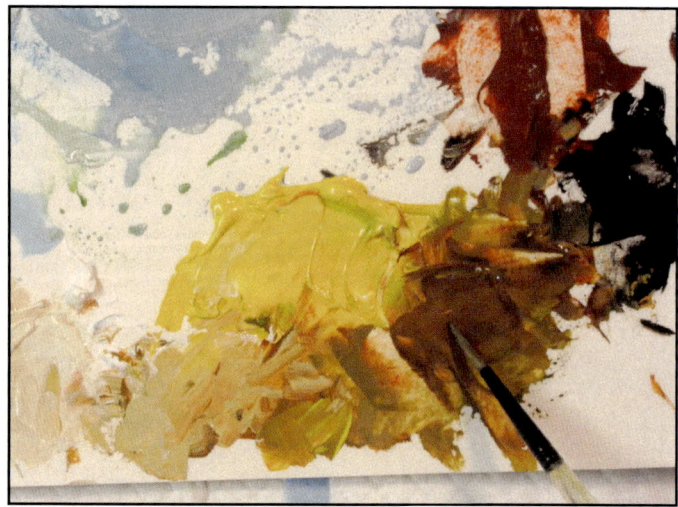

Step 24 Make the Hansa more brown with a small addition of Burnt Sienna and black.

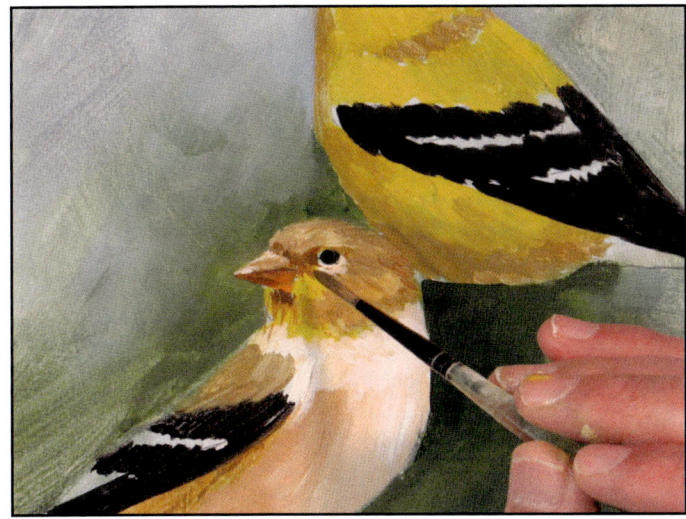

Step 25 Add some dark brown around the beak to contrast her beak. Then stroke some under the eye ring to make it come forward.

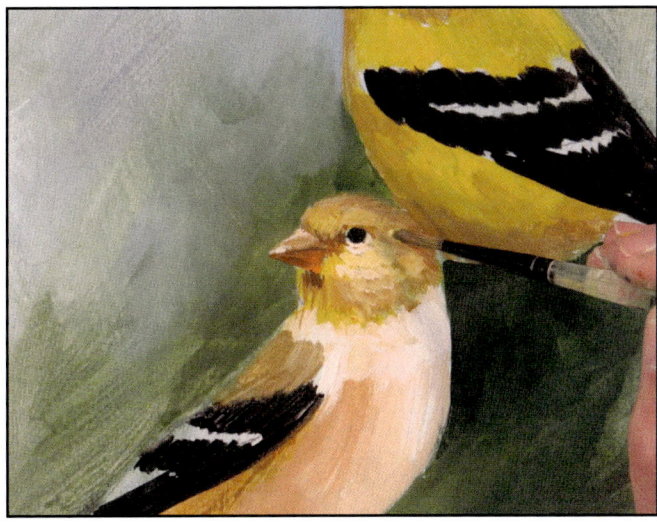

Step 26 Lighten the cheek area with smaller strokes. Remember she will have lots of detail compared to him.

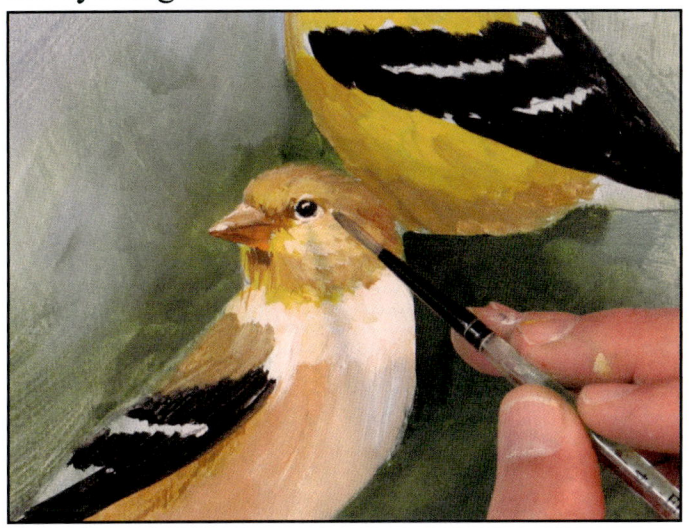

Step 27 Add the shine to the eye and tap some additional lights into the eye ring.

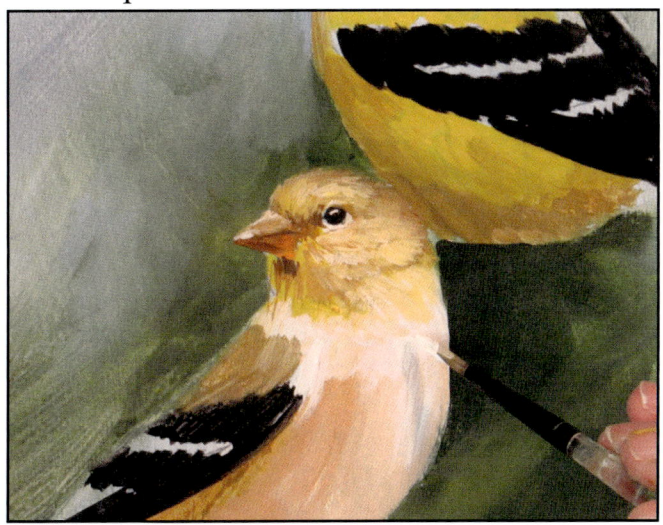

Step 28 Lighten the color and add some light feathers strokes to the neck area. Stroke down on top the mantle to set the wing.

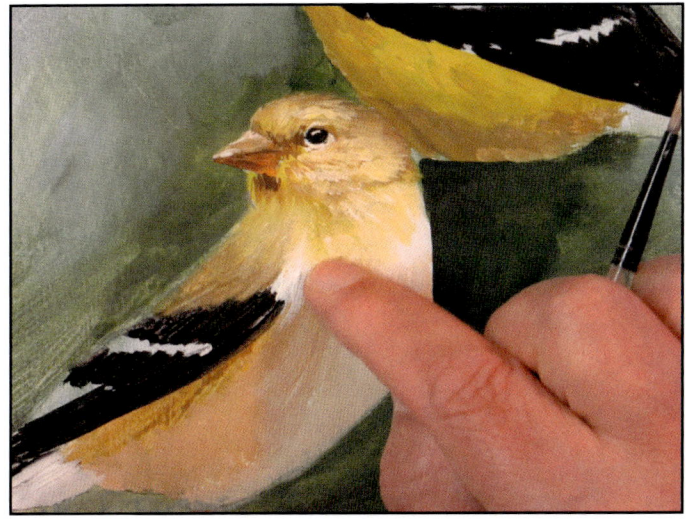

Step 29   Soften some of the color with your finger. Let her head have most interest.

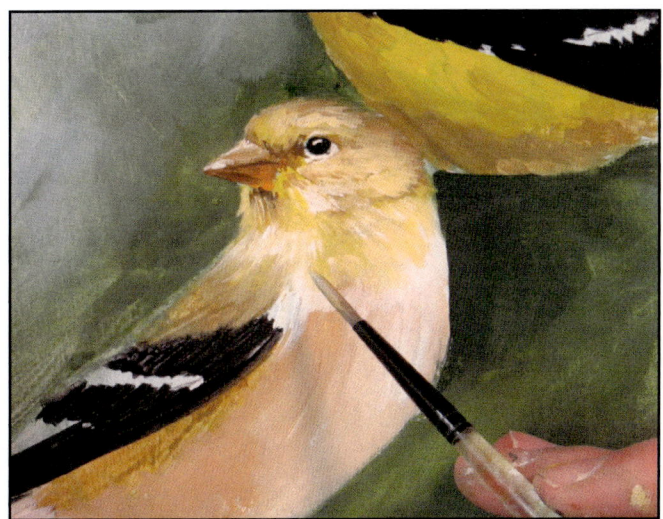

Step 30 Restate some feathers. I usually do this several times to establish the look.

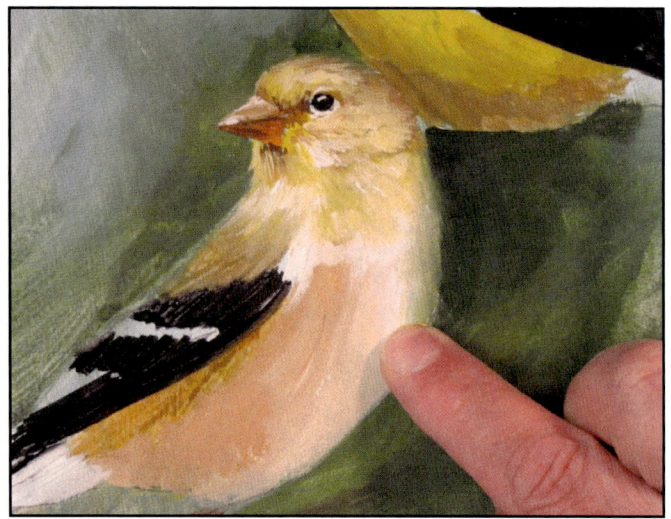

Step 31 Soften down the body with your finger establishing the movement of the feathers.

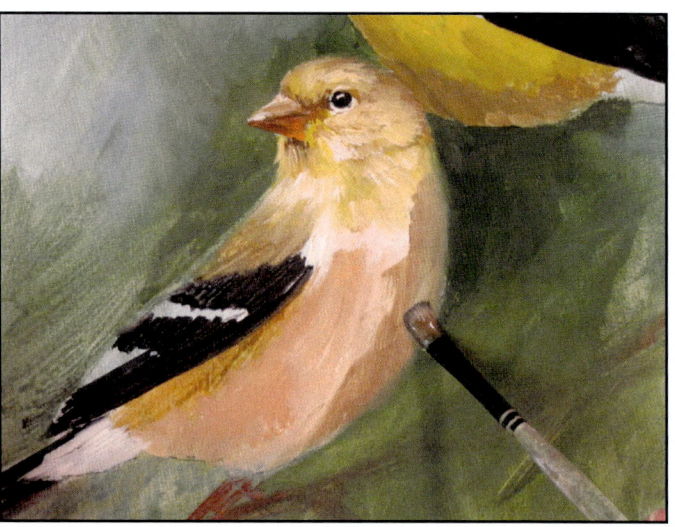

Step 32 Add some dark tan color down the right side. This will make her appear more round and help recede the right side.

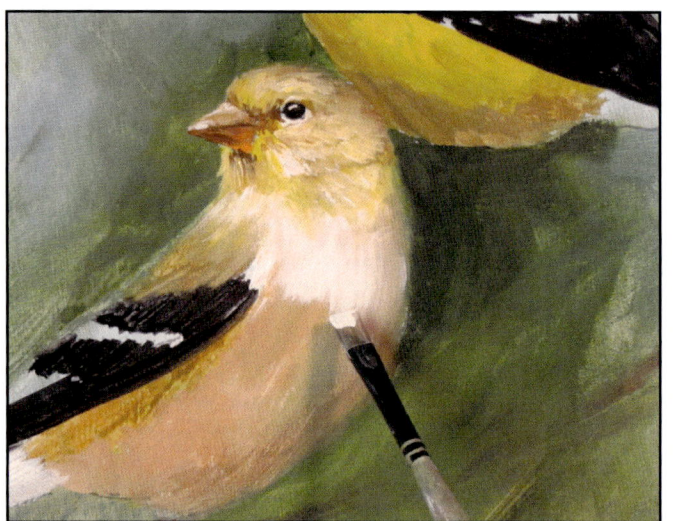

Step 33 Using the flat lighten with white add some body feathers. Use a little longer stroke and keep soft compared to head.

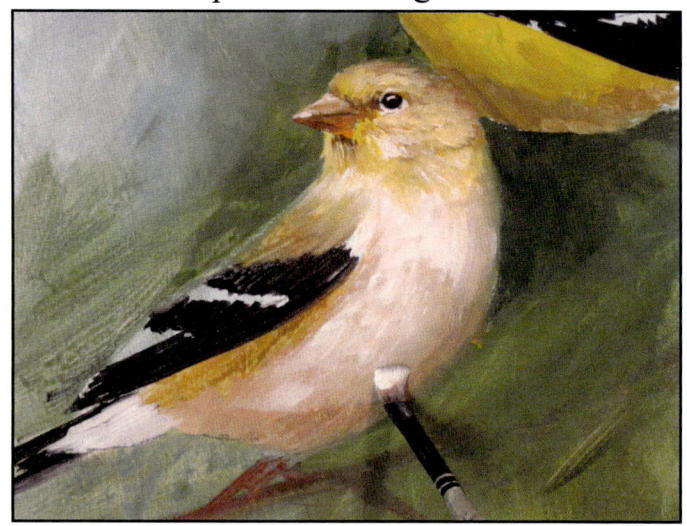

Step 34 Work the strokes down the body softening and letting the color run out of the brush as you stroke to make softer feathers.

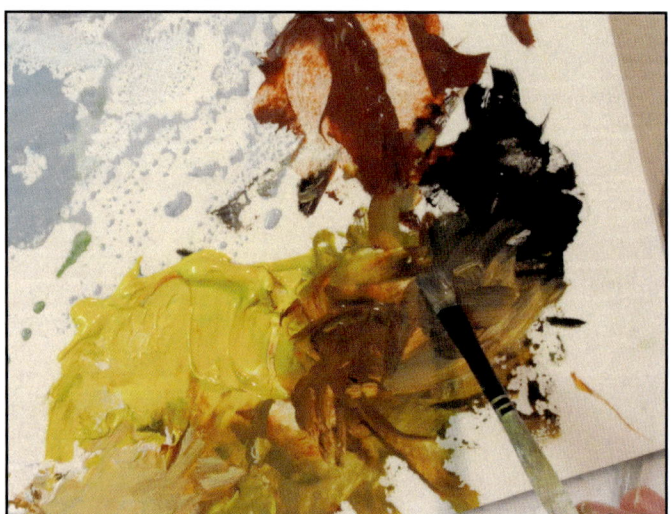

Step 35 Darken the color a little with some Burnt Sienna and touch black.

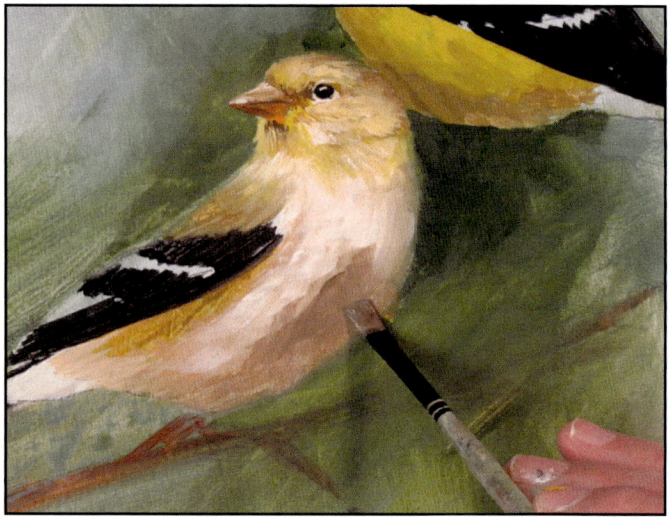

Step 36 Add the darker tan to the middle of the body as a large shadow for the breast.

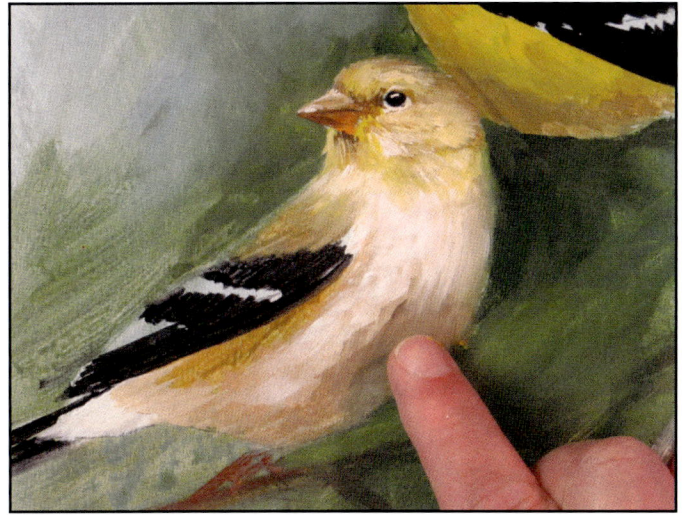

Step 37 Soften the shadow into the other lights with your finger, establishing the movement of the feathers.

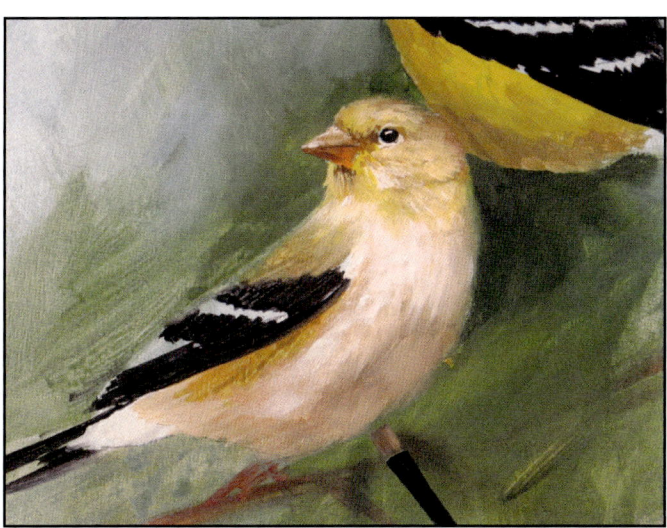

Step 38 Use the chisel of the flat to establish more movement of the feathers.

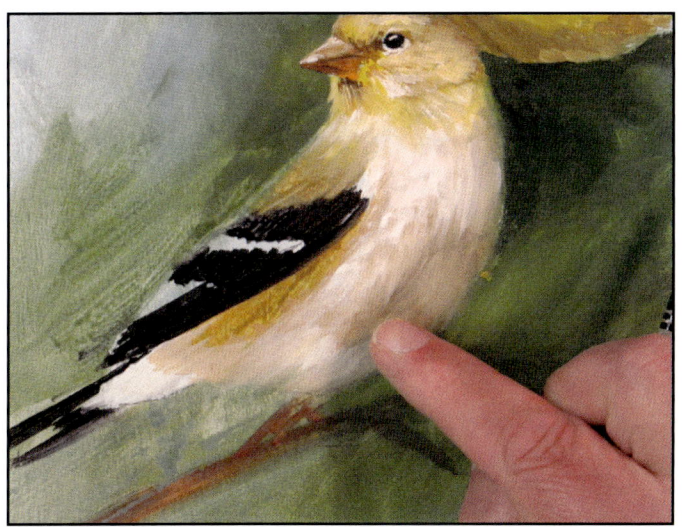

Step 39 Soften the strokes into the shadow. I do this many times... Feather with brush then soften with fingers.

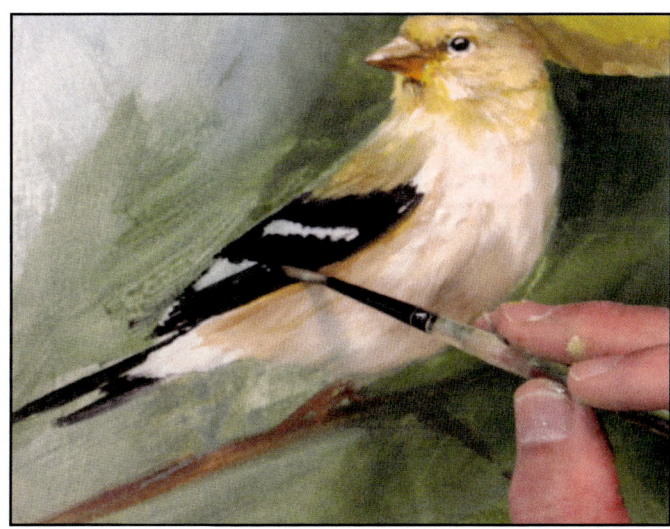

Step 40 Restate some of the darks for the wings with black and dirty tan on the brush.

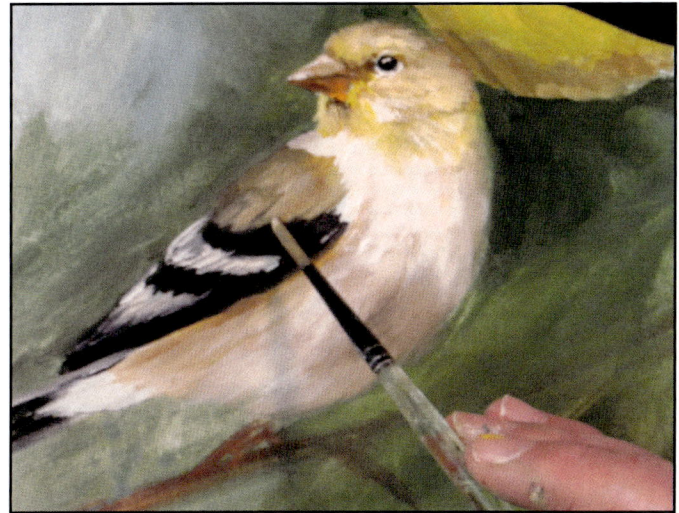

Step 41 Lighten the tan with some white and establish more movement on the mantle.

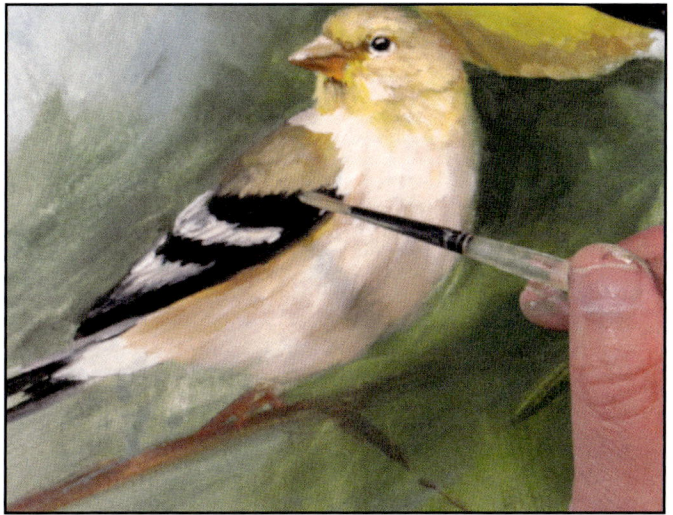

Step 42 Use the tip of the round and drag some tan over the wet black for feathers.

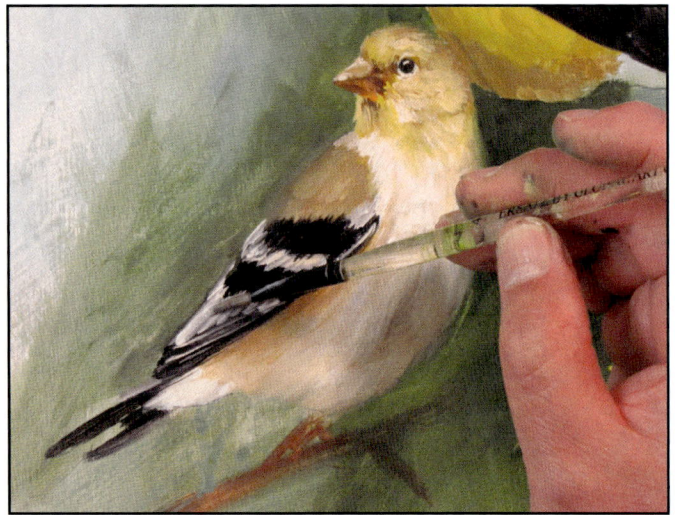
Step 43 Use tan and white and the tip of the brush to feather the light areas on the wing. If you get too much restate the black.

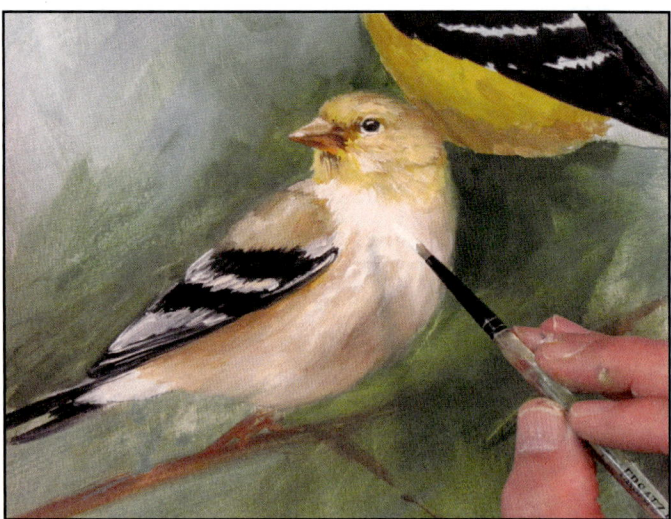
Step 44 Return to the whites and make sure they are heavy before we move to the male goldfinch.

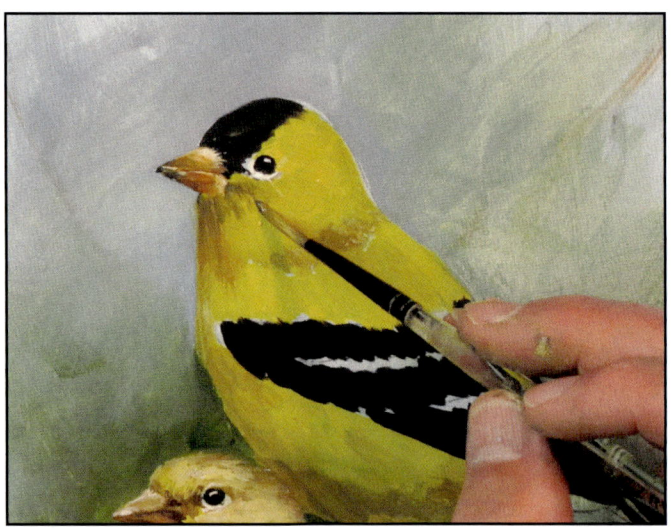
Step 45 Add some shadow to the head with Hansa darkend with touch Burnt Sienna and black. Add around the neck area.

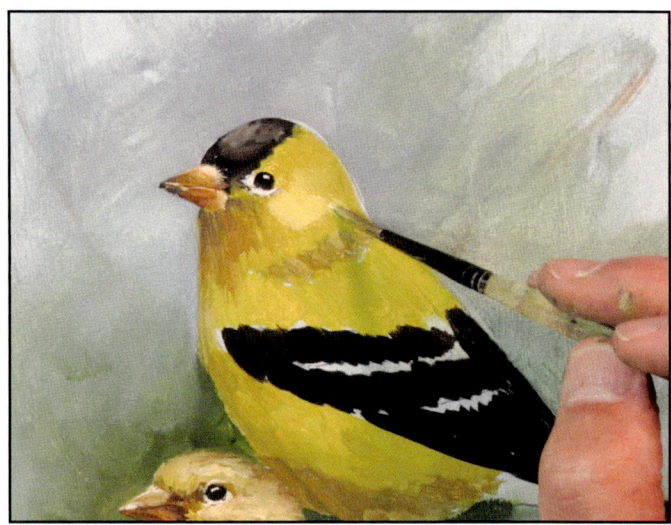
Step 46 Lighten Hansa with white and add the cheek area of the head. Keep a little soft in relation to the female.

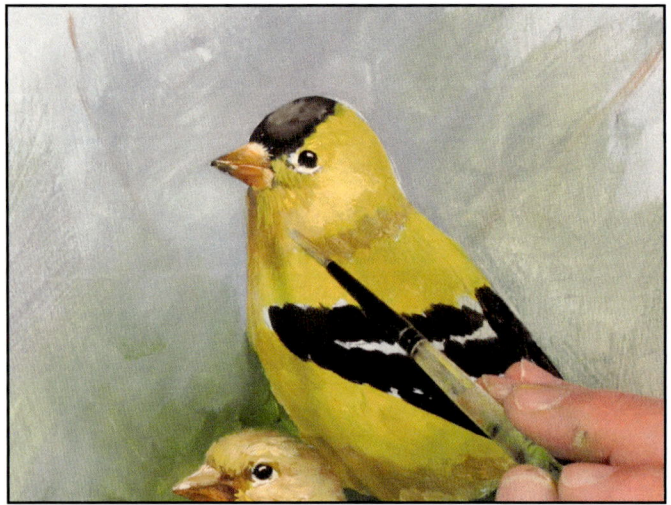
Step 47 Bring some of the light down the neck to soften the neck shadows.

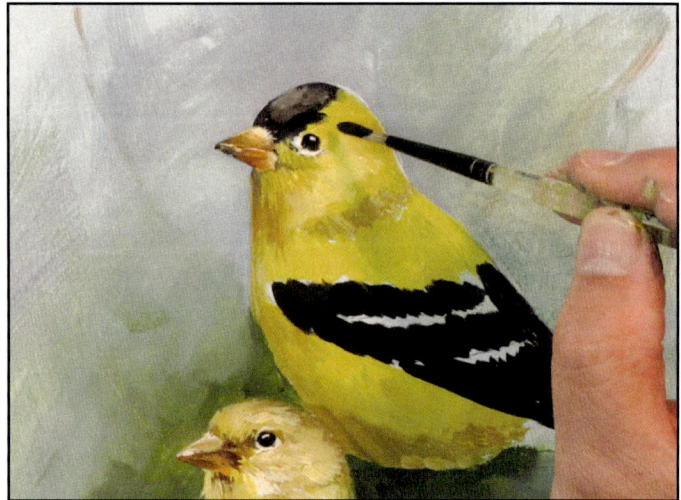
Step 48 Restate the darks on top his head with some black, pulling over the yellows.

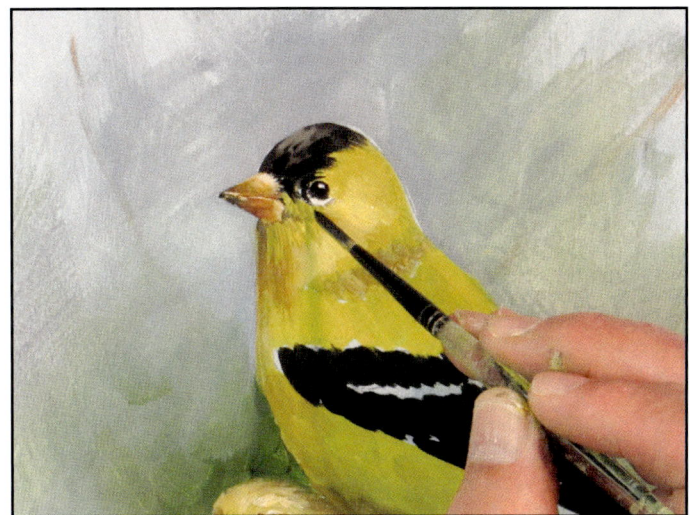

Step 49 Tap some light yellow around the beak. Then restate black and then yellow again to add interest.

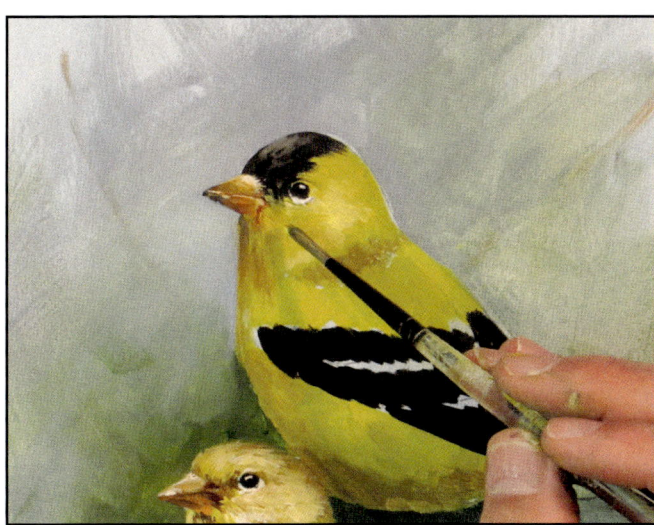

Step 50 Soften the colors with the brush. Remember not to give him more feather interest than her.

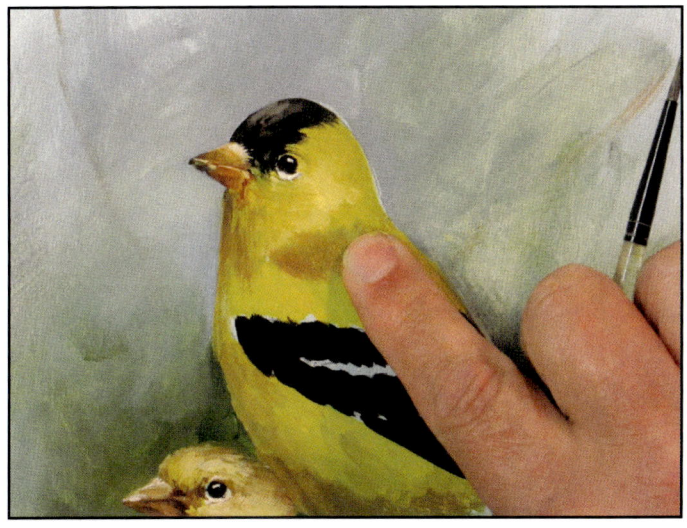

Step 51 Restate shadows with dark tan and soften with you finger.

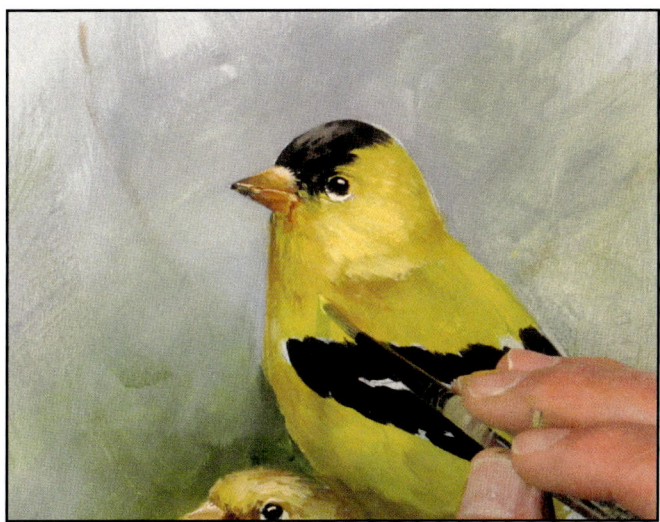

Step 52 Add some light yellow feathers again in that area and then soften with your finger.

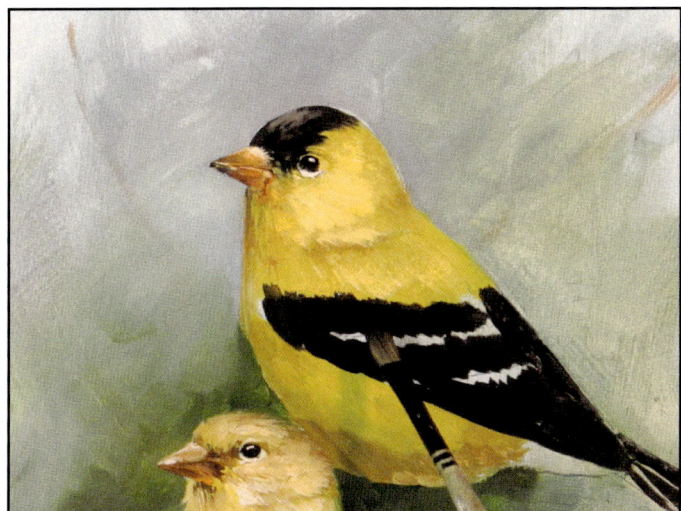

Step 53 Restate the black on the wings running some into the yellow for feathers.

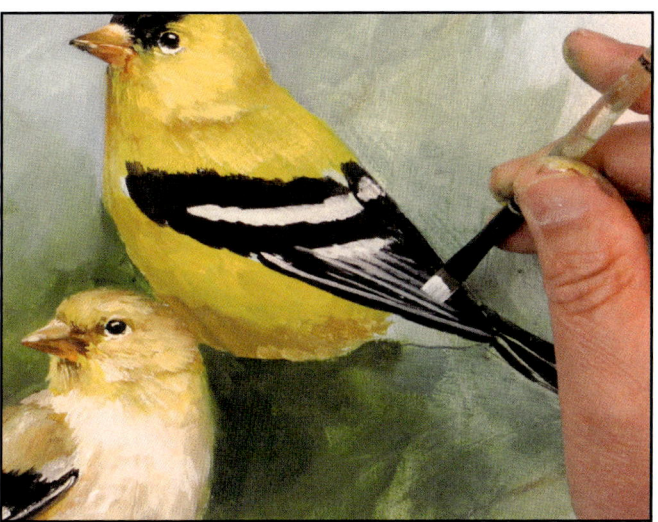

Step 54 Use the chisel of the small flat to make the primary, secondary coverts.

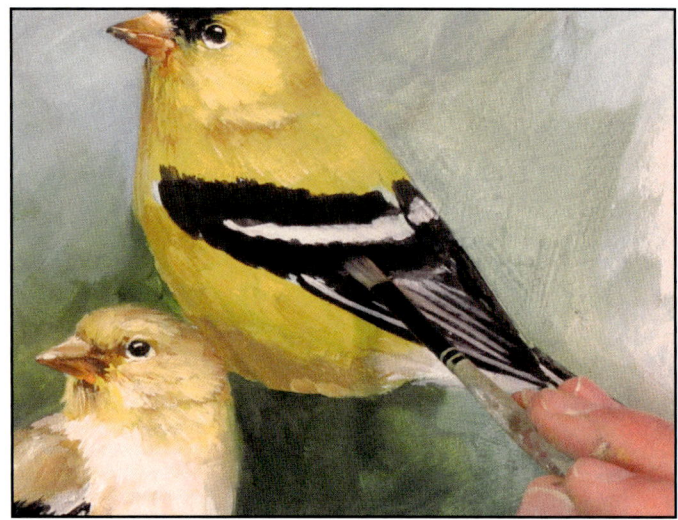

Step 55 Restate the black on the wings of the bird. This is to make wet, but extend some into the white areas of the wing.

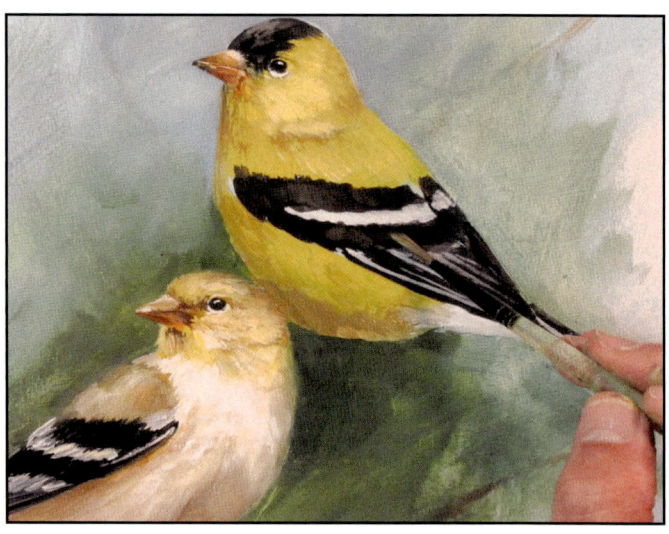

Step 56 Add some brownish grey to the black areas of the wings to add movement and feathers.

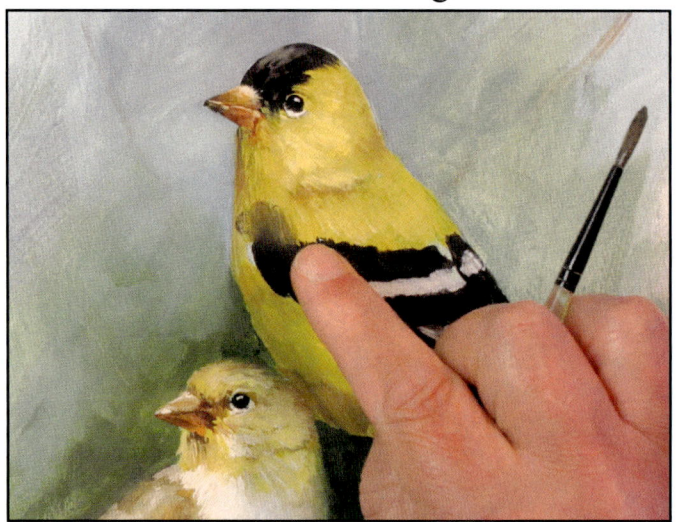

Step 57 Add some brownish grey to the front of the mantel to shadow, then soften with your finger.

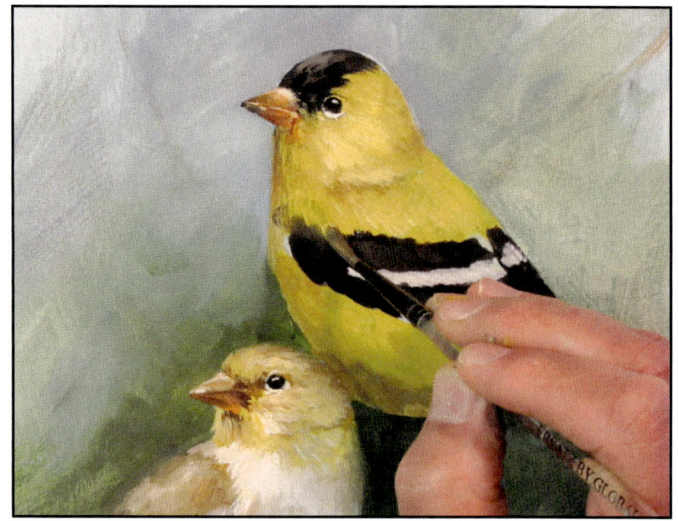

Step 58 Pull some strokes of light yellow down over the shadow you just applied to give the look of feathers.

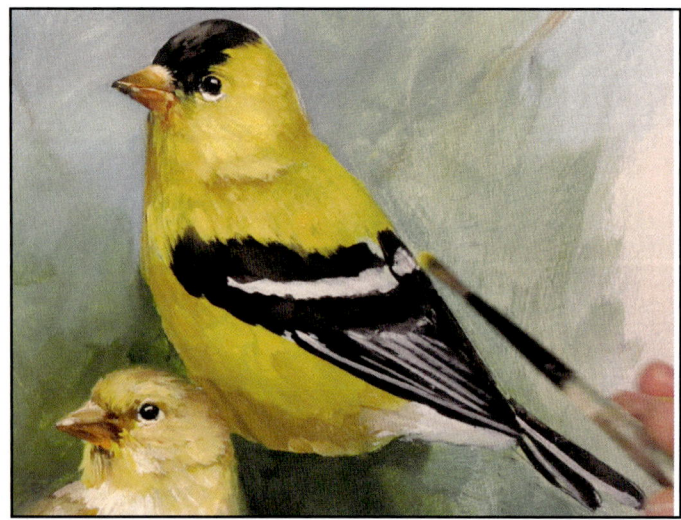

Step 59 Notice the uneven edge of the black and yellow. Pull feathers different lengths.

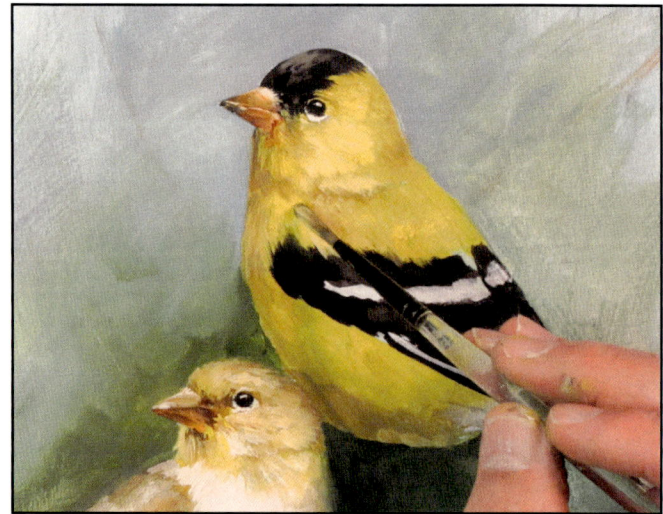

Step 60 Restate some shadows to the neck area and then restate some lights to refine.

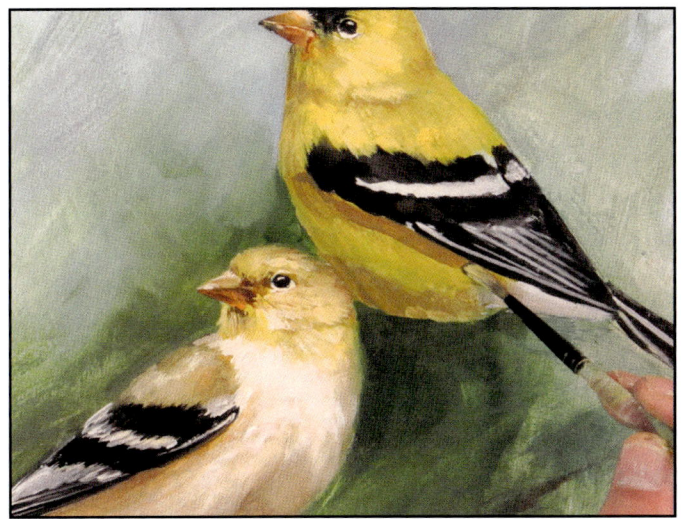

Step 61 Add some shadow under the wind of the male with the darker tan color from the female. This adds harmony as well as shadow.

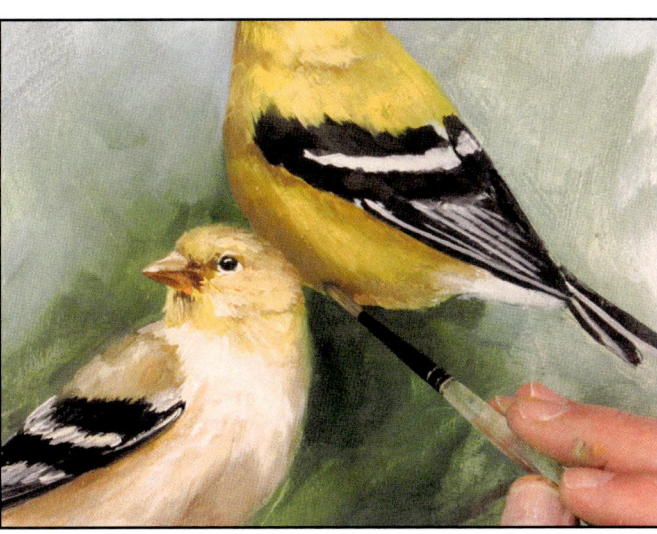

Step 62 Darken the color of the right side which not only increases roundness, but will push the female's head forward.

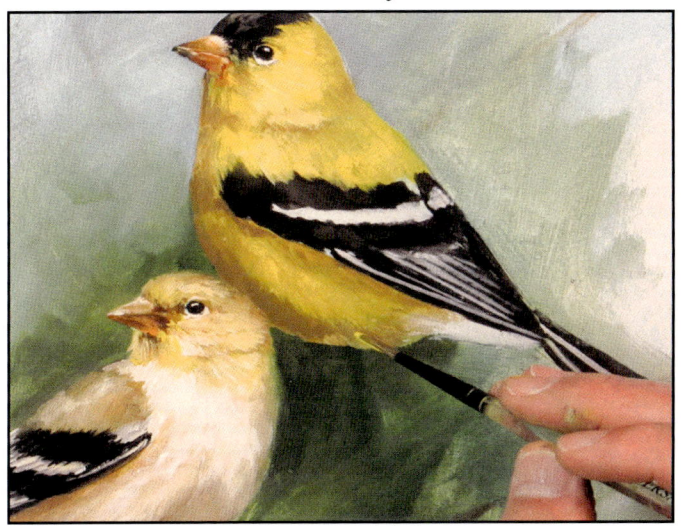

Step 63 Begin to feather over the shadows you just applied with some lighter Hansa and # 4 round.

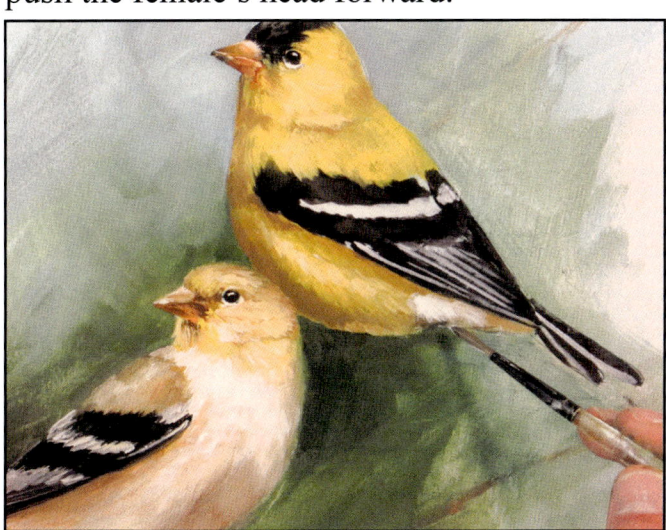

Step 64   Add the white feathers to the base of the tail with short feather strokes.

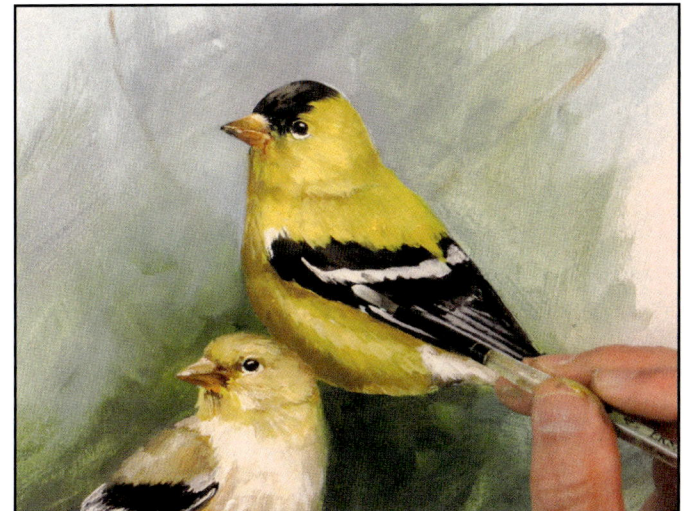

Step 65   Reinforce the white bands on the wings with more white.

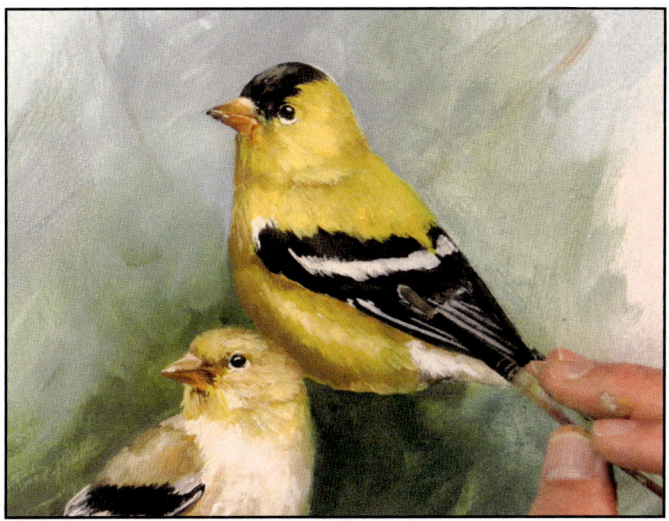

Step 66 Add some streaks of white to the wing with the point and chisel of the round.

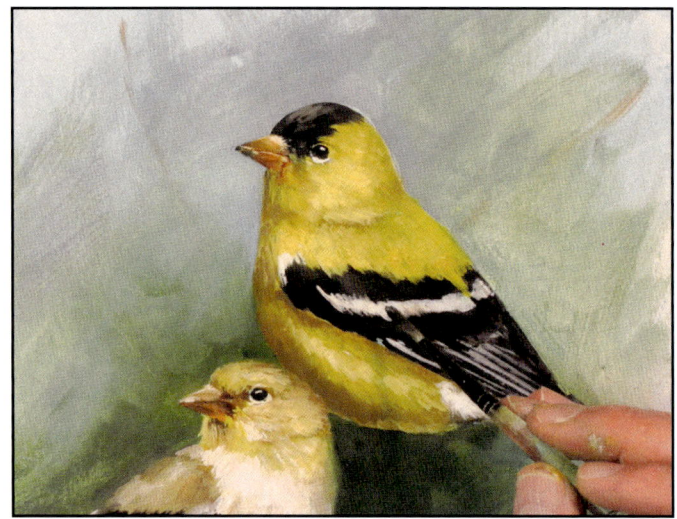

Step 67 Pull the white bands different lengths and restate the black if needed to vary the feathers.

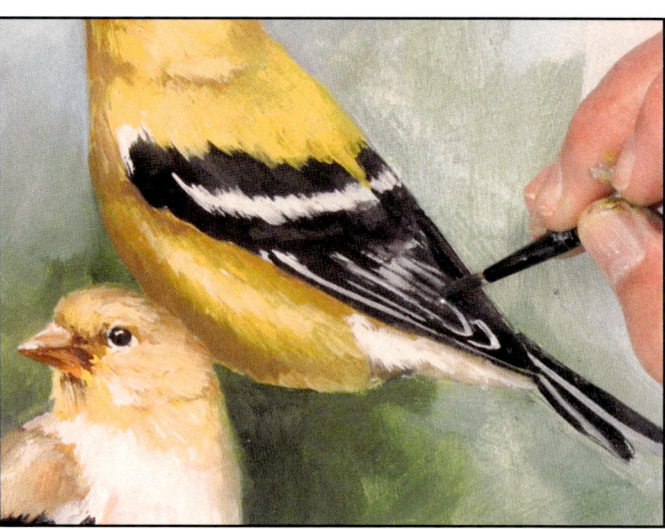

Step 68 Use the point of the round to add the covert details. Paint on the various feathers.

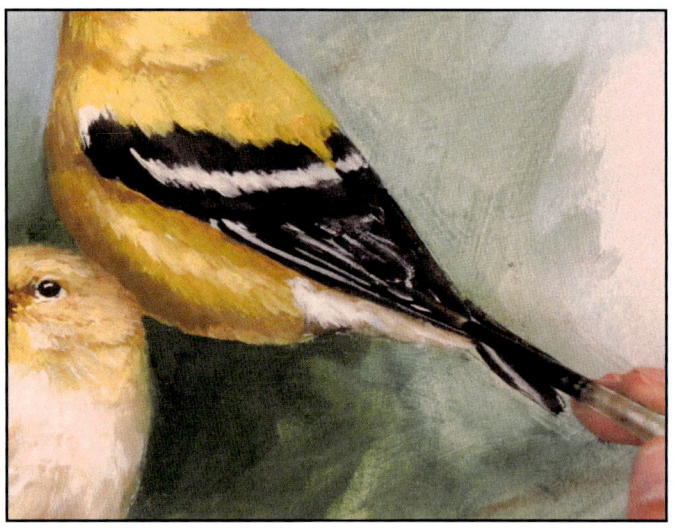

Step 69 Mottle the brush with some black and paint out some of the white to refine the detail on the feathers.

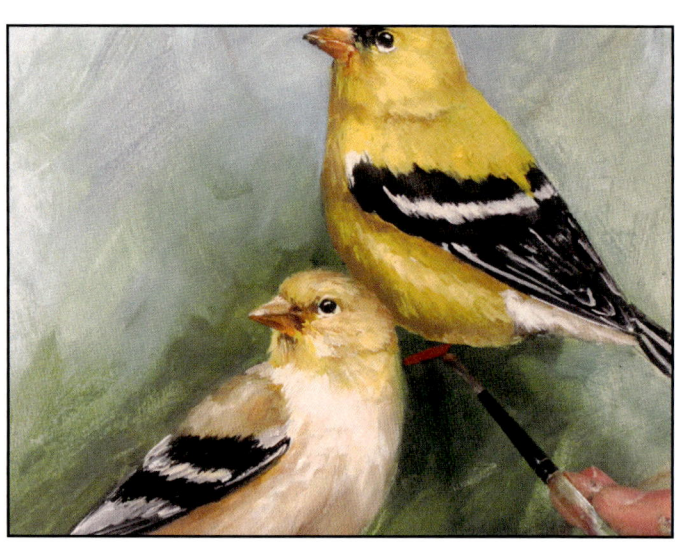

Step 70 Add the suggestion of his leg with some Burnt Sienna.

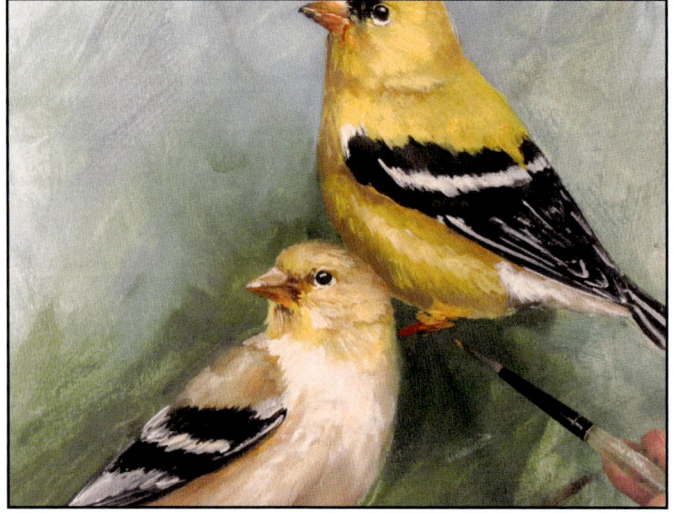

Step 71 Feather over the leg with some Hansa Yellow.

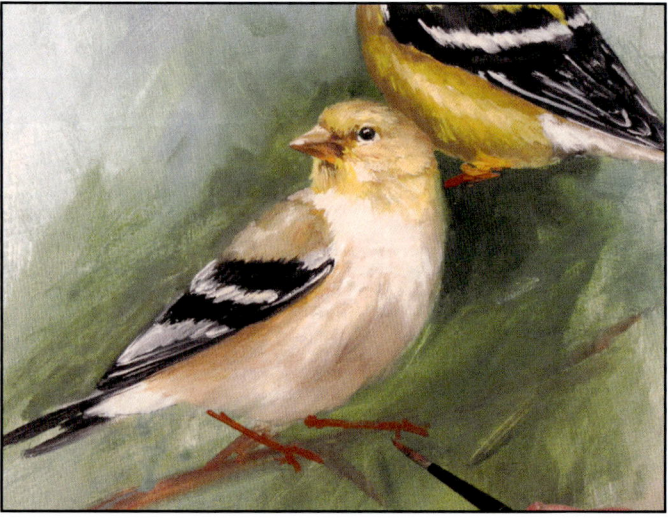

Step 72 Add the legs to the female with some Burnt Sienna.

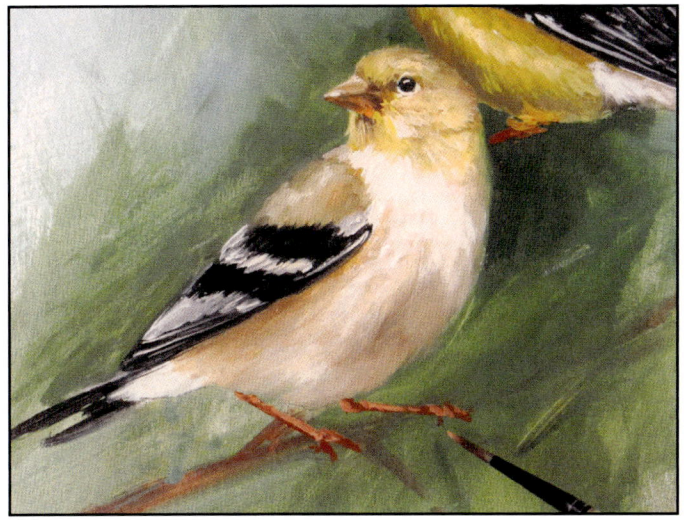

Step 73 Mottle the Burnt Sienna lighter with a touch of white and Hansa, then add some highlights to the legs.

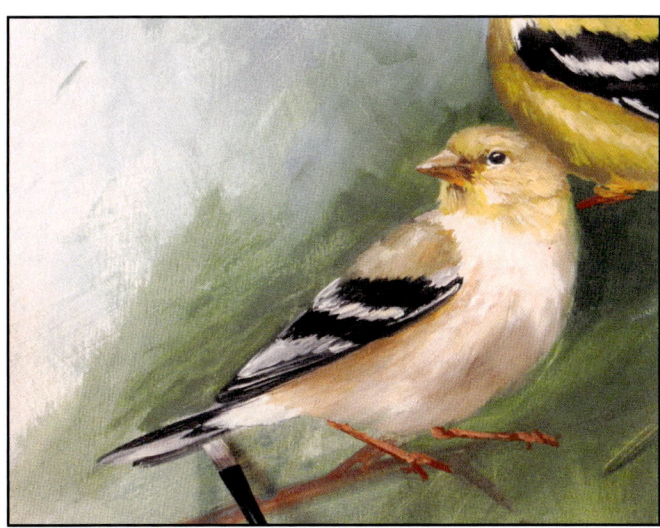

Step 74 Use the chisel of the small flat and add some lights to the tail feathers.

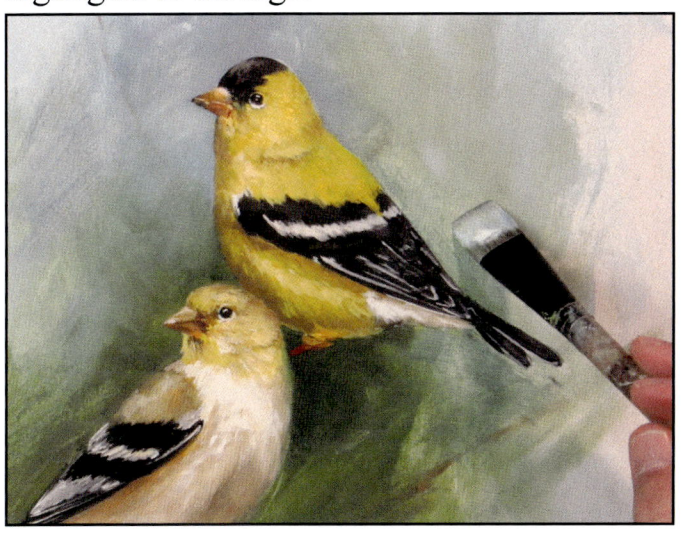

Step 75 Using the larger flat, make the sky behind the male more opaque. This will help push him forward.

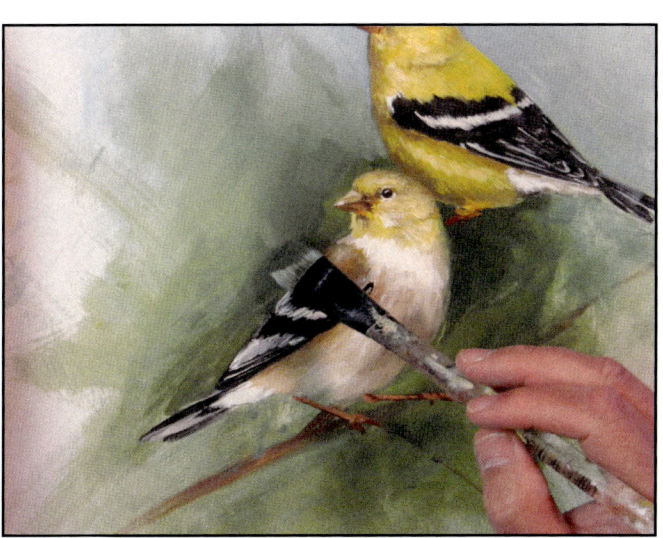

Step 76 Mottle the brush with some green and add behind the female to push her forward.

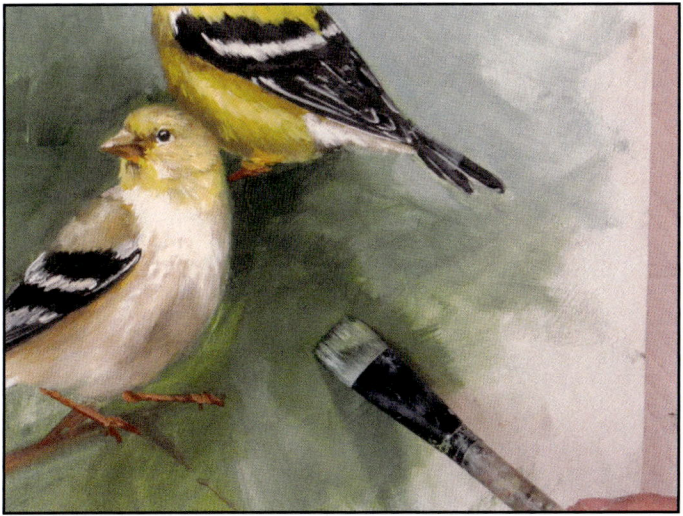

Step 77 Brighten the color with some Hansa and white and add below the female.

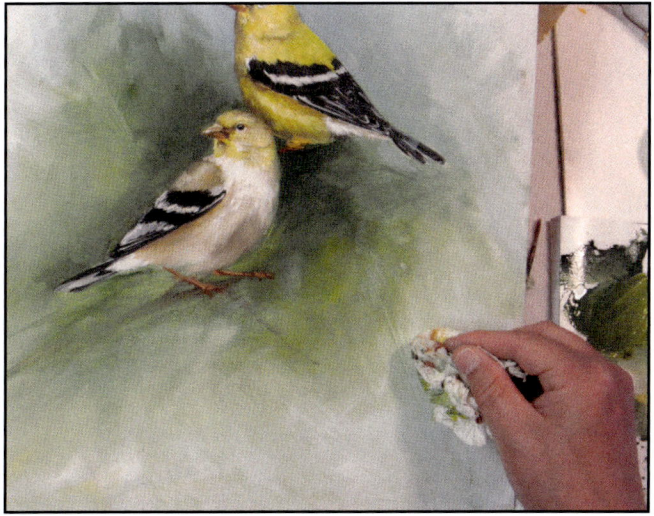

Step 78 To vignette the birds, wipe the green off with a paper towel to soften edges.

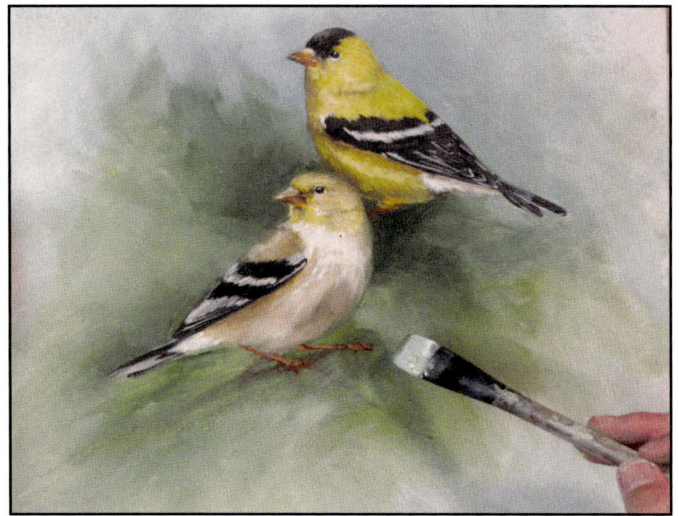

Step 79 Mottle the greens a little lighter and streak into the greens for interest.

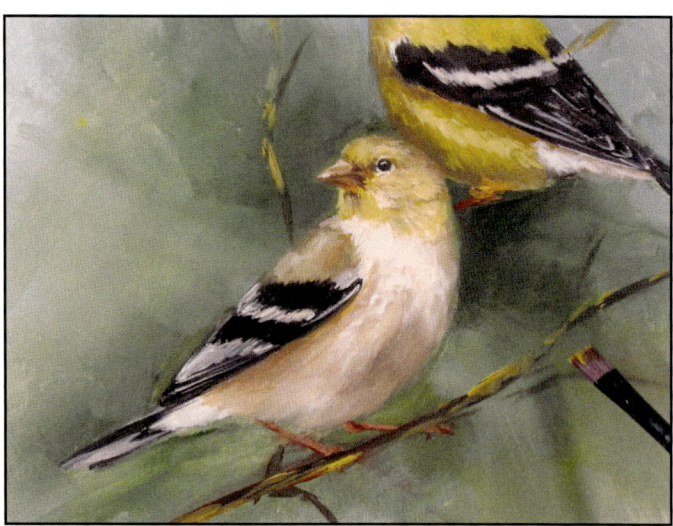

Step 80 Restate the branches with some browns and Hansa. Lighten with white and tap highlights.

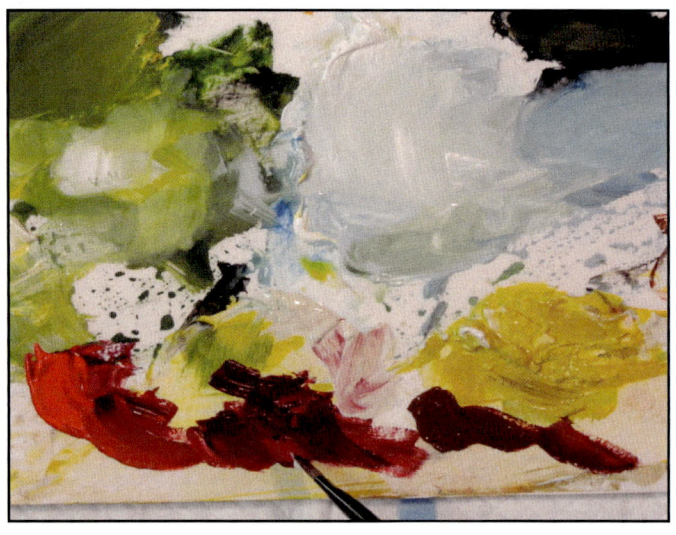

Step 81 Mottle a flat with both reds. When we paint the small flowers it is very important to vary the colors on the brush.

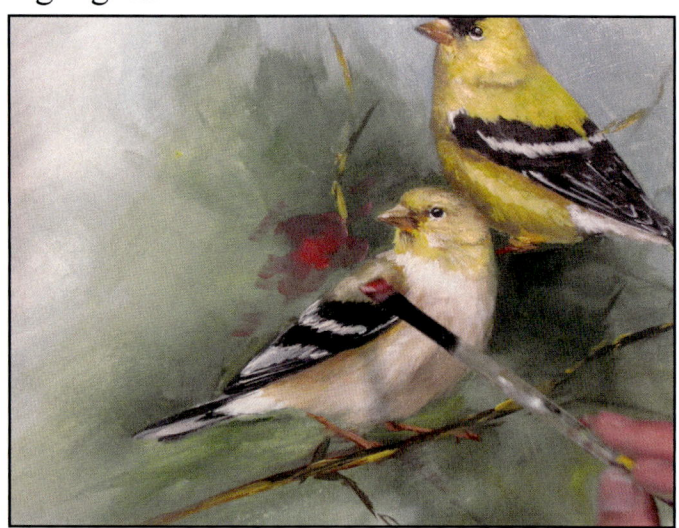

Step 82 Begin to set the reds into the wet paint both greens and sky.

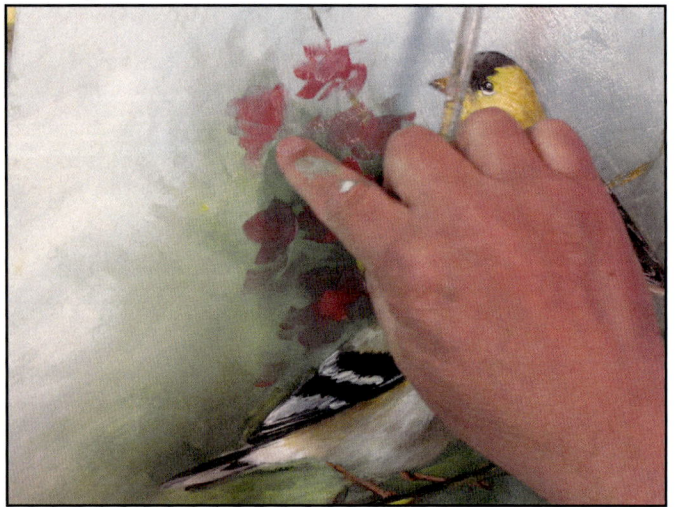

Step 83 Soften the flowers with your finger. This is especially important in the back.

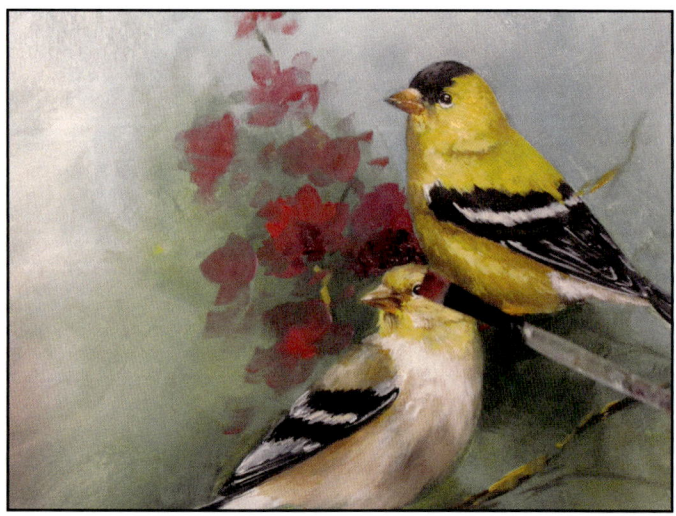

Step 84 Add some darker colors to the reds with some Red Violet.

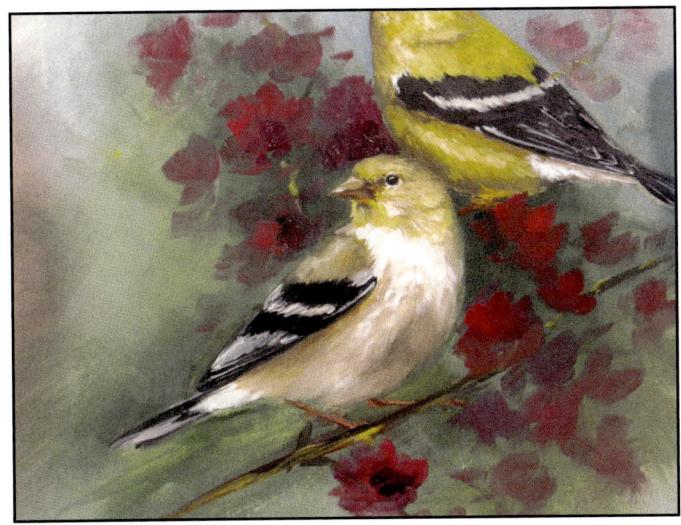
Step 85 Mottle the brush into more Nap. Red Light and touch white and add lighter brighter touches to the blossoms in front.

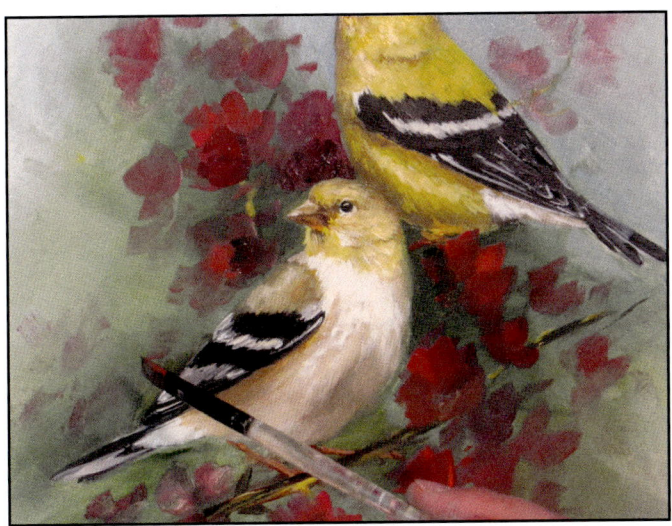
Step 86 Think of the blossoms for depth. Do not lighten every one.

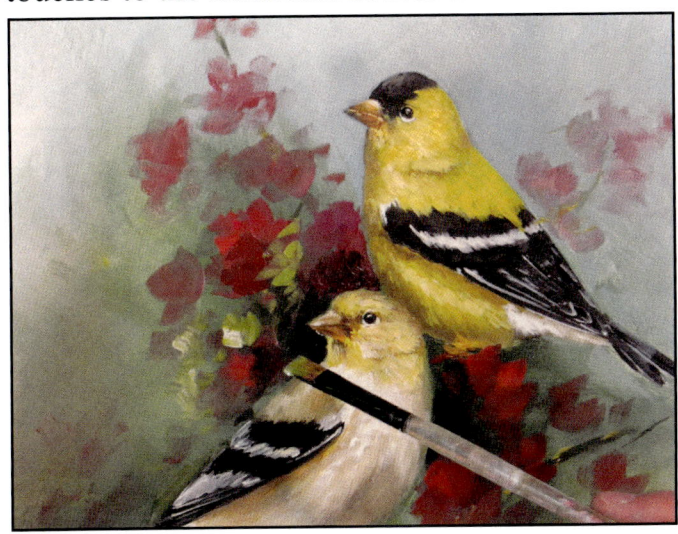
Step 87 Mottle the brush with Hansa, greens and white. Add some lights to the forwards leaves. Keep casual and taps. See final photo.

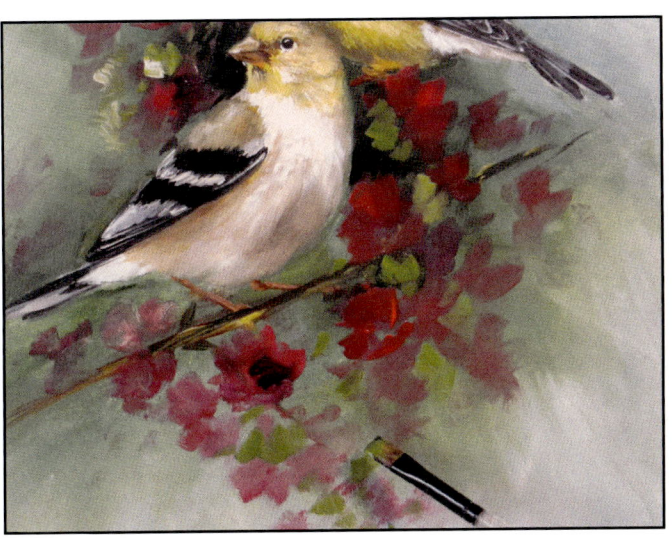
Step 88 Continue adding greens to the lower section mottling the greens into the background and softening with your finger.

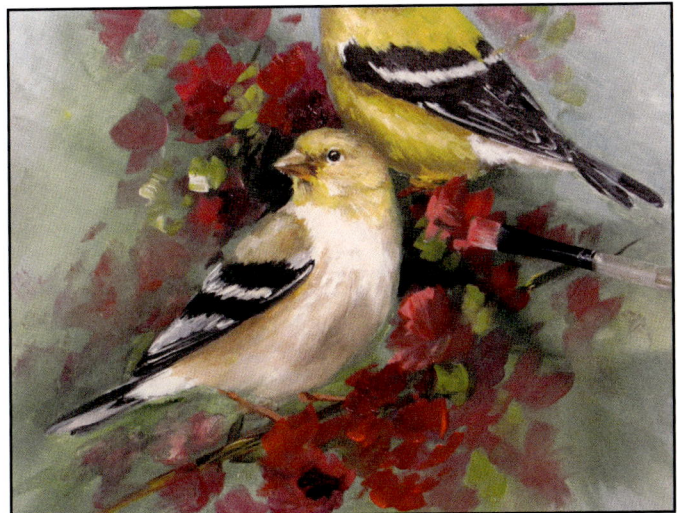
Step 89 Mottle reds lighter with touches of white and add to some flowers.

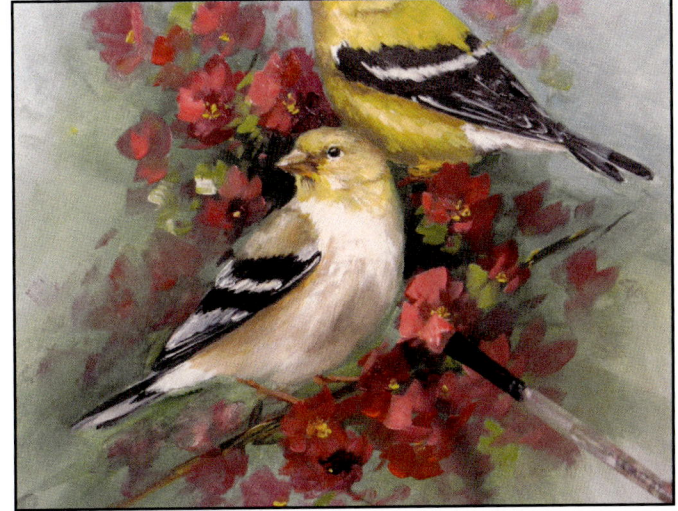
Step 90 Continue lightening, add yellow taps to centers to finish... Enjoy!

Goldfinches Enlarge Pattern 120% for Original Size

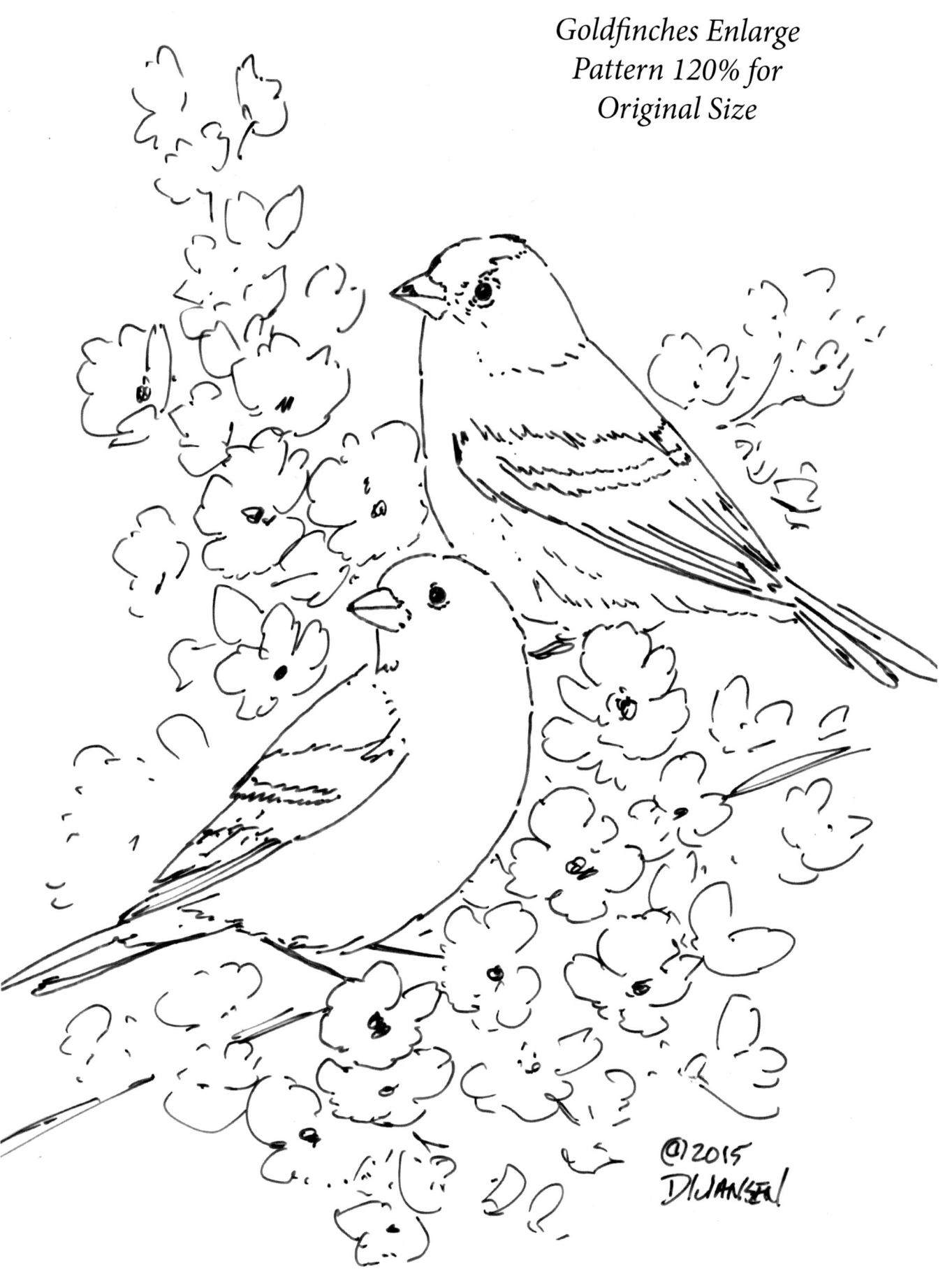

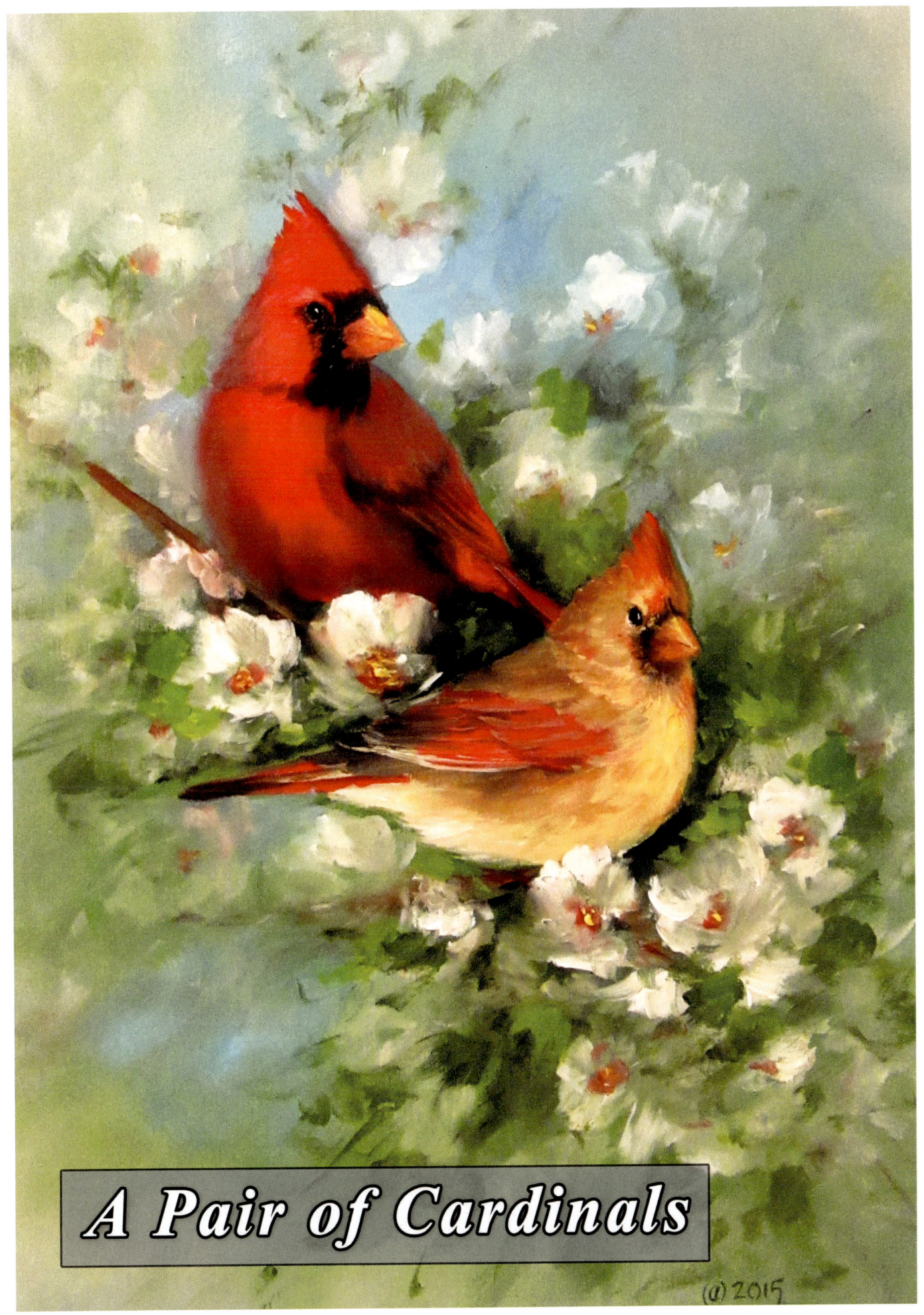

A Pair of Cardinals- Painting Sfumato

Our garden here in Pennsylvania is blessed with many pairs of Cardinals. Sometimes you can look at the feeders and see over 20 at a time. I love to watch them. You can see the male from hundreds of feet away with their bright red wings and body. While many enjoy the vibrant reds of the male, I love the soft yellow greens of the female. To me, she is one of the prettiest birds in nature.

For this lesson I thought it would be fun to put the brighter male in the back. However, about 3/4 of the way into the painting I began to have trouble with my plan and had to rethink the technique. Having a bright red bird in the back that contrasted strongly with the greens from the leaves made the female disappear. So after so quick reflection, I used a technique that Da Vinci made popular.

Sfumato is where the artist will use a smoky color or version the background to soften the color and intensity changes within an element. Towards the end of the painting, I stroke softer color over the edges of the male to make him softer. This did 2 things for the painting. The male Cardinal not only soften and receded, he also became thinner and more attractive.

Over the years I have discovered many things about color. One thing is the eye's ability to see a color without having to make the entire object that color. For example, when I paint a white blossom, I do not make the entire blossom white. It only gets white highlights and the eye sees the rest of the blossom as tones and values of white. The same thing will happen to this cardinal. It doesn't take a lot of red for the eye to read the cardinal as red. The more intense red you place on the male cardinal, the further forward he comes in the painting. Only a small section of him needs to be red, while the rest can be softer, causing him to recede. Thus, sfumato. Try in on other paintings. The technique works and is an amazing addition to our tools as an artist. Let's give it a try!

Paint It Simply Palette
Base Color- White
Palette Colors

Naphthol Red Light	Titanium White
Red Violet	Medium White
Carbon Black	Base Brown
Phthalo Blue	Pine Green
Hansa Yellow	Burnt Sienna

Wood Surface
Linen covered wood panel about 14 Inch X 18 Inch to fit picture frame. Can also use canvas panel.

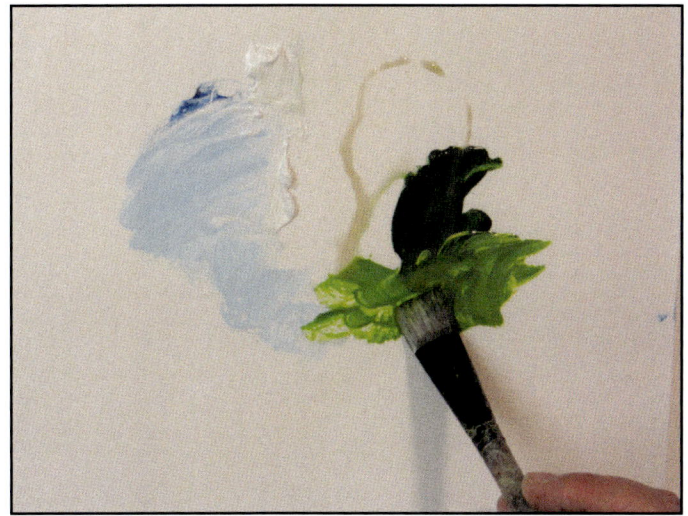
Step 1 Base white, transfer design like the others, then mottle blues, white Pine Green and Hansa.

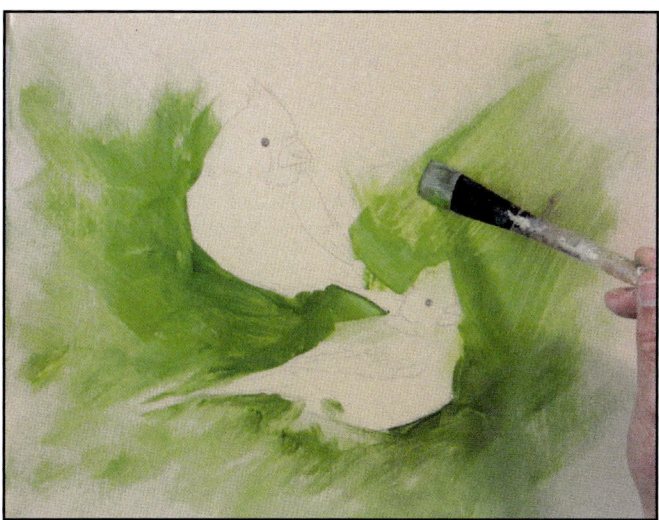
Step 2 Begin painting around the cardinals with the mottled greens.

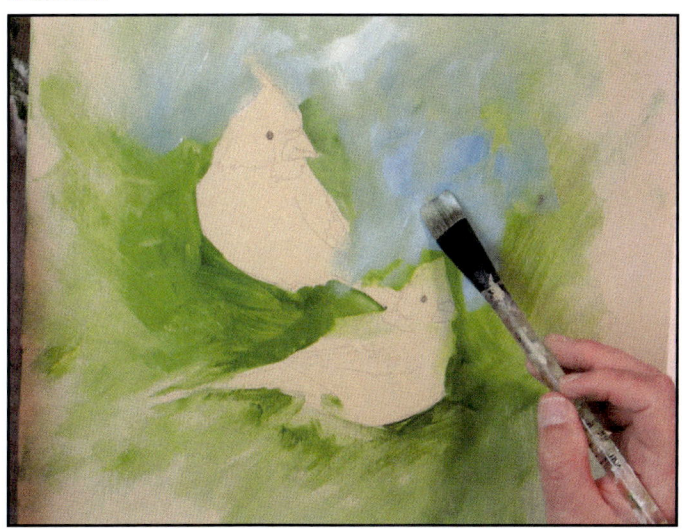
Step 3 Mottle the brush with blues and whites and base around the top of the birds to indicate the sky.

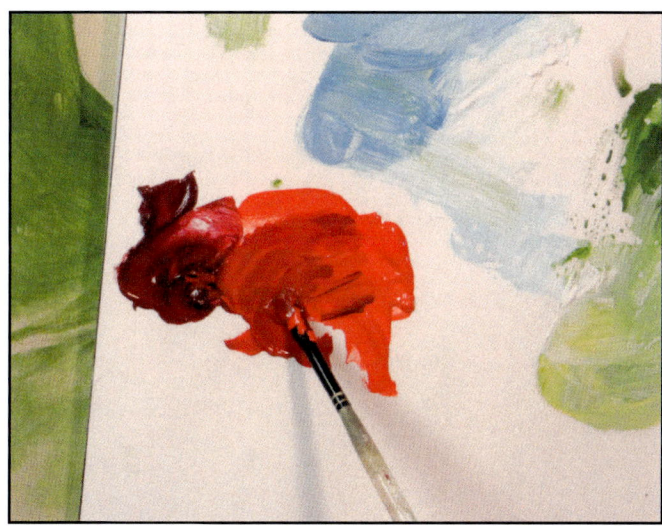
Step 4 Mottle both reds together on the palette. Red Violet and Nap. Red Light. Use small flat.

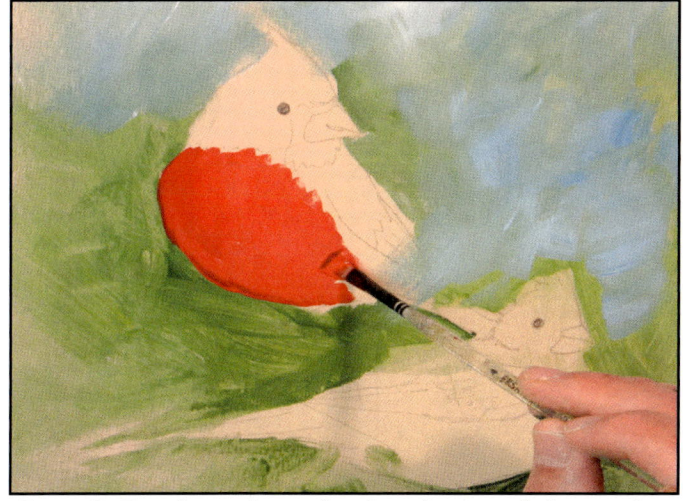
Step 5 Begin to base in the shape of the male cardinal.

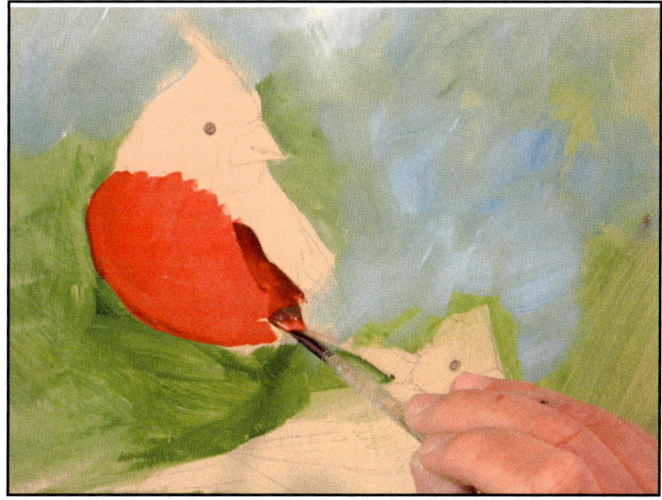
Step 6 Shadow under the wing with some Red Violet.

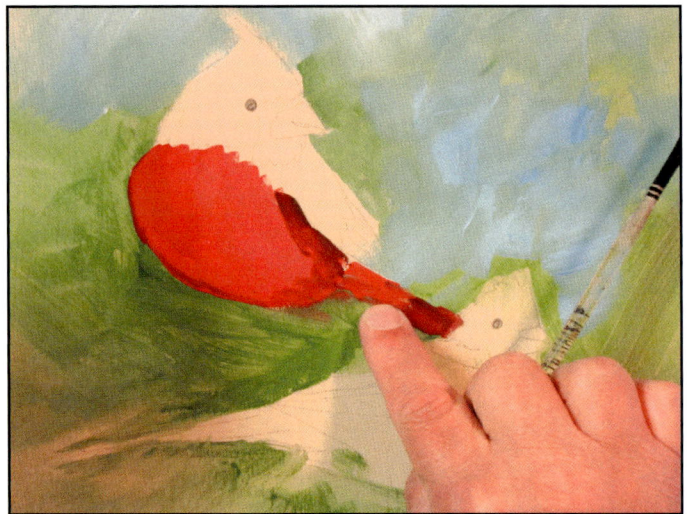

Step 7 Add the tail and then soften the exchange between the colors with short movements of your finger.

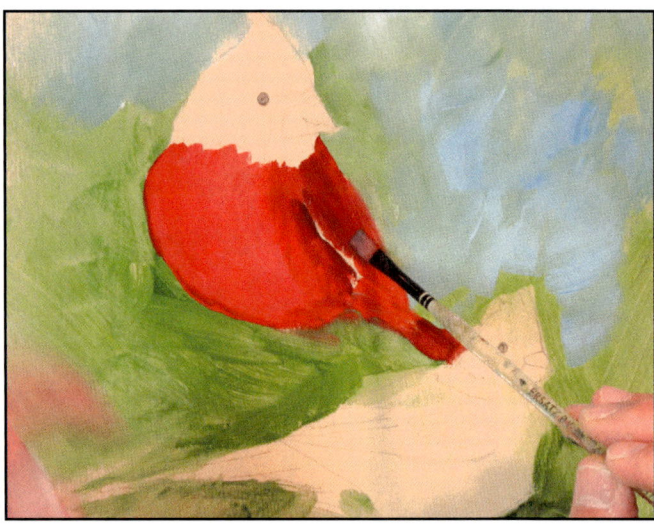

Step 8 Leave a small space between the wing and body to see the pattern. Make the wing a little darker with Red Violet.

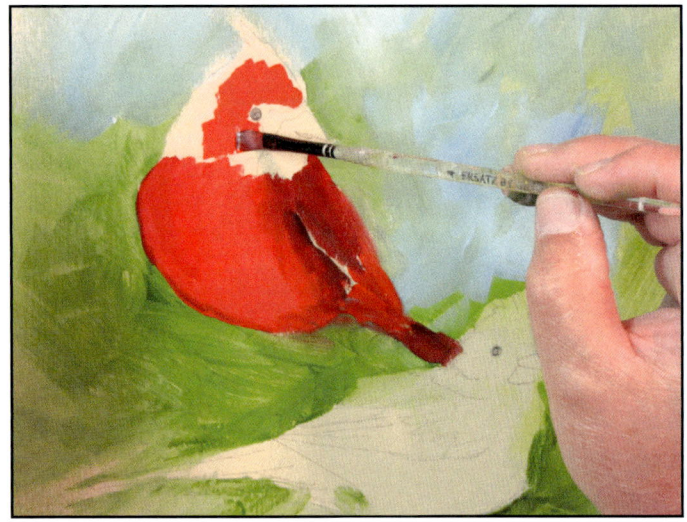

Step 9 Lighten the color more with Nap. Red Light and base in the head with shape following strokes.

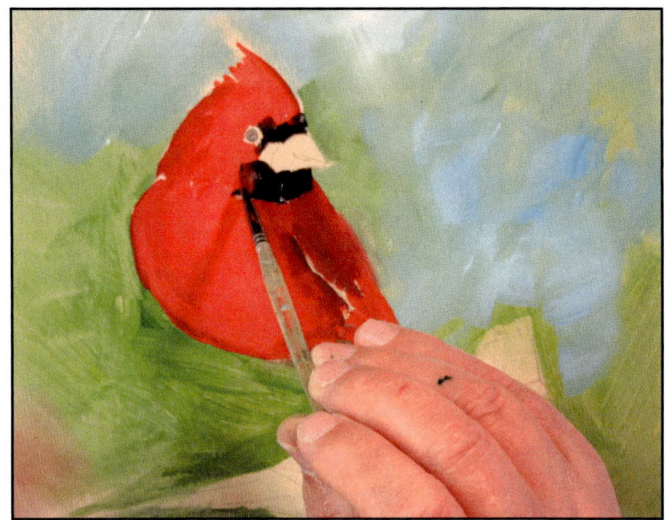

Step 10 Mottle the brush with black and add the black to the face and neck.

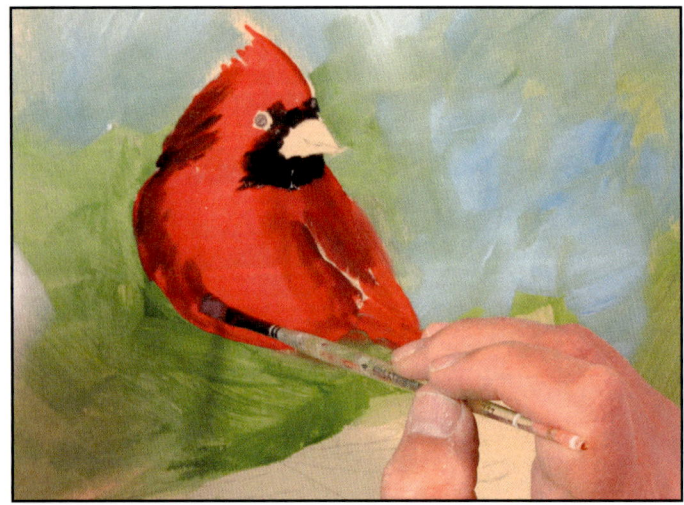

Step 11 Mottle the black with some Red Violet and shadow the side of the cardinal.

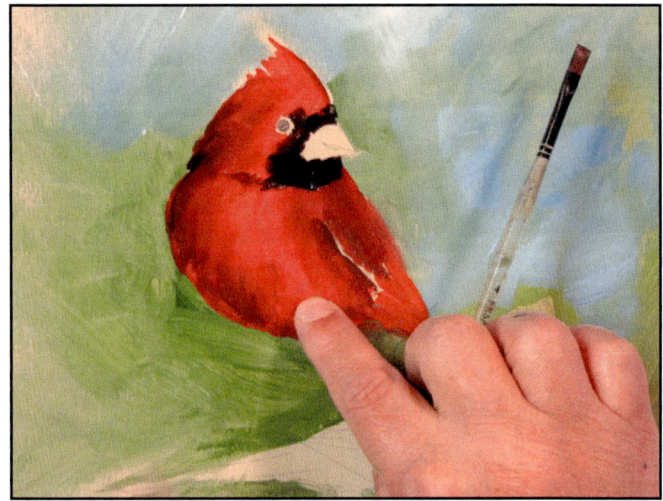

Step 12 Walk the color across the body from the left and then soften with your finger.

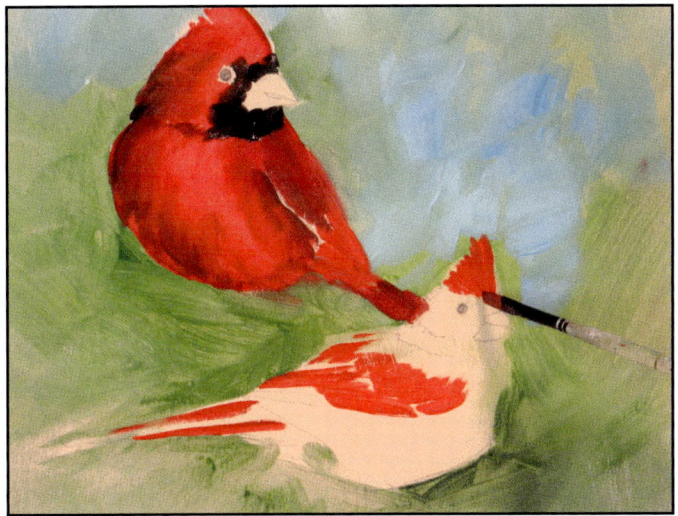

Step 13 Mottle the reds and begin basing in the areas shown in the female cardinal.

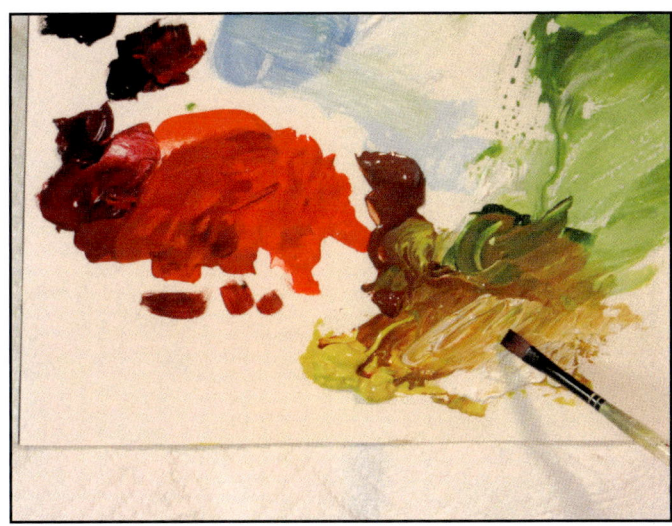

Step 14 Mottle the Hansa with some Burnt Sienna and touch green to tone the color. She is a little toned yellow green.

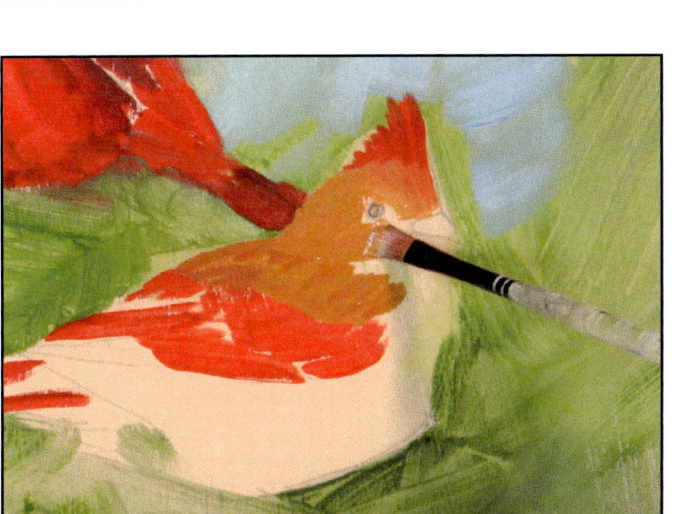

Step 15 Begin to base in the mantle and her head with this toned yellow, slightly green color.

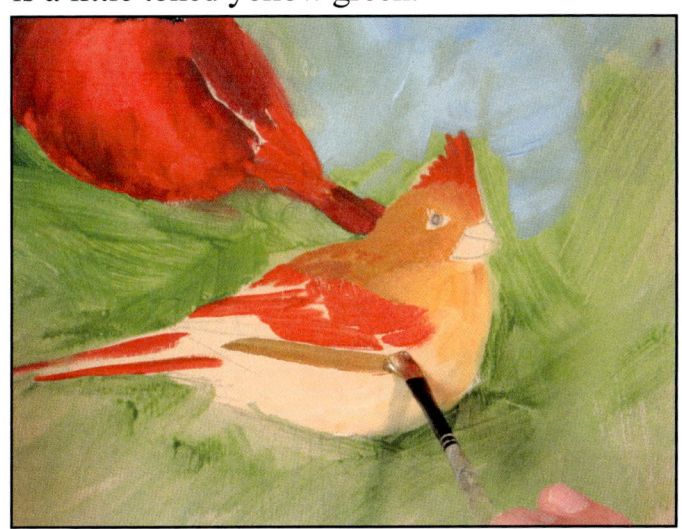

Step 16 Darken the color with a little more Burnt Sienna and shadow under her wing.

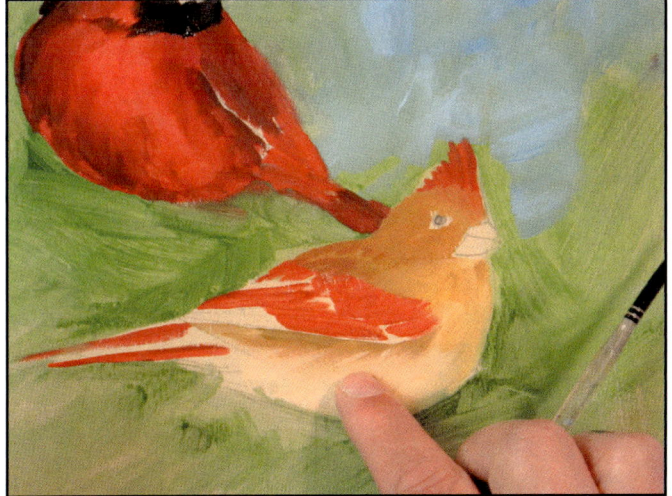

Step 17 Soften the edge of the shadow with your finger.

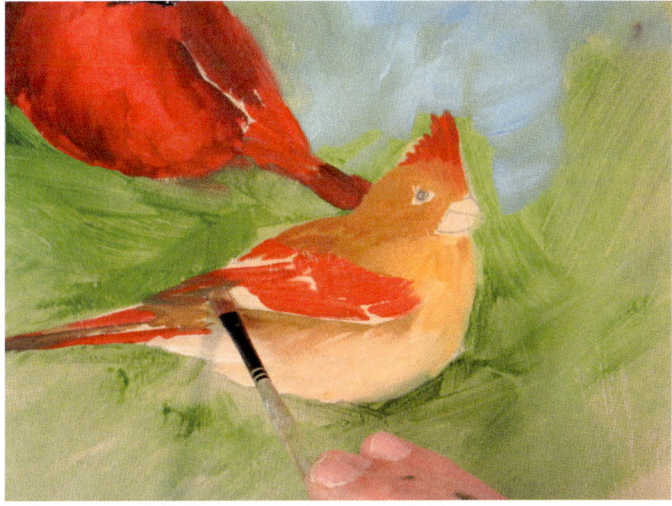

Step 18 Add some additional Burnt Sienna and then green and shadow tips of wing.

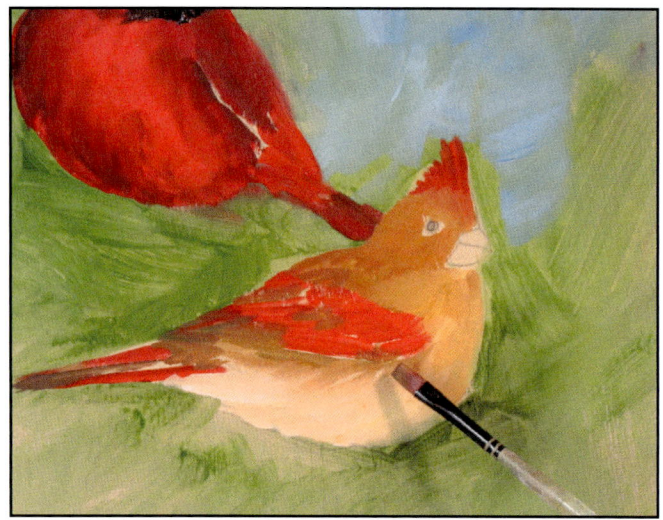

Step 19 Add some of that darker color under the wing.

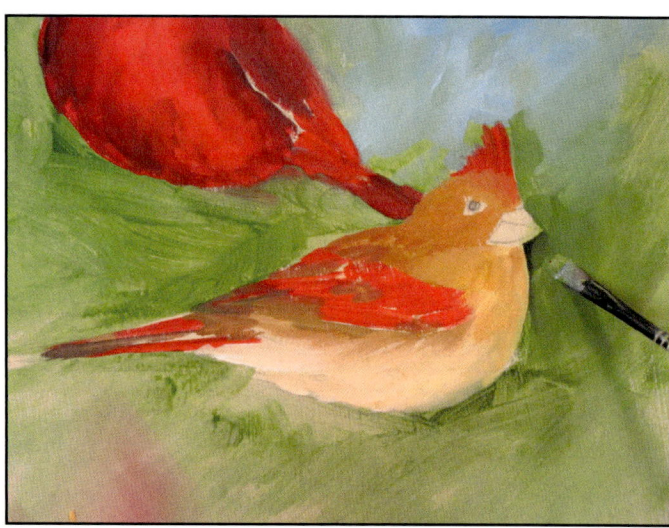

Step 20 Mottle the greens darker with some black and add next to her to bring her forward.

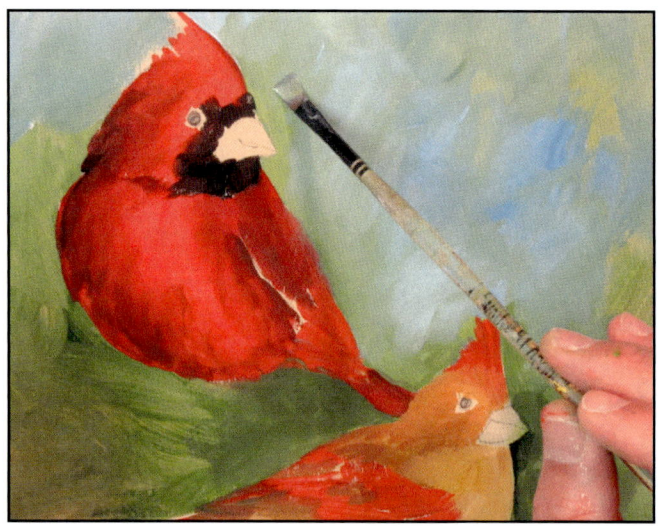

Step 21 Mottle the greens and sky color and add around the male to help bring him forward.

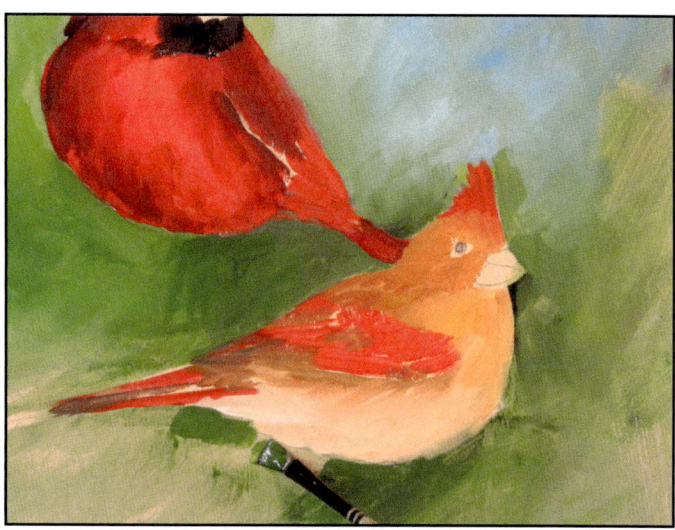

Step 22 Add some additional green under the female to bring her forward.

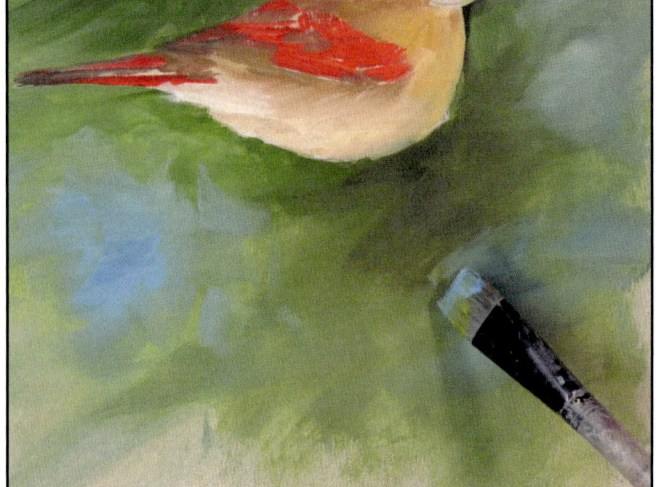

Step 23 Mottle the blue with white and add some into the green to make sky areas.

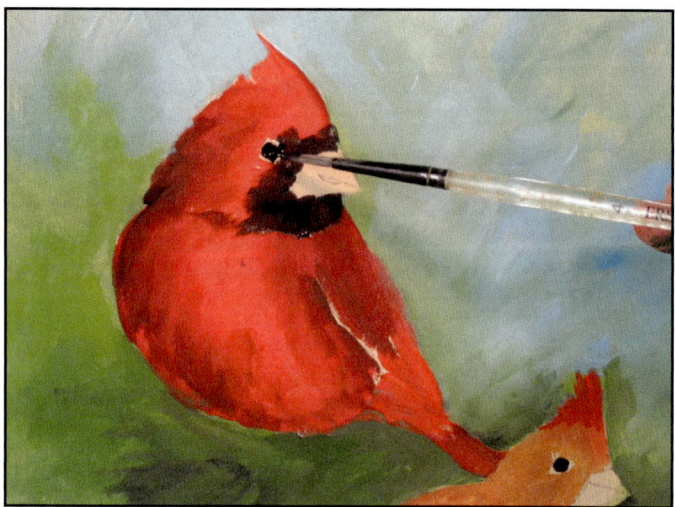

Step 24 Add the black to the eye of the male and female with small round or liner.

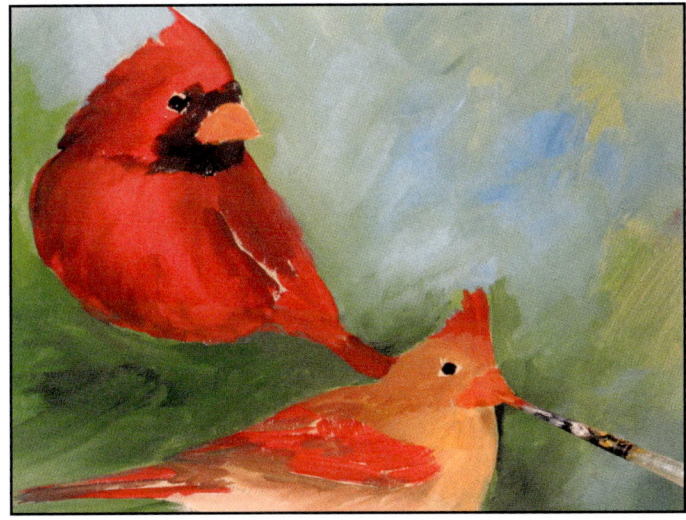
Step 25 Mottle an orange with red and yellow and then add to the beaks of the cardinals.

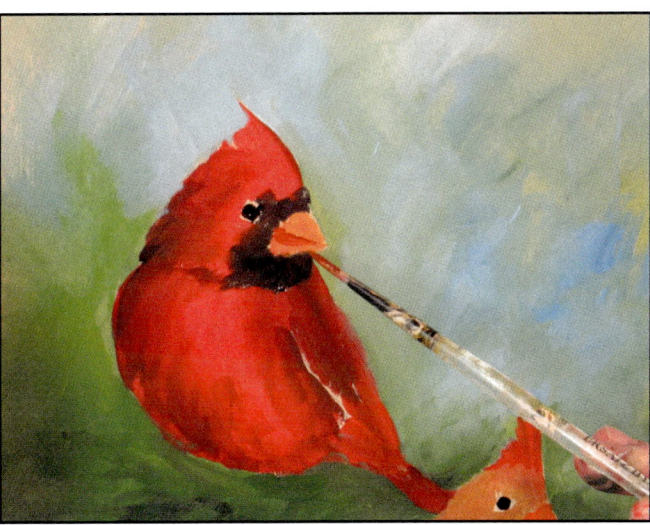
Step 26 Darken the orange with more red and touch Red Violet and add the shadow to the beaks.

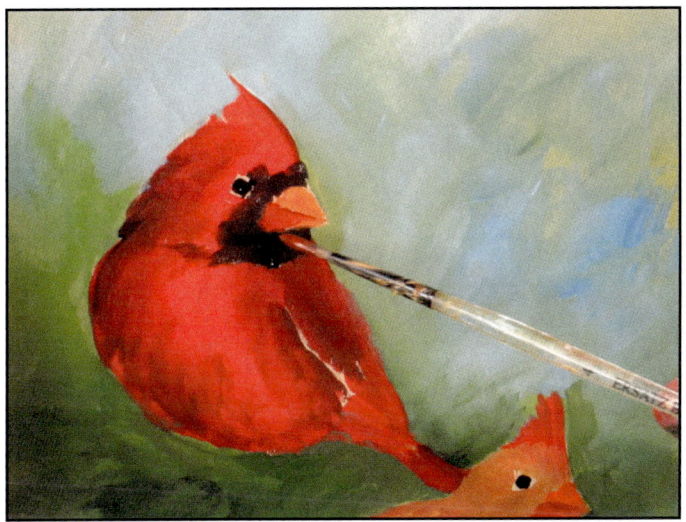
Step 27 Mottle the shadow into the black from the faces.

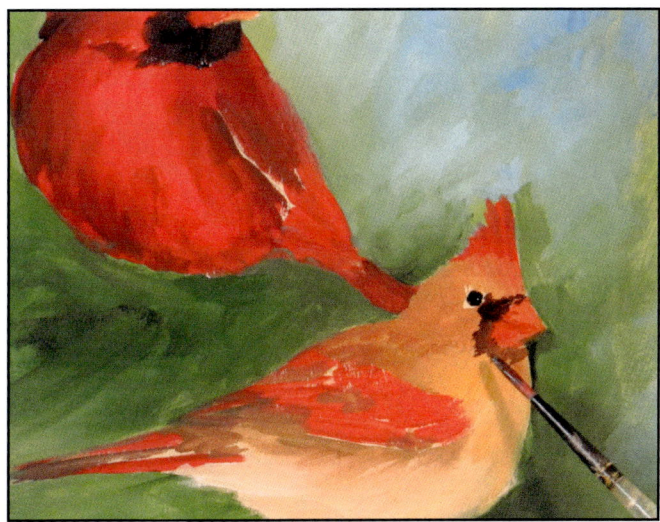
Step 28 Mottle the female beak shadow into the face as well.

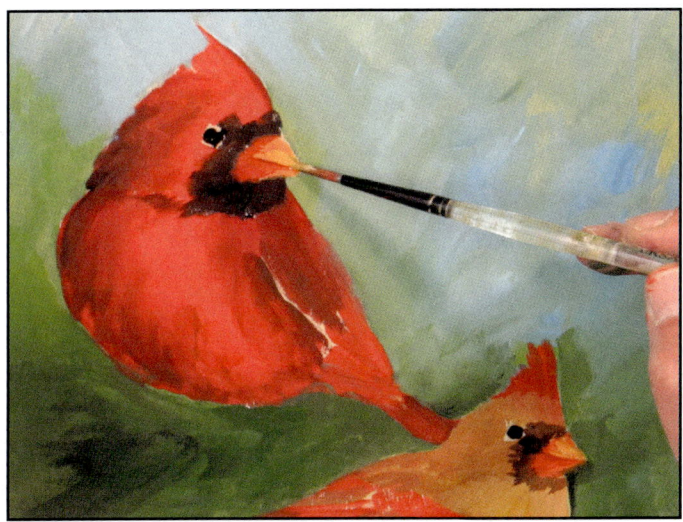
Step 29 Lighten the color with some Hansa and add to the top beak.

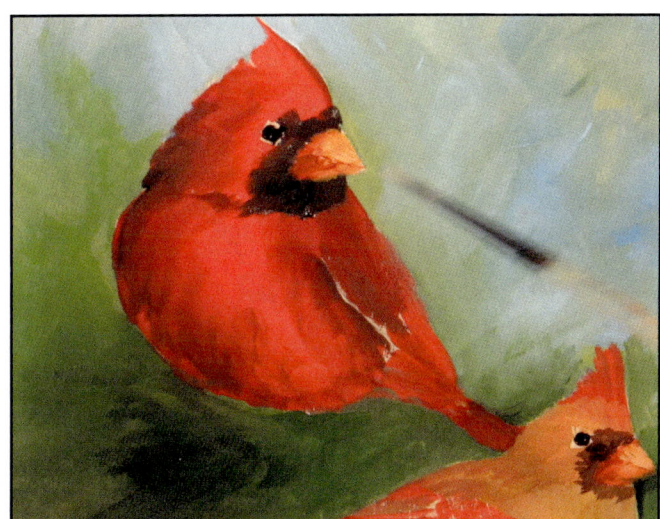
Step 30 Work the colors several times to add interest.

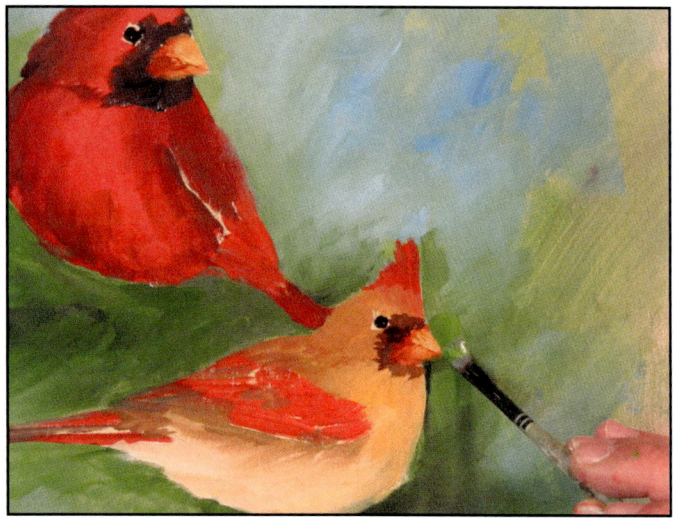

Step 31 Use the greens to clean up the edges of the beaks.

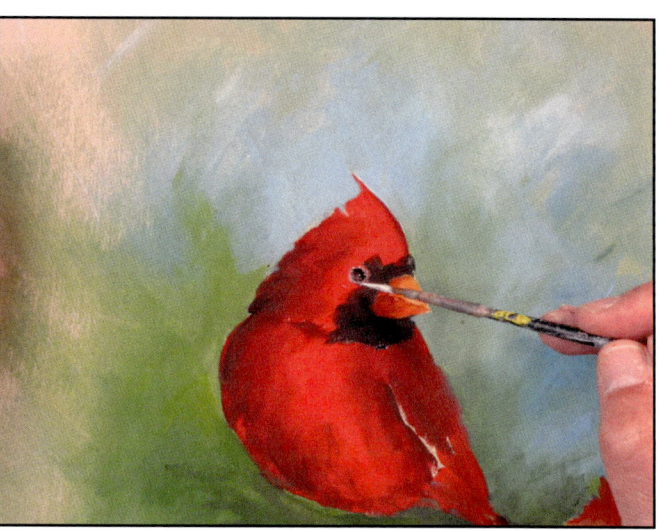

Step 32 Add the white eye ring and details around the eye.

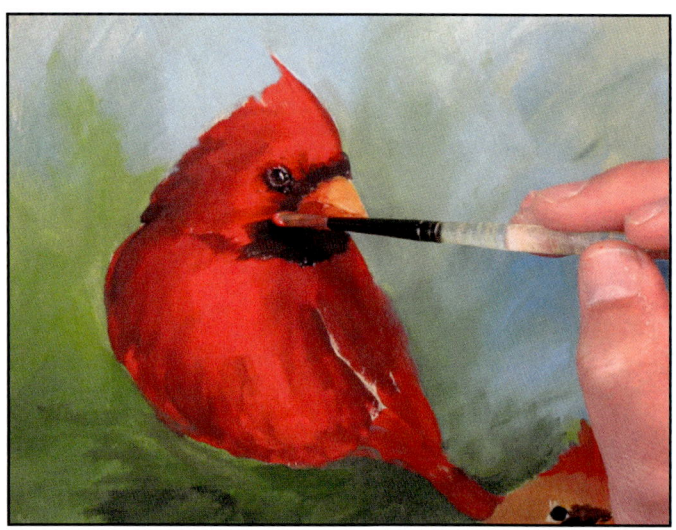

Step 33 Mottle the small round with more reds and begin the small feathers on the face.

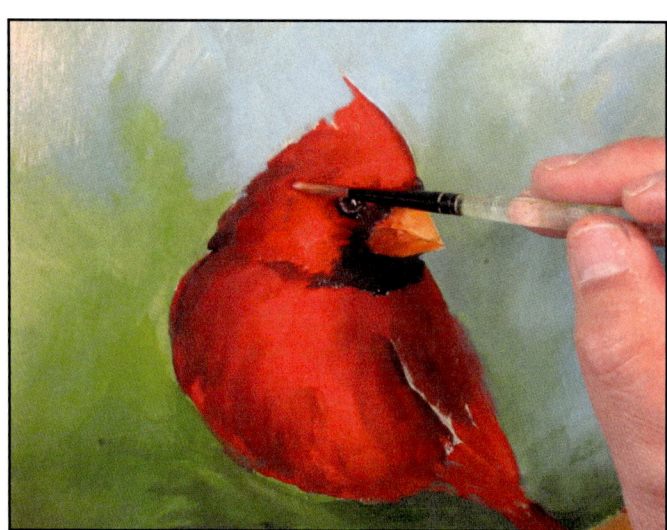

Step 34 Soften the colors into the shadows on the side of the head.

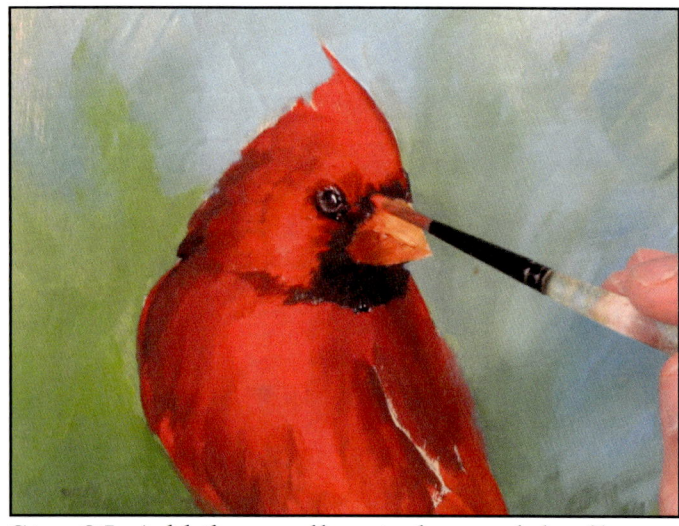

Step 35 Add the smaller strokes and details around the beak areas.

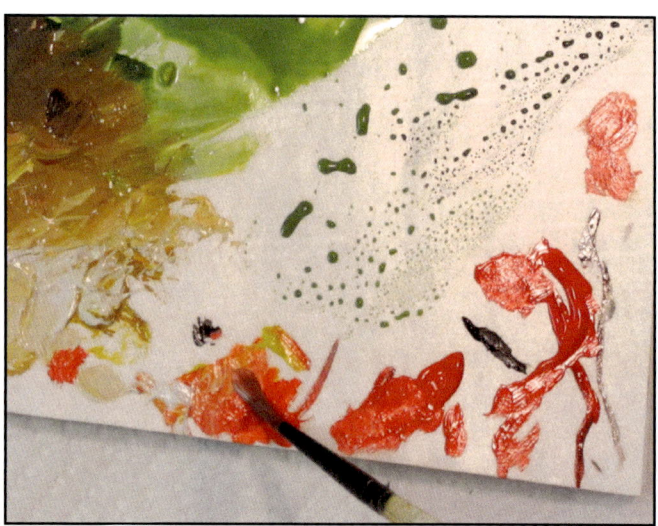

Step 36 Mottle the red lighter with Hansa and touch white. Not too much white.

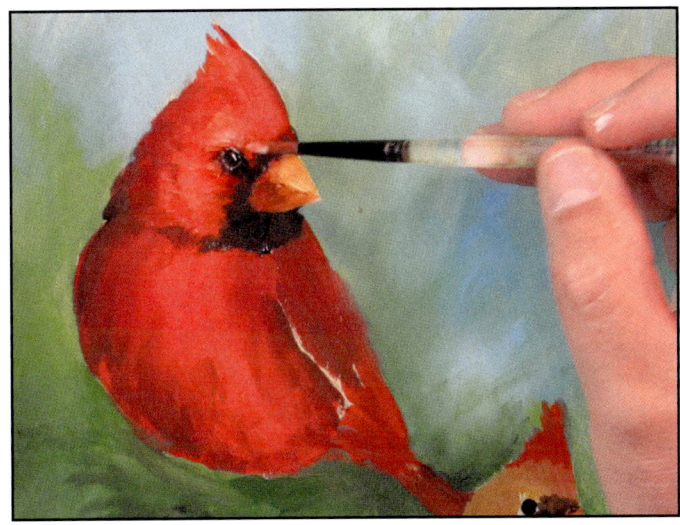

Step 37 Add some strokes to the head above the eye to create roundness.

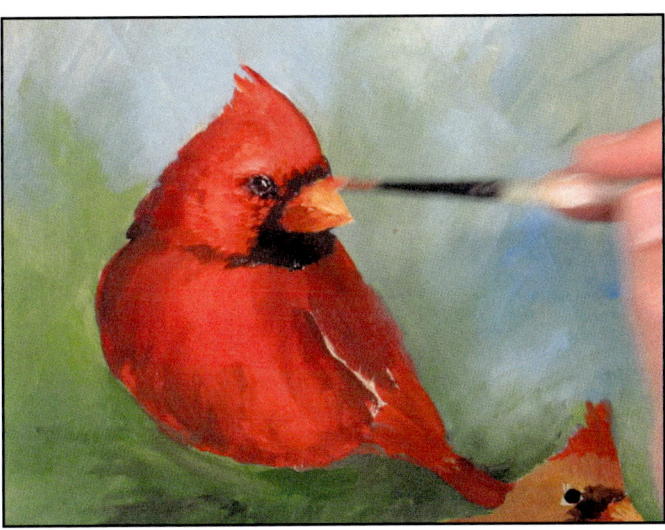

Step 38 Work the details. Clean up the edges.

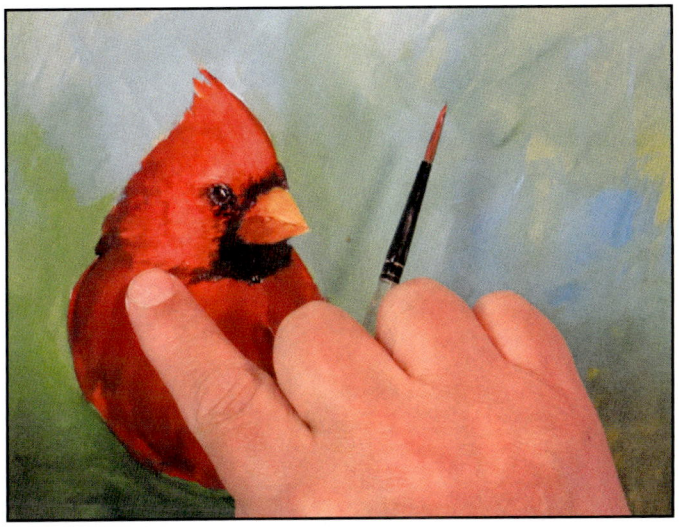

Step 39 Begin creating the feathers down the head and into the neck.

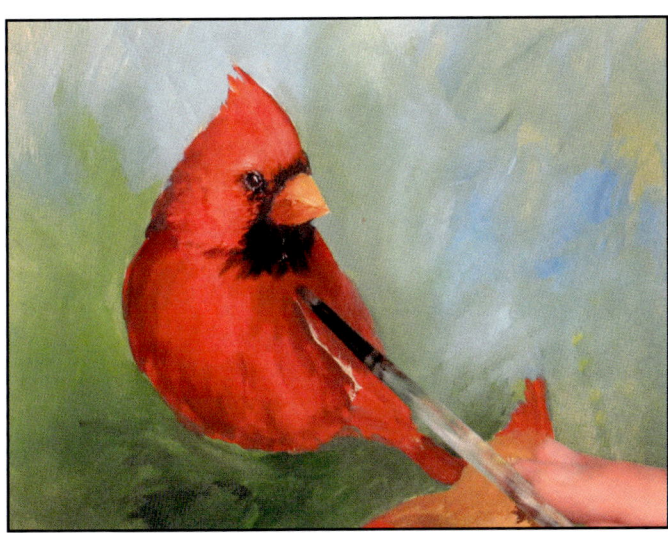

Step 40 Start down the body and onto the mantle making various feather strokes.

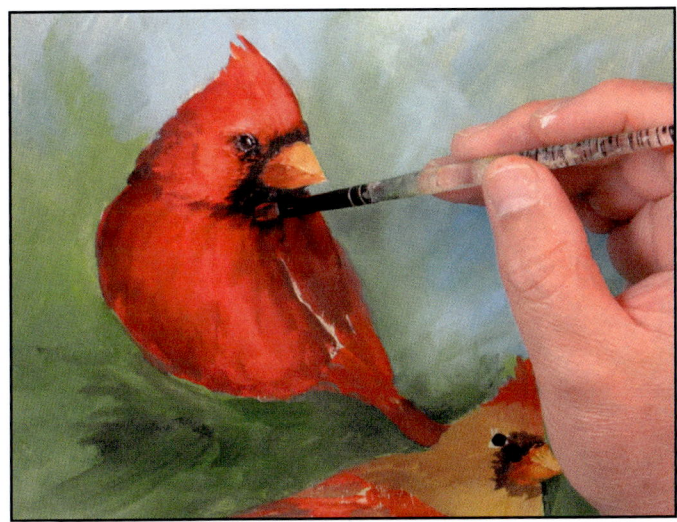

Step 41 Mottle back into the black and work the colors back and forth.

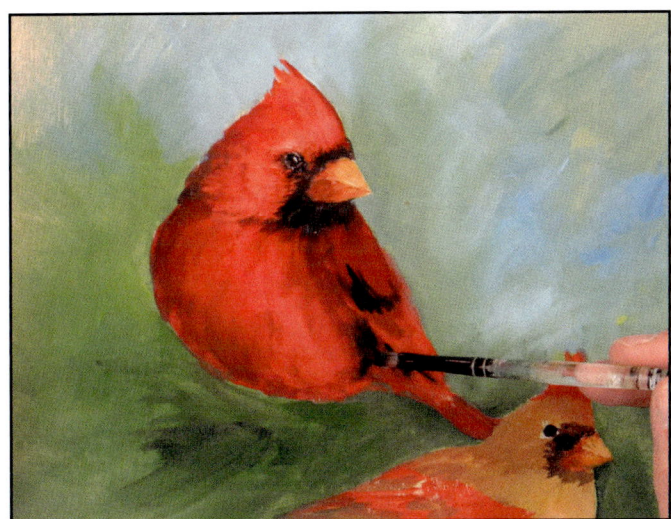

Step 42 Add the black to the wings and under wings and feather with reds.

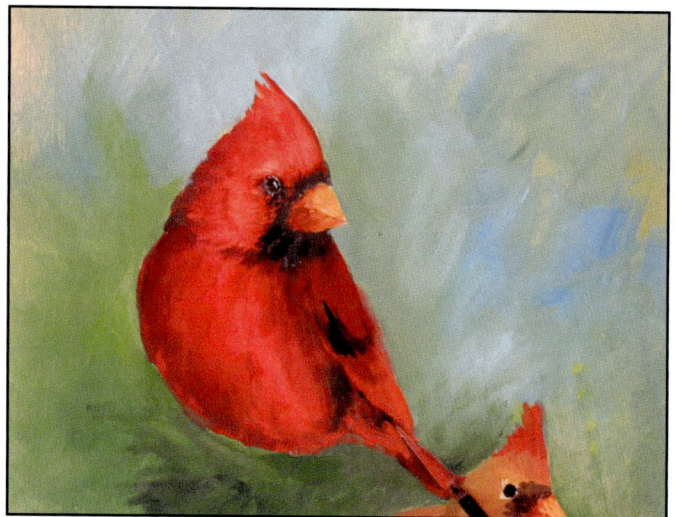

Step 43 Continue feathering down the tail, remember to increase length of feathers down the body.

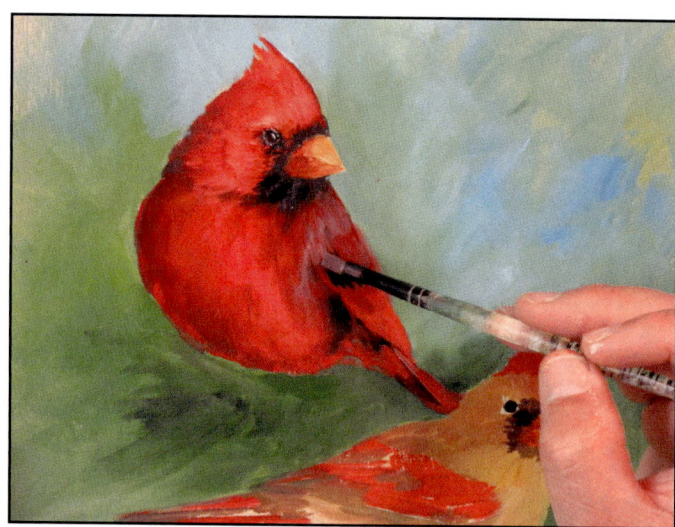

Step 44 Add a touch of white to the red and black, make a almost grey color. Begin to add some light greyish feathers to the mantle.

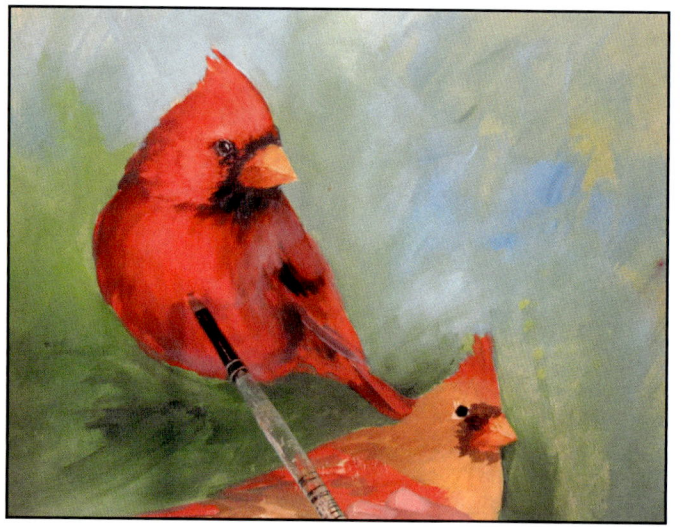

Step 45 Add some of the greyish feathers to the body following the contours.

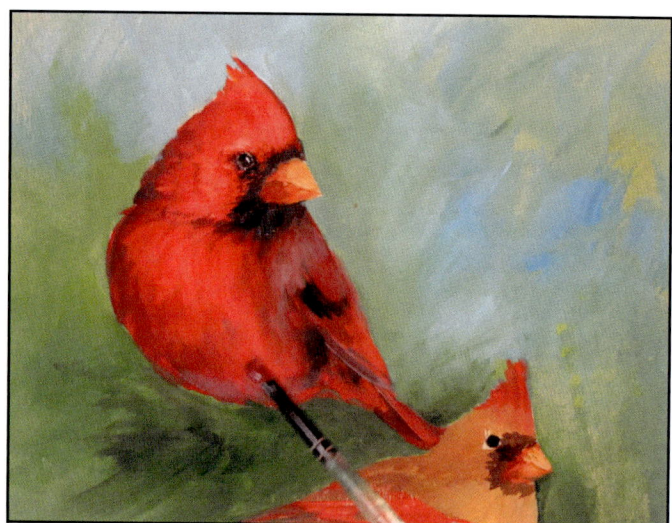

Step 46 Soften the greys with some darker red feathers.

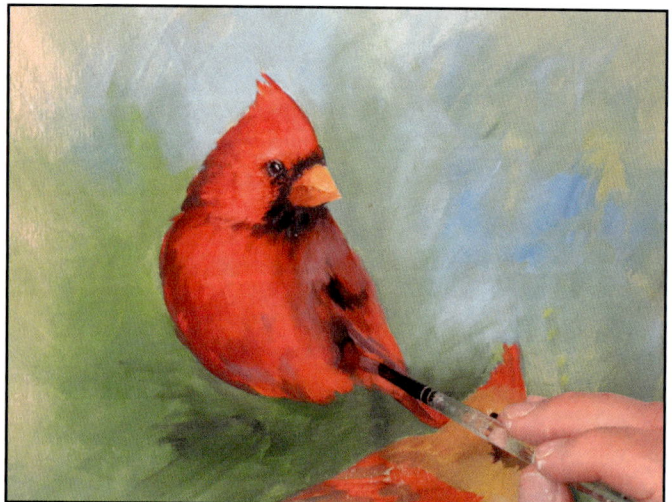

Step 47 Soften the edges of the black with the red feathers.

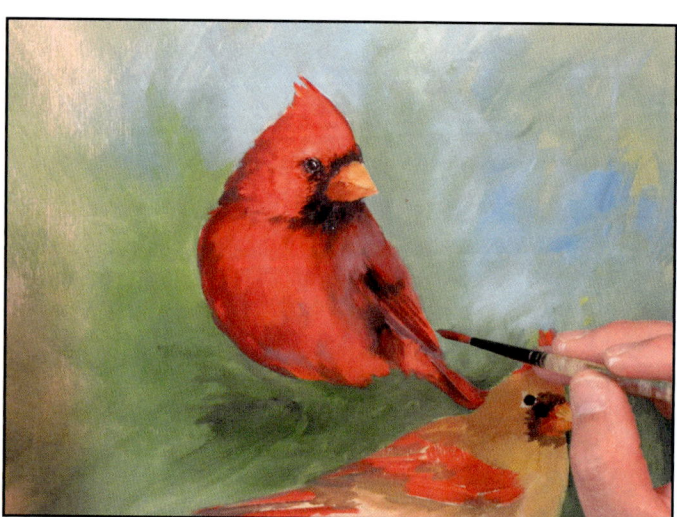

Step 48 Add some darker red lines to suggest the primary coverts of the wing.

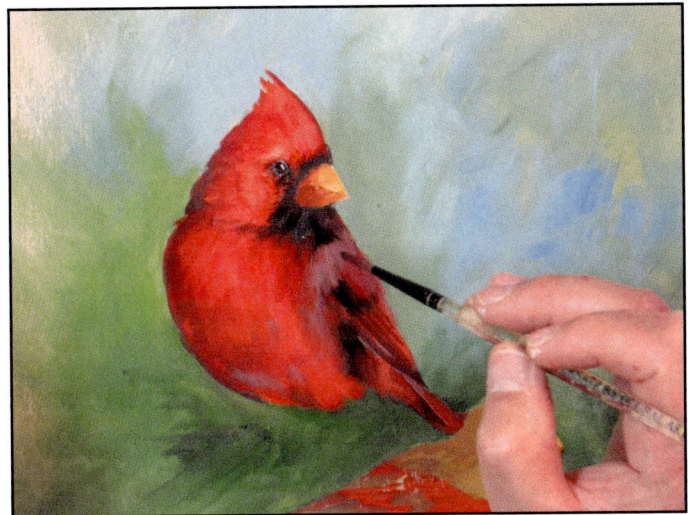

Step 49 Detail the black and reds, working back and forth with the colors to feather the neck and mantle.

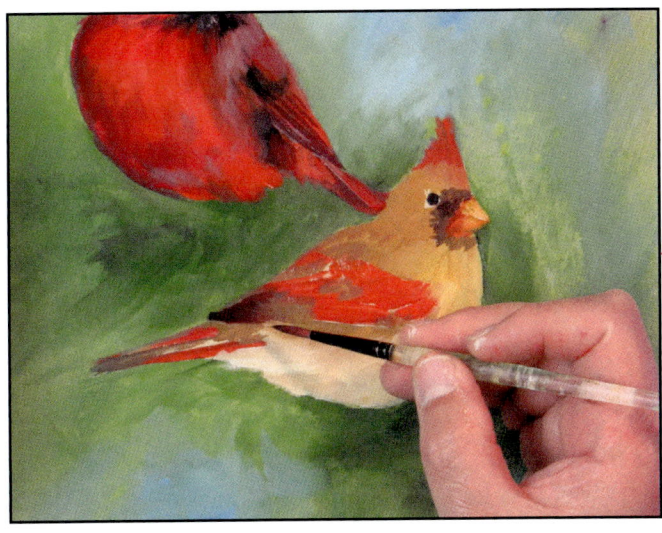

Step 50 Time to feather the female. Start with the tan colors and begin feathering with slightly lighter color.

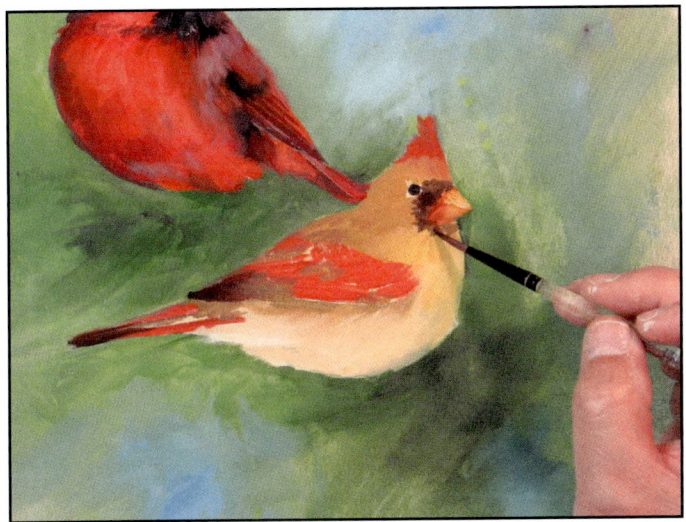

Step 51 Feather around the shadows of the beak and work into the light tan color.

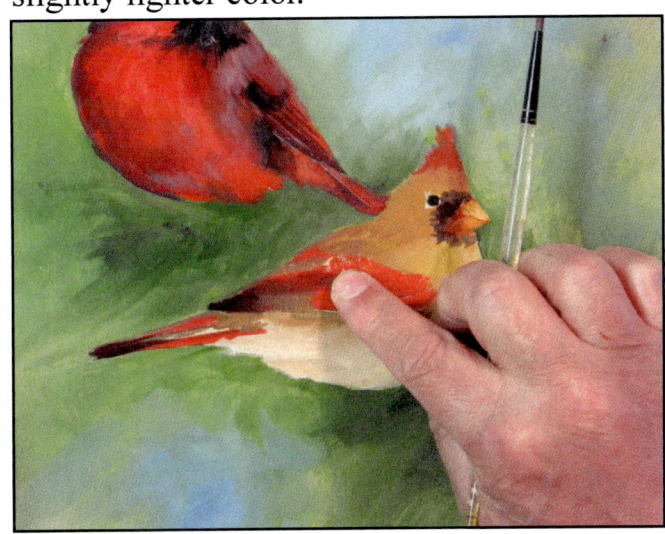

Step 52 Soften some of the tan into the reds of the wing and then soften the movement with your finger.

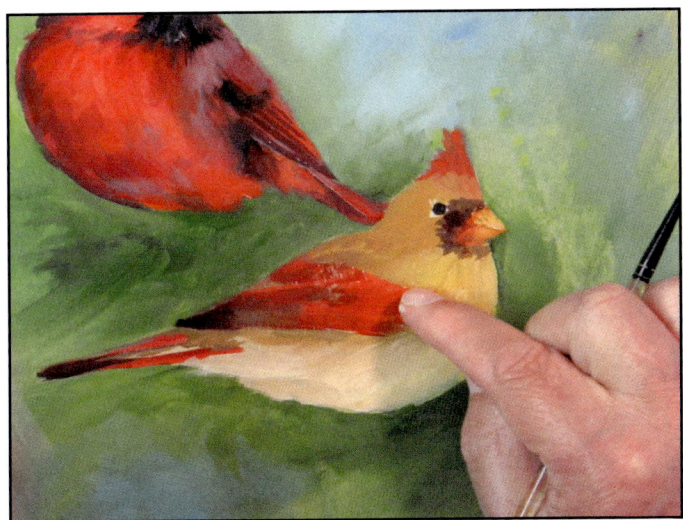

Step 53 Add more reds and then soften then create feather movement with your finger.

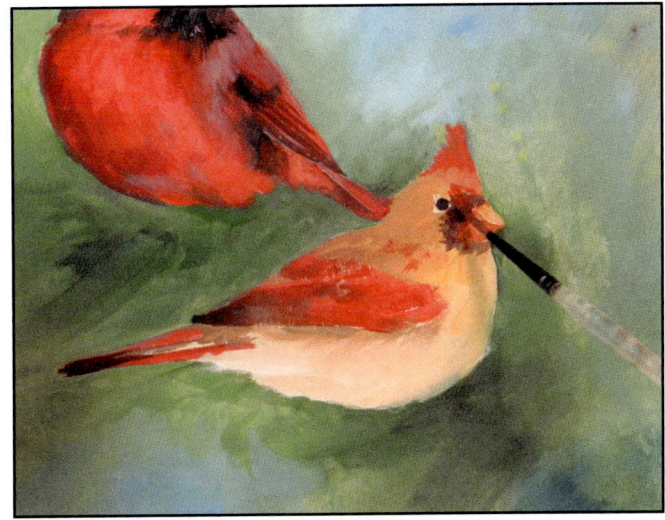

Step 54 Restate the shadows. Work the colors back and forth for interest.

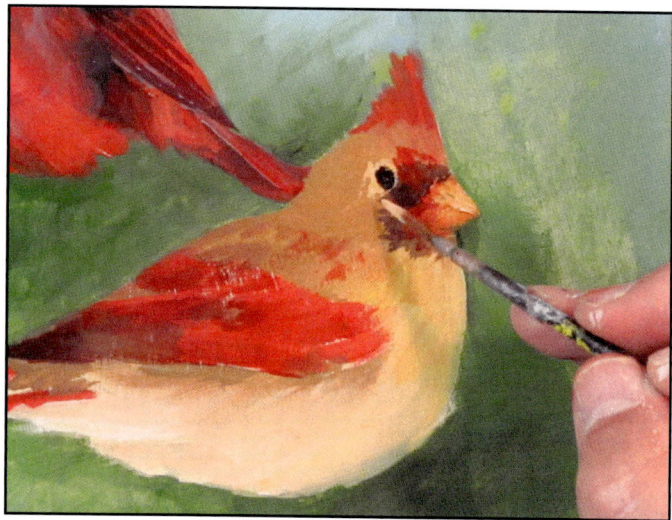

Step 55 Add the light around the eye with light tan.

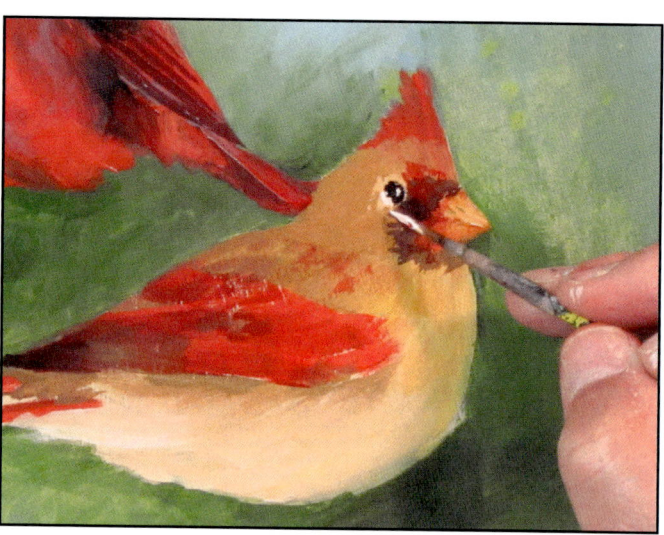

Step 56 Add some white details with the liner and white. Shines and taps to the eye ring.

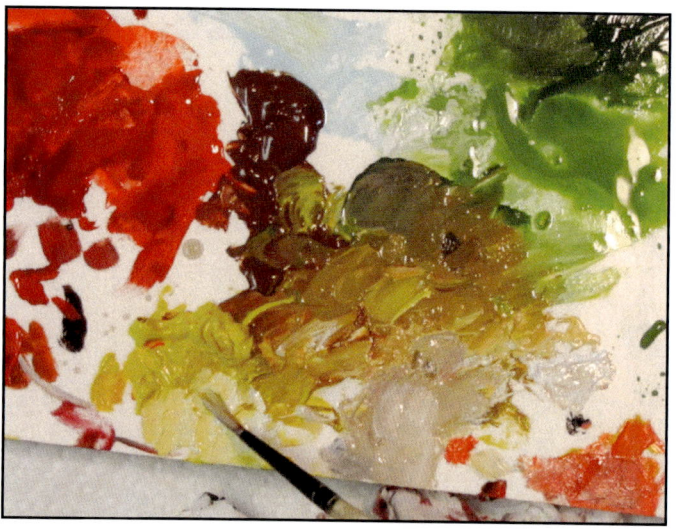

Step 57 Mottle the tans that we have been using with more Hansa and lighten with some white.

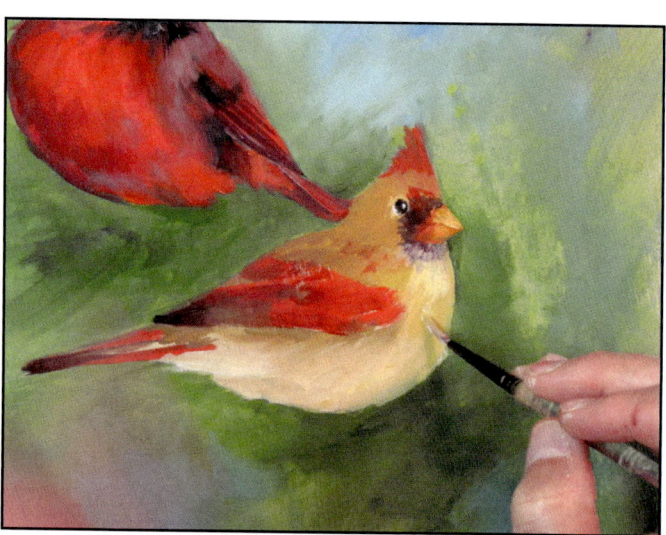

Step 58 Add this to the breast area of the female and feather with short strokes.

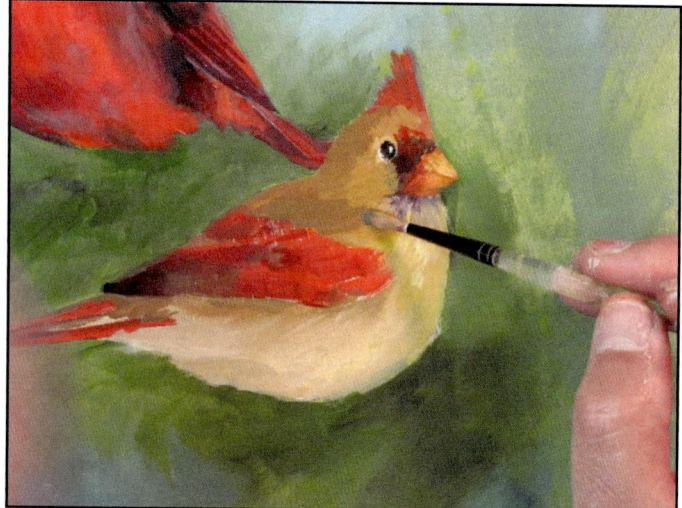

Step 59 Darken the mantle with some darker tan strokes. Then lighten with light feathers.

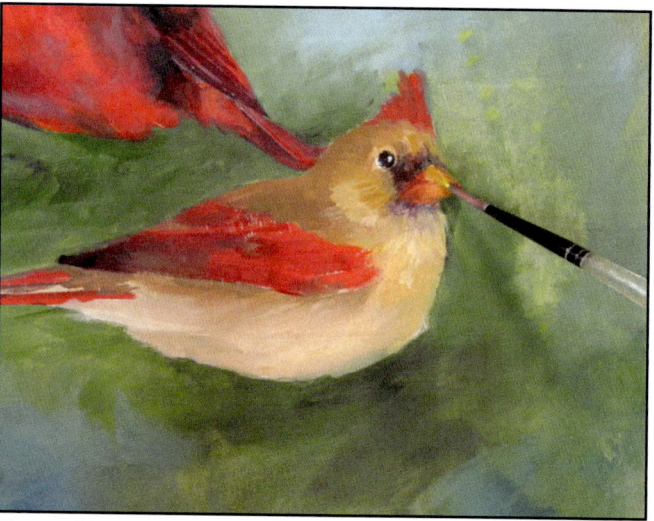

Step 60 Detail the break with light oranges and yellows.

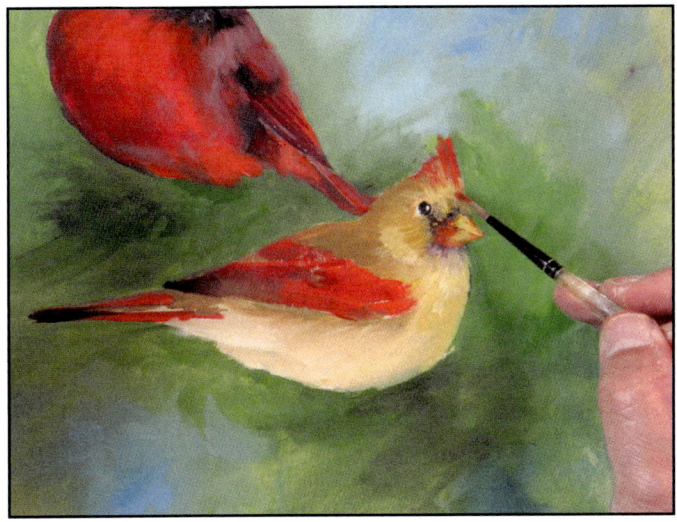

Step 61 Restate the red feathers on top of her head.

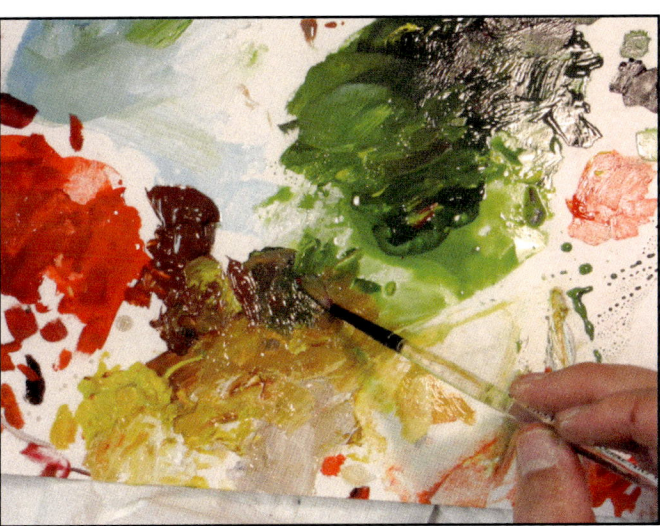

Step 62 Mottle the tan color into the green to change the hue a little.

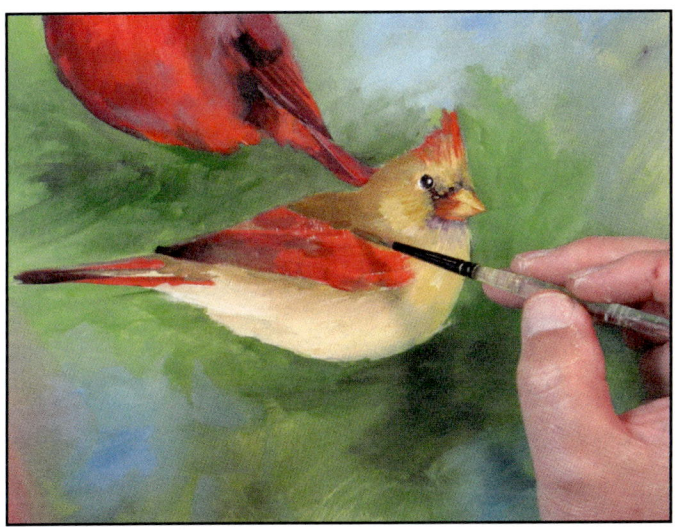

Step 63 Add some of this color to the mantle and darker areas of the wing.

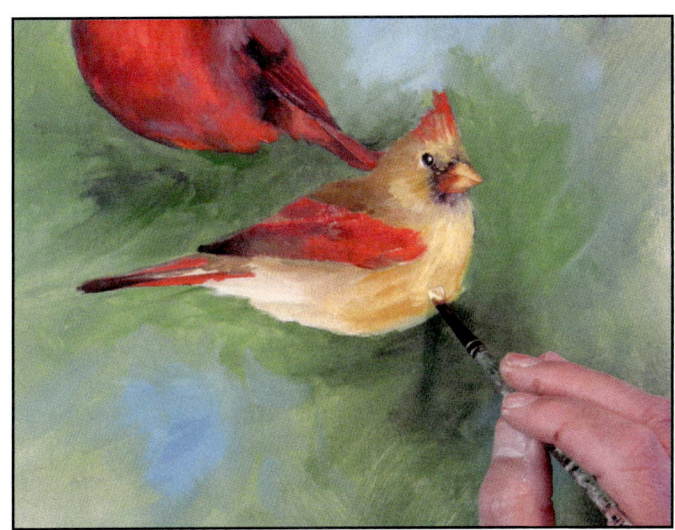

Step 64 Restate the lighter feathers on her breast with tan, yellow and white.

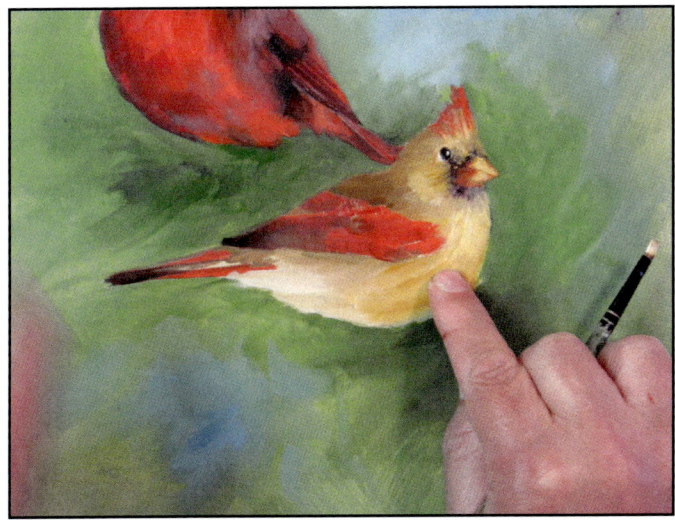

Step 65 Soften the colors down the body with your finger to create feather movement.

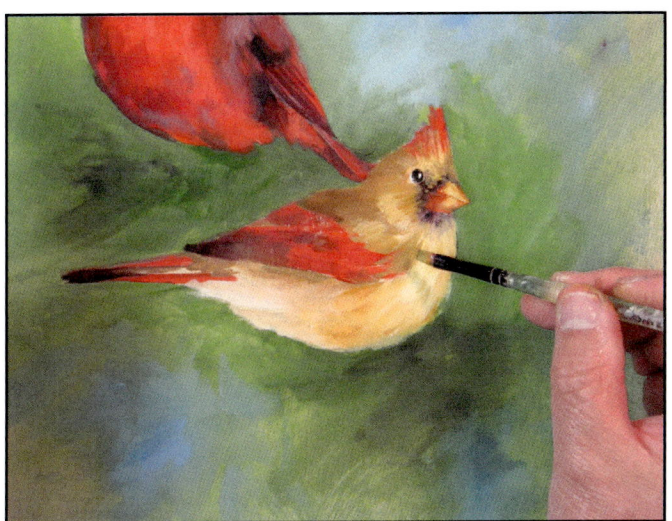

Step 66 Add the mantle detail feathers over the red areas.

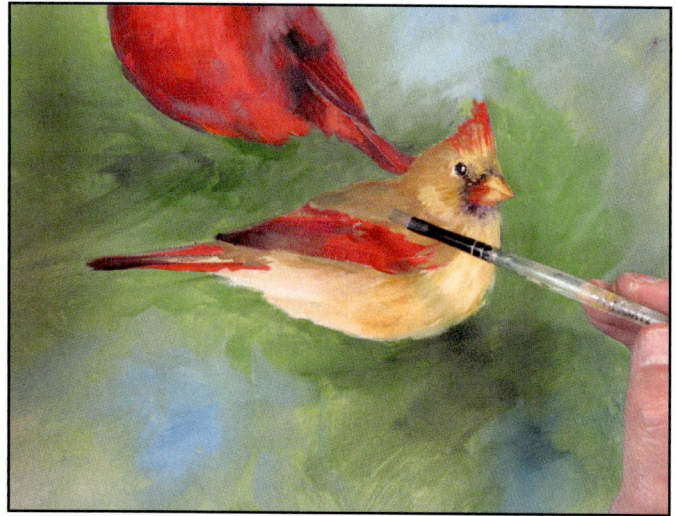

Step 67 Add darks to the mantle. Then add lights to the base of the tail.

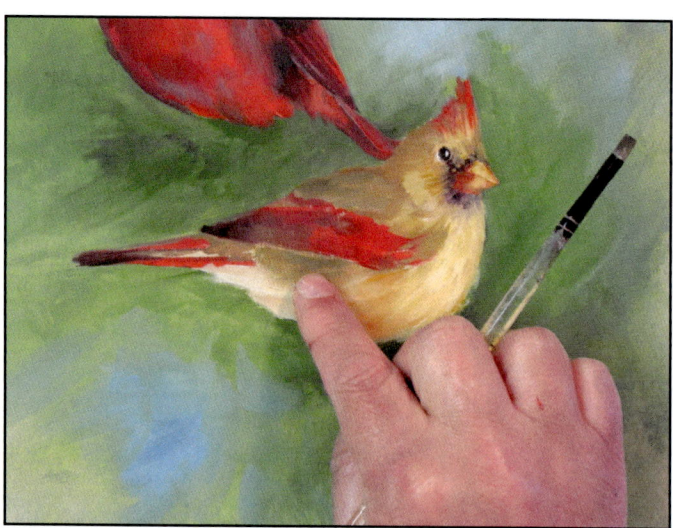

Step 68 Soften the lights of the tail with your finger to create the movement of feathers.

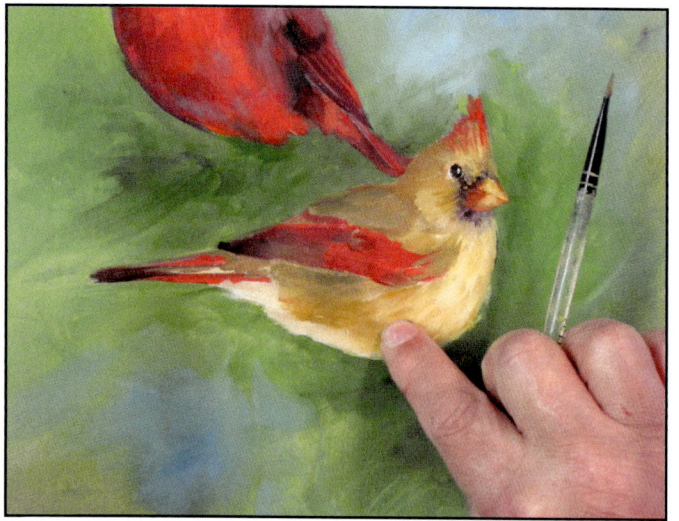

Step 69 Add some more yellows and tans to the body and soften the movement with your finger.

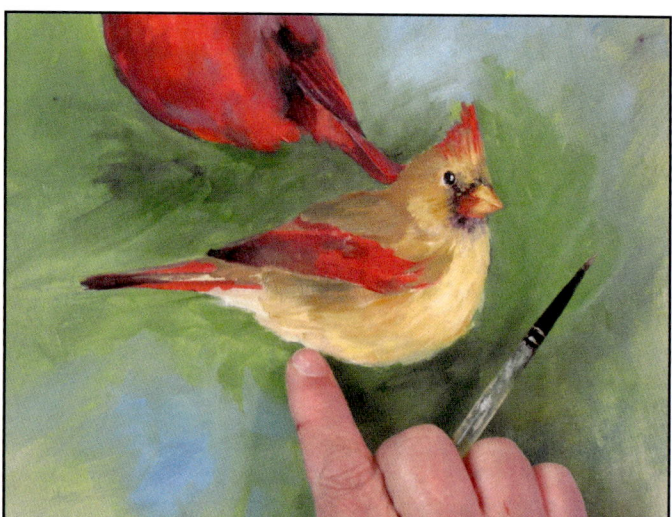

Step 70 Soften the edges of her against the greens with your finger.

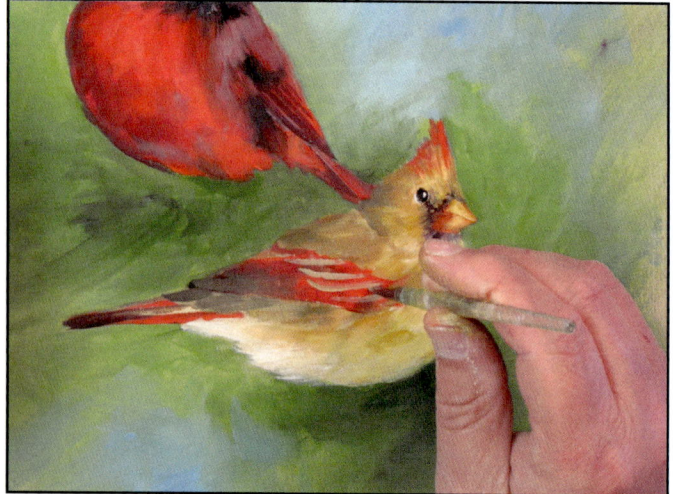

Step 71 Add the light strokes to suggest the flight feathers.

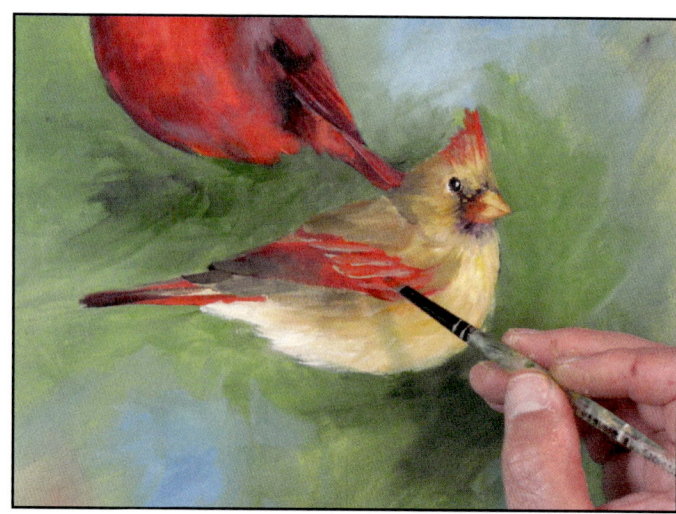

Step 72 Soften the light colors with strokes of red and the round brush.

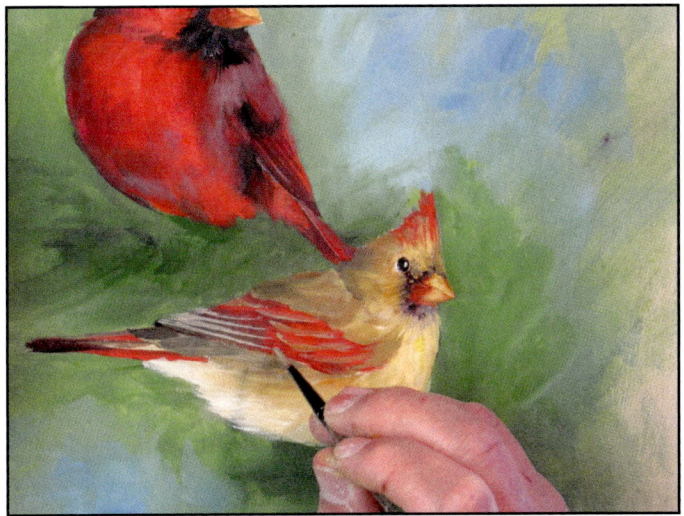

Step 73 Add the lower primary converts with the point of the round and light color.

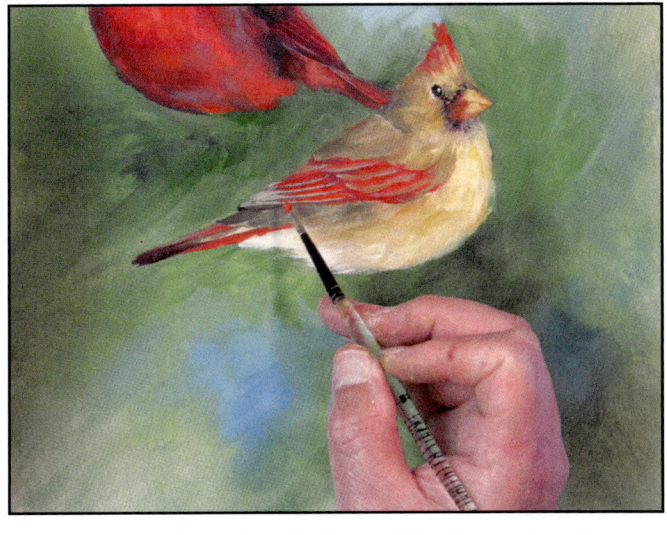

Step 74 Soften the lights with the reds. I repeat several times until I get the desired look of the coverts.

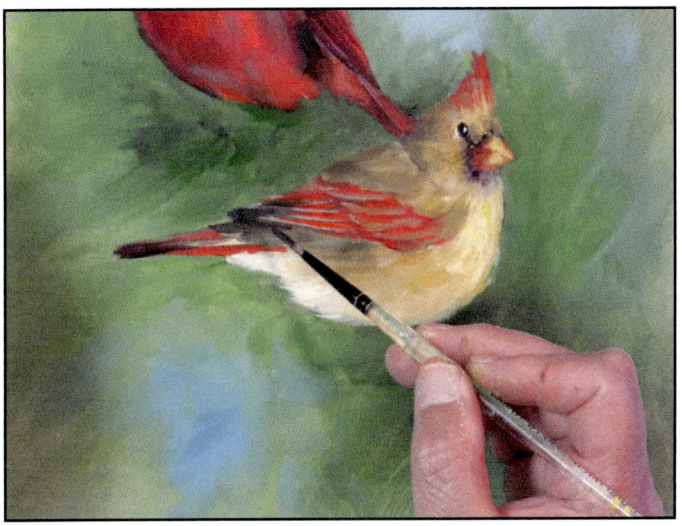

Step 75 Add some darks to the tips of the wings and soften with some reds. Repeat to detail the tips of the wings.

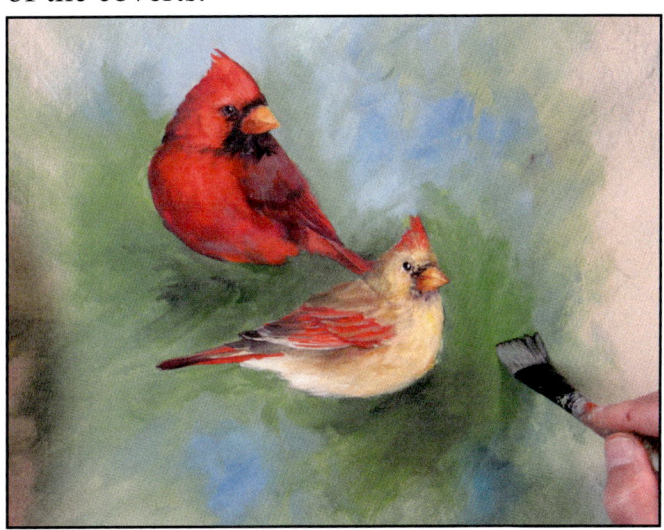

Step 76 Begin the greens outside. Make sure the colors are opaque around the birds so they come forward off the canvas.

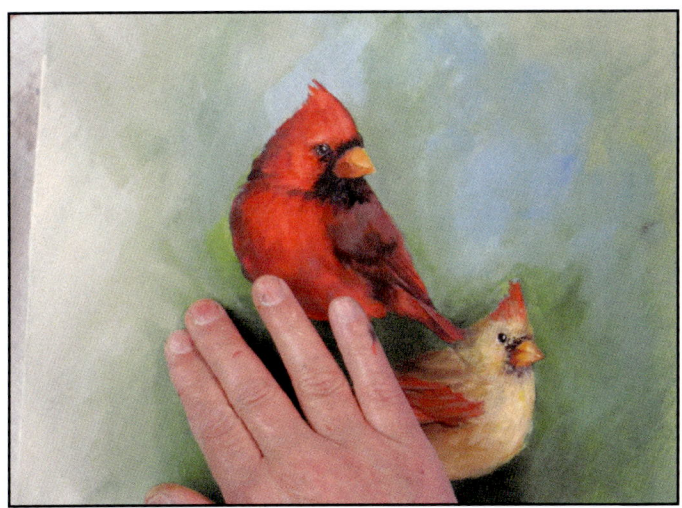

Step 77 Soften the edge of the greens to vignette the canvas.

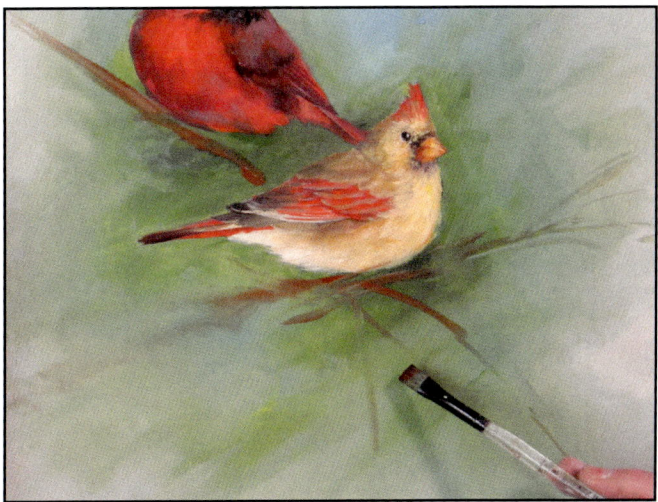

Step 78 Add the suggestions of the branches with Burnt Sienna and the chisel of flat.

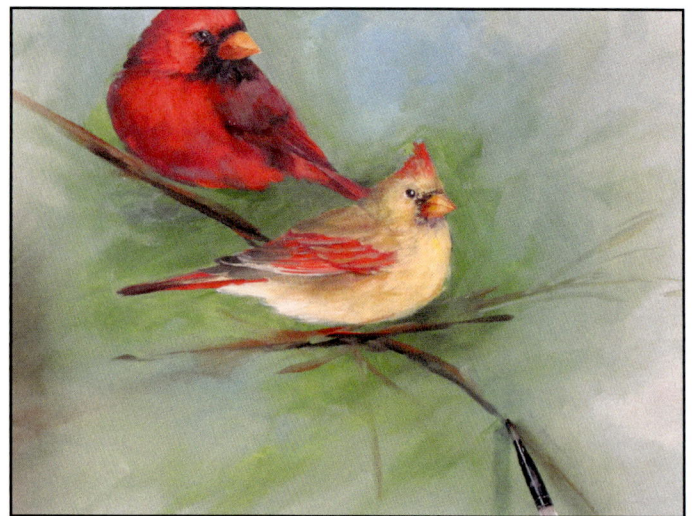

Step 79 Add some shadows to the branches with Burnt Sienna and black.

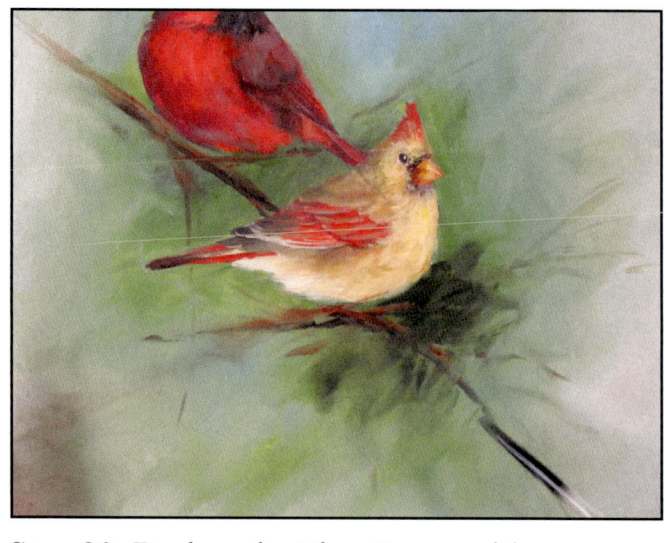

Step 80 Darken the Pine Green with some Black and add some strokes of darker green in to the center below her.

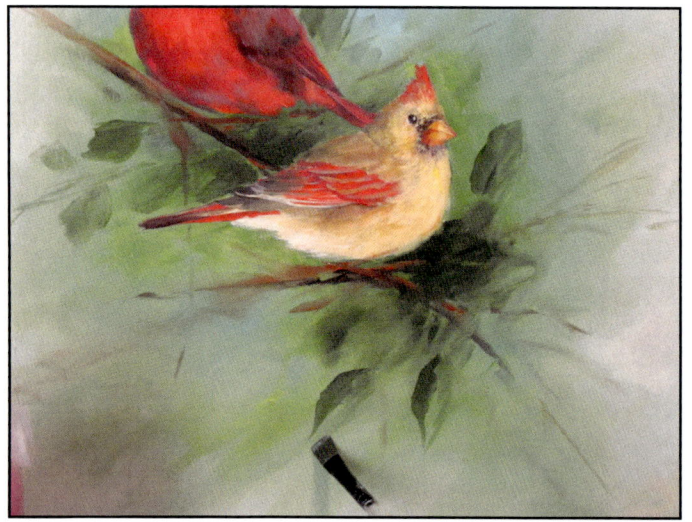

Step 81 Add the shapes of the leaves with the flat and the shadows. Carry the color darker on one side of the leaf as shown.

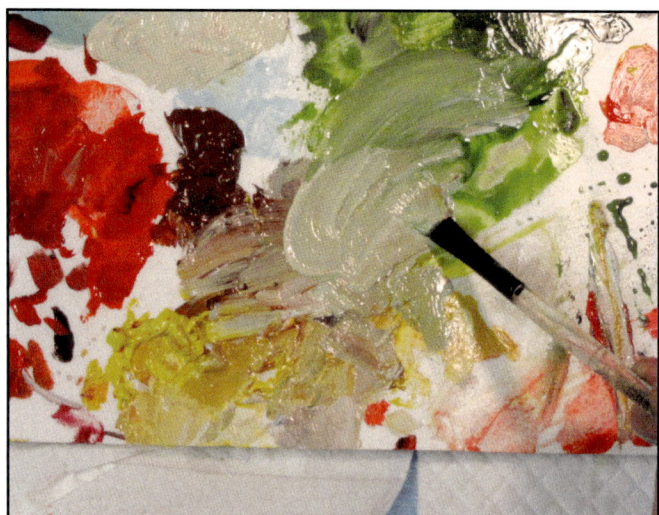

Step 82 Mottle a grey from all the palette colors and then lighten with some white.

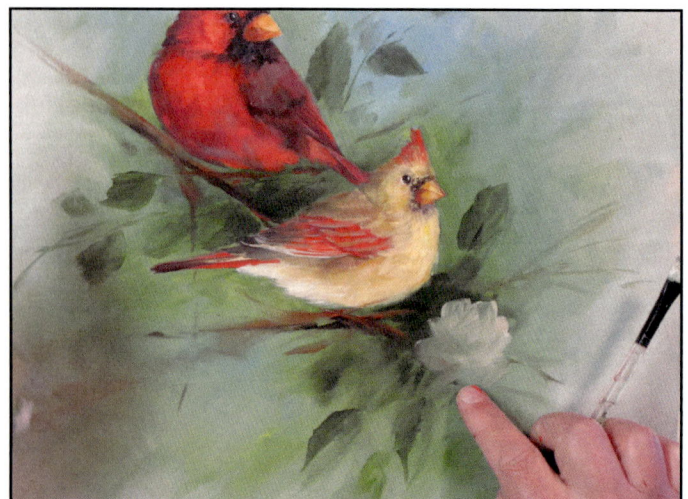

Step 83 This makes the base for the white blossoms. Use your finger to soften.

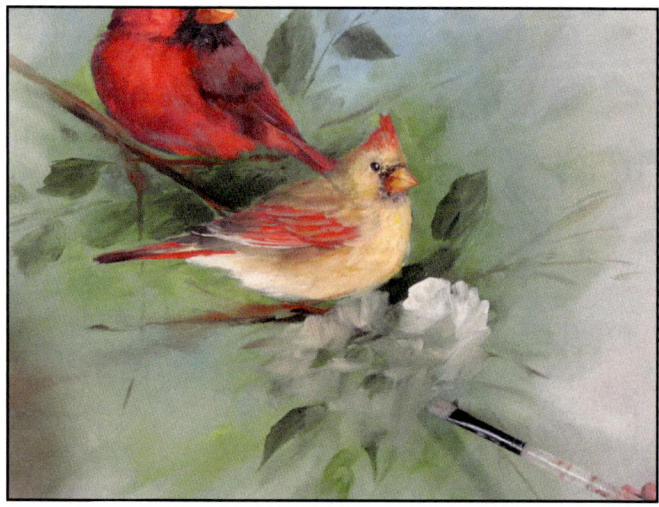

Step 84 Add some additional white to the blossoms to lighten one side.

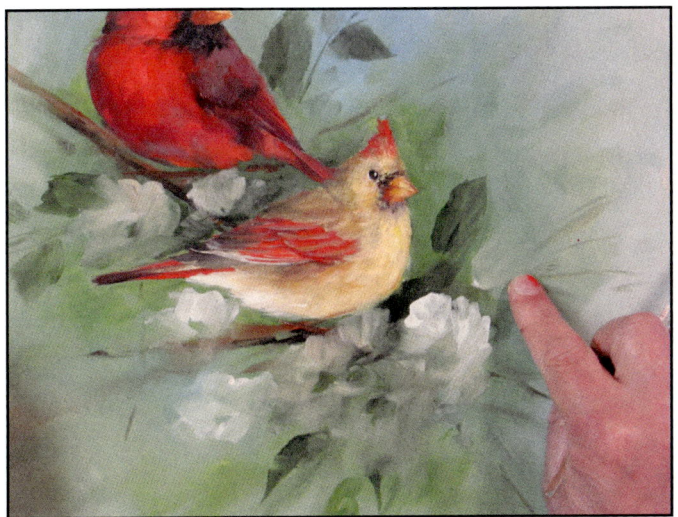

Step 85 Mottle the shapes of the other flowers and keep the ones on the outside soften by using your finger.

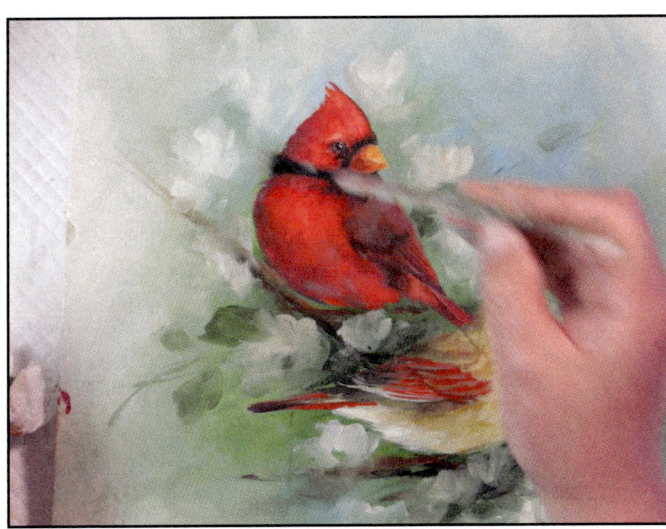

Step 86 Add some soft blossoms behind the head of the male cardinal.

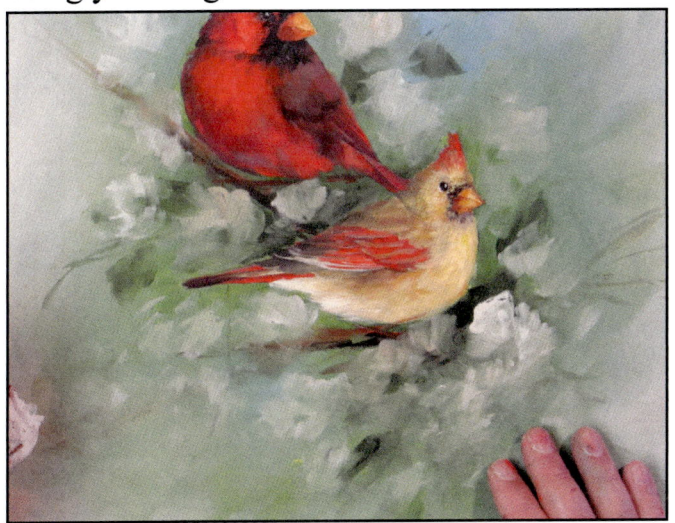

Step 87 Soften the outside ones with your fingers to make them disappear into the vignette.

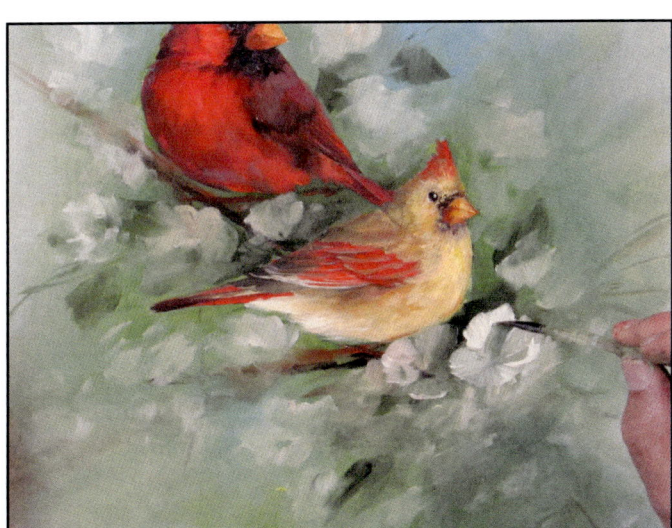

Step 88 Add some additional white to the blossoms in the center to make them come forward.

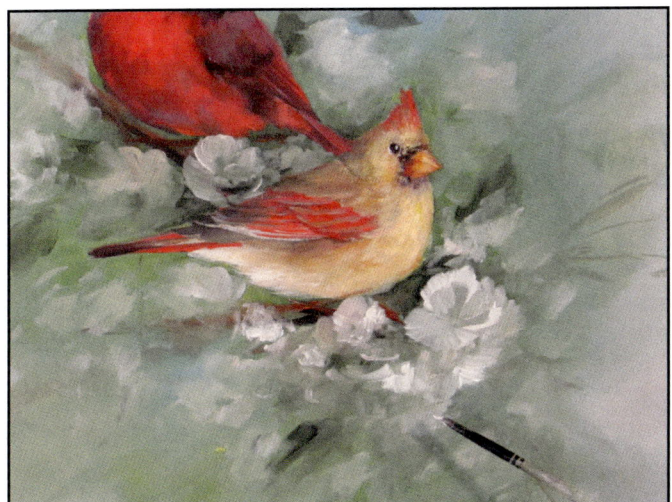

Step 89 Use the corner of the brush to add some petal details to the ones in the center.

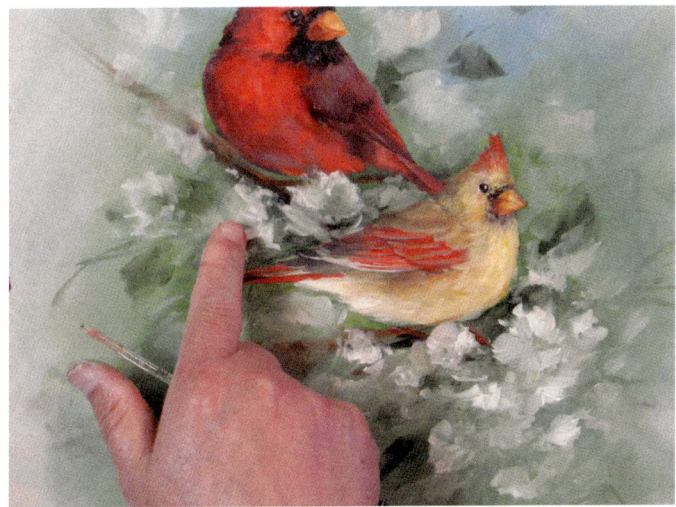

Step 90 Use your finger to soften the outside edges of the petals.

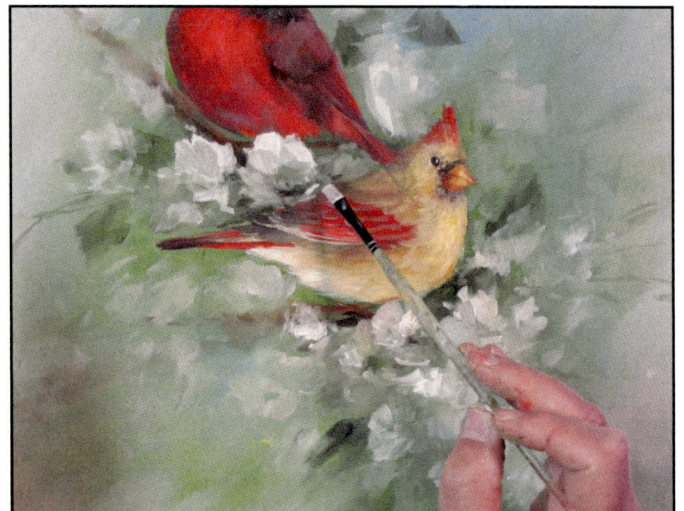
Step 91 Slowly build the blossoms. Add color and then soften with your finger.

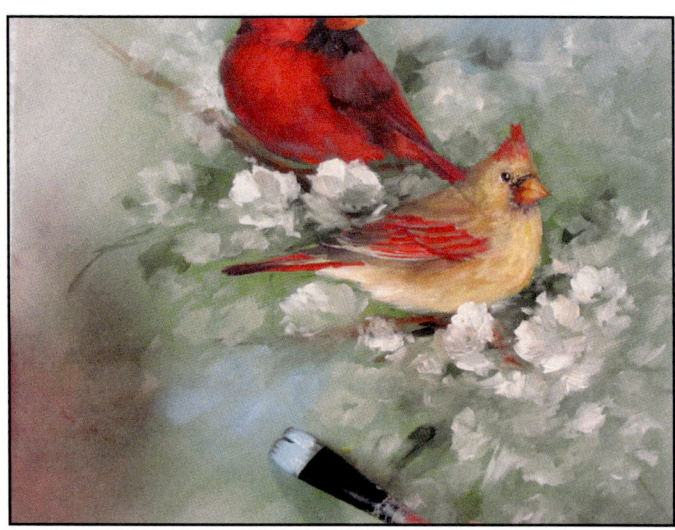
Step 92 Restate some of the base colors. Here I am adding more sky with some mottled light blue.

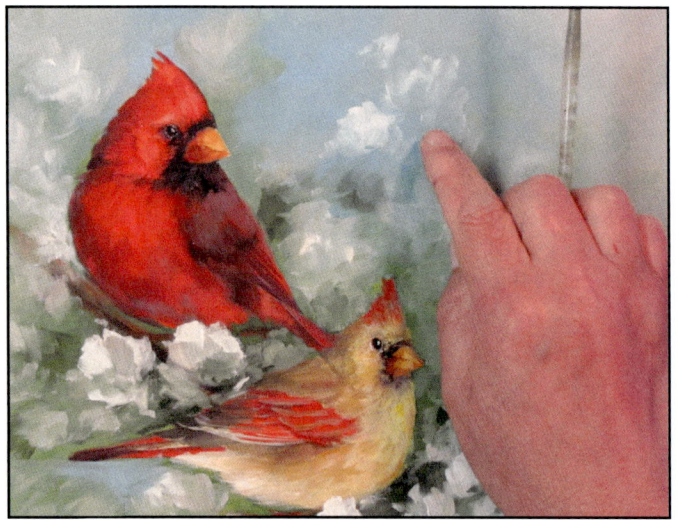
Step 93 Soften the blossoms into the blue at the top.

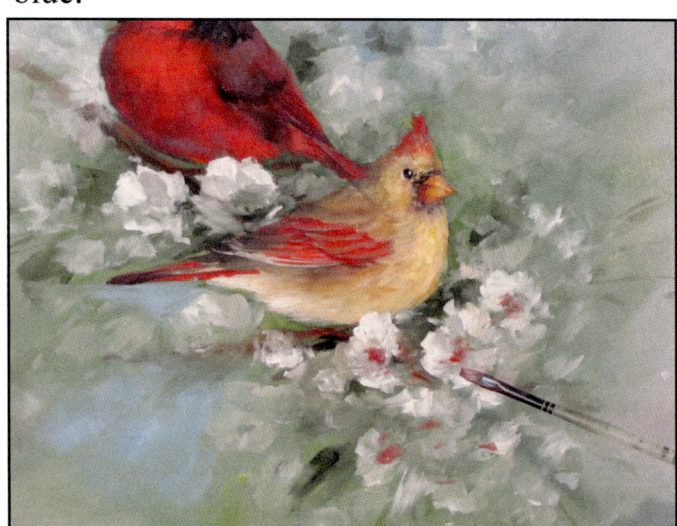
Step 94 Add some reddish centers to the blossom with the corner of the flat.

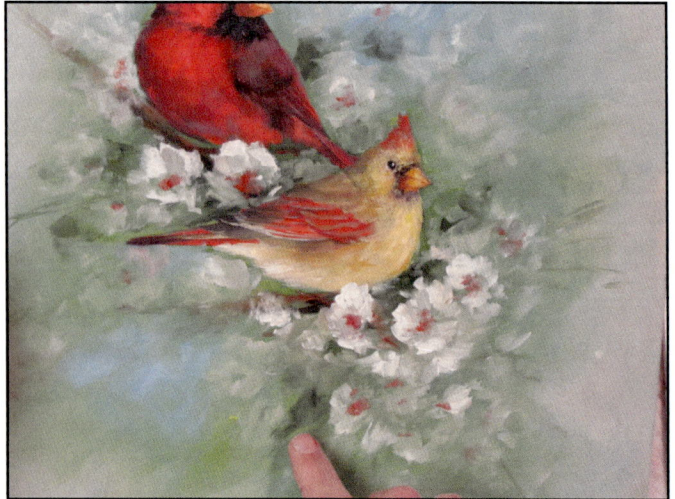
Step 95 Add some greens in between the blossoms and then soften with your finger.

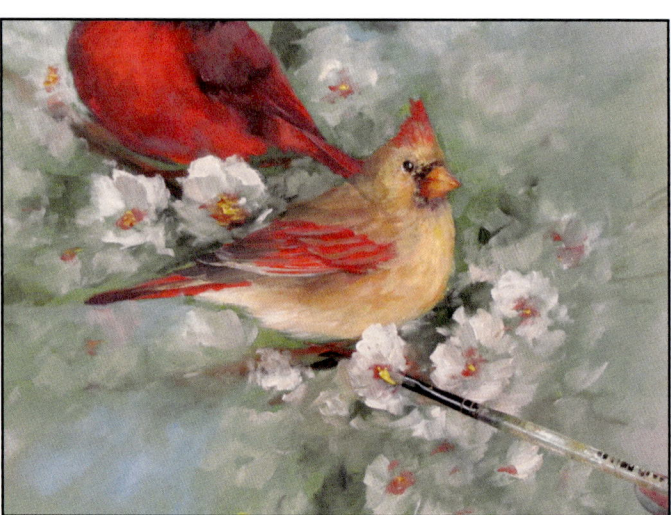
Step 96 Tap some Hansa and white with the corner of the brush into the centers.

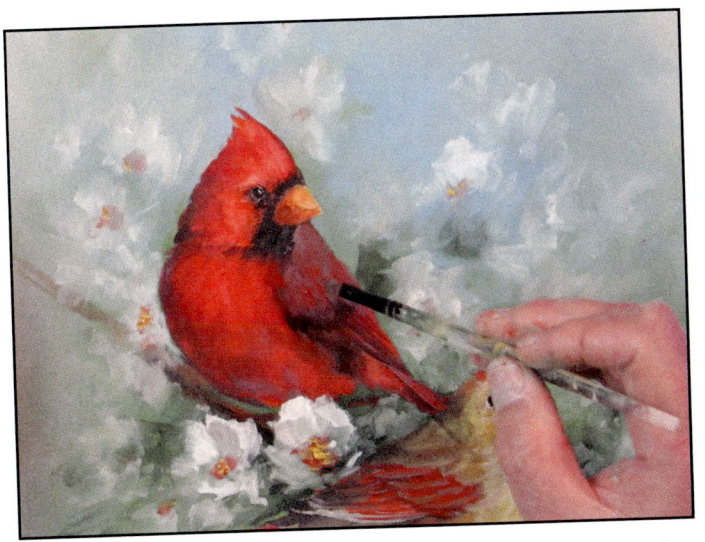

Step 97 Add some greys and lights to the male to restate him after you have painted the blossoms.

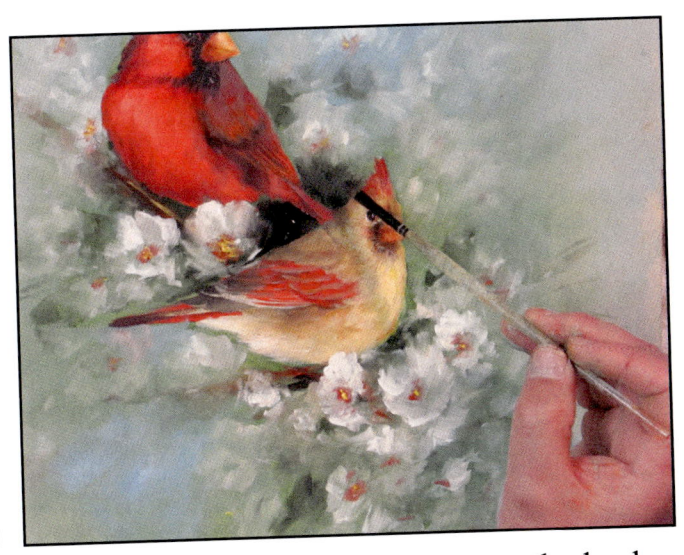

Step 98 Add some darker greens to the back behind the female so the dark brings her light head forward in the painting.

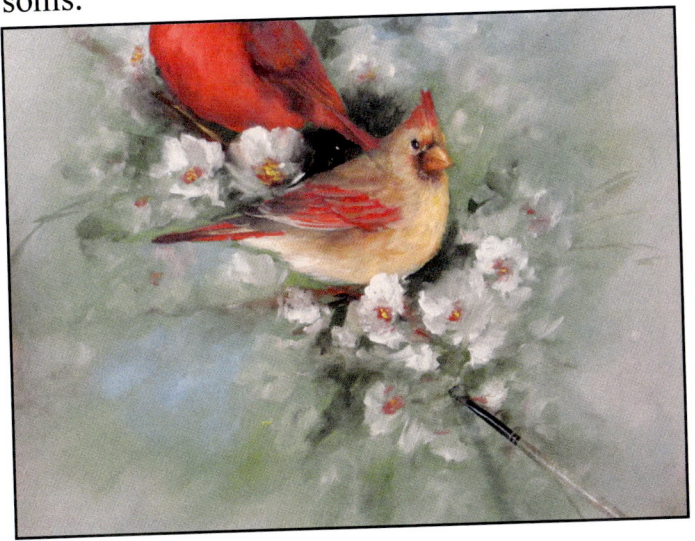

Step 99 Add some suggestions of leaves between the blossoms with a variety of greens. Mottled brush.

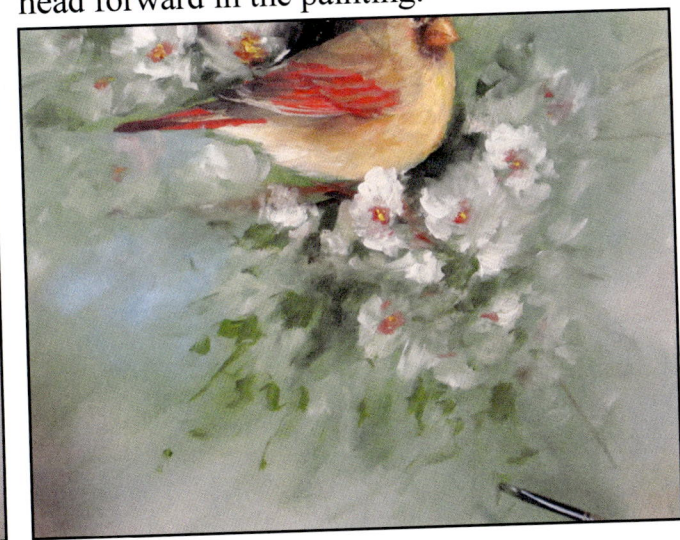

Step 100 Add some smaller greens outside the blossoms to lighten the feeling of the painting.

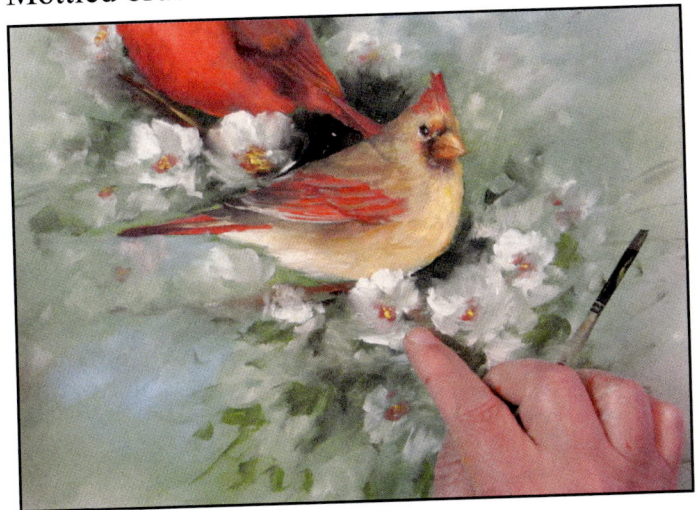

Step 101 Rework the movement on the blossom until you like the contrast.

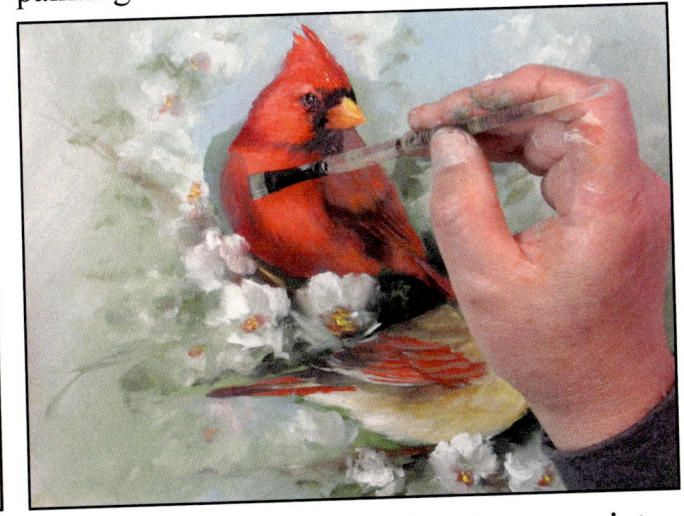

Step 102 Here I am using the sfumato painting technique to soften the right side of him.

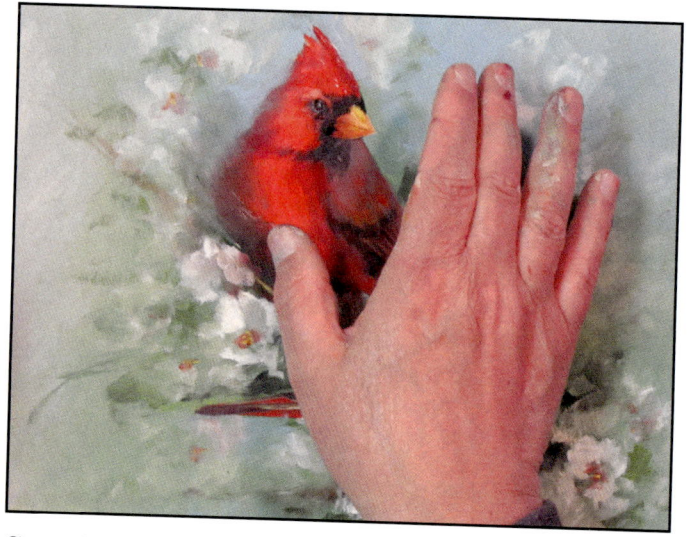

Step 103 Add the background over the right side (sfumato painting technique) then soften with your finger. This reduces intensity.

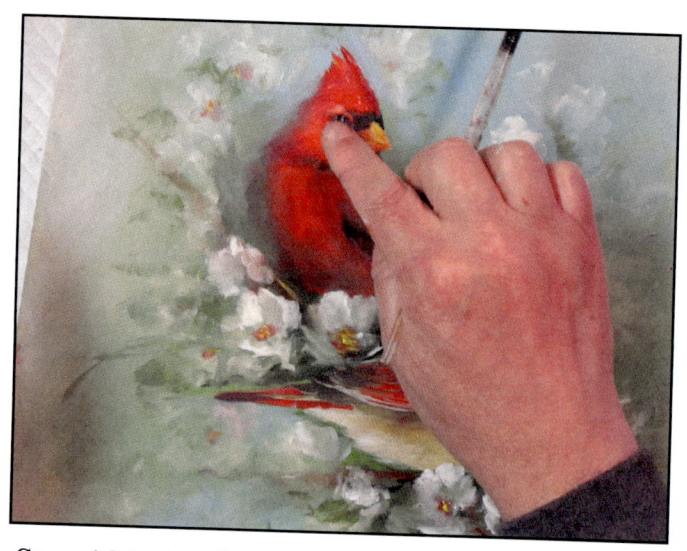

Step 104 Apply some to the top of his head. This will make him set back and appear a little thinner, so she comes forward.

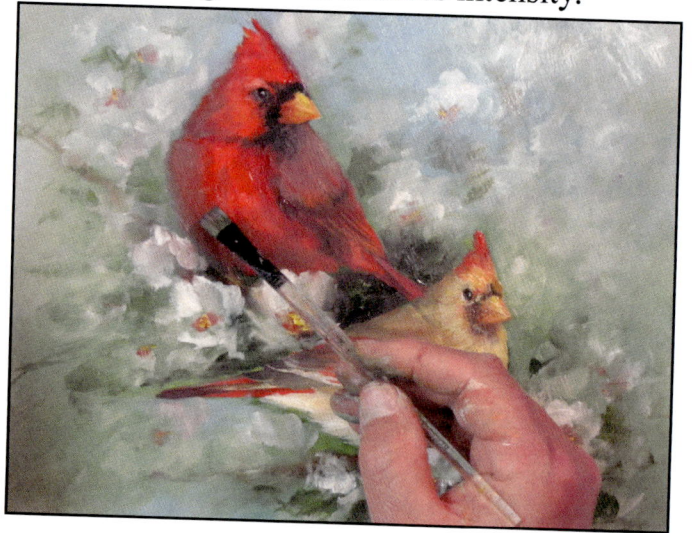

Step 105 Lightly glaze over the edges of him to push back. Work many times until you like the effect.

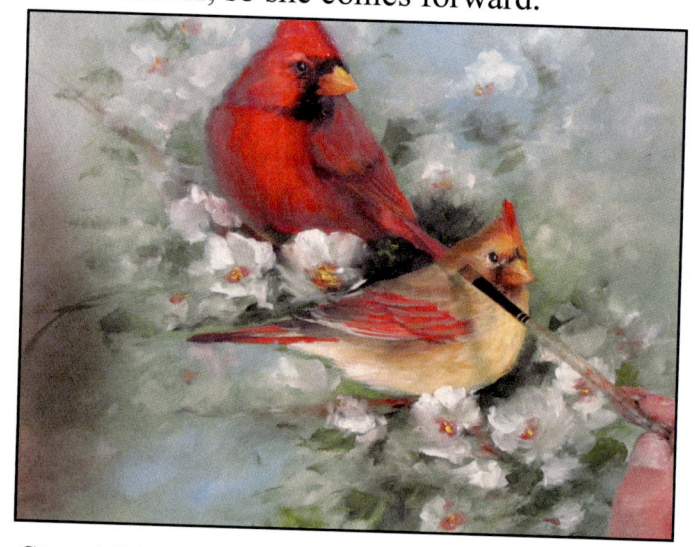

Step 106 Add some additional dark detail to her to help contrast and bring her forward.

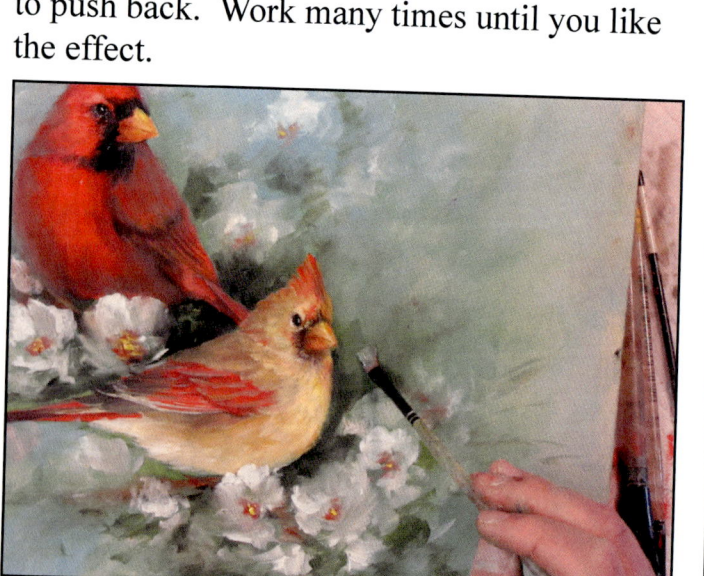

Step 107 Soften the movement of the blossoms so she in most important.

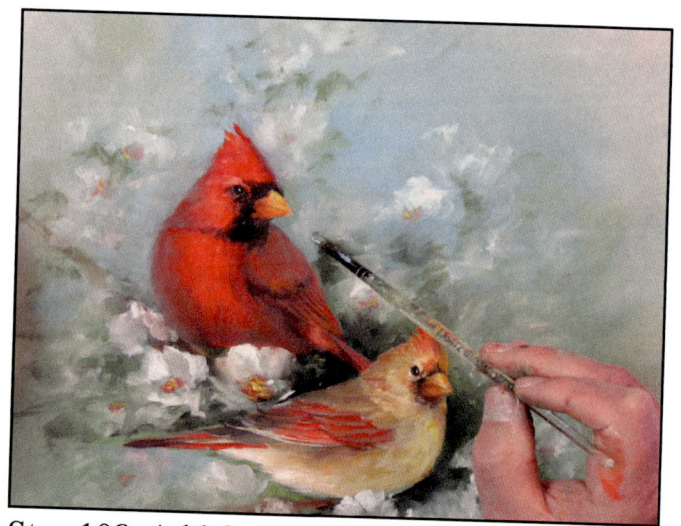

Step 108 Add final soft blossoms to finish. Add as many as desired.......Enjoy!

Cardinals Enlarge Pattern 130% for Original Size

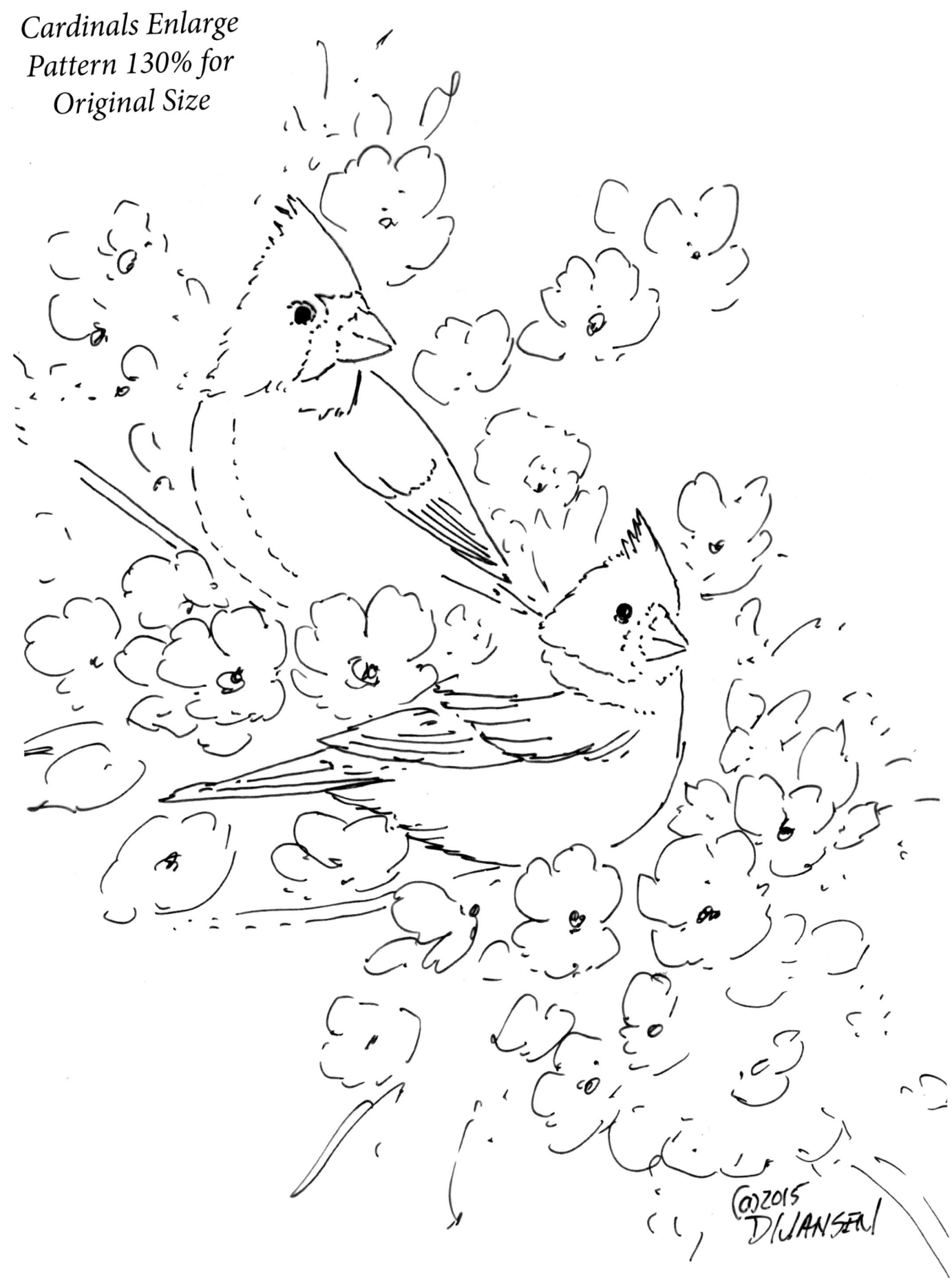

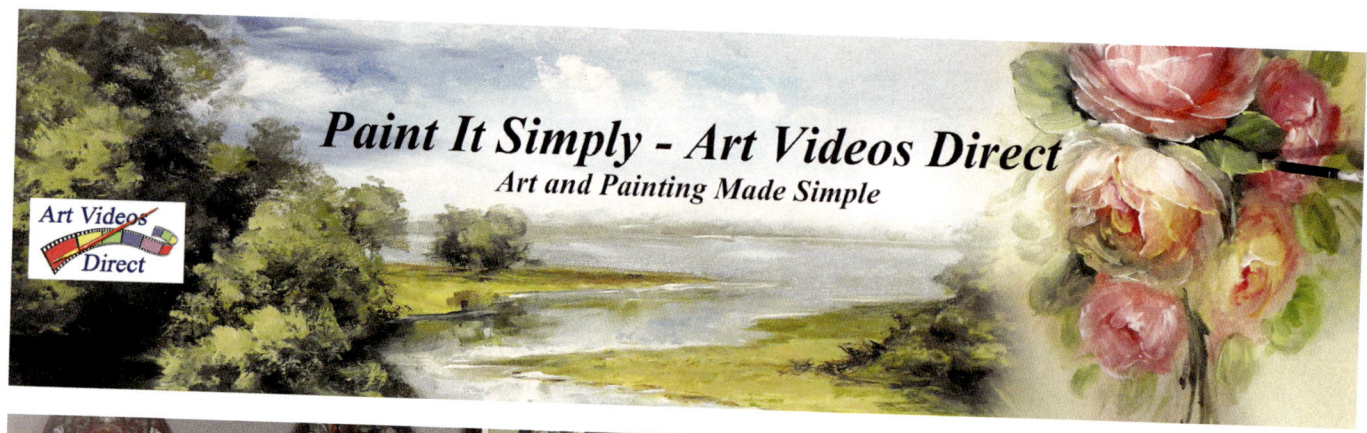

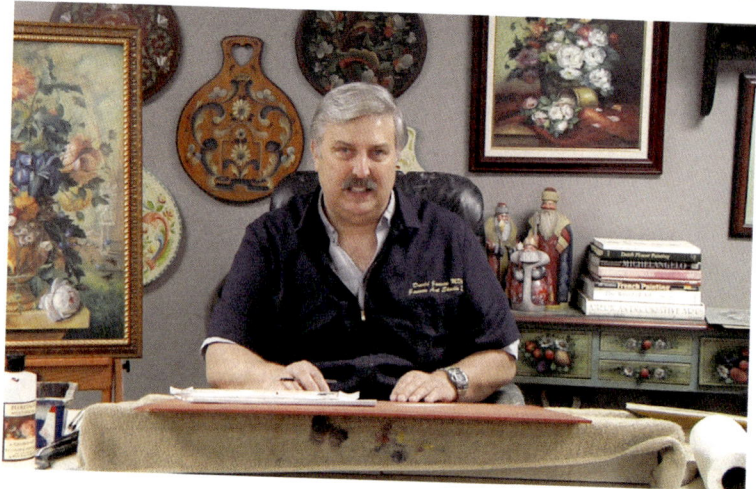

Watch 100's of Videos each month for one low monthly subscription price.

2 week free trial subscription.

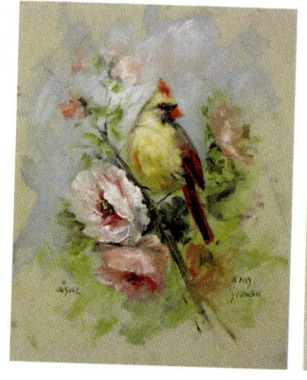 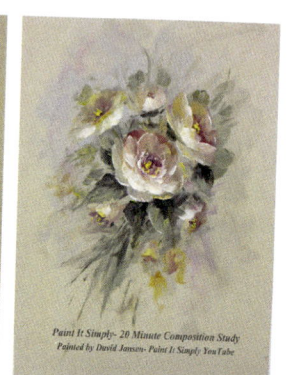

100's of Videos to watch with your monthly subscription. Some new never published. Monthly specials, discounts on art supplies, discounts on video purchases. Rent so to watch and paint. All this and more available to our subscribers!

Visit http://artvideosdirect.com

4 Educational Channels for the same Subscription

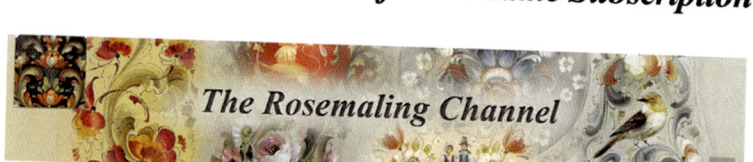
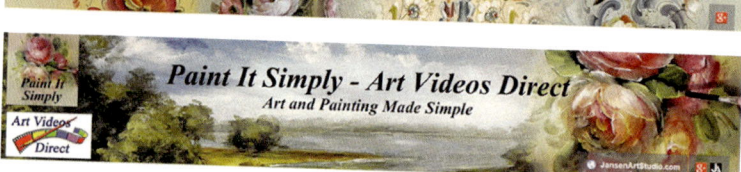
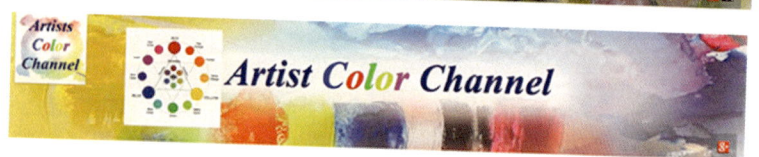

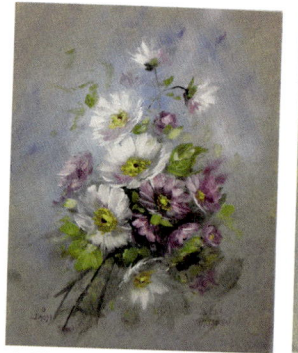 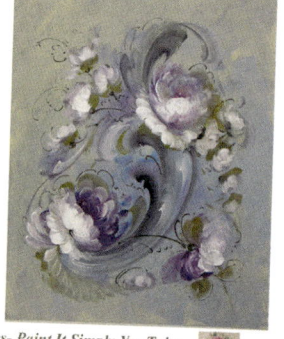

30 Minute Composition Studies- Paint It Simply YouTube
Painted by David Jansen

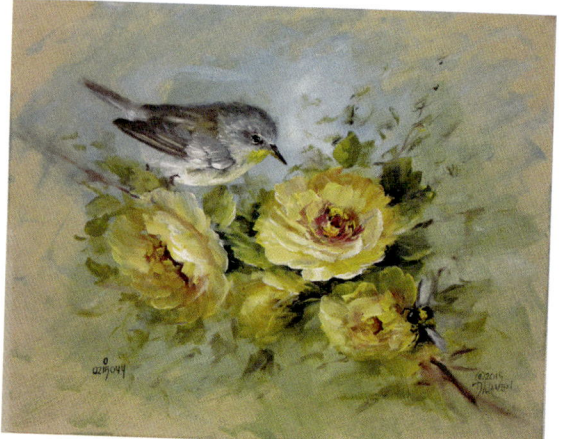

Made in the USA
Middletown, DE
23 May 2021